T H E
Norton Anthology of Poetry

REVISED SHORTER EDITION

THE
Norton Anthology
of Poetry

REVISED SHORTER EDITION

ALEXANDER W. ALLISON
LATE OF THE UNIVERSITY OF MICHIGAN

HERBERT BARROWS
UNIVERSITY OF MICHIGAN

CAESAR R. BLAKE
UNIVERSITY OF TORONTO

ARTHUR J. CARR
WILLIAMS COLLEGE

ARTHUR M. EASTMAN
CARNEGIE-MELLON UNIVERSITY

HUBERT M. ENGLISH, JR.
UNIVERSITY OF MICHIGAN

W · W · NORTON & COMPANY · INC·
NEW YORK

ISBN 0 393 09251 8

PRINTED IN THE UNITED STATES OF AMERICA

1 2 3 4 5 6 7 8 9 0

Contents

>>>->>>->>>->>>-<<<-<<<-<<<-<<<-<<<-<<<-<<<-<<<-<<<-<<<-<<<-<<<-<<<-<<<-<<<-<<<-<<<-<<<-<<<-<<<-<<<-<<<-<<<-<<<-<<<-<<<-<<<

Contents *xxv*

Preface

༺༺༺༺༺༺༺༺༺༺༺༺༺༺༺༺༺༺༺༺༺༺༺༺༺༺༺༺༺༺༺༺༺༺༺

This revision of the Shorter Edition of *The Norton Anthology of Poetry* is intended to broaden, and at the same time refine, the selection of poems through which it represents the grand sweep of poetry in English. Our efforts have been crucially helped by the practical criticism and informed suggestions provided us by many teachers who have used the *Anthology* in their classes. In a real sense, then, this work has been collaborative.

Special attention has been given to the poetry of this century. There are eighteen new modern poets, most of them still active. We have added such major poems as Eliot's "The Waste Land" and the first part of Pound's *Mauberley* sequence. We have included several Canadian poets—as we should have done in the first edition. Three new black poets amplify the presentation of that tradition. In the earlier pages we have made similar, though less striking, augmentations. There are four new women poets, ranging from Anne Bradstreet to Nikki Giovanni. Among the earlier major poems new in this edition are Pope's "Epistle to Dr. Arbuthnot" and Browning's "Soliloquy of the Spanish Cloister."

The Shorter Edition of *The Norton Anthology of Poetry*, like the larger book of poetry in English from which it is compacted, is particularly ample at both ends of the chronological spectrum, the medieval being lyrically richer than is sometimes recognized and the contemporary, denied the endorsement of tradition, meriting a generous if tentative acceptance. All along, the book attempts a discriminating selection of the poets it contains. Long-familiar selections have been re-examined, though without animus, and have sometimes been displaced by works less familiar. Manifestly this edition contains fewer of the long works of the larger edition, but since the goal has been to represent the whole range of verse in English, the long as well as the lyric and epigrammatic, space has still been found for *The Nun's Priest's Tale* and *The Rape of the Lock*, and for whole and self-contained segments from *The Prelude* and *In Memoriam*.

The order is chronological, poets appearing according to the dates of their births (American poets conflated with the British), and their poems according to the dates of their publication in volume form.

These dates follow the poems on the right; when two appear together, they point to significantly different published versions. Dates toward the left, when given, are those of composition.

Texts derive from authoritative editions but have been normalized in spelling and capitalization according to modern American usage—except in the many instances in which changes would significantly obscure meter or meaning. The works of Spenser and the Scottish poets, contrivedly archaic or dialectic in spelling, have been left untouched, as have the oldest of the medieval poems, which would remain to modern eyes almost as opaque after normalizing and modernizing as before. The metrically idiosyncratic Hopkins also remains unchanged. For the normalized text of Chaucer selections (except for "Lack of Steadfastness" and "Against Women Unconstant"), as well as for the notes to them, the editors particularly wish to thank Professor E. T. Donaldson.

Notes, as Dr. Johnson observed, are necessary, but necessary evils. They have been provided for information, not criticism; they gloss words and allusions but refrain, as much as possible, from interpretive comment. A terminal glossary, with prefatory commentary, identifies the technical terms of prosody.

Among the many teachers whose suggestions have aided us in preparing this revision, we particularly wish to thank Professors Daniel Mark Fogel of Cornell University, James McCord of the University of California at Santa Barbara, Paul Magnuson of the University of Pennsylvania, and W. H. New of the University of British Columbia. For their critical assistance with the first edition, we again thank Professors John E. Booty of The Episcopal Theological School, David Brewster of the University of Washington, Robert Dana of Cornell College, Lawrence Dembo of The University of Wisconsin, Donald Finkel of Bennington College, Charles Fuqua of Williams College, Cecil M. McCulley of the College of William and Mary, Robert Pack of Middlebury College, Richard Poirier of Rutgers University, and William C. Pratt of Miami University. And, most especially, we again wish to recognize the saving sanity with which M. H. Abrams guided us at certain perilous junctures, and the sharp eyes, tolerance, and immense helpfulness on which we came regularly to rely from John Francis and John Benedict, and their co-worker at W. W. Norton, Susan Bourla.

It only remains to record the untimely and lamentable death of our friend and colleague, Alexander W. Allison, whose work on the Neoclassics and on the note on prosody add so much to this book.

Note on the Modernizing of Medieval Texts

Changes that have taken place in pronunciation obscure for the modern reader the regular metrical character of some Middle English verse. The most important of these changes is the loss of an unstressed syllable in many word endings. We still pronounce some endings as separate syllables (*roses, wedded*), but for Chaucer the full syllabic value of an ending was available generally, even though its pronunciation was not always mandatory. Moreover, a great many final *—e*'s, vestiges of fuller endings at an earlier stage of the language, were still often pronounced (ə) in the ordinary speech of the day, so that the poet could treat them as syllables or not, according to the requirements of his meter, as *boughte* (pronounced either *bought* or *boughtë*) and *ofte* (pronounced either *oft* or *oftë*).

In modernizing, the editors have tried wherever possible to preserve or devise spellings that do not cut the reader off from the possibility of recovering the original rhythms. A non-modern spelling, especially at the end of a word, means that in the original text there is warrant for supposing that an "extra" syllable might have been pronounced at this point to justify metrical expectation. At the same time the editors have tried to avoid imposing a non-modern reading in those cases where a clear metrical pattern is not manifest.

THE
Norton Anthology of Poetry

REVISED SHORTER EDITION

ANONYMOUS LYRICS OF THE THIRTEENTH AND FOURTEENTH CENTURIES

Now Go'th Sun Under Wood[1]

Nou goth sonne under wode[2]—
Me reweth, Marie, thi faire rode.
Nou goth sonne under tre—
Me reweth, Marie, thi sone and the.

The Cuckoo Song[3]

Sing, cuccu, nu. Sing, cuccu.
Sing, cuccu. Sing, cuccu, nu.

Sumer is i-cumen in—
Lhude sing, cuccu!
5 Groweth sed and bloweth med
And springth the wude nu.
Sing, cuccu!

Awe bleteth after lomb,
Lhouth after calve cu,
10 Bulluc sterteth, bucke verteth—
Murie sing, cuccu!
Cuccu, cuccu.
Wel singes thu, cuccu.
Ne swik thu naver nu!

Steadfast Cross

Stedefast crosse, among all other
Thou art a tree mickle of price;[4]
In branch and flower swilk° another   such
I ne wot° none in wood no rys,°   know / nor thicket
5 Sweete be the nailes and sweete be the tree,
And sweeter be the burden that hanges upon thee.

Bishop Loreless

Bishop loreless,°   without learning
King redeless,°   without counsel
Young men reckless,°   heedless
Old man witless,
5 Woman shameless—
I swear by heaven's king,
Those be five lither thing!°   evil things

1. *Translation:* Now goes the sun under the wood— / I pity, Mary, thy fair face. / Now goes the sun under the tree— / I pity, Mary, thy son and thee.
2. *Wood* and *tree* not only had their modern meanings but also meant *the cross.*
3. *Translation:* Sing, cuckoo, now. Sing, cuckoo. / Sing, cuckoo. Sing, cuckoo, now. Spring is come in— / Sing loud, cuckoo! / The seed grows, the meadow blooms / And the wood now comes into leaf / Sing, cuckoo! The ewe bleats after the lamb, / The cow lows after the calf, / The bullock leaps, the buck breaks wind— / Sing merrily, cuckoo! / Cuckoo, cuckoo. / Well singest thou, cuckoo. / Cease thou never now!
4. Great of worth.

All Night by the Rose

All night by the rose, rose—
All night by the rose I lay;
Dared I not the rose steal,
And yet I bore the flower away.

At a Spring-Well

At a spring-well° under a thorn   spring
There was bote of bale⁵ a little here a-forn;°   before
There beside stands a maid
Full of love i-bound.°   bound
5   Whoso will seek true love,
In her it shall be found.

GEOFFREY CHAUCER
(ca. 1343–1400)

The Nun's Priest's Tale

A poore widwe somdeel stape° in age   advanced
Was whilom° dwelling in a narwe° cotage,   once upon a time / small
Biside a grove, stonding in a dale:
This widwe of which I telle you my tale,
5   Sin thilke° day that she was last a wif,   that same
In pacience ladde° a ful simple lif.   led
For litel was hir catel° and hir rente,°   property / income
By housbondrye° of swich as God hire sente   economy
She foond° hirself and eek hir doughtren two.   provided for
10   Three large sowes hadde she and namo,
Three kin,° and eek a sheep that highte Malle.   cows
Ful sooty was hir bowr° and eek hir halle,   bedroom
In which she eet ful many a sclendre° meel;   scanty
Of poinant° sauce hire needed neveradeel: pungent
15   No daintee morsel passed thurgh hir throte—
Hir diete was accordant to hir cote.°   cottage
Repleccioun° ne made hire nevere sik: overeating
Attempre° diete was al hir physik,°   moderate / medicine
And exercise and hertes suffisaunce.°   contentment
20   The goute lette hire nothing for to daunce,¹
N'apoplexye shente° nat hir heed.°   hurt / head
No win ne drank she, neither whit ne reed:°   red
Hir boord° was served most with whit and blak,²   table
Milk and brown breed, in which she foond no lak;³
25   Seind bacon, and somtime an ey° or twaye,   egg
For she was as it were a manere daye.⁴
A yeerd° she hadde, enclosed al withoute   yard

5. Remedy for evil.
1. The gout didn't hinder her at all from dancing.
2. I.e., milk and bread.
3. Found no fault. "Seind": scorched (i.e., broiled).
4. I.e., a kind of dairymaid.

With stikkes, and a drye dich aboute,
In which she hadde a cok heet° Chauntecleer:　　　　*named*
30　In al the land of crowing nas° his peer.　　　　*was not*
His vois was merier than the merye orgon
On massedayes that in the chirche goon;[5]
Wel sikerer[6] was his crowing in his logge°　　　　*dwelling*
Than is a clok or an abbeye orlogge;°　　　　*timepiece*
35　By nature he knew eech ascensioun
Of th'equinoxial[7] in thilke town:
For whan degrees fifteene were ascended,
Thanne crew° he that it mighte nat been amended.°　　*crowed / improved*
His comb was redder than the fin coral,
40　And batailed° as it were a castel wal;　　　　*battlemented*
His bile° was blak, and as the jeet° it shoon;　　　*bill / jet*
Like asure° were his legges and his toon;°　　　*lapis lazuli / toes*
His nailes whitter° than the lilye flowr,　　　　*whiter*
And lik the burned° gold was his colour.　　　　*burnished*
45　This gentil cok hadde in his governaunce
Sevene hennes for to doon al his plesaunce,°　　　*pleasure*
Whiche were his sustres and his paramours,[8]
And wonder like to him as of colours;
Of whiche the faireste hewed° on hir throte　　　*colored*
50　Was cleped faire damoisele Pertelote:
Curteis she was, discreet, and debonaire,°　　　*meek*
And compaignable,° and bar° hirself so faire,　*companionable / bore*
Sin thilke day that she was seven night old,
That trewely she hath the herte in hold
55　Of Chauntecleer, loken° in every lith.°　　　*locked / limb*
He loved hire so that wel was him therwith.[9]
But swich a joye was it to heere hem singe,
Whan that the brighte sonne gan to springe,
In sweete accord *My Lief is Faren in Londe*[1]—
60　For thilke time, as I have understonde,
Beestes and briddes couden speke and singe.
　　And so bifel that in a daweninge,
As Chauntecleer among his wives alle
Sat on his perche that was in the halle,
65　And next him sat this faire Pertelote,
This Chauntecleer gan gronen in his throte,
As man that in his dreem is drecched° sore.　　　*troubled*
　　And whan that Pertelote thus herde him rore,
She was agast, and saide, "Herte dere,
70　What aileth you to grone in this manere?
Ye been a verray slepere,[2] fy, for shame!"
　　And he answerde and said thus, "Madame,
I praye you that ye take it nat agrief.°　　　　*amiss*
By God, me mette I was in swich meschief[3]
75　Right now, that yit myn herte is sore afright.
Now God," quod he, "my swevene recche aright.[4]
And keepe my body out of foul prisoun!
Me mette how that I romed up and down

---

5. I.e., is played.
6. More reliable.
7. I.e., he knew by instinct each step in the progression of the celestial equator. The celestial equator was thought to make a 360-degree rotation around the earth every 24 hours; therefore a progression of 15 degrees would be equal to the passage of an hour (line 37).
8. His sisters and his mistresses.
9. That he was well contented.
1. A popular song of the time.
2. I.e., sound sleeper.
3. I dreamed that I was in such misfortune.
4. Interpret my dream correctly (i.e., in an auspicious manner).

Within oure yeerd, wher as I sawgh a beest,
80 Was lik an hound and wolde han maad arrest[5]
Upon my body, and han had me deed.[6]
His colour was bitwixe yelow and reed,
And tipped was his tail and bothe his eres
With blak, unlik the remenant° of his heres;°   *rest / hairs*
85 His snoute smal, with glowing yën twaye.
Yit of his look for fere almost I deye:°   *die*
This caused me my groning, doutelees."
    "Avoi,"° quod she, "fy on you, hertelees!°   *fie / coward*
Allas," quod she, "for by that God above,
90 Now han ye lost myn herte and al my love!
I can nat love a coward, by my faith.
For certes, what so any womman saith,
We alle desiren, if it mighte be,
To han housbondes hardy, wise, and free,°   *generous*
95 And secree,° and no nigard, ne no fool,   *discreet*
Ne him that is agast of every tool,°   *weapon*
Ne noon avauntour.° By that God above,   *boaster*
How dorste ye sayn for shame unto youre love
That any thing mighte make you aferd?
100 Have ye no mannes herte and han a beerd?
Allas, and conne° ye been agast of swevenes?°   *can / dreams*
No thing, God woot, but vanitee[7] in swevene is!
Swevenes engendren of replexiouns,[8]
And ofte of fume° and of complexiouns,°   *gas / bodily humors*
105 Whan humours been too habundant in a wight.[9]
Certes, this dreem which ye han met° tonight   *dreamed*
Comth of the grete superfluitee
Of youre rede colera,[1] pardee,
Which causeth folk to dreden° in hir dremes   *fear*
110 Of arwes,° and of fir with rede lemes,°   *arrows / flames*
Of rede beestes, that they wol hem bite,
Of contek,° and of whelpes grete and lite[2]—   *strife*
Right° as the humour of malencolye[3]   *just*
Causeth ful many a man in sleep to crye
115 For fere of blake beres° or boles° blake,   *bears / bulls*
Or elles blake develes wol hem take.
Of othere humours coude I tell also
That werken many a man in sleep ful wo,
But I wol passe as lightly° as I can.   *quickly*
120 Lo, Caton,[4] which that was so wis a man,
Saide he nat thus? 'Ne do no fors of[5] dremes.'
Now, sire," quod she, "whan we flee fro the bemes,[6]
For Goddes love, as take som laxatif.
Up° peril of my soule and of my lif,   *upon*
125 I conseile you the beste, I wol nat lie,
That bothe of colere and of malencolye
Ye purge you; and for° ye shal nat tarye,   *in order that*
Though in this town is noon apothecarye,
I shal myself to herbes techen you,

---

5. Would have laid hold.
6. I.e., killed me.
7. I.e., empty illusion.
8. Dreams have their origin in overeating.
9. I.e., when humors are too abundant in a person. Pertelote's diagnosis is based on the familiar concept that an overabundance of one of the bodily humors in a person affected his temperament.
1. Red bile.
2. And of big and little dogs.
3. I.e., black bile.
4. Dionysius Cato, supposed author of a book of maxims used in elementary education.
5. Pay no attention to.
6. Fly down from the rafters.

130 That shal been for youre hele[7] and for youre prow,
And in oure yeerd tho herbes shal I finde,
The whiche han of hir propretee by kinde°   *nature*
To purge you binethe and eek above;
Foryet° nat this, for Goddes owene love.   *forget*
135 Ye been ful colerik° of complexioun;   *bilious*
Ware° the sonne in his ascencioun   *beware that*
Ne finde you nat repleet° of humours hote;°   *filled / hot*
And if it do, I dar wel laye° a grote   *bet*
That ye shul have a fevere terciane,[8]
140 Or an agu that may be youre bane.°   *death*
A day or two ye shul han digestives
Of wormes, er ye take youre laxatives
Of lauriol, centaure, and fumetere,[9]
Or elles of ellebor° that groweth there,   *hellebore*
145 Of catapuce,° or of gaitres beries,° *caper berry / gaiter berry*
Of herbe-ive° growing in oure yeerd ther merye is.[1]   *herb ivy*
Pekke hem right up as they growe and ete hem in.
Be merye, housbonde, for youre fader kin!
Dredeth no dreem: I can saye you namore."
150   "Madame," quod he, "graunt mercy of youre lore.[2]
But nathelees, as touching daun° Catoun,   *master*
That hath of wisdom swich a greet renown,
Though that he bad no dremes for to drede,
By God, men may in olde bookes rede
155 Of many a man more of auctoritee°   *authority*
Than evere Caton was, so mote I thee,°   *thrive*
That al the revers sayn of his sentence,°   *opinion*
And han wel founden by experience
That dremes been significaciouns
160 As wel of joye as tribulaciouns
That folk enduren in this lif present.
Ther needeth make of this noon argument:
The verray preve[3] sheweth it in deede.
    "Oon of the gretteste auctour[4] that men rede
165 Saith thus, that whilom two felawes wente
On pilgrimage in a ful good entente,
And happed so they comen in a town,
Wher as ther was swich congregacioun
Of peple, and eek so strait of herbergage,[5]
170 That they ne founde as muche as oo cotage
In which they bothe mighte ylogged° be;   *lodged*
Wherfore they mosten° of necessitee   *must*
As for that night departe° compaignye.   *part*
And eech of hem gooth to his hostelrye,
175 And took his logging as it wolde falle.°   *befall*
That oon of hem was logged in a stalle,
Fer° in a yeerd, with oxen of the plough;   *far away*
That other man was logged wel ynough,
As was his aventure° or his fortune,   *lot*
180 That us governeth alle as in commune.
And so bifel that longe er it were day,

---

7. Health; "prow": benefit.
8. Tertian (recurring every other day).
9. Of laureole, centaury, and fumitory. These, and the herbs mentioned in the next lines, were all common medieval medicines used as cathartics.

1. Where it is pleasant.
2. Many thanks for your instruction.
3. Actual experience.
4. I.e., one of the greatest authors (perhaps Cicero).
5. And also such a shortage of lodging.

This man mette° in his bed, ther as he lay,   *dreamed*
How that his felawe gan upon him calle,
And saide, 'Allas, for in an oxes stalle
185 This night I shal be mordred° ther I lie!   *murdered*
Now help me, dere brother, or I die!
In alle haste com to me,' he saide.
"This man out of his sleep for fere abraide,°   *started up*
But whan that he was wakened of his sleep,
190 He turned him and took of this no keep:°   *heed*
Him thoughte his dreem nas but a vanitee.
Thus twies in his sleeping dremed he,
And atte thridde time yit his felawe
Cam, as him thoughte, and saide, 'I am now slawe:°   *slain*
195 Bihold my bloody woundes deepe and wide.
Aris up erly in the morwe tide[6]
And atte west gate of the town,' quod he,
'A carte ful of dong° ther shaltou see,   *dung*
In which my body is hid ful prively:
200 Do thilke carte arresten boldely.[7]
My gold caused my mordre, sooth to sayn'—
And tolde him every point how he was slain,
With a ful pitous face, pale of hewe.
And truste wel, his dreem he foond° ful trewe,   *found*
205 For on the morwe° as soone as it was day,   *morning*
To his felawes in° he took the way,   *lodging*
And whan that he cam to this oxes stalle,
After his felawe he bigan to calle.
"The hostiler° answerde him anoon,   *innkeeper*
210 And saide, 'Sire, youre felawe is agoon:°   *gone away*
As soone as day he wente out of the town.'
"This man gan fallen in suspecioun,
Remembring on his dremes that he mette;°   *dreamed*
And forth he gooth, no lenger wolde he lette,°   *tarry*
215 Unto the west gate of the town, and foond
A dong carte, wente as it were to donge° lond,   *put manure on*
That was arrayed in that same wise
As ye han herd the dede° man devise;   *dead*
And with an hardy herte he gan to crye,
220 'Vengeance and justice of this felonye!
My felawe mordred is this same night,
And in this carte he lith° gaping upright!°   *lies / supine*
I crye out on the ministres,' quod he,
'That sholde keepe and rulen this citee.
225 Harrow,° allas, here lith my felawe slain!'   *help*
What sholde I more unto this tale sayn?
The peple up sterte° and caste the carte to grounde,   *started*
And in the middel of the dong they founde
The dede man that mordred was al newe.[8]
230 "O blisful God that art so just and trewe,
Lo, how that thou biwrayest° mordre alway!   *disclose*
Mordre wol out, that see we day by day:
Mordre is so wlatsom° and abhominable   *loathsome*
To God that is so just and resonable,
235 That he ne wol nat suffre it heled° be,   *concealed*
Though it abide a yeer or two or three.

6. In the morning.   8. Recently.
7. Boldly have this same cart stopped.

Mordre wol out: this my conclusioun.
And right anoon ministres of that town
Han hent° the cartere and so sore him pined,°   seized / tortured
240 And eek the hostiler so sore engined,°   racked
That they biknewe° hir wikkednesse anoon,   confessed
And were anhanged° by the nekke boon.   hanged
Here may men seen that dremes been to drede.[9]
"And certes, in the same book I rede—
245 Right in the nexte chapitre after this—
I gabbe° nat, so have I joye or blis—   lie
Two men that wolde han passed over see
For certain cause into a fer contree,
If that the wind ne hadde been contrarye
250 That made hem in a citee for to tarye,
That stood ful merye upon an haven° side—   harbor's
But on a day again° the even tide   toward
The wind gan chaunge, and blewe right as hem leste:[1]
Jolif° and glad they wenten unto reste,   merry
255 And casten hem[2] ful erly for to saile.
"But to that oo man fil° a greet mervaile;   befell
That oon of hem, in sleeping as he lay,
Him mette[3] a wonder dreem again the day:
Him thoughte a man stood by his beddes side,
260 And him comanded that he sholde abide,
And saide him thus, 'If thou tomorwe wende,
Thou shalt be dreint:° my tale is at an ende.'   drowned
"He wook and tolde his felawe what he mette,
And prayed him his viage° to lette;°   voyage / delay
265 As for that day he prayed him to bide.
"His felawe that lay by his beddes side
Gan for to laughe, and scorned him ful faste.°   hard
'No dreem,' quod he, 'may so myn herte agaste°   terrify
That I wol lette° for to do my thinges.°   delay / business
270 I sette nat a straw by thy dreminges,[4]
For swevenes been but vanitees and japes:[5]
Men dreme alday° of owles or of apes,[6]   constantly
And of many a maze° therwithal—   delusion
Men dreme of thing that nevere was ne shal.[7]
275 But sith I see that thou wolt here abide,
And thus forsleuthen° wilfully thy tide,°   waste / time
Good woot, it reweth me;[8] and have good day.'
And thus he took his leve and wente his way.
But er that he hadde half his cours ysailed—
280 Noot I nat why ne what meschaunce it ailed—
But casuelly the shippes botme rente,[9]
And ship and man under the water wente,
In sighte of othere shippes it biside,
That with hem sailed at the same tide.
285 And therfore, faire Pertelote so dere,
By swiche ensamples olde maistou lere°   learn
That no man sholde been too recchelees°   careless
Of dremes, for I saye thee doutelees
That many a dreem ful sore is for to drede.

9. Worthy of being feared.
1. Just as they wished.
2. Determined.
3. He dreamed.
4. I don't care a straw for your dreamings.
5. Dreams are but illusions and frauds.

6. I.e., of absurdities.
7. I.e., shall be.
8. I'm sorry.
9. I don't know why nor what was the trouble with it—but accidentally the ship's bottom split.

290 "Lo, in the lif of Saint Kenelm[1] I rede—
That was Kenulphus sone, the noble king
Of Mercenrike°—how Kenelm mette a thing   *Mercia*
A lite° er he was mordred on a day.   *little*
His mordre in his avision° he sey.°   *dream / saw*
295 His norice° him expounded everydeel°   *nurse / entirely*
His swevene, and bad him for to keepe him[2] weel
For traison, but he nas but seven yeer old,
And therfore litel tale hath he told
Of any dreem,[3] so holy was his herte.
300 By God, I hadde levere than my sherte[4]
That ye hadde rad° his legende as have I.   *read*
"Dame Pertelote, I saye you trewely,
Macrobeus,[5] that writ the *Avisioun*
In Affrike of the worthy Scipioun,
305 Affermeth° dremes, and saith that they been   *confirms*
Warning of thinges that men after seen.
"And ferthermore, I praye you looketh wel
In the Olde Testament of Daniel,
If he heeld° dremes any vanitee;[6]   *considered*
310 "Rede eek of Joseph[7] and ther shul ye see
Wher° dremes be somtime—I saye nat alle—   *whether*
Warning of thinges that shul after falle.
"Looke of Egypte the king daun Pharao,
His bakere and his botelere° also,   *butler*
315 Wher they ne felte noon effect in dremes.[8]
Whoso wol seeke actes of sondry remes°   *realms*
May rede of dremes many a wonder thing.
"Lo Cresus, which that was of Lyde° king,   *Lydia*
Mette° he nat that he sat upon a tree,   *dreamed*
320 Which signified he sholde anhanged° be?   *hanged*
"Lo here Andromacha, Ectores° wif,   *Hector's*
That day that Ector sholde lese° his lif,   *lose*
She dremed on the same night biforn
How that the lif of Ector sholde be lorn,°   *lost*
325 If thilke° day he wente into bataile;   *that same*
She warned him, but it mighte nat availe:°   *do any good*
He wente for to fighte nathelees,
But he was slain anoon° of Achilles.   *right away*
But thilke tale is al too long to telle,
330 And eek it is neigh day, I may nat dwelle.
Shortly I saye, as for conclusioun,
That I shal han of this avisioun[9]
Adversitee, and I saye ferthermoor
That I ne telle of[1] laxatives no stoor,
335 For they been venimes,° I woot it weel: *poisons*
I hem defye, I love hem neveradeel.°   *not a bit*
"Now lat us speke of mirthe and stinte° al this.   *stop*
Madame Pertelote, so have I blis,
Of oo thing God hath sente me large grace:
340 For whan I see the beautee of youre face—

1. Kenelm succeeded his father as king of
Mercia at the age of 7 but was slain by his
aunt (in 821).
2. Guard himself.
3. Therefore he has set little store by any
dream.
4. I.e., I'd give my shirt.
5. Macrobius wrote a famous commentary on
Cicero's account in *De Republica* of the dream
of Scipio Africanus Minor; the commentary
came to be regarded as a standard authority
on dream lore.
6. See Daniel vii.
7. See Genesis xxxvii.
8. See Genesis xxxix-xli.
9. Divinely inspired dream (as opposed to the
more ordinary "swevene" or "dreem").
1. Set by.

Ye been so scarlet reed° aboute youre yën—   red
It maketh al my drede for to dien.
For also siker° as *In principio*,[2]   certain
Mulier est hominis confusio.[3]
345 Madame, the sentence° of this Latin is,   meaning
'Womman is mannes joye and al his blis.'
For whan I feele anight youre softe side—
Al be it that I may nat on you ride,
For that oure perche is maad so narwe, allas—   delight
350 I am so ful of joye and of solas°
That I defye bothe swevene and dreem."
And with that word he fleigh° down fro the beem,   flew
For it was day, and eek his hennes alle,
And with a "chuk" he gan hem for to calle,
355 For he hadde founde a corn lay in the yeerd.
Real° he was, he was namore aferd:°   regal / afraid
He fethered[4] Pertelote twenty time,
And trad[5] hire as ofte er it was prime.
He looketh as it were a grim leoun,
360 And on his toes he rometh up and down:
Him deined[6] nat to sette his foot to grounde.
He chukketh whan he hath a corn yfounde,
And to him rennen° thanne his wives alle.   run
Thus royal, as a prince is in his halle,
365 Leve I this Chauntecleer in his pasture,
And after wol I telle his aventure.
      Whan that the month in which the world bigan,
That highte March, whan God first maked man,
Was compleet, and passed were also,
370 Sin March bigan, thritty days and two,[7]
Bifel that Chauntecleer in al his pride,
His sevene wives walking him biside,
Caste up his yën to the brighte sonne,
That in the signe of Taurus hadde yronne
375 Twenty degrees and oon and somwhat more,
And knew by kinde,° and by noon other lore,   nature
That it was prime, and crew with blisful stevene.°   voice
"The sonne," he saide, "is clomben[8] up on hevene
Fourty degrees and oon and more, ywis.
380 Madame Pertelote, my worldes blis,
Herkneth thise blisful briddes° how they singe,   birds
And see the fresshe flowres how they springe:
Ful is myn herte of revel and solas."
But sodeinly him fil° a sorweful cas,°   befell / chance
385 For evere the latter ende of joye is wo—
God woot that worldly joye is soone ago,
And if a rethor° coude faire endite,   rhetorician
He in a cronicle saufly° mighte it write,   safely
As for a soverein notabilitee.[9]
390 Now every wis man lat him herkne me:
This storye is also° trewe, I undertake,   as

2. A tag from the Gospel of St. John which gives the essential premises of Christianity: "In the beginning was the Word."
3. Woman is man's ruination.
4. I.e., embraced.
5. Trod, copulated with; "prime": 9 A.M.
6. He deigned.
7. The rhetorical time-telling is perhaps burlesque; it can be read as yielding the date

April 3, though May 3 seems intended from lines 374–75: on May 3 the sun would have passed some twenty degrees through Taurus (the Bull), the second sign of the zodiac; the sun would be forty degrees from the horizon at 9 o'clock in the morning.
8. Has climbed.
9. Indisputable fact.

As is the book of *Launcelot de Lake*,[1]
That wommen holde in ful greet reverence.
Now wol I turne again to my sentence.°   **main point**

395   A colfox[2] ful of sly iniquitee,
That in the grove hadde woned° yeres three,   **dwelled**
By heigh imaginacion forncast,[3]
The same night thurghout the hegges° brast°   **hedges / burst**
Into the yeerd ther Chauntecleer the faire
400   Was wont, and eek his wives, to repaire;
And in a bed of wortes° stille he lay   **cabbages**
Til it was passed undren° of the day,   **midmorning**
Waiting his time on Chauntecleer to falle,
As gladly doon thise homicides alle,
405   That in await liggen to mordre[4] men.
O false mordrour, lurking in thy den!
O newe Scariot![5] Newe Geniloun!
False dissimilour!° O Greek Sinoun,[6]   **dissembler**
That broughtest Troye al outrely° to sorwe!   **utterly**
410   O Chauntecleer, accursed be that morwe°   **morning**
That thou into the yeerd flaugh° fro the bemes!   **flew**
Thou were ful wel ywarned by thy dremes
That thilke day was perilous to thee;
But what that God forwoot° moot° needes be,   **foreknows / must**
415   After° the opinion of certain clerkes: **according to**
Witnesse on him that any parfit° clerk is   **perfect**
That in scole is greet altercacioun
In this matere, and greet disputisoun,°   **disputation**
And hath been of an hundred thousand men.
420   But I ne can nat bulte° it to the bren,°   **sift / husks**
As can the holy doctour Augustin,
Or Boece, or the bisshop Bradwardin[7]—
Wheither that Goddes worthy forwiting°   **foreknowledge**
Straineth me nedely[8] for to doon a thing
425   ("Nedely" clepe I simple necessitee),
Or elles if free chois be graunted me
To do that same thing or do it nought,
Though God forwoot° it er that I was wrought;   **foreknew**
Or if his witing° straineth neveradeel,   **knowledge**
430   But by necessitee condicionel[9]—
I wol nat han to do of swich matere:
My tale is of a cok, as ye may heere,
That took his conseil of his wif with sorwe,
To walken in the yeerd upon that morwe
435   That he hadde met° the dreem that I you tolde.   **dreamed**
Wommenes conseils been ful ofte colde,[1]
Wommanes conseil broughte us first to wo,
And made Adam fro Paradis to go,
Ther as he was ful merye and wel at ese.
440   But for I noot° to whom it mighte displese   **don't know**

1. Romances of the courteous knight Lancelot of the Lake were very popular.
2. Fox with black markings.
3. Predestined by divine planning.
4. That lie in ambush to murder.
5. Judas Iscariot. "Geniloun" is Ganelon, who betrayed Roland to the Saracens (in the medieval French epic *The Song of Roland*).
6. Sinon, who persuaded the Trojans to take the Greeks' wooden horse into their city—with, of course, the result that the city was destroyed.

7. St. Augustine, Boethius (6th-century Roman philosopher, whose *Consolation of Philosophy* was translated by Chaucer), and Thomas Bradwardine (Archbishop of Canterbury, died 1349) were all concerned with the interrelationship between man's free will and God's foreknowledge.
8. Constrains me necessarily.
9. Boethius' "conditional necessity" permitted a large measure of free will.
1. I.e., baneful.

If I conseil of wommen wolde blame,
Passe over, for I saide it in my game°—   *sport*
Rede auctours where they trete of swich matere,
And what they sayn of wommen ye may heere—
445 Thise been the cokkes wordes and nat mine:
I can noon harm of no womman divine.°   *guess*
    Faire in the sond° to bathe hire merily   *sand*
Lith° Pertelote, and alle hir sustres by,   *lies*
Again° the sonne, and Chauntecleer so free°   *in / noble*
450 Soong° merier than the mermaide in the see—   *sang*
For Physiologus[2] saith sikerly
How that they singen wel and merily.
    And so bifel that as he caste his yë
Among the wortes on a boterflye,°   *butterfly*
455 He was war of this fox that lay ful lowe.
No thing ne liste him[3] thanne for to crowe,
But cride anoon "Cok cok!" and up he sterte,°   *started*
As man that[4] was affrayed in his herte—
For naturelly a beest desireth flee
460 Fro his contrarye[5] if he may it see,
Though he nevere erst° hadde seen it with his yë.   *before*
This Chauntecleer, whan he gan him espye,
He wolde han fled, but that the fox anoon
Saide, "Gentil sire, allas, wher wol ye goon?
465 Be ye afraid of me that am youre freend?
Now certes, I were worse than a feend
If I to you wolde° harm or vilainye.   *meant*
I am nat come youre conseil° for t'espye,   *secrets*
But trewely the cause of my cominge
470 Was only for to herkne how that ye singe:
For trewely, ye han as merye a stevene°   *voice*
As any angel hath that is in hevene.
Therwith ye han in musik more feelinge
Than hadde Boece,[6] or any that can singe.
475 My lord your fader—God his soule blesse!—
And eek youre moder, of hir gentilesse,°   *gentility*
Han in myn hous ybeen, to my grete ese.
And certes sire, ful fain° wolde I you plese.   *gladly*
    "But for men speke of singing, I wol saye,
480 So mote I brouke[7] wel mine yën twaye,
Save ye, I herde nevere man so singe
As dide youre fader in the morweninge.
Certes, it was of herte[8] al that he soong.°   *sang*
And for to make his vois the more strong,
485 He wolde so paine him[9] that with bothe his yën
He moste winke,[1] so loude wolde he cryen;
And stonden on his tiptoon therwithal,
And strecche forth his nekke long and smal;
And eek he was of swich discrecioun
490 That ther nas no man in no regioun
That him in song or wisdom mighte passe.
I have wel rad° in *Daun Burnel the Asse*[2]   *read*

2. Supposed author of a bestiary, a book of
moralized zoology describing both natural and
supernatural animals (including mermaids).
3. He wished.
4. Like one who.
5. I.e., his natural enemy.
6. Boethius also wrote a treatise on music.

7. So might I enjoy the use of.
8. Heartfelt.
9. Take pains.
1. He had to shut his eyes.
2. Master Brunellus, a discontented donkey,
was the hero of a 12th-century satirical poem
by Nigel Wireker.

Among his vers how that ther was a cok,
For a preestes sone yaf him a knok[3]
495 Upon his leg whil he was yong and nice,°   *foolish*
He made him for to lese° his benefice.[4]   *lose*
But certain, ther nis no comparisoun
Bitwixe the wisdom and discrecioun
Of youre fader and of his subtiltee.
500 Now singeth, sire, for sainte° charitee!   *holy*
Lat see, conne° ye youre fader countrefete?"°   *can / imitate*
    This Chauntecleer his winges gan to bete,
As man that coude his traison nat espye,
So was he ravisshed with his flaterye.
505   Allas, ye lordes, many a fals flatour°   *flatterer*
Is in youre court, and many a losengeour,°   *deceiver*
That plesen you wel more, by my faith,
Than he that soothfastnesse° unto you saith!   *truth*
Redeth Ecclesiaste[5] of flaterye.
510 Beeth war, ye lordes, of hir trecherye.
    This Chauntecleer stood hye upon his toos,
Strecching his nekke, and heeld his yën cloos,
And gan to crowe loude for the nones;°   *occasion*
And daun Russel the fox sterte° up atones,   *jumped*
515 And by the gargat° hente° Chauntecleer,   *throat / seized*
And on his bak toward the wode him beer,°   *bore*
For yit ne was ther no man that him sued.°   *followed*
    O destinee that maist nat been eschued!°   *eschewed*
Allas that Chauntecleer fleigh° fro the bemes!   *flew*
520 Allas his wif ne roughte nat of[6] dremes!
And on a Friday fil° al this meschaunce!   *befell*
    O Venus that art goddesse of plesaunce,
Sin that thy servant was this Chauntecleer,
And in thy service dide al his power—
525 More for delit than world[7] to multiplye—
Why woldestou suffre him on thy day[8] to die?
    O Gaufred,[9] dere maister soverein,
That, whan thy worthy king Richard was slain
With shot,[1] complainedest his deeth so sore,
530 Why ne hadde I now thy sentence and thy lore,[2]
The Friday for to chide as diden ye?
For on a Friday soothly slain was he.
Thanne wolde I shewe you how that I coulde plaine°   *lament*
For Chauntecleres drede and for his paine.
535   Certes, swich cry ne lamentacioun
Was nevere of ladies maad whan Ilioun°   *Ilium, Troy*
Was wonne, and Pyrrus[3] with his straite swerd,
Whan he hadde hent° King Priam by the beerd   *seized*
And slain him, as saith us *Eneidos*,[4]
540 As maden alle the hennes in the cloos,°   *yard*
Whan they hadde seen of Chauntecleer the sighte.
    But sovereinly° Dame Pertelote shrighte°   *splendidly / shrieked*

---

3. Because a priest's son gave him a knock.
4. The offended cock neglected to crow so that his master, now grown to manhood, overslept, missing his ordination and losing his benefice.
5. The Book of Ecclesiasticus, in the Apocrypha.
6. Didn't care for.
7. I.e., population.
8. Friday is Venus' day.

9. Geoffrey of Vinsauf, a famous medieval rhetorician, who wrote a lament on the death of Richard I in which he scolded Friday, the day on which the king died.
1. I.e., a missile.
2. Thy wisdom and thy learning.
3. Pyrrhus was the Greek who slew Priam, king of Troy. "Straite": rigorous, unsparing.
4. As the *Aeneid* tells us.

Ful louder than dide Hasdrubales[5] wif
Whan that hir housbonde hadde lost his lif,
545 And that the Romains hadden brend° Cartage: *burned*
She was so ful of torment and of rage°   *madness*
That wilfully unto the fir she sterte,°   *jumped*
And brende hirselven with a stedefast herte.
    O woful hennes, right so criden ye
550 As, whan that Nero brende the citee
Of Rome, criden senatoures wives
For that hir housbondes losten alle hir lives:[6]
Withouten gilt this Nero hath hem slain.
Now wol I turne to my tale again.
555   The sely° widwe and eek hir doughtres two   *innocent*
Herden thise hennes crye and maken wo,
And out at dores sterten° they anoon,   *leaped*
And sien° the fox toward the grove goon,   *saw*
And bar upon his bak the cok away,
560 And criden, "Out, harrow,° and wailaway,   *help*
Ha, ha, the fox," and after him they ran,
And eek with staves many another man;
Ran Colle oure dogge, and Talbot and Gerland,[7]
And Malkin with a distaf in hir hand,
565 Ran cow and calf, and eek the verray hogges,
Sore aferd° for berking of the dogges   *frightened*
And shouting of the men and wommen eke.
They ronne° so hem thoughte hir herte breke;[8]   *ran*
They yelleden as feendes doon in helle;
570 The dokes° criden as men wolde hem quelle;°   *ducks / kill*
The gees for fere flowen° over the trees;   *flew*
Out of the hive cam the swarm of bees;
So hidous was the noise, a, benedicite,°   *bless me*
Certes, he Jakke Straw[9] and him meinee°   *company*
575 Ne made nevere shoutes half so shrille
Whan that they wolden any Fleming kille,
As thilke day was maad upon the fox:
Of bras they broughten bemes° and of box,°   *trumpets / boxwood*
Of horn, of boon,° in whiche they blewe and pouped,[1] *bone*
580 And therwithal they skriked° and they houped°—   *shrieked / whooped*
It seemed as that hevene sholde falle.
    Now goode men, I praye you herkneth alle:
Lo, how Fortune turneth° sodeinly   *reverses, overturns*
The hope and pride eek of hir enemy.
585 This cok that lay upon the foxes bak,
In al his drede unto the fox he spak,
And saide, "Sire, if that I were as ye,
Yit sholde I sayn, as wis° God helpe me,   *surely*
'Turneth ayain, ye proude cherles alle!
590 A verray pestilence upon you falle!
Now am I come unto this wodes side,
Maugree your heed,[2] the cok shal here abide.
I wol him ete, in faith, and that anoon.'"
    The fox answerde, "In faith, it shal be doon."

5. Hasdrubal was king of Carthage when it was destroyed by the Romans.
6. According to the legend, Nero not only set fire to Rome (in A.D. 64) but also put many senators to death.
7. Two other dogs.
8. Would break.
9. One of the leaders of the Peasant's Revolt in 1381, which was partially directed against the Flemings living in London.
1. Tooted.
2. Despite your head—i.e., despite anything you can do.

595 And as he spak that word, al sodeinly
　　The cok brak from his mouth deliverly,°　　　　*nimbly*
　　And hye upon a tree he fleigh° anoon.　　　　　*flew*
　　　　And whan the fox sawgh that he was agoon,
　　"Allas," quod he, "O Chauntecleer, allas!
600 I have to you," quod he, "ydoon trespas,
　　In as muche as I maked you aferd
　　Whan I you hente° and broughte out of the yeerd.　　*seized*
　　But sire, I dide it in no wikke° entente:　　　　*wicked*
　　Come down, and I shal telle you what I mente.
605 I shal saye sooth to you, God help me so."
　　　　"Nay thanne," quod he, "I shrewe° us bothe two:　　*curse*
　　But first I shrewe myself, bothe blood and bones,
　　If thou bigile me ofter than ones;
　　Thou shalt namore thurgh thy flaterye
610 Do° me to singe and winken with myn yë.　　　　*cause*
　　For he that winketh whan he sholde see,
　　Al wilfully, God lat him nevere thee."°　　　　*thrive*
　　　　"Nay," quod the fox, "but God yive him meschaunce
　　That is so undiscreet of governaunce°　　　　*self-control*
615 That jangleth° whan he sholde holde his pees."　　*chatters*
　　　　Lo, swich it is for to be recchelees°　　　　*careless*
　　And necligent and truste on flaterye.
　　But ye that holden this tale a folye
　　As of a fox, or of a cok and hen,
620 Taketh the moralitee, goode men.
　　For Saint Paul saith that al that writen is
　　To oure doctrine it is ywrit, ywis:[3]
　　Taketh the fruit, and lat the chaf be stille.
　　Now goode God, if that it be thy wille,
625 As saith my lord, so make us alle goode men,
　　And bringe us to his hye blisse. Amen.

To Rosamond

　　Madame, ye been of alle beautee shrine
　　As fer as cercled is the mapemounde:[4]
　　For as the crystal glorious ye shine,
　　And like ruby been youre cheekes rounde.
5　Therwith ye been so merye and so jocounde
　　That at a revel whan that I see you daunce
　　It is an oinement unto my wounde,
　　Though ye to me ne do no daliaunce.[5]

　　For though I weepe of teres ful a tine,°　　　　*tub*
10　Yit may that wo myn herte nat confounde;
　　Youre semy° vois, that ye so smale outtwine,[6]　　*small*
　　Maketh my thought in joye and blis habounde:°　　*abound*
　　So curteisly I go with love bounde
　　That to myselfe I saye in my penaunce,[7]
15　"Suffiseth me to love you, Rosemounde,
　　Though ye to me ne do no daliaunce."

---

3. See Romans xv.4.
4. I.e., to the farthest circumference of the map of the world.

5. I.e., show me no encouragement.
6. That you so delicately spin out.
7. I.e., pangs of unrequited love.

Was nevere pik walwed in galauntine[8]
As I in love am walwed and ywounde,
For which ful ofte I of myself divine
20 That I am trewe Tristam[9] the secounde;
My love may not refreide nor affounde;[1]
I brenne° ay in amorous plesaunce: *burn*
Do what you list, I wol youre thral° be founde,   *slave*
Though ye to me ne do no daliaunce.

Truth

Flee fro the prees° and dwelle with soothfastnesse;   *crowd*
Suffise° thyn owene thing, though it be smal;   *let suffice*
For hoord hath[2] hate, and climbing tikelnesse;°   *insecurity*
Prees hath envye, and wele° blent° overal.   *prosperity / blinds*
5 Savoure° no more than thee bihoove shal;   *relish*
Rule wel thyself that other folk canst rede:°   *advise*
And Trouthe shal delivere,[3] it is no drede.°   *doubt*

Tempest thee nought al crooked to redresse[4]
In trust of hire[5] that turneth as a bal;
10 Muche wele stant in litel bisinesse;[6]
Be war therfore to spurne ayains an al.[7]
Strive nat as dooth the crokke° with the wal.   *pot*
Daunte° thyself that dauntest otheres deede: *master*
And Trouthe shal delivere, it is no drede.

15 That thee is sent, receive in buxomnesse;°   *obedience*
The wrastling for the world axeth° a fal;   *asks for*
Here is noon hoom, here nis but wildernesse:
Forth, pilgrim, forth! Forth, beest, out of thy stall
Know thy countree, looke up, thank God of al.
20 Hold the heigh way and lat thy gost° thee lede: *spirit*
And Trouthe shal delivere, it is no drede.

Therfore, thou Vache,[8] leve thyn olde wrecchednesse
Unto the world; leve[9] now to be thral.
Crye him mercy that of his heigh goodnesse
25 Made thee of nought, and in especial
Draw unto him, and pray in general,
For thee and eek for othere, hevenelich meede:°   *reward*
And Trouthe shal delivere, it is no drede.

Complaint to His Purse

To you, my purs, and to noon other wight,
Complaine I, for ye be my lady dere.
I am so sory, now that ye be light,
For certes, but if[3] ye make me hevy cheere,

---

8. Pike rolled in galantine sauce.
9. The famous lover of Isolt (Iseult, Isolde) in medieval legend, renowned for his constancy.
1. Cool nor chill.
2. Hoarding causes.
3. I.e., truth shall make you free.
4. Do not disturb yourself to straighten all that's crooked.

5. Fortune, who turns like a ball in that she is always presenting a different aspect to men.
6. Peace of mind stands in little anxiety.
7. I.e., to kick against the pricks.
8. Probably Sir Philip de la Vache, with a pun on the French for "cow."
9. I.e., cease.
3. Unless.

5 Me were as lief⁴ be laid upon my beere;°   *bier*
For which unto youre mercy thus I crye:
Beeth hevy again, or elles moot° I die.   *must*

Now voucheth sauf this day er it be night
That I of you the blisful soun may heere,
10 Or see youre colour, lik the sonne bright,
That of yelownesse hadde nevere peere.
Ye be my life, ye be myn hertes steere,°   *rudder, guide*
Queene of confort and of good compaignye:
Beeth hevy again, or elles moot I die.

15 Ye purs, that been to me my lives light
And saviour, as in this world down here,
Out of this tonne⁵ helpe me thurgh your might,
Sith that ye wol nat be my tresorere;°   *disburser*
For I am shave as neigh° as any frere.°   *close / friar*
20 But yit I praye unto youre curteisye:
Beeth hevy again, or elles moot I die.

Envoy to Henry IV

O conquerour of Brutus Albioun,⁶
Which that by line and free eleccioun
Been verray king, this song to you I sende:
25 And ye, that mowen° alle oure harmes amende,   *may*
Have minde upon my supplicacioun.

Against Women Unconstant

Madame, for youre newefangelnesse,⁷
Many a servant have ye put out of grace.
I take my leve of your unstedefastnesse,
For wel I woot,° whil ye have lives space,   *know*
5 Ye can not love ful half yeer in a place,
To newe thing youre lust° is ay° so keene;   *appetite / always*
In stede of blew, thus may ye were al greene.⁸

Right as a mirour nothing may enpresse,
But, lightly as it cometh, so mote° it pace,°   *must / pass*
10 So fareth youre love, youre werkes bereth witnesse.
Ther is no faith that may your herte enbrace;
But, as a wedercok, that turneth his face
With every wind, ye fare, and this is seene;
In stede of blew, thus may ye were al greene.

15 Ye might be shrined, for youre brotelnesse,⁹
Bet than Dalida, Criseide or Candace;¹
For ever in chaunging stant youre sikernesse;°   *constancy*
That tache° may no wight fro your herte arace.°   *blemish / uproot*
If ye lese oon, ye can wel twain purchace.
20 Al light for somer,² ye woot wel what I mene,
In stede of blew, thus may ye were al greene.

4. I'd just as soon.
5. Tun., meaning "predicament."
6. Britain (Albion) was supposed to have been founded by Brutus, the grandson of Aeneas, the founder of Rome.
7. Fondness for novelty.
8. Blue stands for constancy, green for change.
9. Brittleness, fickleness.
1. Respectively, Samson's betrayer (Delilah), Troilus's faithless mistress, and Alexander's temptress to sloth.

Merciless Beauty

1

Youre yën two wol slee° me sodeinly: *slay*
I may the beautee of hem nat sustene,°   *withstand*
So woundeth it thurghout myn herte keene.°   *keenly*

And but° youre word wol helen hastily   *unless*
5 Myn hertes wounde, whil that it is greene,[3]
    Youre yën two wol slee me sodeinly:
    I may the beautee of hem nat sustene.

Upon my trouthe, I saye you faithfully
That ye been of my lif and deeth the queene,
10 For with my deeth the trouthe shal be seene.
    Youre yën two wol slee me sodeinly:
    I may the beautee of hem nat sustene,
    So woundeth it thurghout myn herte keene.

2

So hath youre beautee fro youre herte chaced
15 Pitee, that me ne availeth nought to plaine:°   *complain*
    For Daunger halt[4] youre mercy in his chaine.

Giltelees my deeth thus han ye me purchaced;°   *procured*
I saye you sooth, me needeth nought to feine:°   *dissemble*
    So hath youre beautee fro youre herte chaced
20   Pitee, that me ne availeth nought to plaine.

Allas, that nature hath in you compaced°   *enclosed*
So greet beautee that no man may attaine
To mercy, though he sterve° for the paine.   *die*
    So hath youre beautee fro youre herte chaced
25   Pitee, that me ne availeth nought to plaine:
    For Daunger halt youre mercy in his chaine.

3

Sin I fro Love escaped am so fat,
I nevere thenke° to been in his prison lene: *intend*
Sin I am free, I counte him nat a bene.[5]

30 He may answere and saye right this and that;
I do no fors,[6] I speke right as I mene:
    Sin I fro Love escaped am so fat,
    I nevere thenke to been in his prison lene.

Love hath my name ystrike° out of his sclat,°   *struck / slate*
35 And he is strike out of my bookes clene
For everemo; ther is noon other mene.°   *solution*
    Sin I fro Love escaped am so fat,
    I nevere thenke to been in his prison lene:
    Sin I am free, I counte him nat a bene.

2. To travel "light for summer" as opposed to heavy for winter suggests ease of movement, readiness for change.
3. I.e., fresh.
4. Haughtiness holds.
5. I don't consider him worth a bean.
6. I don't care.

CHARLES D'ORLÉANS
(1391–1465)

My Ghostly Father

My ghostly° father, I me confess,   spiritual
  First to God and then to you,
    That at a window (wot° ye how)   know
I stole a kiss of great sweetness,
5 Which done was out° advisedness,   without
  But it is done, not undone, now,
My ghostly father, I me confess,
  First to God and then to you.
But I restore it shall doubtless
10   Again, if so be that I mow,°   may
  And that, God, I make a vow,
And else I ask forgiveness—
My ghostly father, I me confess,
  First to God and then to you.

The Smiling Mouth

The smiling mouth and laughing eyen gray,
The breastes round and long small armes twain,
  The handes smooth, the sides straight and plain,
Your feetes lit°—what should I further say?   little
5 It is my craft° when ye are far away   practice
  To muse thereon in stinting° of my pain—   soothing
The smiling mouth and laughing eyen gray,
  The breastes round and long small armes twain.
So would I pray you, if I durst or may,
10   The sight to see as I have seen,
  Forwhy° that craft me is most fain,°   because / pleasing
And will be to the hour in which I day°—   die
The smiling mouth and laughing eyen gray,
  The breastes round and long small armes twain.

Oft in My Thought

Oft in my thought full busily have I sought,
  Against the beginning of this fresh new year,
What pretty thing that I best given ought
  To her that was mine hearte's lady dear;
5   But all that thought bitane° is fro° me clear   taken / from
    Since death, alas, hath closed her under clay
And hath this world fornaked° with her here—   stripped bare
    God have her soul, I can no better say.

But for to keep in custom, lo, my thought,
10   And of my seely° service the manere,   simple
In showing als° that I forget her not   also
  Unto each wight I shall to my powere
  This dead[7] her serve with masses and prayere;

---

7. Dead person, the deceased. *Her* is redundant, as is one of the *its* in line 27.

For all too foul a shame were me, mafay,°   *by my faith*
15   Her to forget this time that nigheth near—
God have her soul, I can no better say.

To her profit now nis° there to be bought   *is not*
None other thing all° will I buy it dear;   *although*
Wherefore, thou Lord that lordest all aloft,
20   My deedes take, such as goodness steer,
And crown her, Lord, within thine heavenly sphere
As for most truest lady, may I say,
Most good, most fair, and most benign of cheer°—   *countenance*
God have her soul, I can no better say.

25   When I her praise, or praising of her hear,
Although it whilom° were to me pleasere,   *formerly*
It fill enough it doth mine heart today,
And doth° me wish I clothed had my bier—   *makes*
God have her soul, I can no better say.

ANONYMOUS LYRICS OF THE FIFTEENTH CENTURY

Adam Lay I-bounden

Adam lay i-bounden, bounden in a bond;
Foure thousand winter thought he not too long.
And all was for an apple, an apple that he took,
As clerkes finden written in theire book.

5   Ne hadde the apple take been,[1] the apple taken been,
Ne hadde never our Lady aye been Heaven's queen.
Blessed be the time that apple taken was,
Therefore we may singen, *"Deo gracias!"*[2]

I Sing of a Maiden

I sing of a maiden
That is makeless:°   *mateless, matchless*
King of alle kinges
To° her son she ches.°   *for / chose*

5   He came also° stille   *as*
Where his mother was
As dew in Aprille
That falleth on the grass.

He came also stille
10   To his mother's bower
As dew in Aprille
That falleth on the flower.

He came also stille
Where his mother lay
15   As dew in Aprille
That falleth on the spray.

---

1. I.e., if the apple had not been taken.   2. Thanks be to God.

Mother and maiden
   Was never none but she—
Well may such a lady
20   Godes mother be.

This Endris Night

   This endris[4] night
   I saw a sight,
     A star as bright as day,
    And ever among[5]
5   A maiden sung,
     "Lullay, by, by, lullay."

That lovely lady sat and sung,
   And to her child said,
"My Son, my Brother, my Father dear,
10   Why liest thou thus in hay?
    My sweete brid,°   *bird*
    Thus it is betid,°   *happened*
     Though thou be king verray;°   *in truth*
    But nevertheless
15   I will not cesse°   *cease*
     To sing 'By, by, lullay.' "

The child then spake in his talking,
   And to his mother said,
"I am kenned° for Heaven's King   *known*
20   In crib though I be laid,
    For angels bright
    Done° to me light,   *gave*
     Thou knowest it is no nay;
    And of[6] that sight
25   Thou mayst be light[7]
     To sing 'By, by, lullay.' "

"Now, sweet Son, since thou art king,
   Why art thou laid in stall?
Why ne thou ordained thy bedding
30   In some great kinge's hall?
    Methinketh it is right
    That king or knight
     Should lie in good array,
    And then among°   *in that circumstance*
35   It were no wrong
     To sing 'By, by, lullay.' "

"Mary mother, I am thy child,
   Though I be laid in stall;
Lords and dukes shall worship me,
40   And so shall kinges all.
    Ye shall well see
    That kinges three

4. "This endris": the other.
5. "Ever among": every now and then.

6. I.e., because of.
7. "Thou mayst be light": feel free.

Shall come the Twelfth Day.
For this behest°   *promise*
45   Give me thy breast
    And sing 'By, by, lullay.' "

"Now tell me, sweet Son, I thee pray,
  Thou are me lief° and dear,   *beloved*
How should I keep thee to thy pay°   *liking*
50   And make thee glad of cheer?°   *face*
  For all thy will
  I would fulfill,
    Thou wottest full well in fay,°   *faith*
  And for all this
55   I will thee kiss
    And sing 'By, by, lullay.' "

"My dear mother, when time it be,
  Thou take me up on loft,
And set me upon thy knee,
60   And handle me full soft,
  And in thy arm
  Thou hill° me warm,   *cover*
    And keepe night and day;
  If I weep
65   And may not sleep,
    Then sing 'By, by, lullay.' "

"Now, sweet Son, since it is so,
  That all thing is at thy will,
I pray thee, grante me a boon,
70   If it be both right and skill:°   *reason*
  That child or man
  That will or can
    Be merry upon my day,
  To bliss them bring,
75   And I shall sing
    'Lullay, by, by, lullay.' "

O! Mankind

O! Mankind,
Have in thy mind
My passion° smart,°   *suffering / bitter*
And thou shalt find
5 Me full kind—
Lo! here my heart.

I Have Labored Sore

I have labored sore and suffered death,
And now I rest and draw my breath;
But I shall come and call right soon
Heaven and earth and hell to doom;°   *judgment*
5 And then shall know both devil and man
What I was and what I am.

Jesus' Wounds So Wide

Jesus' wounds so wide
Be wells of life to the good,
Namely° the stround° of° his side
That ran full breme° on the rood.°

5   If thee list to drink,
To flee from the fiends of hell,
Bow thou down to the brink
And meekly taste of the well.

particularly / stream / from
fiercely / cross

I Have a Gentle Cock

I have a gentle° cock,
  Croweth me day;
He doth me risen[8] early
  My matins for to say.

noble

5   I have a gentle cock,
  Comen he is of great;°
His comb is of red coral,
  His tail is of jet.

lofty lineage

I have a gentle cock,
10 Comen he is of kind;°
His comb is of red coral,
  His tail is of inde.°

good stock

indigo

His legges be of azure,
  So gentle and so small;
15 His spurres are of silver white
  Into the wortewale.[9]

His eyen are of crystal,
  Locked° all in amber;
And every night he percheth him
20 In my lady's chamber.

set

Jolly Jankin

"Kyrie, so kyrie,"
Jankin singeth murie,°
With "Aleison."[1]

merrily

As I went on Yule Day
5 In our procession,
Knew I jolly Jankin
By his merry tone.
    Kyrieleison.

8. "Doth me risen": makes me rise.
9. Up to the root.
1. *Kyrie eleison*, a prayer, "Lord have mercy"; the Epistle (line 13), a reading from Paul or one of the Prophets; the *Sanctus* (line 19), a prayer of rejoicing, "Holy, Holy, Holy"; and the *Agnus* (line 29), an invocation of the Lamb of God are early, middle, and late parts of the divine office (line 9) or Mass.

Jankin began the office
10 On the Yule Day,
And yet methinketh it does me good,
So merry gan he say,
   "Kyrieleison."

Jankin read the 'Pistle
15 Full fair and full well,
And yet methinketh it does me good,
As ever have I sel.[2]
   Kyrieleison.

Jankin at the Sanctus
20 Cracketh a merry note,
And yet methinketh it does me good—
I payed for his coat.
   Kyrieleison.

Jankin cracketh notes
25 An hundred on a knot,°   *at a time*
And yet he hacketh° them smaller   *chops up*
Than wortes° to the pot.   *herbs*
   Kyrieleison.

Jankin at the Agnus
30 Beareth the pax-bred;[3]
He twinkled but said nought,
And on my foot he tread.
   Kyrieleison.

Benedicamus Domino,[4]
35 Christ from shame me shield;
Deo gracias thereto—[5]
Alas! I go with child.
   Kyrieleison.

God, That Madest All Things

God, that madest all things of nought[3]
And with thy precious blood us bought,
   Mercy, help, and grace.
As thou art very god and man,
5 And of thy side thy blood ran,
   Forgive us our trespass.
The world, our flesh, the fiend our foe
Maketh us mis-think, mis-speak, mis-do—
   All thus we fall in blame.
10 Of all our sinnes, less and more,
Sweete Jesu, us rueth sore.
   Mercy, for thine holy name.

---

2. I.e., as ever I (hope to) have good luck.
3. A tablet ("bred": board) bearing a representation of the Crucifixion, kissed by the priests celebrating the Mass, then by the congregation. "Pax": (the kiss of) peace.
4. Let us bless the Lord.
5. Thanks be to God, as well.
3. I.e., from nothing.

I Wend to Death

I wend to death, knight stith in stour;[4]
Through fight in field I won the flower;
No fights me taught the death to quell—
I wend to death, sooth I you tell.

5 I wend to death, a king iwis;°   indeed
What helpes honor or worlde's bliss?
Death is to man the kinde° way—   natural
I wende to be clad in clay.

I wend to death, clerk full of skill,
10 That could with words men mar and dill.[5]
Soon has me made the death an end.
Be ware with[6] me! To death I wend.

Timor Mortis

In what estate° so ever I be   condition
Timor mortis conturbat me.[7]

As I went on a merry morning,
I heard a bird both weep and sing.
5 This was the tenor of her talking:
"*Timor mortis conturbat me.*"

I asked that bird what she meant.
"I am a musket° both fair and gent;°   male sparrowhawk / gentle
For dread of death I am all shent.:°   ruined
10 *Timor mortis conturbat me.*

"When I shall die, I know no day;
What country or place I cannot say;
Wherefore this song sing I may:
Timor mortis conturbat me.

15 "Jesu Christ, when he should die,
To his Father he gan say,
'Father,' he said, 'in Trinity,
Timor mortis conturbat me.'

"All Christian people, behold and see:
20 This world is but a vanity
And replete with necessity.
Timor mortis conturbat me.

"Wake I or sleep, eate or drink,
When I on my last end do think,
25 For greate fear my soul do shrink:
Timor mortis conturbat me.

---

4. "Stith in stour": stout in battle.
5. Mar and keep secret; i.e., expose or conceal.
6. "Be ware with": take warning from.
7. The title phrase comes from the Office of the Dead: "*Peccantem me quotidie et non poenitentem timor mortis conturbat me. Quia in inferno nulla est redemptio misere mei Deus et salva me.*" (Since I have been sinning daily and repenting not, *the fear of death distresses me.* Since in hell there is no redemption, have pity on me, God, and save me.)

"God grant us grace him for to serve,
And be at our end when we sterve,°   *die*
And from the fiend he us preserve.
30   *Timor mortis conturbat me.*

A God and Yet a Man?

A god and yet a man?
   A maid and yet a mother?
Wit wonders what wit can
   Conceive this or the other.

5   A god and can he die?
   A dead man, can he live?
What wit can well reply?
   What reason reason give?

God, truth itself, doth teach it.
10   Man's wit sinks too far under
By reason's power to reach it.
   Believe and leave° to wonder.   *cease*

The Corpus Christi[8] Carol

Lully, lullay, lully, lullay,
   The falcon hath born my make° away.   *mate*

He bore him up, he bore him down,
He bore him into an orchard brown.

5   In that orchard there was a hall
That was hanged with purple and pall.°   *rich fabric*

And in that hall there was a bed,
It was hanged with gold so red.

And in that bed there lieth a knight,
10   His woundes bleeding day and night.

By that bed's side there kneeleth a may°   *maiden*
And she weepeth both night and day.

And by that bed's side there standeth a stone,
Corpus Christi written thereon.

Western Wind

Western wind, when will thou blow,
   The small rain down can rain?
Christ, if my love were in my arms
   And I in my bed again!

8. "Corpus Christi": the body of Christ.

A Lyke-Wake[9] Dirge

This ae° night, this ae night,   one
  Every night and all,
Fire and sleet[1] and candle-light,
  And Christ receive thy saul.°   soul

5 When thou from hence away are past,
To Whinny-muir[2] thou comest at last:

If ever thou gavest hosen and shoon,
Sit thee down and put them on:

If hosen and shoon thou ne'er gavest nane,
10 The whins shall prick thee to the bare bane:

From Whinny-muir when thou mayst pass,
To Brig° o' Dread thou comest at last: bridge

From Brig o' Dread when thou mayst pass,
To purgatory fire thou comest at last:

15 If ever thou gavest meat or drink,
The fire shall never make thee shrink:

If meat or drink thou ne'er gavest nane,
The fire will burn thee to the bare bane:

This ae night, this ae night,
20 Fire and sleet and candle-light,

Jolly Good Ale and Old

Back and side go bare, go bare,
  Both foot and hand go cold;
But, belly, God send thee good ale enough,
  Whether it be new or old.

5 I cannot eat but little meat,
  My stomach is not good;
But sure I think that I can drink
  With him that wears a hood.[3]
Though I go bare, take ye no care,
10 I am nothing a-cold;
I stuff my skin so full within
  Of jolly good ale and old.

I love no roast but a nut-brown toast,[4]
  And a crab° laid in the fire;   crab apple
15 A little bread shall do me stead,°   service
  Much bread I not desire.

---

9. The night watch (*wake*) kept over a corpse (*lyke*).
1. Salt, sometimes placed with earth on the breast of the dead as emblematic of soul and body.

2. Prickly-moor. *Whin* is a name given to various prickly shrubs: furze, heather, buckthorn.
3. I.e., as much as any friar.
4. Used as a sop with ale or wine.

No frost nor snow, no wind, I trow,°   *trust*
    Can hurt me if it would,
I am so wrapped and throughly° lapped°   *thoroughly / swathed*
20   Of° jolly good ale and old.   *in*

And Tib, my wife, that as her life
    Loveth well good ale to seek,
Full oft drinks she till ye may see
    The tears run down her cheek.
25 Then doth she troll° to me the bowl,   *pass*
    Even as a maltworm° should,   *toper*
And saith, "Sweetheart, I took my part
    Of this jolly good ale and old."

Now let them drink till they nod and wink,
30   Even as good fellows should do;
They shall not miss to have the bliss
    Good ale doth bring men to.
And all poor souls that have scoured bowls
    Or have them lustily trolled—
35 God save the lives of them and their wives,
    Whether they be young or old.

WILLIAM DUNBAR
(ca. 1460–ca. 1525)

Lament for the Makaris°   *poets*

I that in heill° was and gladness,   *health*
Am troublit now with great seikness,
And feeblit with infirmity:
    Timor Mortis conturbat me.[1]

5 Our plesance here is all vain-glory
This false warld is bot transitory,
The flesh is brukill,° the Fiend is sle;°   *frail/sly*
    Timor Mortis conturbat me.

The state of man dois change and vary,
10 Now sound, now seik, now blyth, now sary,
Now dansand merry, now like to die;
    Timor Mortis conturbat me.

No state in erd here standis siccar;°   *securely*
As with the wind wavis the wicker,°   *willow*
15 Wavis this warldis vanitie;
    Timor Mortis conturbat me.

Unto the deid gois all Estatis,
Princes, Prelatis, and Potestatis,°   *potentates*
Baith rich and puir of all degree;
20   *Timor Mortis conturbat me.*

---

1. "The fear of death confounds me," a line from the Office for the Dead. Cf. the anon- ymous 15th-century poem with the same re- frain on p. **24**.

He takis the knichtis into the field,
Enarmit under helm and shield;
Victor he is at all mêlée;
  Timor Mortis conturbat me.

25 That strang unmerciful tyrand
Takis on the moderis breist soukand°   *sucking*
The babe, full of benignite;
  Timor Mortis conturbat me.

He takis the champion in the stour,°   *battle*
30 The capitane closit in the tour,
The lady in bour full of beautie;
  Timor Mortis conturbat me.

He sparis no lord for his puissance,
Na clerk° for his intelligence;   *scholar*
35 His awful straik may no man flee;
  Timor Mortis conturbat me.

Art magicianis, and astrologis,°   *astrologers*
Rethoris,° logicianis, and theologis,   *rhetoricians*
Them helpis no conclusionis sle;
40 *Timor Mortis conturbat me.*

In medicine the most° practicianis,   *greatest*
Leechis,° surigianis, and phisicianis,   *doctors*
Them-self fra deid° may not supple;°   *death/help*
  Timor Mortis conturbat me.

45 I see that makaris amang the lave°   *remainder*
Playis here their pageant, syne° gois to grave; *then*
Sparit is nocht their facultie;
  Timor Mortis conturbat me.

He has done piteously devour
50 The noble Chaucer, of makaris flour,
The Monk of Bery, and Gower, all three;
  Timor Mortis conturbat me.

The gude Sir Hew of Eglintoun,
And eik° Heriot, and Wintoun,   *also*
55 He has ta'en out of this countrie;
  Timor Mortis conturbat me.

That scorpion fell has done infec'
Maister John Clerk and James Affleck,
Fra ballad-making and tragedie;
60 *Timor Mortis conturbat me.*

Holland and Barbour he has bereavit;
Alas! that he nought with us leavit
Sir Mungo Lockhart of the Lea;
  Timor Mortis conturbat me.

2. A hero of Arthurian romance.

65   Clerk of Tranent eke he has ta'en,
      That made the Aunteris° of Gawain; ²   *adventures*
      Sir Gilbert Hay endit has he;
        Timor Mortis conturbat me.

      He has Blind Harry, and Sandy Traill
70   Slain with his shour of mortal hail,
      Whilk° Patrick Johnstoun micht nocht flee;   *which*
        Timor Mortis conturbat me.

      He has reft° Merser endite,°   *taken from/talent*
      That did in luve so lively write,
75   So short, so quick, of sentence hie;
        Timor Mortis conturbat me.

      He has ta'en Roull of Aberdeen,
      And gentle Roull of Corstorphin;
      Two better fellowis did no man see;
80   *Timor Mortis conturbat me.*

      In Dunfermline he has done roune°   *whisper*
      With Maister Robert Henryson;
      Sir John the Ross embraced has he;
        Timor Mortis conturbat me.

85   And he has now ta'en, last of a',
      Gude gentle Stobo and Quintin Shaw,
      Of wham all wichtis° has pitie: *creatures*
        Timor Mortis conturbat me.

      Gude Maister Walter Kennedy
90   In point of deid lies verily,
      Great ruth° it were that so suld be;   *pity*
        Timor Mortis conturbat me.

      Sen he has all my brether ta'en,
      He will nocht lat me live alane,
95   On force I maun° his next prey be;   *must*
        Timor Mortis conturbat me.

      Sen for the deid remead° is none,   *remedy*
      Best is that we for deid dispone,°   *prepare*
      Eftir our deid that live may we;
100   *Timor Mortis conturbat me.*

                                                                       1508

JOHN SKELTON
(1460–1529)

My Darling Dear, My Daisy Flower

With lullay, lullay, like a child,
Thou sleepest too long, thou art beguiled.

My darling dear, my daisy flower,
 Let me, quod° he, lie in your lap.   *quoth*
5 Lie still, quod she, my paramour,
 Lie still hardely,° and take a nap.   *indeed*
His head was heavy, such was his hap,°   *luck*
All drowsy dreaming, drowned in sleep,
That of his love he took no keep.

10 With ba, ba, ba!¹ and bas,° bas, bas!   *kiss*
 She cherished him both cheek and chin,
That he wist° never where he was: *knew*
 He had forgotten all deadly sin.
 He wanted wit her love to win:
15 He trusted her payment and lost all his pay;
She left him sleeping and stole away.

The rivers rough, the waters wan,
 She sparéd not to wet her feet;
She waded over, she found a man
20 That halséd° her heartily and kissed her sweet: *embraced*
 Thus after her cold she caught a heat.
My love, she said, routeth° in his bed;   *roots*
Ywis° he hath an heavy head.   *for certain*

What dreamest thou, drunkard, drowsy pate?
25 Thy lust° and liking is from thee gone;   *desire*
Thou blinkard blowbowl,² thou wakest too late,
 Behold thou liest, luggard,° alone.   *sluggard*
 Well may thou sigh, well may thou groan,
To deal with her so cowardly:
30 Ywis, pole hatchet,° she bleared thine eye.   *blockhead*

To Mistress Margaret Hussey

Merry Margaret,
 As midsummer flower,
Gentle as falcon
Or hawk of the tower:³
5 With solace and gladness,
Much mirth and no madness,
All good and no badness;
 So joyously,
 So maidenly,
10 So womanly
 Her demeaning
 In every thing,
 Far, far passing
 That I can indite,
15 Or suffice to write
Of Merry Margaret
 As midsummer flower,
Gentle as falcon
Or hawk of the tower.

1. The "by" of *lullaby.*
2. Blinking sot.

3. Hawk trained to fly high (*tower*).

20   As patient and still
And as full of good will
As fair Isaphill,[4]
Coriander,[5]
Sweet pomander,[6]
25   Good Cassander,[7]
Steadfast of thought,
Well made, well wrought,
Far may be sought
Ere that ye can find
30   So courteous, so kind
As Merry Margaret,
    This midsummer flower,
Gentle as falcon
Or hawk of the tower.

KING HENRY VIII
(1491–1547)

Green Groweth the Holly

Green groweth the holly,
So doth the ivy.
Though winter blasts blow never so high,
Green groweth the holly.

5   As the holly groweth green,
    And never changeth hue,
So I am, ever hath been,
    Unto my lady true.

As the holly groweth green
10   With ivy all alone
When flowers cannot be seen
    And greenwood leaves be gone,

Now unto my lady,
    Promise to her I make
15   From all other only
    To her I me betake.

Adieu, mine owne lady,
    Adieu, my speciäll,
Who hath my heart truely,
20   Be sure, and ever shall.

4. Hypsipyle, princess of Lemnos, savior of
her father's life, comforter of the Argives,
mother of twins by Jason.
5. An aromatic herb.
6. A mixture of perfumed or aromatic sub-
stances made into a ball.
7. Cassandra, daughter of Priam and Hecuba;
according to myth her beauty bedazzled Apollo
himself, who conferred on her the gift of
prophecy.

POPULAR BALLADS

Riddles Wisely Expounded[1]

1

There was a knicht riding frae° the east,   *from*
  Sing the cather banks, the bonnie brume[2]
Wha had been wooing at monie a place.
  And ye may beguile a young thing soon.

2

5 He came unto a widow's door,
And speird° where her three dochters were.   *asked*

3

"The auldest ane's to a washing gane,
The second's to a baking gane.

4

The youngest ane's to a wedding gane,
10 And it will be nicht or° she be hame."   *ere*

5

He sat him doun upon a stane,
Till thir° three lasses came tripping hame.   *these*

6

The auldest ane's to the bed making,
And the second ane's to the sheet spreading.

7

15 The youngest ane was bauld and bricht,
And she was to lie wi' this unco° knicht.   *stranger*

8

"Gin° ye will answer me questions ten,   *if*
The morn ye sall° be made my ain.   *shall*

9

"O what is higher nor the tree?
20 And what is deeper nor the sea?

10

"Or what is heavier nor the lead?
And what is better nor the bread?

11

"O what is whiter nor the milk?
Or what is safter nor the silk?

12

25 "Or what is sharper nor a thorn?
Or what is louder nor a horn?

13

"Or what is greener nor the grass?
Or what is waur° nor a woman was?"   *worse*

14

"O heaven is higher nor the tree,
30 And hell is deeper nor the sea.

1. Ballad versions are conventionally identified by the number and letter assigned them in the monumental collection, *The English and Scottish Popular Ballads*, 1892–98, edited by Francis James Child. "Riddles Wisely Expounded" is No. 1.C.
2. Hemp (cather) and broom are wildflowers to which folklore attributed properties pertinent to young love. Hempseed, sown on Hallowe'en, permitted a sight, over the left shoulder, of one's true love; broom, associated with witchcraft, provided oracular revelation in matters of the heart.

15
"O sin is heavier nor the lead,
The blessing's better nor the bread.
16
"The snaw is whiter nor the milk,
And the down is safter nor the silk.
17
35 "Hunger is sharper nor a thorn,
And shame is louder nor a horn.
18
"The pies³ are greener nor the grass,
And Clootie's⁴ waur nor a woman was."
19
As soon as she the fiend did name,
40 He flew awa' in a blazing flame.

Lord Randal⁵

1
"O where ha' you been, Lord Randal, my son?
And where ha' you been, my handsome young man?"
"I ha' been at the greenwood; mother, mak my bed soon,
For I'm wearied wi' huntin', and fain wad° lie down."   *would*
2
5 "And wha met ye there, Lord Randal, my son?
And wha met you there, my handsome young man?"
"O I met wi' my true-love; mother, mak my bed soon,
For I'm wearied wi' huntin', and fain wad lie down."
3
"And what did she give you, Lord Randal, my son?
10 And what did she give you, my handsome young man?"
"Eels fried in a pan; mother, mak my bed soon,
For I'm wearied wi' huntin', and fain wad lie down."
4
"And wha gat your leavin's, Lord Randal, my son?
And wha gat your leavin's, my handsome young man?"
15 "My hawks and my hounds; mother, mak my bed soon,
For I'm wearied wi' huntin', and fain wad lie down."
5
"And what becam of them, Lord Randal, my son?
And what becam of them, my handsome young man?"
"They stretched their legs out and died; mother, mak my bed soon,
20 For I'm wearied wi' huntin', and fain wad lie down."
6
"O I fear you are poisoned, Lord Randal, my son!
I fear you are poisoned, my handsome young man!"
"O yes, I am poisoned; mother, mak my bed soon,
For I'm sick at the heart, and I fain wad lie down."
7
25 "What d' ye leave to your mother, Lord Randal, my son?
What d'ye leave to your mother, my handsome young man?"
"Four and twenty milk kye°; mother, mak my bed soon,   *kine, cattle*
For I'm sick at the heart, and I fain wad lie down."

---

3. A name given to various species of wood-pecker.
4. Like "Hornie" and "Old Nick," a familiar name for the devil.
5. Child, No. 12.A.

8

"What d' ye leave to your sister, Lord Randal, my son?
30   What d' ye leave to your sister, my handsome young man?"
"My gold and my silver; mother, mak my bed soon,
For I'm sick at the heart, and I fain wad lie down."

9

"What d' ye leave to your brother, Lord Randal, my son?
What d' ye leave to your brother, my handsome young man?"
35   "My houses and my lands; mother, mak my bed soon,
For I'm sick at the heart, and I fain wad lie down."

10

"What d' ye leave to your true-love, Lord Randal, my son?
What d' ye leave to your true-love, my handsome young man?"
"I leave her hell and fire; mother, mak my bed soon,
40   For I'm sick at the heart, and I fain wad lie down."

Edward[6]

1

"Why does your brand° sae° drap wi' bluid,   *sword / so*
        Edward, Edward,
Why does your brand sae drap wi' bluid,
        And why sae sad gang° ye, O?"   *go*
5   "O I ha'e killed my hawk sae guid,
        Mither, mither,
O I ha'e killed my hawk sae guid,
        And I had nae mair but he, O."

2

"Your hawke's bluid was never sae reid,°   *red*
10   Edward, Edward,
Your hawke's bluid was never sae reid,
        My dear son I tell thee, O."
"O I ha'e killed my reid-roan steed,
        Mither, mither,
15   O I ha'e killed my reid-roan steed,
        That erst was sae fair and free, O."

3

"Your steed was auld, and ye ha'e gat mair,
        Edward, Edward,
Your steed was auld, and ye ha'e gat mair,
20   Some other dule° ye drie,° O."   *grief / suffer*
"O I ha'e killed my fader dear,
        Mither, mither,
O I ha'e killed my fader dear,
        Alas, and wae° is me, O!"   *woe*

4

25   "And whatten° penance wul ye drie for that,   *what sort of*
        Edward, Edward?
And whatten penance wul ye dree for that,
        My dear son, now tell me O?"
"I'll set my feet in yonder boat,
30   Mither, mither,
I'll set my feet in yonder boat,
        And I'll fare over the sea, O."

6. Child, No. 13.B.

5

"And what wul ye do wi' your towers and your ha',
 Edward, Edward?
35 And what wul ye do wi' your towers and your ha',
 That were sae fair to see, O?"
"I'll let them stand tul they down fa',
 Mither, mither,
I'll let them stand tul they down fa',
40   For here never mair maun° I be, O."   *must*

6

"And what wul ye leave to your bairns° and your wife, *children*
 Edward, Edward?
And what wul ye leave to your bairns and your wife,
 Whan ye gang over the sea, O?"
45 "The warlde's room,[7] let them beg thrae° life,   *through*
 Mither, mither,
The warlde's room, let them beg thrae life,
 For them never mair wul I see, O."

7

"And what wul ye leave to your ain mither dear,
50   Edward, Edward?
And what wul ye leave to your ain mither dear,
 My dear son, now tell me, O?"
"The curse of hell frae° me sall° ye bear,   *from / shall*
 Mither, mither,
55 The curse of hell frae me sall ye bear,
 Sic° counsels ye gave to me, O."   *such*

Hind Horn[8]

1

In Scotland there was a baby born,
 Lill lal, etc.
And his name it was called young Hind Horn.
 With a fal lal, etc.

2

5 He sent a letter to our king.
That he was in love with his daughter Jean.

3

He's gi'en to her a silver wand,
With seven living lavrocks° sitting thereon.   *larks*

4

She's gi'en to him a diamond ring,
10 With seven bright diamonds set therein.

5

"When this ring grows pale and wan,
You may know by it my love is gane."

6

One day as he looked his ring upon,
He saw the diamonds pale and wan.

7

15 He left the sea and came to land,
And the first that he met was an old beggar man.

8

"What news, what news?" said young Hind Horn;
"No news, no news," said the old beggar man.

---

7. I.e., the wide world.   8. Child, No. 17.A.

9
"No news," said the beggar, "no news at a',
20   But there is a wedding in the king's ha'.

10
"But there is a wedding in the king's ha',
That has halden these forty days and twa."

11
"Will ye lend me your begging coat?
And I'll lend you my scarlet cloak.

12
25   "Will you lend me your beggar's rung?°   *staff*
And I'll gi'e you my steed to ride upon.

13
"Will you lend me your wig o' hair,
To cover mine, because it is fair?"

14
The auld beggar man was bound for the mill,
30   But young Hind Horn for the king's hall.

15
The auld beggar man was bound for to ride,
But young Hind Horn was bound for the bride.

16
When he came to the king's gate,
He sought a drink for Hind Horn's sake.

17
35   The bride came down with a glass of wine,
When he drank out the glass, and dropped in the ring.

18
"O got ye this by sea or land?
Or got ye it off a dead man's hand?"

19
I got not it by sea, I got it by land,
40   And I got it, madam, out of your own hand."

20
"O I'll cast off my gowns of brown,
And beg wi' you frae° town to town.   *from*

21
"O I'll cast off my gowns of red,
And I'll beg wi' you to win my bread."

22
45   "Ye needna cast off your gowns of brown,
For I'll make you lady o' many a town.

23
"Ye needna cast off your gowns of red,
It's only a sham, the begging o' my bread."

24
The bridegroom he had wedded the bride,
50   But young Hind Horn he took her to bed.

St. Stephen and Herod[9]

1
Saint Stephene was a clerk
    In King Herodes' hall,
And served him of° bread and cloth   *for*
    As every king befall.[1]

9. Child, No. 22.

1. "As is appropriate to every king"
[Donaldson's note].

2

5 Stephen out of kitchen came
    With boare's head in hand;
He saw a star was fair and bright
    Over Bedlem° stand.   *Bethlehem*

3

He cast adown the boare's head
10   And went into the hall:
"I forsake thee, King Herodes,
    And thy workes all.

4

"I forsake thee, King Herodes,
    And thy workes all:
15 There is a child in Bedlem born
    Is better than we all."

5

"What aileth thee, Stephene?
    What is thee befall?
Lacketh thee either meat or drink
20   In King Herodes' hall?"

6

"Lacketh me neither meat ne drink
    In King Herodes' hall:
There is a child in Bedlem born
    Is better than we all."

7

25 "What aileth thee, Stephen? Art thou wode,°   *mad*
    Or thou 'ginnest to breed?[2]
Lacketh thee either gold or fee°   *property*
    Or any riche weed?"°   *clothing*

8

"Lacketh me neither gold ne fee
30   Ne none riche weed:
There is a child in Bedlem born
    Shall help us at our need."

9

"That is also sooth,[3] Stephen,
    Also sooth, iwis,°   *certainly*
35 As this capon crowe shall
    That li'th° here in my dish."

10

That word was not so soone said,
    That word in that hall,
The capon crew *Christus natus est*[4]
40   Among the lordes all.

11

"Riseth up, my tormentors,
    By two and all be one,
And leadeth Stephen out of this town,
    And stoneth him with stone."

12

45 Tooken they Stephene,
    And stoned him in the way;°   *road*
And therefore is his even° on   *eve*
    Christe's owen day.

2. I.e., getting strange notions as pregnant women do.   3. "Also sooth": as true.
                                                         4. Christ is born.

The Three Ravens[5]

1

There were three ravens sat on a tree,
   Down a down, hay down, hay down
There were three ravens sat on a tree,
   With a down
5 There were three ravens sat on a tree,
They were as black as they might be.
   With a down derry, derry, derry, down, down.

2

The one of them said to his mate,
"Where shall we our breakfast take?"

3

10 "Down in yonder greene field,
There lies a knight slain under his shield.

4

"His hounds they lie down at his feet,
So well they can their master keep.

5

"His hawks they fly so eagerly,°   *fiercely*
15 There's no fowl dare him come nigh."

6

Down there comes a fallow[6] doe,
As great with young as she might go.

7

She lift up his bloody head
And kissed his wounds that were so red.

8

20 She got him up upon her back
And carried him to earthen lake.°   *pit*

9

She buried him before the prime;[7]
She was dead herself ere even-song time.

10

God send every gentleman
25 Such hawks, such hounds, and such a leman.   *lover, sweetheart*

The Twa Corbies[8]

1

As I was walking all alane,
I heard twa corbies making a mane;°   *moan*
The tane° unto the t'other say,   *one*
"Where sall° we gang° and dine to-day?" *shall / go*

2

5 "In behint you auld fail° dike,   *turf*
I wot there lies a new slain knight;
And naebody kens° that he lies there,   *knows*
But his hawk, his hound, and lady fair.

5. Child, No. 26.
6. A species of deer distinguished by color (fallow: pale brownish or reddish yellow)
from the red deer.
7. The first hour of the day, sunrise.
8. Child, No. 26. "Corbies" are ravens.

3
"His hound is to the hunting gane,
10 His hawk to fetch the wild-fowl hame,
His lady's ta'en another mate,
So we may mak our dinner sweet.

4
"Ye'll sit on his white hause-bane,°
And I'll pike° out his bonny blue een;°
15 Wi' ae° lock o' his gowden° hair
We'll theek° our nest when it grows bare.

neck-bone
pick / eyes
one / golden
thatch

5
"Mony a one for him makes mane,
But nane sall ken where he is gane;
O'er his white banes, when they are bare,
20 The wind sall blaw for evermair."

Dives and Lazarus[4]

1
As it fell out upon a day,
    Rich Dives he made a feast,
And he invited all his friends,
    And gentry of the best.

2
5 Then Lazarus laid him down and down,
    And down at Dives' door:
"Some meat, some drink, brother Dives,
    Bestow upon the poor."

3
"Thou art none of my brother, Lazarus,
10   That lies begging at my door;
No meat nor drink will I give thee,
    Nor bestow upon the poor."

4
Then Lazarus laid him down and down,
    And down at Dives' wall:
15 "Some meat, some drink, brother Dives,
    Or with hunger starve I shall."

5
"Thou art none of my brother, Lazarus,
    That lies begging at my wall;
No meat nor drink will I give thee,
20   But with hunger starve you shall."

6
Then Lazarus laid him down and down,
    And down at Dives' gate:
"Some meat, some drink, brother Dives,
    For Jesus Christ his sake."

7
25 "Thou art none of my brother, Lazarus,
    That lies begging at my gate;
No meat nor drink will I give thee,
    For Jesus Christ his sake."

4. Child, No. 56.A. See Luke xvi.19–31.

8

Then Dives sent out his merry men,
   To whip poor Lazarus away;
30 They had no power to strike a stroke,
   But flung their whips away.

9

Then Dives sent out his hungry dogs,
   To bite him as he lay;
35 They had no power to bite at all,
   But licked his sores away.

10

As it fell out upon a day,
   Poor Lazarus sickened and died;
Then came two angels out of heaven
40   His soul therein to guide.

11

"Rise up, rise up, brother Lazarus,
   And go along with me;
For you've a place prepared in heaven,
   To sit on an angel's knee."

12

45 As it fell out upon a day,
   Rich Dives sickened and died;
Then came two serpents out of hell,
   His soul therein to guide.

13

"Rise up, rise up, brother Dives,
50   And go with us to see
A dismal place, prepared in hell,
   From which thou canst not flee."

14

Then Dives looked up with his eyes,
   And saw poor Lazarus blest:
55 "Give me one drop of water, brother Lazarus,
   To quench my flaming thirst.

15

"Oh had I as many years to abide
   As there are blades of grass,
Then there would be an end, but now
60   Hell's pains will ne'er be past.

16

"Oh was I now but alive again,
   The space of one half hour!
Oh that I had my peace secure!
   Then the devil should have no power."

Sir Patrick Spens[5]

1

The king sits in Dumferling town,
   Drinking the blude-reid° wine: *blood-red*
"O whar will I get guid sailor,
   To sail this ship of mine?"

5. Child, No. 58.A.

2

5 Up and spak an eldern knicht,
    Sat at the king's richt knee:
"Sir Patrick Spens is the best sailor
    That sails upon the sea."

3

The king has written a braid° letter   *broad*
10   And signed it wi' his hand,
And sent it to Sir Patrick Spens,
    Was walking on the sand.

4

The first line that Sir Patrick read,
    A loud lauch° lauched he;   *laugh*
15 The next line that Sir Patrick read,
    The tear blinded his ee.°   *eye*

5

"O wha is this has done this deed,
    This ill deed done to me,
To send me out this time o' the year,
20   To sail upon the sea?

6

"Mak haste, mak haste, my mirry men all,
    Our guid ship sails the morn."
"O say na sae,° my master dear,   *so*
    For I fear a deadly storm.

7

25 "Late, late yestre'en I saw the new moon
    Wi' the auld moon in hir arm,
And I fear, I fear, my dear master,
    That we will come to harm."

8

O our Scots nobles were richt laith°   *loath*
30   To weet° their cork-heeled shoon,°   *wet / shoes*
But lang or° a' the play were played   *before*
    Their hats they swam aboon.[6]

9

O lang, lang may their ladies sit,
    Wi' their fans into their hand,
35 Or ere they see Sir Patrick Spens
    Come sailing to the land.

10

O lang, lang may the ladies stand
    Wi' their gold kems° in their hair,   *combs*
Waiting for their ain dear lords,
40   For they'll see them na mair.

11

Half o'er, half o'er to Aberdour
    It's fifty fadom deep,
And there lies guid Sir Patrick Spens
    Wi' the Scots lords at his feet.

---

6. I.e., their hats swam above (them).

The Unquiet Grave[7]

1

"The wind doth blow today, my love,
    And a few small drops of rain;
I never had but one true-love,
    In cold grave she was lain.

2

"I'll do as much for my true-love
    As any young man may;
I'll sit and mourn all at her grave
    For a twelvemonth and a day."

3

The twelvemonth and a day being up,
    The dead began to speak:
"Oh who sits weeping on my grave,
    And will not let me sleep?"

4

" 'T is I, my love, sits on your grave,
    And will not let you sleep;
For I crave one kiss of your clay-cold lips,
    And that is all I seek."

5

"You crave one kiss of my clay-cold lips,
    But my breath smells earthy strong;
If you have one kiss of my clay-cold lips,
    Your time will not be long.

6

" 'T is down in yonder garden green,
    Love, where we used to walk,
The finest flower that e'er was seen
    Is withered to a stalk.

7

"The stalk is withered dry, my love,
    So will our hearts decay;
So make yourself content, my love,
    Till God calls you away."

The Wife of Usher's Well[8]

1

There lived a wife at Usher's Well,
    And a wealthy wife was she;
She had three stout and stalwart sons,
    And sent them o'er the sea.

2

They hadna been a week from her,
    A week but barely ane,
Whan word came to the carlin° wife   peasant
    That her three sons were gane.

7. Child, No. 78.A.   8. Child, No. 79.A.

3

They hadna been a week from her,
    A week but barely three,
Whan word came to the carlin wife
    That her sons she'd never see.

4

"I wish the wind may never cease,
    Nor fashes° in the flood,   *troubles*
Till my three sons come hame to me,
    In earthly flesh and blood."

5

It fell about the Martinmass,[9]
    When nights are lang and mirk,
The carlin wife's three sons came hame,
    And their hats were o' the birk.°   *birch*

6

It neither grew in syke° nor ditch,   *trench*
    Nor yet in any sheugh;°   *furrow*
But at the gates o' Paradise,
    That birk grew fair eneugh.

7

"Blow up the fire, my maidens,
    Bring water from the well;
For a' my house shall feast this night,
    Since my three sons are well."

8

And she has made to them a bed,
    She's made it large and wide,
And she's ta'en her mantle her about,
    Sat down at the bed-side.

9

Up then crew the red, red cock,
    And up and crew the gray;
The eldest to the youngest said,
    " 'T is time we were away."

10

The cock he hadna crawed but once,
    And clapped his wings at a',
When the youngest to the eldest said,
    "Brother, we must awa'.

11

"The cock doth craw, the day doth daw,
    The channerin'° worm doth chide;   *fretting*
Gin° we be missed out o' our place,   *if*
    A sair° pain we maun° bide.   *sore / must*

12

"Fare ye weel, my mother dear!
    Fareweel to barn and byre!°   *cowhouse*
And fare ye weel, the bonny lass,
    That kindles my mother's fire!"

9. The feast of St. Martin (the martyred Pope Martin I, died 655), November 11.

Bonny Barbara Allan[1]

1

It was in and about the Martinmas[2] time,
  When the green leaves were a falling,
That Sir John Græme, in the West Country,
  Fell in love with Barbara Allan.

2

5 He sent his man down through the town,
  To the place where she was dwelling:
"O haste and come to my master dear,
  Gin° ye be Barbara Allan."   *if*

3

O hooly,° hooly rose she up,   *slowly, gently*
10 To the place where he was lying,
And when she drew the curtain by:
  "Young man, I think you're dying."

4

"O it's I'm sick, and very, very sick,
  And 'tis a' for Barbara Allan."
15 "O the better for me ye s'° never be,   *ye shall*
  Though your heart's blood were a-spilling.

5

"O dinna° ye mind, young man," said she,   *don't*
  "When ye was in the tavern a drinking,
That ye made the healths gae° round and round,   *go*
20 And slighted Barbara Allan?"

6

He turned his face unto the wall,
  And death was with him dealing:
"Adieu, adieu, my dear friends all,
  And be kind to Barbara Allan."

7

25 And slowly, slowly raise she up,
  And slowly, slowly left him,
And sighing said, she could not stay,
  Since death of life had reft him.

8

She had not gane a mile but twa,
30 When she heard the dead-bell ringing,
And every jow° that the dead-bell geid,°   *stroke / gave*
  It cried, "Woe to Barbara Allan!"

9

"O mother, mother, make my bed!
  O make it saft and narrow!
35 Since my love died for me to-day,
  I'll die for him to-morrow."

---

1. Child, No. 84.A.
2. The feast of St. Martin (the martyred   Pope Martin I, died 655), November 11.

Johnie Armstrong[4]

1

There dwelt a man in fair Westmoreland,
   Johnie Armstrong men did him call,
He had neither lands nor rents coming in,
   Yet he kept eight score men in his hall.

2

5 He had horse and harness for them all,
   Goodly steeds were all milk-white;
O the golden bands an about their necks,
   And their weapons, they were all alike.

3

News then was brought unto the king
10   That there was sic° a one as he,   *such*
That livéd lyke a bold outlaw,
   And robbéd all the north country.

4

The king he writ an a letter then,
   A letter which was large and long;
15 He signéd it with his owne hand,
   And he promised to do him no wrong.

5

When this letter came Johnie untill,
   His heart it was as blythe as birds on the tree:
"Never was I sent for before any king,
20   My father, my grandfather, nor none but me.

6

"And if we go the king before,
   I would we went most orderly;
Every man of you shall have his scarlet cloak,
   Laced with silver laces three.

7

25 "Every one of you shall have his velvet coat,
   Laced with silver lace so white;
O the golden bands an about your necks,
   Black hats, white feathers, all alike."

8

By the morrow morning at ten of the clock,
30   Towards Edinburgh gone was he,
And with him all his eight score men;
   Good Lord, it was a goodly sight for to see!

9

When Johnie came before the king,
   He fell down on his knee;
35 "O pardon, my sovereign leige," he said,
   "O pardon my eight score men and me!"

10

"Thou shalt have no pardon, thou traitor strong,
  For thy eight score men nor thee;
For tomorrow morning by ten of the clock,
40   Both thou and them shall hang on the gallow-tree."

11

But Johnie looked over his left shoulder,
  Good Lord, what a grevious look looked he!
Saying, "Asking grace of a graceless face—
  Why there is none for you nor me."

12

45 But Johnie had a bright sword by his side,
  And it was made of the metal so free,[5]
That had not the king stepped his foot aside,
  He had smitten his head from his fair body.

13

Saying, "Fight on, my merry men all,
50 And see that none of you be ta'en;
For rather than men shall say we were hanged,
  Let them report how we were slain."

14

Then, God wot, fair Edinburgh rose,
  And so beset poor Johnie round,
55 That fourscore and ten of Johnie's best men
  Lay gasping all upon the ground.

15

Then like a mad man Johnie laid about,
  And like a mad man then fought he,
Until a false Scot came Johnie behind,
60 And run him through the fair body.

16

Saying, "Fight on, my merry men all,
  And see that none of you be ta'en;
For I will stand by and bleed but awhile,
  And then will I come and fight again."

17

65 News then was brought to young Johnie Armstrong,
  As he stood by his nurse's knee,
Who vowed if e'er he lived for to be a man,
  O' the treacherous Scots revenged he'd be.

Mary Hamilton[6]

1

Word's gane to the kitchen,
  And word's gane to the ha',
That Marie Hamilton gangs° wi' bairn°   *goes / child*
  To the hichest° Stewart of a'.   *highest*

2

5 He's courted her in the kitchen,
  He's courted her in the ha',
He's courted her in the laigh cellar,[7]
  And that was warst of a'.

---

5. "Free" has a range of meanings: noble, ready, workable.

6. Child, No. 173.A.
7. "Laigh cellar": low cellar, basement.

3

She's tied it in her apron
10   And she's thrown it in the sea;
Says, "Sink ye, swim ye, bonny wee babe!
    You'll ne'er get mair o' me."

4

Down then cam the auld queen,
    Goud° tassels tying her hair: *gold*
15 "O Marie, where's the bonny wee babe
    That I heard greet sae sair?"[8]

5

"There was never a babe intill° my room,   *in*
    As little designs to be;
It was but a touch o' my sair side,
20   Come o'er my fair body."

6

"O Marie, put on your robes o' black,
    Or else your robes o' brown,
For ye maun° gang wi' me the night,   *must*
    To see fair Edinbro' town."

7

25 "I winna° put on my robes o' black,   *won't*
    Nor yet my robes o' brown;
But I'll put on my robes o' white,
    To shine through Edinbro' town."

8

When she gaed° up the Cannogate,[9]   *went*
30   She laughed loud laughters three;
But when she cam down the Cannogate
    The tear blinded her ee.°   *eye*

9

When she gaed up the Parliament stair,
    The heel cam aff her shee;
35 And lang or° she cam down again   *before*
    She was condemned to dee.

10

When she cam down the Cannogate,
    The Cannogate sae free,
Many a lady looked o'er her window,
40   Weeping for this lady.

11

"Ye need nae weep for me," she says,
    "Ye need nae weep for me;
For had I not slain mine own sweet babe,
    This death I wadna dee.

12

45 "Bring me a bottle of wine," she says,
    "The best that e'er ye ha'e,
That I may drink to my weil-wishers,
    And they may drink to me.

---

8. "Greet sae sair": cry so sorely.
9. The Cannogate is the Edinburgh street leading uphill from Holyrood House (where the queen and the "four Maries" of line 69 lived) to the Tolbooth, which was both jail and judicial chamber and, on occasion, the place where Parliament (line 33) sat.

13

"Here's a health to the jolly sailors,
50   That sail upon the main;
    Let them never let on to my father and mother
        But what I'm coming hame.

14

"Here's a health to the jolly sailors,
        That sail upon the sea;
55 Let them never let on to my father and mother
        That I cam here to dee.

15

"Oh little did my mother think,
        The day she cradled me,
    What lands I was to travel through,
60   What death I was to dee.

16

"Oh little did my father think,
        The day he held up me,
    What lands I was to travel through,
        What death I was to dee.

17

65 "Last night I washed the queen's feet,
        And gently laid her down;
    And a' the thanks I've gotten the night[1]
        To be hanged in Edinbro' town!

18

    "Last night there was four Maries,
70   The night there'll be but three;
    There was Marie Seton, and Marie Beton,
        And Marie Carmichael, and me."

Bonnie George Campbell[2]

1

High upon Highlands,
    And laigh° upon Tay,[3]   *low*
Bonnie George Campbell
    Rode out on a day.

2

5 He saddled, he bridled,
    And gallant rode he,
And hame cam his guid horse,
    But never cam he.

3

Out cam his mother dear,
10   Greeting° fu' sair,°   *weeping / sore[ly]*
And out cam his bonnie bride,
    Riving° her hair.   *tearing*

4

"The meadow lies green,
    The corn is unshorn,
15 But bonnie George Campbell
    Will never return."

1. I.e., tonight.
2. Child, No. 210.C.
3. The longest river in Scotland, coming down from the Highlands into the Lowlands and entering the North Sea at Perth.

5

Saddled and bridled
  And booted rode he,
A plume in his helmet,
20   A sword at his knee.

6

But toom° cam his saddle,   *empty*
  All bloody to see,
Oh, hame cam his guid horse,
  But never cam he!

Get Up and Bar the Door[4]

1

It fell about the Martinmas[5] time,
  And a gay time it was then,
When our goodwife got puddings to make,
  And she's boiled them in the pan.

2

5   The wind sae° cauld blew south and north,   *so*
  And blew into the floor;
Quoth our goodman to our goodwife,
  "Gae° out and bar the door."   *go*

3

"My hand is in my hussyfskap.°   *housewifery*
10   Goodman, as ye may see;
An° it should nae be barred this hundred year,   *if*
  It s'° no be barred for me."   *shall*

4

They made a paction 'tween them twa,
  They made it firm and sure,
15   That the first word whae'er should speak,
  Should rise and bar the door.

5

Then by there came two gentlemen,
  At twelve o'clock at night,
And they could neither see house nor hall,
20   Nor coal nor candle-light.

6

"Now whether is this a rich man's house,
  Or whether is it a poor?"
But ne'er a word wad° ane o' them speak,   *would*
  For barring of the door.

7

25   And first they ate the white puddings,
  And then they ate the black;
Though muckle° thought the goodwife to hersel,   *much, a lot*
  Yet ne'er a word she spak.

8

Then said the one unto the other,
30   "Here, man, tak ye my knife;
Do ye tak aff° the auld man's beard,   *off*
  And I'll kiss the goodwife."

---

4. Child, No. 275.A.
5. The feast of St. Martin (the martyred Pope Martin I, died 655), November 11.

9

"But there's nae water in the house,
    And what shall we do then?"
35   "What ails ye at⁶ the pudding-broo,°   *-broth*
    That boils into the pan?"

10

O up then started our goodman,
    An angry man was he:
"Will ye kiss my wife before my een,°   *eyes*
40   And scad° me wi' pudding-bree?"°   *scald / -broth*

11

Then up and started our goodwife,
    Gied° three skips on the floor: *gave*
"Goodman, you've spoken the foremost word,
    Get up and bar the door."

The Bitter Withy

1

As it fell out on a holy day,
    The drops of rain did fall, did fall,
Our Saviour asked leave of his mother Mary
    If he might go play at ball.

2

5   "To play at ball, my own dear son,
    It's time you was going or gone,
But be sure let me hear no complain of you,
    At night when you do come home."

3

It was upling scorn and downling scorn,⁷
10   Oh, there he met three jolly jerdins;°   *boys?*
Oh, there he asked the jolly jerdins
    If they would go play at ball.

4

"Oh, we are lords' and ladies' sons,
    Born in bower or in hall,
15 And you are some poor maid's child
    Borned in an ox's stall."

5

"If you are lords' and ladies' sons,
    Borned in bower or in hall,
Then at last I'll make it appear
20   That I am above you all."

6

Our Saviour built a bridge with the beams of the sun,
    And over it he gone, he gone he.
And after followed the three jolly jerdins,
    And drownded they were all three.

7

25 It was upling scorn and downling scorn,
    The mothers of them did whoop and call,
Crying out, "Mary mild, call home your child,
    For ours are drownded all."

6. I.e., what's the matter with.
7. There was scorn everywhere (*upling, downling*).

8

Mary mild, Mary mild, called home her child,
30 And laid our Saviour across her knee,
And with a whole handful of bitter withy°   *willow*
She gave him slashes three.

9

Then he says to his mother, "Oh! the withy, oh! the withy,
The bitter withy that causes me to smart, to smart,
35 Oh! the withy, it shall be the very first tree
That perishes at the heart."

THOMAS WYATT
(1503–1542)

The Long Love That in My Thought Doth Harbor[1]

The long love that in my thought doth harbor,
And in my heart doth keep his residence,
Into my face presseth with bold pretense
And there encampeth, spreading his banner.
5 She that me learns° to love and suffer   *teaches*
And wills that my trust and lust's negligence
Be reined by reason, shame, and reverence
With his hardiness takes displeasure.
Wherewithal unto the heart's forest he fleeth,
10 Leaving his enterprise with pain and cry,
And there him hideth, and not appeareth.
What may I do, when my master feareth,
But in the field with him to live and die?
For good is the life ending faithfully.

1557

Whoso List To Hunt[2]

Whoso list to hunt, I know where is an hind,
But as for me, alas, I may no more;
The vain travail hath wearied me so sore,
I am of them that furthest come behind.
5 Yet may I by no means my wearied mind
Draw from the deer, but as she fleeth afore
Fainting I follow; I leave off therefore,
Since in a net I seek to hold the wind.
Who list her hunt, I put him out of doubt,
10 As well as I, may spend his time in vain.
And graven with diamonds in letters plain,
There is written her fair neck round about,
"*Noli me tangere*,[3] for Caesar's I am,
And wild for to hold, though I seem tame."

Egerton Ms.

1. Translated from Petrarch. Compare the translation by the Earl of Surrey, *Love That Doth Reign and Live Within My Thought*.
2. This poem, like many of Wyatt's, existed only in manuscript form until comparatively recently. In place of a date of publication, the manuscript source is given for all such poems in this selection.
3. Touch me not.

My Galley Charged with Forgetfulness

My galley charged[4] with forgetfulness
  Thorough sharp seas in winter nights doth pass
'Tween rock and rock; and eke° mine enemy, alas,   *also*
That is my lord, steereth with cruelness;
5 And every oar a thought in readiness,
  As though that death were light in such a case.
An endless wind doth tear the sail apace
  Of forced sighs, and trusty fearfulness.
A rain of tears, a cloud of dark disdain,
10 Hath done the wearied cords great hinderance;
  Wreathed with error and eke with ignorance,
The stars be hid that led me to this pain;
  Drowned is reason that should me consort,
  And I remain despairing of the port.

1557

They Flee from Me

They flee from me, that sometime did me seek,
With naked foot stalking in my chamber.
I have seen them, gentle, tame, and meek,
That now are wild, and do not remember
5 That sometime they put themselves in danger
To take bread at my hand; and now they range,
Busily seeking with a continual change.

Thanked be Fortune it hath been otherwise,
Twenty times better; but once in special,
10 In thin array, after a pleasant guise,
When her loose gown from her shoulders did fall,
And she me caught in her arms long and small,°   *slender*
And therewith all sweetly did me kiss
And softly said, "Dear heart, how like you this?"

15 It was no dream, I lay broad waking.
But all is turned, thorough my gentleness,
Into a strange fashion of forsaking;
And I have leave to go, of her goodness,
And she also to use newfangleness.
20 But since that I so kindely[5] am served,
I fain would know what she hath deserved.

1557

My Lute, Awake!

My lute, awake! Perform the last
Labor that thou and I shall waste,
And end that I have now begun;
For when this song is sung and past,
5 My lute, be still, for I have done.

4. Wyatt's meter is so often irregular that it
is difficult to say with certainty when he in-
tended an *-ed* ending to be pronounced as a
second syllable and when not. Hence no at-
tempt has been made to mark syllabic endings
with an accent in any of Wyatt's poems, al-
though in this particular poem such endings
appear to be intended in lines 1, 8, 11, and 13.
5. I.e., in the normal way of womankind, an
older meaning that does not exclude the modern
meaning of "kindly."

As to be heard where ear is none,
As lead to grave° in marble stone,   *engrave*
My song may pierce her heart as soon.
Should we then sigh or sing or moan?
10 No, no, my lute, for I have done.

The rocks do not so cruelly
Repulse the waves continually
As she my suit and affection.
So that I am past remedy,
15 Whereby my lute and I have done.

Proud of the spoil that thou hast got
Of simple hearts, thorough love's shot;
By whom, unkind, thou hast them won,
Think not he hath his bow forgot,
20 Although my lute and I have done.

Vengeance shall fall on thy disdain
That makest but game on earnest pain.
Think not alone under the sun
Unquit° to cause thy lovers plain,   *unrequited*
25 Although my lute and I have done.

Perchance thee lie withered and old
The winter nights that are so cold,
Plaining in vain unto the moon.
Thy wishes then dare not be told.
30 Care then who list,° for I have done.   *likes*

And then may chance thee to repent
The time that thou hast lost and spent
To cause thy lovers sigh and swoon.
Then shalt thou know beauty but lent,
35 And wish and want as I have done.

Now cease, my lute. This is the last
Labor that thou and I shall waste,
And ended is that we begun.
Now is this song both sung and past;
40 My lute, be still, for I have done.

                                                                      1557

HENRY HOWARD, EARL OF SURREY
(ca. 1517–1547)

The Soote Season

The soote° season, that bud and bloom forth brings,   *sweet*
With green hath clad the hill and eke° the vale;   *also*
The nightingale with feathers new she sings;
The turtle° to her make° hath told her tale.   *turtledove / mate*
5 Summer is come, for every spray now springs;
The hart hath hung his old head on the pale;

The buck in brake his winter coat he flings,
The fishes float with new repairéd scale;
The adder all her slough away she slings,
10   The swift swallow pursueth the flies small;
The busy bee her honey now she mings.°   remembers
Winter is worn, that was the flowers' bale.°   harm
And thus I see among these pleasant things,
Each care decays, and yet my sorrow springs.

1557

Love, That Doth Reign and Live Within My Thought[1]

Love, that doth reign and live within my thought,
And built his seat within my captive breast,
Clad in the arms wherein with me he fought,
Oft in my face he doth his banner rest.
5   But she that taught me love and suffer pain,
My doubtful hope and eke my hot desire
With shamefast° look to shadow and refrain,   shamefaced
Her smiling grace converteth straight to ire.
And coward Love, then, to the heart apace
10   Taketh his flight, where he doth lurk and plain,°   complain
His purpose lost, and dare not show his face.
For my lord's guilt thus faultless bide I pain,
Yet from my lord shall not my foot remove:
Sweet is the death that taketh end by love.

1557

Although I Had a Check

Although I had a check,
   To give the mate is hard;
For I have found a neck,°   nook
   To keep my men in guard.
5   And you that hardy are
   To give so great assay°   assault
Unto a man of war
   To drive his men away,

I rede° you take good heed,   advise
10   And mark this foolish verse;
For I will so provide
   That I will have your fers.°   queen
And when your fers is had
   And all your war is done,
15   Then shall yourself be glad
   To end that you begun.

For if by chance I win
   Your person in the field,
Too late then come you in,
20   Yourself to me to yield.

---

1. Translated from Petrarch. Compare the translation by Sir Thomas Wyatt, *The Long Love That in My Thought Doth Harbor.*

For I will use my power
    As captain full of might,
And such I will devour
    As use to show me spite.

25 And for because you gave
    Me check in such degree
This vantage, lo, I have:
    Now check, and guard to thee.
Defend it if thou may,
30   Stand stiff in thine estate;
For sure I will assay,°   *try*
    If I can give thee mate.

                                    1557

GEORGE GASCOIGNE
(ca. 1535–1577)

And If I Did What Then?

"And if I did what then?
Are you aggrieved therefore?
The sea hath fish for every man,
And what would you have more?"

5 Thus did my mistress once
    Amaze my mind with doubt,
And popped a question for the nonce
    To beat my brains about.

Whereto I thus replied:
10 "Each fisherman can wish
That all the sea at every tide
    Were his alone to fish.

And so did I, in vain;
    But since it may not be,
15 Let such fish there as find the gain,
    And leave the loss for me.

And with such luck and loss
    I will content myself,
Till tides of turning time may toss
20 Such fishers on the shelf.

And when they stick on sands,
    That every man may see,
Then will I laugh and clap my hands,
    As they do now at me."

                                    1573

Gascoigne's Lullaby

Sing lullaby, as women do,
Wherewith they bring their babes to rest,
And lullaby can I sing too,
As womanly as can the best.
5 With lullaby they still the child,
And if I be not much beguiled,
Full many wanton babes have I,
Which must be stilled with lullaby.

First, lullaby, my youthful years,
10 It is now time to go to bed,
For crooked age and hoary hairs
Have won the haven within my head.
With lullaby then, youth, be still,
With lullaby content they will,
15 Since courage quails and comes behind,
Go sleep, and so beguile thy mind.

Next, lullaby, my gazing eyes,
Which wonted were to glance apace.
For every glass may now suffice
20 To show the furrows in my face.
With lullaby then wink awhile,
With lullaby your looks beguile.
Let no fair face nor beauty bright
Entice you eft° with vain delight.   *after*

25 And lullaby, my wanton will,
Let reason's rule now rein thy thought,
Since all too late I find by skill
How dear I have thy fancies bought.
With lullaby now take thine ease,
30 With lullaby thy doubts appease.
For trust to this, if thou be still,
My body shall obey thy will.

Eke° lullaby, my loving boy,   *also*
My little Robin, take thy rest.
35 Since age is cold and nothing coy,°   *lascivious*
Keep close thy coin, for so is best.
With lullaby be thou content,
With lullaby thy lusts relent.
Let others pay which° hath mo° pence;   *who/more*
40 Thou art too poor for such expense.

Thus, lullaby, my youth, mine eyes,
My will, my ware, and all that was.
I can no mo delays devise,
But welcome pain, let pleasure pass.
45 With lullaby now take your leave,
With lullaby your dreams deceive,
And when you rise with waking eye,
Remember Gascoigne's lullaby.

1573

SIR WALTER RALEGH
(ca. 1552–1618)

The Nymph's Reply to the Shepherd[1]

If all the world and love were young,
And truth in every shepherd's tongue,
These pretty pleasures might me move
To live with thee and be thy love.

5   Time drives the flocks from field to fold
When rivers rage and rocks grow cold,
And Philomel° becometh dumb;   *the nightingale*
The rest complains of cares to come.

The flowers do fade, and wanton fields
10 To wayward winter reckoning yields;
A honey tongue, a heart of gall,
Is fancy's spring, but sorrow's fall.

Thy gowns, thy shoes, thy beds of roses,
Thy cap, thy kirtle,[2] and thy posies
15 Soon break, soon wither, soon forgotten—
In folly ripe, in reason rotten.

Thy belt of straw and ivy buds,
Thy coral clasps and amber studs,
All these in me no means can move
20 To come to thee and be thy love.

But could youth last and love still breed,
Had joys no date[3] nor age no need,
Then these delights my mind might move
To live with thee and be thy love.

1600

The Passionate Man's Pilgrimage

Give me my scallop-shell[4] of quiet,
My staff of faith to walk upon,
My scrip[5] of joy, immortal diet,
My bottle of salvation,
5   My gown of glory, hope's true gage,°   *pledge*
And thus I'll take my pilgrimage.

Blood must be my body's balmer,
No other balm will there be given,
Whilst my soul like a white palmer[6]
10 Travels to the land of heaven,
Over the silver mountains,
Where spring the nectar fountains;

1. Written in reply to Christopher Marlowe's *The Passionate Shepherd to His Love*.
2. A long dress, often worn under an outer garment.
3. I.e., terminal date.
4. A scallop shell or something resembling it was worn as the sign of a pilgrim.
5. Pilgrim's knapsack or bag.
6. A person wearing a palm leaf as a sign that he had made a pilgrimage to the Holy Land.

And there I'll kiss
The bowl of bliss,
15   And drink my eternal fill
On every milken hill.
My soul will be a-dry before,
But after it will ne'er thirst more;
And by the happy blissful way
20   More peaceful pilgrims I shall see
That have shook off their gowns of clay
And go appareled fresh like me.
I'll bring them first
To slake their thirst,
25   And then to taste those nectar suckets,°   *confections*
At the clear wells
Where sweetness dwells,
Drawn up by saints in crystal buckets.

And when our bottles and all we
30   Are filled with immortality,
Then the holy paths we'll travel,
Strewed with rubies·thick as gravel,
Ceilings of diamonds, sapphire floors,
High walls of coral, and pearl bowers,
35   From thence to heaven's bribeless hall
Where no corrupted voices brawl,
No conscience molten into gold,
Nor forged accusers bought and sold,
No cause deferred, nor vain-spent journey,
40   For there Christ is the king's attorney,
Who pleads for all, without degrees,
And he hath angels,[7] but no fees.
When the grand twelve million jury
Of our sins and sinful fury,
45   'Gainst our souls black verdicts give,
Christ pleads his death, and then we live.
Be thou my speaker, taintless pleader,
Unblotted lawyer, true proceeder;
Thou movest salvation even for alms,
50   Not with a bribed lawyer's palms.
And this is my eternal plea
To him that made heaven, earth, and sea,
Seeing my flesh must die so soon,
And want a head to dine next noon,
55   Just at the stroke when my veins start and spread,
Set on my soul an everlasting head.
Then am I ready, like a palmer fit,
To tread those blest paths which before I writ.

1604

---

7. A punning reference to the gold coin of that name, ten shillings in value.

Nature, That Washed Her Hands in Milk

Nature, that washed her hands in milk,
And had forgot to dry them,
Instead of earth took snow and silk,
At love's request to try them,
5   If she a mistress could compose
To please love's fancy out of those.

Her eyes he would should be of light,
A violet breath, and lips of jelly;
Her hair not black, nor overbright,
10   And of the softest down her belly;
As for her inside he'd have it
Only of wantonness and wit.

At love's entreaty such a one
Nature made, but with her beauty
15   She hath framed a heart of stone;
So as love, by ill destiny,
Must die for her whom nature gave him,
Because her darling would not save him.

But time (which nature doth despise,
20   And rudely gives her love the lie,
Makes hope a fool, and sorrow wise)
His hands do neither wash nor dry;
But being made of steel and rust,
Turns snow and silk and milk to dust.

25   The light, the belly, lips, and breath,
He dims, discolors, and destroys;
With those he feeds but fills not death,
Which sometimes were the food of joys.
Yea, time doth dull each lively wit,
30   And dries all wantonness with it.

Oh, cruel time! which takes in trust
Our youth, our joys, and all we have,
And pays us but with age and dust;
Who in the dark and silent grave
35   When we have wandered all our ways
Shuts up the story of our days.[8]

                                          ca. 1610

---

8. Another version of this stanza, traditionally supposed to have been written by Ralegh on the night before his execution, was published in 1628. In it the first three words are changed to "Even such is time," and the following couplet is added: "And from which earth, and grave, and dust/The Lord shall raise me up, I trust." The poem as a whole existed only in manuscript form until 1902.

EDMUND SPENSER
(ca. 1552–1599)

From Amoretti

Sonnet 67

Lyke as a huntsman after weary chace,
Seeing the game from him escapt away,
Sits downe to rest him in some shady place,
With panting hounds beguiléd of their pray:
5 So after long pursuit and vaine assay,
When I all weary had the chace forsooke,
The gentle deare returnd the selfe-same way,
Thinking to quench her thirst at the next brooke.
There she beholding me with mylder looke,
10 Sought not to fly, but fearelesse still did bide:
Till I in hand her yet halfe trembling tooke,
And with her owne goodwill hir fyrmely tyde.
Strange thing me seemd to see a beast so wyld,
So goodly wonne with her owne will beguyld.

Sonnet 68

Most glorious Lord of lyfe, that on this day,[1]
Didst make thy triumph over death and sin:
And having harrowd hell,[2] didst bring away
Captivity thence captive us to win:[3]
5 This joyous day, deare Lord, with joy begin,
And grant that we for whom thou diddest dye
Being with thy deare blood clene washt from sin,
May live for ever in felicity.
And that thy love we weighing worthily,
10 May likewise love thee for the same againe:
And for thy sake that all lyke deare didst buy,
With love may one another entertayne.
So let us love, deare love, lyke as we ought,
Love is the lesson which the Lord us taught.[4]

Sonnet 70

Fresh spring the herald of loves mighty king,
In whose cote armour° richly are displayd   *coat of arms*
All sorts of flowers the which on earth do spring
In goodly colours gloriously arrayd.
5 Goe to my love, where she is carelesse layd,
Yet in her winters bowre not well awake:
Tell her the joyous time wil not be staid
Unless she doe him by the forelock take.[5]

---

1. Easter.
2. A reference to the apocryphal account of Christ's descent into hell, after his crucifixion, in order to rescue the captive souls of the just.
3. "When he ascended up on high, he led captivity captive" (Ephesians iv.8).
4. "This is my commandment, That ye love one another, as I have loved you" (John xv.12).
5. "To take time by the forelock" is to act promptly.

Bid her therefore her selfe soone ready make,
10 To wayt on love amongst his lovely crew:
Where every one that misseth then her make,°   *mate*
Shall be by him amearst° with penance dew.   *punished*
Make hast therefore sweet love, whilest it is prime,°   *spring*
For none can call againe the passéd time.

Sonnet 75

One day I wrote her name upon the strand,
But came the waves and washéd it away:
Agayne I wrote it with a second hand,°   *a second time*
But came the tyde, and made my paynes his pray.
5 "Vayne man," sayd she, "that doest in vaine assay,
A mortall thing so to immortalize,
For I my selve shall lyke to this decay,
And eek° my name bee wypéd out lykewize."   *also*
"Not so," quod° I, "let baser things devize°   *quoth / plan*
10 To dy in dust, but you shall live by fame:
My verse your vertues rare shall eternize,
And in the hevens wryte your glorious name.
Where whenas death shall all the world subdew,
Our love shall live, and later life renew."

Epithalamion[6]

Ye learned sisters[7] which have oftentimes
Beene to me ayding, others to adorne:
Whom ye thought worthy of your gracefull rymes,
That even the greatest did not greatly scorne
5 To heare theyr names sung in your simple layes,
But joyéd in theyr prayse.
And when ye list your owne mishaps to mourne,
Which death, or love, or fortunes wreck did rayse,
Your string could soone to sadder tenor° turne,   *strain*
10 And teach the woods and waters to lament
Your dolefull dreriment.
Now lay those sorrowfull complaints aside,
And having all your heads with girland crownd,
Helpe me mine owne loves prayses to resound,
15 Ne let the same of any be envíde:
So Orpheus[8] did for his owne bride,
So I unto my selfe alone will sing,
The woods shall to me answer and my Eccho ring.

Early before the worlds light giving lampe,
20 His golden beame upon the hils doth spred,
Having disperst the nights unchearefull dampe,
Doe ye awake, and with fresh lustyhed
Go to the bowre° of my belovéd love,   *bedchamber*
My truest turtle dove,
25 Bid her awake; for Hymen[9] is awake,

---

6. The title (literally "at the bridal chamber") is the Greek word for "wedding song." Spenser's poem was published with the *Amoretti*.
7. The Muses, sources of inspiration.
8. Whose music was said to move even inanimate objects and to change foul weather to fair.
9. The Greek god of the wedding feast, represented as a young man bearing a torch ("Tead") and leading a "maske" or procession.

And long since ready forth his maske to move,
With his bright Tead that flames with many a flake,°   spark
And many a bachelor to waite on him,
In theyr fresh garments trim.
30 Bid her awake therefore and soone her dight,°   dress
For lo the wishéd day is come at last,
That shall for al the paynes and sorrowes past,
Pay to her usury of long delight:
And whylest she doth her dight,
35 Doe ye to her of joy and solace° sing,   pleasure
That all the woods may answer and your eccho ring.

Bring with you all the Nymphes that you can heare[1]
Both of the rivers and the forrests greene:
And of the sea that neighbours to her neare,
40 Al with gay girlands goodly wel beseene.
And let them also with them bring in hand,
Another gay girland
For my fayre love of lillyes and of roses,
Bound truelove wize with a blew silke riband.
45 And let them make great store of bridale poses,°   posies
And let them eeke bring store of other flowers
To deck the bridale bowers.
And let the ground whereas her foot shall tread,
For feare the stones her tender foot should wrong
50 Be strewed with fragrant flowers all along,
And diapred lyke the discolored mead.[2]
Which done, doe at her chamber dore awayt,
For she will waken strayt,°   straightway
The whiles doe ye this song unto her sing,
55 The woods shall to you answer and your Eccho ring.

Ye Nymphes of Mulla[3] which with carefull heed,
The silver scaly trouts doe tend full well,
And greedy pikes which use therein to feed,
(Those trouts and pikes all others doo excell)
60 And ye likewise which keepe the rushy lake,
Where none doo fishes take,
Bynd up the locks the which hang scatterd light,
And in his waters which your mirror make,
Behold your faces as the christall bright,
65 That when you come whereas my love doth lie,
No blemish she may spie.
And eke ye lightfoot mayds which keepe the deere,
That on the hoary mountayne use to towre,[4]
And the wylde wolves which seeke them to devoure,
70 With your steele darts doo chace from comming neer
Be also present heere,
To helpe to decke her and to help to sing,
That all the woods may answer and your eccho ring.

Wake, now my love, awake; for it is time,
75 The Rosy Morne long since left Tithones bed,[5]
All ready to her silver coche to clyme,

1. I.e., that can hear you.
2. And variegated like the many-colored meadow.
3. The Awbeg River in Ireland, near Spenser's home.
4. A hawking term meaning "to climb high."
5. The dawn, personified in mythology as the goddess Eos or Aurora, was the wife of Tithonus.

And Phoebus gins to shew his glorious hed.
Hark how the cheerefull birds do chaunt theyr laies
And carroll of loves praise.
80 The merry Larke hir mattins sings aloft.
The thrush replyes, the Mavis descant[6] playes,
The Ouzell shrills, the Ruddock warbles soft,
So goodly all agree with sweet consent,
To this dayes merriment.
85 Ah my deere love why doe ye sleepe thus long,
When meeter were that ye should now awake,
T' awayt the comming of your joyous make,°   mate
And hearken to the birds lovelearnéd song,
The deawy leaves among.
90 For they of joy and pleasance to you sing,
That all the woods them answer and theyr eccho ring.

My love is now awake out of her dreame,
And her fayre eyes like stars that dimméd were
With darksome cloud, now shew theyr goodly beams
95 More bright then Hesperus° his head doth rere.   evening star
Come now ye damzels, daughters of delight,
Helpe quickly her to dight,
But first come ye fayre houres which were begot
In Joves sweet paradice, of Day and Night,
100 Which doe the seasons of the yeare allot,
And al that ever in this world is fayre
Doe make and still° repayre.   continually
And ye three handmayds of the Cyprian Queene,[7]
The which doe still adorne her beauties pride,
105 Helpe to addorne my beautifullest bride:
And as ye her array, still throw betweene°   at intervals
Some graces to be seene,
And as ye use to Venus, to her sing,
The whiles the woods shal answer and your eccho ring.

110 Now is my love all ready forth to come,
Let all the virgins therefore well awayt,
And ye fresh boyes that tend upon her groome
Prepare your selves; for he is comming strayt.
Set all your things in seemely good aray
115 Fit for so joyfull day,
The joyfulst day that ever sunne did see.
Faire Sun, shew forth thy favourable ray,
And let thy lifull° heat not fervent be   lifegiving
For feare of burning her sunshyny face,
120 Her beauty to disgrace.°   spoil
O fayrest Phoebus, father of the Muse,
If ever I did honour thee aright,
Or sing the thing, that mote° thy mind delight,   might
Doe not thy servants simple boone° refuse,   request
125 But let this day let this one day be myne,
Let all the rest be thine.
Then I thy soverayne prayses loud wil sing,
That all the woods shal answer and theyr eccho ring.

---

6. Melodic counterpart. The mavis, ouzell (or
European blackbird), and ruddock (or robin)
are all varieties of thrush.
7. Venus, whose handmaids were the three

Graces: Aglaia, Thalia, and Euphrosyne. Their
names mean "the brilliant one," "she who
brings flowers," and "she who rejoices the
heart."

Harke how the Minstrels gin to shrill aloud
130 Their merry Musick that resounds from far
      The pipe, the tabor,° and the trembling Croud,°   *drum / viol*
      That well agree withouten breach or jar.°   *discord*
      But most of all the Damzels doe delite,
      When they their tymbrels° smyte,   *tambourines*
135 And thereunto doe daunce and carrol sweet,
      That all the sences they doe ravish quite,
      The whyles the boyes run up and downe the street,
      Crying aloud with strong confuséd noyce,
      As if it were one voyce.
140 *Hymen iô*[8] *Hymen, Hymen* they do shout,
      That even to the heavens theyr shouting shrill
      Doth reach, and all the firmament doth fill,
      To which the people standing all about,
      As in approvance doe thereto applaud
145 And loud advaunce her laud,
      And evermore they *Hymen Hymen* sing,
      That al the woods them answer and theyr eccho ring.

      Loe where she comes along with portly° pace   *stately*
      Lyke Phoebe[9] from her chamber of the East,
150 Arysing forth to run her mighty race,
      Clad all in white, that seemes° a virgin best.   *befits*
      So well it her beseemes that ye would weene
      Some angell she had beene.
      Her long loose yellow locks lyke golden wyre,
155 Sprinckled with perle, and perling° flowres a tweene,   *intermingling*
      Doe lyke a golden mantle her attyre,
      And being crownéd with a girland greene,
      Seeme lyke some mayden Queene.
      Her modest eyes abashéd to behold
160 So many gazers, as on her do stare,
      Upon the lowly ground affixéd are.
      Ne dare lift up her countenance too bold,
      But blush to heare her prayses sung so loud,
      So farre from being proud.
165 Nathlesse° doe ye still loud her prayses sing.   *nevertheless*
      That all the woods may answer and your eccho ring.

      Tell me ye merchants daughters did ye see
      So fayre a creature in your towne before,
      So sweet, so lovely, and so mild as she,
170 Adornd with beautyes grace and vertues store,°   *wealth*
      Her goodly eyes lyke Saphyres shining bright,
      Her forehead yvory white,
      Her cheekes lyke apples which the sun hath rudded,
      Her lips lyke cherryes charming men to byte,
175 Her brest like to a bowle of creame uncrudded,°   *uncurdled*
      Her paps lyke lyllies budded,
      Her snowie necke lyke to a marble towre,
      And all her body lyke a pallace fayre,
      Ascending uppe with many a stately stayre,
180 To honors seat and chastities sweet bowre.

---

8. A shout of joy or triumph (Greek).   9. Another name for the moon goddess Diana.

Why stand ye still ye virgins in amaze,
Upon her so to gaze,
Whiles ye forget your former lay to sing,
To which the woods did answer and your eccho ring.

185 But if ye saw that which no eyes can see,
The inward beauty of her lively spright,°   *spirit*
Garnisht with heavenly guifts of high degree,
Much more then would ye wonder at that sight,
And stand astonisht lyke to those which red°   *saw*
190 Medusaes mazeful hed.[1]
There dwels sweet love and constant chastity,
Unspotted fayth and comely womanhood,
Regard of honour and mild modesty,
There vertue raynes as Queene in royal throne,
195 And giveth lawes alone.
The which the base affections° doe obay,   *lowly emotions*
And yeeld theyr services unto her will,
Ne thought of thing uncomely ever may
Thereto approch to tempt her mind to ill.
200 Had ye once seene these her celestial threasures,
And unrevealéd pleasures,
Then would ye wonder and her prayses sing,
That al the woods should answer and your eccho ring.

Open the temple gates unto my love,
205 Open them wide that she may enter in,
And all the postes adorne as doth behove,[2]
And all the pillours deck with girlands trim,
For to recyve this Saynt with honour dew,
That commeth in to you.
210 With trembling steps and humble reverence,
She commeth in, before th' almighties vew,
Of her ye virgins learne obedience,
When so ye come into those holy places,
To humble your proud faces:
215 Bring her up to th' high altar, that she may
The sacred ceremonies there partake,
The which do endlesse matrimony make,
And let the roring Organs loudly play
The praises of the Lord in lively notes,
220 The whiles with hollow throates
The Choristers the joyous Antheme sing,
That al the woods may answere and their eccho ring.

Behold whiles she before the altar stands
Hearing the holy priest that to her speakes
225 And blesseth her with his two happy hands,
How the red roses flush up in her cheekes,
And the pure snow with goodly vermill° stayne,   *vermilion*
Like crimsin dyde in grayne,[3]
That even th' Angels which continually,
230 About the sacred Altare doe remaine,
Forget their service and about her fly,

1. The Gorgon Medusa had serpents for hair;   2. I.e., as is fitting.
whoever looked upon her was turned to stone.   3. I.e., dyed with colorfast dye.

Ofte peeping in her face that seemes more fayre,
The more they on it stare.
But her sad° eyes still fastened on the ground,   sober
235 Are governéd with goodly modesty,
That suffers not one looke to glaunce awry,
Which may let in a little thought unsownd.
Why blush ye love to give to me your hand,
The pledge of all our band?°   bond
240 Sing ye sweet Angels, Alleluya sing,
That all the woods may answere and your eccho ring.

Now al is done; bring home the bride againe,
Bring home the triumph of our victory,
Bring home with you the glory of her gaine,⁴
245 With joyance bring her and with jollity.
Never had man more joyfull day then this,
Whom heaven would heape with blis.
Make feast therefore now all this live long day,
This day for ever to me holy is,
250 Poure out the wine without restraint or stay,
Poure not by cups, but by the belly full,
Poure out to all that wull,°   will
And sprinkle all the postes and wals with wine,
That they may sweat, and drunken be withall.
255 Crowne ye God Bacchus with a coronall,°   garland
And Hymen also crowne with wreathes of vine,
And let the Graces daunce unto the rest;
For they can doo it best:
The whiles the maydens doe theyr carroll sing,
260 To which the woods shal answer and theyr eccho ring.

Ring ye the bels, ye yong men of the towne,
And leave your wonted labors for this day:
This day is holy; doe ye write it downe,
That ye for ever it remember may.
265 This day the sunne is in his chiefest hight,
With Barnaby the bright,⁵
From whence declining daily by degrees,
He somewhat loseth of his heat and light,
When once the Crab⁶ behind his back he sees.
270 But for this time it ill ordainéd was,
To chose the longest day in all the yeare,
And shortest night, when longest fitter weare:
Yet never day so long, but late° would passe.   finally
Ring ye the bels, to make it weare away,
275 And bonefiers make all day,
And daunce about them, and about them sing:
That all the woods may answer, and your eccho ring.

Ah when will this long weary day have end,
And lende me leave to come unto my love?
280 How slowly do the houres theyr numbers spend?
How slowly does sad Time his feathers move?

4. I.e., of gaining her.
5. St. Barnabas's day (July 11) was also the
day of the summer solstice in the calendar in
use during Spenser's time.

6. Cancer the Crab, the fourth constellation
in the zodiac, through which the sun passes
in July.

Hast thee O fayrest Planet to thy home[7]
Within the Westerne fome:
Thy tyred steedes long since have need of rest.
²⁸⁵ Long though it be, at last I see it gloome,
And the bright evening star with golden creast
Appeare out of the East.
Fayre childe of beauty, glorious lampe of love
That all the host of heaven in rankes doost lead,
²⁹⁰ And guydest lovers through the nightés dread,
How chearefully thou lookest from above,
And seemst to laugh atweene thy twinkling light
As joying in the sight
Of these glad many which for joy doe sing,
²⁹⁵ That all the woods them answer and their eccho ring.

Now ceasse ye damsels your delights forepast;
Enough is it, that all the day was youres:
Now day is doen, and night is nighing fast:
Now bring the Bryde into the brydall boures.
³⁰⁰ Now night is come, now soone her disaray,
And in her bed her lay;
Lay her in lillies and in violets,
And silken courteins over her display,
And odourd sheetes, and Arras° coverlets.   *tapestry*
³⁰⁵ Behold how goodly my faire love does ly
In proud humility;
Like unto Maia,[8] when as Jove her tooke,
In Tempe, lying on the flowry gras,
Twixt sleepe and wake, after she weary was,
³¹⁰ With bathing in the Acidalian brooke.
Now it is night, ye damsels may be gon,
And leave my love alone,
And leave likewise your former lay to sing:
The woods no more shal answere, nor your eccho ring.

³¹⁵ Now welcome night, thou night so long expected,°   *awaited*
That long daies labour doest at last defray,°   *requite*
And all my cares, which cruell love collected,
Hast sumd in one, and cancelléd for aye:
Spread thy broad wing over my love and me,
³²⁰ That no man may us see,
And in thy sable mantle us enwrap,
From feare of perrill and foule horror free.
Let no false treason seeke us to entrap,
Nor any dread disquiet once annoy
³²⁵ The safety of our joy:
But let the night be calme and quietsome,
Without tempestuous storms or sad afray:°   *dark terror*
Lyke as when Jove with fayre Alcmena[9] lay,
When he begot the great Tirynthian groome:
³³⁰ Or lyke as when he with thy selfe did lie,
And begot Majesty.
And let the mayds and yongmen cease to sing:
Ne let the woods them answer, nor theyr eccho ring.

---

7. In Ptolemaic astronomy, still often accepted in Spenser's time, the sun was one of the planets, which revolved about the earth.
8. The most beautiful of the Pleiades, who by Jove became the mother of the god Hermes.
9. The mother of Hercules, who as groom or servant to the king of Tiryns performed twelve prodigious labors.

Let no lamenting cryes, nor dolefull teares,
335 Be heard all night within nor yet without:
Ne let false whispers, breeding hidden feares,
Breake gentle sleepe with misconceivéd dout.°   *fear*
Let no deluding dreames, nor dreadful sights
Make sudden sad affrights;
340 Ne let housefyres, nor lightnings helpelesse harmes,
Ne let the Pouke,[1] nor other evill sprights,
Ne let mischívous witches with theyr charmes,
Ne let hob Goblins, names whose sence we see not,
Fray us with things that be not.
345 Let not the shriech Oule, nor the Storke be heard:
Nor the night Raven that still° deadly yels,   *continually*
Nor damnéd ghosts cald up with mighty spels,
Nor griesly vultures make us once affeard:
Ne let th' unpleasant Quyre of Frogs still croking
350 Make us to wish theyr choking.
Let none of these theyr drery accents sing;
Ne let the woods them answer, nor theyr eccho ring.

But let stil Silence trew night watches keepe,
That sacred peace may in assurance rayne,
355 And tymely sleep, when it is tyme to sleepe,
May poure his limbs forth on your pleasant playne,
The whiles an hundred little wingéd loves,°   *cupids*
Like divers fethered doves,
Shall fly and flutter round about your bed,
360 And in the secret darke, that none reproves,
Their prety stealthes shal worke, and snares shal spread
To filch away sweet snatches of delight,
Conceald through covert night.
Ye sonnes of Venus, play your sports at will,
365 For greedy pleasure, carelesse of your toyes,°   *amorous sports*
Thinks more upon her paradise of joyes,
Then what ye do, albe it good or ill.
All night therefore attend your merry play,
For it will soone be day:
370 Now none doth hinder you, that say or sing,
Ne will the woods now answer, nor your Eccho ring.

Who is the same, which at my window peepes?
Or whose is that faire face, that shines so bright,
Is it not Cinthia,[2] she that never sleepes,
375 But walkes about high heaven al the night?
O fayrest goddesse, do thou not envý
My love with me to spy:
For thou likewise didst love, though now unthought,[3]
And for a fleece of woll,° which privily,   *wool*
380 The Latmian shephard once unto thee brought,

---

1. Puck, also called Hobgoblin. The same
Puck appears as the merely mischievous Robin
Goodfellow in Shakespeare's *A Midsummer
Night's Dream.*
2. Yet another name for the moon goddess
Diana.
3. The moon was often regarded as a symbol
of virginity, in spite of several myths recount-
ing her amours. In the next three lines
Spenser, perhaps mistakenly, blends the story
about Pan, who loved Diana disguised in
the fleece of a white ram, with the story of
Endymion ("The Latmian shephard"), whom
Diana visited nightly in his sleep.

His pleasures with thee wrought.
Therefore to us be favorable now;
And sith of wemens labours thou hast charge,[4]
And generation goodly dost enlarge,
385 Encline thy will t' effect our wishfull vow,
And the chast wombe informe with timely seed,
That may our comfort breed:
Till which we cease our hopefull hap to sing,
Ne let the woods us answere, nor our Eccho ring.

390 And thou great Juno, which with awful° might   *awe-inspiring*
The lawes of wedlock still dost patronize,
And the religion° of the faith first plight   *sanctity*
With sacred rites hast taught to solemnize:
And eeke for comfort often calléd art
395 Of women in their smart,°   *pains of childbirth*
Eternally bind thou this lovely band,
And all thy blessings unto us impart.
And thou glad Genius,[5] in whose gentle hand,
The bridale bowre and geniall° bed remaine,   *marriage*
400 Without blemish or staine,
And the sweet pleasures of theyr loves delight
With secret ayde doest succour and supply,
Till they bring forth the fruitfull progeny,
Send us the timely fruit of this same night.
405 And thou fayre Hebe,[6] and thou Hymen free,
Grant that it may so be.
Til which we cease your further prayse to sing,
Ne any woods shal answer, nor your Eccho ring.

And ye high heavens, the temple of the gods,
410 In which a thousand torches flaming bright
Doe burne, that to us wretched earthly clods,
In dreadful darknesse lend desiréd light;
And all ye powers which in the same remayne,
More then we men can fayne,°   *imagine*
415 Poure out your blessing on us plentiously,
And happy influence upon us raine,
That we may raise a large posterity,
Which from the earth, which they may long possesse,
With lasting happinesse,
420 Up to your haughty pallaces may mount,
And for the guerdon° of theyr glorious merit   *reward*
May heavenly tabernacles there inherit,
Of blessed Saints for to increase the count.
So let us rest, sweet love, in hope of this,
425 And cease till then our tymely joyes to sing,
The woods no more us answer, nor our eccho ring.

4. Lucina, the goddess of childbirth, is often identified with both Diana and Juno (see lines 394–95).
5. The universal god of generation. By invoking both Juno and Genius as patrons of the marriage bed, Spenser draws also on the belief that each individual is watched over from birth by a tutelary spirit called "a Genius" (for boys) or "a Juno" (for girls).
6. Daughter of Juno and goddess of youth.

Song made in lieu of many ornaments,
With which my love should duly have bene dect,
Which cutting off through hasty accidents,
430   Ye would not stay your dew time to expect,
But promist both to recompens,
Be unto her a goodly ornament,
And for short time an endlesse moniment.

1595

JOHN LYLY
(1554–1606)

Cupid and My Campaspe

Cupid and my Campaspe played
At cards for kisses; Cupid paid.
He stakes his quiver, bow, and arrows,
His mother's[1] doves and team of sparrows,
5   Loses them too; then down he throws
The coral of his lip, the rose
Growing on 's cheek (but none knows how),
With these the crystal of his brow,
And then the dimple of his chin:
10   All these did my Campaspe win.
At last he set her both his eyes;
She won, and Cupid blind did rise.
Oh Love! has she done this to thee?
What shall, alas, become of me?

1632

Oh, For a Bowl of Fat Canary

Oh, for a bowl of fat Canary,
Rich Palermo, sparkling Sherry,
Some nectar else, from Juno's dairy;[2]
Oh, these draughts would make us merry!

5   Oh, for a wench (I deal in faces,
And in other daintier things);
Tickled am I with her embraces,
Fine dancing in such fairy rings.

Oh, for a plump fat leg of mutton,
10   Veal, lamb, capon, pig, and coney;°   rabbit
None is happy but a glutton,
None an ass but who wants money.

Wines indeed and girls are good,
But brave victuals feast the blood;
15   For wenches, wine, and lusty cheer,
Jove would leap down to surfeit here.

1640

1. I.e., Venus'.
2. Nectar, the drink of the gods, was some-
times thought to resemble mead, a drink made
from milk and honey; hence it might be re-
garded figuratively as coming from the
"dairy" of Juno, the queen of the gods.

SIR PHILIP SIDNEY
(1554–1586)

Ye Goatherd Gods[1]

STREPHON.[2] Ye goatherd gods, that love the grassy mountains,
　　　　　Ye nymphs which haunt the springs in pleasant valleys,
　　　　　Ye satyrs joyed with free and quiet forests,
　　　　　Vouchsafe your silent ears to plaining music,
5　　　　 Which to my woes gives still an early morning,
　　　　　And draws the dolor on till weary evening.

KLAIUS.　O Mercury,[3] foregoer to the evening,
　　　　　O heavenly huntress of the savage mountains,
　　　　　O lovely star, entitled of the morning,
10　　　　While that my voice doth fill these woeful valleys,
　　　　　Vouchsafe your silent ears to plaining music,
　　　　　Which oft hath Echo tired in secret forests.

STREPHON.　I, that was once free burgess° of the forests,　　　　*citizen*
　　　　　Where shade from sun, and sport I sought in evening,
15　　　　I, that was once esteemed for pleasant music,
　　　　　Am banished now among the monstrous mountains
　　　　　Of huge despair, and foul affliction's valleys,
　　　　　Am grown a screech owl to myself each morning.

KLAIUS.　I, that was once delighted every morning,
20　　　　Hunting the wild inhabiters of forests,
　　　　　I, that was once the music of these valleys,
　　　　　So darkened am that all my day is evening,
　　　　　Heartbroken so, that molehills seem high mountains
　　　　　And fill the vales with cries instead of music.

25　STREPHON.　Long since, alas, my deadly swannish[4] music
　　　　　Hath made itself a crier of the morning,
　　　　　And hath with wailing strength climbed highest mountains;
　　　　　Long since my thoughts more desert be than forests,
　　　　　Long since I see my joys come to their evening,
30　　　　And state° thrown down to overtrodden valleys.　　　　*high position*

KLAIUS.　Long since the happy dwellers of these valleys
　　　　　Have prayed me leave my strange exclaiming music,
　　　　　Which troubles their day's work and joys of evening;
　　　　　Long since I hate the night, more hate the morning,
35　　　　Long since my thoughts chase me like beasts in forests
　　　　　And make me wish myself laid under mountains.

1. The poem is in the form of a double sestina, two sets of six six-line stanzas, with a triplet concluding the whole. The same six key words end the lines of each stanza; their order is always a permutation of the order in the stanza just preceding: the pattern is 6 1 5 2 4 3, i.e., the last word of line 1 of any stanza is always the same as the last word of line 6 in the preceding stanza. Line 2 always ends like the preceding stanza's line 1; line 3 like line 5; line 4 like line 2; line 5 like line 4; and line 6 like line 3. All six key words appear in the triplet in the same order as that of the first and seventh stanzas.
2. Strephon and Klaius are shepherds in Sidney's heroic romance *Arcadia*, in which this poem appears.
3. The evening star. The "heavenly huntress" is the goddess Diana, the moon.
4. The swan was supposed to sing only just before it died.

STREPHON.   Meseems° I see the high and stately mountains   *it seems to me*
Transform themselves to low dejected valleys;
Meseems I hear in these ill-changéd forests
40   The nightingales do learn of owls their music;
Meseems I feel the comfort of the morning
Turned to the mortal serene⁵ of an evening.

KLAIUS.   Meseems I see a filthy cloudy evening
As soon as sun begins to climb the mountains;
45   Meseems I feel a noisome° scent, the morning   *offensive*
When I do smell the flowers of these valleys;
Meseems I hear, when I do hear sweet music,
The dreadful cries of murdered men in forests.

STREPHON.   I wish to fire the trees of all these forests;
50   I give the sun a last farewell each evening;
I curse the fiddling finders-out of music;
With envy I do hate the lofty mountains
And with despite despise the humble valleys;
I do detest night, evening, day, and morning.

55   KLAIUS.   Curse to myself my prayer is, the morning;
My fire is more than can be made with forests,
My state more base than are the basest valleys.
I wish no evenings more to see, each evening;
Shaméd, I hate myself in sight of mountains
60   And stop mine ears, lest I grow mad with music.

STREPHON.   For she whose parts maintained a perfect music,
Whose beauties shined more than the blushing morning,
Who much did pass° in state the stately mountains,   *surpass*
In straightness passed the cedars of the forests,
65   Hath cast me, wretch, into eternal evening
By taking her two suns from these dark valleys.

KLAIUS.   For she, with whom compared, the Alps are valleys,
She, whose least word brings from the spheres their music,
At whose approach the sun rose in the evening,
70   Who where she went bare° in her forehead morning,   *bore*
Is gone, is gone, from these our spoiléd forests,
Turning to deserts our best pastured mountains.

STREPHON.   These mountains witness shall, so shall these valleys,
KLAIUS.   These forests eke,° made wretched by our music,   *also*
75   Our morning hymn this is, and song at evening.
                                        1577–80   1593

The Nightingale

The nightingale, as soon as April bringeth
Unto her rested sense a perfect waking,
While late bare earth, proud of new clothing, springeth,
Sings out her woes, a thorn her song-book making,
5   And mournfully bewailing,
Her throat in tunes expresseth
What grief her breast oppresseth

5. Damp evening air, thought to produce sickness ("mortal": deadly). The stress is on the first syllable.

For Tereus' force on her chaste will prevailing.[6]
Oh Philomela fair, Oh take some gladness,
10 That here is juster cause of plaintful sadness:
Thine earth now springs, mine fadeth;
Thy thorn without, my thorn my heart invadeth.

Alas, she hath no other cause of anguish
But Tereus' love, on her by strong hand wroken,[7]
15 Wherein she suffering, all her spirits languish;
Full womanlike complains her will was broken.
But I, who daily craving,
Cannot have to content me,
Have more cause to lament me,
20 Since wanting is more woe than too much having.
O Philomela fair, O take some gladness,
That here is juster cause of plaintful sadness:
Thine earth now springs, mine fadeth;
Thy thorn without, my thorn my heart invadeth.

                                            1581   1598

Ring Out Your Bells

Ring out your bells, let mourning shows be spread,
For Love is dead.
All Love is dead, infected
With plague of deep disdain;
5 Worth as naught worth rejected,
And Faith fair scorn[8] doth gain.
From so ungrateful fancy,
From such a female franzy,°   *frenzy*
From them that use men thus,
10 Good Lord, deliver us!

Weep, neighbors, weep; do you not hear it said
That Love is dead?
His deathbed peacock's folly,
His winding sheet is shame,
15 His will false-seeming holy,
His sole exec'tor blame.
From so ungrateful . . .

Let dirge be sung and trentals[9] rightly read,
For Love is dead.
20 Sir Wrong his tomb ordaineth
My mistress, marble heart,
Which epitaph containeth,
"Her eyes were once his dart."
From so ungrateful . . .

25 Alas, I lie, rage hath this error bred;
Love is not dead.
Love is not dead, but sleepeth
In her unmatchéd mind,
Where she his counsel keepeth,

---

6. Tereus, the ravisher of Philomela, cut out her tongue to keep her from accusing him. Transformed into a nightingale, she expressed her grief in song.

7. Old past participle of *wreak*, "to urge or force upon."
8. Scorn from the fair.
9. A series of thirty masses for the dead.

30   Till due desert she find.
Therefore from so vile fancy,
To call such wit a franzy,
Who Love can temper thus,
Good Lord, deliver us!

1581   1598

From Astrophel and Stella

1

Loving in truth, and fain° in verse my love to show,   *eager*
That the dear she might take some pleasure of my pain,
Pleasure might cause her read, reading might make her know,
Knowledge might pity win, and pity grace obtain,
5   I sought fit words to paint the blackest face of woe:
Studying inventions fine, her wits to entertain,
Oft turning others' leaves, to see if thence would flow
Some fresh and fruitful showers upon my sunburned brain.
But words came halting forth, wanting Invention's stay;
10   Invention, Nature's child, fled stepdame Study's blows;
And others' feet still seemed but strangers in my way.
Thus, great with child to speak, and helpless in my throes,
Biting my truant pen, beating myself for spite:
"Fool," said my Muse to me, "look in thy heart, and write."

25

The wisest scholar of the wight most wise
By Phoebus' doom,[1] with sugared sentence says
That Virtue, if it once met with our eyes,
Strange flames of love it in our souls would raise;
5   But, for that° man with pain this truth descries,   *because*
While he each thing in sense's balance weighs,
And so nor will nor can behold those skies
Which inward sun to heroic mind displays,
Virtue of late, with virtuous care to stir
10   Love of herself, takes Stella's shape, that she
To mortal eyes might sweetly shine in her.
It is most true, for since I her did see,
Virtue's great beauty in that face I prove,°   *experience*
And find th'effect, for I do burn in love.

31

With how sad steps, Oh Moon, thou climb'st the skies,
How silently, and with how wan a face!
What, may it be that even in heav'nly place
That busy archer[2] his sharp arrows tries?
5   Sure, if that long-with-love-acquainted eyes
Can judge of love, thou feel'st a lover's case;
I read it in thy looks: thy languished grace,
To me that feel the like, thy state descries.
Then even of fellowship, Oh Moon, tell me,
10   Is constant love deemed there but want of wit?

1. Judgment. The "wight most wise" was
Socrates, so called by the oracle of Apollo
(Phoebus) at Delphi. His "wisest scholar," or
pupil, was Plato, who (in *Phaedrus* 250D) pro-
vides the basis for lines 3-8.
2. I.e., Cupid.

Are beauties there as proud as here they be?
Do they above love to be loved, and yet
Those lovers scorn whom that love doth possess?
Do they call virtue there ungratefulness?

48

Soul's joy, bend not those morning stars from me,
Where virtue is made strong by beauty's might,
Where love is chasteness, pain doth learn delight,
And humbleness grows one with majesty.
5 Whatever may ensue, O let me be
Co-partner of the riches of that sight;
Let not mine eyes be hell-driv'n from that light;
O look, O shine, O let me die and see.
For though I oft my self of them bemoan,
10 That through my heart their beamy darts be gone,
Whose cureless wounds even now most freshly bleed,
Yet since my death wound is already got,
Dear killer, spare not thy sweet cruel shot;
A kind of grace it is to slay with speed.

GEORGE PEELE
(1557–1596)

His Golden Locks Time Hath to Silver Turned[3]

His golden locks time hath to silver turned;
  Oh, time too swift, oh, swiftness never ceasing!
His youth 'gainst time and age hath ever spurned,°   **kicked**
  But spurned in vain; youth waneth by increasing.
5 Beauty, strength, youth, are flowers but fading seen;
Duty, faith, love, are roots, and ever green.

His helmet now shall make a hive for bees,
  And lover's sonnets turned to holy psalms,
A man-at-arms must now serve on his knees,
10   And feed on prayers, which are age his[4] alms;
But though from court to cottage he depart,
His saint is sure of his unspotted heart.

And when he saddest sits in homely cell,
  He'll teach his swains this carol for a song:
15 Blest be the hearts that wish my sovereign well,
  Cursed be the souls that think her any wrong!
Goddess, allow this aged man his right,
To be your beadsman[5] now, that was your knight.

1590

---

3. This poem refers to Sir Henry Lee, for
years Queen Elizabeth's champion in courtly
jousts or contests of arms. At the age of sixty,
too old to take part in the queen's birthday
tournament of 1590, he retired in favor of a
younger man.
4. "Age his": age's.
5. One who offers prayers for the soul of another.

MARK ALEXANDER BOYD
(1563–1601)

Fra Bank to Bank

Fra bank to bank, fra wood to wood I rin,
  Ourhailit° with my feeble fantasie;   *overwhelmed*
  Like til a leaf that fallis from a tree,
Or til a reed ourblawin with the win'.

5   Twa gods [1] guidis me; the ane of them is blin',
  Yea and a bairn° brocht up in vanitie;   *child*
  The next a wife° ingenrit of the sea,   *woman*
And lichter° nor° a dauphin with her fin.   *more wanton/than*

Unhappy is the man for evermair
10 That tills the sand and sawis° in the air;   *sows*
  But twice unhappier is he, I lairn,
That feedis in his hairt a mad desire,
And follows on a woman throw the fire,
  Led by a blind and teachit by a bairn.

MICHAEL DRAYTON
(1563–1631)

From Idea

To the Reader of these Sonnets

Into these loves who but for passion looks,
At this first sight here let him lay them by
And seek elsewhere, in turning other books,
Which better may his labor satisfy.
5 No far-fetched sigh shall ever wound my breast,
Love from mine eye a tear shall never wring,
Nor in *Ah me*'s my whining sonnets dressed,
A libertine, fantastically I sing.
My verse is the true image of my mind,
10 Ever in motion, still desiring change;
And as thus to variety inclined,
So in all humors sportively I range:
  My muse is rightly of the English strain,
  That cannot long one fashion entertain.
61
Since there's no help, come let us kiss and part;
Nay, I have done, you get no more of me,
And I am glad, yea glad with all my heart
That thus so cleanly I myself can free;
5 Shake hands forever, cancel all our vows,
And when we meet at any time again,

---

1. Venus, goddess of love, supposedly born from the sea, and Cupid, her blind son.

Be it not seen in either of our brows
That we one jot of former love retain.
Now at the last gasp of love's latest breath,
10 When, his pulse failing, passion speechless lies,
When faith is kneeling by his bed of death,
And innocence is closing up his eyes,
     Now if thou wouldst, when all have given him over,
     From death to life thou mightst him yet recover.

          63

Truce, gentle love, a parley now I crave,
Methinks 'tis long since first these wars begun;
Nor thou nor I the better yet can have;
Bad is the match where neither party won.
5   I offer free conditions of fair peace,
My heart for hostage that it shall remain;
Discharge our forces, here let malice cease,
So for my pledge thou give me pledge again.
Or if no thing but death will serve thy turn,
10 Still thirsting for subversion of my state,
Do what thou canst, raze, massacre, and burn,
Let the world see the utmost of thy hate;
     I send defiance, since if overthrown,
     Thou vanquishing, the conquest is mine own.

                                            1619

CHRISTOPHER MARLOWE
(1564–1593)

The Passionate Shepherd to His Love[2]

Come live with me and be my love,
And we will all the pleasures prove°   *try*
That valleys, groves, hills, and fields,
Woods, or steepy mountain yields.

5   And we will sit upon the rocks,
Seeing the shepherds feed their flocks,
By shallow rivers to whose falls
Melodious birds sing madrigals.

And I will make thee beds of roses
10 And a thousand fragrant posies,
A cap of flowers, and a kirtle
Embroidered all with leaves of myrtle;

A gown made of the finest wool
Which from our pretty lambs we pull;
15 Fair lined slippers for the cold,
With buckles of the purest gold;

2. See the response by Sir Walter Ralegh, *The Nymph's Reply to the Shepherd.*

A belt of straw and ivy buds,
With coral clasps and amber studs:
And if these pleasures may thee move,
20   Come live with me, and be my love.

The shepherds' swains shall dance and sing
For thy delight each May morning:
If these delights thy mind may move,
Then live with me and be my love.

1599, 1600

WILLIAM SHAKESPEARE
(1564–1616)

From Sonnets

18

Shall I compare thee to a summer's day?
Thou art more lovely and more temperate:
Rough winds do shake the darling buds of May,
And summer's lease hath all too short a date:
5   Sometimes too hot the eye of heaven shines,
And often is his gold complexion dimmed;
And every fair from fair sometimes declines,
By chance or nature's changing course untrimmed;[1]
But thy eternal summer shall not fade,
10   Nor lose possession of that fair thou ow'st;°   ownest
Nor shall death brag thou wander'st in his shade,
When in eternal lines to time thou grow'st:
So long as men can breathe, or eyes can see,
So long lives this, and this gives life to thee.

30

When to the sessions[2] of sweet silent thought
I summon up remembrance of things past,
I sigh the lack of many a thing I sought,
And with old woes new wail my dear time's waste:
5   Then can I drown an eye, unused to flow,
For precious friends hid in death's dateless° night,   endless
And weep afresh love's long since canceled woe,
And moan the expense° of many a vanished sight: loss
Then can I grieve at grievances foregone,
10   And heavily from woe to woe tell o'er
The sad account of fore-bemoanéd moan,
Which I new pay as if not paid before.
But if the while I think on thee, dear friend,
All losses are restored and sorrows end.

64

When I have seen by time's fell° hand defaced   destroying
The rich-proud cost of outworn buried age;
When sometime° lofty towers I see down-razed,   formerly
And brass eternal slave to mortal rage;
5   When I have seen the hungry ocean gain

---

1. Divested of its beauty.   2. Sittings of a court.

Advantage on the kingdom of the shore,
And the firm soil win of the watery main,
Increasing store with loss, and loss with store;
When I have seen such interchange of state,
10 Or state itself confounded to decay,
Ruin hath taught me thus to ruminate,
That time will come and take my love away.
This thought is as a death, which cannot choose
But weep to have that which it fears to lose.

65

Since brass, nor[3] stone, nor earth, nor boundless sea
But sad mortality o'er-sways their power,
How with this rage shall beauty hold a plea,
Whose action is no stronger than a flower?
5 O, how shall summer's honey breath hold out
Against the wreckful siege of battering days,
When rocks impregnable are not so stout,
Nor gates of steel so strong, but Time decays?
O fearful meditation! where, alack,
10 Shall Time's best jewel from Time's chest lie hid?
Or what strong hand can hold his swift foot back?
Or who his spoil of beauty can forbid?
O, none, unless this miracle have might,
That in black ink my love may still shine bright.

73

That time of year thou mayst in me behold
When yellow leaves, or none, or few, do hang
Upon those boughs which shake against the cold,
Bare ruined choirs, where late the sweet birds sang.
5 In me thou see'st the twilight of such day
As after sunset fadeth in the west;
Which by and by black night doth take away,
Death's second self, that seals up all in rest.
In me thou see'st the glowing of such fire,
10 That on the ashes of his youth doth lie,
As the deathbed whereon it must expire,
Consumed with that which it was nourished by.
This thou perceiv'st, which makes thy love more strong,
To love that well which thou must leave ere long.

107

Not mine own fears, nor the prophetic soul
Of the wide world dreaming on things to come,
Can yet the lease of my true love control,
Supposed as forfeit to a cónfined doom.
5 The mortal moon[4] hath her eclipse endured,
And the sad augurs mock their own presage;
Incertainties now crown themselves assured,
And peace proclaims olives of endless age.
Now with the drops of this most balmy time
10 My love looks fresh, and death to me subscribes,°   *submits*
Since, spite of him, I'll live in this poor rhyme,
While he insults o'er dull and speechless tribes:
And thou in this shalt find thy monument,
When tyrants' crests and tombs of brass are spent.

---

3. I.e., since there is neither brass nor.
4. Queen Elizabeth, whose sixty-third year
had been anticipated by astrologers ("augurs")
as a time of disaster.

116

Let me not to the marriage of true minds
Admit impediments. Love is not love
Which alters when it alteration finds,
Or bends with the remover to remove:
5   Oh, no! it is an ever-fixéd mark,
That looks on tempests and is never shaken;
It is the star to every wandering bark,
Whose worth's unknown, although his height be taken.[5]
Love's not Time's fool, though rosy lips and cheeks
10   Within his bending sickle's compass come;
Love alters not with his brief hours and weeks.
But bears it out even to the edge of doom.[6]
If this be error and upon me proved,
I never writ, nor no man ever loved.

129

Th' expense of spirit in a waste of shame
Is lust in action; and till action, lust
Is perjured, murderous, bloody, full of blame,
Savage, extreme, rude, cruel, not to trust;
5   Enjoyed no sooner but despiséd straight:
Past reason hunted; and no sooner had,
Past reason hated, as a swallowed bait,
On purpose laid to make the taker mad:
Mad in pursuit, and in possession so;
10   Had, having, and in quest to have, extreme;
A bliss in proof,[7] and proved, a very woe;
Before, a joy proposed; behind, a dream.
All this the world well knows; yet none knows well
To shun the heaven that leads men to this hell.

130

My mistress' eyes are nothing like the sun;
Coral is far more red than her lips' red;
If snow be white, why then her breasts are dun;
If hairs be wires, black wires grow on her head.
5   I have seen roses damasked,° red and white,   *variegated*
But no such roses see I in her cheeks;
And in some perfumes is there more delight
Than in the breath that from my mistress reeks.
I love to hear her speak, yet well I know
10   That music hath a far more pleasing sound;
I grant I never saw a goddess go;°   *walk*
My mistress, when she walks, treads on the ground.
And yet, by heaven, I think my love as rare
As any she belied with false compare.

146

Poor soul, the center of my sinful earth,
Lord of[8] these rebel powers that thee array,°   *dress, deck out*
Why dost thou pine within and suffer dearth,
Painting thy outward walls so costly gay?
5   Why so large cost, having so short a lease,
Dost thou upon thy fading mansion spend?
Shall worms, inheritors of this excess,

---

5. I.e., although its elevation may be meas-
ured.
6. Judgment Day, the end of the world.
7. I.e., in the experience.

8. The original text repeats "My sinful
earth," apparently a mistake, in place of "Lord
of" at the beginning of this line. Other possi-
bilities have been suggested, e.g., "Rebuke,"
"Thrall to," "Pressed by."

Eat up thy charge? Is this thy body's end?
Then, soul, live thou upon thy servant's loss,
10   And let that pine to aggravate° thy store;   *increase*
Buy terms divine in selling hours of dross;
Within be fed, without be rich no more.
So shalt thou feed on death, that feeds on men,
And death once dead, there's no more dying then.

When Daisies Pied[9]

Spring

When daisies pied and violets blue
    And ladysmocks all silver-white
And cuckoobuds of yellow hue
    Do paint the meadows with delight,
5   The cuckoo then, on every tree,
Mocks married men;[1] for thus sings he,
                Cuckoo;
Cuckoo, cuckoo: Oh word of fear.
Unpleasing to a married ear!

10   When shepherds pipe on oaten straws,
    And merry larks are plowmen's clocks,
When turtles tread,[2] and rooks, and daws,
    And maidens bleach their summer smocks,
The cuckoo then, on every tree,
15   Mocks married men; for thus sings he,
                Cuckoo;
Cuckoo, cuckoo: Oh word of fear,
Unpleasing to a married ear!

Winter

When icicles hang by the wall
20   And Dick the shepherd blows his nail[3]
And Tom bears logs into the hall,
    And milk comes frozen home in pail.
When blood is nipped and ways be foul,
Then nightly sings the staring owl,
25   Tu-who;
Tu-whit, tu-who: a merry note,
While greasy Joan doth keel[4] the pot.

When all aloud the wind doth blow,
    And coughing drowns the parson's saw,°   *wise saying*
30   And birds sit brooding in the snow,
    And Marian's nose looks red and raw,
When roasted crabs° hiss in the bowl,   *crab apples*
Then nightly sings the staring owl,
                Tu-who;
35   Tu-whit, tu-who: a merry note
While greasy Joan doth keel the pot.

                                    1595?   1598

---

9. From *Love's Labour's Lost.*
1. The cuckoo's song was often fanci-
fully as "Cuckold!"

2. I.e., when turtledoves mate.
3. I.e., breathes on his fingers to warm them.
4. Keep from boiling over by stirring.

Under the Greenwood Tree[5]

Under the greenwood tree
Who loves to lie with me,
And turn his merry note
Unto the sweet bird's throat,
5 Come hither, come hither, come hither:
    Here shall he see
    No enemy
But winter and rough weather.

Who doth ambition shun
10 And loves to live i' the sun,
Seeking the food he eats,
And pleased with what he gets,
Come hither, come hither, come hither:
    Here shall he see
    No enemy
But winter and rough weather.

1599?   1623

Fear No More the Heat o' the Sun[6]

Fear no more the heat o' the sun,
  Nor the furious winter's rages;
Thou thy worldly task hast done,
  Home art gone, and ta'en thy wages:
5 Golden lads and girls all must,
As chimney-sweepers, come to dust.

Fear no more the frown o' the great;
  Thou art past the tyrant's stroke;
Care no more to clothe and eat;
10   To thee the reed is as the oak:
The scepter, learning, physic, must
All follow this, and come to dust.

Fear no more the lightning flash,
  Nor the all-dreaded thunder stone;[7]
15 Fear not slander, censure rash;
  Thou hast finished joy and moan:
All lovers young, all lovers must
Consign to thee, and come to dust.

No exorciser harm thee!
20 Nor no witchcraft charm thee!
Ghost unlaid forbear thee!
Nothing ill come near thee!
Quiet consummation have;
And renownéd be thy grave!

1610?   1623

---

5. From *As You Like It.*
6. From *Cymbeline.*

7. Thunder was thought to be caused by mete-
orites falling from the sky.

When Daffodils Begin to Peer[8]

When daffodils begin to peer,
  With heigh! the doxy° over the dale,   *trollop, mistress*
Why, then comes in the sweet o' the year;
  For the red blood reigns in the winter's pale.[9]

5 The white sheet bleaching on the hedge,
  With heigh! the sweet birds, Oh, how they sing!
Doth set my pugging° tooth on edge;   *thieving*
  For a quart of ale is a dish for a king.

The lark, that tirra-lirra chants,
  With heigh! with heigh! the thrush and the jay,
10 Are summer songs for me and my aunts,°   *sweethearts*
  While we lie tumbling in the hay.

                             1611   1623

Full Fathom Five[10]

Full fathom five thy father lies;
  Of his bones are coral made;
Those are pearls that were his eyes:
  Nothing of him that doth fade,
5 But doth suffer a sea change
Into something rich and strange.
Sea nymphs hourly ring his knell:
  Ding-dong.
Hark! now I hear them—Ding-dong, bell.

                             1611   1623

THOMAS CAMPION
(1567–1620)

My Sweetest Lesbia[1]

My sweetest Lesbia, let us live and love,
And though the sager sort our deeds reprove,
Let us not weigh them. Heaven's great lamps do dive
Into their west, and straight again revive,
5 But soon as once set is our little light,
Then must we sleep one ever-during night.

If all would lead their lives in love like me,
Then bloody swords and armor should not be;
No drum nor trumpet peaceful sleeps should move,
10 Unless alarm came from the camp of love.
But fools do live, and waste their little light,
And seek with pain their ever-during night.

---

8. From *The Winter's Tale.*
9. Territory, as well as lack of color.
10. From *The Tempest.*
1. The Roman poet Catullus sang the praises

of his Lesbia in a poem here imitated and
partly translated by Campion. Compare Ben
Jonson's adaptation of the same poem in *Song:
To Celia.*

When timely death my life and fortune ends,
Let not my hearse be vexed with mourning friends,
15   But let all lovers, rich in triumph, come
And with sweet pastimes grace my happy tomb;
And Lesbia, close up thou my little light,
And crown with love my ever-during night.

1601

Follow Thy Fair Sun

Follow thy fair sun, unhappy shadow;
Though thou be black as night,
And she made all of light,
Yet follow thy fair sun, unhappy shadow.

5   Follow her whose light thy light depriveth;
Though here thou liv'st disgraced,
And she in heaven is placed,
Yet follow her whose light the world reviveth!

Follow those pure beams whose beauty burneth,
10   That so have scorched thee,
As thou still black must be,
Till her kind beams thy black to brightness turneth.

Follow her while yet her glory shineth;
There comes a luckless night,
15   That will dim all her light;
And this the black unhappy shade divineth.

Follow still since so thy fates ordained;
The sun must have his shade,
Till both at once do fade;
20   The sun still proved,° the shadow still disdained.   °approved

1601

When Thou Must Home

When thou must home to shades of underground,
And there arrived, a new admiréd guest,
The beauteous spirits do engirt thee round,
White Iope, blithe Helen,[2] and the rest,
5   To hear the stories of thy finished love
From that smooth tongue whose music hell can move,

Then wilt thou speak of banqueting delights,
Of masques and revels which sweet youth did make,
Of tourneys and great challenges of knights,
10   And all these triumphs for thy beauty's sake;
When thou hast told these honors done to thee,
Then tell, Oh tell, how thou didst murther me.

1601

2. Iope or Cassiopeia and Helen of Troy, the   second for beauty and fickleness.
first renowned for beauty and vanity, the

Rose-cheeked Laura

Rose-cheeked Laura, come,
Sing thou smoothly with thy beauty's
Silent music, either other
    Sweetly gracing.

5 Lovely forms do flow
From concent° divinely framed;   *sounds in harmony*
Heav'n is music, and thy beauty's
    Birth is heavenly.

These dull notes we sing
10 Discords need for helps to grace them;
Only beauty purely loving
    Knows no discord,

But still moves delight,
Like clear springs renewed by flowing,
15 Ever perfect, ever in them-
    Selves eternal.

                                  1602

Now Winter Nights Enlarge

Now winter nights enlarge
    The number of their hours;
And clouds their storms discharge
    Upon the airy towers.
5 Let now the chimneys blaze
    And cups o'erflow with wine,
Let well-tuned words amaze
    With harmony divine.
Now yellow waxen lights
10   Shall wait on honey love
While youthful revels, masques, and courtly sights
    Sleep's leaden spells remove.

This time doth well dispense
    With[3] lovers' long discourse;
15 Much speech hath some defense,
    Though beauty no remorse.
All do not all things well;
    Some measures comely tread,
Some knotted riddles tell,
20   Some poems smoothly read.
The summer hath his joys,
    And winter his delights;
Though love and all his pleasures are but toys,
    They shorten tedious nights.

                                    1617

---

3. Put up with, deal indulgently with.

Thrice Toss These Oaken Ashes

Thrice toss these oaken ashes in the air,
Thrice sit thou mute in this enchanted chair;
Then thrice three times tie up this truelove's knot,
And murmur soft "She will, or she will not."

5   Go burn these poisonous weeds in yon blue fire,
These screech-owl's feathers and this prickling briar,
This cypress gathered at a dead man's grave,
That all thy fears and cares an end may have.

Then come, you fairies, dance with me a round;
10   Melt her hard heart with your melodious sound.
In vain are all the charms I can devise:
She hath an art to break them with her eyes.

1617

There Is a Garden in Her Face

There is a garden in her face,
Where roses and white lilies grow,
A heavenly paradise is that place,
Wherein all pleasant fruits do flow.
5   There cherries grow, which none may buy
Till "Cherry ripe!"[4] themselves do cry.

Those cherries fairly do enclose
Of orient pearl a double row,
Which when her lovely laughter shows,
10   They look like rosebuds filled with snow.
Yet them nor peer nor prince can buy,
Till "Cherry ripe!" themselves do cry.

Her eyes like angels watch them still;
Her brows like bended bows do stand,
15   Threatening with piercing frowns to kill
All that attempt with eye or hand
Those sacred cherries to come nigh,
Till "Cherry ripe!" themselves do cry.

1617

THOMAS NASHE
(1567–1601)

Spring, the Sweet Spring

Spring, the sweet spring, is the year's pleasant king,
Then blooms each thing, then maids dance in a ring,
Cold doth not sting, the pretty birds do sing:
    Cuckoo, jug-jug, pu-we, to-witta-woo![6]

4. A London street vendor's cry.   lapwing, owl.
6. Bird songs of the cuckoo, nightingale,

5 The palm and may make country houses gay,
  Lambs frisk and play, the shepherds pipe all day,
  And we hear aye birds tune this merry lay:
    Cuckoo, jug-jug, pu-we, to-witta-woo!

  The fields breathe sweet, the daisies kiss our feet,
10 Young lovers meet, old wives a-sunning sit,
  In every street these tunes our ears do greet:
    Cuckoo, jug-jug, pu-we, to-witta-woo!
      Spring, the sweet spring!

1600

A Litany in Time of Plague

  Adieu, farewell, earth's bliss;
  This world uncertain is;
  Fond° are life's lustful joys;   *foolish*
  Death proves them all but toys;°   *trifles*
5 None from his darts can fly;
  I am sick, I must die.
    Lord, have mercy on us!

  Rich men, trust not in wealth,
  Gold cannot buy you health;
10 Physic himself must fade.
  All things to end are made,
  The plague full swift goes by;
  I am sick, I must die.
    Lord, have mercy on us!

15 Beauty is but a flower
  Which wrinkles will devour;
  Brightness falls from the air;
  Queens have died young and fair;
  Dust hath closed Helen's eye.
20 I am sick, I must die.
    Lord, have mercy on us!

  Strength stoops unto the grave,
  Worms feed on Hector brave;
  Swords may not fight with fate,
25 Earth still holds ope her gate.
  "Come, come!" the bells do cry.
  I am sick, I must die.
    Lord, have mercy on us.

  Wit with his wantonness
30 Tasteth death's bitterness;
  Hell's executioner
  Hath no ears for to hear
  What vain art can reply.
  I am sick, I must die.
35   Lord, have mercy on us.

  Haste, therefore, each degree,
  To welcome destiny;
  Heaven is our heritage,

Earth but a player's stage;
40 Mount we unto the sky.
I am sick, I must die.
    Lord, have mercy on us.

                    1592   1600

JOHN DONNE
(1572–1631)

Song

Go and catch a falling star,
  Get with child a mandrake root,[1]
Tell me where all past years are,
  Or who cleft the Devil's foot,
5 Teach me to hear mermaids singing,
Or to keep off envy's stinging,
          And find
          What wind
Serves to advance an honest mind.

10 If thou beest born to strange sights,
  Things invisible to see,
Ride ten thousand days and nights,
  Till age snow white hairs on thee.
Thou, when thou return'st, wilt tell me
15 All strange wonders that befell thee,
          And swear
          Nowhere
Lives a woman true, and fair.

If thou find'st one, let me know,
20 Such a pilgrimage were sweet;
Yet do not, I would not go,
  Though at next door we might meet;
Though she were true when you met her,
And last till you write your letter,
25   Yet she
          Will be
False, ere I come, to two, or three.

                                    1633

Woman's Constancy

Now thou hast loved me one whole day,
Tomorrow when thou leav'st, what wilt thou say?
Wilt thou then antedate some new-made vow?
          Or say that now
5 We are not just those persons which we were?
Or, that oaths made in reverential fear
Of love, and his wrath, any may forswear?

---

1. The large, forked root of the mandrake, roughly resembling a human body, was often credited with human attributes. As a medicine, it was supposed to promote conception.

Or, as true deaths true marriages untie,
  So lovers' contracts, images of those,
10 Bind but till sleep, death's image, them unloose?
    Or, your own end to justify,
For having purposed change, and falsehood, you
Can have no way but falsehood to be true?
Vain lunatic,[2] against these 'scapes I could
15   Dispute, and conquer, if I would,
        Which I abstain to do,
For by tomorrow, I may think so too.

1633

The Sun Rising

    Busy old fool, unruly sun,
      Why dost thou thus,
Through windows and through curtains call on us?
Must to thy motions lovers' seasons run?
5   Saucy pedantic wretch, go chide
      Late school boys and sour prentices,
  Go tell court huntsmen that the king will ride,
    Call country ants to harvest offices;
Love, all alike, no season knows nor clime,
10 Nor hours, days, months, which are the rags of time.

    Thy beams, so reverend and strong
      Why shouldst thou think?
I could eclipse and cloud them with a wink,
But that I would not lose her sight so long;
15   If her eyes have not blinded thine,
      Look, and tomorrow late tell me,
  Whether both th' Indias[3] of spice and mine
    Be where thou leftst them, or lie here with me.
Ask for those kings whom thou saw'st yesterday,
20 And thou shalt hear, All here in one bed lay.

    She's all states, and all princes, I,
      Nothing else is.
Princes do but play us; compared to this,
All honor's mimic, all wealth alchemy.[4]
25   Thou, sun, art half as happy as we,
      In that the world's contracted thus;
  Thine age asks ease, and since thy duties be
    To warm the world, that's done in warming us.
Shine here to us, and thou art everywhere;
30 This bed thy center is, these walls, thy sphere.

1633

The Canonization

For God's sake hold your tongue, and let me love,
  Or chide my palsy, or my gout,
My five gray hairs, or ruined fortune, flout,
  With wealth your state, your mind with arts improve,

---

2. The word has for Donne the additional meaning of *inconstant* or *fickle*, since lunacy (from *luna*, moon) was supposed to be affected by the changing phases of the moon.

3. India and the West Indies, whence came spices and gold, respectively.
4. I.e., a fraud.

5   Take you a course, get you a place,
         Observe His Honor, or His Grace,
   Or the King's real, or his stampéd face[5]
      Contémplate; what you will, approve,°   *try*
      So you will let me love.

10   Alas, alas, who's injured by my love?
         What merchant's ships have my sighs drowned?
   Who says my tears have overflowed his ground?
      When did my colds a forward spring remove?
         When did the heats which my veins fill
15   Add one more to the plaguy bill?[6]
   Soldiers find wars, and lawyers find out still
         Litigious men, which quarrels move,
         Though she and I do love.

   Call us what you will, we're made such by love;
20   Call her one, me another fly,
   We're tapers too, and at our own cost die,[7]
      And we in us find th' eagle and the dove.[8]
         The phoenix[9] riddle hath more wit°   *sense*
         By us: we two being one, are it.
25   So, to one neutral thing both sexes fit.
      We die and rise the same, and prove
      Mysterious by this love.

   We can die by it, if not live by love,
      And if unfit for tombs and hearse
30   Our legend be, it will be fit for verse;
      And if no piece of chronicle we prove,
         We'll build in sonnets pretty rooms;
         As well a well-wrought urn becomes
   The greatest ashes, as half-acre tombs;
35   And by these hymns, all shall approve
      Us canonized for love:

   And thus invoke us: You whom reverend love
      Made one another's hermitage;
   You, to whom love was peace, that now is rage;
40   Who did the whole world's soul contract, and drove
         Into the glasses of your eyes
         (So made such mirrors, and such spies,
   That they did all to you epitomize)
      Countries, towns, courts: Beg from above
45   A pattern of your love!

                                                                    1633

Song

   Sweetest love, I do not go
      For weariness of thee,
   Nor in hope the world can show
      A fitter love for me;

---

5. I.e., on coins.
6. Weekly list of plague victims.
7. Death was a popular metaphor for sexual intercourse in the 17th century. "At our own cost" reflects the common superstition that each act of lovemaking shortened one's life by a day.
8. Common symbols of strength and peace.
9. A legendary bird, the only one of its kind, represented as living five hundred years in the Arabian desert, being consumed in fire, then rising anew from its own ashes.

5   But since that I
Must die at last, 'tis best
To use myself in jest,
    Thus by feigned deaths to die.

Yesternight the sun went hence,
10   And yet is here today;
He hath no desire nor sense,
    Nor half so short a way:
        Then fear not me,
But believe that I shall make
15 Speedier journeys, since I take
    More wings and spurs than he.

O how feeble is man's power,
    That if good fortune fall,
Cannot add another hour,
20   Nor a lost hour recall!
        But come bad chance,
And we join to'it[10] our strength,
And we teach it art and length,
    Itself o'er us to'advance.

25 When thou sigh'st, thou sigh'st not wind,
    But sigh'st my soul away;
When thou weep'st, unkindly kind,
    My life's blood doth decay.
        It cannot be
30 That thou lov'st me, as thou say'st,
If in thine my life thou waste;
    Thou art the best of me.

Let not thy divining heart
    Forethink me any ill;
35 Destiny may take thy part,
    And may thy fears fulfill;
        But think that we
Are but turned aside to sleep;
They who one another keep
40   Alive, ne'er parted be.

                                1633

A Valediction: Of Weeping

        Let me pour forth
My tears before thy face whilst I stay here,
For thy face coins them, and thy stamp they bear,
And by this mintage they are something worth,
5   For thus they be
        Pregnant of thee;
Fruits of much grief they are, emblems of more;
When a tear falls, that Thou falls which it bore,
So thou and I are nothing then, when on a diverse shore.

10. Donne frequently uses an apostrophe between words to indicate that the neighboring syllables are fused in pronunciation and counted as one metrically. Such contractions occur only under certain phonetic conditions (e.g., when one word ends, and the next begins, with a vowel). They continue to be common in modern speech, although in writing we now limit use of the apostrophe to those contractions which omit letters from the usual spelling of the words (*you're, don't*).

10
        On a round ball
A workman that hath copies by, can lay
An Europe, Afric, and an Asïa,
And quickly make that, which was nothing, all,
        So doth each tear
15
        Which thee doth wear,[1]
A globe, yea world, by that impression grow,
Till thy tears mixed with mine do overflow
This world; by waters sent from thee, my heaven dissolvéd so.

        O more than moon,
20
Draw not up seas to drown me in thy sphere;
Weep me not dead, in thine arms, but forbear
To teach the sea what it may do too soon.
        Let not the wind
        Example find
25
To do me more harm than it purposeth;
Since thou and I sigh one another's breath,
Whoe'er sighs most is cruelest, and hastes the other's death.

        1633

A Valediction: Forbidding Mourning

As virtuous men pass mildly'away,
    And whisper to their souls to go,
Whilst some of their sad friends do say
    The breath goes now, and some say, No;

5
So let us melt, and make no noise,
    No tear-floods, nor sigh-tempests move,
'Twere profanation of our joys
    To tell the laity our love.

Moving of th' earth brings harms and fears,
10
    Men reckon what it did and meant;
But trepidation of the spheres,[2]
    Though greater far, is innocent.

Dull sublunary[3] lovers' love
    (Whose soul is sense) cannot admit
15
Absence, because it doth remove
    Those things which elemented it.

But we by'a love so much refined
    That our selves know not what it is,
Inter-assuréd of the mind,
20
    Care less, eyes, lips, and hands to miss.

Our two souls therefore, which are one,
    Though I must go, endure not yet
A breach, but an expansion,
    Like gold to airy thinness beat.

---

1. I.e., doth wear thee.
2. A trembling of the celestial spheres, hypothesized by Ptolemaic astronomers to account for unpredicted variations in the paths of the heavenly bodies.
3. Beneath the moon; earthly—hence, changeable.

25 If they be two, they are two so
    As stiff twin compasses are two;
Thy soul, the fixed foot, makes no show
    To move, but doth, if th' other do.

    And though it in the center sit,
30   Yet when the other far doth roam,
It leans and hearkens after it,
    And grows erect, as that comes home.

Such wilt thou be to me, who must
    Like th' other foot, obliquely run;
35 Thy firmness makes my circle⁴ just,
    And makes me end where I begun.

1633

The Ecstasy⁵

Where, like a pillow on a bed,
    A pregnant bank swelled up to rest
The violet's reclining head,
    Sat we two, one another's best.
5 Our hands were firmly cémented
    With a fast balm, which thence did spring.
Our eye-beams twisted, and did thread
    Our eyes upon one double string;
So to'intergraft our hands, as yet
10   Was all the means to make us one;
And pictures in our eyes to get°   *beget*
    Was all our propagation.
As 'twixt two equal armies, Fate
    Suspends uncertain victory,
15 Our souls (which to advance their state,
    Were gone out) hung 'twixt her and me.
And whilst our souls negotiate there,
    We like sepulchral statues lay;
All day the same our postures were,
20   And we said nothing all the day.
If any, so by love refined
    That he soul's language understood,
And by good love were grown all mind,
    Within convenient distance stood,
25 He (though he knew not which soul spake,
    Because both meant, both spake the same)
Might thence a new concoction⁶ take,
    And part far purer than he came.
This ecstasy doth unperplex,
30   We said, and tell us what we love;
We see by this it was not sex;
    We see we saw not what did move;
But as all several° souls contain   *separate*
    Mixture of things, they know not what,

4. The circle was a symbol of perfection; with a dot in the middle, it was also the alchemist's symbol for gold.
5. Literally, "a standing out." The term was used by religious mystics to describe the experience in which the soul seemed to leave the body and rise superior to it in a state of heightened awareness.
6. Mixture of diverse elements refined by heat (alchemical term).

35 Love these mixed souls doth mix again,
     And makes both one, each this and that.
  A single violet transplant,
     The strength, the colour, and the size
  (All which before was poor, and scant)
40   Redoubles still, and multiplies.
  When love, with one another so
     Interinanimates two souls,
  That abler soul, which thence doth flow,
     Defects of loneliness controls.
45 We then, who are this new soul, know,
     Of what we are composed, and made,
  For, th' atomies° of which we grow,   *atoms*
     Are souls, whom no change can invade.
  But O alas, so long, so far
50   Our bodies why do we forbear?
  They're ours, though they're not we; we are
     Th' intelligences, they the spheres.[7]
  We owe them thanks because they thus,
     Did us to us at first convey,
55 Yielded their forces, sense, to us,
     Nor are dross to us, but allay.°   *alloy*
  On man heaven's influence works not so
     But that it first imprints the air,[8]
  So soul into the soul may flow,
60   Though it to body first repair.
  As our blood labors to beget
     Spirits as like souls as it can,[9]
  Because such fingers need to knit
     That subtle knot which makes us man:
65 So must pure lovers' souls descend
     To' affections, and to faculties
  Which sense may reach and apprehend;
     Else a great Prince in prison lies.
  To'our bodies turn we then, that so
70   Weak men on love revealed may look;
  Love's mysteries in souls do grow,
     But yet the body is his book.
  And if some lover, such as we,
     Have heard this dialogue of one,
75 Let him still mark us; he shall see
     Small change when we're to bodies gone.

                        1633

The Funeral

Whoever comes to shroud me, do not harm
     Nor question much
That subtle wreath of hair which crowns my arm;
  The mystery, the sign you must not touch,

---

7. The nine orders of angels ("intelligences") were believed to govern the nine spheres of Ptolemaic astronomy.
8. Influences from the heavenly bodies were conceived of as being transmitted through the medium of the air; also, angels were thought to assume bodies of air in their dealings with men.
9. "Spirits" were vapors believed to permeate the blood and to mediate between the body and the soul.

5   For 'tis my outward soul,
Viceroy to that, which then to heaven being gone,
        Will leave this to control,
And keep these limbs, her provinces, from dissolution.

For if the sinewy thread my brain lets fall
10   Through every part
Can tie those parts and make me one of all;
These hairs, which upward grew, and strength and art
        Have from a better brain,
Can better do'it; except she meant that I
15   By this should know my pain,
As prisoners then are manacled, when they're condemned to die.

Whate'er she meant by 'it, bury it with me,
        For since I am
Love's martyr, it might breed idolatry,
20 If into other's hands these relics came;
        As 'twas humility
To'afford to it all that a soul can do,
        So 'tis some bravery,
That since you would save none of me, I bury some of you.

                                    1633

The Relic

When my grave is broke up again
Some second guest to entertain[1]
(For graves have learned that woman-head°   *womanhood*
To be to more than one a bed),
5   And he that digs it, spies
A bracelet of bright hair about the bone,
        Will he not let'us alone,
And think that there a loving couple lies,
Who thought that this device might be some way
10 To make their souls, at the last busy day,[2]
Meet at this grave, and make a little stay?

If this fall in a time, or land,
Where mis-devotion doth command,
Then he that digs us up, will bring
15   Us to the Bishop and the King,
        To make us relics; then
Thou shalt be'a Mary Magdalen,[3] and I
        A something else thereby;
All women shall adore us, and some men;
20 And since at such time, miracles are sought,
I would have that age by this paper taught
What miracles we harmless lovers wrought.

---

1. Re-use of a grave, after an interval of years, was a common 17th-century practice.
2. Judgment Day, when all parts of the body would be reassembled and reunited with the soul in the resurrection.

3. The woman out of whom Christ had cast seven devils (Luke viii.2), traditionally identified with the repentant prostitute of Luke vii.37–50.

First, we loved well and faithfully,
Yet knew not what we loved, nor why,
25   Difference of sex no more we knew,
Than our guardian angels do;
Coming and going, we
Perchance might kiss, but not between those meals;
Our hands ne'er touched the seals,
Which nature, injured by late law, sets free:
30   These miracles we did; but now, alas,
All measure and all language I should pass,
Should I tell what a miracle she was.

1633

Good Friday, 1613. Riding Westward

Let man's soul be a sphere, and then, in this,
Th' intelligence that moves,[2] devotion is,
And as the other spheres, by being grown
Subject to foreign motions, lose their own,
5   And being by others hurried every day,
Scarce in a year their natural form obey;
Pleasure or business, so, our souls admit
For their first mover, and are whirled by it.
Hence is 't, that I am carried towards the West
10   This day, when my soul's form bends towards the East.
There I should see a Sun, by rising, set,
And by that setting endless day beget:
But that Christ on this cross did rise and fall,
Sin had eternally benighted all.
15   Yet dare I'almost be glad I do not see
That spectacle, of too much weight for me.
Who sees God's face, that is self-life, must die;
What a death were it then to see God die?
It made his own lieutenant, Nature, shrink;
20   It made his footstool crack, and the sun wink.[3]
Could I behold those hands which span the poles,
And tune all spheres at once, pierced with those holes?
Could I behold that endless height which is
Zenith to us, and to'our antipodes,[4]
25   Humbled below us? Or that blood which is
The seat of all our souls, if not of His,
Make dirt of dust, or that flesh which was worn
By God, for his apparel, ragg'd and torn?
If on these things I durst not look, durst I
30   Upon his miserable mother cast mine eye,
Who was God's partner here, and furnished thus
Half of that sacrifice which ransomed us?
Though these things, as I ride, be from mine eye,
They're present yet unto my memory,
35   For that looks towards them; and Thou look'st towards me,

2. An angel was believed to govern the movements of each of the nine celestial spheres in Ptolemaic astronomy. Each sphere, in addition to its own motion, was influenced by the motions of those outside it ("foreign motions," line 4), the outermost being known as the *primum mobile*, "first mover" (line 8).

3. "Thus saith the Lord * * * the earth is my footstool" (Isaiah lxvi.1). An earthquake and an eclipse accompanied the crucifixion of Jesus (Matthew xxvii.45, 51).
4. The zenith is that part of the heavens directly above any point on earth; the antipodes are that part of the earth diametrically opposite such a point.

O Saviour, as Thou hang'st upon the tree.
I turn my back to Thee but to receive
Corrections, till Thy mercies bid Thee leave.
O think me worth Thine anger; punish me;
40 Burn off my rusts and my deformity;
Restore Thine image so much, by Thy grace,
That Thou may'st know me, and I'll turn my face.

1633

From Holy Sonnets

1

Thou hast made me, and shall Thy work decay?
Repair me now, for now mine end doth haste;
I run to death, and death meets me as fast,
And all my pleasures are like yesterday.
5 I dare not move my dim eyes any way,
Despair behind, and death before doth cast
Such terror, and my feeble flesh doth waste
By sin in it, which it towards hell doth weigh.
Only Thou art above, and when towards Thee
10 By Thy leave I can look, I rise again;
But our old subtle foe so tempteth me
That not one hour myself I can sustain.
Thy grace may wing me to prevent his art,
And Thou like adamant° draw mine iron heart.

loadstone
1635

7

At the round earth's imagined corners, blow
Your trumpets, angels;[5] and arise, arise
From death, you numberless infinities
Of souls, and to your scattered bodies go;
5 All whom the flood did, and fire shall,[6] o'erthrow,
All whom war, dearth, age, agues, tyrannies,
Despair, law, chance hath slain, and you whose eyes
Shall behold God, and never taste death's woe.[7]
But let them sleep, Lord, and me mourn a space;
10 For, if above all these, my sins abound,
'Tis late to ask abundance of Thy grace
When we are there. Here on this lowly ground,
Teach me how to repent; for that's as good
As if Thou'hadst sealed my pardon with Thy blood.

1633

9

If poisonous minerals, and if that tree
Whose fruit threw death on else immortal us,
If lecherous goats, if serpents envious
Cannot be damned, alas, why should I be?
5 Why should intent or reason, born in me,
Make sins, else equal, in me more heinous?
And mercy being easy and glorious

---

5. "* * * I saw four angels standing on the four corners of the earth, holding the four winds of the earth * * *" (Revelation vii.1).
6. At the end of the world, "* * * the elements shall melt with fervent heat, the earth also and the works that are therein shall be burned up" (II Peter iii.10).

7. "But I tell you of a truth, there be some standing here, which shall not taste of death, till they see the kingdom of God" (Christ's words to his disciples, Luke ix.27).

To God, in his stern wrath why threatens he?
But who am I, that dare dispute with thee,
10   O God? Oh! of thine only worthy blood,
And my tears, make a heavenly Lethean[8] flood,
And drown in it my sins' black memory.
That thou remember them, some claim as debt;
I think it mercy if thou wilt forget.

1633

10

Death, be not proud, though some have callèd thee
Mighty and dreadful, for thou are not so;
For those whom thou think'st thou dost overthrow
Die not, poor Death, nor yet canst thou kill me.
5   From rest and sleep, which but thy pictures be,
Much pleasure; then from thee much more must flow,
And soonest our best men with thee do go,
Rest of their bones, and soul's delivery.
Thou'art slave to fate, chance, kings, and desperate men,
10   And dost with poison, war, and sickness dwell,
And poppy'or charms can make us sleep as well
And better than thy stroke; why swell'st thou then?
One short sleep past, we wake eternally
And death shall be no more; Death, thou shalt die.

1633

14

Batter my heart, three-personed God; for You
As yet but knock, breathe, shine, and seek to mend;
That I may rise and stand, o'erthrow me,'and bend
Your force to break, blow, burn, and make me new.
5   I, like an usurped town, to'another due,
Labor to'admit You, but O, to no end;
Reason, Your viceroy'in me, me should defend,
But is captíved, and proves weak or untrue.
Yet dearly'I love You,'and would be lovéd fain,
10   But am betrothed unto Your enemy.
Divorce me,'untie or break that knot again;
Take me to You, imprison me, for I,
Except You'enthrall me, never shall be free,
Nor ever chaste, except You ravish me.

1633

Hymn to God My God, in My Sickness

Since I am coming to that holy room
    Where, with Thy choir of saints for evermore,
I shall be made Thy music; as I come
    I tune the instrument here at the door,
5   And what I must do then, think here before.

Whilst my physicians by their love are grown
    Cosmographers, and I their map, who lie
Flat on this bed, that by them may be shown

8. Lethe was a river in the classical under-   forget the past.
world; drinking of its waters caused one to

That this is my southwest discovery[7]
10 *Per fretum febris*, by these straits to die,

I joy, that in these straits, I see my West;[8]
For, though their currents yield return to none,
What shall my West hurt me? As West and East
In all flat maps (and I am one) are one,
15 So death doth touch the resurrection.

Is the Pacific Sea my home? Or are
The Eastern riches? Is Jerusalem?
Anyan,° and Mágellan, and Gíbraltar,   **Bering Straits**
All straits, and none but straits, are ways to them,
20 Whether where Japhet dwelt, or Cham, or Shem.[9]

We think that Paradise and Calvary,
Christ's cross, and Adam's tree, stood in one place;
Look, Lord, and find both Adams met in me;
As the first Adam's sweat surrounds my face,
25 May the last Adam's blood my soul embrace.

So, in his purple wrapped, receive me, Lord;
By these his thorns give me his other crown;
And, as to others' souls I preached Thy word,
Be this my text, my sermon to mine own:
30 Therefore that he may raise the Lord throws down.[10]

                                                        1635

BEN JONSON
(1573–1637)

To the Reader

Pray thee, take care, that tak'st my book in hand,
To read it well: that is, to understand.

                                                        1616

To Doctor Empirick

When men a dangerous disease did 'scape
Of old, they gave a cock to Aesculape;[1]
Let me give two, that doubly am got free
From my disease's danger, and from thee.

                                                        1616

---

7. Magellan had discovered the straits which bear his name in 1520. They lie at the southern tip of South America and are hence southwest from England. *"Per fretum febris"*: through the straits of fever.
8. "* * * strait is the gate, and narrow is the way, which leadeth unto life * * *" (Matthew vii.14). "West": i.e., death.
9. The three sons of Noah, who settled in Europe, Africa, and Asia respectively after the Flood.
10. Adapted from Psalms cxlvi.8: "* * * the Lord raiseth them that are bowed down."
1. Aesculapius, the Roman god of medicine and healing.

On My First Daughter

Here lies, to each her parents' ruth,°   sorrow
Mary, the daughter of their youth;
Yet all heaven's gifts being heaven's due,
It makes the father less to rue.
5   At six months' end she parted hence
With safety of her innocence;
Whose soul heaven's queen, whose name she bears,
In comfort of her mother's tears,
Hath placed amongst her virgin-train:
10 Where, while that severed doth remain,
This grave partakes the fleshly birth;
Which cover lightly, gentle earth!

                                                                        1616

On My First Son

Farewell, thou child of my right hand,[2] and joy;
My sin was too much hope of thee, loved boy:
Seven years thou'wert lent to me, and I thee pay,
Exacted by thy fate, on the just day.[3]
5   O could I lose all father now! for why
Will man lament the state he should envý,
To have so soon 'scaped world's and flesh's rage,
And, if no other misery, yet age?
Rest in soft peace, and asked, say, "Here doth lie
10 Ben Jonson his best piece of poetry."
For whose sake henceforth all his vows be such
As what he loves may never like too much.

                                                                        1616

To Fool or Knave

Thy praise or dispraise is to me alike:
One doth not stroke me, nor the other strike.

                                                                        1616

On English Monsieur

Would you believe, when you this mónsieur[4] see,
That his whole body should speak French, not he?
That so much scarf of France, and hat, and feather,
And shoe, and tie, and garter should come hether,°   hither
5   And land on one whose face durst never be
Toward the sea farther than Half-Way Tree?[5]
That he, untraveled, should be French so much
As Frenchmen in his company should seem Dutch?
Or had his father, when he did him get,
10 The French disease,[6] with which he labors yet?
Or hung some mónsieur's picture on the wall,

2. A literal translation of the Hebrew Ben-
iamin, the boy's name.
3. Jonson's son died on his seventh birthday
in 1603.
4. Stress on first syllable; often spelled monser
in Jonson's time, suggesting an Anglicized

pronunciation.
5. Perhaps a landmark between London and
Dover, where a traveler would embark for
France.
6. I.e., syphilis.

By which his dam conceived him, clothes and all?
Or is it some French statue? No: 'T doth move,
And stoop, and cringe. O then, it needs must prove
15 The new French tailor's motion,° monthly made,   *puppet*
Daily to turn in Paul's,⁷ and help the trade.

1616

Inviting a Friend to Supper

Tonight, grave sir, both my poor house, and I
Do equally desire your company;
Not that we think us worthy such a guest,
But that your worth will dignify our feast
5 With those that come, whose grace may make that seem
Something, which else could hope for no esteem.
It is the fair acceptance, sir, creates
The entertainment perfect, not the cates.°   *food*
Yet shall you have, to rectify your palate,
10 An olive, capers, or some better salad
Ushering the mutton; with a short-legged hen,
If we can get her, full of eggs, and then
Lemons, and wine for sauce; to these a cony°   *rabbit*
Is not to be despaired of, for our money;
15 And, though fowl now be scarce, yet there are clerks,
The sky not falling, think we may have larks.⁸
I'll tell you of more, and lie, so you will come:
Of partridge, pheasant, woodcock, of which some
May yet be there, and godwit,⁹ if we can;
20 Knot, rail, and ruff too. Howsoe'er, my man
Shall read a piece of Virgil, Tacitus,
Livy, or of some better book to us,
Of which we'll speak our minds, amidst our meat;
And I'll profess no verses to repeat.
25 To this, if aught appear which I not know of,
That will the pastry, not my paper, show of.
Digestive¹ cheese and fruit there sure will be;
But that which most doth take my Muse and me,
Is a pure cup of rich Canary wine,
30 Which is the Mermaid's² now, but shall be mine;
Of which had Horace, or Anacreon tasted,
Their lives, as do their lines, till now had lasted.
Tobacco,³ nectar, or the Thespian spring,
Are all but Luther's beer⁴ to this I sing.
35 Of this we will sup free, but moderately,
And we will have no Pooley, or Parrot⁵ by,
Nor shall our cups make any guilty men;
But, at our parting we will be as when
We innocently met. No simple word
40 That shall be uttered at our mirthful board,
Shall make us sad next morning or affright
The liberty that we'll enjoy tonight.

1616

7. St. Paul's Cathedral in London. In the 17th century St. Paul's was a popular gathering place; merchants hired men to walk up and down in the yard advertising their wares.
8. According to an old proverb, "When the sky falls we shall have larks."
9. The godwit, knot, rail, and ruff are all wading birds related to the curlew or sandpiper. They were formerly regarded as delicacies.
1. Promoting or aiding digestion.
2. A famous tavern—a favorite haunt of Jonson's.
3. Smoking was often called "drinking tobacco."
4. German beer, considered inferior.
5. Notorious government informers.

On Gut

Gut eats all day and lechers all the night;
So all his meat he tasteth over twice;
And, striving so to double his delight,
He makes himself a thoroughfare of vice.
5   Thus in his belly can he change a sin:
Lust it comes out, that gluttony went in.

1616

Epitaph on Salomon Pavy, a Child of Queen Elizabeth's Chapel[6]

Weep with me, all you that read
    This little story,
And know, for whom a tear you shed,
    Death's self is sorry.
5   'Twas a child, that so did thrive
    In grace and feature,
As Heaven and Nature seemed to strive
    Which owned the creature.
Years he numbered scarce thirteen
10   When Fates turned cruel,
Yet three filled zodiacs[7] had he been
    The stage's jewel,
And did act, what now we moan,
    Old men so duly,
15 As, sooth, the Parcae[8] thought him one,
    He played so truly.
So, by error, to his fate
    They all consented;
But viewing him since (alas, too late)
20   They have repented.
And have sought, to give new birth,
    In baths to steep him;[9]
But, being so much too good for earth,
    Heaven vows to keep him.

1616

To Penshurst[1]

Thou art not, Penshurst, built to envious show,
Of touch° or marble; nor canst boast a row   *touchstone, basanite*
Of polished pillars, or a roof of gold;
Thou hast no lantern,[2] whereof tales are told,
5   Or stair, or courts; but stand'st an ancient pile,
And, these grudged at, art reverenced the while.
Thou joy'st in better marks, of soil, of air,
Of wood, of water; therein thou art fair.
Thou hast thy walks for health, as well as sport;

6. The Children of Queen Elizabeth's Chapel were a company of boy actors. Salomon Pavy had acted in Jonson's plays.
7. I.e., three years.
8. The three Fates, who determined men's destinies.

9. Aeson, the father of Jason, was made young again by a magic bath prepared by Jason's wife Medea.
1. The country estate of the Sidney family, in Kent.
2. A glassed or open structure raised above the roof of a house.

10 Thy mount, to which the dryads° do resort,   *wood nymphs*
   Where Pan and Bacchus their high feasts have made,
   Beneath the broad beech and the chestnut shade;
   That taller tree, which of a nut was set
   At his great birth[3] where all the Muses met.
15 There in the writhéd bark are cut the names
   Of many a sylvan,° taken with his flames;   *forest dweller*
   And thence the ruddy satyrs oft provoke
   The lighter fauns to reach thy Lady's Oak.
   Thy copse too, named of Gamage,[4] thou hast there,
20 That never fails to serve thee seasoned deer
   When thou wouldst feast or exercise thy friends.
   The lower land, that to the river bends,
   Thy sheep, thy bullocks, kine, and calves do feed;
   The middle grounds thy mares and horses breed.
25 Each bank doth yield thee conies;° and the tops,   *rabbits*
   Fertile of wood, Ashore and Sidney's copse,
   To crown thy open table, doth provide
   The purpled pheasant with the speckled side;
   The painted partridge lies in every field,
30 And for thy mess is willing to be killed.
   And if the high-swollen Medway[5] fail thy dish,
   Thou hast thy ponds, that pay thee tribute fish,
   Fat aged carps that run into thy net,
   And pikes, now weary their own kind to eat,
35 As loath the second draught or cast to stay,°   *await*
   Officiously° at first themselves betray;   *dutifully*
   Bright eels that emulate them, and leap on land
   Before the fisher, or into his hand.
   Then hath thy orchard fruit, thy garden flowers,
40 Fresh as the air, and new as are the hours.
   The early cherry, with the later plum,
   Fig, grape, and quince, each in his time doth come;
   The blushing apricot and woolly peach
   Hang on thy walls, that every child may reach.
45 And though thy walls be of the country stone,
   They're reared with no man's ruin, no man's groan;
   There's none that dwell about them wish them down;
   But all come in, the farmer and the clown,°   *countryman*
   And no one empty-handed, to salute
50 Thy lord and lady, though they have no suit.
   Some bring a capon, some a rural cake,
   Some nuts, some apples; some that think they make
   The better cheeses bring them, or else send
   By their ripe daughters, whom they would commend
55 This way to husbands, and whose baskets bear
   An emblem of themselves in plum or pear.
   But what can this (more than express their love)
   Add to thy free provisions, far above
   The need of such? whose liberal board doth flow
60 With all that hospitality doth know;
   Where comes no guest but is allowed to eat,
   Without his fear, and of thy lord's own meat;
   Where the same beer and bread, and selfsame wine,

---

3. Sir Philip Sidney's, November 30, 1554.   owner of Penshurst.
4. Barbara Gamage, wife of Sir Robert Sid-   5. The local river.
ney, Philip's younger brother and the current

That is his lordship's shall be also mine,
And I not fain° to sit (as some this day   obliged
At great men's tables), and yet dine away.
Here no man tells° my cups; nor, standing by,   counts
A waiter doth my gluttony envý,
But gives me what I call, and lets me eat;
He knows below he shall find plenty of meat.
Thy tables hoard not up for the next day;
Nor, when I take my lodging, need I pray
For fire, or lights, or livery;° all is there,   provisions
As if thou then wert mine, or I reigned here:
There's nothing I can wish, for which I stay.
That found King James when, hunting late this way
With his brave son, the prince, they saw thy fires
Shine bright on every hearth, as the desires
Of thy Penates⁶ had been set on flame
To entertain them; or the country came
With all their zeal to warm their welcome here.
What (great I will not say, but) sudden cheer
Didst thou then make 'em! and what praise was heaped
On thy good lady then, who therein reaped
The just reward of her high housewifery;
To have her linen, plate, and all things nigh,
When she was far; and not a room but dressed
As if it had expected such a guest!
These, Penshurst, are thy praise, and yet not all.
Thy lady's noble, friutful, chaste withal.
His children thy great lord may call his own,
A fortune in this age but rarely known.
They are, and have been, taught religion; thence
Their gentler spirits have sucked innocence.
Each morn and even they are taught to pray,
With the whole household, and may, every day,
Read in their virtuous parents' noble parts
The mysteries of manners, arms, and arts.
Now, Penshurst, they that will proportion° thee   compare
With other edifices, when they see
Those proud, ambitious heaps, and nothing else,
May say their lords have built, but thy lord dwells.

1616

Song: To Celia

Drink to me only with thine eyes,
And I will pledge with mine;
Or leave a kiss but in the cup,
And I'll not look for wine.
The thirst that from the soul doth rise,
Doth ask a drink divine:
But might I of Jove's nectar sup,
I would not change for thine.

6. Roman household gods.

I sent thee late a rosy wreath,
10　Not so much honoring thee,
As giving it a hope, that there
It could not withered be.
But thou thereon did'st only breathe,
And sent'st it back to me;
15　Since when it grows and smells, I swear,
Not of itself, but thee.

1616

Slow, Slow, Fresh Fount[7]

Slow, slow, fresh fount, keep time with my salt tears;
Yet slower, yet, O faintly, gentle springs!
List to the heavy part the music bears,
Woe weeps out her division,[8] when she sings.
5　　　Droop herbs and flowers;
　　　Fall grief in showers;
Our beauties are not ours. O, I could still,
Like melting snow upon some craggy hill,
　　　Drop, drop, drop, drop,
10　Since nature's pride is now a withered daffodil.

1600

Still to Be Neat[9]

Still to be neat, still to be dressed,
As you were going to a feast;
Still to be powdered, still perfumed;
Lady, it is to be presumed,
5　Though art's hid causes are not found,
All is not sweet, all is not sound.

Give me a look, give me a face
That makes simplicity a grace;
Robes loosely flowing, hair as free;
10　Such sweet neglect more taketh me
Then all th' adulteries of art.
They strike mine eyes, but not my heart.

1609

Though I Am Young and Cannot Tell[1]

Though I am young, and cannot tell
　Either what Death or Love is well,
Yet I have heard they both bear darts,
　And both do aim at human hearts.
5　And then again, I have been told
　Love wounds with heat, as Death with cold;
So that I fear they do but bring
　Extremes to touch, and mean one thing.

---

7. From *Cynthia's Revels*, sung by Echo for Narcissus, who fell in love with his own reflection and was changed into the flower that bears his name. The daffodil (line 11) is a species of narcissus.
8. Part in a song.
9. From *The Silent Woman*.
1. From *The Sad Shepherd*.

As in a ruin we it call
10 One thing to be blown up, or fall;
Or to our end like way may have
By a flash of lightning, or a wave;
So Love's inflaméd shaft or brand
May kill as soon as Death's cold hand;
15 Except Love's fires the virtue have
To fright the frost out of the grave.

1641

To the Memory of My Beloved, the Author Mr. William Shakespeare

AND WHAT HE HATH LEFT US[2]

To draw no envy, Shakespeare, on thy name,
Am I thus ample to thy book and fame,
While I confess thy writings to be such
As neither man nor Muse can praise too much.
5 'Tis true, and all men's suffrage.° But these ways   consent
Were not the paths I meant unto thy praise:
For silliest ignorance on these may light,
Which, when it sounds at best, but echoes right;
Or blind affection,° which doth ne'er advance   feeling
10 The truth, but gropes, and urgeth all by chance;
Or crafty malice might pretend this praise,
And think to ruin where it seemed to raise.
These are as some infamous bawd or whore
Should praise a matron. What could hurt her more?
15 But thou art proof against them, and, indeed,
Above th' ill fortune of them, or the need.
I therefore will begin. Soul of the age!
The applause! delight! the wonder of our stage!
My Shakespeare, rise; I will not lodge thee by
20 Chaucer or Spenser, or bid Beaumont lie
A little further to make thee a room:[3]
Thou art a monument without a tomb,
And art alive still while thy book doth live,
And we have wits to read and praise to give.
25 That I not mix thee so, my brain excuses,
I mean with great, but disproportioned° Muses;   not comparable
For, if I thought my judgment were of years,
I should commit thee surely with thy peers,
And tell how far thou didst our Lyly outshine,
30 Or sporting Kyd, or Marlowe's mighty line.[4]
And though thou hadst small Latin and less Greek,
From thence to honor thee I would not seek
For names, but call forth thund'ring Aeschylus,
Euripides, and Sophocles to us,

2. Prefixed to the first folio edition of Shakespeare's works, 1623.
3. Chaucer, Spenser, and Beaumont are all buried in Westminster Abbey.
4. John Lyly, Thomas Kyd, and Christopher Marlowe, all Elizabethan dramatists.

35 Pacuvius, Accius, him of Cordova dead,[5]
To life again, to hear thy buskin[6] tread
And shake a stage; or, when thy socks were on,
Leave thee alone for the comparison
Of all that insolent Greece or haughty Rome
40 Sent forth, or since did from their ashes come.
Triumph, my Britain; thou hast one to show
To whom all scenes° of Europe homage owe.　　　　*stages*
He was not of an age, but for all time!
And all the Muses still were in their prime
45 When like Apollo he came forth to warm
Our ears, or like a Mercury to charm.
Nature herself was proud of his designs,
And joyed to wear the dressing of his lines,
Which were so richly spun, and woven so fit,
50 As, since, she will vouchsafe no other wit:
The merry Greek, tart Aristophanes,
Neat Terence, witty Plautus[7] now not please,
But antiquated and deserted lie,
As they were not of Nature's family.
55 Yet must I not give Nature all; thy Art,
My gentle Shakespeare, must enjoy a part.
For though the poet's matter Nature be,
His Art doth give the fashion; and that he
Who casts to write a living line must sweat
60 (Such as thine are) and strike the second heat
Upon the muses' anvil; turn the same,
And himself with it, that he thinks to frame,
Or for the laurel he may gain a scorn;
For a good poet's made as well as born.
65 And such wert thou! Look how the father's face
Lives in his issue, even so the race
Of Shakespeare's mind and manners brightly shines
In his well-turnéd and true-filéd lines,
In each of which he seems to shake a lance,
70 As brandished at the eyes of ignorance.
Sweet swan of Avon, what a sight it were
To see thee in our waters yet appear,
And make those flights upon the banks of Thames
That so did take Eliza and our James![8]
75 But stay; I see thee in the hemisphere
Advanced and made a constellation there!
Shine forth, thou star of poets, and with rage
Or influence[9] chide or cheer the drooping stage,
Which, since thy flight from hence, hath mourned like night,
80 And despairs day, but for thy volume's light.

1623

---

5. Marcus Pacuvius and Lucius Accius were Roman tragedians of the second century B.C.; "him of Cordova" is the Roman tragedian Seneca of the first century A.D.
6. The high-heeled boot worn by Greek tragic actors; the "sock" or light shoe was worn in comedies.
7. Aristophanes (Greek) and Terence and Plautus (Roman) were comic writers of the fourth to second centuries B.C.
8. Queen Elizabeth and King James.
9. A supposed emanation of power from stars.

JOHN WEBSTER
(1580–1625)

Call for the Robin Redbreast and the Wren

Call for the robin redbreast and the wren,
Since o'er shady groves they hover,
And with leaves and flowers do cover
The friendless bodies of unburied men.
5   Call unto his funeral dole°   *sorrow*
The ant, the field mouse, and the mole,
To rear him hillocks that shall keep him warm,
And, when gay tombs are robbed, sustain no harm;
But keep the wolf far thence, that's foe to men,
10 For with his nails he'll dig them up again.

                                                   1612

Hark, Now Everything Is Still

Hark, now everything is still;
The screech owl and the whistler shrill
Call upon our dame aloud,
And bid her quickly don her shroud.
5 Much you had of land and rent;
Your length in clay's now competent.
A long war disturbed your mind;
Here your perfect peace is signed.
Of what is 't fools make such vain keeping?
10 Sin their conception, their birth weeping,
Their life a general mist of error,
Their death a hideous storm of terror.
Strew your hair with powders sweet,
Don clean linen, bathe your feet,
15 And, the foul fiend more to check,
A crucifix let bless your neck.
'Tis now full tide, 'tween night and day,
End your groan and come away.

                                                   1623

ROBERT HERRICK
(1591–1674)

The Argument[1] of His Book

I sing of brooks, of blossoms, birds, and bowers,
Of April, May, of June, and July flowers.
I sing of Maypoles, hock carts, wassails, wakes,[2]
Of bridegrooms, brides, and of their bridal cakes.

---

1. I.e., subject matter.
2. The hock cart brought in the last load of   the harvest. "Wakes": parish festivals as well as watches over the dead.

5   I write of youth, of love, and have access
    By these to sing of cleanly wantonness.
    I sing of dews, of rains, and, piece by piece,
    Of balm, of oil, of spice, and ambergris.
    I sing of times trans-shifting, and I write
10 How roses first came red and lilies white.
    I write of groves, of twilights, and I sing
    The court of Mab[3] and of the fairy king.
    I write of hell; I sing (and ever shall)
    Of heaven, and hope to have it after all.

1648

The Scare-Fire [3a]

  Water, water I desire,
  Here's a house of flesh on fire;
  Ope' the fountains and the springs,
  And come all to bucketings.
5 What ye cannot quench, pull down,
  Spoil a house to save a town:
  Better 'tis that one should fall,
  Than by one to hazard all.

1648

Delight in Disorder

  A sweet disorder in the dress
  Kindles in clothes a wantonness.
  A lawn about the shoulders thrown
  Into a fine distractiön;
5 An erring lace, which here and there
  Enthralls the crimson stomacher;[4]
  A cuff neglectful, and thereby
  Ribbons to flow confusedly;
  A winning wave, deserving note,
10 In the tempestuous petticoat;
  A careless shoestring, in whose tie
  I see a wild civility;
  Do more bewitch me than when art
  Is too precise in every part.

1648

Corinna's Going A-Maying

  Get up! get up for shame! the blooming morn
  Upon her wings presents the god unshorn.[5]
    See how Aurora[6] throws her fair
    Fresh-quilted colors through the air:
5   Get up, sweet slug-a-bed, and see
    The dew bespangling herb and tree.
  Each flower has wept and bowéd toward the east
  Above an hour since, yet you not dressed;
    Nay, not so much as out of bed?
10   When all the birds have matins said,

---

3. Queen of the fairies.
3a. A sudden conflagration.
4. An ornamental piece worn under the open

(and often laced) front of a bodice.
5. I.e., Apollo, god of the sun.
6. Goddess of the dawn.

And sung their thankful hymns, 'tis sin,
Nay, profanation to keep in,
Whenas a thousand virgins on this day
Spring, sooner than the lark, to fetch in May.[7]

15 Rise, and put on your foliage, and be seen
To come forth, like the springtime, fresh and green,
And sweet as Flora.[8] Take no care
For jewels for your gown or hair;
Fear not; the leaves will strew
20 Gems in abundance upon you;
Besides, the childhood of the day has kept,
Against[9] you come, some orient pearls unwept;
Come and receive them while the light
Hangs on the dew-locks of the night,
25 And Titan[1] on the eastern hill
Retires himself, or else stands still
Till you come forth. Wash, dress, be brief in praying:
Few beads[2] are best when once we go a-Maying.

Come, my Corinna, come; and, coming mark
30 How each field turns a street, each street a park
Made green and trimmed with trees; see how
Devotion gives each house a bough
Or branch: each porch, each door ere this,
An ark, a tabernacle is,
35 Made up of whitethorn neatly interwove,
As if here were those cooler shades of love.
Can such delights be in the street
And open fields, and we not see 't?
Come, we'll abroad; and let's obey
40 The proclamation made for May,
And sin no more, as we have done, by staying;
But, my Corinna, come, let's go a-Maying.

There's not a budding boy or girl this day
But is got up and gone to bring in May;
45 A deal of youth, ere this, is come
Back, and with whitethorn laden home.
Some have dispatched their cakes and cream
Before that we have left to dream;
And some have wept, and wooed, and plighted troth,
50 And chose their priest, ere we can cast off sloth.
Many a green-gown has been given,
Many a kiss, both odd and even,
Many a glance, too, has been sent
From out the eye, love's firmament;
55 Many a jest told of the keys betraying
This night, and locks picked; yet we're not a-Maying.

Come, let us go while we are in our prime,
And take the harmless folly of the time.
We shall grow old apace, and die
60 Before we know our liberty.

---

7. Boughs of white hawthorn, traditionally gathered to decorate streets and houses on May Day.
8. Goddess of flowers.

9. I.e., in readiness for the time when. "Orient": lustrous, glowing.
1. The sun.
2. I.e., prayers.

Our life is short, and our days run
  As fast away as does the sun;
And, as a vapor or a drop of rain
Once lost, can ne'er be found again;
65   So when or you or I are made
  A fable, song, or fleeting shade,
  All love, all liking, all delight
  Lies drowned with us in endless night.
Then while time serves, and we are but decaying,
70 Come, my Corinna, come, let's go a-Maying.

1648

To the Virgins, to Make Much of Time

Gather ye rosebuds while ye may,
  Old time is still a-flying;
And this same flower that smiles today
  Tomorrow will be dying.

5 The glorious lamp of heaven, the sun,
  The higher he's a-getting,
The sooner will his race be run,
  And nearer he's to setting.

That age is best which is the first,
10   When youth and blood are warmer;
But being spent, the worse, and worst
  Times still succeed the former.

Then be not coy, but use your time,
  And, while ye may, go marry;
15 For, having lost but once your prime,
  You may forever tarry.

1648

Upon a Child That Died

Here she lies, a pretty bud,
Lately made of flesh and blood,
Who as soon fell fast asleep
As her little eyes did peep.
5 Give her strewings, but not stir
The earth that lightly covers her.

1648

To Daffodils

Fair daffodils, we weep to see
  You haste away so soon:
As yet the early-rising sun
  Has not attained his noon.
5   Stay, stay,
  Until the hasting day
    Has run
  But to the evensong;
And, having prayed together, we
10   Will go with you along.

We have short time to stay as you;
　　We have as short a spring;
As quick a growth to meet decay,
　　As you or anything.
15　　　We die,
　　As your hours do, and dry
　　　　Away
　　Like to the summer's rain;
Or as the pearls of morning's dew,
20　　Ne'er to be found again.

1648

His Prayer to Ben Jonson

When I a verse shall make,
　　Know I have prayed thee,
For old religion's sake,
　　Saint Ben, to aid me.

5　Make the way smooth for me,
　　When I, thy Herrick,
Honoring thee, on my knee
　　Offer my lyric.

Candles I'll give to thee,
10　　And a new altar;
And thou, Saint Ben, shalt be
　　Writ in my psalter.

1648

Upon a Child

Here a pretty baby lies
Sung asleep with lullabies:
Pray be silent, and not stir
Th' easy earth that covers her.

1648

Upon Julia's Clothes

Whenas in silks my Julia goes,
Then, then, methinks, how sweetly flows
That liquefaction of her clothes.

Next, when I cast mine eyes, and see
5　That brave vibration, each way free,
O, how that glittering taketh me!

1648

Upon Prue, His Maid

In this little urn is laid
Prudence Baldwin, once my maid,
From whose happy spark here let
Spring the purple violet.

1648

Upon Ben Jonson

Here lies Jonson with the rest
Of the poets; but the best.
Reader, would'st thou more have known?
Ask his story, not this stone.
5   That will speak what this can't tell
Of his glory. So farewell.

1648

An Ode for Him

Ah, Ben!
Say how or when
Shall we, thy guests,
Meet at those lyric feasts
5   Made at the Sun,
The Dog, the Triple Tun,[3]
Where we such clusters had
As made us nobly wild, not mad;
And yet each verse of thine
10 Outdid the meat, outdid the frolic wine.

My Ben!
Or come again,
Or send to us
Thy wit's great overplus;
15   But teach us yet
Wisely to husband it,
Lest we that talent spend,
And having once brought to an end
That precious stock, the store
20 Of such a wit the world should have no more.

1648

To His Conscience

Can I not sin, but thou wilt be
My private protonotary?[1]
Can I not woo thee to pass by
A short and sweet iniquity?
5   I'll cast a mist and cloud upon
My delicate transgression,
So utter dark, as that no eye
Shall see the hugged impiety.
Gifts blind the wise,[2] and bribes do please,
10 And wind° all other witnesses;   *pervert*
And wilt not thou, with gold, be tied
To lay thy pen and ink aside?
That in the murk° and tongueless night,   *murky*
Wanton I may, and thou not write?

---

3. The names of taverns.
1. Chief recorder in a law court.
2. Deuteronomy xvi.19: ". . . a gift doth blind the eyes of the wise, and pervert the words of the righteous."

15 It will not be; and therefore now,
For times to come, I'll make this vow:
From aberrations to live free;
So I'll not fear the judge or thee.

1648

The White Island, or Place of the Blest

In this world, the isle of dreams,
While we sit by sorrow's streams,
Tears and terrors are our themes
    Reciting:

5 But when once from hence we fly,
More and more approaching nigh
Unto young eternity,
    Uniting:

In that whiter island, where
10 Things are evermore sincere;
Candor° here and luster there   *whiteness*
    Delighting:

There no monstrous fancies shall
Out of hell an horror call,
15 To create, or cause at all,
    Affrighting.

There, in calm and cooling sleep
We our eyes shall never steep,
But eternal watch shall keep,
20   Attending

Pleasures, such as shall pursue
Me immortalized, and you;
And fresh joys, as never too
    Have ending.

1648

HENRY KING
(1592–1669)

The Exequy

Accept, thou shrine of my dead saint,
Instead of dirges, this complaint;
And for sweet flowers to crown thy hearse,
Receive a strew of weeping verse
5 From thy grieved friend, whom thou might'st see
Quite melted into tears for thee.

Dear loss! since thy untimely fate
My task hath been to meditate

On thee, on thee; thou art the book,
10 The library whereon I look,
Though almost blind. For thee, loved clay,
I languish out, not live, the day,
Using no other exercise
But what I practice with mine eyes;
15 By which wet glasses I find out
How lazily time creeps about
To one that mourns: this, only this,
My exercise and business is.
So I compute the weary hours
20 With sighs dissolvéd into showers.

Nor wonder if my time go thus
Backward and most preposterous;
Thou hast benighted me, thy set
This eve of blackness did beget,
25 Who wast my day, though overcast
Before thou hadst thy noontide passed;
And I remember must in tears,
Thou scarce hadst seen so many years
As day tells hours. By thy clear sun
30 My love and fortune first did run;
But thou wilt never more appear
Folded within my hemisphere,
Since both thy light and motïon
Like a fled star is fallen and gone;
35 And 'twixt me and my soul's dear wish
An earth now interposéd is,
Which such a strange eclipse doth make
As ne'er was read in almanac.

I could allow thee for a time
40 To darken me and my sad clime;
Were it a month, a year, or ten,
I would thy exile live till then,
And all that space my mirth adjourn,
So thou wouldst promise to return;
45 And putting off thy ashy shroud,
At length disperse this sorrow's cloud.

But woe is me! the longest date
Too narrow is to calculate
These empty hopes; never shall I
50 Be so much blest as to descry
A glimpse of thee, till that day come
Which shall the earth to cinders doom,
And a fierce fever must calcine[1]
The body of this world—like thine,
55 My little world! That fit of fire
Once off, our bodies shall aspire
To our souls' bliss; then we shall rise
And view ourselves with clearer eyes
In that calm region where no night
60 Can hide us from each other's sight.

1. Reduce to dust by heat.

Meantime, thou hast her, earth: much good
May my harm do thee. Since it stood
With heaven's will I might not call
Her longer mine, I give thee all
65 My short-lived right and interest
In her whom living I loved best;
With a most free and bounteous grief
I give thee what I could not keep.
Be kind to her, and prithee look
70 Thou write into thy doomsday book
Each parcel of this rarity
Which in thy casket shrined doth lie.
See that thou make thy reckoning straight,
And yield her back again by weight;
75 For thou must audit on thy trust
Each grain and atom of this dust,
As thou wilt answer Him that lent,
Not gave thee, my dear monument.

So close the ground, and 'bout her shade
80 Black curtains draw; my bride is laid.

Sleep on, my love, in thy cold bed,
Never to be disquieted!
My last good-night! Thou wilt not wake
Till I thy fate shall overtake;
85 Till age, or grief, or sickness must
Marry my body to that dust
It so much loves; and fill the room
My heart keeps empty in thy tomb.
Stay for me there; I will not fail
90 To meet thee in that hollow vale.
And think not much of my delay;
I am already on the way,
And follow thee with all the speed
Desire can make, or sorrows breed.
95 Each minute is a short degree,
And every hour a step towards thee.
At night when I betake to rest,
Next morn I rise nearer my west
Of life, almost by eight hours' sail,
100 Than when sleep breathed his drowsy gale.

Thus from the sun my bottom° steers,   vessel
And my day's compass downward bears;
Nor labor I to stem the tide
Through which to thee I swiftly glide.

105 'Tis true, with shame and grief I yield,
Thou like the van° first took'st the field,   vanguard
And gotten hast the victory
In thus adventuring to die
Before me, whose more years might crave
110 A just precédence in the grave.
But hark! my pulse like a soft drum
Beats my approach, tells thee I come;
And slow howe'er my marches be,
I shall at last sit down by thee.

¹¹⁵ The thought of this bids me go on,
And wait my dissolutïon
With hope and comfort. Dear (forgive
The crime), I am content to live
Divided, with but half a heart,
¹²⁰ Till we shall meet and never part.

1657

A Contemplation Upon Flowers

Brave flowers, that I could gallant it like you,
And be as little vain;
You come abroad and make a harmless show,
And to your beds of earth again;
5 You are not proud, you know your birth,
For your embroidered garments are from earth.

You do obey your months and times, but I
Would have it ever spring;
My fate would know no winter, never die,
10 Nor think of such a thing;
Oh that I could my bed of earth but view,
And smile and look as cheerfully as you.

Oh teach me to see death and not to fear,
But rather to take truce;
15 How often have I seen you at a bier,
And there look fresh and spruce;
You fragrant flowers then teach me that my breath
Like yours may sweeten and perfume my death.

ca. 1660

GEORGE HERBERT
(1593–1633)

Redemption

Having been tenant long to a rich lord,
Not thriving, I resolvéd to be bold,
And make a suit unto him, to afford°   *grant*
A new small-rented lease, and cancel the old.

5 In heaven at his manor I him sought;
They told me there that he was lately gone
About some land, which he had dearly bought
Long since on earth, to take possessïon.

I straight returned, and knowing his great birth,
10 Sought him accordingly in great resorts;
In cities, theaters, gardens, parks, and courts;
At length I heard a ragged noise and mirth
Of thieves and murderers; there I him espied,
Who straight, *Your suit is granted*, said, and died.

1633

Easter Wings

Lord, who createdst man in wealth and store,°   *abundance*
    Though foolishly he lost the same,
        Decaying more and more
           Till he became
5   Most poor:
             With thee
          O let me rise
      As larks, harmoniously,
    And sing this day thy victories:
10 Then shall the fall further the flight in me.

My tender age in sorrow did begin;
    And still with sicknesses and shame
        Thou didst so punish sin,
           That I became
15   Most thin.
             With thee
          Let me combine,
    And feel this day[1] thy victory;
    For, if I imp[2] my wing on thine,
20 Affliction shall advance the flight in me.

                    1633

Prayer (I)

Prayer, the church's banquet, angels' age,
    God's breath in man returning to his birth,
    The soul in paraphrase, heart in pilgrimage,
The Christian plummet sounding heaven and earth;

5 Engine against th' Almighty, sinner's tower,
    Reverséd thunder, Christ-side-piercing spear,
    The six-days' world[3] transposing in an hour,
A kind of tune, which all things hear and fear;

Softness, and peace, and joy, and love, and bliss,
10   Exalted manna, gladness of the best,
    Heaven in ordinary,[4] man well dressed,
The Milky Way, the bird of Paradise,

    Church bells beyond the stars heard, the soul's blood,
    The land of spices; something understood.

                    1633

---

1. The words "this day," which are superfluous in the metrical scheme of the poem, were perhaps included in the early editions to emphasize the occasion, Easter. They are omitted, however, in the only surviving manuscript book of Herbert's poems.
2. A term from falconry: additional feathers were "imped" or grafted onto the wing of a hawk to improve its powers of flight.
3. God created the world in six days (Genesis i). Also, of course, the six weekdays might be thought of as a "world" distinct from that of the Sabbath.
4. In the everyday course of things. More specifically, *ordinary* also meant a daily allowance of food or an established order or form, as of the divine service.

Jordan (I)[5]

Who says that fictions only and false hair
Become a verse? Is there in truth no beauty?
Is all good structure in a winding stair?
May no lines pass, except they do their duty
5   Not to a true, but painted chair?[6]

Is it no verse, except enchanted groves
And sudden arbors[7] shadow coarse-spun lines?
Must purling streams refresh a lover's loves?
Must all be veiled while he that reads, divines,
10   Catching the sense at two removes?

Shepherds are honest people; let them sing:
Riddle who list, for me, and pull for prime:[8]
I envy no man's nightingale or spring;
Nor let them punish me with loss of rhyme,
15   Who plainly say, *My God, My King.*

1633

Church Monuments

While that my soul repairs to her devotion,
Here I intomb my flesh, that it betimes
May take acquaintance of this heap of dust;
To which the blast of death's incessant motion,
5   Fed with the exhalation of our crimes,
Drives all at last. Therefore I gladly trust

My body to this school, that it may learn
To spell his elements, and find his birth
Written in dusty heraldry and lines;
10   Which dissolution sure doth best discern,
Comparing dust with dust, and earth with earth.
These laugh at jet, and marble put for signs,

To sever the good fellowship of dust,
And spoil the meeting. What shall point out them,
15   When they shall bow, and kneel, and fall down flat
To kiss those heaps, which now they have in trust?
Dear flesh, while I do pray, learn here thy stem
And true descent, that when thou shalt grow fat

And wanton in thy cravings, thou mayst know
20   That flesh is but the glass which holds the dust
That measures all our time; which also shall
Be crumbled into dust. Mark, here below
How tame these ashes are, how free from lust,
That thou mayst fit thyself against thy fall.

1633

5. A river in the Holy Land, the cleansing waters of which cured leprosy (II Kings v.10).
6. It was customary to bow or "do one's duty" to the king's chair of state even when unoccupied.
7. One aim of garden design was to incorporate attractive features in such a way that they would be revealed unexpectedly in the course of a walk.
8. Draw for a winning card.

The Windows

Lord, how can man preach thy eternal word?
  He is a brittle crazy° glass;   *flawed*
Yet in thy temple thou dost him afford
  This glorious and transcendent place,
5   To be a window, through thy grace.

But when thou dost anneal in glass thy story,
  Making thy life to shine within
The holy preachers, then the light and glory
  More reverend grows, and more doth win;
10   Which else shows waterish, bleak, and thin.

Doctrine and life, colors and light, in one
  When they combine and mingle, bring
A strong regard and awe; but speech alone
  Doth vanish like a flaring thing,
15   And in the ear, not conscience, ring.

                                                    1633

Virtue

Sweet day, so cool, so calm, so bright,
  The bridal of the earth and sky:
The dew shall weep thy fall tonight;
  For thou must die.

5 Sweet rose, whose hue, angry and brave,
  Bids the rash gazer wipe his eye:
Thy root is ever in its grave,
  And thou must die.

Sweet spring, full of sweet days and roses,
10 A box where sweets° compacted lie;   *perfumes*
My music shows ye have your closes,[9]
  And all must die.

Only a sweet and virtuous soul,
  Like seasoned timber, never gives;
15 But though the whole world turn to coal,[1]
  Then chiefly lives.

                                                    1633

Artillery

As I one evening sat before my cell,
Methought[2] a star did shoot into my lap.
I rose and shook my clothes, as knowing well
That from small fires comes oft no small mishap;

---

9. A close is a cadence, the conclusion of
a musical strain.

1. An allusion to Judgment Day, when the
world will end in a general conflagration.
2. It seemed to me.

5 When suddenly I heard one say,
"Do as thou usest, disobey,
Expel good motions from thy breast,
Which have the face of fire, but end in rest."

I, who had heard of music in the spheres,
10 But not of speech in stars, began to muse;
But turning to my God, whose ministers
The stars and all things are: "If I refuse,
    Dread Lord," said I, "so oft my good,
    Then I refuse not ev'n with blood
15   To wash away my stubborn thought;
For I will do or suffer what I ought.

"But I have also stars and shooters too,
Born where thy servants both artilleries use.
My tears and prayers night and day do woo
20 And work up to thee; yet thou dost refuse.
    Not but I am (I must say still)
    Much more obliged to do thy will
    Than thou to grant mine; but because
Thy promise now hath ev'n set thee thy laws.

25 "Then we are shooters both, and thou dost deign
To enter combat with us, and contest
With thine own clay. But I would parley fain:
Shun not my arrows, and behold my breast.
    Yet if thou shunnest, I am thine:
30   I must be so, if I am mine.
    There is no articling° with thee: *negotiating*
I am but finite, yet thine infinitely."

                                                      1633

The Collar

I struck the board° and cried, "No more;   *table*
    I will abroad!
What? shall I ever sigh and pine?
My lines and life are free, free as the road,
5   Loose as the wind, as large as store.°   *abundance*
        Shall I be still in suit?
Have I no harvest but a thorn
To let me blood, and not restore
What I have lost with cordial° fruit?   *life-giving*
10   Sure there was wine
Before my sighs did dry it; there was corn
    Before my tears did drown it.
    Is the year only lost to me?
    Have I no bays³ to crown it,
15 No flowers, no garlands gay? All blasted?
        All wasted?
Not so, my heart; but there is fruit,
    And thou hast hands.
Recover all thy sigh-blown age

---

3. A laurel garland symbolizing honor or renown.

20 On double pleasures: leave thy cold dispute
Of what is fit and not. Forsake thy cage,
  Thy rope of sands,
Which petty thoughts have made, and made to thee
 Good cable, to enforce and draw,
25   And be thy law,
While thou didst wink and wouldst not see.
  Away! take heed;
  I will abroad.
Call in thy death's-head⁴ there; tie up thy fears.
30   He that forbears
 To suit and serve his need,
  Deserves his load."
But as I raved and grew more fierce and wild
 At every word,
35 Methought I heard one calling, *Child!*
And I replied, *My Lord.*

1633

The Forerunners

The harbingers⁵ are come. See, see their mark:
White is their color, and behold my head.
But must they have my brain? Must they dispark⁶
Those sparkling notions, which therein were bred?
5 Must dullness turn me to a clod?
Yet have they left me, *Thou art still my God.*

Good men ye be, to leave me my best room,
Ev'n all my heart, and what is lodgéd there:
I pass not,° I, what of the rest become,   *I care not*
10 So *Thou art still my God* be out of fear.
 He will be pleaséd with that ditty;
And if I please him, I write fine and witty.

Farewell sweet phrases, lovely metaphors.
But will ye leave me thus? When ye before
15 Of stews and brothels only knew the doors,
Then did I wash you with my tears, and more,
 Brought you to church well dressed and clad:
My God must have my best, ev'n all I had.

Lovely enchanting language, sugar-cane,
20 Honey of roses, wither wilt thou fly?
Hath some fond lover 'ticed thee to thy bane?
And wilt thou leave the church and love a sty?
 Fie, thou wilt soil thy broidered coat,
And hurt thyself, and him that sings the note.

25 Let foolish lovers, if they will love dung,
With canvas, not with arras, clothe their shame:
Let folly speak in her own native tongue.

4. A representation of a human skull intended to serve as a *memento mori*, a reminder that all men must die.
5. The advance agents of the king and his party on a royal progress or tour. They marked with chalk the doors of those dwellings where the court would be accommodated.
6. I.e., *dis-park*, to turn out, as of a park; there may also be a play on *dis-spark* (from "sparkling notions" in the next line).

True beauty dwells on high: ours is a flame
    But borrowed thence to light us thither.
30 Beauty and beauteous words should go together.

Yet if you go, I pass not; take your way:
For *Thou art still my God* is all that ye
Perhaps with more embellishment can say.
Go, birds of spring: let winter have his fee;
35   Let a bleak paleness chalk the door,
So all within be livelier than before.

1633

Discipline

Throw away thy rod,
Throw away thy wrath:
      O my God,
Take the gentle path.

5 For my heart's desire
Unto thine is bent:
      I aspire
To a full consent.

Not a word or look
10 I affect to own,
      But by book,
And thy book alone.

Though I fail, I weep:
Though I halt in pace,
15   Yet I creep
To the throne of grace.

Then let wrath remove;
Love will do the deed:
      For with love
20 Stony hearts will bleed.

Love is swift of foot;
Love's a man of war,[7]
      And can shoot,
And can hit from far.

25 Who can 'scape his bow?
That which wrought on thee,
      Brought thee low,
Needs must work on me.

Throw away thy rod;
30 Though man frailties hath,
      Thou art God:
Throw away thy wrath.

1633

7. "The Lord is a man of war" (Exodus xv.3).

Love (III)

Love bade me welcome: yet my soul drew back,
    Guilty of dust and sin.
But quick-eyed Love, observing me grow slack
    From my first entrance in,
5 Drew nearer to me, sweetly questioning
    If I lacked anything.

"A guest," I answered, "worthy to be here":
    Love said, "You shall be he."
"I, the unkind, ungrateful? Ah, my dear,
10   I cannot look on thee."
Love took my hand, and smiling did reply,
    "Who made the eyes but I?"

"Truth, Lord; but I have marred them; let my shame
    Go where it doth deserve."
15 "And know you not," says Love, "who bore the blame?"
    "My dear, then I will serve."
"You must sit down," says Love, "and taste my meat."
    So I did sit and eat.

1633

JAMES SHIRLEY
(1596–1666)

The Glories of Our Blood and State

The glories of our blood and state
Are shadows, not substantial things;
There is no armor against fate;
Death lays his icy hand on kings.
5   Scepter and crown
    Must tumble down
And in the dust be equal made
With the poor crooked scythe and spade.

Some men with swords may reap the field
10 And plant fresh laurels where they kill,
But their strong nerves at last must yield;
They tame but one another still.
    Early or late
    They stoop to fate
15 And must give up their murmuring breath,
When they, pale captives, creep to death.

The garlands wither on your brow,
Then boast no more your mighty deeds;
Upon death's purple altar now
20 See where the victor-victim bleeds.
    Your heads must come
    To the cold tomb;
Only the actions of the just
Smell sweet and blossom in their dust.

1659

THOMAS CAREW
(1598?–1639?)

A Song

Ask me no more where Jove bestows,
When June is past, the fading rose;
For in your beauty's orient deep,
These flowers, as in their causes,[1] sleep.

5 Ask me no more whither do stray
The golden atoms of the day;
For in pure love heaven did prepare
Those powders to enrich your hair.

Ask me no more whither doth haste
10 The nightingale when May is past;
For in your sweet dividing[2] throat
She winters, and keeps warm her note.

Ask me no more where those stars light,
That downwards fall in dead of night;
15 For in your eyes they sit, and there
Fixéd become, as in their sphere.

Ask me no more if east or west
The phoenix[3] builds her spicy nest;
For unto you at last she flies,
20 And in your fragrant bosom dies.

1640

Mediocrity in Love Rejected

Give me more love, or more disdain;
    The torrid or the frozen zone
Bring equal ease unto my pain;
    The temperate affords me none:
5 Either extreme, of love or hate,
Is sweeter than a calm estate.

Give me a storm; if it be love,
    Like Danaë in that golden shower,[4]
I swim in pleasure; if it prove
10   Disdain, that torrent will devour
My vulture hopes; and he's possessed
Of heaven that's but from hell released.
    Then crown my joys, or cure my pain;
    Give me more love or more disdain.

1640

---

1. Aristotelian philosophy regarded that from which a thing is made or comes into being as the "material cause" of the thing.
2. Executing a "division," an embellished musical phrase.
3. A legendary bird, the only one of its kind, represented as living five hundred years in the Arabian desert, being consumed in fire, then rising anew from its own ashes.
4. Danaë, imprisoned by her father in a house of bronze, was visited by Zeus in a shower of gold. The result of their union was the hero Perseus.

An Elegy upon the Death of the Dean of Paul's, Dr. John Donne

Can we not force from widowed poetry,
Now thou art dead, great Donne, one elegy
To crown thy hearse? Why yet did we not trust,
Though with unkneaded dough-baked prose, thy dust,
5   Such as the unscissored[5] lect'rer from the flower
Of fading rhetoric, short-lived as his hour,
Dry as the sand that measures it,[6] should lay
Upon the ashes on the funeral day?
Have we nor tune, nor voice? Didst thou dispense
10   Through all our language both the words and sense?
'Tis a sad truth. The pulpit may her plain
And sober Christian precepts still retain;
Doctrines it may, and wholesome uses, frame,
Grave homilies and lectures; but the flame
15   Of thy brave soul, that shot such heat and light
As burnt our earth and made our darkness bright,
Committed holy rapes upon our will,
Did through the eye the melting heart distil,
And the deep knowledge of dark truths so teach
20   As sense might judge what fancy could not reach,
Must be desired forever. So the fire
That fills with spirit and heat the Delphic choir,[7]
Which, kindled first by thy Promethean[8] breath,
Glowed here a while, lies quenched now in thy death.
25   The Muses' garden, with pedantic weeds
O'erspread, was purged by thee; the lazy seeds
Of servile imitation thrown away,
And fresh invention planted; thou didst pay
The debts of our penurious bankrupt age;
30   Licentious thefts, that make poetic rage
A mimic fury, when our souls must be
Possessed, or with Anacreon's ecstasy,
Or Pindar's,[9] not their own; the subtle cheat
Of sly exchanges, and the juggling feat
35   Of two-edged words, or whatsoever wrong
By ours was done the Greek or Latin tongue,
Thou hast redeemed, and opened us a mine
Of rich and pregnant fancy, drawn a line
Of masculine expression, which had good
40   Old Orpheus[1] seen, or all the ancient brood
Our superstitious fools admire, and hold
Their lead more precious than thy burnished gold,
Thou hadst been their exchequer, and no more
They in each other's dung had searched for ore.
45   Thou shalt yield no precédence, but of time
And the blind fate of language, whose tuned chime

5. I.e., with uncut hair.
6. I.e., the sand in an hourglass.
7. Ie., the choir of poets. Delphi was the site of an oracle of Apollo, the god of poetry.
8. The fire which Prometheus stole from the gods for the benefit of mankind was some-

times interpreted as man's vital spirit.
9. Anacreon and Pindar were famous Greek poets.
1. In Greek mythology, the son of one of the Muses and the greatest of poets and musicians.

More charms the outward sense; yet thou mayest claim
From so great disadvantage greater fame,
Since to the awe of thy imperious wit
50 Our troublesome language bends, made only fit
With her tough thick-ribbed hoops, to gird about
Thy giant fancy, which had proved too stout
For their soft melting phrases. As in time
They had the start, so did they cull the prime
55 Buds of invention many a hundred year,
And left the rifled fields, besides the fear
To touch their harvest; yet from those bare lands
Of what is only thine, thy only hands
(And that their smallest work) have gleanéd more
60 Than all those times and tongues could reap before.
   But thou art gone, and thy strict laws will be
Too hard for libertines in poetry.
They will recall the goodly exiled train
Of gods and goddesses, which in thy just reign
65 Were banished nobler poems; now with these
The silenced tales i' th' *Metamorphoses*[2]
Shall stuff their lines and swell the windy page,
Till verse, refined by thee in this last age,
Turn ballad-rhyme, or those old idols be
70 Adored again with new apostasy.
   O pardon me, that break with untuned verse
The reverend silence that attends thy hearse,
Whose solemn awful murmurs were to thee,
More than these faint lines, a loud elegy,
75 That did proclaim in a dumb eloquence
The death of all the arts, whose influence,
Grown feeble, in these panting numbers lies
Gasping short-winded accents, and so dies:
So doth the swiftly turning wheel not stand
80 In th' instant we withdraw the moving hand,
But some small time retain a faint weak course
By virtue of the first impulsive force;
And so whilst I cast on thy funeral pile
Thy crown of bays,[3] oh, let it crack awhile
85 And spit disdain, till the devouring flashes
Suck all the moisture up; then turn to ashes.
   I will not draw thee envy to engross
All thy perfections, or weep all the loss;
Those are too numerous for one elegy,
90 And this too great to be expressed by me.
Let others carve the rest; it shall suffice
I on thy grave this epitaph incise:

Here lies a king, that ruled as he thought fit
The universal monarchy of wit;
95 *Here lie two flamens,° and both those the best:*   priests
Apollo's first, at last the true God's priest.

1633, 1640

2. Earlier poets had drawn heavily on the stories in Ovid's *Metamorphoses* for the materials of their poetry.

3. In classical times a crown of bays or laurel was the reward of the victor in a poetic competition.

JOHN MILTON
(1608–1674)

Lycidas

IN THIS MONODY[1] THE AUTHOR BEWAILS A LEARNED FRIEND, UNFORTUNATELY DROWNED IN HIS PASSAGE FROM CHESTER ON THE IRISH SEAS, 1637. AND BY OCCASION FORETELLS THE RUIN OF OUR CORRUPTED CLERGY, THEN IN THEIR HEIGHT.

Yet once more, O ye laurels[2] and once more
Ye myrtles brown,° with ivy never sere,°   *dark / withered*
I come to pluck your berries harsh and crude,°   *unripe*
And with forced fingers rude,
5   Shatter your leaves before the mellowing year.
Bitter constraint, and sad occasion dear,°   *severe*
Compels me to disturb your season due;
For Lycidas is dead, dead ere his prime,
Young Lycidas, and hath not left his peer.
10 Who would not sing for Lycidas? He knew
Himself to sing, and build the lofty rhyme.
He must not float upon his watery bier
Unwept, and welter° to the parching wind,   *roll about*
Without the meed° of some melodious tear.   *tribute*
15   Begin then, sisters of the sacred well[3]
That from beneath the seat of Jove doth spring,
Begin, and somewhat loudly sweep the string.
Hence with denial vain, and coy excuse;
So may some gentle Muse°   *poet*
20 With lucky words favor my destined urn,
And as he passes turn,
And bid fair peace be to my sable shroud.
For we were nursed upon the selfsame hill,
Fed the same flock, by fountain, shade, and rill.
25   Together both, ere the high lawns° appeared   *pastures*
Under the opening eyelids of the morn,
We drove afield, and both together heard
What time the grayfly winds her sultry horn,
Battening° our flocks with the fresh dews of night,   *fattening*
30 Oft till the star that rose at evening bright
Toward Heaven's descent had sloped his westering wheel.
Meanwhile the rural ditties were not mute,
Tempered to th' oaten flute,
Rough satyrs danced, and fauns with cloven heel
35 From the glad sound would not be absent long,
And old Damoetas[4] loved to hear our song.
    But O the heavy change, now thou art gone,
Now thou art gone, and never must return!
Thee, shepherd, thee the woods and desert caves,
40 With wild thyme and the gadding° vine o'ergrown,   *wandering*

1. An elegy or dirge sung by a single voice. The "learned friend" was Edward King, Milton's fellow student at Cambridge.
2. The laurel, myrtle, and ivy were all traditional materials for poetic garlands.
3. The Muses. The well sacred to them was Aganippe, at the foot of Mt. Helicon, where they danced about the altar of Jove.
4. A conventional pastoral name, here perhaps referring to one of the tutors at Cambridge.

And all their echoes mourn.
The willows and the hazel copses green
Shall now no more be seen,
Fanning their joyous leaves to thy soft lays.
45 As killing as the canker to the rose,
Or taint-worm to the weanling herds that graze,
Or frost to flowers that their gay wardrobe wear,
When first the white thorn blows;°   *blooms*
Such, Lycidas, thy loss to shepherd's ear.
50   Where were ye, nymphs, when the remorseless deep
Closed o'er the head of your loved Lycidas?
For neither were ye playing on the steep,
Where your old Bards, the famous Druids lie,
Nor on the shaggy top of Mona high,
55 Nor yet where Deva spreads her wizard stream:⁵
Ay me! I fondly° dream—   *foolishly*
Had ye been there—for what could that have done?
What could the Muse⁶ herself that Orpheus bore,
The Muse herself, for her inchanting son
60 Whom universal Nature did lament,
When by the rout that made the hideous roar,
His gory visage down the stream was sent,
Down the swift Hebrus to the Lesbian shore?
Alas! What boots° it with uncessant care   *profits*
65 To tend the homely slighted shepherd's trade,
And strictly meditate the thankless Muse?
Were it not better done as others use,
To sport with Amaryllis⁷ in the shade,
Or with the tangles of Neaera's hair?
70 Fame is the spur that the clear spirit doth raise
(That last infirmity of noble mind)
To scorn delights, and live laborious days;
But the fair guerdon° when we hope to find,   *reward*
And think to burst out into sudden blaze,
75 Comes the blind Fury⁸ with th' abhorréd shears,
And slits the thin spun life. "But not the praise,"
Phoebus⁹ replied, and touched my trembling ears;
"Fame is no plant that grows on mortal soil,
Nor in the glistering foil¹
80 Set off to th' world, nor in broad rumor lies,
But lives and spreads aloft by those pure eyes,
And perfect witness of all-judging Jove;
As he pronounces lastly on each deed,
Of so much fame in Heaven expect thy meed."
85   O fountain Arethuse,² and thou honored flood,
Smooth-sliding Mincius, crowned with vocal reeds,
That strain I heard was of a higher mood.

---

5. The "steep" is probably the mountain Kerig-y-Druidion in northern Wales, a Druid burial ground. Mona is the Isle of Anglesey, Deva the River Dee, called "wizard" because its changes of course were supposed to foretell the country's fortune. All three places are just south of that part of the Irish Sea where King was drowned.
6. Calliope, the Muse of epic poetry. Her son Orpheus, the greatest of all poets and musicians, was torn limb from limb by a band of Thracian Maenads, who flung his head into the River Hebrus, whence it drifted across the Aegean to the island of Lesbos.

7. A conventional pastoral name, like "Neaera" in the next line.
8. Atropos, the third of the three Fates, who cut the thread of a man's life after it had been spun and measured by her sisters.
9. Apollo, god of poetic inspiration.
1. The setting for a gem, especially one that enhances the appearance of an inferior or false stone.
2. A fountain in Sicily, associated with the pastoral poems of Theocritus. The Mincius is a river in Italy described in one of Virgil's pastorals.

But now my oat³ proceeds,
And listens to the herald of the sea⁴
90 That came in Neptune's plea.
He asked the waves, and asked the felon winds,
"What hard mishap hath doomed this gentle swain?"
And questioned every gust of rugged wings
That blows from off each beakèd promontory;
95 They knew not of his story,
And sage Hippotades⁵ their answer brings,
That not a blast was from his dungeon strayed,
The air was calm, and on the level brine,
Sleek Panope⁶ with all her sisters played.
100 It was that fatal and perfidious bark
Built in th' eclipse, and rigged with curses dark,
That sunk so low that sacred head of thine.
    Next Camus,⁷ reverend sire, went footing slow,
His mantle hairy, and his bonnet sedge,
105 Inwrought with figures dim, and on the edge
Like to that sanguine flower inscribed with woe.⁸
"Ah! who hath reft," quoth he, "my dearest pledge?"
Last came and last did go
The pilot of the Galilean lake,⁹
110 Two massy keys he bore of metals twain
(The golden opes, the iron shuts amain).
He shook his mitered locks, and stern bespake:
"How well could I have spared for thee, young swain,
Enow° of such as for their bellies' sake,   enough
115 Creep and intrude, and climb into the fold!
Of other care they little reckoning make,
Than how to scramble at the shearers' feast,
And shove away the worthy bidden guest.
Blind mouths! That scarce themselves know how to hold
120 A sheep-hook, or have learned aught else the least
That to the faithful herdsman's art belongs!
What recks it them?¹ What need they? They are sped;
And when they list, their lean and flashy° songs   insipid
Grate on their scrannel° pipes of wretched straw.   meager
125 The hungry sheep look up, and are not fed,
But swoln with wind, and the rank mist they draw,
Rot inwardly, and foul contagion spread,
Besides what the grim wolf with privy paw²
Daily devours apace, and nothing said.
130 But that two-handed engine at the door
Stands ready to smite once, and smite no more."³
    Return, Alpheus,⁴ the dread voice is past,

3. Oaten pipe, song.
4. The merman Triton, who came to plead his master Neptune's innocence of Lycidas' death.
5. Aeolus, son of Hippotas and god of the winds.
6. One of the Nereids, daughters of Nereus, the Old Man of the Sea.
7. The god of the river Cam, representing Cambridge University.
8. The hyacinth, created by Apollo from the blood of the youth Hyacinthus, whom he had killed by accident with a discus. Certain markings on the flower are supposed to be the letters AIAI ("Alas, alas!"), inscribed there by Apollo.
9. St. Peter, the Galilean fisherman, to whom Christ promised the keys of the kingdom of heaven (Matthew xvi.19). He wears the

bishop's miter (line 112) as the first head of Christ's church.
1. What does it matter to them?
2. I.e., anti-Protestant forces, either Roman Catholic or Anglican.
3. A satisfactory explanation of these two lines has yet to be made, although many have been attempted. Most have taken the "two-handed engine" as an instrument of retribution against those clergy who neglect their responsibilities (such as the ax of reformation; the two-handed sword of the archangel Michael; the two houses of Parliament; death and damnation).
4. A river god who fell in love with the nymph Arethusa. When she fled to Sicily he pursued her by diving under the sea and coming up in the island. There she was turned into a fountain (see line 85) and their waters mingled.

That shrunk thy streams; return, Sicilian muse,
And call the vales, and bid them hither cast
135 Their bells and flowerets of a thousand hues.
Ye valleys low where the mild whispers use,°   *frequent*
Of shades and wanton winds, and gushing brooks,
On whose fresh lap the swart star⁵ sparely looks,
Throw hither all your quaint enameled eyes,
140 That on the green turf suck the honeyed showers,
And purple all the ground with vernal flowers.
Bring the rathe° primrose that forsaken dies,   *early*
The tufted crow-toe, and pale jessamine,
The white pink, and the pansy freaked° with jet,   *mottled*
145 The glowing violet,
The musk-rose, and the well attired woodbine.
With cowslips wan that hang the pensive head,
And every flower that sad embroidery wears:
Bid amaranthus⁶ all his beauty shed,
150 And daffadillies fill their cups with tears,   *bier*
To strew the laureate hearse° where Lycid lies.
For so to interpose a little ease,
Let our frail thoughts dally with false surmise.
Ay me! Whilst thee the shores and sounding seas
155 Wash far away, where'er thy bones are hurled,
Whether beyond the stormy Hebrides,
Where thou perhaps under the whelming tide
Visit'st the bottom of the monstrous world;
Or whether thou, to our moist vows denied,
160 Sleep'st by the fable of Bellerus old,⁷
Where the great vision of the guarded mount
Looks toward Namancos and Bayona's hold;
Look homeward angel now, and melt with ruth:°   *pity*
And, O ye dolphins, waft the hapless youth.
165   Weep no more, woeful shepherds, weep no more,
For Lycidas your sorrow is not dead,
Sunk though he be beneath the watery floor,
So sinks the day-star° in the ocean bed,   *sun*
And yet anon repairs his drooping head,
170 And tricks° his beams, and with new-spangled ore,°   *dresses / gold*
Flames in the forehead of the morning sky:
So Lycidas sunk low, but mounted high,
Through the dear might of him that walked the waves,
Where other groves, and other streams along,
175 With nectar pure his oozy locks he laves,
And hears the unexpressive° nuptial song,⁸   *inexpressible*
In the blest kingdoms meek of joy and love.
There entertain him all the saints above,
In solemn troops and sweet societies
180 That sing, and singing in their glory move,
And wipe the tears forever from his eyes.
Now, Lycidas, the shepherds weep no more;
Henceforth thou art the genius° of the shore,   *local divinity*
In thy large recompense, and shalt be good

5. Sirius, the Dog Star, thought to have a swart or malignant influence.
6. A legendary flower, supposed never to fade.
7. A legendary figure supposedly buried at Land's End in Cornwall. The "mount" of the next line is St. Michael's Mount at the tip of Land's End, "guarded" by the archangel Michael, who gazes southward toward Nemancos and the stronghold of Bayona in northwestern Spain.
8. Milton may have been thinking of the "marriage supper of the Lamb" mentioned in Revelation xix.9.

185 To all that wander in that perilous flood.
     Thus sang the uncouth° swain to th' oaks and rills,   *unlettered*
     While the still morn went out with sandals gray;
     He touched the tender stops of various quills,[9]
     With eager thought warbling his Doric[1] lay:
190 And now the sun had stretched out all the hills,
     And now was dropped into the western bay;
     At last he rose, and twitched his mantle blue:
     Tomorrow to fresh woods, and pastures new.

                                                               1637

On the Morning of Christ's Nativity

1

     This is the month, and this the happy morn,
     Wherein the Son of Heaven's Eternal King,
     Of wedded maid and virgin mother born,
     Our great redemption from above did bring;
5   For so the holy sages[2] once did sing,
         That he our deadly forfeit[3] should release,
     And with his Father work us a perpetual peace.

2

     That glorious form, that light unsufferable,
     And that far-beaming blaze of majesty,
10   Wherewith he wont at Heaven's high council-table
     To sit the midst of Trinal Unity,
     He laid aside, and, here with us to be,
         Forsook the courts of everlasting day,
     And chose with us a darksome house of mortal clay.

3

15   Say, Heavenly Muse,[4] shall not thy sacred vein
     Afford a present to the Infant God?
     Hast thou no verse, no hymn, or solemn strain,
     To welcome him to this his new abode,
     Now while the heaven, by the Sun's team untrod,
20   Hath took no print of the approaching light,
     And all the spangled host keep watch in squadrons
         bright?

4

     See how from far upon the eastern road
     The star-led wizards[5] haste with odors sweet!
     Oh run, prevent° them with thy humble ode,   *go before*
25   And lay it lowly at his blessed feet;
     Have thou the honor first thy Lord to greet,
         And join thy voice unto the angel choir
     From out his secret altar touched with hallowed fire.

The Hymn

1

     It was the winter wild,
30   While the heaven-born child
     All meanly wrapt in the rude manger lies;
         Nature, in awe to him,

---

9. The individual reeds in a set of Panpipes.
1. Pastoral, because Doric was the dialect of the Greek pastoral writers Theocritus, Bion, and Moschus.
2. I.e., the Hebrew prophets.
3. The penalty of death, occasioned by the sin of Adam.
4. Urania, the Muse of Astronomy, later identified with divine wisdom and treated by Milton as the source of creative inspiration.
5. The "wise men from the east" (Matthew ii.1).

Had doffed her gaudy trim,
With her great Master so to sympathize:
35   It was no season then for her
To wanton with the Sun, her lusty paramour.

2

Only with speeches fair
She woos the gentle air
To hide her guilty front with innocent snow,
40   And on her naked shame,
Pollute with sinful blame,
The saintly veil of maiden white to throw;
Confounded, that her Maker's eyes
Should look so near upon her foul deformities.

3

45   But he, her fears to cease,
Sent down the meek-eyed Peace:
She, crowned with olive green, came softly sliding
Down through the turning sphere,[6]
His ready harbinger,   *dove*
50   With turtle wing the amorous clouds dividing;
And, waving wide her myrtle wand,
She strikes a universal peace through sea and land.

4

No war, or battle's sound,
Was heard the world around;
55   The idle spear and shield were high uphung;
The hookéd chariot[7] stood,
Unstained with hostile blood;
The trumpet spake not to the arméd throng;
And kings sat still with awful eye,
60 As if they surely knew their sovran Lord was by.

5

But peaceful was the night
Wherein the Prince of Light
His reign of peace upon the earth began.
The winds, with wonder whist,°   *hushed*
65   Smoothly the waters kissed,
Whispering new joys to the mild Ocean,
Who now hath quite forgot to rave,
While birds of calm[8] sit brooding on the charméd wave.

6

The stars, with deep amaze,
70   Stand fixed in steadfast gaze,
Bending one way their precious influence,[9]
And will not take their flight,
For all the morning light,
Or Lucifer[1] that often warned them thence;
75 But in their glimmering orbs[2] did glow,
Until their Lord himself bespake, and bid them go.

---

6. The heavens as a whole, which "turn" once daily about the earth because of the earth's rotation.
7. War chariots were sometimes armed with sickle-like hooks projecting from the hubs of the wheels.
8. Halcyons or kingfishers, which in ancient times were believed to build floating nests at sea about the time of the winter solstice, and to calm the waves during the incubation of their young.

9. Medieval astrologers believed that stars emitted an ethereal liquid ("influence") that had the power to nourish or otherwise affect all things on earth.
1. Probably the morning star, although Milton sometimes uses the word for the sun.
2. The concentric crystalline spheres of Ptolemaic astronomy. Each sphere was supposed to contain one or more of the heavenly bodies in its surface and to revolve about the earth.

7

And, though the shady gloom
Had given day her room,
The Sun himself withheld his wonted speed,
80   And hid his head for shame,
As his inferior flame
The new-enlightened world no more should need:
He saw a greater Sun appear
Than his bright throne or burning axletree could bear.

8

85   The shepherds on the lawn,   *meadow*
Or ere the point of dawn,
Sat simply chatting in a rustic row;
Full little thought they than°   *then*
That the mighty Pan³
90   Was kindly come to live with them below:
Perhaps their loves, or else their sheep,
Was all that did their silly° thoughts so busy keep.   *simple*

9

When such music sweet
Their hearts and ears did greet
95   As never was by mortal finger strook,°   *struck*
Divinely-warbled voice
Answering the stringéd noise,
As all their souls in blissful rapture took:
The air, such pleasure loth to lose,
100   With thousand echoes still prolongs each heavenly close.°   *cadence*

10

Nature, that heard such sound
Beneath the hollow round
Of Cynthia's seat⁴ the airy region thrilling,
Now was almost won
105   To think her part was done,
And that her reign had here its last fulfilling:
She knew such harmony alone
Could hold all Heaven and Earth in happier uniön.

11

At last surrounds their sight
110   A globe of circular light,
That with long beams the shamefaced Night arrayed;
The helméd cherubim
And sworded seraphim⁵
Are seen in glittering ranks with wings displayed,
115   Harping loud and solemn quire,
With unexpressive° notes, to Heaven's new-born Heir.   *inexpressible*

12

Such music (as 'tis said)
Before was never made,
But when of old the sons of morning sung,⁶
120   While the Creator great
His constellations set,

3. The Greek shepherd god Pan (whose name means "all") was often associated with Christ.
4. I.e., beneath the sphere of the moon.
5. Seraphim and cherubim (both are plural forms) are the two highest of the nine orders of angels in the medieval classification.
6. Job speaks of the creation of the universe as the time "when the morning stars sang together, and all the sons of God shouted for joy" (Job xxxviii.7).

And the well-balanced world on hinges hung,
And cast the dark foundations deep,
And bid the weltering waves their oozy channel keep.

13

125   Ring out, ye crystal spheres,
     Once bless our human ears,
If ye have power to touch our senses so;
     And let your silver chime
     Move in melodious time;
130   And let the bass of heaven's deep organ blow;
And with your ninefold harmony
Make up full consort to th' angelic symphony.

14

     For, if such holy song
     Enwrap our fancy long,
135   Time will run back and fetch the age of gold;[7]
     And speckled vanity
     Will sicken soon and die;
And leprous sin will melt from earthly mold;
And Hell itself will pass away,
140   And leave her dolorous mansions to the peering day.

15

     Yea, Truth and Justice then
     Will down return to men,
Orbed in a rainbow; and, like glories wearing,
     Mercy will sit between,
145   Throned in celestial sheen,
With radiant feet the tissued clouds down steering;
And Heaven, as at some festival,
Will open wide the gates of her high palace-hall.

16

     But wisest Fate says no,
150   This must not yet be so;
The Babe lies yet in smiling infancy
     That on the bitter cross
     Must redeem our loss,
So both himself and us to glorify:
155   Yet first, to those ychained[8] in sleep,
The wakeful° trump of doom must thunder through the   *awakening*
     deep,

17

     With such a horrid clang
     As on Mount Sinai rang,[9]
While the red fire and smoldering clouds outbrake:
160   The aged Earth, aghast,
     With terror of that blast,
Shall from the surface to the center shake,
When, at the world's last sessïon,
The dreadful Judge in middle air shall spread his throne.

---

7. The Romans believed that Saturn, after his dethronement by Jupiter, fled to Italy and there brought in the Golden Age, a time of perfect peace and happiness.
8. Milton uses the archaic form of the past participle, common in Chaucer and imitated by Spenser, in which *y-* represents a reduced form of the Old English prefix *ge-*.
9. Moses received the Ten Commandments on Mount Sinai: "* * * there were thunders and lightnings * * * and the voice of the trumpet exceeding loud" (Exodus xix.16).

18

165 And then at last our bliss
Full and perfect is,
But now begins; for from this happy day
Th' old Dragon° under ground,   *Satan*
In straiter limits bound,
170 Not half so far casts his usurpéd sway,
And, wroth to see his kingdom fail,
Swinges° the scaly horror of his folded tail.   *lashes*

19

The Oracles are dumb;
No voice or hideous hum
175 Runs through the archéd roof in words deceiving.
Apollo from his shrine
Can no more divine,
With hollow shriek the steep of Delphos leaving.
No nightly trance, or breathéd spell,
180 Inspires the pale-eyed priest from the prophetic cell.

20

The lonely mountains o'er,
And the resounding shore,
A voice of weeping heard and loud lament;
From haunted spring, and dale
185 Edged with poplar pale,
The parting genius° is with sighing sent;   *local spirit*
With flower-inwoven tresses torn
The Nymphs in twilight shade of tangled thickets mourn.

21

In consecrated earth,
190 And on the holy hearth,
The Lars[1] and Lemures moan with midnight plaint;
In urns and altars round,
A drear and dying sound
Affrights the flamens° at their service quaint;°   *priests / elaborate*
195 And the chill marble seems to sweat,
While each peculiar power forgoes his wonted seat.

22

Peor[2] and Baälim
Forsake their temples dim,
With that twice-battered God of Palestine;[3]
200 And mooned Ashtaroth,[4]
Heaven's queen and mother both,
Now sits not girt with tapers' holy shine:
The Libyc Hammon[5] shrinks his horn;
In vain the Tyrian maids their wounded Thammuz mourn.[6]

---

1. Tutelary gods or spirits of the ancient Romans associated with particular places. Lemures were hostile spirits of the unburied dead.
2. Baal or Baal-Peor, the highest Canaanite god, whose shrine was at Mount Peor. Baalim (the plural form) were lesser gods related to him.
3. Dagon, god of the Philistines, whose statue twice fell to the ground before the ark of the Lord (I Samuel v.1–4).
4. Astarte, a Phoenician goddess identified with the moon.
5. The Egyptian god Ammon, represented as a horned ram. He had a famous temple and oracle at an oasis in the Libyan desert.
6. The death of the god Thammuz, Ashtaroth's lover, symbolized the coming of winter. The Tyrian (Phoenician) women mourned for him in an annual ceremony.

23

205   And sullen Moloch,[7] fled,
      Hath left in shadows dread
His burning idol all of blackest hue;
      In vain with cymbals' ring
      They call the grisly king,
210   In dismal dance about the furnace blue;
The brutish gods of Nile as fast,
Isis, and Orus, and the dog Anubis,[8] haste.

24

      Nor is Osiris seen
      In Memphian grove or green,
215   Trampling the unshowered grass with lowings loud;
      Nor can he be at rest
      Within his sacred chest;
Nought but profoundest Hell can be his shroud;
      In vain, with timbreled anthems dark,
220   The sable-stoléd sorcerers bear his worshiped ark.

25

      He feels from Juda's land
      The dreaded Infant's hand;
The rays of Bethlehem blind his dusky eyn;°   *eyes*
      Nor all the gods beside
225   Longer dare abide,
Not Typhon[9] huge ending in snaky twine:
Our Babe, to show his Godhead true,
Can in his swaddling bands control the damnéd crew.

26

      So, when the sun in bed,
230   Curtained with cloudy red,
Pillows his chin upon an orient° wave,   *eastern*
      The flocking shadows pale
      Troop to th' infernal jail;
Each fettered ghost slips to his several grave,
235 And the yellow-skirted fays
Fly after the night-steeds, leaving their moon-loved maze.

27

      But see! the Virgin blest
      Hath laid her Babe to rest.
Time is our tedious song should here have ending:
240   Heaven's youngest-teeméd star[1]
      Hath fixed her polished car,
Her sleeping Lord with handmaid lamp attending;
And all about the courtly stable
Bright-harnessed angels sit in order serviceable.

                                      1629   1645

7. A pagan god to whom children were sacrificed. Their cries were drowned out by the clang of cymbals.
8. The Egyptian goddess Isis was represented as a cow, the gods Orus and Anubis as a hawk and a dog (hence "brutish"). Osiris (line 213) the creator, who had a shrine at Memphis, was represented as a bull.
9. A hundred-headed monster destroyed by Zeus.
1. I.e., newest-born star, the star that guided the wise men, now imagined as having halted its "car" or chariot over the manger.

When I Consider How My Light Is Spent[6]

When I consider how my light is spent
  Ere half my days, in this dark world and wide,
  And that one talent which is death to hide[7]
  Lodged with me useless, though my soul more bent
5 To serve therewith my Maker, and present
  My true account, lest he returning chide;
  "Doth God exact day-labor, light denied?"
  I fondly° ask; but Patience to prevent   *foolishly*
That murmur, soon replies, "God doth not need
10   Either man's work or his own gifts; who best
  Bear his mild yoke, they serve him best. His state
Is kingly. Thousands at his bidding speed
  And post o'er land and ocean without rest:
  They also serve who only stand and wait."

                        ca. 1652   1673

On the Late Massacre in Piedmont[8]

Avenge, O Lord, thy slaughtered saints, whose bones
  Lie scattered on the Alpine mountains cold,
  Even them who kept thy truth so pure of old
  When all our fathers worshiped stocks° and stones,[9]   *idols*
5 Forget not: in thy book record their groans
  Who were thy sheep and in their ancient fold
  Slain by the bloody Piedmontese that rolled
  Mother with infant down the rocks. Their moans
The vales redoubled to the hills, and they
10   To Heaven. Their martyred blood and ashes sow
  O'er all th' Italian fields where still doth sway
The triple tyrant:[1] that from these may grow
  A hundredfold, who having learnt thy way
  Early may fly the Babylonian woe.[2]

                          1655   1673

Lawrence[3] of Virtuous Father

Lawrence, of virtuous father virtuous son,
  Now that the fields are dank, and ways are mire,
  Where shall we sometimes meet, and by the fire
  Help waste a sullen day, what may be won
5 From the hard season gaining? Time will run

---

6. Milton had become totally blind in 1651.
7. An allusion to the parable of the talents, in which the servant who buried the single talent his lord had given him, instead of investing it, was deprived of all he had and cast "into outer darkness" at the lord's return (Matthew xxv.14–30).
8. Some 1700 members of the Protestant Waldensian sect in the Piedmont in northwestern Italy died as a result of a treacherous attack by the Duke of Savoy's forces on Easter Day, 1655.
9. The Waldenses had existed as a sect, first within the Catholic Church and then as here-

tics, since the 12th century. They were particularly critical of materialistic tendencies in the Church.
1. The Pope, whose tiara has three crowns.
2. Babylon, as a city of luxury and vice, was often linked with the Papal Court by Protestants, who took the destruction of the city described in Revelation xviii as an allegory of the fate in store for the Roman Church.
3. Edward Lawrence, a friend of Milton's though twenty-five years his junior, was the son of Henry Lawrence, Lord President of the Council of State at the time this sonnet was written.

On smoother, till Favonius[4] reinspire
   The frozen earth, and clothe in fresh attire
   The lily and rose, that neither sowed nor spun.[5]
What neat repast shall feast us, light and choice,
10   Of Attic[6] taste, with wine, whence we may rise
   To hear the lute well touched, or artful voice
Warble immortal notes and Tuscan air?
   He who of those delights can judge, and spare
   To interpose them oft, is not unwise.

ca. 1655   1673

Cyriack,[7] Whose Grandsire

Cyriack, whose grandsire on the royal bench
   Of British Themis,[8] with no mean applause,
   Pronounced, and in his volumes taught, our laws,
   Which others at their bar so often wrench,
5 Today deep thoughts resolve with me to drench
   In mirth that after no repenting draws;
   Let Euclid rest, and Archimedes pause,
   And what the Swede intend, and what the French.
To measure life learn thou betimes,° and know   *early*
10   Toward solid good what leads the nearest way;
   For other things mild Heaven a time ordains,
And disapproves that care, though wise in show,
   That with superfluous burden loads the day,
   And, when God sends a cheerful hour, refrains.

ca. 1655   1673

Methought I Saw

Methought I saw my late espoused saint[9]
   Brought to me like Alcestis[1] from the grave,
   Whom Jove's great son to her glad husband gave,
   Rescued from Death by force, though pale and faint.
5 Mine, as whom washed from spot of child-bed taint
   Purification in the Old Law did save,[2]
   And such, as yet once more I trust to have
   Full sight of her in heaven without restraint,
Came vested all in white, pure as her mind.
10   Her face was veiled; yet to my fancied sight
   Love, sweetness, goodness, in her person shined
So clear as in no face with more delight.
   But O, as to embrace me she inclined,
   I waked, she fled, and day brought back my night.

ca. 1658   1673

4. The Latin name of the west wind.
5. "Consider the lilies of the field, how they grow; they toil not, neither do they spin" (Matthew vi.28).
6. Athenian; i.e., delicate, discriminating.
7. Cyriack Skinner, a pupil of Milton's and grandson of Sir Edward Coke, the great jurist who had been Chief Justice of the King's Bench under James I.
8. The Greek goddess of justice.
9. The "saint," or soul in heaven, is Milton's second wife, Katherine Woodcock, to whom he had been married less than two years (hence "late espoused") when she died in 1658. Since Milton had become blind in 1651, it is almost certain that he had never seen his wife.
1. The wife who is brought back from the dead to her husband Admetus by Hercules ("Jove's great son") in Euripides' *Alcestis*.
2. Hebrew law (Leviticus xii) prescribed certain sacrificial rituals for the purification of women after childbirth.

SIR JOHN SUCKLING
(1609–1642)

Song

Why so pale and wan, fond lover?
　　Prithee, why so pale?
Will, when looking well can't move her,
　　Looking ill prevail?
5　　　Prithee, why so pale?

Why so dull and mute, young sinner?
　　Prithee, why so mute?
Will, when speaking well can't win her,
　　Saying nothing do 't?
10　　　Prithee, why so mute?

Quit, quit, for shame; this will not move,
　　This cannot take her.
If of herself she will not love,
　　Nothing can make her:
15　　The devil take her!

1638

Out upon It!

Out upon it! I have loved
　　Three whole days together;
And am like to love three more,
　　If it prove fair weather.

5　Time shall molt away his wings,
　　Ere he shall discover
In the whole wide world again
　　Such a constant lover.

But the spite on 't is, no praise
10　　Is due at all to me:
Love with me had made no stays
　　Had it any been but she.

Had it any been but she,
　　And that very face,
15　There had been at least ere this
　　A dozen dozen in her place.

1659

ANNE BRADSTREET
(ca. 1612–1672)

The Vanity of All Worldly Things

As he [1] said vanity, so vain say I,
Oh! vanity, O vain all under sky;
Where is the man can say, "Lo, I have found
On brittle earth a consolation sound"?
5   What is't in honor to be set on high?
No, they like beasts and sons of men shall die,
And whilst they live, how oft doth turn their fate;
He's now a captive that was king of late.
What is't in wealth great treasures to obtain?
10   No, that's but labor, anxious care, and pain.
He heaps up riches, and he heaps up sorrow,
It's his today, but who's his heir tomorrow?
What then? Content in pleasures canst thou find?
More vain than all, that's but to grasp the wind.
15   The sensual senses for a time they please,
Meanwhile the conscience rage, who shall appease?
What is't in beauty? No that's but a snare,
They're foul enough today, that once were fair.
What is't in flow'ring youth, or manly age?
20   The first is prone to vice, the last to rage.
Where is it then, in wisdom, learning, arts?
Sure if on earth, it must be in those parts;
Yet these the wisest man of men did find
But vanity, vexation of mind.
25   And he that knows the most doth still bemoan
He knows not all that here is to be known.
What is it then? to do as stoics tell,
Nor laugh, nor weep, let things go ill or well?
Such stoics are but stocks, such teaching vain,
30   While man is man, he shall have ease or pain.
If not in honor, beauty, age, nor treasure,
Nor yet in learning, wisdom, youth, nor pleasure,
Where shall I climb, sound, seek, search, or find
That *summum bonum* [2] which may stay my mind?
35   There is a path no vulture's eye hath seen,
Where lion fierce, nor lion's whelps have been,
Which leads unto that living crystal fount,
Who drinks thereof, the world doth nought account.
The depth and sea have said "'tis not in me,"
40   With pearl and gold it shall not valued be,
For sapphire, onyx, topaz who would change;
It's hid from eyes of men, they count it strange.
Death and destruction the fame hath heard,
But where and what it is, from heaven's declared;
45   It brings to honor which shall ne'er decay,

---

1. The preacher of Ecclesiastes i.2: "Vanity
of vanity, saith the Preacher, vanity of   vanities; all is vanity."
2. The highest good (Latin).

It stores with wealth which time can't wear away.
It yieldeth pleasures far beyond conceit,
And truly beautifies without deceit.
Nor strength, nor wisdom, nor fresh youth shall fade,
50   Nor death shall see, but are immortal made.
This pearl of price, this tree of life, this spring,
Who is possessed of shall reign a king.
Nor change of state nor cares shall ever see,
But wear his crown unto eternity.
55   This satiates the soul, this stays the mind,
And all the rest, but vanity we find.

1650

A Letter to Her Husband, Absent upon Public Employment

My head, my heart, mine eyes, my life, nay, more,
My joy, my magazine of earthly store,
If two be one, as surely thou and I,
How stayest thou there, whilst I at Ipswich lie?
5   So many steps, head from the heart to sever,
If but a neck, soon should we be together.
I, like the Earth this season, mourn in black,
My Sun is gone so far in's zodiac,
Whom whilst I' joyed, nor storms, nor frost I felt,
10   His warmth such frigid colds did cause to melt.
My chilled limbs now numbed lie forlorn;
Return, return, sweet Sol, from Capricorn; [3]
In this dead time, alas, what can I more
Than view those fruits which through thy heat I bore?
15   Which sweet contentment yield me for a space,
True living pictures of their father's face.
O strange effect! now thou art southward gone,
I weary grow the tedious day so long;
But when thou northward to me shalt return,
20   I wish my Sun may never set, but burn
Within the Cancer [4] of my glowing breast,
The welcome house of him my dearest guest.
Where ever, ever stay, and go not thence,
Till nature's sad decree shall call thee hence;
25   Flesh of thy flesh, bone of thy bone,
I here, thou there, yet both but one.

1678

3. When the sun "enters" the constellation Capricorn, it is at its furthest south. This occurs at the winter solstice, the shortest day and longest night of the year in the northern hemisphere.
4. The sun is in Cancer at the summer solstice.

RICHARD CRASHAW
(1613–1649)

A Hymn to the Name and Honor of the Admirable Saint Teresa[3]

FOUNDRESS OF THE REFORMATION OF THE DISCALCED[4] CARMELITES, BOTH MEN AND WOMEN. A WOMAN FOR ANGELICAL HEIGHT OF SPECU-LATION, FOR MASCULINE COURAGE OF PERFORMANCE, MORE THAN A WOMAN; WHO YET A CHILD OUTRAN MATURITY, AND DURST PLOT A MARTYRDOM.

Love, thou art absolute sole lord
Of life and death. To prove the word,
We'll now appeal to none of all
Those thy old soldiers, great and tall,
5   Ripe men of martyrdom, that could reach down
With strong arms their triumphant crown;
Such as could with lusty breath
Speak loud into the face of death
Their great Lord's glorious name; to none
10 Of those whose spacious bosoms spread a throne
For Love at large to fill. Spare blood and sweat,
And see Him take a private seat;
Making His mansion in the mild
And milky soul of a soft child.
15   Scarce has she learnt to lisp the name
Of Martyr, yet she thinks it shame
Life should so long play with that breath
Which spent can buy so brave a death.
She never undertook to know
20 What death with love should have to do;
Nor has she e'er yet understood
Why to show love she should shed blood;
Yet though she cannot tell you why,
She can love and she can die.
25   Scarce has she blood enough to make
A guilty sword blush for her sake;
Yet has she a heart dares hope to prove
How much less strong is death than love.
     Be love but there, let poor six years
30 Be posed with the maturest fears
Man trembles at, you straight shall find
Love knows no nonage, nor the mind.
'Tis love, not years or limbs, that can
Make the martyr or the man.

3. The remarkable Spanish mystic (1515–82), canonized in 1622. Her autobiography records how, at the age of six, she ran away from home to convert the Moors. In later visions she saw a seraph with a fire-tipped golden dart who pierced her heart repeatedly, causing simultaneously intense pain and joy. It is these "wounds of love" that constitute the "death more mystical and high" referred to in line 76.
4. Barefoot.

35   Love touched her heart, and lo it beats
      High, and burns with such brave heats,
      Such thirsts to die, as dares drink up
      A thousand cold deaths in one cup.
      Good reason, for she breathes all fire;
40   Her weak breast heaves with strong desire
      Of what she may with fruitless wishes
      Seek for amongst her mother's kisses.
         Since 'tis not to be had at home,
      She'll travel to a martyrdom.
45   No home for hers confesses she
      But where she may a martyr be.
         She'll to the Moors and trade with them
      For this unvalued° diadem.   invaluable
      She'll offer them her dearest breath,
50   With Christ's name in 't, in change for death.
      She'll bargain with them, and will give
      Them God, teach them how to live
      In Him; or, if they this deny,
      For Him she'll teach them how to die.
55   So shall she leave amongst them sown
      Her Lord's blood, or at least her own.
         Farewell then, all the world, adieu!
      Teresa is no more for you.
      Farewell, all pleasures, sports, and joys,
60   Never till now esteeméd toys;
      Farewell, whatever dear may be,
      Mother's arms, or father's knee;
      Farewell house and farewell home,
      She's for the Moors and martyrdom!
65   Sweet, not so fast! lo, thy fair Spouse
      Whom thou seek'st with so swift vows
      Calls thee back, and bids thee come
      T' embrace a milder martyrdom.
         Blest powers forbid thy tender life
70   Should bleed upon a barbarous knife;
      Or some base hand have power to rase°   cut
      Thy breast's chaste cabinet, and uncase
      A soul kept there so sweet; oh no,
      Wise Heav'n will never have it so.
75   Thou art Love's victim, and must die
      A death more mystical and high;
      Into Love's arms thou shalt let fall
      A still surviving funeral.
      His is the dart must make the death
80   Whose stroke shall taste thy hallowed breath;
      A dart thrice dipped in that rich flame
      Which writes thy Spouse's radiant name
      Upon the roof of heaven, where aye
      It shines, and with a sovereign ray
85   Beats bright upon the burning faces
      Of souls which in that name's sweet graces
      Find everlasting smiles. So rare,
      So spiritual, pure, and fair
      Must be th' immortal instrument
90   Upon whose choice point shall be sent

A life so loved; and that there be
Fit executioners for thee,
The fair'st and first-born sons of fire,
Blest seraphim, shall leave their choir
95 And turn Love's soldiers, upon thee
To exercise their archery.
    Oh, how oft shalt thou complain
Of a sweet and subtle pain,
Of intolerable joys,
100 Of a death, in which who dies
Loves his death and dies again,
And would for ever so be slain,
And lives and dies, and knows not why
To live, but that he thus may never leave to die!
105   How kindly will thy gentle heart
Kiss the sweetly killing dart!
And close in his embraces keep
Those delicious wounds, that weep
Balsam to heal themselves with. Thus
110 When these thy deaths, so numerous,
Shall all at last die into one,
And melt thy soul's sweet mansion;
Like a soft lump of incense, hasted
By too hot a fire, and wasted
115 Into perfuming clouds, so fast
Shalt thou exhale to heaven at last
In a resolving sigh; and then,
Oh, what? Ask not the tongues of men;
Angels cannot tell; suffice,
120 Thyself shall feel thine own full joys
And hold them fast for ever. There,
So soon as thou shalt first appear,
The moon of maiden stars, thy white
Mistress, attended by such bright
125 Souls as thy shining self, shall come
And in her first ranks make thee room;
Where 'mongst her snowy family
Immortal welcomes wait for thee.
    Oh, what delight when revealed life shall stand
130 And teach thy lips heaven with his hand,
On which thou now mayst to thy wishes
Heap up thy consecrated kisses.
What joys shall seize thy soul when she,
Bending her blessed eyes on thee,
135 Those second smiles of heaven, shall dart
Her mild rays through thy melting heart!
    Angels, thy old friends, there shall greet thee,
Glad at their own home now to meet thee.
    All thy good works which went before
140 And waited for thee at the door
Shall own thee there, and all in one
Weave a constellatïon
Of crowns, with which the King, thy Spouse,
Shall build up thy triumphant brows.
145   All thy old woes shall now smile on thee,
And thy pains sit bright upon thee;

All thy sorrows here shall shine,
All thy sufferings be divine;
Tears shall take comfort and turn gems,
150 And wrongs repent to diadems.
Even thy deaths shall live, and new
Dress the soul that erst they slew;
Thy wounds shall blush to such bright scars
As keep account of the Lamb's wars.
155   Those rare works where thou shalt leave writ
Love's noble history, with wit
Taught thee by none but Him, while here
They feed our souls, shall clothe thine there.
Each heavenly word by whose hid flame
160 Our hard hearts shall strike fire, the same
Shall flourish on thy brows, and be
Both fire to us and flame to thee,
Whose light shall live bright in thy face
By glory, in our hearts by grace.
165   Thou shalt look round about and see
Thousands of crowned souls throng to be
Themselves thy crown; sons of thy vows,
The virgin-births with which thy sovereign Spouse
Made fruitful thy fair soul, go now
170 And with them all about thee, bow
To Him. "Put on," He'll say, "put on,
My rosy love, that, thy rich zone
Sparkling with the sacred flames
Of thousand souls whose happy names
175 Heav'n keeps upon thy score. Thy bright
Life brought them first to kiss the light
That kindled them to stars." And so
Thou with the Lamb, thy Lord, shalt go,
And whereso'er He sets His white
180 Steps, walk with Him those ways of light
Which who in death would live to see
Must learn in life to die like thee.

1652

RICHARD LOVELACE
(1618–1658)

To Althea, from Prison

When Love with unconfinéd wings
Hovers within my gates,
And my divine Althea brings
To whisper at the grates;
5 When I lie tangled in her hair
And fettered to her eye,
The gods[1] that wanton in the air
Know no such liberty.

---

1. Most 17th-century versions read "birds" for "gods."

10 When flowing cups run swiftly round,
   With no allaying Thames,[2]
   Our careless heads with roses bound,
   Our hearts with loyal flames;
   When thirsty grief in wine we steep,
15 When healths and draughts go free,
   Fishes, that tipple in the deep,
   Know no such liberty.

   When, like committed° linnets, I   caged
   With shriller throat shall sing
   The sweetness, mercy, majesty,
20 And glories of my King;
   When I shall voice aloud how good
   He is, how great should be,
   Enlargéd winds, that curl the flood,
   Know no such liberty.

25 Stone walls do not a prison make,
   Nor iron bars a cage;
   Minds innocent and quiet take
   That for an hermitage.
   If I have freedom in my love,
30 And in my soul am free,
   Angels alone, that soar above,
   Enjoy such liberty.

                                                                 1649

To Lucasta, Going to the Wars

   Tell me not, sweet, I am unkind
   That from the nunnery
   Of thy chaste breast and quiet mind,
   To war and arms I fly.

5 True, a new mistress now I chase,
   The first foe in the field;
   And with a stronger faith embrace
   A sword, a horse, a shield.

   Yet this inconstancy is such
10 As you too shall adore;
   I could not love thee, dear, so much,
   Loved I not honor more.

                                                                 1649

The Grasshopper

TO MY NOBLE FRIEND, MR. CHARLES COTTON

   O thou that swing'st upon the waving hair
      Of some well-filléd oaten beard,
   Drunk every night with a delicious tear
      Dropped thee from heaven, where now th' art reared;

2. I.e., without dilution (the Thames River flows through London).

⁵ The joys of earth and air are thine entire,
   That with thy feet and wings dost hop and fly;
And, when thy poppy° works, thou dost retire   *sleeping potion*
   To thy carved acorn-bed to lie.

   Up with the day, the sun thou welcom'st then,
¹⁰   Sport'st in the gilt plats° of his beams,   *hair braids*
And all these merry days mak'st merry men,
   Thyself, and melancholy streams.

   But ah, the sickle! Golden ears are cropped;
   Ceres and Bacchus[3] bid good night;
¹⁵ Sharp, frosty fingers all your flowers have topped,
   And what scythes spared, winds shave off quite.

   Poor verdant fool, and now green ice! thy joys,
   Large and as lasting as thy perch of grass,
Bid us lay in 'gainst winter rain, and poise°   *balance*
²⁰   Their floods with an o'erflowing glass.

   Thou best of men and friends! we will create
   A genuine summer in each other's breast,
And spite of this cold time and frozen fate,
   Thaw us a warm seat to our rest.

²⁵ Our sacred hearths shall burn eternally,
   As vestal flames;[4] the North Wind, he
Shall strike his frost-stretched wings, dissolve, and fly
   This Etna[5] in epitome.

   Dropping December shall come weeping in,
³⁰   Bewail th' usurping of his reign:
But when in showers of old Greek[6] we begin,
   Shall cry he hath his crown again!

   Night, as clear Hesper,[7] shall our tapers whip
   From the light casements where we play,
³⁵ And the dark hag from her black mantle strip,
   And stick there everlasting day.

   Thus richer than untempted kings are we,
   That, asking nothing, nothing need:
Though lord of all what seas embrace, yet he
⁴⁰   That wants himself is poor indeed.

                           1649

3. The grain and the grape, from Ceres, goddess of the harvest, and Bacchus, god of wine.
4. The vestal virgins, consecrated to the Roman goddess Vesta, kept a sacred fire burning perpetually on her altar.
5. A Sicilian volcano.
6. Old Greek wine.
7. The morning star.

ANDREW MARVELL
(1621–1678)

The Coronet

When for the thorns with which I long, too long,
   With many a piercing wound,
   My Savior's head have crowned,
I seek with garlands to redress that wrong;
5   Through every garden, every mead,
I gather flowers (my fruits are only flowers)
   Dismantling all the fragrant towers°   *high headdresses*
That once adorned my shepherdess's head.
And now when I have summed up all my store,
10   Thinking (so I myself deceive)
   So rich a chaplet° thence to weave   *garland*
As never yet the king of glory wore;
   Alas I find the serpent old
   That, twining in his speckled breast,
15   About the flowers disguised does fold,
   With wreaths of fame and interest.
Ah, foolish man, that wouldst debase with them,
And mortal glory, heaven's diadem!
   But Thou who only couldst the serpent tame,
20   Either his slippery knots at once untie,
And disentangle all his winding snare;
Or shatter too with him my curious° frame,°   *elaborate/structure*
And let these wither, so that he may die,
Though set with skill and chosen out with care,
25   That they, while Thou on both their spoils dost tread,
May crown Thy feet, that could not crown Thy head.

                                       1681

Bermudas

   Where the remote Bermudas ride,
In th' ocean's bosom unespied,
From a small boat that rowed along,
The listening winds received this song:
5   "What should we do but sing His praise,
That led us through the watery maze
Unto an isle so long unknown,
And yet far kinder than our own?
Where He the huge sea monsters wracks,°   *casts ashore*
10   That lift the deep upon their backs;
He lands us on a grassy stage,
Safe from the storms, and prelate's rage.[1]
He gave us this eternal spring

1. Marvell indicates Puritan sympathies by associating the wrath of prelates with storms at sea.

Which here enamels everything,
15 And sends the fowls to us in care,
On daily visits through the air;
He hangs in shades the orange bright,
Like golden lamps in a green night,
And does in the pomegranates close
20 Jewels more rich than Ormus² shows;
He makes the figs our mouths to meet,
And throws the melons at our feet;
But apples° plants of such a price,   *pineapples*
No tree could ever bear them twice;
25 With cedars, chosen by His hand,
From Lebanon, He stores the land;
And makes the hollow seas, that roar,
Proclaim the ambergris³ on shore;
He cast (of which we rather boast)
30 The Gospel's pearl upon our coast,
And in these rocks for us did frame
A temple, where to sound His name.
O! let our voice His praise exalt,
Till it arrive at heaven's vault,
35 Which, thence (perhaps) rebounding, may
Echo beyond the Mexique Bay."⁴
        Thus sung they in the English boat,
An holy and a cheerful note;
And all the way, to guide their chime,
40 With falling oars they kept the time.

                                                    1681

The Nymph Complaining for the Death of Her Fawn⁵

The wanton troopers riding by
Have shot my fawn, and it will die.
Ungentle men! they cannot thrive
To kill thee. Thou ne'er didst alive
5   Them any harm, alas! nor could
Thy death yet do them any good.
I'm sure I never wished them ill,
Nor do I for all this, nor will;
But if my simple prayers may yet
10 Prevail with heaven to forget
Thy murder, I will join my tears,
Rather than fail. But, O my fears!
It cannot die so. Heaven's King
Keeps register of everything,
15 And nothing may we use in vain;
Even beasts must be with justice slain,
Else men are made their deodands.⁶
Though they should wash their guilty hands

2. An island off Persia whence gems were exported.
3. A soapy secretion of the sperm whale, gathered on beaches and used in perfumes.
4. I.e., the Gulf of Mexico.
5. "Complaining" means "uttering a poetic lament." Marvell's original spelling "Faun" (for "Fawn") creates an ambiguous expectation, perhaps deliberately.
6. In English law, a deodand was an animal (or object) which, having caused a person's death, was forfeited to the crown to be applied to pious uses.

In this warm life-blood, which doth part
20 From thine, and wound me to the heart,
Yet could they not be clean, their stain
Is dyed in such a purple° grain.°   *brilliant / hue*
There is not such another in
The world to offer for their sin.
25   Unconstant Sylvio, when yet
I had not found him counterfeit,
One morning (I remember well)
Tied in this silver chain and bell,
Gave it to me: nay, and I know
30 What he said then; I'm sure I do:
Said he, "Look how your huntsman here
Hath taught a fawn to hunt his *dear*."
But Sylvio soon had me beguiled;
This waxéd tame, while he grew wild,
35 And quite regardless of my smart,
Left me his fawn, but took his heart.
    Thenceforth I set myself to play
My solitary time away
With this, and very well content,
40 Could so mine idle life have spent;
For it was full of sport, and light
Of foot and heart, and did invite
Me to its game: it seemed to bless
Itself in me; how could I less
45 Than love it? Oh, I cannot be
Unkind to a beast that loveth me.
    Had it lived long, I do not know
Whether it too might have done so
As Sylvio did; his gifts might be
50 Perhaps as false, or more, than he;
But I am sure, for aught that I
Could in so short a time espy,
Thy love was far more better than
The love of false and cruel men.
55   With sweetest milk and sugar, first
I it at mine own fingers nursed;
And as it grew, so every day
It waxed more white and sweet than they.
It had so sweet a breath! And oft
60 I blushed to see its foot more soft
And white, shall I say than my hand?
Nay, any lady's of the land.
    It is a wondrous thing how fleet
'Twas on those little silver feet;
65 With what a pretty skipping grace
It oft would challenge me the race;
And when 't had left me far away,
'Twould stay, and run again, and stay;
For it was nimbler much than hinds,
70 And trod as if on the four winds.
    I have a garden of my own,
But so with roses overgrown,
And lilies, that you would it guess

To be a little wilderness;
75   And all the springtime of the year
It only loved to be there.
Among the beds of lilies I
Have sought it oft, where it should lie,
Yet could not, till itself would rise,
80   Find it, although before mine eyes;
For, in the flaxen lilies' shade,
It like a bank of lilies laid.
Upon the roses it would feed,
Until its lips e'en seemed to bleed;
85   And then to me 'twould boldly trip,
And print those roses on my lip.
But all its chief delight was still
On roses thus itself to fill,
And its pure virgin limbs to fold
90   In whitest sheets of lilies cold:
Had it lived long, it would have been
Lilies without, roses within.
　　O help! O help! I see it faint
And die as calmly as a saint!
95   See how it weeps! the tears do come
Sad, slowly dropping like a gum.
So weeps the wounded balsam; so
The holy frankincense[7] doth flow;
The brotherless Heliades[8]
100   Melt in such amber tears as these.
　　I in a golden vial will
Keep these two crystal tears, and fill
It till it do o'erflow with mine;
Then place it in Diana's shrine.
105   　　Now my sweet fawn is vanished to
Whither the swans and turtles° go,　　　　　　　　　*turtledoves*
In fair Elysium to endure,
With milk-white lambs and ermines pure.
O do not run too fast; for I
110   Will but bespeak° thy grave, and die.　　　　　　　*address*
　　First, my unhappy statue shall
Be cut in marble, and withal,
Let it be weeping too; but there
The engraver sure his art may spare;
115   For I so truly thee bemoan
That I shall weep, though I be stone,
Until my tears, still dropping, wear
My breast, themselves engraving there.
There at my feet shalt thou be laid,
120   Of purest alabaster made;
For I would have thine image be
White as I can, though not as thee.

1681

7. Frankincense, called holy because it is burned in religious ceremonies, is the aromatic gum of an African tree.
8. A name denoting children of Helios, the sun god. Phaethon, the brother referred to, had ventured to drive his father's chariot (the sun) and had been struck dead by Zeus when his wild career endangered the earth. His sisters wept for him until they were turned into poplar trees and their tears into amber.

To His Coy Mistress

    Had we but world enough, and time,
This coyness, lady, were no crime.
We would sit down, and think which way
To walk, and pass our long love's day.
5 Thou by the Indian Ganges' side
Shoudst rubies[9] find; I by the tide
Of Humber[1] would complain. I would
Love you ten years before the flood,
And you should, if you please, refuse
10 Till the conversion of the Jews.[2]
My vegetable[3] love should grow
Vaster than empires and more slow;
An hundred years should go to praise
Thine eyes, and on thy forehead gaze;
15 Two hundred to adore each breast,
But thirty thousand to the rest;
An age at least to every part,
And the last age should show your heart.
For, lady, you deserve this state,°   *dignity*
20 Nor would I love at lower rate.
    But at my back I always hear
Time's wingéd chariot hurrying near;
And yonder all before us lie
Deserts of vast eternity.
25 Thy beauty shall no more be found;
Nor, in thy marble vault, shall sound
My echoing song; then worms shall try
That long-preserved virginity,
And your quaint° honor turn to dust,   *over-subtle*
30 And into ashes all my lust:
The grave's a fine and private place,
But none, I think, do there embrace.
    Now therefore, while the youthful hue
Sits on thy skin like morning glow,[4]
35 And while thy willing soul transpires°   *breathes out*
At every pore with instant fires,
Now let us sport us while we may,
And now, like amorous birds of prey,
Rather at once our time devour
40 Than languish in his slow-chapped° power.   *slow-jawed*
Let us roll all our strength and all
Our sweetness up into one ball,
And tear our pleasures with rough strife
Thorough the iron gates[5] of life:
45 Thus, though we cannot make our sun
Stand still,[6] yet we will make him run.

1681

9. Rubies are talismans, preserving virginity.
1. The Humber flows through Marvell's native town of Hull.
2. To occur, as tradition had it, at the end of recorded history.
3. A technical term: "possessing, like plants, the power of growth but not of consciousness"; in context, "being magnified without conscious nurture."
4. In these rhyme-words (originally spelled *hew* and *glew*) the vowel sounds are probably similar and possibly identical: an *eh* gliding into an *oo*.
5. The obscurity "iron gates" suggests that the "ball" of line 42 has become a missile from a siege gun, battering its way into a citadel.
6. We lack, that is, the power of Zeus, who, to prolong his enjoyment of the mortal Alcmena, arrested the diurnal course and created a week-long night.

The Garden

How vainly men themselves amaze°   *perplex*
To win the palm, the oak, or bays,[8]
And their incessant° labors see   *unceasing*
Crowned from some single herb, or tree,
5   Whose short and narrow-vergéd[9] shade
Does prudently their toils upbraid;
While all flowers and all trees do close°   *join*
To weave the garlands of repose!

Fair Quiet, have I found thee here,
10   And Innocence, thy sister dear?
Mistaken long, I sought you then
In busy companies of men.
Your sacred plants,° if here below,   *cuttings*
Only among the plants will grow;
15   Society is all but rude[1]
To this delicious solitude.

No white nor red was ever seen
So amorous as this lovely green.
Fond lovers, cruel as their flame,
20   Cut in these trees their mistress' name:
Little, alas, they know or heed
How far these beauties hers exceed!
Fair trees, wheresoe'er your barks I wound,
No name shall but your own be found.

25   When we have run our passion's heat,°   *course*
Love hither makes his best retreat.
The gods, that mortal beauty chase,
Still in a tree did end their race:
Apollo hunted Daphne so,
30   Only that she might laurel grow;
And Pan did after Syrinx speed,
Not as a nymph, but for a reed.[2]

What wondrous life is this I lead!
Ripe apples drop about my head;
35   The luscious clusters of the vine
Upon my mouth do crush their wine;
The nectarine and curious° peach   *exquisite*
Into my hands themselves do reach;
Stumbling on melons, as I pass,
40   Insnared with flowers, I fall on grass.

8. The wreaths awarded, respectively, for athletic, civic, and poetic accomplishments.
9. Confined, not spreading luxuriantly like the living branch.
1. I.e., all merely barbarous.

2. In the original myths, as told by Ovid, the nymphs frustrated the pursuing gods by turning into the plants named. In Marvell's version, the gods intended the transformations.

Meanwhile the mind, from pleasure less,
Withdraws into its happiness;[3]
The mind, that ocean where each kind
Does straight its own resemblance find;[4]
45 Yet it creates, transcending these,
Far other worlds and other seas,
Annihilating all that's made
To a green thought in a green shade.

Here at the fountain's sliding foot,
50 Or at some fruit tree's mossy root,
Casting the body's vest° aside,   garment
My soul into the boughs does glide:
There, like a bird, it sits and sings,
Then whets[5] and combs its silver wings,
55 And, till prepared for longer flight,
Waves in its plumes the various° light.   iridescent

Such was that happy garden-state,
While man there walked without a mate:
After a place so pure and sweet,
60 What other help could yet be meet![5a]
But 'twas beyond a mortal's share
To wander solitary there:
Two paradises 'twere in one
To live in paradise alone.

65 How well the skillful gardener drew
Of flowers and herbs this dial[6] new,
Where, from above, the milder sun
Does through a fragrant zodiac run;
And as it works, th' industrious bee
70 Computes its time as well as we!
How could such sweet and wholesome hours
Be reckoned but with herbs and flowers?

1681

HENRY VAUGHAN
(1622–1695)

The Retreat

Happy those early days! when I
Shined in my angel infancy.
Before I understood this place
Appointed for my second race,
5 Or taught my soul to fancy aught
But a white, celestial thought;

---

3. I.e., its own intellectual happiness is a greater pleasure than the taste of fruits.
4. Every land creature was thought to have its counterpart sea creature.
5. Sharpens its beak. But birds apparently whetting their beaks are actually cleaning them.
5a. God created Eve because "for Adam there was not found an help meet for him" (Genesis ii.20).
6. A plantation of flowers forming a dial face, perhaps surrounding an actual sundial.

When yet I had not walked above
A mile or two from my first love,
And looking back, at that short space,
10 Could see a glimpse of His bright face;
When on some gilded cloud or flower
My gazing soul would dwell an hour,
And in those weaker glories spy
Some shadows of eternity;
15 Before I taught my tongue to wound
My conscience with a sinful sound,
Or had the black art to dispense
A several° sin to every sense,   separate
But felt through all this fleshly dress
20 Bright shoots of everlastingness.
O, how I long to travel back,
And tread again that ancient track!
That I might once more reach that plain
Where first I left my glorious train,
25 From whence th' enlightened spirit sees
That shady city of palm trees.
But, ah! my soul with too much stay
Is drunk, and staggers in the way.
Some men a forward motion love;
30 But I by backward steps would move,
And when this dust falls to the urn,
In that state I came, return.

1650

They Are All Gone into the World of Light!

They are all gone into the world of light!
  And I alone sit lingering here;
Their very memory is fair and bright,
  And my sad thoughts doth clear.

5 It glows and glitters in my cloudy breast
  Like stars upon some gloomy grove,
Or those faint beams in which this hill is dressed
  After the sun's remove.

I see them walking in an air of glory,
10   Whose light doth trample on my days;
My days, which are at best but dull and hoary,
  Mere glimmering and decays.

O holy hope, and high humility,
  High as the heavens above!
15 These are your walks, and you have showed them me
  To kindle my cold love.

Dear, beauteous death! the jewel of the just,
  Shining nowhere but in the dark;
What mysteries do lie beyond thy dust,
20   Could man outlook that mark!°   boundary

He that hath found some fledged bird's nest may know
    At first sight if the bird be flown;
But what fair well or grove he sings in now,
    That is to him unknown.

25 And yet, as angels in some brighter dreams
    Call to the soul when man doth sleep,
So some strange thoughts transcend our wonted themes,
    And into glory peep.

If a star were confined into a tomb,
30   Her captive flames must needs burn there;
But when the hand that locked her up gives room,
    She'll shine through all the sphere.

O Father of eternal life, and all
    Created glories under Thee!
35 Resume° Thy spirit from this world of thrall   *take back*
    Into true liberty!

Either disperse these mists, which blot and fill
    My perspective° still as they pass;   *telescope*
Or else remove me hence unto that hill
40   Where I shall need no glass.

                                      1655

The Timber

Sure thou didst flourish once! and many springs,
Many bright mornings, much dew, many showers
Passed o'er thy head; many light hearts and wings,
Which now are dead, lodged in thy living bowers.

5 And still a new succession sings and flies;
Fresh groves grow up, and their green branches shoot
Toward the old and still enduring skies,
While the low violet thrives at their root.

But thou beneath the sad and heavy line
10 Of death, doth waste all senseless, cold, and dark;
Where not so much as dreams of light may shine,
Nor any thought of greenness, leaf, or bark.

And yet (as if some deep hate and dissent,
Bred in thy growth betwixt high winds and thee,
15 Were still alive) thou dost great storms resent
Before they come, and know'st how near they be.[1]

Else all at rest thou liest, and the fierce breath
Of tempests can no more disturb thy ease;
But this thy strange resentment after death
20 Means° only those who broke in life thy peace.   *is directed at*

---

1. An allusion to foxfire, the eerie phosphores- cially before a storm.
cent light given off by decaying wood, espe-

So murdered man, when lovely life is done
And his blood freezed, keeps in the center still
Some secret sense, which makes the dead blood run
At his approach, that did the body kill.

25 And is there any murderer worse than sin?
Or any storms more foul than a lewd life?
Or what resentient[2] can work more within
Than true remorse, when with past sins at strife?

He that hath left life's vain joys and vain care,
30 And truly hates to be detained on earth,
Hath got an house where many mansions are,[3]
And keeps his soul unto eternal mirth.

But though thus dead unto the world, and ceased
From sin, he walks a narrow, private way;
35 Yet grief and old wounds make him sore displeased,
And all his life a rainy, weeping day.

For though he would forsake the world, and live
As mere° a stranger, as men long since dead;   *total*
Yet joy itself will make a right soul grieve
40 To think he should be so long vainly led.

But as shades set off light, so tears and grief
(Though of themselves but a sad blubbered story)
By showing the sin great, show the relief
Far greater, and so speak my Saviour's glory.

45 If my way lies through deserts and wild woods,
Where all the land with scorching heat is curst,
Better the pools should flow with rain and floods
To fill my bottle, than I die with thirst.

Blest showers they are, and streams sent from above
50 Begetting virgins where they use to flow;
And trees of life no other water love;[4]
These upper springs, and none else make them grow.

But these chaste fountains flow not till we die;
Some drops may fall before, but a clear spring
55 And ever running, till we leave° to fling   *cease*
Dirt in her way, will keep above the sky.

1655

2. That which causes a change of heart.
3. "In my Father's house are many mansions"
(John xiv.2). "Mansions": rooms.
4. "And he shewed me a pure river of water
of life, clear as crystal, proceeding out of the
throne of God and of the Lamb. In the midst
of the street of it, and on either side of the
river, was there the tree of life * * * " (Rev-
elation xxii.1–2).

The Waterfall

With what deep murmurs through time's silent stealth
Doth thy transparent, cool, and watery wealth
    Here flowing fall,
    And chide, and call,
5 As if his liquid, loose retinue stayed
Lingering, and were of this steep place afraid,
    The common pass
    Where, clear as glass,
    All must descend—
10   Not to an end,
But quickened by this deep and rocky grave,
Rise to a longer course more bright and brave.°   *sparkling*

    Dear stream! dear bank, where often I
    Have sat and pleased my pensive eye,
15   Why, since each drop of thy quick° store   *living*
    Runs thither whence it flowed before,
    Should poor souls fear a shade or night,
    Who came, sure, from a sea of light?
    Or since those drops are all sent back
20   So sure to thee, that none doth lack,
    Why should frail flesh doubt any more
    That what God takes He'll not restore?

    O useful element and clear!
    My sacred wash and cleanser here,[5]
25   My first consignor unto those
    Fountains of life where the Lamb goes![6]
    What sublime truths and wholesome themes
    Lodge in thy mystical deep streams!
    Such as dull man can never find
30   Unless that Spirit lead his mind
    Which first upon thy face did move,[7]
    And hatched all with His quickening love.
    As this loud brook's incessant fall
    In streaming rings restagnates° all,   *becomes stagnant*
35   Which reach by course the bank, and then
    Are no more seen, just so pass men.
    O my invisible estate,
    My glorious liberty,[8] still late!
    Thou art the channel my soul seeks,
40   Not this with cataracts and creeks.

                          1655

---

5. I.e., through baptism.
6. "For the Lamb which is in the midst of the throne shall feed them, and shall lead them unto living fountains of waters: and God shall wipe away all tears from their eyes" (Revelation vii.17).

7. "And the Spirit of God moved upon the face of the waters" (Genesis i.2).
8. "Because the creature itself also shall be delivered from the bondage of corruption into the glorious liberty of the children of God" (Romans viii.21).

JOHN DRYDEN
(1631–1700)

Song from *Troilus and Cressida*

1

Can life be a blessing,
　Or worth the possessing,
Can life be a blessing, if love were away?
Ah, no! though our love all night keep us waking,
5 And though he torment us with cares all the day,
　Yet he sweetens, he sweetens our pains in the taking;
There's an hour at the last, there's an hour to repay.

2

In every possessing
　The ravishing blessing,
10 In every possessing the fruit of our pain,
　Poor lovers forget long ages of anguish,
Whate'er they have suffered and done to obtain;
　'Tis a pleasure, a pleasure to sigh and to languish,
When we hope, when we hope to be happy again.

1679

Mac Flecknoe

OR A SATIRE UPON THE
TRUE-BLUE-PROTESTANT POET, T. S.[1]

All human things are subject to decay,
And when fate summons, monarchs must obey.
This Flecknoe found, who, like Augustus,[2] young
Was called to empire, and had governed long;
5 In prose and verse, was owned, without dispute,
Through all the realms of Nonsense, absolute.
This aged prince, now flourishing in peace,
And blest with issue of a large increase,
Worn out with business, did at length debate
10 To settle the succession of the state;
And, pondering which of all his sons was fit
To reign, and wage immortal war with wit,[3]
Cried: " 'Tis resolved; for nature pleads that he
Should only rule, who most resembles me.
15 Sh———[4] alone my perfect image bears,
Mature in dullness from his tender years:
Sh——— alone, of all my sons, is he

1. Thomas Shadwell (1640–92), a comic play-
wright of respectable talents, who considered
himself the dramatic heir of Ben Jonson. He
was vain, corpulent, and probably overbearing
in manner. Dryden names him *Mac* (son of)
Flecknoe, making him heir not of Jonson but
of the recently dead Irish priest Richard
Flecknoe, a poet at once tiresome and prolific.
The subtitle (presumably added when the
poem, itself non-political, was published in
1682) acknowledges a political controversy fed
by Dryden's poems *Absalom and Achitophel*
and *The Medal* (a satire on Shaftesbury's ac-
quittal) and Shadwell's rejoinder *The Medal
of John Bayes* (John Dryden). Shadwell be-
longed to the Whig party, the political haven
of dissenting Protestants.
2. Augustus became Roman emperor at thirty-
two and reigned for forty years.
3. *Wit*, here as in other poems of the time,
variously denotes the intellect, the poetic
imagination, and a general sprightliness of
mind.
4. A transparent pretense to anonymity, ad-
mitting here and there a scatological sug-
gestion.

Sworn by his sire a mortal foe to Rome,[9]
So Sh—— swore, nor should his vow be vain,
115 That he till death true dullness would maintain;
And, in his father's right, and realm's defense,
Ne'er to have peace with wit, nor truce with sense.
The king himself the sacred unction° made,   ointment
As king by office, and as priest by trade.
120 In his sinister[1] hand, instead of ball,
He placed a mighty mug of potent ale;
Love's Kingdom[2] to his right he did convey,
At once his scepter, and his rule of sway;
Whose righteous lore the prince had practiced young,
125 And from whose loins recorded *Psyche* sprung.
His temples, last, with poppies[3] were o'erspread,
That nodding seemed to consecrate his head.
Just at that point of time, if fame not lie,
On his left hand twelve reverend owls did fly.
130 So Romulus, 'tis sung, by Tiber's brook,
Presage of sway from twice six vultures took.[4]
The admiring throng loud acclamations make,
And omens of his future empire take.
The sire then shook the honors° of his head,   locks
135 And from his brows damps° of oblivion shed   vapors
Full on the filial dullness: long he stood,
Repelling from his breast the raging god;
At length burst out in this prophetic mood:
     "Heavens bless my son, from Ireland let him reign
140 To far Barbadoes on the western main;[5]
Of his dominion may no end be known,
And greater than his father's be his throne;
Beyond *Love's Kingdom* let his stretch his pen!"
He paused, and all the people cried, "Amen."
145 Then thus continued he: "My son, advance
Still in new imprudence, new ignorance.
Success let others teach, learn thou from me
Pangs without birth, and fruitless industry.
Let *Virtuosos* in five years be writ;
150 Yet not one thought accuse thy toil of wit.
Let gentle George[6] in triumph tread the stage,
Make Dorimant betray, and Loveit rage;
Let Cully, Cockwood, Fopling, charm the pit,
And in their folly show the writer's wit.
155 Yet still thy fools shall stand in thy defense,
And justify their author's want of sense.
Let 'em be all by thy own model made
Of dullness, and desire no foreign aid;
That they to future ages may be known,
160 Not copies drawn, but issue of thy own.
Nay, let thy men of wit too be the same,

---

9. Hannibal, the Carthaginian general who invaded Italy, was dedicated to his hatred of Rome (it was said) at the age of nine.
1. In British coronations the monarch holds in his left ("sinister") hand a globe surmounted by a cross.
2. A "pastoral tragicomedy" by Flecknoe, apparently visualized by Dryden as a rolled-up manuscript held like a scepter.
3. Connoting both intellectual heaviness and Shadwell's addiction to opiates.

4. When the site which Romulus had chosen for Rome was visited by twelve vultures, or twice as many as had visited the site picked by his brother Remus, the kingship ("sway") of Romulus was presaged.
5. I.e., a realm of empty ocean.
6. George Etherege (ca. 1635–91), playwright who set the tone for stylish Restoration comedy; Dryden proceeds to name five of his characters.

All full of thee, and differing but in name.
But let no alien S—dl—y[7] interpose,
To lard with wit thy hungry *Epsom* prose.
165 And when false flowers of rhetoric thou wouldst cull,
Trust nature, do not labor to be dull;
But write thy best, and top; and, in each line,
Sir Formal's[8] oratory will be thine:
Sir Formal, though unsought, attends thy quill,
170 And does thy northern dedications[9] fill.
Nor let false friends seduce thy mind to fame,
By arrogating Jonson's hostile name.
Let father Flecknoe fire thy mind with praise,
And uncle Ogilby thy envy raise.
175 Thou art my blood, where Jonson has no part:
What share have we in nature, or in art?
Where did his wit on learning fix a brand,
And rail at arts he did not understand?
Where made he love in Prince Nicander's vein,
180 Or swept the dust in *Psyche's* humble strain?[1]
Where sold he bargains,[2] 'whip-stitch, kiss my arse,'
Promised a play and dwindled to a farce?
When did his Muse from Fletcher scenes purloin,
As thou whole Eth'rege dost transfuse to thine?
185 But so transfused, as oil on water's flow,
His always floats above, thine sinks below.
This is thy province, this thy wondrous way,
New humors to invent for each new play:
This is that boasted bias of thy mind,
190 By which one way, to dullness, 'tis inclined;
Which makes thy writings lean on one side still,
And, in all changes, that way bends thy will.
Nor let thy mountain-belly make pretense
Of likeness; thine's a tympany[3] of sense.
195 A tun of man in thy large bulk is writ,
But sure thou'rt but a kilderkin of wit.[4]
Like mine, thy gentle numbers feebly creep;
Thy tragic Muse gives smiles, thy comic sleep.
With whate'er gall thou sett'st thyself to write,
200 Thy inoffensive satires never bite.
In thy felonious heart though venom lies,
It does but touch thy Irish pen, and dies.
Thy genius calls thee not to purchase fame
In keen iambics,[5] but mild anagram.
205 Leave writing plays, and choose for thy command
Some peaceful province in acrostic land.
There thou may'st wings display and altars raise,
And torture one poor word ten thousand ways.[6]
Or, if thou wouldst thy different talent suit,
210 Set thy own songs, and sing them to thy lute."

---

7. Sir Charles Sedley (ca. 1639–1701), Restoration wit who had contributed a prologue and (Dryden suggests) a part of the text to Shadwell's *Epsom Wells*.
8. Sir Formal Trifle was an inflated orator in *The Virtuoso*.
9. I.e., to Shadwell's patron the Duke of Newcastle, whose seat was in northern England.
1. Nicander pays court to the title character Psyche in Shadwell's opera.

2. A "bargain" is a gross rejoinder to an innocent question. The rest of the line, itself a kind of bargain, echoes a farcical character in *The Virtuoso*.
3. A swelling caused by air.
4. Tuns are big casks; kilderkins, little ones.
5. The meter of (Greek) satire; hence satire itself.
6. Ingenuities like those mentioned, frequent in the early century, had been put away as trivial.

He said: but his last words were scarcely heard ⎤
For Bruce and Longville had a trap prepared,   ⎬
And down they sent the yet declaiming bard.[7] ⎦
Sinking he left his drugget robe behind,
15   Borne upwards by a subterranean wind.
The mantle fell to the young prophet's part,[8]
With double portion of his father's art.

                                              ca. 1679   1682

To the Memory of Mr. Oldham[9]

Farewell, too little, and too lately known,
Whom I began to think and call my own:
For sure our souls were near allied, and thine
Cast in the same poetic mold with mine.
5   One common note on either lyre did strike,
And knaves and fools we both abhorred alike.
To the same goal did both our studies° drive;   *endeavors*
The last set out the soonest did arrive.
Thus Nisus[1] fell upon the slippery place,
10   While his young friend performed° and won the race.   *completed*
O early ripe! to thy abundant store
What could advancing age have added more?
It might (what nature never gives the young)
Have taught the numbers° of thy native tongue.   *metrics*
15   But satire needs not those, and wit will shine
Through the harsh cadence of a rugged line:
A noble error, and but seldom made,
When poets are by too much force betrayed.
Thy generous fruits, though gathered ere their prime, ⎤
20   Still showed a quickness,° and maturing time   ⎬   *pungency*
But mellows what we write to the dull sweets of rhyme. ⎦
Once more, hail and farewell; farewell, thou young,
But ah too short, Marcellus[2] of our tongue;
Thy brows with ivy, and with laurels bound;
25   But fate and gloomy night encompass thee around.[3]

                                                                 1684

Song from *Cleomenes*

1

No, no, poor suffering heart, no change endeavor,
Choose to sustain the smart, rather than leave her;
My ravished eyes behold such charms about her,
I can die with her, but not live without her;
5   One tender sigh of hers to see me languish,
Will more than pay the price of my past anguish:
Beware, O cruel fair, how you smile on me,
'Twas a kind look of yours that has undone me.

---

7. These characters in *The Virtuoso* so trap Sir Formal Trifle.
8. Like the prophet Elijah's mantle falling on Elisha. See II Kings ii, or Cowley's elegy on Crashaw, line 66n.
9. John Oldham (1653–83), author of *Satires Upon the Jesuits*, was a promising young poet, harsh (partly by calculation) in metrics and manner, but earnest and vigorous.
1. A foot racer in Virgil's *Aeneid;* his young friend Euryalus came from behind to reach the goal before him (V.315 ff.).
2. Augustus Caesar's nephew, who died at twenty after a meteoric military career.
3. The Roman elegiac phrase "Hail and farewell!" in line 22; the mention of Marcellus (line 23) and of the classical poet's wreath (line 24); and the echo of Virgil's lament for Marcellus (see *Aeneid* VI.566) conspire to Romanize Oldham.

2

Love has in store for me one happy minute,
10 And she will end my pain, who did begin it;
Then no day void of bliss, or pleasure, leaving,
Ages shall slide away without perceiving:
Cupid shall guard the door, the more to please us,
And keep out Time and Death, when they would seize us;
15 Time and Death shall depart, and say, in flying,
Love has found out a way to live by dying.

1692

THOMAS TRAHERNE
(1637–1674)

Wonder

How like an angel came I down!
    How bright are all things here!
When first among His works I did appear
    Oh, how their glory me did crown!
5 The world resembled His eternity,
        In which my soul did walk;
    And everything that I did see
        Did with me talk.

The skies in their magnificence,
10   The lively, lovely air,
Oh, how divine, how soft, how sweet, how fair!
    The stars did entertain my sense,
And all the works of God, so bright and pure,
        So rich and great did seem,
15   As if they ever must endure
        In my esteem.

A native health and innocence
        Within my bones did grow;
And while my God did all His glories show,
20   I felt a vigor in my sense
That was all spirit. I within did flow
        With seas of life, like wine;
    I nothing in the world did know
        But 'twas divine.

25 Harsh ragged objects were concealed;
        Oppressions, tears, and cries,
Sins, griefs, complaints, dissensions, weeping eyes
    Were hid, and only things revealed
Which heavenly spirits and the angels prize.
30   The state of innocence
    And bliss, not trades and poverties,
        Did fill my sense.

The streets were paved with golden stones,
        The boys and girls were mine,
35 Oh, how did all their lovely faces shine!
    The sons of men were holy ones,

In joy and beauty they appeared to me,
  And everything I found,
 While like an angel I did see,
40   Adorned the ground.

 Rich diamond and pearl and gold
  In every place was seen;
Rare splendors, yellow, blue, red, white, and green,
 Mine eyes did everywhere behold.
45 Great wonders clothed with glory did appear,
  Amazement was my bliss,
 That and my wealth met everywhere;
   No joy to° this!   *compared to*

 Cursed and devised proprieties,[1]
50 With envy, avarice,
And fraud, those fiends that spoil even paradise,
 Flew from the splendor of mine eyes;
And so did hedges, ditches, limits, bounds:
  I dreamed not aught of those,
55 But wandered over all men's grounds,
  And found repose.

 Proprieties themselves were mine,
  And hedges ornaments;
Walls, boxes, coffers, and their rich contents
60 To make me rich combine.
Clothes, ribbons, jewels, laces, I esteemed
 My joys by others worn:
 For me they all to wear them seemed
  When I was born.

            1903

Shadows in the Water

In unexperienced infancy
Many a sweet mistake doth lie:
Mistake though false, intending° true; *directing to*
A seeming somewhat more than view;
5 That doth instruct the mind
 In things that lie behind,
And many secrets to us show
Which afterwards we come to know.

 Thus did I by the water's brink
10 Another world beneath me think;
And while the lofty spacious skies
Reverséd there, abused mine eyes,
 I fancied other feet
 Came mine to touch or meet;
15 As by some puddle I did play
Another world within it lay.

1. Proprietorships, devised or bequeathed in a will.

Beneath the water people drowned,
Yet with another heaven crowned,
In spacious regions seemed to go
20   As freely moving to and fro:
    In bright and open space
    I saw their very face;
Eyes, hands, and feet they had like mine;
Another sun did with them shine.

25   'Twas strange that people there should walk,
And yet I could not hear them talk:
That through a little watery chink,
Which one dry ox or horse might drink,
    We other worlds should see,
30   Yet not admitted be;
And other confines there behold
Of light and darkness, heat and cold.

I called them oft, but called in vain;
No speeches we could entertain:
35   Yet did I there expect to find
Some other world, to please my mind.
    I plainly saw by these
    A new antipodes,[2]
Whom, though they were so plainly seen,
40   A film kept off that stood between.

By walking men's reverséd feet
I chanced another world to meet;
Though it did not to view exceed
A phantom, 'tis a world indeed,
45   Where skies beneath us shine,
    And earth by art divine
Another face presents below,
Where people's feet against ours go.

Within the regions of the air,
50   Compassed about with heavens fair,
Great tracts of land there may be found
Enriched with fields and fertile ground;
    Where many numerous hosts
    In those far distant coasts,
55   For other great and glorious ends
Inhabit, my yet unknown friends.

O ye that stand upon the brink,
Whom I so near me through the chink
With wonder see: what faces there,
60   Whose feet, whose bodies, do ye wear?
    I my companions see
    In you, another me.
They seeméd others, but are we;
Our second selves these shadows be.

2. People living at a diametrically opposite point on the globe (literally, "with the feet opposite").

65   Look how far off those lower skies
     Extend themselves! scarce with mine eyes
     I can them reach. O ye my friends,
     What secret borders on those ends?
       Are lofty heavens hurled
70   'Bout your inferior world?
     Are yet the representatives
     Of other peoples' distant lives?

     Of all the playmates which I knew
     That here I do the image view
75   In other selves, what can it mean?
     But that below the purling stream
       Some unknown joys there be
       Laid up in store for me;
     To which I shall, when that thin skin
80   Is broken, be admitted in.

                             ca. 1665   1910

EDWARD TAYLOR
(ca. 1642–1729)

Meditation 8[1]

I kenning° through astronomy divine   *discerning, knowing*
   The world's bright battlement, wherein I spy
A golden path my pencil cannot line,
   From that bright throne unto my threshold lie.
5   And while my puzzled thoughts about it pore
     I find the bread of life in it at my door.

When that this bird of paradise put in
   This wicker cage (my corpse)[2] to tweedle° praise   *sing*
Had pecked the fruit forbad, and so did fling
10   Away its food, and lost its golden days,
     It fell into celestial famine sore,
     And never could attain a morsel more.

Alas! alas! Poor bird, what wilt thou do?
   The creatures' field no food for souls e'er gave.
15 And if thou knock at angels' doors they show
    An empty barrel; they no soul bread have.
     Alas! Poor bird, the world's white loaf is done,
     And cannot yield thee here the smallest crumb.

In this sad state, God's tender bowels[3] run
20   Out streams of grace; and he to end all strife
   The purest wheat in heaven, his dear, dear son
    Grinds, and kneads up into this bread of life.
     Which bread of life from heaven down came and stands
     Dished on my table up by angels' hands.

---

1. Based on John vi.51: "I am the living bread which came down from heaven: if any man eat of this bread, he shall live for ever: and the bread that I will give is my flesh, which I will give for the life of the world."

2. In this context, the living body.
3. I.e., God's powers of mercy and compassion.

²⁵ Did God mould up this bread in heaven, and bake,
    Which from his table came, and to thine goeth?
Doth he bespeak thee thus: This soul bread take;
    Come eat thy fill of this thy God's white loaf?
It's food too fine for angels, yet come, take
³⁰   And eat thy fill: it's heaven's sugar cake.

What grace is this knead in this loaf? This thing
    Souls are but petty things it to admire.
Ye angels, help. This fill would to the brim
    Heaven's whelmed-down[4] crystal meal bowl, yea and higher,
³⁵ This bread of life dropped in thy mouth, doth cry:
    Eat, eat me, soul, and thou shalt never die.

1684   1937

The Glory of and Grace in the Church Set Out

    Come now behold
Within this knot[5] what flowers do grow,
    Spangled like gold,
Whence wreaths of all perfumes do flow.
⁵ Most curious° colors of all sorts you shall   *amazing*
With all sweet spirits° scent. Yet that's not all.   *odors*

    Oh! Look, and find
These choicest flowers most richly sweet
    Are disciplined
¹⁰   With artificial angels meet.[6]
An heap of pearls is precious; but they shall,
When set by art, excel. Yet that's not all.

    Christ's spirit showers
Down in his word, and sacraments
    Upon these flowers
¹⁵ The clouds of grace divine contents.
Such things of wealthy blessings on them fall
As make them sweetly thrive. Yet that's not all.

    Yet still behold!
²⁰ All flourish not at once. We see
    While some unfold
Their blushing leaves, some buds there be.
Here's faith, glory, charity in flower, which call
On yonders in the bud. Yet that's not all.

²⁵   But as they stand
Like beauties reeking in° perfume   *giving off*
    A divine hand
Doth hand them up to glory's room,
Where each in sweetened songs all praises shall
³⁰ Sing all o'er heaven for aye. And that's but all.

1937

---

4. Turned over upon something so as to cover it.
5. Plot of ground, or planting-bed.

6. "Artificial angels meet": i.e., appropriate angel-artificers.

Upon Wedlock, and Death of Children

A curious knot God made in paradise,
   And drew it out enameled° neatly fresh.   *variously colored*
It was the truelove knot, more sweet than spice
   And set with all the flowers of grace's dress.
5   Its wedding knot, that ne'er can be untied;
   No Alexander's sword[7] can it divide.

The slips here planted, gay and glorious grow,
   Unless an hellish breath do singe their plumes.
Here primrose, cowslips, roses, lilies blow
10   With violets and pinks that void° perfumes: *give off, exude*
   Whose beauteous leaves o'er laid with honey-dew,
   And chanting birds chirp out sweet music true.

When in this knot I planted was, my stock°   *stem*
   Soon knotted, and a manly flower out brake.
15   And after it my branch again did knot;
   Brought out another flower its sweet breathed mate.
   One knot gave one t'other the t'other's place;
   Whence chuckling smiles fought in each other's face.

But oh! a glorious hand from glory came
20   Guarded with angels, soon did crop this flower
Which almost tore the root up of the same
   At that unlooked for, dolesome, darksome hour.
   In prayer to Christ perfumed it did ascend,
   And angels bright did it to heaven tend.

25   But pausing on't, this sweet perfumed my thought,
   Christ would in glory have a flower, choice, prime,
And having choice, chose this my branch forth brought.
   Lord take't. I thank thee, thou takest aught of mine,
   It is my pledge in glory; part of me
30   Is now in it, Lord, glorified with thee.

But praying o'er my branch, my branch did sprout
   And bore another manly flower, and gay;
And after that another, sweet, brake out,
   The which the former hand soon got away.
35   But oh! the tortures, vomit, screechings, groans,
   And six weeks fever would pierce hearts like stones.

Grief o'er doth flow, and nature fault would find
   Were not thy will, my spell charm, joy, and gem;
That as I said, I say, take, Lord, they're thine.
40   I piecemeal pass to glory bright in them.
   I joy, may I sweet flowers for glory breed,
   Whether thou getst them green, or let them seed.

1937

---

7. Gordius, king of Phrygia, devised a complicated knot to be undone only by him who was to rule Asia. Alexander the Great cut the knot with a blow of his sword.

Upon a Spider Catching a Fly

Thou sorrow, venom elf:
   Is this thy play,
To spin a web out of thyself
   To catch a fly?
5   For why?

I saw a pettish° wasp   *peevish, petulant*
   Fall foul therein,
Whom yet thy whorl-pins[8] did not clasp
   Lest he should fling
10   His sting.

But as afraid, remote
   Didst stand hereat
And with thy little fingers stroke
   And gently tap
15   His back.

Thus gently him didst treat
   Lest he should pet,
And in a froppish,° waspish heat   *fretful*
   Should greatly fret
20   Thy net.

Whereas the silly fly,
   Caught by its leg
Thou by the throat tookst hastily
   And hind the head
25   Bite dead.

This goes to pot,[9] that not
   Nature doth call.
Strive not above what strength hath got
   Lest in the brawl
30   Thou fall.

This fray seems thus to us.
   Hell's spider gets
His entrails spun to whip-cords[10] thus,
   And wove to nets
35   And sets.

To tangle Adam's race
   In's strategems
To their destructions, spoiled, made base
   By venom things,
40   Damned sins.

---

8. Technically, the flywheel holding the thread on the spindle of a spinning wheel; here, the spider's legs.

9. As in the modern sense, deteriorates.
10. Strong cord or binding, like that made of hemp or catgut.

But mighty, gracious Lord
   Communicate
Thy grace to break the cord, afford
   Us glory's gate
45   And state.

We'll nightingale sing like
   When perched on high
In glory's cage, thy glory, bright,
   And thankfully,
50   For joy.

1939

JONATHAN SWIFT
(1667–1745)

Frances Harris's Petition

TO THEIR EXCELLENCIES THE LORDS JUSTICES OF
IRELAND,[1] WRITTEN IN THE YEAR 1701

The humble petition of Frances Harries,
Who must starve and die a maid if it miscarries;
Humbly sheweth, that I went to warm myself in Lady Betty's
   chamber, because I was cold;
And I had in a purse seven pound, four shillings, and sixpence,
   besides farthings, in money and gold;
5 So because I had been buying things for my lady last night,
I was resolved to tell° my money, to see if it was right.   *count*
Now, you must know, because my trunk has a very bad lock,
Therefore all the money I have, which, God knows, is a very
   small stock,
I keep in my pocket, tied about my middle, next my smock.
10 So when I went to put up my purse, as God would have it,
   my smock was unripped,
And instead of putting it into my pocket, down it slipped;
Then the bell rung, and I went down to put my lady to bed;
And, God knows, I thought my money was as safe as my
   maidenhead.
So, when I came up again, I found my pocket feel very light;
15 But when I searched, and missed my purse, Lord! I thought
   I should have sunk outright.
"Lord! madam," says Mary,[2] "how d'ye do?"—"Indeed," says I,
   "never worse:
But pray, Mary, can you tell what I have done with my purse?"
"Lord help me!" says Mary, "I never stirred out of this place!"
"Nay," said I, "I had it in Lady Betty's chamber, that's a
   plain case."
20 So Mary got me to bed, and covered me up warm:

1. The Lord Justice chiefly involved was the Earl of Berkeley, whom Swift served in the capacity of chaplain from 1699 to 1701. Berkeley's daughter ("Lady Betty"), Frances Harris's mistress, was then a girl of sixteen. The other domestics in the poem are identifiable members of Berkeley's household.
2. A housemaid.

However, she stole away my garters, that I might do myself
no harm.
So I tumbled and tossed all night, as you may very well think,
But hardly ever set my eyes together, or slept a wink.
So I was a-dreamed, methought, that I went and searched the
folks round,
25 And in a corner of Mrs. Dukes's[3] box, tied in a rag, the
money was found.
So next morning we told Whittle,[4] and he fell a-swearing:
Then my dame Wadgar[5] came, and she, you know, is thick
of hearing.
"Dame," said I, as loud as I could bawl, "do you know what
a loss I have had?"
30 "Nay," says she, "my Lord Colway's[6] folks are all very sad:
For my Lord Dromedary[7] comes a Tuesday without fail."
"Pugh!" said I, "but that's not the business that I ail."
Says Cary,[8] says he, "I have been a servant this five and twenty
years come spring,
And in all the places I lived I never heard of such a thing."
"Yes," says the steward,[9] "I remember when I was at my
Lord Shrewsbury's,
35 Such a thing as this happened, just about the time of
gooseberries."
So I went to the party suspected, and I found her full of grief:
(Now, you must know, of all things in the world I hate a thief.)
However, I was resolved to bring the discourse slily about:
"Mrs. Dukes," said I, "here's an ugly accident has happened out:
40 'Tis not that I value the money three skips of a louse;
But the thing I stand upon is the credit of the house.
'Tis true, seven pound, four shillings, and sixpence, makes a
great hole in my wages:
Besides, as they say, service is no inheritance in these ages.
Now, Mrs. Dukes, you know, and everybody understands,
45 That though 'tis hard to judge, yet money can't go without
hands."
"The devil take me!" said she (blessing herself), "if ever
I saw't!"
So she roared like a bedlam,° as though I had called her   *mad person*
all to naught.
So, you know, what could I say to her any more?
I e'en left her, and came away as wise as I was before.
50 Well; but then they would have had me gone to the
cunning man:°   *fortune-teller*
"No," said I, " 'tis the same thing, the Chaplain[1] will be
here anon."
So the Chaplain came in. Now the servants say he is my
sweetheart,
Because he's always in my chamber, and I always take his part.
So, as the devil would have it, before I was aware, out I blundered,
55 "Parson," said I, "can you cast a nativity[2] when a body's
plundered?"

3. Wife to one of the footmen.
4. The Earl of Berkeley's valet.
5. The old housekeeper.
6. A mispronunciation of "Galway," the Lord
Justice whose term coincided with Berkeley's.
7. Drogheda, a newly appointed Lord Justice.
8. Clerk of the kitchen.
9. One Ferris, whom Swift elsewhere called "a
scoundrel dog."
1. Swift himself.
2. Discover things by astrology.

(Now you must know, he hates to be called Parson, like the
    devil!)
"Truly," says he, "Mrs. Nab, it might become you to be
    more civil;
If your money be gone, as a learned Divine[3] says, d'ye see,
You are no text for my handling; so take that from me:
60 I was never taken for a conjurer before, I'd have you to know."
"Lord!" said I, "don't be angry, I am sure I never thought
    you so;
You know I honor the cloth; I design to be a parson's wife;
I never took one in your coat[4] for a conjurer in all my life."
With that he twisted his girdle at me like a rope, as who
    should say,
65 "Now you may go hang yourself for me," and so went away.
Well: I thought I should have swooned. "Lord!" said I, "what
    shall I do?
I have lost my money, and shall lose my true love too."
Then my lord called me: "Harry," said my lord, "don't cry;
I'll give you something toward thy loss." "And," says my lady,
    "so will I."
70 "Oh! but," said I, "what if, after all, the Chaplain won't
    come to?"
For that, he said (an't please your Excellencies) I must
    petition you.
The premises tenderly considered, I desire your Excellencies'
    protection,
And that I may have a share in next Sunday's collection;
And, over and above, that I may have your Excellencies' letter,
75 With an order for the Chaplain aforesaid, or, instead of him,
    a better:
And then your poor petitioner, both night and day,
Or the Chaplain (for 'tis his trade) as in duty bound, shall
    ever pray.

1701   1709

A Description of a City Shower

Careful observers may foretell the hour
(By sure prognostics) when to dread a shower:
While rain depends,° the pensive cat gives o'er   *impends*
Her frolics, and pursues her tail no more.
5 Returning home at night, you'll find the sink°   *sewer*
Strike your offended sense with double stink.
If you be wise, then go not far to dine;
You'll spend in coach hire more than save in wine.
A coming shower your shooting corns presage,
10 Old achés throb, your hollow tooth will rage.
Sauntering in coffeehouse is Dulman° seen;   *dull-man*
He damns the climate and complains of spleen.°   *melancholy*
    Meanwhile the South,° rising with dabbled wings,   *south wind*
A sable cloud athwart the welkin° flings,   *sky*
15 That swilled more liquor than it could contain,
And, like a drunkard, gives it up again.

---

3. Conjecturally, a Dr. Bolton, who had been   4. I.e., clerical garb.
advanced in the Church before Swift.

Brisk Susan whips her linen from the rope,
While the first drizzling shower is borne aslope:
Such is that sprinkling which some careless quean°   wench
20 Flirts on you from her mop, but not so clean:
You fly, invoke the gods; then turning, stop
To rail; she singing, still whirls on her mop.
Not yet the dust had shunned the unequal strife,
But, aided by the wind, fought still for life,
25 And wafted with its foe by violent gust,
'Twas doubtful which was rain and which was dust.
Ah! where must needy poet seek for aid,
When dust and rain at once his coat invade?
Sole coat, where dust cemented by the rain
30 Erects the nap, and leaves a mingled stain.
    Now in contiguous drops the flood comes down,
Threatening with deluge this devoted° town.   doomed
To shops in crowds the daggled° females fly,   spattered
Pretend to cheapen° goods, but nothing buy.   price
35 The Templar° spruce, while every spout's abroach,°   law student / running
Stays till 'tis fair, yet seems to call a coach.
The tucked-up sempstress walks with hasty strides,
While streams run down her oiled umbrella's sides.
Here various kinds, by various fortunes led,
40 Commence acquaintance underneath a shed.
Triumphant Tories and desponding Whigs[5]
Forget their feuds, and join to save their wigs.
Boxed in a chair° the beau impatient sits,   sedan chair
While spouts run clattering o'er the roof by fits,
45 And ever and anon with frightful din
The leather[6] sounds; he trembles from within.
So when Troy chairmen bore the wooden steed,
Pregnant with Greeks impatient to be freed
(Those bully Greeks, who, as the moderns do,
50 Instead of paying chairmen, run them through),
Laocoön struck the outside with his spear,
And each imprisoned hero quaked for fear.[7]
    Now from all parts the swelling kennels° flow,   gutters
And bear their trophies with them as they go:
55 Filth of all hues and odors seem to tell
What street they sailed from, by their sight and smell.
They, as each torrent drives with rapid force,
From Smithfield or St. Pulchre's shape their course,
And in huge confluence joined at Snow Hill ridge,
60 Fall from the conduit prone to Holborn Bridge.[8]
Sweepings from butchers' stalls, dung, guts, and blood,
Drowned puppies, stinking sprats,° all drenched in mud,   }herring
Dead cats, and turnip tops, come tumbling down the flood.

1710

5. The Tories (Swift's party) had recently assumed power.
6. Leather roof of the sedan chair.
7. In *Aeneid* II, Laocoön so struck the side of the Trojan horse, frightening the Greeks within.
8. The sewage system referred to is fed first by the refuse of the Smithfield cattle market and drains at last into the open Fleet Ditch at Holborn Bridge.

ISAAC WATTS
(1674–1748)

The Day of Judgment

AN ODE ATTEMPTED IN ENGLISH SAPPHIC[1]

When the fierce north wind with his airy forces
Rears up the Baltic to a foaming fury,
And the red lightning with a storm of hail comes
                Rushing amain down,

5 How the poor sailors stand amazed and tremble,
While the hoarse thunder, like a bloody trumpet,
Roars a loud onset to the gaping waters,
                Quick to devour them!

Such shall the noise be and the wild disorder,
10 (If things eternal may be like these earthly)
Such the dire terror, when the great Archangel
                Shakes the creation,

Tears the strong pillars of the vault of heaven,
Breaks up old marble, the repose of princes;
15 See the graves open, and the bones arising,
                Flames all around 'em!

Hark, the shrill outcries of the guilty wretches!
Lively bright horror and amazing anguish
Stare through their eyelids, while the living worm lies
20   Gnawing within them.

Thoughts like old vultures prey upon their heart-strings,
And the smart twinges, when the eye beholds the
Lofty Judge frowning, and a flood of vengeance
                Rolling afore him.

25 Hopeless immortals! how they scream and shiver,
While devils push them to the pit wide-yawning
Hideous and gloomy, to receive them headlong
                Down to the center.

Stop here, my fancy: (all away ye horrid
30 Doleful ideas); come, arise to Jesus;
How He sits God-like! and the saints around him
                Throned, yet adoring!

Oh may I sit there when he comes triumphant
Dooming the nations! then ascend to glory
35 While our hosannas all along the passage
                Shout the Redeemer.

                                    1706

---

1. See Glossary, entry on **Sapphic strophe**, at the end of this anthology.

A Cradle Hymn

Hush, my dear, lie still and slumber;
Holy angels guard thy bed!
Heavenly blessings without number
Gently falling on thy head.

5   Sleep, my babe; thy food and raiment,
House and home thy friends provide;
All without thy care or payment,
All thy wants are well supplied.

How much better thou'rt attended
10 Than the Son of God could be,
When from Heaven he descended,
And became a child like thee!

Soft and easy is thy cradle;
Coarse and hard thy Saviour lay,
15 When his birth-place was a stable,
And his softest bed was hay.

Blessed Babe! what glorious features,
Spotless fair, divinely bright!
Must he dwell with brutal creatures?
20 How could angels bear the sight?

Was there nothing but a manger
Cursèd sinners could afford,
To receive the heavenly Stranger?
Did they thus affront their Lord?

25 Soft, my child; I did not chide thee,
Though my song might sound too hard;
'Tis thy $\left\{ \begin{array}{l} \text{Mother}^2 \\ \text{Nurse that} \end{array} \right\}$ sits beside thee
And her arm shall be thy guard.

Yet to read the shameful story,
30 How the Jews abused their King,
How they served the Lord of Glory,
Makes me angry while I sing.

See the kinder shepherds round him,
Telling wonders from the sky;
35 There they sought him, there they found him,
With his Virgin-Mother by.

See the lovely Babe a-dressing;
Lovely Infant, how he smiled!
When he wept, the Mother's blessing
40 Soothed and hushed the holy Child.

Lo, he slumbers in his manger,
Where the hornèd oxen fed;

2. "Here you may use the words *Brother, Sister, Neighbor, Friend*, &c" [Watts's note].

Peace, my darling, here's no danger,
  Here's no ox anear thy bed.

45 'Twas to save thee, child, from dying,
  Save my dear from burning flame,
  Bitter groans, and endless crying,
  That my blest Redeemer came.

Mayst thou live to know and fear him,
50 Trust and love him all thy days!
  Then go dwell forever near him,
  See his face, and sing his praise!

I could give thee thousand kisses,
  Hoping what I most desire;
55 Not a mother's fondest wishes
  Can to greater joys aspire.

                            1720

JOHN GAY
(1685–1732)

Sweet William's Farewell to Black-eyed Susan

A BALLAD

All in the Downs[1] the fleet was moored,
  The streamers waving in the wind,
When black-eyed Susan came aboard.
  "Oh! where shall I my true love find?
5 Tell me, ye jovial sailors, tell me true,
If my sweet William sails among the crew."

William, who high upon the yard
  Rocked with the billow to and fro,
Soon as her well-known voice he heard,
10   He sighed and cast his eyes below;
The cord slides swiftly through his glowing hands,
And quick as lightning on the deck he stands.

So the sweet lark, high-poised in air,
  Shuts close his pinions to his breast,
15 (If, chance, his mate's shrill call he hear)
    And drops at once into her nest.
The noblest Captain in the British fleet
Might envy William's lip those kisses sweet.

"O Susan, Susan, lovely dear,
20   My vows shall ever true remain;
Let me kiss off that falling tear;
    We only part to meet again.
Change, as ye list, ye winds! my heart shall be
The faithful compass that still points to thee.

1. An anchorage up the English Channel from Dover.

25 "Believe not what the landmen say,
　　　Who tempt with doubts thy constant mind;
　　They'll tell thee, sailors, when away,
　　　In every port a mistress find.
　　Yes, yes, believe them when they tell thee so,
30 For thou art present wheresoe'er I go.

　　"If to far India's coast we sail,
　　　Thy eyes are seen in diamonds bright,
　　Thy breath is Afric's spicy gale,
　　　Thy skin is ivory, so white.
35 Thus every beauteous object that I view,
　　Wakes in my soul some charm of lovely Sue.

　　"Though battle call me from thy arms,
　　　Let not my pretty Susan mourn;
　　Though cannons roar, yet safe from harms.
40 　　William shall to his dear return.
　　Love turns aside the balls that round me fly,
　　Lest precious tears should drop from Susan's eye."

　　The boatswain gave the dreadful word,
　　　The sails their swelling bosom spread,
45 No longer must she stay aboard;
　　　They kissed, she sighed, he hung his head;
　　Her lessening boat unwilling rows to land;
　　"Adieu!" she cries, and waved her lily hand.

1720

ALEXANDER POPE
(1688–1744)

The Rape of the Lock

AN HEROI-COMICAL POEM[1]

Nolueram, Belinda, tuos violare capillos;
sed juvat hoc precibus me tribuisse tuis.[2]
　　　　　　　—MARTIAL

Canto I

　　What dire offense from amorous causes springs,
What mighty contests rise from trivial things,
I sing—This verse to Caryll, Muse! is due:
This, even Belinda may vouchsafe to view:
5 Slight is the subject, but not so the praise,
If she inspire, and he approve my lays.
　　Say what strange motive, Goddess! could compel
A well-bred lord to assault a gentle belle?

1. Based on an actual incident. A young man, Lord Petre, had sportively cut off a lock of a Miss Arabella Fermor's hair. She and her family were angered by the prank, and Pope's friend John Caryll (line 3), a relative of Lord Petre's, asked the poet to turn the incident into jest, so that good relations (and possibly negotiations toward a marriage between the principals) might be resumed. Pope responded by treating the incident in a mock epic or "heroi-comical poem." The epic conventions first encountered are the immediate statement of the topic, which the poet says he will "sing" as if in oral recitation, and the request to the Muse (line 7) to grant him the necessary insight.
2. "I did not want, Belinda, to violate your locks, but it pleases me to have paid this tribute to your prayers." Miss Fermor did not in fact request the poem.

Oh, say what stranger cause, yet unexplored,
10 Could make a gentle belle reject a lord?
In tasks so bold can little men engage,
And in soft bosoms dwells such mighty rage?
    Sol through white curtains shot a timorous ray,
And oped those eyes that must eclipse the day.[3]
15 Now lapdogs give themselves the rousing shake,
And sleepless lovers just at twelve awake:
Thrice rung the bell, the slipper knocked the ground,[4]
And the pressed watch returned a silver sound.[5]
Belinda still her downy pillow pressed,
20 Her guardian Sylph[6] prolonged the balmy rest:
'Twas he had summoned to her silent bed
The morning dream that hovered o'er her head.
A youth more glittering than a birthnight beau[7]
(That even in slumber caused her cheek to glow)
25 Seemed to her ear his winning lips to lay,
And thus in whispers said, or seemed to say:
"Fairest of mortals, thou distinguished care
Of thousand bright inhabitants of air!
If e'er one vision touched thy infant thought,
30 Of all the nurse and all the priest have taught,
Of airy elves by moonlight shadows seen,
The silver token, and the circled green,[8]
Or virgins visited by angel powers,
With golden crowns and wreaths of heavenly flowers,
35 Hear and believe! thy own importance know,
Nor bound thy narrow views to things below.
Some secret truths, from learned pride concealed,
To maids alone and children are revealed:
What though no credit doubting wits may give?
40 The fair and innocent shall still believe.
Know, then, unnumbered spirits round thee fly,
The light militia of the lower sky:
These, though unseen, are ever on the wing,
Hang o'er the box, and hover round the Ring.[9]
45 Think what an equipage thou hast in air,
And view with scorn two pages and a chair.°   *sedan chair*
As now your own, our beings were of old,
And once enclosed in woman's beauteous mold;
Thence, by a soft transition, we repair
50 From earthly vehicles[1] to these of air.
Think not, when woman's transient breath is fled,
That all her vanities at once are dead:
Succeeding vanities she still regards,
And though she plays no more, o'erlooks the cards.
55 Her joy in gilded chariots,° when alive,   *carriages*
And love of ombre,[2] after death survive.

3. The eyes of lovely young women—though Belinda herself is still asleep.
4. These are two ways of summoning servants.
5. In the darkened beds, one discovered the approximate time by a watch which chimed the hour and quarter-hour when the stem was pressed.
6. Air-spirit. He accounts for himself in the lines below.
7. Courtier dressed for a royal birthday celebration.

8. The silver token is the coin left by a fairy or elf, and the circled green is a ring of bright green grass, supposed dancing circle of fairies.
9. The box is a theater box; the Ring, the circular carriage course in Hyde Park.
1. Mediums of existence, with a side glance at the fondness of young women for riding in carriages.
2. A popular card game, pronounced *omber*.

For when the Fair in all their pride expire,
To their first elements their souls retire:[3]
The sprites of fiery termagants in flame
60 Mount up, and take a Salamander's name.
Soft yielding minds to water glide away,
And sip, with Nymphs, their elemental tea.[4]
The graver prude sinks downward to a Gnome,
In search of mischief still on earth to roam.
65 The light coquettes in Sylphs aloft repair,
And sport and flutter in the fields of air.
   "Know further yet; whoever fair and chaste
Rejects mankind, is by some Sylph embraced:
For spirits, freed from mortal laws, with ease
70 Assume what sexes and what shapes they please.[5]
What guards the purity of melting maids,
In courtly balls, and midnight masquerades,
Safe from the treacherous friend, the daring spark,
The glance by day, the whisper in the dark,
75 When kind occasion prompts their warm desires,
When music softens, and when dancing fires?
'Tis but their Sylph, the wise Celestials know,
Though Honor is the word with men below.
   "Some nymphs there are, too conscious of their face,
80 For life predestined to the Gnomes' embrace.
These swell their prospects and exalt their pride,
When offers are disdained, and love denied:
Then gay ideas° crowd the vacant brain,   *imaginings*
While peers, and dukes, and all their sweeping train,
85 And garters, stars, and coronets[6] appear,
And in soft sounds, 'your Grace' salutes their ear.
'Tis these that early taint the female soul,
Instruct the eyes of young coquettes to roll,
Teach infant cheeks a bidden blush to know,
90 And little hearts to flutter at a beau.
   "Oft, when the world imagine women stray,
The Sylphs through mystic mazes guide their way,
Through all the giddy circle they pursue,
And old impertinence expel by new.
95 What tender maid but must a victim fall
To one man's treat, but for another's ball?
When Florio speaks what virgin could withstand,
If gentle Damon did not squeeze her hand?
With varying vanities, from every part,
100 They shift the moving toyshop of their heart;
Where wigs with wigs, with sword-knots sword-knots strive,[7]
Beaux banish beaux, and coaches coaches drive.
This erring mortals levity may call;
Oh, blind to truth! the Sylphs contrive it all.

3. Namely, to fire, water, earth, and air, the four elements of the old cosmology and the several habitats (in the Rosicrucian myths upon which Pope embroiders) of four different kinds of "spirit." Envisaging these spirits as the transmigrated souls of different kinds of women, Pope causes termagants (scolds) to become fire-spirits or Salamanders (line 60); irresolute women to become water-spirits or Nymphs (line 62); prudes, or women who delight in rejection and negation, to become earth-spirits or Gnomes (line 64); and coquettes to become air-spirits or Sylphs. Since "nymph" could designate either a water-spirit or (in literary usage) a young lady, Pope permits his water-spirits to claim tea as their native element (line 62) and to keep their former company at tea-parties.
4. Pronounced *tay*.
5. Like Milton's angels (*Paradise Lost* I.423 ff.).
6. Insignia of rank and court status.
7. Sword-Knots are ribbons tied to hilts. The verbal repetition and the tangled syntax recall descriptions of the throng and press of battle appearing in English translations of classical epic.

05   "Of these am I, who thy protection claim,
A watchful sprite, and Ariel is my name.
Late, as I ranged the crystal wilds of air,
In the clear mirror of thy ruling star
I saw, alas! some dread event impend,
10 Ere to the main this morning sun descend,
But Heaven reveals not what, or how, or where:
Warned by the Sylph, O pious maid, beware!
This to disclose is all thy guardian can:
Beware of all, but most beware of Man!"
15   He said; when Shock,[8] who thought she slept too long,
Leaped up, and waked his mistress with his tongue.
'Twas then, Belinda, if report say true,
Thy eyes first opened on a billet-doux;[9]
Wounds, charms, and ardors were no sooner read,
120 But all the vision vanished from thy head.
   And now, unveiled, the toilet stands displayed,
Each silver vase in mystic order laid.
First, robed in white, the nymph intent adores,
With head uncovered, the cosmetic powers.
125 A heavenly image in the glass[1] appears;
To that she bends, to that her eyes she rears.
The inferior priestess, at her altar's side,
Trembling begins the sacred rites of pride.
Unnumbered treasures ope at once, and here
130 The various offerings of the world appear;
From each she nicely culls with curious toil,
And decks the goddess with the glittering spoil.
This casket India's glowing gems unlocks,
And all Arabia[2] breathes from yonder box.
135 The tortoise here and elephant unite,
Transformed to combs, the speckled and the white.
Here files of pins extend their shining rows,
Puffs, powders, patches, Bibles, billet-doux.
Now awful Beauty put on all its arms;
140 The fair each moment rises in her charms,
Repairs her smiles, awakens every grace,
And calls forth all the wonders of her face;
Sees by degrees a purer blush arise,
And keener lightnings quicken in her eyes.
145 The busy Sylphs surround their darling care,
These set the head, and those divide the hair,
Some fold the sleeve, whilst others plait the gown;
And Betty's praised for labors not her own.

Canto II

   Not with more glories, in the ethereal plain,
The sun first rises o'er the purpled main,
Than, issuing forth, the rival of his beams[3]
Launched on the bosom of the silver Thames.
5 Fair nymphs and well-dressed youths around her shone,
But every eye was fixed on her alone.

8. A name for lapdogs (like "Poll" for parrots); they looked like little "shocks" of hair.
9. A love letter. The affected language of the fashionable love letter is exhibited in the next line.
1. The mirror. Her image is the object of veneration, the "goddess" named later. Belinda presides over the appropriate rites. **Betty, her** maid, is the "inferior priestess."
2. Source of perfumes.
3. I.e., Belinda. She is en route to Hampton Court, a royal palace some twelve miles up the river Thames from London.

On her white breast a sparkling cross she wore,
Which Jews might kiss, and infidels adore.
Her lively looks a sprightly mind disclose,
Quick as her eyes, and as unfixed as those:
Favors to none, to all she smiles extends;
Oft she rejects, but never once offends.
Bright as the sun, her eyes the gazers strike,
And, like the sun, they shine on all alike.
Yet graceful ease, and sweetness void of pride,
Might hide her faults, if belles had faults to hide:
If to her share some female errors fall,
Look on her face, and you'll forget 'em all.
   This nymph, to the destruction of mankind,
Nourished two locks which graceful hung behind
In equal curls, and well conspired to deck
With shining ringlets the smooth ivory neck.
Love in these labyrinths his slaves detains,
And mighty hearts are held in slender chains.
With hairy springes° we the birds betray,   *snares*
Slight lines of hair surprise the finny prey,
Fair tresses man's imperial race ensnare,
And beauty draws us with a single hair.
   The adventurous Baron the bright locks admired,
He saw, he wished, and to the prize aspired.
Resolved to win, he meditates the way,
By force to ravish, or by fraud betray;
For when success a lover's toil attends,
Few ask if fraud or force attained his ends.
   For this, ere Phoebus rose, he had implored
Propitious Heaven, and every power adored,
But chiefly Love—to Love an altar built,
Of twelve vast French romances, neatly gilt.
There lay three garters, half a pair of gloves,
And all the trophies of his former loves.
With tender billet-doux he lights the pyre,
And breathes three amorous sighs to raise the fire.
Then prostrate falls, and begs with ardent eyes
Soon to obtain, and long possess the prize:
The powers gave ear, and granted half his prayer,
The rest the winds dispersed in empty air.
   But now secure the painted vessel glides,
The sunbeams trembling on the floating tides,
While melting music steals upon the sky,
And softened sounds along the waters die.
Smooth flow the waves, the zephyrs gently play,
Belinda smiled, and all the world was gay.
All but the Sylph—with careful thoughts oppressed,
The impending woe sat heavy on his breast.
He summons straight his denizens° of air;   *inhabitants*
The lucid squadrons round the sails repair:°   *assemble*
Soft o'er the shrouds aërial whispers breathe
That seemed but zephyrs to the train beneath.
Some to the sun their insect-wings unfold,
Waft on the breeze, or sink in clouds of gold.
Transparent forms too fine for mortal sight,

Their fluid bodies half dissolved in light,
Loose to the wind their airy garments flew,
Thin glittering textures of the filmy dew,[4]
65 Dipped in the richest tincture of the skies,
Where light disports in ever-mingling dyes,
While every beam new transient colors flings,
Colors that change whene'er they wave their wings.
Amid the circle, on the gilded mast,
70 Superior by the head was Ariel placed;   *brilliant*
His purple° pinions opening to the sun,
He raised his azure wand, and thus begun:
    "Ye Sylphs and Sylphids, to your chief give ear!
Fays, Fairies, Genii, Elves, and Daemons, hear!
75 Ye know the spheres and various tasks assigned
By laws eternal to the aërial kind.
Some in the fields of purest ether play,
And bask and whiten in the blaze of day.
Some guide the course of wandering orbs on high,
80 Or roll the planets through the boundless sky.
Some less refined, beneath the moon's pale light
Pursue the stars that shoot athwart the night,
Or suck the mists in grosser air below,
Or dip their pinions in the painted bow,°   *rainbow*
85 Or brew fierce tempests on the wintry main,
Or o'er the glebe° distill the kindly rain.   *farmland*
Others on earth o'er human race preside,
Watch all their ways, and all their actions guide:
Of these the chief the care of nations own,
90 And guard with arms divine the British Throne.
    "Our humbler province is to tend the Fair,
Not a less pleasing, though less glorious care:
To save the powder from too rude a gale,
Nor let the imprisoned essences exhale;
95 To draw fresh colors from the vernal flowers;
To steal from rainbows e'er they drop in showers
A brighter wash;° to curl their waving hairs,   *(cosmetic) wash*
Assist their blushes, and inspire their airs;
Nay oft, in dreams invention we bestow,
100 To change a flounce, or add a furbelow.
    "This day black omens threat the brightest fair,
That e'er deserved a watchful spirit's care;
Some dire disaster, or by force or slight,
But what, or where, the Fates have wrapped in night:
105 Whether the nymph shall break Diana's law,[5]
Or some frail china jar receive a flaw,
Or stain her honor or her new brocade,
Forget her prayers, or miss a masquerade,
Or lose her heart, or necklace, at a ball;
110 Or whether Heaven has doomed that Shock must fall.
Haste, then, ye spirits! to your charge repair:
The fluttering fan be Zephyretta's care;
The drops° to thee, Brillante, we consign;   *earrings*
And, Momentilla, let the watch be thine;,

4. The supposed material of spider webs.   5. Of chastity.

115 Do thou, Crispissa,[6] tend her favorite Lock;
      Ariel himself shall be the guard of Shock.
        "To fifty chosen Sylphs, of special note,
      We trust the important charge, the petticoat;
      Oft have we known that sevenfold fence to fail,
120 Though stiff with hoops, and armed with ribs of whale.
      Form a strong line about the silver bound,
      And guard the wide circumference around.
        "Whatever spirit, careless of his charge,
      His post neglects, or leaves the fair at large,
125 Shall feel sharp vengeance soon o'ertake his sins,
      Be stopped in vials, or transfixed with pins,
      Or plunged in lakes of bitter washes lie,
      Or wedged whole ages in a bodkin's° eye;   large needle's
      Gums and pomatums shall his flight restrain,
130 While clogged he beats his silken wings in vain,
      Or alum styptics with contracting power
      Shrink his thin essence like a riveled° flower: shriveled
      Or, as Ixion[7] fixed, the wretch shall feel
      The giddy motion of the whirling mill,°   cocoa-mill
135 In fumes of burning chocolate shall glow,
      And tremble at the sea that froths below!"
        He spoke; the spirits from the sails descend;
      Some, orb in orb, around the nymph extend;
      Some thread the mazy ringlets of her hair;
140 Some hang upon the pendants of her ear:
      With beating hearts the dire event they wait,
      Anxious, and trembling for the birth of Fate.

            Canto III

        Close by those meads, forever crowned with flowers,
      Where Thames with pride surveys his rising towers,
      There stands a structure of majestic frame,[8]
      Which from the neighboring Hampton takes its name.
5   Here Britain's statesmen oft the fall foredoom
      Of foreign tyrants and of nymphs at home;
      Here thou, great Anna! whom three realms obey,
      Dost sometimes counsel take—and sometimes tea.
        Hither the heroes and the nymphs resort,
10   To taste awhile the pleasures of a court;
      In various talk the instructive hours they passed,
      Who gave the ball, or paid the visit last;
      One speaks the glory of the British Queen,
      And one describes a charming Indian screen;
15   A third interprets motions, looks, and eyes;
      At every word a reputation dies.
      Snuff, or the fan, supply each pause of chat,
      With singing, laughing, ogling, and all that.
        Meanwhile, declining from the noon of day,
20   The sun obliquely shoots his burning ray;
      The hungry judges soon the sentence sign,
      And wretches hang that jurymen may dine;
      The merchant from the Exchange° returns in peace,   stock market
      And the long labors of the toilet cease.
25   Belinda now, whom thirst of fame invites,

---

6. To "crisp" is to curl (hair).   eternally to a turning wheel.
7. For an affront to Juno, Ixion was bound   8. Hampton Court.

Burns to encounter two adventurous knights,
At ombre[9] singly to decide their doom,
And swells her breast with conquests yet to come.
Straight the three bands prepare in arms° to join,   *combat*
30 Each band the number of the sacred nine.
Soon as she spreads her hand, the aërial guard
Descend, and sit on each important card:
First Ariel perched upon a Matadore,
Then each according to the rank they bore;
35 For Sylphs, yet mindful of their ancient race,
Are, as when women, wondrous fond of place.
    Behold, four Kings in majesty revered,
With hoary whiskers and a forky beard;
And four fair Queens whose hands sustain a flower,
40 The expressive emblem of their softer power;
Four Knaves in garbs succinct,[1] a trusty band,
Caps on their heads, and halberts in their hand;
And parti-colored troops, a shining train,
Draw forth to combat on the velvet plain.
45   The skillful nymph reviews her force with care;
"Let Spades be trumps!" she said, and trumps they were.
    Now move to war her sable Matadores,
In show like leaders of the swarthy Moors.
Spadillio first, unconquerable lord!
50 Led off two captive trumps, and swept the board.
As many more Manillio forced to yield,
And marched a victor from the verdant field.
Him Basto followed, but his fate more hard
Gained but one trump and one plebeian card.
55 With his broad saber next, a chief in years,
The hoary Majesty of Spades appears,
Puts forth one manly leg, to sight revealed,
The rest his many-colored robe concealed.
The rebel Knave, who dares his prince engage,
60 Proves the just victim of his royal rage.
Even mighty Pam,[2] that kings and queens o'erthrew
And mowed down armies in the fights of loo,
Sad chance of war! now distitute of aid,
Falls undistinguished by the victor Spade.
65   Thus far both armies to Belinda yield;
Now to the Baron fate inclines the field.
His warlike amazon her host invades,
The imperial consort of the crown of Spades.
The Club's black tyrant first her victim died,
70 Spite of his haughty mien and barbarous pride.

9. This game is like three-handed bridge with some features of poker added. From a deck lacking 8's, 9's and 10's, nine cards are dealt to each player (linc 30) and the rest put in a central pool. A declarer called the *Ombre* (Spanish *hombre*, man) commits himself to taking more tricks than either of his opponents individually; hence Belinda would "encounter two knights *singly*." Declarer, followed by the other players, then selects discards and replenishes his hand with cards drawn sight unseen from the pool (line 45). He proceeds to name his trumps (line 46). The three principal trumps, called *Matadors* (line 47), always include the black aces. When spades are declared, the Matadors are, in order of value, the ace of spades (called *Spadille,* line 49), the deuce of spades (called *Manille,* line 51), and the ace of clubs (called *Basto,* line 53). The remaining spades fill out the trump suit. In the game here described, Belinda leads out her high trumps (lines 49–56), but the suit breaks badly (line 54); the Baron retains the queen (line 67), with which he presently trumps her king of clubs (line 69). He then leads high diamonds until she is on the verge of a set (called *Codille,* line 92). But she makes her bid at the last trick (line 94), taking his ace of hearts with her king (line 95), this being, in ombre, the highest card in the heart suit. The game is played on a green velvet cloth (line 44).
1. Hemmed up short, not flowing.
2. The jack of clubs, paramount trump in the game of loo.

What boots the regal circle on his head,
His giant limbs, in state unwieldy spread?
That long behind he trails his pompous robe,
And of all monarchs only grasps the globe?
75   The Baron now his Diamonds pours apace;
The embroidered King who shows but half his face,
And his refulgent Queen, with powers combined
Of broken troops an easy conquest find.
Clubs, Diamonds, Hearts, in wild disorder seen,
80   With throngs promiscuous strew the level green.
Thus when dispersed a routed army runs,
Of Asia's troops, and Afric's sable sons,
With like confusion different nations fly,
Of various habit,° and of various dye,°   dress / color
85   The pierced battalions disunited fall
In heaps on heaps; one fate o'erwhelms them all.
    The Knave of Diamonds tries his wily arts,
And wins (oh, shameful chance!) the Queen of Hearts.
At this, the blood the virgin's cheek forsook,
90   A livid paleness spreads o'er all her look;
She sees, and trembles at the approaching ill,
Just in the jaws of ruin, and Codille,
And now (as oft in some distempered state)
On one nice trick depends the general fate.
95   An Ace of Hearts steps forth: the King unseen
Lurked in her hand, and mourned his captive Queen.
He springs to vengeance with an eager pace,
And falls like thunder on the prostrate Ace.
The nymph exulting fills with shouts the sky,
100   The walls, the woods, and long canals[3] reply.
    O thoughtless mortals! ever blind to fate,
Too soon dejected, and too soon elate:
Sudden these honors shall be snatched away,
And cursed forever this victorious day.
105   For lo! the board with cups and spoons is crowned,
The berries crackle, and the mill turns round;[4]
On shining altars of Japan[5] they raise
The silver lamp; the fiery spirits blaze:
From silver spouts the grateful liquors glide,
110   While China's earth[6] receives the smoking tide.
At once they gratify their scent and taste,
And frequent cups prolong the rich repast.
Straight hover round the fair her airy band;
Some, as she sipped, the fuming liquor fanned,
115   Some o'er her lap their careful plumes displayed,
Trembling, and conscious of the rich brocade.
Coffee (which makes the politician wise,
And see through all things with his half-shut eyes)
Sent up in vapors to the Baron's brain
120   New stratagems, the radiant Lock to gain.
Ah, cease, rash youth! desist ere 'tis too late,
Fear the just Gods, and think of Scylla's fate![7]
Changed to a bird, and sent to flit in air,
She dearly pays for Nisus' injured hair!

3. Passages between avenues of trees.
4. As coffee beans are roasted and ground.
5. Lacquered tables.
6. Ceramic cups.
7. Scylla cut from the head of her father

Nisus the lock of hair on which his life depended and gave it to her lover Minos of Crete, who was Scylla's enemy. For this she was turned into a sea-bird relentlessly pursued by an eagle.

125 But when to mischief mortals bend their will,
How soon they find fit instruments of ill!
Just then, Clarissa drew with tempting grace
A two-edged weapon from her shining case:
So ladies in romance assist their knight,
130 Present the spear, and arm him for the fight.
He takes the gift with reverence, and extends
The little engine on his fingers' ends;
This just behind Belinda's neck he spread,
As o'er the fragrant steams she bends her head.
135 Swift to the Lock a thousand sprites repair,
A thousand wings, by turns, blow back the hair,
And thrice they twitched the diamond in her ear,
Thrice she looked back, and thrice the foe drew near.
Just in that instant, anxious Ariel sought
140 The close recesses of the virgin's thought;
As on the nosegay in her breast reclined,
He watched the ideas rising in her mind,
Sudden he viewed, in spite of all her art,
An earthly lover lurking at her heart.
145 Amazed, confused, he found his power expired,[8]
Resigned to fate, and with a sigh retired.
  The Peer now spreads the glittering forfex° wide,   *scissors*
To enclose the Lock; now joins it, to divide.
Even then, before the fatal engine closed,
150 A wretched Sylph too fondly interposed;
Fate urged the shears, and cut the Sylph in twain
(But airy substance soon unites again):[9]
The meeting points the sacred hair dissever
From the fair head, forever, and forever!
155   Then flashed the living lightning from her eyes,
And screams of horror rend the affrighted skies.
Not louder shrieks to pitying heaven are cast,
When husbands, or when lapdogs breathe their last;
Or when rich china vessels fallen from high,
160 In glittering dust and painted fragments lie!
"Let wreaths of triumph now my temples twine,"
The victor cried, "the glorious prize is mine!
While fish in streams, or birds delight in air,
Or in a coach and six the British Fair,
165 As long as *Atalantis*[1] shall be read,
Or the small pillow grace a lady's bed,
While visits shall be paid on solemn days,
When numerous wax-lights in bright order blaze,[2]
While nymphs take treats, or assignations give,
170 So long my honor, name, and praise shall live!
What Time would spare, from Steel receives its date,°   *termination*
And monuments, like men, submit to fate!
Steel could the labor of the Gods destroy,[3]
And strike to dust the imperial towers of Troy;
175 Steel could the works of mortal pride confound,
And hew triumphal arches to the ground.
What wonder then, fair nymph! thy hairs should feel,
The conquering force of unresisted Steel?"

8. Belinda, being strongly attracted to the
Baron (line 144), can no longer merely co-
quette. She hence passes beyond Ariel's
control.
9. Again as with Milton's angels (*Paradise
Lost* VI.329-31).

1. A set of memoirs which, under thin dis-
guise, recounted actual scandals.
2. Attending the formal evening visits of the
previous line.
3. Troy (named in the next line) was built by
Apollo and Poseidon.

Canto IV

But anxious cares the pensive nymph oppressed,
And secret passions labored in her breast.
Not youthful kings in battle seized alive,
Not scornful virgins who their charms survive,
5   Not ardent lovers robbed of all their bliss,
Not ancient ladies when refused a kiss,
Not tyrants fierce that unrepenting die,
Not Cynthia when her manteau's⁴ pinned awry,
E'er felt such rage, resentment, and despair,
10   As thou, sad virgin! for thy ravished hair.
 For, that sad moment, when the Sylphs withdrew
And Ariel weeping from Belinda flew,
Umbriel,⁵ a dusky, melancholy sprite
As ever sullied the fair face of light,
15   Down to the central earth, his proper scene,
Repaired to search the gloomy Cave of Spleen.⁶
Swift on his sooty pinions flits the Gnome,
And in a vapor reached the dismal dome.
No cheerful breeze this sullen region knows,
20   The dreaded east is all the wind that blows.
Here in a grotto, sheltered close from air,
And screened in shades from day's detested glare,
She sighs forever on her pensive bed,
Pain at her side, and Megrim° at her head.   *migraine*
25   Two handmaids wait the throne: alike in place,
But differing far in figure and in face.
Here stood Ill-Nature like an ancient maid,
Her wrinkled form in black and white arrayed;
With store of prayers for mornings, nights, and noons,
30   Her hand is filled; her bosom with lampoons.°   *slanders*
 There Affectation, with a sickly mien,
Shows in her cheek the roses of eighteen,
Practiced to lisp, and hang the head aside,
Faints into airs, and languishes with pride,
35   On the rich quilt sinks with becoming woe,
Wrapped in a gown, for sickness and for show.
The fair ones feel such maladies as these,
When each new nightdress gives a new disease.
 A constant vapor o'er the palace flies,
40   Strange phantoms rising as the mists arise;
Dreadful as hermit's dreams in haunted shades,
Or bright as visions of expiring maids.
Now glaring fiends, and snakes on rolling spires,°   *coils*
Pale specters, gaping tombs, and purple fires;
45   Now lakes of liquid gold, Elysian scenes,
And crystal domes, and angels in machines.⁷
 Unnumbered throngs on every side are seen
Of bodies changed to various forms by Spleen.

4. I.e., robe is.
5. Suggesting *umbra*, shadow; and *umber*, brown. The final *el* of this name is a further reminiscence of Milton's angels: Gabriel, Abdiel, Zophiel.
6. This journey is formally equivalent to Odysseus' and Aeneas' visits to the underworld. "Spleen" refers to the human organ, the supposed seat of melancholy; hence to melancholy itself. Believed to be induced by misty weather such as the east wind brings (lines 18–20), the condition was also called the "vapors." In its severer manifestations it tends toward madness; in its milder forms, it issues in peevishness and suspicion.
7. These images are both 1) the hallucinations of insane melancholy and 2) parodies of stage properties and effects.

Here living teapots stand, one arm held out,
50 One bent; the handle this, and that the spout:
A pipkin[8] there, like Homer's tripod, walks;
Here sighs a jar, and there a goose pie talks;
Men prove with child, as powerful fancy works,
And maids, turned bottles, call aloud for corks.
55   Safe passed the Gnome through this fantastic band,
A branch of healing spleenwort[9] in his hand.
Then thus addressed the Power: "Hail, wayward Queen!
Who rule the sex to fifty from fifteen:
Parent of vapors and of female wit,
60 Who give the hysteric or poetic fit,
On various tempers act by various ways,
Make some take physic, others scribble plays;
Who cause the proud their visits to delay,
And send the godly in a pet to pray.
65 A nymph there is that all thy power disdains,
And thousands more in equal mirth maintains.
But oh! if e'er thy Gnome could spoil a grace,
Or raise a pimple on a beauteous face,
Like citron-waters° matrons' cheeks inflame,   *orange brandy*
70 Or change complexions at a losing game;
If e'er with airy horns I planted heads,[1]
Or rumpled petticoats, or tumbled beds,
Or caused suspicion when no soul was rude,
Or discomposed the headdress of a prude,
75 Or e'er to costive lapdog gave disease,
Which not the tears of brightest eyes could ease,
Hear me, and touch Belinda with chagrin:°   *annoyance*
That single act gives half the world the spleen."
    The Goddess with a discontented air
80 Seems to reject him though she grants his prayer.
A wondrous bag with both her hands she binds,
Like that where once Ulysses held the winds;[2]
There she collects the force of female lungs,
Sighs, sobs, and passions, and the war of tongues.
85 A vial next she fills with fainting fears,
Soft sorrows, melting griefs, and flowing tears.
The Gnome rejoicing bears her gifts away,
Spreads his black wings, and slowly mounts to day.
    Sunk in Thalestris'[3] arms the nymph he found,
90 Her eyes dejected and her hair unbound.
Full o'er their heads the swelling bag he rent,
And all the Furies issued at the vent.
Belinda burns with more than mortal ire,
And fierce Thalestris fans the rising fire.
95 "O wretched maid!" she spreads her hands, and cried
(While Hampton's echoes, "Wretched maid!" replied),
"Was it for this you took such constant care
The bodkin,° comb, and essence to prepare?   *hairpin*
For this your locks in paper durance bound,
100 For this with torturing irons wreathed around?
For this with fillets° strained your tender head,   *bands*

8. An earthen pot; it walks like the three-legged stools which Vulcan made for the gods in *Iliad* XVIII.
9. A kind of fern, purgative of spleen; suggesting the golden bough which Aeneas bore as a passport to Hades in *Aeneid* VI.

1. I.e., made men imagine they were being cuckolded.
2. Aeolus, the wind god, enabled Odysseus so to contain all adverse winds in *Odyssey* X.
3. The name of an Amazon.

And bravely bore the double loads of lead?[4]
Gods! shall the ravisher display your hair,
While the fops envy, and the ladies stare!
105   Honor forbid! at whose unrivaled shrine
Ease, pleasure, virtue, all, our sex resign.
Methinks already I your tears survey,
Already hear the horrid things they say,
Already see you a degraded toast,
110   And all your honor in a whisper lost!
How shall I, then, your helpless fame defend?
'Twill then be infamy to seem your friend!
And shall this prize, the inestimable prize,
Exposed through crystal to the gazing eyes,
115   And heightened by the diamond's circling rays,
On that rapacious hand forever blaze?
Sooner shall grass in Hyde Park Circus[5] grow,
And wits take lodgings in the sound of Bow;[6]
Sooner let earth, air, sea, to chaos fall,
120   Men, monkeys, lapdogs, parrots, perish all!"
    She said; then raging to Sir Plume repairs,
And bids her beau demand the precious hairs
(Sir Plume of amber snuffbox justly vain,
And the nice° conduct° of a clouded cane).   *precise / handling*
125   With earnest eyes, and round unthinking face,
He first the snuffbox opened, then the case,
And thus broke out—"My Lord, why, what the devil!
Zounds! damn the lock! 'fore Gad, you must be civil!
Plague on't! 'tis past a jest—nay prithee, pox!
130   Give her the hair"—he spoke, and rapped his box.
    "It grieves me much," replied the Peer again,
"Who speaks so well should ever speak in vain.
But by this Lock, this sacred Lock I swear
(Which never more shall join its parted hair;
135   Which never more its honors shall renew,
Clipped from the lovely head where late it grew),
That while my nostrils draw the vital air,
This hand, which won it, shall forever wear."
He spoke, and speaking, in proud triumph spread
140   The long-contended honors° of her head.   *ornaments*
    But Umbriel, hateful Gnome, forbears not so;
He breaks the vial whence the sorrows flow.
Then see! the nymph in beauteous grief appears,
Her eyes half languishing, half drowned in tears;
145   On her heaved bosom hung her drooping head,
Which with a sigh she raised, and thus she said:
    "Forever cursed be this detested day,
Which snatched my best, my favorite curl away!
Happy! ah, ten times happy had I been,
150   If Hampton Court these eyes had never seen!
Yet am not I the first mistaken maid,
By love of courts to numerous ills betrayed.
Oh, had I rather unadmired remained
In some lone isle, or distant northern land;

<hr />

4. The means by which Belinda's locks were
fashioned into a ringlet: lead strips held her
curl papers in place.
5. The fashionable carriage course (the
"Ring" of I.44).

6. I.e., the sound of the bells of Bowchurch
in the unfashionable commercial section of
London.

155 Where the gilt chariot never marks the way,
Where none learn ombre, none e'er taste bohea!°   *fine tea*
There kept my charms concealed from mortal eye,
Like roses that in deserts bloom and die.
What moved my mind with youthful lords to roam?
160 Oh, had I stayed, and said my prayers at home!
'Twas this the morning omens seemed to tell,
Thrice from my trembling hand the patch box[7] fell;
The tottering china shook without a wind,
Nay, Poll sat mute, and Shock was most unkind!
165 A Sylph too warned me of the threats of fate,
In mystic visions, now believed too late!
See the poor remnants of these slighted hairs!
My hands shall rend what e'en thy rapine spares.
These in two sable ringlets taught to break,
170 Once gave new beauties to the snowy neck;
The sister lock now sits uncouth, alone,
And in its fellow's fate foresees its own;
Uncurled it hangs, the fatal shears demands,
And tempts once more thy sacrilegious hands.
175 Oh, hadst thou, cruel! been content to seize
Hairs less in sight, or any hairs but these!"

Canto V

She said: the pitying audience melt in tears.
But Fate and Jove had stopped the Baron's ears.
In vain Thalestris with reproach assails,
For who can move when fair Belinda fails?
5 Not half so fixed the Trojan could remain,
While Anna begged and Dido raged in vain.[8]
Then grave Clarissa graceful waved her fan;
Silence ensued, and thus the nymph began:
"Say why are beauties praised and honored most,
10 The wise man's passion, and the vain man's toast?
Why decked with all that land and sea afford,
Why angels called, and angel-like adored?
Why round our coaches crowd the white-gloved beaux,
Why bows the side box from its inmost rows?
15 How vain are all these glories, all our pains,
Unless good sense preserve what beauty gains;
That men may say when we the front box grace,
'Behold the first in virtue as in face!'
Oh! if to dance all night, and dress all day,
20 Charmed the smallpox, or chased old age away,
Who would not scorn what housewife's cares produce,
Or who would learn one earthly thing of use?
To patch, nay ogle, might become a saint,
Nor could it sure be such a sin to paint.
25 But since, alas! frail beauty must decay,
Curled or uncurled, since locks will turn to gray;
Since painted, or not painted, all shall fade,
And she who scorns a man must die a maid;
What then remains but well our power to use,
30 And keep good humor still whate'er we lose?

---

7. A box for ornamental patches to accent the face.
8. Aeneas was determined to leave Carthage for Italy, though the enamored queen Dido raved and her sister Anna pleaded with him to stay.

And trust me, dear, good humor can prevail
When airs, and flights, and screams, and scolding fail.
Beauties in vain their pretty eyes may roll;
Charms strike the sight, but merit wins the soul."9
35   So spoke the dame, but no applause ensued;
Belinda frowned, Thalestris called her prude.
"To arms, to arms!" the fierce virago cries,
And swift as lightning to the combat flies.
All side in parties, and begin the attack;
40   Fans clap, silks rustle, and tough whalebones crack;
Heroes' and heroines' shouts confusedly rise,
And bass and treble voices strike the skies.
No common weapons in their hands are found,
Like Gods they fight, nor dread a mortal wound.
45   So when bold Homer makes the Gods engage,
And heavenly breasts with human passions rage;
'Gainst Pallas, Mars; Latona, Hermes arms;1
And all Olympus rings with loud alarms:
Jove's thunder roars, heaven trembles all around,
50   Blue Neptune storms, the bellowing deeps resound:
Earth shakes her nodding towers, the ground gives way,
And the pale ghosts start at the flash of day!
    Triumphant Umbriel on a sconce's height
Clapped his glad wings, and sat to view the fight:
55   Propped on the bodkin spears, the sprites survey
The growing combat, or assist the fray.
    While through the press enraged Thalestris flies,
And scatters death around from both her eyes,
A beau and witling perished in the throng,
60   One died in metaphor, and one in song.
"O cruel nymph! a living death I bear,"
Cried Dapperwit, and sunk beside his chair.
A mournful glance Sir Fopling upwards cast,
"Those eyes are made so killing"—was his last.
65   Thus on Maeander's flowery margin lies
The expiring swan, and as he sings he dies.
    When bold Sir Plume had drawn Clarissa down,
Chloe stepped in, and killed him with a frown;
She smiled to see the doughty hero slain,
70   But, at her smile, the beau revived again.
    Now Jove suspends his golden scales in air,2
Weighs the men's wits against the lady's hair;
The doubtful beam long nods from side to side;
At length the wits mount up, the hairs subside.
75   See, fierce Belinda on the Baron flies,
With more than usual lightning in her eyes;
Nor feared the chief the unequal fight to try,
Who sought no more than on his foe to die.
    But this bold lord with manly strength endued,
80   She with one finger and a thumb subdued:
Just where the breath of life his nostrils drew,
A charge of snuff the wily virgin threw;

9. Clarissa's address parallels a speech in *Iliad* XII, wherein Sarpedon tells Glaucus that, as leaders of the army, they must justify their privilege by extraordinary prowess.
1. Mars arms against Pallas, and Hermes against Latona in *Iliad* XX. The tangled syntax is supposed to mirror the press of battle.
2. He so weighs the fortunes of war in classical epic.

The Gnomes direct, to every atom just,
The pungent grains of titillating dust.
85 Sudden, with starting tears each eye o'erflows,
And the high dome re-echoes to his nose.
    "Now meet thy fate," incensed Belinda cried,
And drew a deadly bodkin³ from her side.
(The same, his ancient personage to deck,
90 Her great-great-grandsire wore about his neck,
In three seal rings; which after, melted down,
Formed a vast buckle for his widow's gown:
Her infant grandame's whistle next it grew,
The bells she jingled, and the whistle blew;
95 Then in a bodkin graced her mother's hairs,
Which long she wore, and now Belinda wears.)
    "Boast not my fall," he cried, "insulting foe!
Thou by some other shalt be laid as low.
Nor think to die dejects my lofty mind:
100 All that I dread is leaving you behind!
Rather than so, ah, let me still survive,
And burn in Cupid's flames—but burn alive."
    "Restore the Lock!" she cries; and all around
"Restore the Lock!" the vaulted roofs rebound.
105 Not fierce Othello in so loud a strain
Roared for the handkerchief that caused his pain.⁴
But see how oft ambitious aims are crossed,
And chiefs contend till all the prize is lost!
The lock, obtained with guilt, and kept with pain,
110 In every place is sought, but sought in vain:
With such a prize no mortal must be blessed,
So Heaven decrees! with Heaven who can contest?
    Some thought it mounted to the lunar sphere,
Since all things lost on earth are treasured there.
115 There heroes' wits are kept in ponderous vases,
And beaux' in snuffboxes and tweezer cases.
There broken vows and deathbed alms are found,
And lovers' hearts with ends of riband bound,
The courtier's promises, and sick man's prayers,
120 The smiles of harlots, and the tears of heirs,
Cages for gnats, and chains to yoke a flea,
Dried butterflies, and tomes of casuistry.
    But trust the Muse—she saw it upward rise,
Though marked by none but quick, poetic eyes
125 (So Rome's great founder to the heavens withdrew,⁵
To Proculus alone confessed in view);
A sudden star, it shot through liquid° air,   *clear*
And drew behind a radiant trail of hair.
Not Berenice's locks first rose so bright,⁶
130 The heavens bespangling with disheveled light.
The Sylphs behold it kindling as it flies,
And pleased pursue its progress through the skies.
    This the beau monde shall from the Mall⁷ survey,
And hail with music its propitious ray.

3. Here an ornamental hairpin. Its history suggests that of Agamemnon's scepter in *Iliad* II. "Seal rings" (line 91) are for impressing seals on letters and legal documents.
4. In *Othello* III.iv.
5. Romulus was borne heavenward in a stormcloud and later deified.
6. The locks which the Egyptian queen Berenice dedicated to her husband's safe return were turned into a constellation.
7. A fashionable walk which (like Rosamonda's Lake [line 136]) was in St. James's Park.

135   This the blest lover shall for Venus take,
     And send up vows from Rosamonda's Lake.
     This Partridge⁸ soon shall view in cloudless skies,
     When next he looks through Galileo's eyes;
     And hence the egregious wizard shall foredoom
140   The fate of Louis, and the fall of Rome.
        Then cease, bright nymph! to mourn thy ravished hair,
     Which adds new glory to the shining sphere!
     Not all the tresses that fair head can boast,
     Shall draw such envy as the Lock you lost.
145   For, after all the murders of your eye,
     When, after millions slain, yourself shall die:
     When those fair suns shall set, as set they must,
     And all those tresses shall be laid in dust,
     This Lock the Muse shall consecrate to fame,
150   And 'midst the stars inscribe Belinda's name.

                         1712   1714

Epistle to Dr. Arbuthnot¹

   P. Shut, shut the door, good John!² (fatigued, I said),
   Tie up the knocker, say I'm sick, I'm dead.
   The Dog Star³ rages! nay 'tis past a doubt
   All Bedlam, or Parnassus,⁴ is let out:
5 Fire in each eye, and papers in each hand,
   They rave, recite, and madden round the land.
     What walls can guard me, or what shades can hide?
   They pierce my thickets, through my grot⁵ they glide,
   By land, by water, they renew the charge,
10 They stop the chariot, and they board the barge.⁶
   No place is sacred, not the church is free;
   Even Sunday shines no Sabbath day to me:
   Then from the Mint⁷ walks forth the man of rhyme,
   Happy to catch me just at dinner time.
15   Is there a parson, much bemused in beer,
   A maudlin poetess, a rhyming peer,
   A clerk foredoomed his father's soul to cross,
   Who pens a stanza when he should engross?⁸
   Is there who,⁹ locked from ink and paper, scrawls
20 With desperate charcoal round his darkened walls?
   All fly to Twit'nam,° and in humble strain   *Twickenham*
   Apply to me to keep them mad or vain.
   Arthur,¹ whose giddy son neglects the laws,
   Imputes to me and my damned works the cause:
25 Poor Cornus² sees his frantic wife elope,
   And curses wit, and poetry, and Pope.

---

8. A London astrologer who predicted calamities on the enemies of England and Protestantism. "Galileo's eyes": the telescope.
1. John Arbuthnot, former physician to Queen Anne, was Pope's physician, and friend and literary collaborator of Pope, Swift, and Gay. He had asked Pope to moderate his attacks on his personal and literary enemies and was hence a logical person to whom to address an apology for writing satire.
2. Pope's servant, John Serle.
3. The summer star Sirius, attendant upon crazing heat. In ancient Rome, late summer was a season for public recitations of poetry.
4. Bedlam is a hospital for the insane; Mt.

Parnassus, the haunt of the Muses.
5. Pope's "grotto," one entrance to the grounds of his villa at Twickenham.
6. Pope often traveled from Twickenham to London by water.
7. A sanctuary for debtors. They emerged on Sunday, being everywhere immune from arrest on that day.
8. Prepare legal documents.
9. I.e., one who.
1. Arthur Moore, father of James Moore Smythe, a playwright who had plagiarized some lines from Pope.
2. From Latin *cornu*, horn; hence a cuckold.

Friend to my life (which did not you prolong,
The world had wanted many an idle song)
What drop or nostrum° can this plague remove?   *drug*
30 Or which must end me, a fool's wrath or love?
A dire dilemma! either way I'm sped,°   *ruined*
If foes, they write, if friends, they read me dead.
Seized and tied down to judge, how wretched I!
Who can't be silent, and who will not lie.
35 To laugh were want of goodness and of grace,
And to be grave exceeds all power of face.
I sit with sad° civility, I read   *sober*
With honest anguish and an aching head,
And drop at last, but in unwilling ears,
40 This saving counsel, "Keep your piece nine years."[3]
    "Nine years!" cries he, who high in Drury Lane,[4]
Lulled by soft zephyrs through the broken pane,
Rhymes ere he wakes, and prints before term° ends,   *the publishing season*
Obliged by hunger and request of friends:
45 "The piece, you think, is incorrect? why, take it,
I'm all submission, what you'd have it, make it."
    Three things another's modest wishes bound,
My friendship, and a prologue, and ten pound.
    Pitholeon[5] sends to me: "You know his Grace,
50 I want a patron; ask him for a place."
Pitholeon libeled me—"but here's a letter
Informs you, sir, 'twas when he knew no better.
Dare you refuse him? Curll[6] invites to dine,
He'll write a *Journal,* or he'll turn divine."[7]
55 Bless me! a packet.—" 'Tis a stranger sues,
A virgin tragedy, an orphan Muse."
If I dislike it, "Furies, death, and rage!"
If I approve, "Commend it to the stage."
There (thank my stars) my whole commission ends,
60 The players and I are, luckily, no friends.
Fired that the house° reject him, " 'Sdeath, I'll print it,   *playhouse*
And shame the fools—Your interest, sir, with Lintot!"[8]
Lintot, dull rogue, will think your price too much.
"Not, sir, if you revise it, and retouch."
65 All my demurs but double his attacks;
At last he whispers, "Do; and we go snacks."°   *shares*
Glad of a quarrel, straight I clap the door,
"Sir, let me see your works and you no more."
    'Tis sung, when Midas' ears began to spring
70 (Midas, a sacred person and a king),
His very minister who spied them first
(Some say his queen) was forced to speak, or burst.[9]
And is not mine, my friend, a sorer case,
When every coxcomb perks them in my face?

---

3. Horace's advice (*Ars Poetica,* 386–89).
4. The theater district, where the speaker occupies a garret.
5. "A foolish poet of Rhodes, who pretended much to Greek" [Pope's note]. He stands for Leonard Welsted, translator of Longinus and an enemy of Pope's.
6. Edmund Curll, an unscrupulous publisher; the bookseller principally derided in the *Dunciad* (above).
7. Referring to attacks on Pope in *The London Journal* and (perhaps) to Welsted's theological writing.
8. Bernard Lintot, an early publisher of Pope's.
9. King Midas, preferring Pan's music to Apollo's, was given ass's ears by the affronted god. His barber (in Chaucer's version of the tale, his wife) discovered the ears and, fairly bursting with the secret, whispered it into a hole in the ground. It is suggested that the prime minister (Walpole) and Queen Caroline know that George II is an ass.

75   A. Good friend, forbear! you deal in dangerous things.
        I'd never name queens, ministers, or kings;
        Keep close to ears, and those let asses prick;
        'Tis nothing——— P. Nothing? if they bite and kick?
        Out with it, *Dunciad!* let the secret pass,
80   That secret to each fool, that he's an ass:
        The truth once told (and wherefore should we lie?)
        The queen of Midas slept, and so may I.
            You think this cruel? take it for a rule,
        No creature smarts so little as a fool.
85   Let peals of laughter, Codrus![1] round thee break,
        Thou unconcerned canst hear the mighty crack.
        Pit, box, and gallery in convulsions hurled,
        Thou stand'st unshook amidst a bursting world.
        Who shames a scribbler? break one cobweb through,
90   He spins the slight, self-pleasing thread anew:
        Destroy his fib or sophistry, in vain;
        The creature's at his dirty work again,
        Throned in the center of his thin designs,
        Proud of a vast extent of flimsy lines.
95   Whom have I hurt? has poet yet or peer
        Lost the arched eyebrow or Parnassian sneer?
        And has not Colley[2] still his lord and whore?
        His butchers Henley? his freemasons Moore?[3]
        Does not one table Bavius still admit?
100   Still to one bishop Philips seem a wit?
        Still Sappho——— A. Hold! for God's sake—you'll offend.
        No names—be calm—learn prudence of a friend.
        I too could write, and I am twice as tall;
        But foes like these!——— P. One flatterer's worse than all.
105   Of all mad creatures, if the learn'd are right,
        It is the slaver kills, and not the bite.
        A fool quite angry is quite innocent:
        Alas! 'tis ten times worse when they repent.
            One dedicates in high heroic prose,
110   And ridicules beyond a hundred foes;
        One from all Grub Street[4] will my fame defend,
        And, more abusive, calls himself my friend.
        This prints my letters,[5] that expects a bribe,
        And others roar aloud, "Subscribe, subscribe!"[6]
115   There are, who to my person pay their court:
        I cough like Horace, and, though lean, am short;
        Ammon's great son° one shoulder had too high,   *Alexander the Great*
        Such Ovid's nose, and "Sir! you have an eye—"
        Go on, obliging creatures, make me see
120   All that disgraced my betters met in me.
        Say for my comfort, languishing in bed,
        "Just so immortal Maro° held his head":   *Virgil*
        And when I die, be sure you let me know
        Great Homer died three thousand years ago.

---

1. A poet ridiculed by Virgil and Juvenal.
2. Colley Cibber, poet laureate.
3. John Henley ("Orator Henley") was an independent preacher with a mass following. James Moore Smythe was a member of the Masonic order. Bavius (line 99) is a bad poet referred to by Virgil. The Bishop of Armagh employed Ambrose Philips (line 100 [called "Namby-Pamby" by the wits]) as his secretary. "Sappho" (line 101) is Lady Mary Wortley Montagu.
4. The traditional haunt of hack writers.
5. As Curll had done without permission.
6. Pay for copies in advance of publication.

25 Why did I write? what sin to me unknown
Dipped me in ink, my parents', or my own?
As yet a child, nor yet a fool to fame,
I lisped in numbers, for the numbers came.
I left no calling for this idle trade,
30 No duty broke, no father disobeyed.
The Muse but served to ease some friend, not wife,
To help me through this long disease, my life,
To second, Arbuthnot! thy art and care,
And teach the being° you preserved, to bear.   *life*
35 A. But why then publish? P. Granville the polite,[7]
And knowing Walsh, would tell me I could write;
Well-natured Garth inflamed with early praise,
And Congreve loved, and Swift endured my lays;
The courtly Talbot, Somers, Sheffield, read;
40 Even mitered Rochester[8] would nod the head,
And St. John's[9] self (great Dryden's friends before)
With open arms received one poet more.
Happy my studies, when by these approved!
Happier their author, when by these beloved!
45 From these the world will judge of men and books,
Not from the Burnets, Oldmixons, and Cookes.[1]
   Soft were my numbers; who could take offense
While pure description held the place of sense?
Like gentle Fanny's[2] was my flowery theme,
50 A painted mistress, or a purling stream.
Yet then did Gildon[3] draw his venal quill;
I wished the man a dinner, and sat still.
Yet then did Dennis[4] rave in furious fret;
I never answered, I was not in debt.
55 If want provoked, or madness made them print,
I waged no war with Bedlam or the Mint.
   Did some more sober critic come abroad?
If wrong, I smiled; if right, I kissed the rod.
Pains, reading, study are their just pretense,
60 And all they want is spirit, taste, and sense.
Commas and points they set exactly right,
And 'twere a sin to rob them of their mite.
Yet ne'er one sprig of laurel graced these ribalds,
From slashing Bentley down to piddling Tibbalds.[5]
65 Each wight who reads not, and but scans and spells,
Each word-catcher that lives on syllables,
Even such small critics some regard may claim,
Preserved in Milton's or in Shakespeare's name.
Pretty! in amber to observe the forms
70 Of hairs, or straws, or dirt, or grubs, or worms!
The things, we know, are neither rich nor rare,
But wonder how the devil they got there.

7. There follow the names of poets and men of letters, Pope's early friends. They were literary elder statesmen, chiefly, who had befriended Dryden in the preceding century.
8. The Bishop of Rochester.
9. Pronounced *sinjin.*
1. Thomas Burnet, John Oldmixon and Arthur Cooke had all attacked Pope or his works.
2. Lord Hervey, satirized as Sporus in lines 305 ff.
3. Charles Gildon, a critic who had, as Pope believed, written against him "venally," to curry favor with Addison. (See line 209n. below.)
4. John Dennis, who wrote a furious condemnation of Pope's *Essay on Criticism.*
5. Richard Bentley, a classical scholar, had edited *Paradise Lost* with undue license on the ground that Milton was blind and never saw his text. Lewis Theobald, no wit but a closer scholar than Pope, had exposed the faults of Pope's edition of Shakespeare in a subsequent edition of his own.

Were others angry? I excused them too;
Well might they rage; I gave them but their due.
175 A man's true merit 'tis not hard to find;
But each man's secret standard in his mind,
That casting weight[6] pride adds to emptiness,
This, who can gratify? for who can guess?
The bard whom pilfered pastorals renown,
180 Who turns a Persian tale for half a crown,[7]
Just writes to make his barrenness appear,
And strains from hard-bound brains eight lines a year:
He, who still wanting, though he lives on theft,
Steals much, spends little, yet has nothing left;
185 And he who now to sense, now nonsense leaning,
Means not, but blunders round about a meaning:
And he whose fustian's so sublimely bad,
It is not poetry, but prose run mad:
All these, my modest satire bade translate,
190 And owned that nine such poets made a Tate.[8]
How did they fume, and stamp, and roar, and chafe!
And swear, not Addison himself was safe.

Peace to all such! but were there one whose fires
True Genius kindles, and fair Fame inspires;
195 Blessed with each talent and each art to please,
And born to write, converse, and live with ease:
Should such a man, too fond to rule alone,
Bear, like the Turk, no brother near the throne;[9]
View him with scornful, yet with jealous eyes,
200 And hate for arts that caused himself to rise;
Damn with faint praise, assent with civil leer,
And without sneering, teach the rest to sneer;
Willing to wound, and yet afraid to strike,
Just hint a fault, and hesitate dislike;
205 Alike reserved to blame or to commend,
A timorous foe, and a suspicious friend;
Dreading even fools; by flatterers besieged,
And so obliging that he ne'er obliged;
Like Cato, give his little senate laws,[1]
210 And sit attentive to his own applause;
While wits and Templars° every sentence raise,   *law students*
And wonder with a foolish face of praise—
Who but must laugh, if such a man there be?
Who would not weep, if Atticus[2] were he?

215 What though my name stood rubric° on the walls?   *in red letters*
Or plastered posts, with claps,° in capitals?   *posters*
Or smoking forth, a hundred hawkers' load,
On wings of winds came flying all abroad?
I sought no homage from the race that write;
220 I kept, like Asian monarchs, from their sight:
Poems I heeded (now berhymed so long)
No more than thou, great George! a birthday song.
I ne'er with wits or witlings passed my days
To spread about the itch of verse and praise;

---

6. Weight tipping the scales.
7. Ambrose Philips (named in line 100), who had competed with the youthful Pope as a pastoral poet; author of *Persian Tales*.
8. Nahum Tate, successor to Dryden as poet laureate.
9. The Ottoman Emperors, Europeans believed, regularly killed their principal kins-

men upon ascending the throne.
1. Addison (author of the immensely popular tragedy *Cato*) presided over an admiring company of political and literary partisans at Button's Coffee House.
2. A friend of Cicero's; here a pseudonym for Addison.

225 Nor like a puppy daggled through the town
     To fetch and carry sing-song up and down;
     Nor at rehearsals sweat, and mouthed, and cried,
     With handkerchief and orange at my side;
     But sick of fops, and poetry, and prate,
230 To Bufo left the whole Castalian state.[3]
         Proud as Apollo on his forkéd hill,[4]
     Sat full-blown Bufo, puffed by every quill;
     Fed with soft dedication all day long,
     Horace and he went hand in hand in song.
235 His library (where busts of poets dead
     And a true Pindar stood without a head)
     Received of wits an undistinguished race,
     Who first his judgment asked, and then a place:
     Much they extolled his pictures, much his seat,°   *estate*
240 And flattered every day, and some days eat:°   *ate*
     Till grown more frugal in his riper days,
     He paid some bards with port, and some with praise;
     To some a dry° rehearsal was assigned,   *without performance*
     And others (harder still) he paid in kind.[5]
245 Dryden alone (what wonder?) came not nigh;
     Dryden alone escaped this judging eye:
     But still the great have kindness in reserve;
     He helped to bury whom he helped to starve.
         May some choice patron bless each gray goose quill!°   *quill pen*
250 May every Bavius have his Bufo still!
     So when a statesman wants a day's defense,
     Or Envy holds a whole week's war with Sense,
     Or simple Pride for flattery makes demands,
     May dunce by dunce be whistled off my hands!
255 Blessed be the great! for those they take away,
     And those they left me—for they left me Gay;[6]
     Left me to see neglected genius bloom,
     Neglected die, and tell it on his tomb;
     Of all thy blameless life the sole return
260 My verse, and Queensberry weeping o'er thy urn!
     Oh, let me live my own, and die so too!
     ("To live and die is all I have to do")
     Maintain a poet's dignity and ease,
     And see what friends, and read what books I please;
265 Above a patron, though I condescend
     Some times to call a minister my friend.
     I was not born for courts or great affairs;
     I pay my debts, believe, and say my prayers,
     Can sleep without a poem in my head,
270 Nor know if Dennis be alive or dead.
         Why am I asked what next shall see the light?
     Heavens! was I born for nothing but to write?
     Has life no joys for me? or (to be grave)
     Have I no friend to serve, no soul to save?
275 "I found him close with Swift"—"Indeed? no doubt,"
     Cries prating Balbus, "something will come out."
     'Tis all in vain, deny it as I will.

3. Pope leaves Bufo the whole republic of let-
ters, named from the spring Castalia, which
was sacred to Apollo and the Muses. Bufo is
perhaps a composite of Lord Halifax and
"Bubo," Bubb Dodington.
4. The twin peaks of Parnassus.

5. I.e., he read them his poetry in turn.
6. John Gay, author of *The Beggar's Opera,*
associate of Pope and Swift; befriended (line
260) by the Duke and Duchess of Queens-
berry.

"No, such a genius never can lie still,"
And then for mine obligingly mistakes
280 The first lampoon Sir Will or Bubo[7] makes.
Poor guiltless I! and can I choose but smile,
When every coxcomb knows me by my style?
　　Cursed be the verse, how well soe'er it flow,
That tends to make one worthy man my foe,
285 Give Virtue scandal, Innocence a fear,
Or from the soft-eyed virgin steal a tear!
But he who hurts a harmless neighbor's peace,
Insults fallen worth, or Beauty in distress,
Who loves a lie, lame Slander helps about,
290 Who writes a libel, or who copies out:
That fop whose pride affects a patron's name,
Yet absent, wounds an author's honest fame;
Who can your merit selfishly approve,
And show the sense of it without the love;
295 Who has the vanity to call you friend,
Yet wants the honor, injured, to defend;
Who tells whate'er you think, whate'er you say,
And, if he lie not, must at least betray:
Who to the dean and silver bell can swear,
300 And sees at Cannons what was never there:[8]
Who reads but with a lust to misapply,
Make satire a lampoon, and fiction, lie:
A lash like mine no honest man shall dread,
But all such babbling blockheads in his stead.
305 　　Let Sporus[9] tremble—— A. What? that thing of silk,
Sporus, that mere white curd of ass's milk?
Satire or sense, alas! can Sporus feel?
Who breaks a butterfly upon a wheel?
　　P. Yet let me flap this bug with gilded wings,
310 This painted child of dirt, that stinks and stings;
Whose buzz the witty and the fair annoys,
Yet wit ne'er tastes, and beauty ne'er enjoys;
So well-bred spaniels civilly delight
In mumbling of the game they dare not bite.
315 Eternal smiles his emptiness betray,
As shallow streams run dimpling all the way.
Whether in florid impotence he speaks,
And, as the prompter breathes, the puppet squeaks;
Or at the ear of Eve,[1] familiar toad,
320 Half froth, half venom, spits himself abroad,
In puns, or politics, or tales, or lies,
Or spite, or smut, or rhymes, or blasphemies.
His wit all seesaw between *that* and *this*, ⎫
Now high, now low, now master up, now miss, ⎬
325 And he himself one vile antithesis. ⎭

7. Sir William Yonge or Bubb Dodington. Both were Pope's political adversaries as well as, in some degree, silly men.
8. In his *Epistle to Burlington*, Pope satirized "Timon's Villa," an estate where a silver bell and an obsequious dean invite worshipers to an overstuffed chapel. Mischief-makers had identified this estate with Cannons, the ostentatious home of Pope's well-wisher the Duke of Chandos.
9. Roman eunuch, victim of the Emperor Nero's perversions; in the poem, Lord Hervey, a foppish and effeminate courtier who was Pope's personal, political, and literary enemy. He attested his frailty by drinking ass's milk as a tonic.
1. Like Satan in Eden (*Paradise Lost* IV. 790 ff.). Hervey was Queen Caroline's confidant; the word *familiar* suggests a demonic ministrant.

Amphibious thing! that acting either part,
The trifling head or the corrupted heart,
Fop at the toilet, flatterer at the board,
Now trips a lady, and now struts a lord.
30 Eve's tempter thus the rabbins° have expressed,   *Hebrew scholars*
A cherub's face, a reptile all the rest;
Beauty that shocks you, parts° that none will trust,   *talents*
Wit that can creep, and pride that licks the dust.
     Not Fortune's worshiper, nor Fashion's fool,
35 Not Lucre's° madman, nor Ambition's tool,   *Money's*
Not proud, nor servile, be one poet's praise,
That if he pleased, he pleased by manly ways:
That flattery, even to kings, he held a shame,
And thought a lie in verse or prose the same:
40 That not in fancy's maze he wandered long,
But stooped[2] to truth, and moralized his song:
That not for fame, but Virtue's better end,
He stood the furious foe, the timid friend,
The damning critic, half approving wit,
45 The coxcomb hit, or fearing to be hit;
Laughed at the loss of friends he never had,
The dull, the proud, the wicked, and the mad;
The distant threats of vengeance on his head,
The blow unfelt, the tear he never shed;
50 The tale revived, the lie so oft o'erthrown,
The imputed trash, and dullness not his own;
The morals blackened when the writings 'scape,
The libeled person, and the pictured shape;[3]
Abuse on all he loved, or loved him, spread,
55 A friend in exile, or a father dead;
The whisper,[4] that to greatness still too near,
Perhaps yet vibrates on his sovereign's ear—
Welcome for thee, fair Virtue! all the past!
For thee, fair Virtue! welcome even the last!
60   A. But why insult the poor, affront the great?
P. A knave's a knave to me in every state:
Alike my scorn, if he succeed or fail,
Sporus at court, or Japhet[5] in a jail,
A hireling scribbler, or a hireling peer,
65 Knight of the post[6] corrupt, or of the shire,
If on a pillory, or near a throne,
He gain his prince's ear, or lose his own.
     Yet soft by nature, more a dupe than wit,
Sappho can tell you how this man was bit:°   *deceived*
70 This dreaded satirist Dennis will confess
Foe to his pride, but friend to his distress:[7]
So humble, he has knocked at Tibbald's door,
Has drunk with Cibber, nay, has rhymed for Moore.
Full ten years slandered, did he once reply?

2. Swooped down perceiving prey (a term from falconry).
3. Cartoons were drawn of Pope's hunched posture.
4. Hervey's whisper to Queen Caroline.
5. Japhet Crook, a forger; his ears were cropped for his crime (line 367).
6. "Knight of the post": professional witness.
7. Pope contributed to a benefit performance for the aging Dennis.

375   Three thousand suns went down on Welsted's lie.[8]
      To please a mistress one aspersed his life;
      He lashed him not, but let her be his wife.
      Let Budgell charge low Grub Street on his quill,
      And write whate'er he pleased, except his will;[9]
380   Let the two Curlls, of town and court,[1] abuse
      His father, mother, body, soul, and muse.
      Yet why? that father held it for a rule,
      It was a sin to call our neighbor fool;
      That harmless mother thought no wife a whore:
385   Hear this, and spare his family, James Moore!
      Unspotted names, and memorable long,
      If there be force in virtue, or in song.
        Of gentle blood (part shed in honor's cause,
      While yet in Britain honor had applause)
390   Each parent sprung—— A. What fortune, pray?—— P. Their own,
      And better got than Bestia's[2] from the throne.
      Born to no pride, inheriting no strife,
      Nor marrying discord in a noble wife,
      Stranger to civil and religious rage,
395   The good man walked innoxious through his age.
      No courts he saw, no suits would ever try,
      Nor dared an oath, nor hazarded a lie.[3]
      Unlearn'd, he knew no schoolman's subtle art,
      No language but the language of the heart.
400   By nature honest, by experience wise,
      Healthy by temperance, and by exercise;
      His life, though long, to sickness passed unknown,
      His death was instant, and without a groan.
      Oh, grant me thus to live, and thus to die!
405   Who sprung from kings shall know less joy than I.
        O friend! may each domestic bliss be thine!
      Be no unpleasing melancholy mine:
      Me, let the tender office long engage,
      To rock the cradle of reposing Age,
410   With lenient arts extend a mother's breath,
      Make Languor smile, and smooth the bed of Death,
      Explore the thought, explain the asking eye,
      And keep a while one parent from the sky!
      On cares like these if length of days attend,
415   May Heaven, to bless those days, preserve my friend,
      Preserve him social, cheerful, and serene,
      And just as rich as when he served a Queen![4]
      A. Whether that blessing be denied or given,
      Thus far was right—the rest belongs to Heaven.

1735

---

8. A hint that Pope had contributed to the death of the "Unfortunate Lady" celebrated in the *Elegy* above. (The lady seems actually to have been a fiction.)
9. Budgell (perhaps falsely) attributed to Pope a squib in the *Grub-Street Journal* charging that Budgell had forged a will.
1. Edmund Curll, the publisher; and Lord Hervey.
2. A Roman consul who was bribed to arrange a dishonorable peace; in the poem, probably the Duke of Marlborough.
3. He did not take the special oath required of Catholics wanting to enter public life or the professions, nor did he evade by falsehood the restrictions on Catholics.
4. Arbuthnot, who had sought no professional profit as physician to Queen Anne, continued to earn the same income after her death.

SAMUEL JOHNSON
(1709–1784)

On the Death of Dr. Robert Levet[1]

Condemned to Hope's delusive mine,
   As on we toil from day to day,
By sudden blasts, or slow decline,
   Our social comforts drop away.

5 Well tried through many a varying year,
   See Levet to the grave descend;
Officious,° innocent, sincere,   *dutiful*
   Of every friendless name the friend.

Yet still he fills Affection's eye,
10   Obscurely wise, and coarsely kind;
Nor, lettered Arrogance, deny
   Thy praise to merit unrefined.

When fainting Nature called for aid,
   And hovering Death prepared the blow,
15 His vigorous remedy displayed
   The power of art without the show.

In Misery's darkest cavern known,
   His useful care was ever nigh,
Where hopeless Anguish poured his groan,
20   And lonely Want retired to die.

No summons mocked by chill delay,
   No petty gain disdained by pride,
The modest wants of every day
   The toil of every day supplied.

25 His virtues walked their narrow round,
   Nor made a pause, nor left a void;
And sure the Eternal Master found
   The single talent[2] well employed.

The busy day, the peaceful night,
30   Unfelt, uncounted, glided by;
His frame was firm, his powers were bright,
   Though now his eightieth year was nigh.

Then with no throbbing fiery pain,
   No cold gradations of decay,
35 Death broke at once the vital chain,
   And freed his soul the nearest way.

                                      1783

1. An unlicensed physician practicing among the poor, who had long lived in Dr. Johnson's house. He was uncouth in appearance and stiff in manner.

2. An allusion to the portion of wealth given in trust in the parable of the talents, Matthew xxv.14–30.

THOMAS GRAY
(1716–1771)

Ode

ON THE DEATH OF A FAVORITE CAT,
DROWNED IN A TUB OF GOLDFISHES

'Twas on a lofty vase's side,
Where China's gayest art had dyed
   The azure flowers that blow;°   *bloom*
Demurest of the tabby kind,
5 The pensive Selima, reclined,
   Gazed on the lake below.

Her conscious tail her joy declared;
The fair round face, the snowy beard,
   The velvet of her paws,
10 Her coat, that with the tortoise vies,
Her ears of jet, and emerald eyes,
   She saw; and purred applause.

Still had she gazed; but 'midst the tide
Two angel forms were seen to glide,
15   The genii° of the stream: *guardian spirits*
Their scaly armor's Tyrian hue
Through richest purple to the view
   Betrayed a golden gleam.[1]

The hapless nymph with wonder saw:
20 A whisker first and then a claw,
   With many an ardent wish,
She stretched in vain to reach the prize.
What female heart can gold despise?
   What cat's averse to fish?

25 Presumptuous maid! with looks intent
Again she stretched, again she bent,
   Nor knew the gulf between.
(Malignant Fate sat by and smiled)
The slippery verge her feet beguiled,
30   She tumbled headlong in.

Eight times emerging from the flood
She mewed to every watery god,
   Some speedy aid to send.
No dolphin came, no Nereid stirred;[2]
35 Nor cruel Tom, nor Susan heard;
   A favorite has no friend!

---

1. "Tyrian" and (in classical reference) "purple" cover a considerable spectrum, including crimson. The fish are seen, through red highlights, as golden.

2. A dolphin appeared to save the singer Arion when he was cast overboard. Nereids are sea-nymphs.

From hence, ye beauties, undeceived,
Know, one false step is ne'er retrieved,
   And be with caution bold.
40 Not all that tempts your wandering eyes
And heedless hearts, is lawful prize;
   Nor all that glisters, gold.

1748

Elegy Written in a Country Churchyard

The curfew tolls the knell of parting day,
   The lowing herd wind slowly o'er the lea,
The plowman homeward plods his weary way,
   And leaves the world to darkness and to me.

5 Now fades the glimmering landscape on the sight,
   And all the air a solemn stillness holds,
Save where the beetle wheels his droning flight,
   And drowsy tinklings lull the distant folds;

Save that from yonder ivy-mantled tower
10   The moping owl does to the moon complain
Of such, as wandering near her secret bower,
   Molest her ancient solitary reign.

Beneath those rugged elms, that yew tree's shade,
   Where heaves the turf in many a moldering heap,
15 Each in his narrow cell forever laid,
   The rude° forefathers of the hamlet sleep.   *rustic*

The breezy call of incense-breathing morn,
   The swallow twittering from the straw-built shed,
The cock's shrill clarion, or the echoing horn,°   *hunting horn*
20   No more shall rouse them from their lowly bed.

For them no more the blazing hearth shall burn,
   Or busy housewife ply her evening care;
No children run to lisp their sire's return,
   Or climb his knees the envied kiss to share.

25 Oft did the harvest to their sickle yield,
   Their furrow oft the stubborn glebe° has broke;   *soil*
How jocund did they drive their team afield!
   How bowed the woods beneath their sturdy stroke!

Let not Ambition mock their useful toil,
30   Their homely joys, and destiny obscure;
Nor Grandeur hear with a disdainful smile
   The short and simple annals of the poor.

The boast of heraldry,[3] the pomp of power,
   And all that beauty, all that wealth e'er gave,
35 Awaits alike the inevitable hour.
   The paths of glory lead but to the grave.

3. I.e., noble family.

Nor you, ye proud, impute to these the fault,
   If Memory o'er their tomb no trophies[4] raise,
Where through the long-drawn aisle and fretted° vault   *ornamented*
40   The pealing anthem swells the note of praise.

Can storied urn[5] or animated° bust   *lifelike*
   Back to its mansion call the fleeting breath?
Can Honor's voice provoke° the silent dust,   *call forth*
   Or Flattery soothe the dull cold ear of Death?

45 Perhaps in this neglected spot is laid
   Some heart once pregnant with celestial fire;
Hands that the rod of empire might have swayed,
   Or waked to ecstasy the living lyre.

But Knowledge to their eyes her ample page
50   Rich with the spoils of time did ne'er unroll;
Chill Penury repressed their noble rage,
   And froze the genial current of the soul.

Full many a gem of purest ray serene,
   The dark unfathomed caves of ocean bear:
55 Full many a flower is born to blush unseen,
   And waste its sweetness on the desert air.

Some village Hampden,[6] that with dauntless breast
   The little tyrant of his fields withstood;
Some mute inglorious Milton here may rest,
60   Some Cromwell guiltless of his country's blood.

The applause of listening senates to command,
   The threats of pain and ruin to despise,
To scatter plenty o'er a smiling land,
   And read their history in a nation's eyes,

65 Their lot forbade: nor circumscribed alone
   Their growing virtues, but their crimes confined;
Forbade to wade through slaughter to a throne,
   And shut the gates of mercy on mankind,

The struggling pangs of conscious truth to hide,
70   To quench the blushes of ingenuous shame,
Or heap the shrine of Luxury and Pride
   With incense kindled at the Muse's flame.

Far from the madding° crowd's ignoble strife,   *milling*
   Their sober wishes never learned to stray;
75 Along the cool sequestered vale of life
   They kept the noiseless tenor of their way.

---

4. Memorials to military heroes; typically, statuary representations of arms captured in battle.
5. Funeral urn with descriptive epitaph.

6. Leader of the opposition to Charles I in the controversy over ship money; killed in battle in the Civil Wars.

Yet even these bones from insult to protect
    Some frail memorial still erected nigh,
With uncouth rhymes and shapeless sculpture decked,
30   Implores the passing tribute of a sigh.

Their name, their years, spelt by the unlettered Muse,
    The place of fame and elegy supply:
And many a holy text around she strews,
    That teach the rustic moralist to die.

85 For who to dumb Forgetfulness a prey,
    This pleasing anxious being e'er resigned,
Left the warm precincts of the cheerful day,
    Nor cast one longing lingering look behind?

On some fond breast the parting soul relies,
90   Some pious drops the closing eye requires;
Even from the tomb the voice of Nature cries,
    Even in our ashes live their wonted fires.

For thee, who mindful of the unhonored dead
    Dost in these lines their artless tale relate;
95 If chance, by lonely contemplation led,
    Some kindred spirit shall inquire thy fate,

Haply some hoary-headed swain may say,
    "Oft have we seen him at the peep of dawn
Brushing with hasty steps the dews away
100   To meet the sun upon the upland lawn.

"There at the foot of yonder nodding beech
    That wreathes its old fantastic roots so high,
His listless length at noontide would he stretch,
    And pore upon the brook that babbles by.

105 "Hard by yon wood, now smiling as in scorn,
    Muttering his wayward fancies he would rove,
Now drooping, woeful wan, like one forlorn,
    Or crazed with care, or crossed in hopeless love.

"One morn I missed him on the customed hill,
110   Along the heath and near his favorite tree;
Another came; nor yet beside the rill,
    Nor up the lawn, nor at the wood was he;

"The next with dirges due in sad array
    Slow through the churchway path we saw him borne.
115 Approach and read (for thou canst read) the lay,
    Graved on the stone beneath yon aged thorn."

      The Epitaph

Here rests his head upon the lap of Earth
    A youth to Fortune and to Fame unknown.
Fair Science° frowned not on his humble birth,   Learning
120   *And Melancholy marked him for her own.*

> Large was his bounty, and his soul sincere,
>   Heaven did a recompense as largely send:
> He gave to Misery all he had, a tear,
>   He gained from Heaven ('twas all he wished) a friend.

125 No farther seek his merits to disclose,
      Or draw his frailties from their dread abode
   (There they alike in trembling hope repose),
      The bosom of his Father and his God.

ca. 1742–50   1751

Stanzas to Mr. Bentley[7]

In silent gaze the tuneful choir among,
  Half pleased, half blushing, let the Muse admire,
While Bentley leads her sister-art along,
  And bids the pencil° answer to the lyre.   *painter's brush*

5 See, in their course, each transitory thought
     Fixed by his touch a lasting essence take;
   Each dream, in fancy's airy coloring wrought,
     To local symmetry and life awake!

   The tardy rhymes that used to linger on,
10   To censure cold, and negligent of fame,
   In swifter measures animated run,
     And catch a luster from his genuine flame.

   Ah! could they catch his strength, his easy grace,
     His quick creation, his unerring line;
15 The energy of Pope they might efface,
     And Dryden's harmony submit to mine.

   But not to one in this benighted age
     Is that diviner inspiration given,
   That burns in Shakespeare's or in Milton's page,
20   The pomp and prodigality of Heaven.

   As when, conspiring in the diamond's blaze,
     The meaner gems that singly charm the sight
   Together dart their intermingled rays,
     And dazzle with a luxury of light.

25 Enough for me, if to some feeling breast,
     My lines a secret sympathy [impart;]
   And as their pleasing influence [is confessed,]
     A sigh of soft reflection [stirs the heart.]

ca. 1752   1775

7. Written while Richard Bentley was preparing the designs for *Six Poems by Mr. T. Gray.* The manuscript in which this poem was preserved was torn in its lower right-hand corner. The missing words are here conjecturally supplied in brackets.

WILLIAM COLLINS
(1721–1759)

Ode Written in the Beginning of the Year 1746[1]

How sleep the brave who sink to rest
By all their country's wishes blest!
When Spring, with dewy fingers cold,
Returns to deck their hallowed mold,
5   She there shall dress a sweeter sod
Than Fancy's feet have ever trod.

By fairy hands their knell is rung,
By forms unseen their dirge is sung;
There Honor comes, a pilgrim gray,
10   To bless the turf that wraps their clay,
And Freedom shall awhile repair,
To dwell a weeping hermit there!

                                                        1746

Ode to Evening

If aught of oaten stop,[2] or pastoral song,
May hope, chaste Eve, to soothe thy modest ear,
    Like thy own solemn springs,
    Thy springs and dying gales,
5   O nymph reserved, while now the bright-haired sun
Sits in yon western tent, whose cloudy skirts,
    With brede° ethereal wove,   *braid*
    O'erhang his wavy bed:
Now air is hushed, save where the weak-eyed bat,
10   With short shrill shriek flits by on leathern wing,
    Or where the beetle winds
    His small but sullen horn,
As oft he rises 'midst the twilight path,
Against the pilgrim° borne in heedless hum: *wayfarer*
15   Now teach me, maid composed,
    To breathe some softened strain,
Whose numbers, stealing through thy darkening vale,
May not unseemly with its stillness suit,
    As, musing slow, I hail
20   Thy genial loved return!
For when thy folding-star[3] arising shows
His paly circlet, at his warning lamp
    The fragrant Hours, and elves
    Who slept in flowers the day,
25   And many a nymph who wreaths her brows with sedge,
And sheds the freshening dew, and, lovelier still,
    The pensive Pleasures sweet,
    Prepare thy shadowy car.

1. The poem celebrates Englishmen who fell
resisting the pretender to the throne ("Bonnie
Prince Charlie," the grandson of James II)
in the previous year.

2. "If any modulation of a (shepherd's)
reed."
3. The evening star, which, when it becomes
visible, tells the shepherd to drive his flock to
the sheepfold.

Then lead, calm votaress, where some sheety lake
30 Cheers the lone heath, or some time-hallowed pile
        Or upland fallows gray
        Reflect its last cool gleam.
But when chill blustering winds, or driving rain,
Forbid my willing feet, be mine the hut
35   That from the mountain's side
        Views wilds, and swelling floods,
And hamlets brown, and dim-discovered spires,
And hears their simple bell, and marks o'er all
        Thy dewy fingers draw
40   The gradual dusky veil.
While Spring shall pour his showers, as oft he wont,
And bathe thy breathing tresses, meekest Eve;
        While Summer loves to sport
        Beneath thy lingering light;
45 While sallow Autumn fills thy lap with leaves;
Or Winter, yelling through the troublous air,
        Affrights thy shrinking train,
        And rudely rends thy robes;
        So long, sure-found beneath the sylvan shed,[4]
50 Shall Fancy, Friendship, Science, rose-lipped Health,
        Thy gentlest influence own,
        And hymn thy favorite name!

                                            1746, 1748

CHRISTOPHER SMART
(1722–1771)

From Jubilate Agno[1]

For I will consider my Cat Jeoffry.
For he is the servant of the Living God, duly and daily serving him.
For at the first glance of the glory of God in the East he worships in his way.
700 For is this done by wreathing his body seven times round with elegant
        quickness.
For then he leaps up to catch the musk,[2] which is the blessing of God upon
        his prayer.
For he rolls upon prank to work it in.
For having done duty and received blessing he begins to consider himself.
For this he performs in ten degrees.
705 For first he looks upon his forepaws to see if they are clean.
For secondly he kicks up behind to clear away there.
For thirdly he works it upon stretch with the forepaws extended.
For fourthly he sharpens his paws by wood.
For fifthly he washes himself.
710 For sixthly he rolls upon wash.
For seventhly he fleas himself, that he may not be interrupted upon the beat.[3]
For eighthly he rubs himself against a post.
For ninthly he looks up for his instructions.

4. I.e., securely attained beneath the shelter of the forest.
1. "Rejoice in the Lamb"; i.e., in Jesus, the Lamb of God; written while Smart was confined for insanity.
2. Perhaps a scented plant, played with like catnip.
3. Upon his daily round, possibly of hunting.

For tenthly he goes in quest of food.

15 For having considered God and himself he will consider his neighbor.

For if he meets another cat he will kiss her in kindness.

For when he takes his prey he plays with it to give it a chance.

For one mouse in seven escapes by his dallying.

For when his day's work is done his business more properly begins.

20 For he keeps the Lord's watch in the night against the adversary.

For he counteracts the powers of darkness by his electrical skin and glaring eyes.

For he counteracts the Devil, who is death, by brisking about the life.

For in his morning orisons he loves the sun and the sun loves him.

For he is of the tribe of Tiger.

25 For the Cherub Cat is a term of the Angel Tiger.[4]

For he has the subtlety and hissing of a serpent, which in goodness he suppresses.

For he will not do destruction if he is well-fed, neither will he spit without provocation.

For he purrs in thankfulness when God tells him he's a good Cat.

For he is an instrument for the children to learn benevolence upon.

30 For every house is incomplete without him, and a blessing is lacking in the spirit.

For the Lord commanded Moses concerning the cats at the departure of the Children of Israel from Egypt.

For every family had one cat at least in the bag.[5]

For the English Cats are the best in Europe.

For he is the cleanest in the use of his forepaws of any quadruped.

35 For the dexterity of his defense is an instance of the love of God to him exceedingly.

For he is the quickest to his mark of any creature.

For he is tenacious of his point.

For he is a mixture of gravity and waggery.

For he knows that God is his Saviour.

40 For there is nothing sweeter than his peace when at rest.

For there is nothing brisker than his life when in motion.

For he is of the Lord's poor, and so indeed is he called by benevolence perpetually—Poor Jeoffry! poor Jeoffry! the rat has bit thy throat.

For I bless the name of the Lord Jesus that Jeoffry is better.

For the divine spirit comes about his body to sustain it in complete cat.

45 For his tongue is exceeding pure so that it has in purity what it wants in music.

For he is docile and can learn certain things.

For he can sit up with gravity, which is patience upon approbation.

For he can fetch and carry, which is patience in employment.

For he can jump over a stick, which is patience upon proof positive.

50 For he can spraggle upon waggle at the word of command.

For he can jump from an eminence into his master's bosom.

For he can catch the cork and toss it again.

For he is hated by the hypocrite and miser.

For the former is afraid of detection.

55 For the latter refuses the charge.

For he camels his back to bear the first notion of business.

For he is good to think on, if a man would express himself neatly.

For he made a great figure in Egypt for his signal services.

---

4. Smart apparently thinks of Jeoffry as an immature or diminutive phase of a larger creature—cherubs being by artistic convention small and childlike.

5. The Israelites took with them silver and gold ornaments and raiment, as well as flocks and herds (Exodus xi.2 and xii.32,35). Smart adds the cats.

For he killed the Icneumon rat, very pernicious by land.[6]
760 For his ears are so acute that they sting again.
For from this proceeds the passing quickness of his attention.
For by stroking of him I have found out electricity.
For I perceived God's light about him both wax and fire.
For the electrical fire is the spiritual substance which God sends from heaven
    to sustain the bodies both of man and beast.
765 For God has blessed him in the variety of his movements.
For, though he cannot fly, he is an excellent clamberer.
For his motions upon the face of the earth are more than any other
    quadruped.
For he can tread to all the measures upon the music.
For he can swim for life.
780 For he can creep.

ca. 1760   1939

OLIVER GOLDSMITH
(1730–1774)

When Lovely Woman Stoops to Folly

When lovely woman stoops to folly,
    And finds too late that men betray,
What charm can soothe her melancholy,
    What art can wash her guilt away?

5 The only art her guilt to cover,
    To hide her shame from every eye,
To give repentance to her lover,
    And wring his bosom—is to die.

1766

WILLIAM COWPER
(1731–1800)

Epitaph on a Hare

Here lies, whom hound did ne'er pursue,
    Nor swifter greyhound follow,
Whose foot ne'er tainted morning dew,
    Nor ear heard huntsman's hallo',

5 Old Tiney, surliest of his kind,
    Who, nursed with tender care,
And to domestic bounds confined,
    Was still a wild jack-hare.

6. The rats encountered by Jeoffry may have impressed Smart as resembling mongooses (one sense of *ichneumon*); or there may be some reference to the ichneumon fly, a wasp-like insect parasitic upon caterpillers.

Though duly from my hand he took
   His pittance every night,
10 He did it with a jealous look,
   And, when he could, would bite.

His diet was of wheaten bread,
   And milk, and oats, and straw,
15 Thistles, or lettuces instead,
   With sand to scour his maw.

On twigs of hawthorn he regaled,° **feasted**
   On pippins' russet peel;
And, when his juicy salads failed,
20   Sliced carrot pleased him well.

A Turkey carpet was his lawn,[3]
   Whereon he loved to bound,
To skip and gambol like a fawn,
   And swing his rump around.

25 His frisking was at evening hours,
   For then he lost his fear;
But most before approaching showers,
   Or when a storm drew near.

Eight years and five round-rolling moons
30   He thus saw steal away,
Dozing out all his idle noons,
   And every night at play.

I kept him for his humor's sake,
   For he would oft beguile
35 My heart of thoughts that made it ache,
   And force me to a smile.

But now, beneath this walnut-shade
   He finds his long, last home,
And waits in snug concealment laid,
40   Till gentler Puss shall come.

He,[4] still more agéd, feels the shocks
   From which no care can save,
And, partner once of Tiney's box,
   Must soon partake his grave.

1783   1784

The Castaway

Obscurest night involved the sky,
   The Atlantic billows roared,
When such a destined wretch as I,
   Washed headlong from on board,
5 Of friends, of hope, of all bereft,
   His floating home forever left.

---

3. Cowper exercised his hares on his parlor carpet of Turkey red.

4. Puss, the longest-lived of Cowper's three hares.

No braver chief could Albion boast
  Than he with whom he went,[6]
Nor ever ship left Albion's coast,
10   With warmer wishes sent.
He loved them both, but both in vain,
Nor him beheld, nor her again.

Not long beneath the whelming brine,
  Expert to swim, he lay;
15 Nor soon he felt his strength decline,
  Or courage die away;
But waged with death a lasting strife,
Supported by despair of life.

He shouted; nor his friends had failed
20   To check the vessel's course,
But so the furious blast prevailed,
  That, pitiless perforce,
They left their outcast mate behind,
And scudded still before the wind.

25 Some succor yet they could afford;
  And, such as storms allow,
The cask, the coop, the floated cord,
  Delayed not to bestow.
But he (they knew) nor ship, nor shore,
30 Whate'er they gave, should visit more.

Nor, cruel as it seemed, could he
  Their haste himself condemn,
Aware that flight, in such a sea,
  Alone could rescue them;
35 Yet bitter felt it still to die
Deserted, and his friends so nigh.

He long survives, who lives an hour
  In ocean, self-upheld;
And so long he, with unspent power,
40   His destiny repelled;
And ever, as the minutes flew,
Entreated help, or cried, "Adieu!"

At length, his transient respite past,
  His comrades, who before
45 Had heard his voice in every blast,
  Could catch the sound no more.
For then, by toil subdued, he drank
The stifling wave, and then he sank.

No poet wept him; but the page
50   Of narrative sincere,
That tells his name, his worth, his age,
  Is wet with Anson's tear.
And tears by bards or heroes shed
Alike immortalize the dead.

6. Namely, George, Lord Anson, who told the castaway's story in his *Voyage Round the World* (1748).

5   I therefore purpose not, or dream,
      Descanting on his fate,
To give the melancholy theme
     A more enduring date:
But misery still delights to trace
10 Its semblance in another's case.

No voice divine the storm allayed,
     No light propitious shone,
When, snatched from all effectual aid,
     We perished, each alone;
15 But I beneath a rougher sea,
And whelmed in deeper gulfs than he.

                      1799   1803

WILLIAM BLAKE
(1757–1827)

From POETICAL SKETCHES

To the Muses[1]

Whether on Ida's[2] shady brow,
     Or in the chambers of the East,
The chambers of the sun, that now
     From antient melody have ceas'd;

5   Whether in Heav'n ye wander fair,
     Or the green corners of the earth,
Or the blue regions of the air,
     Where the melodious winds have birth;

Whether on chrystal rocks ye rove,
10   Beneath the bosom of the sea
Wand'ring in many a coral grove,
     Fair Nine, forsaking Poetry!

How have you left the antient love
     That bards of old enjoy'd in you!
15 The languid strings do scarcely move!
     The sound is forc'd, the notes are few!

                               1783

Song

How sweet I roam'd from field to field,
     And tasted all the summer's pride,
'Till I the prince of love beheld,
     Who in the sunny beams did glide!

---

1. Nine goddesses who, in Greek myth, preside over the arts and sciences, especially poetry.

2. Mountain in Asia Minor, distant from the mountains sacred to the Muses (Helicon and Parnassus) in Greece.

5   He shew'd me lilies for my hair,
          And blushing roses for my brow;
       He led me through his gardens fair,
          Where all his golden pleasures grow.

       With sweet May dews my wings were wet,
10   And Phoebus fir'd my vocal rage;[3]
       He caught me in his silken net,
          And shut me in his golden cage.

       He loves to sit and hear me sing,
          Then, laughing, sports and plays with me;
15   Then stretches out my golden wing,
          And mocks my loss of liberty.

                                                  1783

To the Evening Star

       Thou fair-hair'd angel of the evening,
       Now, while the sun rests on the mountains, light
       Thy bright torch of love; thy radiant crown
       Put on, and smile upon our evening bed!
5   Smile on our loves; and, while thou drawest the
       Blue curtains of the sky, scatter thy silver dew
       On every flower that shuts its sweet eyes
       In timely sleep. Let thy west wind sleep on
       The lake; speak silence with thy glimmering eyes,
10   And wash the dusk with silver. Soon, full soon,
       Dost thou withdraw; then the wolf rages wide,
       And the lion glares thro' the dun forest:
       The fleeces of our flocks are cover'd with
       Thy sacred dew: protect them with thine influence.[4]

                                                  1783

From Songs of Innocence

Introduction

       Piping down the valleys wild
       Piping songs of pleasant glee
       On a cloud I saw a child,
       And he laughing said to me,

5   "Pipe a song about a Lamb";
       So I piped with merry chear.
       "Piper pipe that song again"—
       So I piped, he wept to hear.

       "Drop thy pipe thy happy pipe
10   Sing thy songs of happy chear";
       So I sung the same again
       While he wept with joy to hear.

---

3. Impassioned song. Phoebus is Apollo, god of
poetic inspiration.

4.. In astrology, the effect that heavenly bodies
exert on earthly things and creatures.

"Piper sit thee down and write
In a book that all may read"—
15 So he vanish'd from my sight.
And I pluck'd a hollow reed,

And I made a rural pen,
And I stain'd the water clear,
And I wrote my happy songs
20 Every child may joy to hear.

1789

The Lamb

Little Lamb, who made thee?
Dost thou know who made thee?
Gave thee life & bid thee feed,
By the stream & o'er the mead;
5 Gave thee clothing of delight,
Softest clothing wooly bright;
Gave thee such a tender voice,
Making all the vales rejoice!
Little Lamb who made thee?
10 Dost thou know who made thee?

Little Lamb I'll tell thee,
Little Lamb I'll tell thee!
He° is calléd by thy name,   *Christ*
For he calls himself a Lamb:
15 He is meek & he is mild,
He became a little child:
I a child & thou a lamb,
We are calléd by his name.
Little Lamb God bless thee.
20 Little Lamb God bless thee.

1789

Holy Thursday [I.]

'Twas on a Holy Thursday,[5] their innocent faces clean,
The children[6] walking two & two, in red & blue & green,
Grey headed beadles[7] walkd before with wands as white as snow,
Till into the high dome of Paul's they like Thames' waters flow.

5 O what a multitude they seemd, these flowers of London town!
Seated in companies they sit with radiance all their own.
The hum of multitudes was there, but multitudes of lambs,
Thousands of little boys & girls raising their innocent hands.

Now like a mighty wind they raise to heaven the voice of song,
10 Or like harmonious thunderings the seats of heaven among.
Beneath them sit the aged men, wise guardians of the poor;
Then cherish pity, lest you drive an angel from your door.

1789

5. Probably Ascension Day (40 days after Easter).
6. Here the children of charity schools are depicted in St. Paul's Cathedral, London.
7. Ushers charged with keeping order.

The Little Black Boy

My mother bore me in the southern wild,
And I am black, but O! my soul is white;
White as an angel is the English child:
But I am black as if bereav'd of light.

5 My mother taught me underneath a tree,
And sitting down before the heat of day,
She took me on her lap and kisséd me,
And pointing to the east, began to say:

"Look on the rising sun: there God does live,
10 And gives his light, and gives his heat away;
And flowers and trees and beasts and men receive
Comfort in morning, joy in the noon day.

"And we are put on earth a little space,
That we may learn to bear the beams of love,
15 And these black bodies and this sun-burnt face
Is but a cloud, and like a shady grove.

"For when our souls have learn'd the heat to bear,
The cloud will vanish; we shall hear his voice,
Saying: 'Come out from the grove, my love & care,
20 And round my golden tent like lambs rejoice.' "

Thus did my mother say, and kisséd me;
And thus I say to little English boy:
When I from black and he from white cloud free,
And round the tent of God like lambs we joy,

25 I'll shade him from the heat till he can bear
To lean in joy upon our father's knee;
And then I'll stand and stroke his silver hair,
And be like him, and he will then love me.

                                                    1789

From Songs of Experience

Holy Thursday [II.]

Is this a holy thing to see,
In a rich and fruitful land,
Babes reducd to misery,
Fed with cold and usurous hand?

5 Is that trembling cry a song?
Can it be a song of joy?
And so many children poor?
It is a land of poverty!

And their sun does never shine,
10 And their fields and bleak & bare,
And their ways are fill'd with thorns;
It is eternal winter there.

For where-e'er the sun does shine,
And where-e'er the rain does fall,
15 Babe can never hunger there,
Nor poverty the mind appall.

1794

The Clod & the Pebble

"Love seeketh not Itself to please,
Nor for itself hath any care;
But for another gives its ease,
And builds a Heaven in Hells despair."

5   So sang a little Clod of Clay,
Trodden with the cattle's feet;
But a Pebble of the brook,
Warbled out these metres meet:°   *appropriate*

"Love seeketh only Self to please,
10 To bind another to its delight,
Joys in another's loss of ease,
And builds a Hell in Heaven's despite."

1794

The Sick Rose

O Rose, thou art sick.
The invisible worm
That flies in the night
In the howling storm

5 Has found out thy bed
Of crimson joy,
And his dark secret love
Does thy life destroy.

1794

A Poison Tree

I was angry with my friend:
I told my wrath, my wrath did end.
I was angry with my foe:
I told it not, my wrath did grow.

5 And I waterd it in fears,
Night & morning with my tears;
And I sunnéd it with smiles,
And with soft deceitful wiles.

And it grew both day and night,
10   Till it bore an apple bright.
And my foe beheld it shine,
And he knew that it was mine,

And into my garden stole,
When the night had veild the pole;
15   In the morning glad I see
My foe outstretchd beneath the tree.

1794

The Tyger

Tyger! Tyger! burning bright
In the forests of the night,
What immortal hand or eye
Could frame thy fearful symmetry?

5   In what distant deeps or skies
Burnt the fire of thine eyes?
On what wings dare he aspire?
What the hand, dare seize the fire?

10   And what shoulder, & what art,
Could twist the sinews of thy heart?
And when thy heart began to beat,
What dread hand? & what dread feet?

What the hammer? what the chain?
In what furnace was thy brain?
15   What the anvil? what dread grasp
Dare its deadly terrors clasp?

When the stars threw down their spears,
And water'd heaven with their tears,
Did he smile his work to see?
20   Did he who made the Lamb make thee?

Tyger! Tyger! burning bright
In the forests of the night,
What immortal hand or eye
Dare frame thy fearful symmetry?

1794

Ah Sun-flower

Ah Sun-flower! weary of time,
Who countest the steps of the Sun,
Seeking after that sweet golden clime
Where the traveller's journey is done;

5   Where the Youth pined away with desire,
And the pale Virgin shrouded in snow,
Arise from their graves and aspire,
Where my Sun-flower wishes to go.

1794

The Garden of Love

I went to the Garden of Love,
And saw what I never had seen:
A Chapel was built in the midst,
Where I used to play on the green.

5 And the gates of this Chapel were shut,
And "Thou shalt not" writ over the door;
So I turn'd to the Garden of Love,
That so many sweet flowers bore,

And I saw it was filled with graves,
10 And tomb-stones where flowers should be:
And Priests in black gowns were walking their rounds,
And binding with briars my joys & desires.

1794

London

I wander thro' each charter'd[8] street,
Near where the charter'd Thames does flow,
And mark in every face I meet
Marks of weakness, marks of woe.

5 In every cry of every man,
In every Infant's cry of fear,
In every voice, in every ban,[9]
The mind-forg'd manacles I hear.

How the Chimney-sweeper's cry
10 Every blackning Church appalls;
And the hapless Soldier's sigh
Runs in blood down Palace walls.

But most thro' midnight streets I hear
How the youthful Harlot's curse
15 Blasts the new-born Infant's tear,
And blights with plagues the Marriage hearse.

1794

From SONGS AND BALLADS

I Askéd a Thief

I askéd a thief to steal me a peach,
He turned up his eyes;
I ask'd a lithe lady to lie her down,
Holy & meek she cries.

5 As soon as I went
An angel came.
He wink'd at the thief
And smild at the dame—

8. Mapped out, legally defined, constricted.   9. A law or notice commanding or forbidding; a published penalty.

And without one word said
10 Had a peach from the tree
And still as a maid
Enjoy'd the lady.

1796   1863

Mock on, Mock on, Voltaire, Rousseau

Mock on, Mock on, Voltaire, Rousseau;[1]
Mock on, Mock on, 'tis all in vain.
You throw the sand against the wind,
And the wind blows it back again.

5 And every sand becomes a Gem
Reflected in the beams divine;
Blown back, they blind the mocking Eye,
But still in Israel's paths they shine.

The Atoms of Democritus
10 And Newton's Particles of light[2]
Are sands upon the Red sea shore,[3]
Where Israel's tents do shine so bright.

1800–08   1863

From MILTON

And Did Those Feet

And did those feet in ancient time
Walk upon England's mountains green?
And was the holy Lamb of God
On England's pleasant pastures seen?

5 And did the Countenance Divine
Shine forth upon our clouded hills?
And was Jerusalem builded here,
Among these dark Satanic Mills?[4]

Bring me my Bow of burning gold:
10 Bring me my Arrows of desire:
Bring me my Spear: O clouds unfold!
Bring me my Chariot of fire!

I will not cease from Mental Fight,
Nor shall my Sword sleep in my hand,
15 Till we have built Jerusalem
In England's green & pleasant Land.

1804–10

1. Leaders of the pre-Revolutionary French "Enlightenment"; critics of the established order, here representing thinkers who destroy without creating.
2. Democritus (Greek philosopher, fifth century B.C.) and Sir Isaac Newton (1642–1727), both represented as nonsensically reducing nature to inanimate matter.
3. Where God delivered the Israelites from the Egyptians (Exodus xiv).
4. The primary meaning is "millstone"—two heavy cylindrical stones that grind grain into meal between them; "factory" is an extended meaning.

From JERUSALEM

England! Awake! Awake! Awake!

England! awake! awake! awake!
  Jerusalem thy Sister calls!
Why wilt thou sleep the sleep of death?
  And close her from thy ancient walls.

5
              Thy hills & valleys felt her feet,
                Gently upon their bosoms move:
              Thy gates beheld sweet Zions ways;
                Then was a time of joy and love.

10
           And now the time returns again:
              Our souls exult & Londons towers,
           Receive the Lamb of God to dwell
              In Englands green & pleasant bowers.
                          1804–09   1818

From FOR THE SEXES: *The Gates of Paradise*

To The Accuser who is
The God of This World[5]

Truly My Satan thou art but a Dunce,
And dost not know the Garment from the Man;
Every Harlot was a Virgin once,
Nor canst thou ever change Kate into Nan.

5
Tho thou are Worshipd by the Names Divine
Of Jesus & Jehovah: thou art still
The Son of Morn in weary Night's decline,
The lost Traveller's Dream under the Hill.
                                1793–1818

ROBERT BURNS
(1759–1796)

To a Mouse

ON TURNING HER UP IN HER NEST WITH THE PLOUGH,
NOVEMBER, 1785

Wee, sleekit,° cow'rin, tim'rous beastie,   *sleek*
O, what a panic's in thy breastie!
Thou need na start awa sae hasty,
        Wi' bickering° brattle!°   *hurried / scamper*
5 I wad be laith to rin an' chase thee,
        Wi' murd'ring pattle!°   *plowstaff ("paddle")*

---

5. God conceived of as a harsh taskmaster and merciless judge; Blake rejected this concept as "Satanic."

I'm truly sorry man's dominion
Has broken Nature's social union,
An' justifies that ill opinion
          Which makes thee startle
At me, thy poor earth-born companion,
          An' fellow-mortal!

I doubt na, whiles,° but thou may thieve;   *sometimes*
What then? poor beastie, thou maun° live!   *must*
A daimen° icker° in a thrave°   *random / corn-ear / shock*
          'S a sma' request:
I'll get a blessin wi' the lave,°   *rest*
          And never miss't!

Thy wee bit housie, too, in ruin!
Its silly° wa's the win's are strewin!   *frail*
An' naething, now, to big° a new ane,   *build*
          O' foggage° green!   *mosses*
An' bleak December's winds ensuin,
          Baith snell° an' keen!   *bitter*

Thou saw the fields laid bare and waste,
An' weary winter comin fast,
An' cozie here, beneath the blast,
          Thou thought to dwell,
Till crash! the cruel coulter° past   *plowshare*
          Out thro' thy cell.

That wee bit heap o' leaves an' stibble°   *stubble*
Has cost thee mony a weary nibble!
Now thou's turned out, for a' thy trouble,
          But° house or hald,°   *without / home ("hold")*
To thole° the winter's sleety dribble,   *endure*
          An' cranreuch° cauld!   *hoarfrost*

But, Mousie, thou art no thy lane,[1]
In proving foresight may be vain:
The best laid schemes o' mice an' men
          Gang° aft a-gley.°   *go / astray*
An' lea'e us nought but grief an' pain
          For promised joy.

Still thou art blest, compared wi' me!
The present only toucheth thee:
But och! I backward cast my e'e
          On prospects drear!
An' forward, tho' I canna see,
          I guess an' fear!

          1785, 1786

---

1. "No thy lane": not alone.

Holy Willie's[2] Prayer

O Thou, wha in the heavens dost dwell,
Wha, as it pleases best thysel',
Sends ane to heaven and ten to hell,
      A' for thy glory,
5 And no for ony guid or ill
        They've done afore thee!

I bless and praise thy matchless might,
Whan thousands thou hast left in night,
That I am here afore thy sight,
10   For gifts an' grace
A burnin' an' a shinin' light,
      To a' this place.

What was I, or my generation,
That I should get sic exaltation?
15 I, wha deserve most just damnation,
      For broken laws,
Sax thousand years 'fore my creation,
      Thro' Adam's cause.

When frae my mither's womb I fell,
20 Thou might hae plungéd me in hell,
To gnash my gums, to weep and wail,
      In burnin lakes,
Where damnéd devils roar and yell,
      Chained to their stakes;

25 Yet I am here a chosen sample,
To show thy grace is great and ample;
I'm here a pillar in thy temple,
      Strong as a rock,
A guide, a buckler, an example
30   To a' thy flock.

O Lord, thou kens what zeal I bear,
When drinkers drink, and swearers swear.
And singin' there and dancin' here,
      Wi' great an' sma':
35 For I am keepit by thy fear
      Free frae them a'.

But yet, O Lord! confess I must
At times I'm fashed° wi' fleshy lust;   *troubled*
An' sometimes too, wi' warldly trust,
40   Vile self gets in;
But thou remembers we are dust,
      Defiled in sin.

2. One William Fisher, an elder in the church at Mauchline, the seat of Burns's farm. He habitually censured other men's behavior and doctrine, but was himself rebuked for drunkenness and was suspected of stealing church funds.

O Lord! yestreen,° thou kens, wi' Meg—   *last night*
Thy pardon I sincerely beg;
45 O! may't ne'er be a livin' plague
            To my dishonour,
An' I'll ne'er lift a lawless leg
            Again upon her.

Besides I farther maun allow,
50 Wi' Lizzie's lass, three times I trow—
But, Lord, that Friday I was fou,°   *full (of liquor)*
            When I cam near her,
Or else thou kens thy servant true
            Wad never steer° her.   *touch ("stir")*

55 May be thou lets this fleshly thorn
Beset thy servant e'en and morn
Lest he owre high and proud should turn,
            That he's sae gifted;
If sae, thy hand maun e'en be borne,
60   Until thou lift it.

Lord, bless thy chosen in this place,
For here thou hast a chosen race;
But God confound their stubborn face,
            And blast their name,
65 Wha bring thy elders to disgrace
            An' public shame.

Lord, mind Gawn Hamilton's[3] deserts,
He drinks, an' swears, an' plays at cartes,
Yet has sae mony takin arts
70   Wi' great an' sma',
Frae God's ain priest the people's hearts
            He steals awa'.

An' when we chastened him therefor,
Thou kens how he bred sic a splore°   *row*
75 As set the warld in a roar
            O' laughin' at us;
Curse thou his basket and his store,
            Kail° and potatoes.   *cabbage*

Lord, hear my earnest cry an' pray'r,
80 Against that presbytery o' Ayr;
Thy strong right hand, Lord, make it bare
            Upo' their heads;
Lord, weigh it down, and dinna spare,
            For their misdeeds.

85 O Lord my God, that glib-tongued Aiken,
My very heart and soul are quakin',
To think how we stood sweatin, shakin,
            An' pissed wi' dread,

---

3. Gavin Hamilton, a convivial lawyer friend of Burns's. Accused of Sabbath-breaking and other offenses by the elders of Mauchline church, he was cleared by the Presbytery of Ayr (line 80) with the help of his counsel Robert Aiken (line 85).

Green Grow the Rashes 229

hanging / sneering

90   While he, wi' hingin° lips and snakin,°
           Held up his head.

    Lord in the day of vengeance try him;
    Lord, visit them wha did employ him,
    And pass not in thy mercy by them,
           Nor hear their pray'r:
95   But, for thy people's sake, destroy them,
           And dinna spare.

    But, Lord, remember me and mine
    Wi' mercies temp'ral and divine,
    That I for gear° and grace may shine   *wealth*
100   Excelled by nane,
    And a' the glory shall be thine,
           Amen, Amen!

1785   1808

Green Grow the Rashes

Chorus

    Green grow the rashes,° O;   *tall grasses or rushes*
     Green grow the rashes, O;
    The sweetest hours that e'er I spend,
    Are spent amang the lasses, O!

5   There's nought but care on ev'ry han',
     In ev'ry hour that passes, O:
    What signifies the life o' man,
     An'° 'twere na for the lasses, O.   *if*
           (*Chorus*)

    The warly° race may riches chase,   *worldly*
10   An' riches still may fly them, O;
    An' though at last they catch them fast,
     Their hearts can ne'er enjoy them, O.
           (*Chorus*)

    But gie me a canny° hour at e'en,   *pleasant*
     My arms about my dearie, O;
15   An' warly cares, an' warly men,
     May a' gae tapsalteerie,° O!   *topsy turvy*
           (*Chorus*)

    For you sae douce,° ye sneer at this,   *prudent*
     Ye're nought but senseless asses, O:
    The wisest man[4] the warl' saw,
20   He dearly loved the lasses, O.
           (*Chorus*)

    Auld nature swears, the lovely dears
    Her noblest work she classes, O:
    Her prentice han' she tried on man,
    An' then she made the lasses, O.
           (*Chorus*)

1784   1787

4. King Solomon, who had many wives.

Of A' the Airts[5]

Of a' the airts° the wind can blaw,   *quarters*
 I dearly like the west,
For there the bonie lassie lives,
 The lassie I lo'e best:
5 There's wild woods grow, and rivers row,° *flow*
 And mony a hill between;
But day and night my fancy's flight
 Is ever wi' my Jean.

I see her in the dewy flowers,
10 I see her sweet and fair;
I hear her in the tunefu' birds,
 I hear her charm the air:
There's not a bonie flower that springs
 By fountain, shaw,° or green,   *wood*
15 There's not a bonie bird that sings,
 But minds me o' my Jean.

1788   1790

Bonie Doon

Ye flowery banks o' bonie Doon,
 How can ye blume sae fair?
How can ye chant, ye little birds,
 And I sae fu' o' care?

5 Thou'll break my heart, thou bonie bird,
 That sings upon the bough;
Thou minds me o' the happy days,
 When my fause° luve was true.   *false*

Thou'll break my heart, thou bonie bird,
10 That sings beside thy mate;
For sae I sat, and sae I sang,
 And wist° na o' my fate.   *knew*

Aft hae I roved by bonie Doon
 To see the wood-bine twine,
15 And ilka° bird sang o' its luve,   *every*
 And sae did I o' mine.

Wi' lightsome heart I pu'd a rose
 Frae aff its thorny tree;
And my fause luver staw° my rose   *stole*
20 But left the thorn wi' me.

1791   1792

A Red, Red Rose

O my luve's like a red, red rose,
 That's newly sprung in June;
O my luve's like the melodie
 That's sweetly played in tune.

---

5. Written from Dumfriesshire to Burns's wife, Jean Armour, in Ayrshire, the county to the west.

5   As fair art thou, my bonnie lass,
        So deep in luve am I;
    And I will luve thee still, my dear,
        Till a' the seas gang dry.

    Till a' the seas gang dry, my dear,
10   And the rocks melt wi' the sun:
    O I will love thee still, my dear,
        While the sands o' life shall run.

    And fare thee weel, my only luve,
        And fare thee weel awhile!
15   And I will come again, my luve,
        Though it were ten thousand mile.

1796

WILLIAM WORDSWORTH
(1770–1850)

Lines

COMPOSED A FEW MILES ABOVE TINTERN ABBEY ON REVISITING THE BANKS OF THE WYE DURING A TOUR. JULY 13, 1798[1]

    Five years have passed; five summers, with the length
    Of five long winters! and again I hear
    These waters, rolling from their mountain-springs
    With a soft inland murmur. Once again
5   Do I behold these steep and lofty cliffs,
    That on a wild secluded scene impress
    Thoughts of more deep seclusion; and connect
    The landscape with the quiet of the sky.
    The day is come when I again repose
10 Here, under this dark sycamore, and view
    These plots of cottage ground, these orchard tufts,
    Which at this season, with their unripe fruits,
    Are clad in one green hue, and lose themselves
    'Mid groves and copses. Once again I see
15 These hedgerows, hardly hedgerows, little lines
    Of sportive wood run wild; these pastoral farms,
    Green to the very door; and wreaths of smoke
    Sent up, in silence, from among the trees!
    With some uncertain notice, as might seem
20 Of vagrant dwellers in the houseless woods,
    Or of some Hermit's cave, where by his fire
    The Hermit sits alone.

---

1. Ruins of a medieval abbey situated in the valley of the river Wye, in Monmouthshire, noted for its scenery.

These beauteous forms,
Through a long absence, have not been to me
As is a landscape to a blind man's eye;
²⁵ But oft, in lonely rooms, and 'mid the din
Of towns and cities, I have owed to them,
In hours of weariness, sensations sweet,
Felt in the blood, and felt along the heart;
And passing even into my purer mind,
³⁰ With tranquil restoration—feelings too
Of unremembered pleasure; such, perhaps,
As have no slight or trivial influence
On that best portion of a good man's life,
His little, nameless, unremembered, acts
³⁵ Of kindness and of love. Nor less, I trust,
To them I may have owed another gift,
Of aspect more sublime; that blessed mood,
In which the burthen of the mystery,
In which the heavy and the weary weight
⁴⁰ Of all this unintelligible world,
Is lightened—that serene and blessed mood,
In which the affections gently lead us on—
Until, the breath of this corporeal frame
And even the motion of our human blood
⁴⁵ Almost suspended, we are laid asleep
In body, and become a living soul;
While with an eye made quiet by the power
Of harmony, and the deep power of joy,
We see into the life of things.

                              If this
⁵⁰ Be but a vain belief, yet, oh! how oft—
In darkness and amid the many shapes
Of joyless daylight; when the fretful stir
Unprofitable, and the fever of the world,
Have hung upon the beatings of my heart—
⁵⁵ How oft, in spirit, have I turned to thee,
O sylvan Wye! thou wanderer through the woods,
How often has my spirit turned to thee!

    And now, with gleams of half-extinguished thought,
With many recognitions dim and faint,
⁶⁰ And somewhat of a sad perplexity,
The picture of the mind revives again;
While here I stand, not only with the sense
Of present pleasure, but with pleasing thoughts
That in this moment there is life and food
⁶⁵ For future years. And so I dare to hope,
Though changed, no doubt, from what I was when first
I came among these hills; when like a roe
I bounded o'er the mountains, by the sides
Of the deep rivers, and the lonely streams,
⁷⁰ Wherever nature led—more like a man
Flying from something that he dreads than one
Who sought the thing he loved. For nature then
(The coarser² pleasures of my boyish days,
And their glad animal movements all gone by)

2. I.e., primarily physical.

75 To me was all in all.—I cannot paint
    What then I was. The sounding cataract
    Haunted me like a passion; the tall rock,
    The mountain, and the deep and gloomy wood,
    Their colors and their forms, were then to me
80 An appetite; a feeling and a love,
    That had no need of a remoter charm,
    By thought supplied, nor any interest
    Unborrowed from the eye.—That time is past,
    And all its aching joys are now no more,
85 And all its dizzy raptures. Not for this
    Faint° I, nor mourn nor murmur; other gifts   *become discouraged*
    Have followed; for such loss, I would believe,
    Abundant recompense. For I have learned
    To look on nature, not as in the hour
90 Of thoughtless youth; but hearing oftentimes
    The still, sad music of humanity,
    Nor harsh nor grating, though of ample power
    To chasten and subdue. And I have felt
    A presence that disturbs me with the joy
95 Of elevated thoughts; a sense sublime
    Of something far more deeply interfused,
    Whose dwelling is the light of setting suns,
    And the round ocean and the living air,
    And the blue sky, and in the mind of man:
100 A motion and a spirit, that impels
    All thinking things, all objects of all thought,
    And rolls through all things. Therefore am I still
    A lover of the meadows and the woods,
    And mountains; and of all that we behold
105 From this green earth; of all the mighty world
    Of eye, and ear—both what they half create,
    And what perceive; well pleased to recognize
    In nature and the language of the sense
    The anchor of my purest thoughts, the nurse,
110 The guide, the guardian of my heart, and soul
    Of all my moral being.

                    Nor perchance,
    If I were not thus taught, should I the more
    Suffer my genial spirits° to decay: *vital energies*
    For thou art with me here upon the banks
115 Of this fair river; thou my dearest Friend,[3]
    My dear, dear Friend; and in thy voice I catch
    The language of my former heart, and read
    My former pleasures in the shooting lights
    Of thy wild eyes. Oh! yet a little while
120 May I behold in thee what I was once,
    My dear, dear Sister! and this prayer I make,
    Knowing that Nature never did betray
    The heart that loved her; 'tis her privilege,
    Through all the years of this our life, to lead
125 From joy to joy: for she can so inform
    The mind that is within us, so impress
    With quietness and beauty, and so feed
    With lofty thoughts, that neither evil tongues,

3. Wordsworth's sister Dorothy, who accompanied him on the walking trip here commemorated.

Rash judgments, nor the sneers of selfish men,
130 Nor greetings where no kindness is, nor all
The dreary intercourse of daily life,
Shall e'er prevail against us, or disturb
Our cheerful faith, that all which we behold
Is full of blessings. Therefore let the moon
135 Shine on thee in thy solitary walk;
And let the misty mountain winds be free
To blow against thee: and, in after years,
When these wild ecstasies shall be matured
Into a sober pleasure; when thy mind
140 Shall be a mansion for all lovely forms,
Thy memory be as a dwelling place
For all sweet sounds and harmonies; oh! then,
If solitude, or fear, or pain, or grief
Should be thy portion, with what healing thoughts
145 Of tender joy wilt thou remember me,
And these my exhortations! Nor, perchance—
If I should be where I no more can hear
Thy voice, nor catch from thy wild eyes these gleams
Of past existence—wilt thou then forget
150 That on the banks of this delightful stream
We stood together; and that I, so long
A worshiper of Nature, hither came
Unwearied in that service; rather say
With warmer love—oh! with far deeper zeal
155 Of holier love. Nor wilt thou then forget,
That after many wanderings, many years
Of absence, these steep woods and lofty cliffs,
And this green pastoral landscape, were to me
More dear, both for themselves and for thy sake!

1798

From The Prelude

From *Book I*

Fair seedtime had my soul, and I grew up
Fostered alike by beauty and by fear:
Much favored in my birthplace,[4] and no less
In that belovéd Vale[5] to which erelong
305 We were transplanted—there were we let loose
For sports of wider range. Ere I had told
Ten birthdays, when among the mountain slopes
Frost, and the breath of frosty wind, had snapped
The last autumnal crocus, 'twas my joy
310 With store of springes° o'er my shoulder hung   snares
To range the open heights where woodcocks run
Along the smooth green turf. Through half the night,
Scudding away from snare to snare, I plied
That anxious visitation—moon and stars
315 Were shining o'er my head. I was alone,
And seemed to be a trouble to the peace
That dwelt among them. Sometimes it befell

4. Cockermouth, in the northern part of the   5. Esthwaite, also in the Lakes.
English Lake District.

In these night wanderings, that a strong desire
O'erpowered my better reason, and the bird
320 Which was the captive of another's toil
Became my prey; and when the deed was done
I heard among the solitary hills
Low breathings coming after me, and sounds
Of undistinguishable motion, steps
325 Almost as silent as the turf they trod.

Nor less, when spring had warmed the cultured° Vale,   cultivated
Moved we as plunderers where the mother bird
Had in high places built her lodge; though mean
Our object and inglorious, yet the end
330 Was not ignoble. Oh! when I have hung
Above the raven's nest, by knots of grass
And half-inch fissures in the slippery rock
But ill sustained, and almost (so it seemed)
Suspended by the blast that blew amain,
335 Shouldering the naked crag, oh, at that time
While on the perilous ridge I hung alone,
With what strange utterance did the loud dry wind
Blow through my ear! the sky seemed not a sky
Of earth—and with what motion moved the clouds!

340 Dust as we are, the immortal spirit grows
Like harmony in music; there is a dark
Inscrutable workmanship that reconciles
Discordant elements, makes them cling together
In one society. How strange that all
345 The terrors, pains, and early miseries,
Regrets, vexations, lassitudes interfused
Within my mind, should e'er have borne a part,
And that a needful part, in making up
The calm existence that is mine when I
350 Am worthy of myself! Praise to the end!
Thanks to the means which Nature deigned to employ;
Whether her fearless visitings, or those
That came with soft alarm, like hurtless light
Opening the peaceful clouds; or she may use
355 Severer interventions, ministry
More palpable, as best might suit her aim.

One summer evening (led by her) I found
A little boat tied to a willow tree
Within a rocky cave, its usual home.
360 Straight I unloosed her chain, and stepping in
Pushed from the shore. It was an act of stealth
And troubled pleasure, nor without the voice
Of mountain echoes did my boat move on;
Leaving behind her still, on either side,
365 Small circles glittering idly in the moon,
Until they melted all into one track
Of sparkling light. But now, like one who rows,
Proud of his skill, to reach a chosen point
With an unswerving line, I fixed my view
370 Upon the summit of a craggy ridge,

The horizon's utmost boundary; for above
Was nothing but the stars and the gray sky.
She was an elfin pinnace; lustily
I dipped my oars into the silent lake,
375   And, as I rose upon the stroke, my boat
Went heaving through the water like a swan;
When, from behind that craggy steep till then
The horizon's bound, a huge peak, black and huge,
As if with voluntary power instinct,
380   Upreared its head. I struck and struck again,
And growing still in stature the grim shape
Towered up between me and the stars, and still,
For so it seemed, with purpose of its own
And measured motion like a living thing,
385   Strode after me. With trembling oars I turned,
And through the silent water stole my way
Back to the covert of the willow tree;
There in her mooring place I left my bark,
And through the meadows homeward went, in grave
390   And serious mood; but after I had seen
That spectacle, for many days, my brain
Worked with a dim and undetermined sense
Of unknown modes of being; o'er my thoughts
There hung a darkness, call it solitude
395   Or blank desertion. No familiar shapes
Remained, no pleasant images of trees,
Of sea or sky, no colors of green fields;
But huge and mighty forms, that do not live
Like living men, moved slowly through the mind
400   By day, and were a trouble to my dreams.

      Wisdom and Spirit of the universe!
Thou Soul that art the eternity of thought,
That givest to forms and images a breath
And everlasting motion, not in vain
405   By day or starlight thus from my first dawn
Of childhood didst thou intertwine for me
The passions that build up our human soul;
Not with the mean and vulgar works of man,
But with high objects, with enduring things—
410   With life and nature—purifying thus
The elements of feeling and of thought,
And sanctifying, by such discipline,
Both pain and fear, until we recognize
A grandeur in the beating of the heart.
415   Nor was this fellowship vouchsafed to me
With stinted kindness. In November days,
When vapors rolling down the valley made
A lonely scene more lonesome, among woods,
At noon and 'mid the calm of summer nights,
420   When, by the margin of the trembling lake,
Beneath the gloomy hills homeward I went
In solitude, such intercourse was mine;
Mine was it in the fields both day and night,
And by the waters, all the summer long.

25   And in the frosty season, when the sun
Was set, and visible for many a mile
The cottage windows blazed through twilight gloom,
I heeded not their summons: happy time
It was indeed for all of us—for me
430 It was a time of rapture! Clear and loud
The village clock tolled six—I wheeled about,
Proud and exulting like an untired horse
That cares not for his home. All shod with steel,
We hissed along the polished ice in games
435 Confederate, imitative of the chase
And woodland pleasures—the resounding horn,
The pack loud chiming, and the hunted hare.
So through the darkness and the cold we flew,
And not a voice was idle; with the din
440 Smitten, the precipices rang aloud;
The leafless trees and every icy crag
Tinkled like iron; while far distant hills
Into the tumult sent an alien sound
Of melancholy not unnoticed, while the stars
445 Eastward were sparkling clear, and in the west
The orange sky of evening died away.
Not seldom from the uproar I retired
Into a silent bay, or sportively
Glanced sideway, leaving the tumultuous throng,
450 To cut across the reflex° of a star   *reflection*
That fled, and, flying still before me, gleamed
Upon the glassy plain; and oftentimes,
When we had given our bodies to the wind,
And all the shadowy banks on either side
455 Came sweeping through the darkness, spinning still
The rapid line of motion, then at once
Have I, reclining back upon my heels,
Stopped short; yet still the solitary cliffs
Wheeled by me—even as if the earth had rolled
460 With visible motion her diurnal round!
Behind me did they stretch in solemn train,
Feebler and feebler, and I stood and watched
Till all was tranquil as a dreamless sleep.

    Ye Presences of Nature in the sky
465   And on the earth! Ye Visions of the hills!
And Souls of lonely places! can I think
A vulgar° hope was yours when ye employed   *lowly*
Such ministry, when ye, through many a year
Haunting me thus among my boyish sports,
470 On caves and trees, upon the woods and hills,
Impressed upon all forms the characters
Of danger or desire; and thus did make
The surface of the universal earth
With triumph and delight, with hope and fear,
Work like a sea?

                                1798–1800   1850

She Dwelt Among the Untrodden Ways

She dwelt among the untrodden ways
    Beside the springs of Dove.[6]
A Maid whom there were none to praise
    And very few to love;

5   A violet by a mossy stone
      Half hidden from the eye!
    —Fair as a star, when only one
      Is shining in the sky.

She lived unknown, and few could know
10   When Lucy ceased to be;
But she is in her grave, and, oh,
    The difference to me!

1800

Three Years She Grew

Three years she grew in sun and shower,
Then Nature said, "A lovelier flower
On earth was never sown;
This Child I to myself will take;
5   She shall be mine, and I will make
A Lady of my own.

"Myself will to my darling be
Both law and impulse: and with me
The Girl, in rock and plain,
10   In earth and heaven, in glade and bower,
Shall feel an overseeing power
To kindle or restrain.

"She shall be sportive as the fawn
That wild with glee across the lawn
15   Or up the mountain springs;
And hers shall be the breathing balm,
And hers the silence and the calm
Of mute insensate things.

"The floating clouds their state shall lend
20   To her; for her the willow bend;
Nor shall she fail to see
Even in the motions of the Storm
Grace that shall mold the Maiden's form
By silent sympathy.

25   "The stars of midnight shall be dear
To her; and she shall lean her ear
In many a secret place
Where rivulets dance their wayward round,
And beauty born of murmuring sound
30   Shall pass into her face.

6. Several rivers in England are named Dove.

"And vital feelings of delight
Shall rear her form to stately height,
Her virgin bosom swell;
Such thoughts to Lucy I will give
35 While she and I together live
Here in this happy dell."

Thus Nature spake—the work was done—
How soon my Lucy's race was run!
She died, and left to me
40 This health, this calm, and quiet scene;
The memory of what has been,
And never more will be.

1800

A Slumber Did My Spirit Seal

A slumber did my spirit seal;
    I had no human fears:
She seemed a thing that could not feel
    The touch of earthly years.

5 No motion has she now, no force;
    She neither hears nor sees;
Rolled round in earth's diurnal course,
    With rocks, and stones, and trees.

1800

It Is a Beauteous Evening

It is a beauteous evening, calm and free,
The holy time is quiet as a Nun
Breathless with adoration; the broad sun
Is sinking down in its tranquility;
5 The gentleness of heaven broods o'er the Sea:
Listen! the mighty Being is awake,
And doth with his eternal motion make
A sound like thunder—everlastingly.
Dear Child! dear Girl! that walkest with me here,
10 If thou appear untouched by solemn thought,
Thy nature is not therefore less divine:
Thou liest in Abraham's bosom[7] all the year,
And worship'st at the Temple's inner shrine,[8]
God being with thee when we know it not.

1807

London, 1802

Milton! thou shouldst be living at this hour:
England hath need of thee: she is a fen
Of stagnant waters: altar, sword, and pen,
Fireside, the heroic wealth of hall and bower,
5 Have forfeited their ancient English dower
Of inward happiness. We are selfish men;

7. Where souls in heaven rest (as in Luke, xvi.22).

8. The holy of holies (as in the ancient temple in Jerusalem); where God is present.

Oh! raise us up, return to us again;
And give us manners, virtue, freedom, power.
Thy soul was like a Star, and dwelt apart;
10   Thou hadst a voice whose sound was like the sea:
Pure as the naked heavens, majestic, free,
So didst thou travel on life's common way,
In cheerful godliness; and yet thy heart
The lowliest duties on herself did lay.

1807

Composed upon Westminster Bridge, September 3, 1802

Earth has not anything to show more fair:
Dull would he be of soul who could pass by
A sight so touching in its majesty;
This City now doth, like a garment, wear
5   The beauty of the morning; silent, bare,
Ships, towers, domes, theaters, and temples lie
Open unto the fields, and to the sky;
All bright and glittering in the smokeless air.
Never did sun more beautifully steep
10   In his first splendor, valley, rock, or hill;
Ne'er saw I, never felt, a calm so deep!
The river glideth at his own sweet will:
Dear God! the very houses seem asleep;
And all that mighty heart is lying still!

1807

Nuns Fret Not at Their Convent's Narrow Room

Nuns fret not at their convent's narrow room;
And hermits are contented with their cells;
And students with their pensive citadels;
Maids at the wheel, the weaver at his loom,
5   Sit blithe and happy; bees that soar for bloom,
High as the highest Peak of Furness-fells,[9]
Will murmur by the hour in foxglove bells:
In truth the prison, into which we doom
Ourselves, no prison is: and hence for me,
10   In sundry moods, 'twas pastime to be bound
Within the Sonnet's scanty plot of ground;
Pleased if some Souls (for such there needs must be)
Who have felt the weight of too much liberty,
Should find brief solace there, as I have found.

1807

My Heart Leaps Up

My heart leaps up when I behold
    A rainbow in the sky:
So was it when my life began;
So is it now I am a man;
5   So be it when I shall grow old,
    Or let me die!
The Child is father of the Man;
And I could wish my days to be
Bound each to each by natural piety.

1807

9. Mountains in the English Lake District.

Ode

INTIMATIONS OF IMMORTALITY FROM
RECOLLECTIONS OF EARLY CHILDHOOD

The Child is father of the Man;
And I could wish my days to be
Bound each to each by natural piety.[1]

1

There was a time when meadow, grove, and stream,
The earth, and every common sight,
    To me did seem
    Appareled in celestial light,
5 The glory and the freshness of a dream.
It is not now as it hath been of yore—
    Turn whereso'er I may,
      By night or day,
The things which I have seen I now can see no more.

2

10   The Rainbow comes and goes,
      And lovely is the Rose,
      The Moon doth with delight
Look round her when the heavens are bare,
      Waters on a starry night
15   Are beautiful and fair;
  The sunshine is a glorious birth;
  But yet I know, where'er I go,
That there hath passed away a glory from the earth.

3

Now, while the birds thus sing a joyous song,
20   And while the young lambs bound
     As to the tabor's sound,[2]
To me alone there came a thought of grief:
A timely utterance gave that thought relief,
    And I again am strong:
25 The cataracts blow their trumpets from the steep;
No more shall grief of mine the season wrong;
I hear the Echoes through the mountains throng,
The Winds come to me from the fields of sleep,
    And all the earth is gay;
30   Land and sea
   Give themselves up to jollity,
    And with the heart of May
  Doth every Beast keep holiday—
    Thou Child of Joy,
35 Shout round me, let me hear thy shouts, thou happy Shepherd-boy!

4

Ye blessèd Creatures, I have heard the call
  Ye to each other make; I see
The heavens laugh with you in your jubilee;
40   My heart is at your festival,
    My head hath its coronal,
The fullness of your bliss, I feel—I feel it all.
    Oh, evil day! if I were sullen

1. Final lines of Wordsworth's *My Heart Leaps Up*. 2. "Tabor": a small drum.

While Earth herself is adorning,
45   This sweet May morning,
And the Children are culling
        On every side,
In a thousand valleys far and wide,
Fresh flowers; while the sun shines warm,
50 And the Babe leaps up on his Mother's arm—
        I hear, I hear, with joy I hear!
—But there's a Tree, of many, one,
A single Field which I have looked upon,
Both of them speak of something that is gone:
55   The Pansy at my feet
        Doth the same tale repeat:
Whither is fled the visionary gleam?
Where is it now, the glory and the dream?

                5
Our birth is but a sleep and a forgetting:
60 The Soul that rises with us, our life's Star,
        Hath had elsewhere its setting,
        And cometh from afar:
        Not in entire forgetfulness,
        And not in utter nakedness,
65 But trailing clouds of glory do we come
From God, who is our home:
Heaven lies about us in our infancy!
Shades of the prison-house begin to close
        Upon the growing Boy
70   But he
Beholds the light, and whence it flows,
        He sees it in his joy;
The Youth, who daily farther from the east
        Must travel, still is Nature's Priest,
75   And by the vision splendid
        Is on his way attended;
At length the Man perceives it die away,
And fade into the light of common day.
                6
Earth fills her lap with pleasures of her own;
80 Yearnings she hath in her own natural kind,
And, even with something of a Mother's mind,
        And no unworthy aim,
        The homely° Nurse doth all she can   *simple, kindly*
To make her foster child, her Inmate Man,
85   Forget the glories he hath known,
And that imperial palace whence he came.
                7
Behold the Child among his newborn blisses,
A six-years' Darling of a pygmy size!
See, where 'mid work of his own hand he lies,
90 Fretted° by sallies of his mother's kisses,   *vexed*
With light upon him from his father's eyes!
See, at his feet, some little plan or chart,
Some fragment from his dream of human life,
Shaped by himself with newly-learnèd art;
95   A wedding or a festival,
        A mourning or a funeral;
        And this hath now his heart,

And unto this he frames his song;
  Then will he fit his tongue
100 To dialogues of business, love, or strife;
  But it will not be long
  Ere this be thrown aside,
  And with new joy and pride
The little Actor cons another part;
105 Filling from time to time his "humorous stage"[3]
With all the Persons, down to palsied Age,
That Life brings with her in her equipage;
  As if his whole vocation
  Were endless imitation.
   8
110 Thou, whose exterior semblance doth belie
  Thy Soul's immensity;
Thou best Philosopher, who yet dost keep
Thy heritage, thou Eye among the blind,
That, deaf and silent, read'st the eternal deep,
115 Haunted forever by the eternal mind—
  Mighty Prophet! Seer blest!
  On whom those truths do rest,
Which we are toiling all our lives to find,
In darkness lost, the darkness of the grave;
120 Thou, over whom thy Immortality
Broods like the Day, a Master o'er a Slave,
A Presence which is not to be put by;
Thou little Child, yet glorious in the might
Of heaven-born freedom on thy being's height,
125 Why with such earnest pains dost thou provoke
The years to bring the inevitable yoke,
Thus blindly with thy blessedness at strife?
Full soon thy Soul shall have her earthly freight,
And custom lie upon thee with a weight,
130 Heavy as frost, and deep almost as life!
   9
  O joy! that in our embers
  Is something that doth live,
  That nature yet remembers
  What was so fugitive!
135 The thought of our past years in me doth breed
Perpetual benediction: not indeed
For that which is most worthy to be blest;
Delight and liberty, the simple creed
Of Childhood, whether busy or at rest,
140 With new-fledged hope still fluttering in his breast—
  Not for these I raise
  The song of thanks and praise;
  But for those obstinate questionings
  Of sense and outward things,
145   Fallings from us, vanishings;
  Blank misgivings of a Creature
Moving about in worlds not realized,
High instincts before which our mortal Nature
Did tremble like a guilty Thing surprised;
150   But for those first affections,

3. I.e., playing the parts of characters with various temperaments, called "humors" by Elizabethan poets and playwrights.

Those shadowy recollections,
Which, be they what they may,
Are yet the fountain light of all our day,
Are yet a master light of all our seeing;
155   Uphold us, cherish, and have power to make
Our noisy years seem moments in the being
Of the eternal Silence: truths that wake,
To perish never;
Which neither listlessness, nor mad endeavor,
160   Nor Man nor Boy,
Nor all that is at enmity with joy,
Can utterly abolish or destroy!
Hence in a season of calm weather
Though inland far we be,
165 Our Souls have sight of that immortal sea
Which brought us hither,
Can in a moment travel thither,
And see the Children sport upon the shore,
And hear the mighty waters rolling evermore.
                10
170 Then sing, ye Birds, sing, sing a joyous song!
And let the young Lambs bound
As to the tabor's sound!
We in thought will join your throng,
Ye that pipe and ye that play,
175   Ye that through your hearts today
Feel the gladness of the May!
What though the radiance which was once so bright
Be now forever taken from my sight,
Though nothing can bring back the hour
180 Of splendor in the grass, of glory in the flower;
We will grieve not, rather find
Strength in what remains behind;
In the primal sympathy
Which having been must ever be;
185   In the soothing thoughts that spring
Out of human suffering;
In the faith that looks through death,
In years that bring the philosophic mind.
                11
And O, ye Fountains, Meadows, Hills, and Groves,
190 Forebode not any severing of our loves!
Yet in my heart of hearts I feel your might;
I only have relinquished one delight
To live beneath your more habitual sway.
I love the Brooks which down their channels fret,
195 Even more than when I tripped lightly as they;
The innocent brightness of a newborn Day
Is lovely yet;
The clouds that gather round the setting sun
Do take a sober coloring from an eye
200 That hath kept watch o'er man's mortality;
Another race hath been, and other palms° are won.   *symbols of victory*
Thanks to the human heart by which we live,
Thanks to its tenderness, its joys, and fears,
To me the meanest° flower that blows° can give   *most ordinary / blooms*
205 Thoughts that do often lie too deep for tears.

1802–4   1807

Ode to Duty

Jam non consilio bonus, sed more eo perductus, ut non tantum recte facere possim, sed nisi recte facere non possim.

—SENECA[4]

Stern Daughter of the Voice of God!
O Duty! if that name thou love
Who are a light to guide, a rod
To check the erring, and reprove;
5   Thou, who art victory and law
When empty terrors overawe;
From vain temptations dost set free;
And calm'st the weary strife of frail humanity!

There are who ask not if thine eye
10 Be on them; who, in love and truth,
Where no misgiving is, rely
Upon the genial sense[5] of youth:
Glad Hearts! without reproach or blot;
Who do thy work, and know it not:
15 Oh! if through confidence misplaced
They fail, thy saving arms, dread Power! around them cast.

Serene will be our days and bright,
And happy will our nature be,
When love is an unerring light,
20 And joy its own security.
And they a blissful course may hold
Even now, who, not unwisely bold,
Live in the spirit of this creed;
Yet seek thy firm support, according to their need.

25 I, loving freedom, and untried,
No sport of every random gust,
Yet being to myself a guide,
Too blindly have reposed my trust;
And oft, when in my heart was heard
30 Thy timely mandate, I deferred
The task, in smoother walks to stray;
But thee I now would serve more strictly, if I may.

Through no disturbance of my soul,
Or strong compunction° in me wrought,   *remorse*
35 I supplicate for thy control;
But in the quietness of thought:
Me this unchartered freedom tires;
I feel the weight of chance desires:
My hopes no more must change their name,
40 I long for a repose that ever is the same.

Stern Lawgiver! yet thou dost wear
The Godhead's most benignant grace;
Nor know we anything so fair
As is the smile upon thy face:

4. From the Roman philosopher and dramatist's *Moral Epistles* (CXX.10): "Now am I good not by taking thought but urged on by habit, to this effect: not so much can I act rightly as other than rightly I cannot act."
5. Generous impulse; innate good nature.

45   Flowers laugh before thee on their beds
      And fragrance in thy footing treads;
      Thou dost preserve the stars from wrong
      And the most ancient heavens, through thee, are fresh and strong.

50   To humbler functions, awful Power!
      I call thee: I myself commend
      Unto thy guidance from this hour;
      Oh, let my weakness have an end!
      Give unto me, made lowly wise,
      The spirit of self-sacrifice;
55   The confidence of reason give;
      And in the light of truth thy Bondman let me live!

                                                              1807

I Wandered Lonely As a Cloud

      I wandered lonely as a cloud
      That floats on high o'er vales and hills,
      When all at once I saw a crowd,
      A host, of golden daffodils;
5   Beside the lake, beneath the trees,
      Fluttering and dancing in the breeze.

      Continuous as the stars that shine
      And twinkle on the milky way,
      They stretched in never-ending line
10   Along the margin of a bay:
      Ten thousand saw I at a glance,
      Tossing their heads in sprightly dance.

      The waves beside them danced; but they
      Outdid the sparkling waves in glee;
15   A poet could not but be gay,
      In such a jocund° company;   *cheerful*
      I gazed—and gazed—but little thought
      What wealth the show to me had brought:

      For oft, when on my couch I lie
20   In vacant or in pensive mood,
      They flash upon that inward eye
      Which is the bliss of solitude;
      And then my heart with pleasure fills,
      And dances with the daffodils.

                                                              1807

Elegiac Stanzas[6]

**SUGGESTED BY A PICTURE OF PEELE CASTLE, IN A STORM, PAINTED BY
SIR GEORGE BEAUMONT**

      I was thy neighbor once, thou rugged Pile!
      Four summer weeks I dwelt in sight of thee:
      I saw thee every day; and all the while
      Thy Form was sleeping on a glassy sea.

---

6. In memory of the poet's brother, John, who had recently died in a shipwreck (see lines 36–39).

5   So pure the sky, so quiet was the air!
      So like, so very like, was day to day!
      Whene'er I looked, thy Image still was there;
      It trembled, but it never passed away.

      How perfect was the calm! it seemed no sleep;
10   No mood, which season takes away, or brings:
      I could have fancied that the mighty Deep
      Was even the gentlest of all gentle Things.

      Ah! THEN, if mine had been the Painter's hand,
      To express what then I saw; and add the gleam,
15   The light that never was, on sea or land,
      The consecration, and the Poet's dream;

      I would have planted thee, thou hoary Pile
      Amid a world how different from this!
      Beside a sea that could not cease to smile;
20   On tranquil land, beneath a sky of bliss.

      Thou shouldst have seemed a treasure house divine
      O peaceful years; a chronicle of heaven—
      Of all the sunbeams that did ever shine
      The very sweetest had to thee been given.

25   A Picture had it been of lasting ease,
      Elysian[7] quiet, without toil or strife;
      No motion but the moving tide, a breeze,
      Or merely silent Nature's breathing life.

      Such, in the fond illusion of my heart,
30   Such Picture would I at that time have made,
      And seen the soul of truth in every part,
      A steadfast peace that might not be betrayed.

      So once it would have been—'tis so no more;
      I have submitted to a new control:
35   A power is gone, which nothing can restore;
      A deep distress hath humanized my Soul.

      Not for a moment could I now behold
      A smiling sea, and be what I have been:
      The feeling of my loss will ne'er be old;
40   This, which I know, I speak with mind serene.

      Then, Beaumont, Friend! who would have been the Friend,
      If he had lived, of him whom I deplore,°   *lament*
      This work of thine I blame not, but commend;
      This sea in anger, and that dismal shore.

45   O 'tis a passionate Work!—yet wise and well,
      Well chosen is the spirit that is here;
      That Hulk which labors in the deadly swell,
      This rueful sky, this pageantry of fear!

---

7. In Greek myth the souls of the blest dwelt in the Elysian Fields.

And this huge Castle, standing here sublime,
50 I love to see the look with which it braves,
Cased in the unfeeling armor of old time,
The lightning, the fierce wind, and trampling waves.

Farewell, farewell the heart that lives alone,
Housed in a dream, at distance from the Kind!°   *mankind*
55 Such happiness, wherever it be known,
Is to be pitied; for 'tis surely blind.

But welcome fortitude, and patient cheer,
And frequent sights of what is to be borne!
Such sights, or worse, as are before me here.
60 Not without hope we suffer and we mourn.

1807

The World Is Too Much with Us

The world is too much with us; late and soon,
Getting and spending, we lay waste our powers;
Little we see in Nature that is ours;
We have given our hearts away, a sordid boon!°   *gift*
5   This Sea that bares her bosom to the moon,
The winds that will be howling at all hours,
And are up-gathered now like sleeping flowers,
For this, for everything, we are out of tune;
It moves us not.—Great God! I'd rather be
10 A Pagan suckled in a creed outworn;
So might I, standing on this pleasant lea,
Have glimpses that would make me less forlorn;
Have sight of Proteus rising from the sea;
Or hear old Triton blow his wreathéd horn.8

1807

The Solitary Reaper

Behold her, single in the field,
Yon solitary Highland Lass!
Reaping and singing by herself;
Stop here, or gently pass!
5   Alone she cuts and binds the grain,
And sings a melancholy strain;
O listen! for the Vale profound
Is overflowing with the sound.

No Nightingale did ever chaunt
10 More welcome notes to weary bands
Of travelers in some shady haunt,
Among Arabian sands;

8. In Greek myth Proteus, the "Old Man of the Sea," rises from the sea at midday and can be forced to read the future by anyone who holds him while he takes many frightening shapes. Triton is the son of the sea-god Neptune; the sound of his conch-shell horn calms the waves.

A voice so thrilling ne'er was heard
In springtime from the Cuckoo bird,
15 Breaking the silence of the seas
Among the farthest Hebrides.

Will no one tell me what she sings?—
Perhaps the plaintive numbers flow
For old, unhappy, far-off things,
20 And battles long ago;
Or is it some more humble lay,
Familiar matter of today?
Some natural sorrow, loss, or pain,
That has been, and may be again?

25 Whate'er the theme, the Maiden sang
As if her song could have no ending;
I saw her singing at her work,
And o'er the sickle bending—
I listened, motionless and still;
30 And, as I mounted up the hill,
The music in my heart I bore,
Long after it was heard no more.

1807

Surprised by Joy

Surprised by joy—impatient as the Wind
I turned to share the transport—Oh! with whom
But thee,[9] deep buried in the silent tomb,
That spot which no vicissitude can find?
5 Love, faithful love, recalled thee to my mind—
But how could I forget thee? Through what power,
Even for the least division of an hour,
Have I been so beguiled as to be blind
To my most grievous loss!—That thought's return
10 Was the worst pang that sorrow ever bore,
Save one, one only, when I stood forlorn,
Knowing my heart's best treasure was no more;
That neither present time, nor years unborn
Could to my sight that heavenly face restore.

1815

Mutability

From low to high doth dissolution climb,
And sink from high to low, along a scale
Of awful notes, whose concord shall not fail;
A musical but melancholy chime,
5 Which they can hear who meddle not with crime,
Nor avarice, nor over-anxious care.

9. The poet's daughter Catharine, who died at the age of four, in 1812.

Truth fails not; but her outward forms that bear
The longest date do melt like frosty rime,°   *thin coating*
That in the morning whitened hill and plain
10   And is no more; drop like the tower sublime
Of yesterday, which royally did wear
His crown of weeds, but could not even sustain
Some casual shout that broke the silent air,
Or the unimaginable touch of Time.

1822

Extempore Effusion upon the Death of James Hogg[1]

When first, descending from the moorlands,
I saw the Stream of Yarrow glide
Along a bare and open valley,
The Ettrick Shepherd was my guide.

5   When last along its banks I wandered,
Through groves that had begun to shed
Their golden leaves upon the pathways,
My steps the Border-minstrel[2] led.

The mighty Minstrel breathes no longer,
10   'Mid moldering ruins low he lies;
And death upon the braes° of Yarrow,   *banks*
Has closed the Shepherd-poet's eyes:

Nor has the rolling year twice measured,
From sign to sign, its steadfast course,
15   Since every mortal power of Coleridge[3]
Was frozen at its marvelous source;

The rapt One,[4] of the godlike forehead,
The heaven-eyed creature sleeps in earth:
And Lamb,[5] the frolic and the gentle,
20   Has vanished from his lonely hearth.

Like clouds that rake the mountain summits,
Or waves that own no curbing hand,
How fast has brother followed brother,
From sunshine to the sunless land!

25   Yet I, whose lids from infant slumber
Were earlier raised, remain to hear
A timid voice, that asks in whispers,
"Who next will drop and disappear?"

Our haughty life is crowned with darkness,
30   Like London with its own black wreath,
On which with thee, O Crabbe![6] forth-looking,
I gazed from Hampstead's breezy heath.

1. Scottish poet (1770–1835) born in Ettrick;
for a time he was a shepherd. An *extempore
effusion* is a poem composed rapidly, without
premeditation.
2. Sir Walter Scott, famous Scottish poet and
novelist (1771–1832).
3. Wordsworth's friend and collaborator, who
died in 1834.
4. Coleridge (alluding to his "mystical"
philosophy).
5. Charles Lamb (1775–1834), essayist and
critic, friend of Wordsworth and Coleridge.
6. George Crabbe (1754–1832), poet, acquaint-
ance of Wordsworth.

As if but yesterday departed,
Thou too art gone before; but why,
35 O'er ripe fruit, seasonably gathered,
Should frail survivors heave a sigh?

Mourn rather for that holy Spirit,
Sweet as the spring, as ocean deep;
For her[7] who, ere her summer faded,
40 Has sunk into a breathless sleep.

No more of old romantic sorrows,
For slaughtered Youth or lovelorn Maid!
With sharper grief is Yarrow smitten,
And Ettrick mourns with her their Poet dead.

1835

So Fair, So Sweet, Withal So Sensitive

So fair, so sweet, withal so sensitive,
Would that the little Flowers were born to live,
Conscious of half the pleasure which they give;

That to this mountain-daisy's self were known
5 The beauty of its star-shaped shadow, thrown
On the smooth surface of this naked stone!

And what if hence a bold desire should mount
High as the Sun, that he could take account
Of all that issues from his glorious fount!

10 So might he ken how by his sovereign aid
These delicate companionships are made;
And how he rules the pomp of light and shade;

And were the Sister-power that shines by night
So privileged, what a countenance of delight
15 Would through the clouds break forth on human sight!

Fond fancies! wheresoe'er shall turn thine eye
On earth, air, ocean, or the starry sky,
Converse with Nature in pure sympathy;

All vain desires, all lawless wishes quelled,
20 Be Thou to love and praise alike impelled,
Whatever boon° is granted or withheld.

gift
1845

7. Felicia Hemans (1793–1835), popular poetess, noted for her beauty and conversation.

SAMUEL TAYLOR COLERIDGE
(1772–1834)

Kubla Khan[1]

OR A VISION IN A DREAM. A FRAGMENT

In Xanadu did Kubla Khan
A stately pleasure dome decree:
Where Alph, the sacred river, ran
Through caverns measureless to man
5   Down to a sunless sea.
So twice five miles of fertile ground
With walls and towers were girdled round:
And there were gardens bright with sinuous rills,
Where blossomed many an incense-bearing tree;
10 And here were forests ancient as the hills,
Enfolding sunny spots of greenery.

But oh! that deep romantic chasm which slanted
Down the green hill athwart a cedarn cover!
A savage place! as holy and enchanted
15 As e'er beneath a waning moon was haunted
By woman wailing for her demon lover!
And from this chasm, with ceaseless turmoil seething,
As if this earth in fast thick pants were breathing,
A mighty fountain momently was forced:
20 Amid whose swift half-intermitted burst
Huge fragments vaulted like rebounding hail,
Or chaffy grain beneath the thresher's flail:
And 'mid these dancing rocks at once and ever
It flung up momently the sacred river.
25 Five miles meandering with a mazy motion
Through wood and dale the sacred river ran,
Then reached the caverns measureless to man,
And sank in tumult to a lifeless ocean:
And 'mid this tumult Kubla heard from far
30 Ancestral voices prophesying war!

1. The first *khan*, or ruler, of the Mongol dynasty in 13th-century China. The topography and place-names are fictitious. In a prefatory note to the poem, Coleridge gave the following background: "In the summer of the year 1797, the author, then in ill health, had retired to a lonely farmhouse between Porlock and Linton, on the Exmoor confines of Somerset and Devonshire. In consequence of a slight indisposition, an anodyne had been prescribed, from the effects of which he fell asleep in his chair at the moment that he was reading the following sentence, or words of the same substance, in *Purchas's Pilgrimage:* "Here the Khan Kubla commanded a palace to be built, and a stately garden thereunto. And thus ten miles of fertile ground were inclosed with a wall." The author continued for about three hours in a profound sleep, at least of the external sense, during which time he has the most vivid confidence that he could not have composed less than from two to three hundred lines; if that indeed can be called composition in which all the images rose up before him as *things,* with a parallel production of the correspondent expressions, without any sensation or consciousness of effort. On awaking he appeared to himself to have a distinct recollection of the whole, and taking his pen, ink, and paper, instantly and eagerly wrote down the lines that are here preserved. At this moment he was unfortunately called out by a person on business from Porlock, and detained by him above an hour, and on his return to his room, found, to his no small surprise and mortification, that though he still retained some vague and dim recollection of the general purport of the vision, yet, with the exception of some eight or ten scattered lines and images, all the rest had passed away like the images on the surface of a stream into which a stone has been cast, but, alas! without the after restoration of the latter!"

The shadow of the dome of pleasure
Floated midway on the waves;
Where was heard the mingled measure
From the fountain and the caves.
35 It was a miracle of rare device,
A sunny pleasure dome with caves of ice!

A damsel with a dulcimer[2]
In a vision once I saw:
It was an Abyssinian maid,
40 And on her dulcimer she played,
Singing of Mount Abora.
Could I revive within me
Her symphony and song,
To such a deep delight 'twould win me,
45 That with music loud and long,
I would build that dome in air,
That sunny dome! those caves of ice!
And all who heard should see them there,
And all should cry, Beware! Beware!
50 His flashing eyes, his floating hair!
Weave a circle round him thrice,
And close your eyes with holy dread,
For he on honey-dew hath fed,
And drunk the milk of Paradise.

1797–98   1816

Frost at Midnight

The Frost performs its secret ministry,
Unhelped by any wind. The owlet's cry
Came loud—and hark, again! loud as before.
The inmates of my cottage, all at rest,
5 Have left me to that solitude, which suits
Abstruser musings: save that at my side
My cradled infant[3] slumbers peacefully.
'Tis calm indeed! so calm, that it disturbs
And vexes meditation with its strange
10 And extreme silentness. Sea, hill, and wood,
This populous village! Sea, and hill, and wood,
With all the numberless goings-on of life,
Inaudible as dreams! the thin blue flame
Lies on my low-burnt fire, and quivers not;
15 Only that film,[4] which fluttered on the grate,
Still flutters there, the sole unquiet thing.
Methinks its motion in this hush of nature
Gives it dim sympathies with me who live,
Making it a companionable form,
20 Whose puny flaps and freaks the idling Spirit
By its own moods interprets, everywhere
Echo or mirror seeking of itself,
And makes a toy of Thought.

2. A harp-like instrument.
3. Coleridge's son Hartley.
4. Embers flickering in the grate of a fire-place; in folklore said to forecast the arrival of an unexpected guest; hence called *strangers* (lines 26, 41).

But O! how oft,
How oft, at school, with most believing mind,
25 Presageful,° have I gazed upon the bars,   *foretelling*
To watch that fluttering *stranger!* and as oft
With unclosed lids, already had I dreamt
Of my sweet birthplace, and the old church tower,
Whose bells, the poor man's only music, rang
30 From morn to evening, all the hot Fair-day,[5]
So sweetly, that they stirred and haunted me
With a wild pleasure, falling on mine ear
Most like articulate sounds of things to come!
So gazed I, till the soothing things, I dreamt,
35 Lulled me to sleep, and sleep prolonged my dreams!
And so I brooded all the following morn,
Awed by the stern preceptor's° face, mine eye   *schoolmaster's*
Fixed with mock study on my swimming book:[6]
Save if the door half opened, and I snatched
40 A hasty glance, and still my heart leaped up,
For still I hoped to see the *stranger's* face,
Townsman, or aunt, or sister more beloved,
My playmate when we both were clothed alike![7]

Dear Babe, that sleepest cradled by my side,
45 Whose gentle breathings, heard in this deep calm,
Fill up the interspersèd vacancies
And momentary pauses of the thought!
My babe so beautiful! it thrills my heart
With tender gladness, thus to look at thee,
50 And think that thou shalt learn far other lore,
And in far other scenes! For I was reared
In the great city, pent 'mid cloisters dim,
And saw nought lovely but the sky and stars.
But *thou,* my babe! shalt wander like a breeze
55 By lakes and sandy shores, beneath the crags
Of ancient mountain, and beneath the clouds,
Which image in their bulk both lakes and shores
And mountain crags: so shalt thou see and hear
The lovely shapes and sounds intelligible
60 Of that eternal language, which thy God
Utters, who from eternity doth teach
Himself in all, and all things in himself.
Great universal Teacher! he shall mold
Thy spirit, and by giving make it ask.

65 Therefore all seasons shall be sweet to thee,
Whether the summer clothe the general° earth   *generative, vernal*
With greenness, or the redbreast sit and sing
Betwixt the tufts of snow on the bare branch
Of mossy apple tree, while the nigh thatch
70 Smokes in the sun-thaw; whether the eave-drops fall
Heard only in the trances of the blast,
Or if the secret ministry of frost
Shall hang them up in silent icicles,
Quietly shining to the quiet Moon.

1798

---

5. Market-day, often a time of festivities.
6. I.e., seen unclearly because of emotion.

7. In early childhood, when boys and girls
wore the same kind of infants' clothing.

The Rime of the Ancient Mariner

IN SEVEN PARTS

Facile credo, plures esse Naturas invisibles quam visibiles in rerum universitate. Sed horum [sic] omnium familiam quis nobis enarrabit? et gradus et cognationes et discrimina et singulorum munera? Quid agunt? quae loca habitant? Harum rerum notitiam semper ambivit ingenium humanum, nunquam attigit. Juvat, interea, non diffiteor, quandoque in animo, in tabulâ, majoris et melioris mundi imaginem contemplari: ne mens assuefacta hodiernae vitae minutiis se contrahat nimis, et tota subsidat in pusillas cogitationes. Sed veritati interea invigilandum est, modusque servandus, ut certa ab incertis, diem a nocte, distinguamus.

—T. BURNET[8]

Part I

An ancient Mariner meeteth three Gallants bidden to a wedding feast, and detaineth one.	It is an ancient Mariner And he stoppeth one of three. —"By thy long gray beard and glittering eye, Now wherefore stopp'st thou me?

The Bridegroom's doors are opened wide,   5
And I am next of kin;
The guests are met, the feast is set:
May'st hear the merry din."

He holds him with his skinny hand,
"There was a ship," quoth he.   10
"Hold off! unhand me, graybeard loon!"
Eftsoons° his hand dropped he.   *straightway*

The Wedding Guest is spellbound by the eye of the old seafaring man, and constrained to hear his tale.	He holds him with his glittering eye— The Wedding Guest stood still, 15 And listens like a three years' child: The Mariner hath his will.

The Wedding Guest sat on a stone:
He cannot choose but hear;
And thus spake on that ancient man,
The bright-eyed Mariner.   20

"The ship was cheered, the harbor cleared,
Merrily did we drop
Below the kirk,° below the hill,   *church*

The Mariner tells how the ship sailed southward with a good wind and fair weather, till it reached the line.	Below the lighthouse top. The Sun came up upon the left, 25 Out of the sea came he! And he shone bright, and on the right Went down into the sea.

Higher and higher every day,
Till over the mast at noon—"   30
The Wedding Guest here beat his breast,
For he heard the loud bassoon.

8. From *Archaeologiae Philosophiae*, p. 68. "I can easily believe that there are more invisible than visible beings in the universe. But of their families, degrees, connections, distinctions, and functions, who shall tell us? How do they act? Where are they found? About such matters the human mind has always circled without attaining knowledge. Yet I do not doubt that sometimes it is well for the soul to contemplate as in a picture the image of a larger and better world, lest the mind, habituated to the small concerns of daily life, limit itself too much and sink entirely into trivial thinking. But meanwhile we must be on watch for the truth, avoiding extremes, so that we may distinguish certain from uncertain, day from night." Burnet was a 17th-century English theologian.

*The Wedding
Guest heareth
the bridal music;
but the Mariner
continueth his
tale.*
The bride hath paced into the hall,
Red as a rose is she;
Nodding their heads before her goes   35
The merry minstrelsy.

The Wedding Guest he beat his breast,
Yet he cannot choose but hear;
And thus spake on that ancient man,
The bright-eyed Mariner.   40

*The ship driven
by a storm to-
ward the South
Pole.*
"And now the STORM-BLAST came, and he
Was tyrannous and strong;
He struck with his o'ertaking wings,
And chased us south along.

With sloping masts and dipping prow,   45
As who pursued with yell and blow
Still treads the shadow of his foe,
And forward bends his head,
The ship drove fast, loud roared the blast,
And southward aye we fled.   50

And now there came both mist and snow,
And it grew wondrous cold:
And ice, mast-high, came floating by,
As green as emerald.

*The land of ice,
and of fearful
sounds where no
living thing was
to be seen.*
And through the drifts the snowy clifts°   cliffs 55
Did send a dismal sheen:
Nor shapes of men nor beasts we ken—
The ice was all between.

The ice was here, the ice was there,
The ice was all around: 60
It cracked and growled, and roared and howled,
Like noises in a swound!°   swoon

*Till a great sea
bird, called the
Albatross, came
through the
snow-fog, and
was received
with great joy
and hospitality.*
At length did cross an Albatross,
Thorough the fog it came;
As if it had been a Christian soul,   65
We hailed it in God's name.

It ate the food it ne'er had eat,
And round and round it flew.
The ice did split with a thunder-fit;
The helmsman steered us through!   70

*And lo! the Al-
batross proveth
a bird of good
omen, and fol-
loweth the ship
as it returned
northward
through fog and
floating ice.*
And a good south wind sprung up behind;
The Albatross did follow,
And every day, for food or play,
Came to the mariners' hollo!

In mist or cloud, on mast or shroud,   75
It perched for vespers nine;
Whiles all the night, through fog-smoke white,
Glimmered the white Moon-shine."

The ancient
Mariner inhospi-
tably killeth the
pious bird of
good omen.

"God save thee, ancient Mariner!
From the fiends, that plague thee thus!—
Why look'st thou so?"—With my crossbow
I shot the ALBATROSS.   80

Part II

The Sun now rose upon the right:
Out of the sea came he,
Still hid in mist, and on the left   85
Went down into the sea.

And the good south wind still blew behind,
But no sweet bird did follow,
Nor any day for food or play
Came to the mariners' hollo!   90

His shipmates
cry out against
the ancient Mar-
iner, for killing
the bird of good
luck.

And I had done a hellish thing,
And it would work 'em woe:
For all averred, I had killed the bird
That made the breeze to blow.
Ah wretch! said they, the bird to slay,   95
That made the breeze to blow!

But when the
fog cleared off,
they justify the
same, and thus
make themselves
accomplices in
the crime.

Nor dim nor red, like God's own head,
The glorious Sun uprist:°   *arose*
Then all averred, I had killed the bird
That brought the fog and mist.   100
'Twas right, said they, such birds to slay,
That bring the fog and mist.

The fair breeze
continues; the
ship enters the
Pacific Ocean,
and sails north-
ward, even till it
reaches the Line.

The fair breeze blew, the white foam flew,
The furrow followed free;
We were the first that ever burst   105
Into that silent sea.

The ship hath
been suddenly
becalmed.

Down dropped the breeze, the sails dropped down,
'Twas sad as sad could be;
And we did speak only to break
The silence of the sea!   110

All in a hot and copper sky,
The bloody Sun, at noon,
Right up above the mast did stand,
No bigger than the Moon.

Day after day, day after day,   115
We stuck, nor breath nor motion;
As idle as a painted ship
Upon a painted ocean.

And the Alba-
tross begins to
be avenged.

Water, water, everywhere,
And all the boards did shrink;   120
Water, water, everywhere,
Nor any drop to drink.

The very deep did rot: O Christ!
That ever this should be!
Yea, slimy things did crawl with legs   125
Upon the slimy sea.

About, about, in reel and rout
The death-fires danced at night;
The water, like a witch's oils,
Burnt green, and blue and white.   130

And some in dreams assuréd were

A Spirit had   Of the Spirit that plagued us so;
followed them;   Nine fathom deep he had followed us
one of the invis- From the land of mist and snow.
ible inhabitants
of this planet,
neither departed souls nor angels; concerning whom the learned Jew, Josephus, and the Platonic Con-
stantinopolitan, Michael Psellus, may be consulted. They are very numerous, and there is no climate
or element without one or more.

And every tongue, through utter drought,   135
Was withered at the root;
We could not speak, no more than if
We had been choked with soot.

The shipmates,   Ah! well-a-day! what evil looks
in their sore dis- Had I from old and young!   140
tress, would fain Instead of the cross, the Albatross
throw the whole About my neck was hung.
guilt on the an-
cient Mariner:
in sign whereof they hang the dead sea bird round his neck.

Part III

There passed a weary time. Each throat
Was parched, and glazed each eye.
A weary time! a weary time!   145
How glazed each weary eye,
The ancient Mar- When looking westward, I beheld
iner beholdeth a A something in the sky.
sign in the ele-
ment afar off.

At first it seemed a little speck,
And then it seemed a mist;
It moved and moved, and took at last   150
A certain shape, I wist.°   *knew*

A speck, a mist, a shape, I wist!
And still it neared and neared:
As if it dodged a water sprite,   155
It plunged and tacked and veered.

At its nearer ap- With throats unslaked, with black lips baked,
proach, it seem- We could nor laugh nor wail;
eth him to be a Through utter drought all dumb we stood!
ship; and at a   I bit my arm, I sucked the blood,   160
dear ransom he   And cried, A sail! a sail!
freeth his speech
from the bonds
of thirst.

With throats unslaked, with black lips baked,
Agape they heard me call:
A flash of joy; Gramercy!° they for joy did grin,   *thank heavens!*
And all at once their breath drew in,   165
As they were drinking all.

And horror fol-
lows. For can it
be a ship that
comes onward
without wind or
tide?

See! see! (I cried) she tacks no more!
Hither to work us weal;°   benefit
Without a breeze, without a tide,
She steadies with upright keel!   170

The western wave was all aflame.
The day was well nigh done!
Almost upon the western wave
Rested the broad bright Sun;
When that strange shape drove suddenly   175
Betwixt us and the Sun.

It seemeth him
but the skeleton
of a ship.

And straight the Sun was flecked with bars,
(Heaven's Mother send us grace!)
As if through a dungeon grate he peered
With broad and burning face.   180

And its ribs are
seen as bars on
the face of the
setting Sun.

Alas! (thought I, and my heart beat loud)
How fast she nears and nears!
Are those *her* sails that glance in the Sun,
Like restless gossameres?

The Specter-
Woman and her
Deathmate, and
no other on
board the skele-
ton ship.

Are those *her* ribs through which the Sun   185
Did peer, as through a grate?
And is that Woman all her crew?
Is that a DEATH? and are there two?
Is DEATH that woman's mate?

Like vessel, like
crew!

Her lips were red, *her* looks were free,   190
Her locks were yellow as gold:
Her skin was as white as leprosy,
The Nightmare LIFE-IN-DEATH was she,
Who thicks man's blood with cold.

Death and Life-
in-Death have
diced for the
ship's crew, and
she (the latter)
winneth the an-
cient Mariner.

The naked hulk alongside came,   195
And the twain were casting dice;
"The game is done! I've won! I've won!"
Quoth she, and whistles thrice.

No twilight
within the courts
of the Sun.

The Sun's rim dips; the stars rush out:
At one stride comes the dark;   200
With far-heard whisper, o'er the sea,
Off shot the specter-bark.

At the rising of
the Moon,

We listened and looked sideways up!
Fear at my heart, as at a cup,
My lifeblood seems to sip!   205
The stars were dim, and thick the night,
The steersman's face by his lamp gleamed white;
From the sails the dew did drip—
Till clomb above the eastern bar
The hornéd Moon, with one bright star   210
Within the nether tip.

One after an-
other,

One after one, by the star-dogged Moon,
Too quick for groan or sigh,
Each turned his face with ghastly pang,
And cursed me with his eye.   215

His shipmates
drop down dead.

Four times fifty living men,
(And I heard nor sigh nor groan)
With heavy thump, a lifeless lump,
They dropped down one by one.

But Life-in-
Death begins her
work on the an-
cient Mariner.

The souls did from their bodies fly—   220
They fled to bliss or woe!
And every soul, it passed me by,
Like the whizz of my cross-bow!

Part IV

The Wedding
Guest feareth
that a Spirit is
talking to him;

"I fear thee, ancient Mariner!
I fear thy skinny hand!   225
And thou art long, and lank, and brown,
As is the ribbed sea-sand.

I fear thee and thy glittering eye,
And thy skinny hand, so brown."—

But the ancient
Mariner assureth
him of his bodily
life, and pro-
ceedeth to relate
his horrible pen-
ance.

Fear not, fear not, thou Wedding Guest!   230
This body dropped not down.

Alone, alone, all, all alone,
Alone on a wide wide sea!
And never a saint took pity on
My soul in agony.   235

He despiseth the
creatures of the
calm,

The many men, so beautiful!
And they all dead did lie:
And a thousand thousand slimy things
Lived on; and so did I.

And envieth that
they should live,
and so many lie
dead.

I looked upon the rotting sea,   240
And drew my eyes away;
I looked upon the rotting deck,
And there the dead men lay.

I looked to heaven, and tried to pray;
But or ever a prayer had gushed,   245
A wicked whisper came, and made
My heart as dry as dust.

I closed my lids, and kept them close,
And the balls like pulses beat,
For the sky and the sea, and the sea and the sky   250
Lay like a load on my weary eye,
And the dead were at my feet.

But the curse
liveth for him in
the eye of the
dead men.

The cold sweat melted from their limbs,
Nor rot nor reek did they:
The look with which they looked on me   255
Had never passed away.

An orphan's curse would drag to hell
A spirit from on high;
But oh! more horrible than that
Is the curse in a dead man's eye!   260
Seven days, seven nights, I saw that curse,
And yet I could not die.

The moving Moon went up the sky,
And nowhere did abide:
In his loneliness Softly she was going up,   265
and fixedness he And a star or two beside—
yearneth towards
the journeying
Moon, and the Her beams bemocked the sultry main,
stars that still Like April hoar-frost spread;
sojourn, yet still But where the ship's huge shadow lay,
move onward; The charmèd water burnt alway   270
and everywhere A still and awful red.
the blue sky be-
longs to them,
and is their ap-
pointed rest, and
their native
country and their own natural homes, which they enter unannounced, as lords that are certainly
expected and yet there is a silent joy at their arrival.

By the light of Beyond the shadow of the ship,
the Moon he be- I watched the water snakes:
holdeth God's They moved in tracks of shining white,
creatures of the And when they reared, the elfish light   275
great calm. Fell off in hoary° flakes.   *gray or white*

Within the shadow of the ship
I watched their rich attire:
Blue, glossy green, and velvet black,
They coiled and swam; and every track   280
Was a flash of golden fire.

Their beauty and O happy living things! no tongue
their happiness. Their beauty might declare:
A spring of love gushed from my heart,
He blesseth them And I blessed them unaware: 285
in his heart. Sure my kind saint took pity on me,
And I blessed them unaware.

The spell begins The self-same moment I could pray;
to break. And from my neck so free
The Albatross fell off, and sank   290
Like lead into the sea.

Part V

Oh sleep! it is a gentle thing,
Beloved from pole to pole!
To Mary Queen the praise be given!
She sent the gentle sleep from Heaven,   295
That slid into my soul.

By grace of the The silly° buckets on the deck,   *lowly, harmless*
holy Mother, the That had so long remained,
ancient Mariner I dreamt that they were filled with dew;
is refreshed with And when I awoke, it rained.   300
rain.

My lips were wet, my throat was cold,
My garments all were dank;
Sure I had drunken in my dreams,
And still my body drank.

I moved, and could not feel my limbs: 305
I was so light—almost
I thought that I had died in sleep,
And was a blessèd ghost.

*He heareth
sounds and seeth
strange sights
and commotions
in the sky and
the element.*
And soon I heard a roaring wind: 310
It did not come anear;
But with its sound it shook the sails,
That were so thin and sere.

The upper air burst into life!
And a hundred fire-flags sheen,°   *shone*
To and fro they were hurried about!   315
And to and fro, and in and out,
The wan stars danced between.

And the coming wind did roar more loud,
And the sails did sigh like sedge;[9]
And the rain poured down from one black cloud;   320
The Moon was at its edge.

The thick black cloud was cleft, and still
The Moon was at its side:
Like waters shot from some high crag,
The lightning fell with never a jag,   325
A river steep and wide.

*The bodies of
the ship's crew
are inspirited,
and the ship
moves on;*
The loud wind never reached the ship,
Yet now the ship moved on!
Beneath the lightning and the Moon
The dead men gave a groan.   330

They groaned, they stirred, they all uprose,
Nor spake, nor moved their eyes;
It had been strange, even in a dream,
To have seen those dead men rise.

The helmsman steered, the ship moved on;   335
Yet never a breeze up-blew;
The mariners all 'gan work the ropes,
Where they were wont to do;
They raised their limbs like lifeless tools—
We were a ghastly crew.   340

The body of my brother's son
Stood by me, knee to knèe:
The body and I pulled at one rope,
But he said nought to me.

9. Rushlike plants bordering streams and lakes.

But not by the souls of the men, nor by demons of earth or middle air, but by a blessèd troop of angelic spirits, sent down by the invocation of the guardian saint.

"I fear thee, ancient Mariner!"   345
Be calm, thou Wedding Guest!
'Twas not those souls that fled in pain,
Which to their corses° came again,   *corpses*
But a troop of spirits blest:

For when it dawned—they dropped their arms,   350
And clustered round the mast;
Sweet sounds rose slowly through their mouths,
And from their bodies passed.

Around, around, flew each sweet sound,
Then darted to the Sun;   355
Slowly the sounds came back again,
Now mixed, now one by one.

Sometimes a-dropping from the sky
I heard the sky-lark sing;
Sometimes all little birds that are,   360
How they seemed to fill the sea and air
With their sweet jargoning!°   *warbling*

And now 'twas like all instruments,
Now like a lonely flute;
And now it is an angel's song,   365
That makes the heavens be mute.

It ceased; yet still the sails made on
A pleasant noise till noon,
A noise like of a hidden brook
In the leafy month of June,   370
That to the sleeping woods all night
Singeth a quiet tune.

Till noon we quietly sailed on,
Yet never a breeze did breathe:
Slowly and smoothly went the ship,   375
Moved onward from beneath.

The lonesome Spirit from the South Pole carries on the ship as far as the Line, in obedience to the angelic troop, but still requireth vengeance.

Under the keel nine fathom deep,
From the land of mist and snow,
The spirit slid: and it was he
That made the ship to go.   380
The sails at noon left off their tune,
And the ship stood still also.

The Sun, right up above the mast,
Had fixed her to the ocean:
But in a minute she 'gan stir,   385
With a short uneasy motion—
Backwards and forwards half her length
With a short uneasy motion.

Then like a pawing horse let go,
She made a sudden bound:
It flung the blood into my head, 390
And I fell down in a swound.

The Polar Spirit's fellow demons, the invisible inhabitants of the element, take part in his wrong; and two of them relate, one to the other, that penance long and heavy for the ancient Mariner hath been accorded to the Polar Spirit, who returneth southward.

How long in that same fit I lay,
I have not° to declare;   cannot
But ere my living life returned, 395
I heard and in my soul discerned
Two voices in the air.

"Is it he?" quoth one, "Is this the man?
By him who died on cross,
With his cruel bow he laid full low 400
The harmless Albatross.

The spirit who bideth by himself
In the land of mist and snow,
He loved the bird that loved the man
Who shot him with his bow." 405

The other was a softer voice,
As soft as honey-dew:
Quoth he, "The man hath penance done,
And penance more will do."

Part VI

FIRST VOICE

"But tell me, tell me! speak again, 410
Thy soft response renewing—
What makes that ship drive on so fast?
What is the ocean doing?"

SECOND VOICE

"Still as a slave before his lord,
The ocean hath no blast;
His great bright eye most silently 415
Up to the Moon is cast—

If he may know which way to go;
For she guides him smooth or grim.
See, brother, see! how graciously 420
She looketh down on him."

FIRST VOICE

The Mariner hath been cast into a trance; for the angelic power causeth the vessel to drive northward faster than human life could endure.

"But why drives on that ship so fast,
Without or wave or wind?"

SECOND VOICE

"The air is cut away before,
And closes from behind. 425

Fly, brother, fly! more high, more high!
Or we shall be belated:
For slow and slow that ship will go,
When the Mariner's trance is abated."

The supernatural motion is retarded; the Mariner awakes, and his penance begins anew.

I woke, and we were sailing on　430
As in a gentle weather:
'Twas night, calm night, the moon was high;
The dead men stood together.

All stood together on the deck,
For a charnel-dungeon fitter:　435
All fixed on me their stony eyes,
That in the Moon did glitter.

The pang, the curse, with which they died,
Had never passed away:
I could not draw my eyes from theirs,　440
Nor turn them up to pray.

The curse is finally expiated.

And now this spell was snapped: once more
I viewed the ocean green,
And looked far forth, yet little saw
Of what had else been seen—　445

Like one, that on a lonesome road
Doth walk in fear and dread,
And having once turned round walks on,
And turns no more his head;
Because he knows, a frightful fiend　450
Doth close behind him tread.

But soon there breathed a wind on me,
Nor sound nor motion made:
Its path was not upon the sea,
In ripple or in shade.　455

It raised my hair, it fanned my cheek
Like a meadow-gale of spring—
It mingled strangely with my fears,
Yet it felt like a welcoming.

Swiftly, swiftly flew the ship,　460
Yet she sailed softly too:
Sweetly, sweetly blew the breeze—
On me alone it blew.

And the ancient Mariner beholdeth his native country.

Oh! dream of joy! is this indeed
The lighthouse top I see?　465
Is this the hill? is this the kirk?
Is this mine own countree?

We drifted o'er the harbor-bar,
And I with sobs did pray—
O let me be awake, my God!　470
Or let me sleep alway.

The harbor-bay was clear as glass,
So smoothly it was strewn!
And on the bay the moonlight lay,
And the shadow of the Moon.　475

The rock shone bright, the kirk no less,
That stands above the rock:
The moonlight steeped in silentness
The steady weathercock.

And the bay was white with silent light,   480
Till rising from the same,
Full many shapes, that shadows were,
In crimson colors came.

The angelic spirits leave the dead bodies,

A little distance from the prow
Those crimson shadows were: 485
I turned my eyes upon the deck—
Oh, Christ! what saw I there!

And appear in their own forms of light.

Each corse lay flat, lifeless and flat,
And, by the holy rood!°   *cross of Christ*
A man all light, a seraph°-man,   *angel-like* 490
On every corse there stood.

This seraph-band, each waved his hand:
It was a heavenly sight!
They stood as signals to the land,
Each one a lovely light;   495

This seraph-band, each waved his hand,
No voice did they impart—
No voice; but oh! the silence sank
Like music on my heart.

But soon I heard the dash of oars,   500
I heard the Pilot's cheer;
My head was turned perforce away
And I saw a boat appear.

The Pilot and the Pilot's boy,
I heard them coming fast: 505
Dear Lord in Heaven! it was a joy
The dead men could not blast.

I saw a third—I heard his voice:
It is the Hermit good!
He singeth loud his godly hymns   510
That he makes in the wood.
He'll shrieve[1] my soul, he'll wash away
The Albatross's blood.

Part VII

The Hermit of the Wood

This Hermit good lives in that wood
Which slopes down to the sea.   515
How loudly his sweet voice he rears!
He loves to talk with marineres
That come from a far countree.

---

1. Set free from sin.

He kneels at morn, and noon, and eve—
He hath a cushion plump:
It is the moss that wholly hides
The rotted old oak stump.   520

The skiff-boat neared: I heard them talk,
"Why, this is strange, I trow!
Where are those lights so many and fair,   525
That signal made but now?"

Approacheth the ship with wonder.

"Strange, by my faith!" the Hermit said—
"And they answered not our cheer!
The planks looked warped! and see those sails,
How thin they are and sere!   530
I never saw aught like to them,
Unless perchance it were

Brown skeletons of leaves that lag
My forest-brook along;
When the ivy tod° is heavy with snow,   *bushy clump* 535
And the owlet whoops to the wolf below,
That eats the she-wolf's young."

"Dear Lord! it hath a fiendish look,"
The Pilot made reply,
"I am a-feared"—"Push on, push on!"   540
Said the Hermit cheerily.

The boat came closer to the ship,
But I nor spake nor stirred;
The boat came close beneath the ship,
And straight a sound was heard.   545

The ship suddenly sinketh.

Under the water it rumbled on,
Still louder and more dread:
It reached the ship, it split the bay;
The ship went down like lead.

The ancient Mariner is saved in the Pilot's boat.

Stunned by that loud and dreadful sound,   550
Which sky and ocean smote,
Like one that hath been seven days drowned
My body lay afloat;
But swift as dreams, myself I found
Within the Pilot's boat.   555

Upon the whirl, where sank the ship,
The boat spun round and round;
And all was still, save that the hill
Was telling of the sound.

I moved my lips—the Pilot shrieked   560
And fell down in a fit;
The holy Hermit raised his eyes,
And prayed where he did sit.

I took the oars: the Pilot's boy,
Who now doth crazy go,
Laughed loud and long, and all the while
His eyes went to and fro.
"Ha! ha!" quoth he, "full plain I see,
The Devil knows how to row."

And now, all in my own countree,
I stood on the firm land!
The Hermit stepped forth from the boat,
And scarcely he could stand.

The ancient
Mariner ear-
nestly entreateth
the Hermit to
shrieve him; and
the penance of
life falls on him.

"O shrieve me, shrieve me, holy man!"
The Hermit crossed[2] his brow.
"Say quick," quoth he, "I bid thee say—
What manner of man art thou?"

Forthwith this frame of mine was wrenched
With a woeful agony,
Which forced me to begin my tale;
And then it left me free.

And ever and
anon throughout
his future life
an agony con-
straineth him to
travel from
land to land;

Since then, at an uncertain hour,
That agony returns:
And till my ghastly tale is told,
This heart within me burns.

I pass, like night, from land to land;
I have strange power of speech;
That moment that his face I see,
I know the man that must hear me:
To him my tale I teach.

What loud uproar bursts from that door!
The wedding guests are there:
But in the garden-bower the bride
And bridemaids singing are:
And hark the little vesper bell,
Which biddeth me to prayer!

O Wedding Guest! this soul hath been
Alone on a wide wide sea:
So lonely 'twas, that God himself
Scarce seeméd there to be.

O sweeter than the marriage feast,
'Tis sweeter far to me,
To walk together to the kirk
With a goodly company!

To walk together to the kirk,
And all together pray,
While each to his great Father bends,
Old men, and babes, and loving friends
And youths and maidens gay!

2. Made the sign of the cross upon.

*And to teach, by
his own exam-
ple, love and
reverence to all
things that God
made and loveth.*

Farewell, farewell! but this I tell   610
To thee, thou Wedding Guest!
He prayeth well, who loveth well
Both man and bird and beast.

He prayeth best, who loveth best
All things both great and small;   615
For the dear God who loveth us,
He made and loveth all.

The Mariner, whose eye is bright,
Whose beard with age is hoar,
Is gone: and now the Wedding Guest   620
Turned from the bridegroom's door.

He went like one that hath been stunned,
And is of sense forlorn:°   *deprived*
A sadder and a wiser man,
He rose the morrow morn.

1798   1817

Dejection: An Ode

Late, late yestreen I saw the new Moon,
With the old Moon in her arms;
And I fear, I fear, my master dear!
We shall have a deadly storm.
Ballad of Sir Patrick Spence

1

Well! If the bard was weather-wise, who made
   The grand old ballad of Sir Patrick Spence,
   This night, so tranquil now, will not go hence
Unroused by winds, that ply a busier trade
5 Than those which mold yon cloud in lazy flakes,
Or the dull sobbing draft, that moans and rakes
Upon the strings of this Aeolian lute,[3]
     Which better far were mute.
   For lo! the New-moon winter-bright!
10   And overspread with phantom light,
   (With swimming phantom light o'erspread
   But rimmed and circled by a silver thread)
I see the old Moon in her lap, foretelling
   The coming-on of rain and squally blast.
15 And oh! that even now the gust were swelling,
   And the slant night shower driving loud and fast!
Those sounds which oft have raised me, whilst they awed,
     And sent my soul abroad,
Might now perhaps their wonted° impulse give,   *usual*
20 Might startle this dull pain, and make it move and live!

2

A grief without a pang, void, dark, and drear,
   A stifled, drowsy, unimpassioned grief,
   Which finds no natural outlet, no relief,
     In word, or sigh, or tear—
25 O Lady! in this wan and heartless mood,

---

3. The wind-harp (named after Aeolus, classi-
cal god of winds) has a sounding board
equipped with a set of strings that vibrate in
response to air currents.

To other thoughts by yonder throstle wooed,
　All this long eve, so balmy and serene,
Have I been gazing on the western sky,
　And its peculiar tint of yellow green:
30 And still I gaze—and with how blank an eye!
And those thin clouds above, in flakes and bars,
That give away their motion to the stars;
Those stars, that glide behind them or between,
Now sparkling, now bedimmed, but always seen:
35 Yon crescent Moon, as fixed as if it grew
In its own cloudless, starless lake of blue;
I see them all so excellently fair,
I see, not feel, how beautiful they are!

3

　　My genial spirits° fail;   *vital energies*
40 　　And what can these avail
To lift the smothering weight from off my breast?
　　It were a vain endeavor,
　　Though I should gaze forever
On that green light that lingers in the west:
45 I may not hope from outward forms to win
The passion and the life, whose fountains are within.

4

O Lady! we receive but what we give,
And in our life alone does Nature live:
Ours is her wedding garment, ours her shroud!
50 　And would we aught behold, of higher worth,
Than that inanimate cold world allowed
To the poor loveless ever-anxious crowd,
　Ah! from the soul itself must issue forth
A light, a glory, a fair luminous cloud
55 　Enveloping the Earth—
And from the soul itself must there be sent
　A sweet and potent voice, of its own birth,
Of all sweet sounds the life and element!

5

O pure of heart! thou need'st not ask of me
60 What this strong music in the soul may be!
What, and wherein it doth exist,
This light, this glory, this fair luminous mist,
This beautiful and beauty-making power.
　Joy, virtuous Lady! Joy that ne'er was given,
65 Save to the pure, and in their purest hour,
Life, and Life's effluence, cloud at once and shower,
Joy, Lady! is the spirit and the power,
Which wedding Nature to us gives in dower
　A new Earth and new Heaven,
70 Undreamt of by the sensual and the proud—
Joy is the sweet voice, Joy the luminous cloud—
　　We in ourselves rejoice!
And thence flows all that charms or ear or sight,
　All melodies the echoes of that voice,
75 All colors a suffusion from that light.

6

There was a time when, though my path was rough,
　This joy within me dallied with distress,
And all misfortunes were but as the stuff

Whence Fancy made me dreams of happiness:
80   For hope grew round me, like the twining vine,
And fruits, and foliage, not my own, seemed mine.
But now afflictions bow me down to earth:
Nor care I that they rob me of my mirth;
       But oh! each visitation
85   Suspends what nature gave me at my birth,
       My shaping spirit of Imagination.

For not to think of what I needs must feel,
       But to be still and patient, all I can;
And happly by abstruse research to steal
90   From my own nature all the natural man—
This was my sole resource, my only plan:
Till that which suits a part infects the whole,
And now is almost grown the habit of my soul.

                    7
Hence, viper thoughts, that coil around my mind,
95   Reality's dark dream!
I turn from you, and listen to the wind,
       Which long has raved unnoticed. What a scream
Of agony by torture lengthened out
That lute sent forth! Thou Wind, that rav'st without,
100   Bare crag, or mountain tairn,° or blasted tree,   *pool*
Or pine grove whither woodman never clomb,
Or lonely house, long held—the witches' home,
       Methinks were fitter instruments for thee,
Mad lutanist! who in this month of showers,
105 Of dark-brown gardens, and of peeping flowers,
Mak'st devils' yule,[4] with worse than wintry song,
The blossoms, buds, and timorous leaves among.
       Thou actor, perfect in all tragic sounds!
Thou mighty poet, e'en to frenzy bold!
110   What tell'st thou now about?
       'Tis of the rushing of an host in rout,
With groans, of trampled men, with smarting wounds—
At once they groan with pain, and shudder with the cold!
But hush! there is a pause of deepest silence!
115 And all that noise, as of a rushing crowd,
With groans, and tremulous shudderings—all is over—
       It tells another tale, with sounds less deep and loud!
              A tale of less affright,
              And tempered with delight,
120 As Otway's[5] self had framed the tender lay—
              'Tis of a little child
              Upon a lonesome wild,
Not far from home, but she hath lost her way:
And now moans low in bitter grief and fear,
125 And now screams loud, and hopes to make her mother hear.
                    8
'Tis midnight, but small thoughts have I of sleep:
Full seldom may my friend such vigils keep!
Visit her, gentle Sleep! with wings of healing,
       And may this storm be but a mountain birth,

---

4. A winter storm in spring; hence, an unnatu-
ral or "devils'" Christmas.

5. A 17th-century English dramatist, noted for
his power to evoke pathos.

130   May all the stars hang bright above her dwelling,
        Silent as though they watched the sleeping Earth!
          With light heart may she rise,
          Gay fancy, cheerful eyes,
          Joy lift her spirit, joy attune her voice;
135   To her may all things live, from pole to pole,
        Their life the eddying of her living soul!
          O simple spirit, guided from above,
        Dear Lady! friend devoutest of my choice,
        Thus mayest thou ever, evermore rejoice.

                                        1802   1817

WALTER SAVAGE LANDOR
(1775–1864)

Rose Aylmer[1]

Ah what avails the sceptered race,
    Ah what the form divine!
What every virtue, every grace!
    Rose Aylmer, all were thine.
5   Rose Aylmer, whom these wakeful eyes
        May weep, but never see,
    A night of memories and of sighs
        I consecrate to thee.

                                        1806, 1831, 1846

Mild Is the Parting Year, and Sweet

Mild is the parting year, and sweet
    The odor of the falling spray;
Life passes on more rudely fleet,
    And balmless is its closing day.

5   I wait its close, I court its gloom,
        But mourn that never must there fall
    Or on my breast or on my tomb
        The tear that would have soothed it all.

                                        1831, 1846

Past Ruined Ilion Helen[2] Lives

Past ruined Ilion Helen lives,
    Alcestis[3] rises from the shades;
Verse calls them forth; 'tis verse that gives
    Immortal youth to mortal maids.

5   Soon shall Oblivion's deepening veil
        Hide all the peopled hills you see,
    The gay, the proud, while lovers hail
        In distant ages you and me.

---

1. The Honorable Rose Whitworth Aylmer (1779–1800), whom Landor had known in Wales, died suddenly in Calcutta on March 2, 1800.
2. Helen of Troy ("Ilion").

3. Alcestis sacrificed her life for her husband, who was stricken with a mortal illness. She acted in accordance with Apollo's promise that he might thus be saved; she was then brought back from the underworld by Hercules.

10   The tear for fading beauty check,
     For passing glory cease to sigh;
  One form shall rise above the wreck,
     One name, Ianthe, shall not die.

1831

Dirce

Stand close around, ye Stygian set,[4]
    With Dirce in one boat conveyed!
Or Charon, seeing may forget
    That he is old and she a shade.

1831, 1846

To My Child Carlino[5]

*They are verses written by a gentleman who resided long in this country,
and who much regretted the necessity of leaving it.*
—BOCCACCIO

Carlino! what art thou about, my boy?
Often I ask that question, though in vain;
For we are far apart: ah! therefore 'tis
I often ask it; not in such a tone
5 As wiser fathers do, who know too well.
Were we not children, you and I together?
Stole we not glances from each other's eyes?
Swore we not secrecy in such misdeeds?
Well could we trust each other. Tell me, then,
10 What thou art doing. Carving out thy name,
Or haply mine, upon my favorite seat,
With the new knife I sent thee oversea?
Or hast thou broken it, and hid the hilt
Among the myrtles, starred with flowers, behind?
15 Or under that high throne whence fifty lilies
(With sworded tuberoses dense around)
Lift up their heads at once . . . not without fear
That they were looking at thee all the while?
    Does Cincirillo follow thee about?
20 Inverting one swart foot suspensively,
And wagging his dread jaw, at every chirp
Of bird above him on the olive-branch?
Frighten him then away! 'twas he who slew
Our pigeons, our white pigeons, peacock-tailed,
25 That feared not you and me . . . alas, nor him!
I flattened his striped sides along my knee,
And reasoned with him on his bloody mind,
Till he looked blandly, and half-closed his eyes
To ponder on my lecture in the shade.
30 I doubt his memory much, his heart a little,
And in some minor matters (may I say it?)
Could wish him rather sager. But from thee
God hold back wisdom yet for many years!
Whether in early season or in late
35 It always comes high priced. For thy pure breast
I have no lesson; it for me has many.

---

4. The shades of the dead who were ferried by
Charon over the river Styx to Hades.
5. The poem is addressed to Charles Savage

Landor (1825–1917), youngest of Landor's
three sons, at a time when Landor was in
England and the three boys were in Italy.

Come, throw it open then! What sports, what cares
(Since there are none too young for these) engage
Thy busy thoughts? Are you again at work,
40 Walter[6] and you, with those sly laborers,
Geppo, Giovanni, Cecco, and Poeta,
To build more solidly your broken dam
Among the poplars, whence the nightingale
Inquisitively watched you all day long?
45 I was not of your council in the scheme,
Or might have saved you silver without end,
And sighs too without number. Art thou gone
Below the mulberry, where that cold pool
Urged to devise a warmer, and more fit
50 For mighty swimmers, swimming three abreast?
Or art thou panting in this summer noon
Upon the lowest step before the hall,
Drawing a slice of watermelon, long
As Cupid's bow, athwart thy wetted lips
(Like one who plays Pan's pipe) and letting drop
The sable seeds from all their separate cells,
And leaving bays profound and rocks abrupt,
Redder than coral round Calypso's[7] cave?

1837   1846

Dying Speech of an Old Philosopher

I strove with none, for none was worth my strife:
 Nature I loved, and, next to Nature, Art:
I warmed both hands before the fire of Life;
 It sinks; and I am ready to depart.

1849

GEORGE GORDON, LORD BYRON
(1788–1824)

Written After Swimming from Sestos to Abydos[1]

1

If, in the month of dark December,
 Leander, who was nightly wont
(What maid will not the tale remember?)
 To cross thy stream, broad Hellespont!

2

5 If, when the wintry tempest roared,
 He sped to Hero, nothing loath,
And thus of old thy current poured,
 Fair Venus! how I pity both!

3

For *me*, degenerate modern wretch,
10 Though in the genial month of May,
My dripping limbs I faintly stretch,
 And think I've done a feat today.

6. Walter Savage Landor (1822–99), the poet's second son.
7. The nymph or goddess who welcomed Odysseus in her island, Ogygia, after the wreck of his ship, and held him there for seven years.

1. The Hellespont, or Dardanelles, is the strait separating Europe from Asia Minor, between Abydos on the Greek shore and Sestos on the Asian. In Greek legend, Leander used to swim from Abydos to visit his sweetheart Hero at Sestos.

4

But since he crossed the rapid tide,
   According to the doubtful story,
15 To woo—and—Lord knows what beside,
   And swam for Love, as I for Glory;

5

'Twere hard to say who fared the best:
   Sad mortals! thus the gods still plague you!
He lost his labor, I my jest;
   For he was drowned, and I've the ague.°

               chills and fever
               1812

The Destruction of Sennacherib[2]

1

The Assyrian came down like the wolf on the fold,
And his cohorts were gleaming in purple and gold;
And the sheen of their spears was like stars on the sea,
When the blue wave rolls nightly on deep Galilee.

2

5 Like the leaves of the forest when summer is green,
That host with their banners at sunset were seen:
Like the leaves of the forest when autumn hath blown,
That host on the morrow lay withered and strown.

3

10 For the Angel of Death spread his wings on the blast,
And breathed in the face of the foe as he passed;
And the eyes of the sleepers waxed deadly and chill,
And their hearts but once heaved, and forever grew still!

4

And there lay the steed with his nostril all wide,
But through it there rolled not the breath of his pride;
15 And the foam of his gasping lay white on the turf,
And cold as the spray of the rock-beating surf.

5

And there lay the rider distorted and pale,
With the dew on his brow, and the rust on his mail:
And the tents wer all silent, the banners alone,
20 The lances unlifted, the trumpet unblown.

6

And the widows of Ashur[3] are loud in their wail,
And the idols are broke in the temple of Baal;[4]
And the might of the Gentile,[5] unsmote by the sword,
Hath melted like snow in the glance of the Lord!

               1815

She Walks in Beauty

1

She walks in beauty, like the night
   Of cloudless climes and starry skies;
And all that's best of dark and bright
   Meet in her aspect and her eyes:
5 Thus mellowed to that tender light
   Which heaven to gaudy day denies.

2. Assyrian king, whose armies, while besieg-   3. Assyria.
ing Jerusalem (701 B.C.), were attacked by a   4. Deity of the Assyrians.
violent plague (II Kings xix.35).   5. Here, Sennacherib; anyone not a Hebrew.

2

One shade the more, one ray the less,
   Had half impaired the nameless grace
Which waves in every raven tress,
10   Or softly lightens o'er her face;
Where thoughts serenely sweet express
   How pure, how dear their dwelling place.

3

And on that cheek, and o'er that brow,
   So soft, so calm, yet eloquent,
15 The smiles that win, the tints that glow,
   But tell of days in goodness spent,
A mind at peace with all below,
A heart whose love is innocent!

1815

Prometheus

Titan! [1] to whose immortal eyes
   The sufferings of mortality,
   Seen in their sad reality,
Were not as things that gods despise;
5 What was thy pity's recompense?
A silent suffering, and intense;
The rock, the vulture, and the chain,
All that the proud can feel of pain,
The agony they do not show,
10 The suffocating sense of woe,
   Which speaks but in its loneliness,
And then is jealous lest the sky
Should have a listener, nor will sigh
   Until its voice is echoless.

15 Titan! to thee the strife was given
   Between the suffering and the will,
   Which torture where they cannot kill;
And the inexorable heaven,
And the deaf tyranny of fate,
20 The ruling principle of hate,
Which for its pleasure doth create
The things it may annihilate,
Refused thee even the boon to die:
The wretched gift eternity
25 Was thine—and thou hast borne it well.
All that the Thunderer wrung from thee
Was but the menace which flung back
On him the torments of thy rack;
The fate thou didst so well foresee,
30 But would not to appease him tell;
And in thy silence [2] was his sentence,
And in his soul a vain repentance,
And evil dread so ill dissembled,
That in his hand the lightnings trembled.

---

1. An ancient Greek deity who stole fire from the heavens and gave it to mankind. His punishment, imposed by Jove ("the Thunderer," line 26) was to be chained to a cliff and torn by vultures so long as he defied Jove.
2. Prometheus knew but would not reveal the secret of Jove's eventual downfall.

35   Thy godlike crime was to be kind,
     To render with thy precepts less
     The sum of human wretchedness,
  And strengthen man with his own mind;
  But baffled as thou wert from high,
40   Still in thy patient energy,
  In the endurance, and repulse
     Of thine impenetrable spirit,
  Which earth and heaven could not convulse,
     A mighty lesson we inherit:
45   Thou art a symbol and a sign
     To mortals of their fate and force;
  Like thee, man is in part divine,
     A troubled stream from a pure source;
  And Man in portions can foresee
50   His own funereal destiny;
  His wretchedness, and his resistance,
  And his sad unallied existence;
  To which his spirit may oppose
  Itself—and equal to all woes,
55   And a firm will, and a deep sense,
  Which even in torture can descry
     Its own concentered recompense,
  Triumphant where it dares defy,
  And making death a victory.

1816

So We'll Go No More A-Roving

1
So we'll go no more a-roving
  So late into the night,
Though the heart be still as loving,
  And the moon be still as bright.

2
5 For the sword outwears its sheath,
  And the soul wears out the breast,
And the heart must pause to breathe,
  And Love itself have rest.

3
Though the night was made for loving,
10   And the day returns too soon,
Yet we'll go no more a-roving
  By the light of the moon.

1817   1836

Stanzas

WHEN A MAN HATH NO FREEDOM TO FIGHT FOR AT HOME

When a man hath no freedom to fight for at home,
  Let him combat for that of his neighbors;
Let him think of the glories of Greece and of Rome,
  And get knocked on his head for his labors.

5   To do good to mankind is the chivalrous plan,
 And is always as nobly requited;
Then battle for freedom wherever you can,
 And, if not shot or hanged, you'll get knighted.

1824

On This Day I Complete My Thirty-sixth Year

Missolonghi,[7] January 22, 1824

'Tis time this heart should be unmoved,
 Since others it hath ceased to move:
Yet, though I cannot be beloved,
  Still let me love!

5   My days are in the yellow leaf;
 The flowers and fruits of love are gone;
The worm, the canker,° and the grief   *deep infection*
  Are mine alone!

The fire that on my bosom preys
10   Is lone as some volcanic isle;
No torch is kindled at its blaze—
  A funeral pile.

The hope, the fear, the jealous care,
 The exalted portion of the pain
15 And power of love, I cannot share,
  But wear the chain.

But 'tis not *thus*—and 'tis not *here*—
 Such thoughts should shake my soul, nor *now*,
Where glory decks the hero's bier,
20   Or binds his brow.

The sword, the banner, and the field,
 Glory and Greece, around me see!
The Spartan, borne upon his shield,
  Was not more free.

25 Awake! (not Greece—she *is* awake!)
 Awake, my spirit! Think through *whom*
Thy life-blood tracks its parent lake,
  And then strike home!

Tread those reviving passions down,
30   Unworthy manhood!—unto thee
Indifferent should the smile or frown
  Of beauty be.

If thou regrett'st thy youth, *why live?*
 The land of honorable death
35 Is here:—up to the field, and give
  Away thy breath!

7. In Greece, where Byron had gone to support the Greek war for independence from Turkey, and where he died, April 19, 1824.

Seek out—less often sought than found—
A soldier's grave, for thee the best;
Then look around, and choose thy ground,
40   And take thy rest.

                                        1824

PERCY BYSSHE SHELLEY
(1792–1822)

Hymn to Intellectual Beauty[1]

1

The awful shadow of some unseen Power
Floats though unseen among us—visiting
This various world with as inconstant wing
As summer winds that creep from flower to flower—
5 Like moonbeams that behind some piny mountain shower,
It visits with inconstant glance
Each human heart and countenance;
Like hues and harmonies of evening—
Like clouds in starlight widely spread—
10 Like memory of music fled—
Like aught that for its grace may be
Dear, and yet dearer for its mystery.

2

Spirit of BEAUTY, that dost consecrate
With thine own hues all thou dost shine upon
15 Of human thought or form—where art thou gone?
Why dost thou pass away and leave our state,
This dim vast vale of tears, vacant and desolate?
Ask why the sunlight not forever
Weaves rainbows o'er yon mountain river,
20 Why aught should fail and fade that once is shown,
Why fear and dream and death and birth
Cast on the daylight of this earth
Such gloom—why man has such a scope
For love and hate, despondency and hope?

3

25 No voice from some sublimer world hath ever
To sage or poet these responses given—
Therefore the names of Daemon, Ghost, and Heaven,
Remain the records of their vain endeavor,
Frail spells—whose uttered charm might not avail to sever,
30 From all we hear and all we see,
Doubt, chance, and mutability.
Thy light alone—like mist o'er mountains driven,
Or music by the night wind sent
Through strings of some still instrument,
35 Or moonlight on a midnight stream,
Gives grace and truth to life's unquiet dream.

---

1. Beauty perceived not by the senses but by spiritual illumination.

4

Love, Hope, and Self-esteem, like clouds depart
And come, for some uncertain moments lent.
Man were immortal, and omnipotent,
40 Didst thou, unknown and awful as thou art,
Keep with thy glorious train° firm state within his heart.   *company*
    Thou messenger of sympathies,
    That wax and wane in lovers' eyes—
Thou—that to human thought art nourishment,
45   Like darkness to a dying flame!
      Depart not as thy shadow came,
      Depart not—lest the grave should be,
Like life and fear, a dark reality.

5

While yet a boy I sought for ghosts, and sped
50   Through many a listening chamber, cave and ruin,
    And starlight wood, with fearful steps pursuing
Hopes of high talk with the departed dead.
I called on poisonous names² with which our youth is fed;
      I was not heard—I saw them not—
55   When musing deeply on the lot
Of life, at that sweet time when winds are wooing
      All vital things that wake to bring
      News of birds and blossoming—
Sudden, thy shadow fell on me;
60 I shrieked, and clasped my hands in ecstasy!

6

I vowed that I would dedicate my powers
    To thee and thine—have I not kept the vow?
    With beating heart and streaming eyes, even now
I call the phantoms of a thousand hours
65 Each from his voiceless grave: they have in visioned bowers
      Of studious zeal or love's delight
      Outwatched with me the envious night—
They know that never joy illumed my brow
      Unlinked with hope that thou wouldst free
70   This world from its dark slavery,
That thou—O awful Loveliness,
Wouldst give whate'er these words cannot express.

7

The day becomes more solemn and serene
    When noon is past—there is a harmony
75   In autumn, and a luster in its sky,
Which through the summer is not heard or seen,
As if it could not be, as if it had not been!
      Thus let thy power, which like the truth
      Of nature on my passive youth
80 Descended, to my onward life supply
      Its calm—to one who worships thee,
      And every form containing thee,
Whom, Spirit fair, thy spells did bind
To fear himself, and love all human kind.

                                                                            1817

---

2. Possibly alluding to attempts to summon spirits of the dead by means of magic rites.

Ozymandias[3]

I met a traveler from an antique land
Who said: Two vast and trunkless legs of stone
Stand in the desert . . . Near them, on the sand,
Half sunk, a shattered visage lies, whose frown,
5 And wrinkled lip, and sneer of cold command,
Tell that its sculptor well those passions read
Which yet survive, stamped on these lifeless things,
The hand that mocked them, and the heart that fed:
And on the pedestal these words appear:
10 "My name is Ozymandias, king of kings:
Look on my works, ye Mighty, and despair!"
Nothing beside remains. Round the decay
Of that colossal wreck, boundless and bare
The lone and level sands stretch far away.

1818

Stanzas Written in Dejection, Near Naples

1

The sun is warm, the sky is clear,
　The waves are dancing fast and bright,
Blue isles and snowy mountains wear
　The purple noon's transparent might,
5 　The breath of the moist earth is light,
Around its unexpanded buds;
　Like many a voice of one delight,
The winds, the birds, the ocean floods,
The City's voice itself is soft like Solitude's.

2

10 I see the Deep's untrampled floor
　With green and purple seaweeds strown;
I see the waves upon the shore,
　Like light dissolved in star-showers, thrown:
　I sit upon the sands alone—
15 The lightning of the noontide ocean
　Is flashing round me, and a tone
Arises from its measured motion;
How sweet! did any heart now share in my emotion.

3

20 Alas! I have nor hope nor health,
　Nor peace within nor calm around,
Nor that content surpassing wealth
　The sage in meditation found,
　And walked with inward glory crowned—
Nor fame, nor power, nor love, nor leisure.
25 　Others I see whom these surround—
Smiling they live, and call life pleasure;
To me that cup has been dealt in another measure.

4

Yet now despair itself is mild,
　Even as the winds and waters are;
30 I could lie down like a tired child,

3. Greek name for the Egyptian monarch Ramses II (13th century B.C.), who is said to have erected a huge statue of himself.

And weep away the life of care
Which I have borne and yet must bear,
Till death like sleep might steal on me,
And I might feel in the warm air
35 My cheek grow cold, and hear the sea
Breathe o'er my dying brain its last monotony.

5

Some might lament that I were cold,
    As I, when this sweet day is gone,
Which my lost heart, too soon grown old,
40   Insults with this untimely moan;
    They might lament—for I am one
Whom men love not—and yet regret,
    Unlike this day, which, when the sun
Shall on its stainless glory set,
Will linger, though enjoyed, like joy in memory yet.

                                        1818   1824

Ode to the West Wind

1

O wild West Wind, thou breath of Autumn's being,
Thou, from whose unseen presence the leaves dead
Are driven, like ghosts from an enchanter fleeing,

Yellow, and black, and pale, and hectic red,
5 Pestilence-stricken multitudes: O thou,
Who chariotest to their dark wintry bed

The wingéd seeds, where they lie cold and low,
Each like a corpse within its grave, until
Thine azure sister of the Spring shall blow

10 Her clarion[4] o'er the dreaming earth, and fill
(Driving sweet buds like flocks to feed in air)
With living hues and odors plain and hill:

Wild Spirit, which art moving everywhere;
Destroyer and preserver; hear, oh, hear!

2

15 Thou on whose stream, mid the steep sky's commotion,
Loose clouds like earth's decaying leaves are shed,
Shook from the tangled boughs of Heaven and Ocean,

Angels[5] of rain and lightning: there are spread
On the blue surface of thine aëry surge,
20 Like the bright hair uplifted from the head

Of some fierce Maenad,[6] even from the dim verge
Of the horizon to the zenith's height,
The locks of the approaching storm. Thou dirge

4. Melodious trumpet-call.
5. In Greek derivation, messengers or divine
messengers.

6. Frenzied dancer, worshipper of Dionysus,
a god of wine and fertility.

Of the dying year, to which this closing night
25 Will be the dome of a vast sepulcher,
Vaulted with all thy congregated might

Of vapors, from whose solid atmosphere
Black rain, and fire, and hail will burst: oh, hear!

3
Thou who didst waken from his summer dreams
30 The blue Mediterranean, where he lay,
Lulled by the coil of his crystálline streams,

Beside a pumice isle in Baiae's bay,[7]
And saw in sleep old palaces and towers
Quivering within the wave's intenser day,

35 All overgrown with azure moss and flowers
So sweet, the sense faints picturing them! Thou
For whose path the Atlantic's level powers

Cleave themselves into chasms, while far below
The sea-blooms and the oozy woods which wear
40 The sapless foliage of the ocean, know

Thy voice, and suddenly grow gray with fear,
And tremble and despoil themselves: oh, hear!

4
If I were a dead leaf thou mightest bear;
If I were a swift cloud to fly with thee;
45 A wave to pant beneath thy power, and share

The impulse of thy strength, only less free
Than thou, O uncontrollable! If even
I were as in my boyhood, and could be

The comrade of thy wanderings over Heaven,
50 As then, when to outstrip thy skyey speed
Scarce seem a vision; I would ne'er have striven

As thus with thee in prayer in my sore need.
Oh, lift me as a wave, a leaf, a cloud!
I fall upon the thorns of life! I bleed!

55 A heavy weight of hours has chained and bowed
One too like thee: tameless, and swift, and proud.

5
Make me thy lyre,[8] even as the forest is:
What if my leaves are falling like its own!
The tumult of thy mighty harmonies

60 Will take from both a deep, autumnal tone,
Sweet though in sadness. Be thou, Spirit fierce,
My spirit! Be thou me, impetuous one!

---

7. Near Naples, Italy.

8. Small harp traditionally used to accompany songs and recited poems.

Drive my dead thoughts over the universe
Like withered leaves to quicken a new birth!
65 And, by the incantation of this verse,

Scatter, as from an unextinguished hearth
Ashes and sparks, my words among mankind!
Be through my lips to unawakened earth

The trumpet of a prophecy! O Wind,
70 If Winter comes, can Spring be far behind?

1820

The Cloud

I bring fresh showers for the thirsting flowers,
    From the seas and the streams;
I bear light shade for the leaves when laid
    In their noonday dreams.
5 From my wings are shaken the dews that waken
        The sweet buds every one,
When rocked to rest on their mother's breast,
        As she dances about the sun.
I wield the flail of the lashing hail,
10   And whiten the green plains under,
And then again I dissolve it in rain,
        And laugh as I pass in thunder.

I sift the snow on the mountains below,
    And their great pines groan aghast;
15 And all the night 'tis my pillow white,
        While I sleep in the arms of the blast.
Sublime on the towers of my skyey bowers,
        Lightning my pilot⁹ sits;
In a cavern under is fettered the thunder,
20   It struggles and howls at fits;°   *intermittently*
Over earth and ocean, with gentle motion,
        This pilot is guiding me,
Lured by the love of the genii that move
        In the depths of the purple sea;
25 Over the rills, and the crags, and the hills,
        Over the lakes and the plains,
Wherever he dream, under mountain or stream,
        The Spirit he loves remains;
And I all the while bask in Heaven's blue smile,
30   Whilst he is dissolving in rains.

The sanguine Sunrise, with his meteor eyes,
        And his burning plumes outspread,
Leaps on the back of my sailing rack,[1]
        When the morning star shines dead;
35 As on the jag of a mountain crag,
        Which an earthquake rocks and swings,
An eagle alit one moment may sit
        In the light of its golden wings.

9. Electrical energy, here represented as direct-
ing the cloud in response to the attraction of

opposite charges ("genii," line 23) under the
sea.
1. Wind-driven clouds.

And when Sunset may breathe, from the lit sea beneath,
40   Its ardors of rest and of love,
And the crimson pall of eve may fall
      From the depth of Heaven above,
With wings folded I rest, on mine aëry nest,
      As still as a brooding dove.

45 That orbéd maiden with white fire laden,
      Whom mortals call the Moon,
Glides glimmering o'er my fleecelike floor,
      By the midnight breezes strewn;
And wherever the beat of her unseen feet,
50   Which only the angels hear,
May have broken the woof° of my tent's thin roof,   *fabric*
      The stars peep behind her and peer;
And I laugh to see them whirl and flee,
      Like a swarm of golden bees,
55 When I widen the rent in my wind-built tent,
      Till the calm rivers, lakes, and seas,
Like strips of the sky fallen through me on high,
      Are each paved with the moon and these.

60 I bind the Sun's throne with a burning zone,°   *belt*
      And the Moon's with a girdle of pearl;
The volcanoes are dim, and the stars reel and swim,
      When the whirlwinds my banner unfurl.
From cape to cape, with a bridgelike shape,
      Over a torrent sea,
65 Sunbeam-proof, I hang like a roof—
      The mountains its columns be.
The triumphal arch through which I march
      With hurricane, fire, and snow,
When the Powers of the air are chained to my chair,
70   Is the million-colored bow;
The sphere-fire above its soft colors wove,
      While the moist Earth was laughing below.

I am the daughter of Earth and Water,
      And the nursling of the Sky;
75 I pass through the pores of the ocean and shores;
      I change, but I cannot die.
For after the rain when with never a stain
      The pavilion of Heaven is bare,
And the winds and sunbeams with their convex° gleams   *upward-arching*
80   Build up the blue dome of air,
I silently laugh at my own cenotaph,[2]
      And out of the caverns of rain,
Like a child from the womb, like a ghost from the tomb,
      I arise and unbuild it again.

                                                      1820

---

2. Monument honoring a person who is buried elsewhere.

[This Is the Day] [1]

This is the day which down the void abysm
At the earth-born's spell yawns for heaven's despotism,[2]
   And conquest is dragged captive through the deep:
Love, from its awful throne of patient power
5 In the wise heart, from the last giddy hour
   Of dread endurance, from the slippery, steep,
And narrow verge of craglike agony, springs
And folds over the world its healing wings.

Gentleness, virtue, wisdom, and endurance,
10 These are the seals of that most firm assurance
   Which bars the pit over destruction's strength;
And if, with infirm hand, eternity,
Mother of many acts and hours, should free
   The serpent [3] that would clasp her with his length;
15 These are the spells by which to reassume
An empire o'er the disentangled doom:

To suffer woes which hope thinks infinite;
To forgive wrongs darker than death or night;
   To defy power, which seems omnipotent;
20 To love, and bear; to hope till hope creates
From its own wreck the thing it contemplates;
   Neither to change, nor falter, nor repent;
This, like thy glory, Titan,[4] is to be
Good, great and joyous, beautiful and free;
This is alone life, joy, empire, and victory.

1820

Adonais[3]

AN ELEGY ON THE DEATH OF JOHN KEATS, AUTHOR OF ENDYMION, HYPERION, ETC.

Ἀστὴρ πρὶν μὲν ἔλαμπες ἐνὶ ζωοῖσιν Ἐῷος·
νῦν δὲ θανὼν λάμπεις Ἔσπερος ἐν φθιμένοις.[4]

—PLATO

1

I weep for Adonais—he is dead!
Oh, weep for Adonais! though our tears
Thaw not the frost which binds so dear a head!
And thou, sad Hour, selected from all years
5 To mourn our loss, rouse thy obscure compeers,

1. The closing speech from Shelley's lyrical drama, *Prometheus Unbound.* Prometheus ("the earth-born," line 2) was an ancient Greek deity who stole fire from the heavens and gave it to mankind. His punishment, imposed by Jupiter, was to be chained to a cliff and torn by vultures so long as he defied Jupiter. Shelley's play relates the fall of Jupiter and the emancipation of Prometheus. This speech is spoken by Demogorgon, a personification of destiny. He is superior to the gods and an agent of liberty.
2. The rule of Jupiter.
3. Symbolizing the constructive power of tyranny.

4. Prometheus.
3. A name derived from *Adonis,* in Greek legend a young hunter beloved of Aphrodite (Venus) and killed by a wild boar. The root meaning of his name, *Adon,* is "the lord," and in the form *Adonai* appears in Hebrew scriptures as a synonym for *God.*
4. "Thou wert the morning star among the living,/Ere thy fair light had fled—/Now, having died, thou art as Hesperus, giving/New splendor to the dead" [Shelley's translation]; Venus is both Hesperus, the evening star, and also the morning star.

And teach them thine own sorrow, say: with me
Died Adonais; till the Future dares
Forget the Past, his fate and fame shall be
An echo and a light unto eternity!

2

10   Where wert thou mighty Mother,[5] when he lay,
When thy Son lay, pierced by the shaft which flies
In darkness? where was lorn Urania
When Adonais died? With veiléd eyes,
'Mid listening Echoes, in her Paradise
15   She sate, while one, with soft enamored breath,
Rekindled all the fading melodies,
With which, like flowers that mock the corse° beneath,   *corpse*
He had adorned and hid the coming bulk of death.

3

Oh, weep for Adonais—he is dead!
20   Wake, melancholy Mother, wake and weep!
Yet wherefore? Quench within their burning bed
Thy fiery tears, and let thy loud heart keep
Like his, a mute and uncomplaining sleep;
For he is gone, where all things wise and fair
25   Descend:—oh, dream not that the amorous Deep
Will yet restore him to the vital air;
Death feeds on his mute voice, and laughs at our despair.

4

Most musical of mourners, weep again!
Lament anew, Urania!—He[6] died,
30   Who was the Sire of an immortal strain,
Blind, old, and lonely, when his country's pride,
The priest, the slave, and the liberticide,
Trampled and mocked with many a loathéd rite
Of lust and blood; he went, unterrified,
35   Into the gulf of death; but his clear Sprite°   *spirit*
Yet reigns o'er earth; the third among the sons of light.[7]

5

Most musical of mourners, weep anew!
Not all to that bright station dared to climb;
And happier they their happiness who knew,
40   Whose tapers yet burn through that night of time
In which suns perished; others more sublime,
Struck by the envious wrath of man or God,
Have sunk, extinct in their refulgent prime;
And some yet live, treading the thorny road,
45   Which leads, through toil and hate, to Fame's serene abode.

6

But now, thy youngest, dearest one, has perished,
The nursling of thy widowhood, who grew,
Like a pale flower by some sad maiden cherished,
And fed with true-love tears, instead of dew;
50   Most musical of mourners, weep anew!
Thy extreme° hope, the loveliest and the last,   *highest, latest*
The bloom, whose petals nipped before they blew
Died on the promise of the fruit, is waste;
The broken lily lies—the storm is overpast.

5. Urania, "heavenly one," Venus invoked as
the Muse of noble poetry. Adonais is repre-
sented as her son.
6. Milton, who also invoked the aid of Urania

(see *Paradise Lost,* I.6–16).
7. Rivaled as a poet by only two predecessors,
Homer and Dante.

7

55 To that high Capital,[8] where kingly Death
Keeps his pale court in beauty and decay,
He came; and bought, with price of purest breath,
A grave among the eternal.—Come away!
Haste, while the vault of blue Italian day
60 Is yet his fitting charnel-roof! while still
He lies, as if in dewy sleep he lay;
Awake him not! surely he takes his fill
Of deep and liquid rest, forgetful of all ill.

8

He will awake no more, oh, never more!—
65 Within the twilight chamber spreads apace
The shadow of white Death, and at the door
Invisible Corruption waits to trace
His extreme way to her dim dwelling-place;
The eternal Hunger sits, but pity and awe
70 Soothe her pale rage, nor dares she to deface
So fair a prey, till darkness and the law
Of change, shall o'er his sleep the mortal curtain draw.

9

Oh, weep for Adonais!—The quick Dreams,
The passion-wingéd Ministers of thought,
75 Who were his flocks, whom near the living streams
Of his young spirit he fed, and whom he taught
The love which was its music, wander not—
Wander no more, from kindling brain to brain,
But droop there, whence they sprung; and mourn their lot
80 Round the cold heart, where, after their sweet pain,
They ne'er will gather strength, or find a home again.

10

And one with trembling hand clasps his cold head,
And fans him with her moonlight wings, and cries,
"Our love, our hope, our sorrow, is not dead;
85 See, on the silken fringe of his faint eyes,
Like dew upon a sleeping flower, there lies
A tear some Dream has loosened from his brain."
Lost Angel of a ruined Paradise!
She knew not 'twas her own; as with no stain
90 She faded, like a cloud which had outwept its rain.

11

One from a lucid urn of starry dew
Washed his light limbs as if embalming them;
Another clipped her profuse locks, and threw
The wreath upon him, like an anadem,°   *garland*
95 Which frozen tears instead of pearls begem;
Another in her willful grief would break
Her bow and wingéd reeds, as if to stem
A greater loss with one which was more weak;
And dull the barbéd fire against his frozen cheek.

12

100 Another Splendor on his mouth alit,
That mouth, whence it was wont to draw the breath
Which gave it strength to pierce the guarded wit,[9]
And pass into the panting heart beneath

---

8. Rome, where Keats died.   9. The defensive analytical mind.

With lightning and with music: the damp death
105   Quenched its caress upon its icy lips;
And, as a dying meteor stains a wreath
Of moonlight vapor, which the cold night clips,°   *envelops*
It flushed through his pale limbs, and passed to its eclipse.

13

And others came . . . Desires and Adorations,
110   Wingéd Persuasions and veiled Destinies,
Splendors, and Glooms, and glimmering Incarnations
Of hopes and fears, and twilight Phantasies;
And Sorrow, with her family of Sighs,
And Pleasure, blind with tears, led by the gleam
115   Of her own dying smile instead of eyes,
Came in slow pomp;—the moving pomp might seem
Like pageantry of mist on an autumnal stream.

14

All he had loved, and molded into thought
From shape, and hue, and odor, and sweet sound,
120   Lamented Adonais. Morning sought
Her eastern watch-tower, and her hair unbound,
Wet with the tears which should adorn the ground,
Dimmed the aërial eyes that kindle day;
Afar the melancholy thunder moaned,
125   Pale Ocean in unquiet slumber lay,
And the wild Winds flew round, sobbing in their dismay.

15

Lost Echo[1] sits amid the voiceless mountains,
And feeds her grief with his remembered lay,
And will no more reply to winds or fountains,
130   Or amorous birds perched on the young green spray,
Or herdsman's horn, or bell at closing day;
Since she can mimic not his lips, more dear
Than those for whose disdain she pined away
Into a shadow of all sounds:—a drear
135   Murmur, between their songs, is all the woodmen hear.

16

Grief made the young Spring wild, and she threw down
Her kindling buds, as if she Autumn were,
Or they dead leaves; since her delight is flown
For whom should she have waked the sullen year?
140   To Phoebus was not Hyacinth[2] so dear,
Nor to himself Narcissus, as to both
Thou, Adonais; wan they stand and sere
Amid the faint companions of their youth,
With dew all turned to tears; odor, to sighing ruth.°   *pity*

17

145   Thy spirit's sister, the lorn nightingale,
Mourns not her mate with such melodious pain;
Not so the eagle, who like thee could scale
Heaven, and could nourish in the sun's domain
Her mighty youth,[3] with morning, doth complain,
150   Soaring and screaming round her empty nest,

---

1. A nymph who loved Narcissus and who pined away into a mere voice when that youth fell in love with his own reflection in a pool.

2. Youth loved by Apollo ("Phoebus"), who killed him by accident.
3. In folklore an eagle could recapture its youth by soaring close to the sun.

As Albion° wails for thee: the curse of Cain[4]   *England*
Light on his head who[5] pierced thy innocent breast,
And scared the angel soul that was its earthly guest!

18

Ah, woe is me! Winter is come and gone,
155 But grief returns with the revolving year;
The airs and streams renew their joyous tone;
The ants, the bees, the swallows reappear;
Fresh leaves and flowers deck the dead Seasons' bier;
The amorous birds now pair in every brake,°   *thicket*
160 And build their mossy homes in field and brere;°   *briar*
And the green lizard, and the golden snake,
Like unimprisoned flames, out of their trance awake.

19

Through wood and stream and field and hill and Ocean,
A quickening life from the Earth's heart has burst
165 As it has ever done, with change and motion,
From the great morning of the world when first
God dawned on Chaos; in its stream immersed
The lamps of Heaven flash with a softer light;
All baser things pant with life's sacred thirst;
170 Diffuse themselves; and spend in love's delight,
The beauty and the joy of their renewéd might.

20

The leprous corpse touched by this spirit tender
Exhales itself in flowers of gentle breath;
Like incarnations of the stars, when splendor
175 Is changed to fragrance, they illumine death
And mock the merry worm that wakes beneath;
Nought we know, dies. Shall that alone which knows
Be as a sword consumed before the sheath
By sightless[6] lightning?—the intense atom[7] glows
180 A moment, then is quenched in a most cold repose.

21

Alas! that all we loved of him should be,
But for our grief, as if it had not been.
And grief itself be mortal! Woe is me!
Whence are we, and why are we? of what scene
185 The actors or spectators? Great and mean
Meet massed in death, who lends what life must borrow.
As long as skies are blue, and fields are green,
Evening must usher night, night urge the morrow,
Month follow month with woe, and year wake year to sorrow.

22

190 *He* will awake no more, oh, never more!
"Wake thou," cried Misery, "childless Mother, rise
Out of thy sleep, and slake, in thy heart's core,
A wound more fierce than his with tears and sighs."
And all the Dreams that watched Urania's eyes,
195 And all the Echoes whom their sister's song

---

4. God's curse upon Cain for having slain his brother Abel was that nothing should grow for him and that he should be homeless (Genesis iii.11–12).
5. The anonymous critic whose venomous re-view of Keats's *Endymion* had hastened, Shelley believed, Keats's death.
6. Unseeing and unseen.
7. Indivisible and indestructible unit of any-thing that exists.

Had held in holy silence, cried, "Arise!"
Swift as a Thought by the snake Memory stung,
From her ambrosial rest the fading Splendor sprung.

23

She rose like an autumnal Night, that springs
200   Out of the East, and follows wild and drear
The golden Day, which, on eternal wings,
Even as a ghost abandoning a bier,
Has left the Earth a corpse. Sorrow and fear
So struck, so roused, so rapt Urania;
205   So saddened round her like an atmosphere
Of stormy mist; so swept her on her way
Even to the mournful place where Adonais lay.

24

Out of her secret Paradise she sped,
Through camps and cities rough with stone, and steel,
210   And human hearts, which to her aery tread
Yielding not, wounded the invisible
Palms of her tender feet where'er they fell:
And barbéd tongues, and thoughts more sharp than they,
Rent the soft Form they never could repel,
215   Whose sacred blood, like the young tears of May,
Paved with eternal flowers that undeserving way.

25

In the death-chamber for a moment Death,
Shamed by the presence of that living Might,
Blushed to annihilation, and the breath
220   Revisited those lips, and life's pale light
Flashed through those limbs, so late her dear delight.
"Leave me not wild and drear and comfortless,
As silent lightning leaves the starless night!
Leave me not!" cried Urania: her distress
225   Roused Death: Death rose and smiled, and met her vain caress.

26

"Stay yet awhile! speak to me once again;
Kiss me, so long but as a kiss may live;
And in my heartless breast and burning brain
That word, that kiss, shall all thoughts else survive,
230   With food of saddest memory kept alive,
Now thou art dead, as if it were a part
Of thee, my Adonais! I would give
All that I am to be as thou now art,
But I am chained to Time, and cannot thence depart!

27

235   "O gentle child, beautiful as thou wert,
Why didst thou leave the trodden paths of men
Too soon, and with weak hands though mighty heart
Dare the unpastured dragon in his den?
Defenseless as thou wert, oh! where was then
240   Wisdom the mirrored shield, or scorn the spear?[8]
Or hadst thou waited the full cycle, when
Thy spirit should have filled its crescent sphere,
The monsters of life's waste had fled from thee like deer.

8. An allusion to Perseus, who killed the monster Medusa, evading her gaze, which could turn him into stone, by using his shield as a mirror.

28

"The herded wolves, bold only to pursue;
245 The obscene ravens, clamorous o'er the dead;
The vultures, to the conqueror's banner true,
Who feed where Desolation first has fed,
And whose wings rain contagion;—how they⁹ fled,
When like Apollo, from his golden bow,
250 The Pythian of the age¹ one arrow sped
And smiled!—The spoilers tempt no second blow,
They fawn on the proud feet that spurn them lying low.

29

"The sun comes forth, and many reptiles spawn;
He sets, and each ephemeral insect then
255 Is gathered into death without a dawn,
And the immortal stars awake again;
So is it in the world of living men:
A godlike mind soars forth, in its delight
Making earth bare and veiling heaven, and when
260 It sinks, the swarms that dimmed or shared its light
Leave to its kindred lamps the spirit's awful night."

30

Thus ceased she: and the mountain shepherds came
Their garlands sere, their magic mantles rent;
The Pilgrim of Eternity,² whose fame
265 Over his living head like Heaven is bent,
An early but enduring monument,
Came, veiling all the lightnings of his song
In sorrow; from her wilds Ierne° sent   *Ireland*
The sweetest lyrist of her saddest wrong,³
270 And love taught grief to fall like music from his tongue.

31

Midst others of less note, came one frail Form,⁴
A phantom among men; companionless
As the last cloud of an expiring storm,
Whose thunder is its knell; he, as I guess,
275 Had gazed on Nature's naked loveliness,
Actaeon-like,⁵ and now he fled astray
With feeble steps o'er the world's wilderness,
And his own thoughts, along that rugged way,
Pursued, like raging hounds, their father and their prey.

32

280 A pardlike⁶ Spirit beautiful and swift—
A Love in desolation masked;—a Power
Girt round with weakness;—it can scarce uplift
The weight of the superincumbent hour;
It is a dying lamp, a falling shower,
285 A breaking billow;—even whilst we speak
Is it not broken? On the withering flower
The killing sun smiles brightly: on a cheek
The life can burn in blood, even while the heart may break.

9. Critics, here characterized as beasts and birds of prey.
1. Byron, Shelley's friend, who attacked the critics in *English Bards and Scotch Reviewers;* here compared to Apollo the Pythian, who slew the monster Python near Delphi.
2. Byron, as author of *Childe Harold's Pilgrimage.*
3. Thomas Moore (1779–1852), poet, author of *Irish Melodies.*
4. Shelley, as poet-mourner, here wearing emblems of the god Dionysus.
5. Actaeon, a young hunter, offended the goddess Diana by discovering her while she was bathing. She transformed him into a stag, and he was torn to pieces by his hounds.
6. Leopard-like; the leopard was sacred to Dionysus.

33

His head was bound with pansies overblown,
290 And faded violets, white, and pied,° and blue;   *multicolored*
And a light spear topped with a cypress cone,
Round whose rude shaft dark ivy-tresses grew
Yet dripping with the forest's noonday dew,
Vibrated, as the ever-beating heart
295 Shook the weak hand that grasped it; of that crew
He came the last, neglected and apart;
A herd-abandoned deer, struck by the hunter's dart.

34

All stood aloof, and at his partial moan[7]
Smiled through their tears; well knew that gentle band
300 Who in another's fate now wept his own;
As in the accents of an unknown land,
He sung new sorrow; sad Urania scanned
The Stranger's mien, and murmured: "Who art thou?"
He answered not, but with a sudden hand
305 Made bare his branded and ensanguined brow,
Which was like Cain's or Christ's—oh! that it should be so!

35

What softer voice is hushed over the dead?
Athwart what brow is that dark mantle thrown?
What form leans sadly o'er the white death-bed,
310 In mockery° of monumental stone,   *imitation*
The heavy heart heaving without a moan?
If it be He,[8] who, gentlest of the wise,
Taught, soothed, loved, honored the departed one;
Let me not vex, with inharmonious sighs,
315 The silence of that heart's accepted sacrifice.

36

Our Adonais has drunk poison—oh!
What deaf and viperous murderer could crown
Life's early cup with such a draught of woe?
The nameless worm[9] would now itself disown:
320 It felt, yet could escape the magic tone
Whose prelude held° all envy, hate and wrong,   *held off*
But what was howling in one breast alone,
Silent with expectation of the song,
Whose master's hand is cold, whose silver lyre unstrung.

37

325 Live thou, whose infamy is not thy fame!
Live! fear no heavier chastisement from me,
Thou noteless blot on a remembered name!
But be thyself, and know thyself to be!
And ever at thy season be thou free
330 To spill the venom when thy fangs o'erflow:
Remorse and Self-contempt shall cling to thee;
Hot Shame shall burn upon thy secret brow,
And like a beaten hound tremble thou shalt—as now.

7. Expressing a bond of sympathy (partiality)   friend of Keats and Shelley.
toward Adonais.   9. Serpent; the anonymous reviewer (see line
8. Leigh Hunt (1784–1859), poet and critic,   152).

38

Nor let us weep that our delight is fled
335   Far from these carrion kites° that scream below;   *scavenger hawks*
He wakes or sleeps with the enduring dead;
Thou canst not soar where he is sitting now.
Dust to the dust! but the pure spirit shall flow
Back to the burning fountain whence it came,
340   A portion of the Eternal, which must glow
Through time and change, unquenchably the same,
Whilst thy¹ cold embers choke the sordid hearth of shame.

39

Peace, peace! he is not dead, he doth not sleep—
He hath awakened from the dream of life—
345   'Tis we, who lost in stormy visions, keep
With phantoms an unprofitable strife,
And in mad trance strike with our spirit's knife
Invulnerable nothings.—*We* decay
Like corpses in a charnel; fear and grief
350   Convulse us and consume us day by day,
And cold hopes swarm like worms within our living clay.

40

He has outsoared the shadow of our night;
Envy and calumny and hate and pain,
And that unrest which men miscall delight,
355   Can touch him not and torture not again;
From the contagion of the world's slow stain
He is secure, and now can never mourn
A heart grown cold, a head grown gray in vain;
Nor, when the spirit's self has ceased to burn,
360   With sparkless ashes load an unlamented urn.

41

He lives, he wakes—'tis Death is dead, not he;
Mourn not for Adonais.—Thou young Dawn,
Turn all thy dew to splendor, for from thee
The spirit thou lamentest is not gone;
365   Ye caverns and ye forests, cease to moan!
Cease ye faint flowers and fountains, and thou Air,
Which like a morning veil thy scarf hadst thrown
O'er the abandoned Earth, now leave it bare
Even to the joyous stars which smile on its despair!

42

370   He is made one with Nature: there is heard
His voice in all her music, from the moan
Of thunder, to the song of night's sweet bird;
He is a presence to be felt and known
In darkness and in light, from herb and stone,
375   Spreading itself where'er that Power may move
Which has withdrawn his being to its own;
Which wields the world with never wearied love,
Sustains it from beneath, and kindles it above.

43

He is a portion of the loveliness
380   Which once he made more lovely: he doth bear
His part, while the one Spirit's plastic° stress   *formative*
Sweeps through the dull dense world, compelling there
All new successions to the forms they wear;

1. The reviewer's.

Torturing the unwilling dross° that checks its flight   *coarse matter*
385   To its own likeness, as each mass may bear;
And bursting in its beauty and its might
From trees and beasts and men into the Heaven's light.

44
The splendors of the firmament of time
May be eclipsed, but are extinguished not;
390   Like stars to their appointed height they climb,
And death is a low mist which cannot blot
The brightness it may veil. When lofty thought
Lifts a young heart above its mortal lair,
And love and life contend in it, for what
395   Shall be its earthly doom, the dead live there
And move like winds of light on dark and stormy air.

45
The inheritors of unfulfilled renown
Rose from their thrones, built beyond mortal thought,
Far in the Unapparent. Chatterton[2]
400   Rose pale, his solemn agony had not
Yet faded from him; Sidney,[3] as he fought
And as he fell and as he lived and loved
Sublimely mild, a Spirit without spot,
Arose; and Lucan,[4] by his death approved:°   *vindicated*
405   Oblivion as they rose shrank like a thing reproved.

46
And many more, whose names on Earth are dark
But whose transmitted effluence cannot die
So long as fire outlives the parent spark,
Rose, robed in dazzling immortality.
410   "Thou art become as one of us," they cry,
"It was for thee yon kingless sphere has long
Swung blind in unascended majesty,
Silent alone amid an Heaven of Song.
Assume thy wingéd throne, thou Vesper of our throng!"

47
415   Who mourns for Adonais? Oh, come forth,
Fond wretch! and know thyself and him aright.
Clasp with thy panting soul the pendulous[5] Earth;
As from a center, dart thy spirit's light
Beyond all worlds, until its spacious might
420   Satiate the void circumference: then shrink
Even to a point within our day and night;
And keep thy heart light lest it make thee sink
When hope has kindled hope, and lured thee to the brink.

48
Or go to Rome, which is the sepulcher,
425   Oh, not of him, but of our joy: 'tis nought
That ages, empires, and religions there
Lie buried in the ravage they have wrought;
For such as he can lend—they borrow not
Glory from those who made the world their prey;

2. Thomas Chatterton (1752–70), a gifted young poet who committed suicide.
3. Sir Philip Sidney (1554–1586), a poet, critic, courtier, and soldier, fatally wounded in battle.
4. Lucan, a young Roman poet, took his own life rather than die under sentence of the notorious emperor Nero, against whom he had conspired.
5. Floating poised in space.

430   And he is gathered to the kings of thought
        Who waged contention with their time's decay,
    And of the past are all that cannot pass away.

49

      Go thou to Rome,—at once the Paradise,
        The grave, the city, and the wilderness;
435   And where its wrecks like shattered mountains rise,
        And flowering weeds, and fragrant copses dress
      The bones of Desolation's nakedness
      Pass, till the Spirit of the spot shall lead
      Thy footsteps to a slope of green access
440   Where, like an infant's smile, over the dead
    A light of laughing flowers along the grass is spread,

50

      And gray walls moulder round, on which dull Time
        Feeds, like slow fire upon a hoary brand;
      And one keen pyramid[6] with wedge sublime,
445   Pavilioning the dust of him who planned
        This refuge for his memory, doth stand
      Like flame transformed to marble; and beneath,
      A field is spread, on which a newer band
      Have pitched in Heaven's smile their camp of death,
450 Welcoming him we lose with scarce extinguished breath.

51

      Here pause: these graves are all too young as yet
        To have outgrown the sorrow which consigned
      Its charge to each; and if the seal is set,
      Here, on one fountain of a mourning mind,
455   Break it not thou! too surely shalt thou find
        Thine own well full, if thou returnest home,
      Of tears and gall. From the world's bitter wind
      Seek shelter in the shadow of the tomb.
  What Adonais is, why fear we to become?

52

460   The One remains, the many change and pass;
        Heaven's light forever shines, Earth's shadows fly;
      Life, like a dome of many-colored glass,
      Stains the white radiance of Eternity,
      Until Death tramples it to fragments.—Die,
465   If thou wouldst be with that which thou dost seek!
        Follow where all is fled!—Rome's azure sky,
      Flowers, ruins, statues, music, words, are weak
  The glory they transfuse with fitting truth to speak.

53

      Why linger, why turn back, why shrink, my Heart?
470   Thy hopes are gone before: from all things here
      They have departed; thou shouldst now depart!
      A light is past from the revolving year,
      And man, and woman; and what still is dear
      Attracts to crush, repels to make thee wither.
475   The soft sky smiles,—the low wind whispers near:
      'Tis Adonais calls! oh, hasten thither,
  No more let life divide what Death can join together.

---

6. Tomb of Gaius Cestius, an officer of ancient Rome, beside the Protestant cemetery where Keats and Shelley are buried.

54

That Light whose smile kindles the Universe,
That Beauty in which all things work and move,
480 That Benediction which the eclipsing Curse
Of birth can quench not, that sustaining Love
Which through the web of being blindly wove
By man and beast and earth and air and sea,
Burns bright or dim, as each are mirrors of
485 The fire for which all thirst; now beams on me,
Consuming the last clouds of cold mortality.

55

The breath whose might I have invoked in song
Descends on me; my spirit's bark is driven,
Far from the shore, far from the trembling throng
490 Whose sails were never to the tempest given;
The massy earth and spheréd skies are riven!
I am borne darkly, fearfully, afar;
Whilst burning through the inmost veil of Heaven,
The soul of Adonais, like a star,
495 Beacons from the abode where the Eternal are.

1821

To Jane:[7] The Keen Stars Were Twinkling

1

The keen stars were twinkling,
And the fair moon was rising among them,
   Dear Jane!
The guitar was tinkling,
5 But the notes were not sweet till you sung them
   Again.

2

As the moon's soft splendor
O'er the faint cold starlight of Heaven
   Is thrown,
10 So your voice most tender
To the strings without soul had then given
   Its own.

3

The stars will awaken,
Though the moon sleep a full hour later,
15   Tonight;
No leaf will be shaken
Whilst the dews of your melody scatter
   Delight.

4

Though the sound overpowers,
20 Sing again, with your dear voice revealing
   A tone
Of some world far from ours,
Where music and moonlight and feeling
   Are one.

1822   1832

7. Jane Williams and her husband Edward were intimate friends of Shelley's.

From Hellas:[8] *Two Choruses*

Worlds on Worlds

Worlds on worlds are rolling ever
    From creation to decay,
Like the bubbles on a river
    Sparkling, bursting, borne away.
5   But they[9] are still immortal
    Who, through birth's orient portal
And death's dark chasm hurrying to and fro,
    Clothe their unceasing flight
    In the brief dust and light
10 Gathered around their chariots as they go;
    New shapes they still may weave,
    New gods, new laws receive,
Bright or dim are they as the robes they last
    On Death's bare ribs had cast.

15   A power from the unknown God,[1]
    A Promethean conqueror,[2] came;
Like a triumphal path he trod
    The thorns of death and shame.
    A mortal shape to him
    Was like the vapor dim
20 Which the orient planet animates with light;
    Hell, Sin, and Slavery came,
    Like bloodhounds mild and tame,
Nor preyed, until their Lord had taken flight;
25   The moon of Mahomet[3]
    Arose, and it shall set:
While blazoned as on Heaven's immortal noon
    The cross leads generations on.

    Swift as the radiant shapes of sleep
30   From one whose dreams are Paradise
Fly, when the fond wretch wakes to weep,
    And Day peers forth with her blank eyes;
    So fleet, so fain, so fair,
    The Powers of earth and air
35 Fled from the folding-star[4] of Bethlehem:
    Apollo, Pan, and Love,
    And even Olympian Jove[5]
Grew weak, for killing Truth had glared on them;
40   Our hills and seas and streams,
    Dispeopled of their dreams,
Their waters turned to blood, their dew to tears,
    Wailed for the golden years.

1822

8. *Hellas,* an ancient name for Greece, is the title of a drama in which Shelley celebrates the contemporary Greek struggle for independence, which he saw as heralding the return of the legendary "Age of Saturn" or "Age of Gold," the first, best period of human history.
9. "The first stanza contrasts the immortality of the living and thinking beings which inhabit the planets, and to use a common and inadequate phrase, *clothe themselves in matter,* with the transience of the noblest manifestations of the external world" [Shelley's note].

1. At Athens St. Paul proclaimed the "unknown god," i.e., the One God of the Hebraic and Christian faiths (Acts xvii.22–28).
2. Christ; likened to the Greek Titan Prometheus, who befriended and suffered for mankind.
3. Crescent moon, symbol of Mohammedanism.
4. Star that rises at the hour when sheep are brought to the fold at evening.
5. Gods worshipped in Greece until Christianity displaced them.

The World's Great Age

The world's great age begins anew,
   The golden years return,
The earth doth like a snake[6] renew
   Her winter weeds[7] outworn:
5 Heaven smiles, and faiths and empires gleam,
Like wrecks of a dissolving dream.

A brighter Hellas rears its mountains
   From waves serener far;
A new Peneus[8] rolls his fountains
10   Against the morning star.
Where fairer Tempes[9] bloom, there sleep
Young Cyclads[1] on a sunnier deep.

A loftier Argo[2] cleaves the main,
   Fraught with a later prize;
15 Another Orpheus[3] sings again,
   And loves, and weeps, and dies.
A new Ulysses leaves once more
Calypso[4] for his native shore.

Oh, write no more the tale of Troy,
20   If earth Death's scroll must be!
Nor mix with Laian rage[5] the joy
   Which dawns upon the free:
Although a subtler Sphinx renew
Riddles of death Thebes never knew.

25 Another Athens shall arise,
   And to remoter time
Bequeath, like sunset to the skies,
   The splendor of its prime;
And leave, if nought so bright may live,
30 All earth can take or Heaven can give.

Saturn and Love their long repose
   Shall burst, more bright and good
Than all who fell, than One who rose,
   Than many unsubdued:[6]
35 Not gold, not blood, their altar dowers,
But votive tears and symbol flowers.

6. Shedding its skin after hibernation, a symbol of regeneration.
7. Clothes, especially mourning garments.
8. Greek river of legendary beauty.
9. Valley of the Peneus.
1. Or Cyclades, islands in the Aegean Sea.
2. In Greek legend, the first of seagoing vessels, on which Jason sailed to gain the "prize" (line 14) of the Golden Fleece.
3. Legendary Greek poet and musician of magical genius whose playing on the lyre caused his wife, Eurydice, to be released from the realm of the dead on condition that he would not look at her until they had reached the upper world. Breaking his pledge at the last moment, he lost her forever.
4. Island-nymph with whom Ulysses (Odysseus) lived for seven years during his return to Ithaca from the Trojan War.
5. Ignorant of his own identity, Oedipus in a rage killed King Laius of Thebes (in fact his father). Oedipus then delivered Thebes from the power of a sphinx by answering her riddles and won Jocasta (in fact his mother) as his wife and queen.
6. Saturn and Love are the restored deities of the "world's great age"; "all who fell" are the deities who "fell" when Christ arose from the dead; the "many unsubdued" are idols still worshipped throughout the world.

Oh, cease! must hate and death return?
   Cease! must men kill and die?
Cease! drain not to its dregs the urn
40   Of bitter prophecy.
The world is weary of the past,
Oh, might it die or rest at last!

1822

JOHN CLARE
(1793–1864)

Badger

When midnight comes a host of dogs and men
Go out and track the badger to his den,
And put a sack within the hole, and lie
Till the old grunting badger passes by.
5 He comes and hears—they let the strongest loose.
The old fox hears the noise and drops the goose.
The poacher shoots and hurries from the cry,
And the old hare half wounded buzzes by.
They get a forkéd stick to bear him down
10 And clap the dogs and take him to the town,
And bait him all the day with many dogs,
And laugh and shout and fright the scampering hogs.
He runs along and bites at all he meets:
They shout and hollo down the noisy streets.

15 He turns about to face the loud uproar
And drives the rebels to their very door.
The frequent stone is hurled where'er they go;
When badgers fight, then everyone's a foe.
The dogs are clapped and urged to join the fray;
20 The badger turns and drives them all away.
Though scarcely half as big, demure and small,
He fights with dogs for hours and beats them all.
The heavy mastiff, savage in the fray,
Lies down and licks his feet and turns away.
25 The bulldog knows his match and waxes cold,
The badger grins and never leaves his hold.
He drives the crowd and follows at their heels
And bites them through—the drunkard swears and reels.

The frighted women take the boys away,
30 The blackguard laughs and hurries on the fray.
He tries to reach the woods, an awkward race,
But sticks and cudgels quickly stop the chase.
He turns again and drives the noisy crowd
And beats the many dogs in noises loud.
35 He drives away and beats them every one,
And then they loose them all and set them on.

He falls as dead and kicked by boys and men,
Then starts and grins and drives the crowd again;
Till kicked and torn and beaten out he lies
40   And leaves his hold and crackles, groans, and dies.

                              1835–37   1920

Gypsies

The snow falls deep; the forest lies alone;
The boy goes hasty for his load of brakes,°   **brushwood**
Then thinks upon the fire and hurries back;
The gypsy knocks his hands and tucks them up,
5   And seeks his squalid camp, half hid in snow,
Beneath the oak which breaks away the wind,
And bushes close in snow like hovel warm;
There tainted mutton wastes upon the coals,
And the half-wasted dog squats close and rubs,
10 Then feels the heat too strong, and goes aloof;
He watches well, but none a bit can spare,
And vainly waits the morsel thrown away.
'Tis thus they live—a picture to the place,
A quiet, pilfering, unprotected race.

                              1837–41   1920

Song: Love Lives Beyond the Tomb

          Love lives beyond
The tomb, the earth, which fades like dew—
          I love the fond,
The faithful, and the true.

5   Love lives in sleep,
'Tis happiness of healthy dreams,
          Eve's dews may weep,
But love delightful seems.

          'Tis seen in flowers,
10 And in the even's pearly dew
          On earth's green hours,
And in the heaven's eternal blue.

          'Tis heard in spring
When light and sunbeams, warm and kind,
15   On angel's wing
Brings love and music to the wind.

          And where's the voice
So young, so beautiful, and sweet
          As nature's choice,
20 Where spring and lovers meet?

          Love lives beyond
The tomb, the earth, the flowers, and dew.
          I love the fond,
The faithful, young, and true.

                              1842–64   1873

First Love

   I ne'er was struck before that hour
     With love so sudden and so sweet,
   Her face it bloomed like a sweet flower
     And stole my heart away complete.
5 My face turned pale as deadly pale.
     My legs refused to walk away,
   And when she looked, what could I ail?
     My life and all seemed turned to clay.

   And then my blood rushed to my face
10   And took my eyesight quite away,
   The trees and bushes round the place
     Seemed midnight at noonday.
   I could not see a single thing,
     Words from my eyes did start—
15 They spoke as chords do from the string,
     And blood burnt round my heart.

   Are flowers the winter's choice?
     Is love's bed always snow?
   She seemed to hear my silent voice,
20   Not love's appeals to know.
   I never saw so sweet a face
     As that I stood before.
   My heart has left its dwelling-place
     And can return no more.

                        1842–64   1920

Farewell

   Farewell to the bushy clump close to the river
   And the flags where the butter-bump° hides in forever;   *bittern*
   Farewell to the weedy nook, hemmed in by waters;
   Farewell to the miller's brook and his three bonny daughters;
5 Farewell to them all while in prison I lie—
   In the prison a thrall sees naught but the sky.

   Shut out are the green fields and birds in the bushes;
   In the prison yard nothing builds, blackbirds or thrushes.
   Farewell to the old mill and dash of the waters,
10 To the miller and, dearer still, to his three bonny daughters.

   In the nook, the larger burdock grows near the green willow;
   In the flood, round the moor-cock dashes under the billow;
   To the old mill farewell, to the lock, pens, and waters,
   To the miller himsel', and his three bonny daughters.

                        1842–64   1920

I Am

I am: yet what I am none cares or knows
My friends forsake me like a memory lost,
I am the self-consumer of my woes—
They rise and vanish in oblivious host,
5 Like shadows in love's frenzied, stifled throes—
And yet I am, and live—like vapors tossed

Into the nothingness of scorn and noise,
Into the living sea of waking dreams,
Where there is neither sense of life or joys,
10 But the vast shipwreck of my life's esteems;
Even the dearest, that I love the best,
Are strange—nay, rather stranger than the rest.

I long for scenes, where man hath never trod,
A place where woman never smiled or wept—
15 There to abide with my Creator, God,
And sleep as I in childhood sweetly slept,
Untroubling, and untroubled where I lie,
The grass below— above the vaulted sky.

1842–64   1865

JOHN KEATS
(1795–1821)

On First Looking into Chapman's Homer[1]

Much have I traveled in the realms of gold,
And many goodly states and kingdoms seen;
Round many western islands have I been
Which bards in fealty° to Apollo[2] hold.   *allegiance*
5 Oft of one wide expanse had I been told
That deep-browed Homer ruled as his demesne;°   *domain*
Yet did I never breathe its pure serene°   *atmosphere*
Till I heard Chapman speak out loud and bold:
Then felt I like some watcher of the skies
10 When a new planet swims into his ken;
Or like stout Cortez[3] when with eagle eyes
He stared at the Pacific—and all his men
Looked at each other with a wild surmise—
Silent, upon a peak in Darien.

1816

On the Sea

It keeps eternal whisperings around
Desolate shores, and with its mighty swell
Gluts twice ten thousand Caverns, till the spell
Of Hecate[4] leaves them their old shadowy sound.

1. Translation of Homer's *Iliad* by George Chapman, a contemporary of Shakespeare's.
2. God of poetic inspiration.
3. Spanish conqueror of Mexico; in fact, Balboa, not Cortez, was the first European to see the Pacific, from Darien, in Panama.
4. Greek goddess associated with witchcraft and the underworld.

5   Often 'tis in such gentle temper found,
     That scarcely will the very smallest shell
       Be moved for days from where it sometime fell,
When last the winds of Heaven were unbound.
     Oh ye! who have your eyeballs vexed and tired,
10   Feast them upon the wideness of the Sea;
       Oh ye! whose ears are dinned with uproar rude,
     Or fed too much with cloying melody—
       Sit ye near some old Cavern's Mouth and brood,
Until ye start, as if the sea nymphs quired!°   *choired*

                                                                          1817

On Sitting Down to Read *King Lear* Once Again

O golden-tongued Romance with serene lute!
     Fair pluméd Siren!° Queen of far away!   *enchantress*
     Leave melodizing on this wintry day,
Shut up thine olden pages, and be mute:
5   Adieu! for once again the fierce dispute
       Betwixt damnation and impassioned clay
       Must I burn through; once more humbly assay
The bitter-sweet of this Shakespearean fruit.
Chief Poet! and ye clouds of Albion,[5]
10   Begetters of our deep eternal theme,
When through the old oak forest I am gone,
     Let me not wander in a barren dream,
But when I am consuméd in the fire,
Give me new Phoenix[6] wings to fly at my desire.

                                        1818   1838

When I Have Fears

When I have fears that I may cease to be
     Before my pen has gleaned my teeming brain,
Before high-piléd books, in charact'ry,°   *written symbols*
     Hold like rich garners the full-ripened grain;
5   When I behold, upon the night's starred face,
     Huge cloudy symbols of a high romance,
And think that I may never live to trace
     Their shadows, with the magic hand of chance;
And when I feel, fair creature of an hour,
10   That I shall never look upon thee more,
Never have relish in the faery° power   *magical*
     Of unreflecting love!—then on the shore
Of the wide world I stand alone, and think
Till Love and Fame to nothingness do sink.

                                        1818   1848

5. Ancient name for England, especially re-
ferring to pre-Roman Britain, the era of King
Lear.

6. Fabled Arabian bird that, after living for
centuries, consumes itself in fire and is reborn.

The Eve of St. Agnes[3]

1

St. Agnes' Eve—Ah, bitter chill it was!
The owl, for all his feathers, was a-cold;
The hare limped trembling through the frozen grass,
And silent was the flock in woolly fold:
5   Numb were the Beadsman's[4] fingers, while he told
His rosary, and while his frosted breath,
Like pious incense from a censer old,
Seemed taking flight for heaven, without a death,
Past the sweet Virgin's picture, while his prayer he saith.

2

10   His prayer he saith, this patient, holy man;
Then takes his lamp, and riseth from his knees,
And back returneth, meager, barefoot, wan,
Along the chapel aisle by slow degrees:
The sculptured dead, on each side, seem to freeze,
15   Imprisoned in black, purgatorial rails:
Knights, ladies, praying in dumb orat'ries,[5]
He passeth by; and his weak spirit fails
To think how they may ache in icy hoods and mails.

3

Northward he turneth through a little door,
20   And scarce three steps, ere Music's golden tongue
Flattered to tears this aged man and poor;
But no—already had his deathbell rung:
The joys of all his life were said and sung:
His was harsh penance on St. Agnes' Eve:
25   Another way he went, and soon among
Rough ashes sat he for his soul's reprieve,
And all night kept awake, for sinners' sake to grieve.

4

That ancient Beadsman heard the prelude soft;
And so it chanced, for many a door was wide,
30   From hurry to and fro. Soon, up aloft,
The silver, snarling trumpets 'gan to chide:
The level chambers, ready with their pride,
Were glowing to receive a thousand guests:
The carvéd angels, ever eager-eyed,
35   Stared, where upon their heads the cornice rests,
With hair blown back, and wings put crosswise on their breasts.

5

At length burst in the argent revelry,[6]
With plume, tiara, and all rich array,
Numerous as shadows haunting faerily
40   The brain, new stuffed, in youth, with triumphs gay
Of old romance. These let us wish away,

---

3. January 20, proverbially the coldest winter night. St. Agnes, martyred in the 4th century A.D., is patroness of virgins. Traditionally, a maiden who observes the ritual of St. Agnes' Eve will see a vision of her husband-to-be.
4. From Middle English *bede,* meaning *prayer.*

A needy dependent, paid a small stipend to pray regularly for his benefactor. "Rosary" (line 6): a string of beads on which a series of short prayers are counted ("told," line 5).
5. Small chapels in a larger one.
6. Brightly-dressed revelers.

And turn, sole-thoughted, to one Lady there,
Whose heart had brooded, all that wintry day,
On love, and winged St. Agnes' saintly care,
45   As she had heard old dames full many times declare.

6

They told her how, upon St. Agnes' Eve,
Young virgins might have visions of delight,
And soft adorings from their loves receive
Upon the honeyed middle of the night,
50   If ceremonies due they did aright;
As, supperless to bed they must retire,
And couch supine their beauties, lily white;
Nor look behind, nor sideways, but require
Of Heaven with upward eyes for all that they desire.

7

55   Full of this whim was thoughtful Madeline:
The music, yearning like a God in pain,
She scarcely heard: her maiden eyes divine,
Fixed on the floor, saw many a sweeping train
Pass by—she heeded not at all: in vain
60   Came many a tiptoe, amorous cavalier,
And back retired; not cooled by high disdain;
But she saw not: her heart was otherwhere:
She sighed for Agnes' dreams, the sweetest of the year.

8

She danced along with vague, regardless eyes,
65   Anxious her lips, her breathing quick and short:
The hallowed hour was near at hand: she sighs
Amid the timbrels,° and the thronged resort   *hand drums*
Of whisperers in anger, or in sport;
'Mid looks of love, defiance, hate, and scorn,
70   Hoodwinked with faery fancy; all amort,[7]
Save to St. Agnes and her lambs unshorn,[8]
And all the bliss to be before tomorrow morn.

9

So, purposing each moment to retire,
She lingered still. Meantime, across the moors,
75   Had come young Porphyro, with heart on fire
For Madeline. Beside the portal doors,
Buttressed from moonlight,[9] stands he, and implores
All saints to give him sight of Madeline,
But for one moment in the tedious hours,
80   That he might gaze and worship all unseen;
Perchance speak, kneel, touch, kiss—in sooth such things have been.

10

He ventures in: let no buzzed whisper tell:
All eyes be muffled, or a hundred swords
Will storm his heart, Love's fev'rous citadel:
85   For him, those chambers held barbarian hordes,
Hyena foemen, and hot-blooded lords,
Whose very dogs would execrations howl
Against his lineage: not one breast affords
Him any mercy, in that mansion foul,
90   Save one old beldame,° weak in body and in soul.   *old woman*

7. Dead; i.e., oblivious.
8. Symbolically associated with St. Agnes; new wool offered at the Mass commemorating the saint was later spun and woven by the nuns (lines 115–117).
9. I.e., concealed in dark shadows.

11

Ah, happy chance! the aged creature came,
Shuffling along with ivory-headed wand,
To where he stood, hid from the torch's flame,
Behind a broad hall-pillar, far beyond
95 The sound of merriment and chorus bland:°   *harmonizing*
He startled her; but soon she knew his face,
And grasped his fingers in her palsied hand,
Saying, "Mercy, Porphyro! hie thee from this place;
They are all here tonight, the whole bloodthirsty race!

12

100 "Get hence! get hence! there's dwarfish Hildebrand;
He had a fever late, and in the fit
He curséd thee and thine, both house and land:
Then there's that old Lord Maurice, not a whit
More tame for his gray hairs—Alas me! flit!
105 Flit like a ghost away."—"Ah, Gossip[1] dear,
We're safe enough; here in this armchair sit,
And tell me how"—"Good Saints! not here, not here;
Follow me, child, or else these stones will be thy bier."

13

He followed through a lowly archéd way,
110 Brushing the cobwebs with his lofty plume,
And as she muttered "Well-a—well-a-day!"
He found him in a little moonlight room,
Pale, latticed, chill, and silent as a tomb.
"Now tell me where is Madeline," said he,
115 "O tell me, Angela, by the holy loom
Which none but secret sisterhood may see,
When they St. Agnes' wool are weaving piously."

14

"St Agnes! Ah! it is St. Agnes' Eve—
Yet men will murder upon holy days:
120 Thou must hold water in a witch's sieve,
And be liege lord of all the Elves and Fays,[2]
To venture so: it fills me with amaze
To see thee, Porphyro!—St. Agnes' Eve!
God's help! my lady fair the conjuror plays[3]
125 This very night: good angels her deceive!
But let me laugh awhile, I've mickle° time to grieve."   *much*

15

Feebly she laugheth in the languid moon,
While Porphyro upon her face doth look,
Like puzzled urchin on an aged crone
130 Who keepeth closed a wondrous riddle-book,
As spectacled she sits in chimney nook.
But soon his eyes grew brilliant, when she told
His lady's purpose; and he scarce could brook°   *check*
Tears, at the thought of those enchantments cold,
135 And Madeline asleep in lap of legends old.

16

Sudden a thought came like a full-blown rose,
Flushing his brow, and in his painéd heart
Made purple riot: then doth he propose
A stratagem, that makes the beldame start:

---

1. Old kinswoman or household retainer.
2. I.e., to hold water in a sieve and to com-
mand elves and fairies ("Fays"), Porphyro
would have to be a magician.
3. I.e., is trying magic spells.

140 "A cruel man and impious thou art:
Sweet lady, let her pray, and sleep, and dream
Alone with her good angels, far apart
From wicked men like thee. Go, go!—I deem
Thou canst not surely be the same that thou didst seem."

17

145 "I will not harm her, by all saints I swear,"
Quoth Porphyro: "O may I ne'er find grace
When my weak voice shall whisper its last prayer,
If one of her soft ringlets I displace,
Or look with ruffian passion in her face:
150 Good Angela, believe me by these tears;
Or I will, even in a moment's space,
Awake, with horrid shout, my foemen's ears,
And beard them, though they be more fanged than wolves and bears."

18

"Ah! why wilt thou affright a feeble soul?
155 A poor, weak, palsy-stricken, churchyard thing,[4]
Whose passing bell[5] may ere the midnight toll;
Whose prayers for thee, each morn and evening,
Were never missed."—Thus plaining,° doth she bring   *complaining*
A gentler speech from burning Porphyro;
160 So woeful and of such deep sorrowing,
That Angela gives promise she will do
Whatever he shall wish, betide her weal or woe.

19

Which was, to lead him, in close secrecy,
Even to Madeline's chamber, and there hide
165 Him in a closet, of such privacy
That he might see her beauty unespied,
And win perhaps that night a peerless bride,
While legioned faeries paced the coverlet,
And pale enchantment held her sleepy-eyed.
170 Never on such a night have lovers met,
Since Merlin paid his Demon all the monstrous debt.[6]

20

"It shall be as thou wishest," said the Dame:
"All cates° and dainties shall be storéd there   *delicacies*
Quickly on this feast[7] night: by the tambour frame[8]
175 Her own lute thou wilt see: no time to spare,
For I am slow and feeble, and scarce dare
On such a catering trust my dizzy head.
Wait here, my child, with patience; kneel in prayer
The while: Ah! thou must needs the lady wed,
180 Or may I never leave my grave among the dead."

21

So saying, she hobbled off with busy fear.
The lover's endless minutes slowly passed:
The dame returned, and whispered in his ear
To follow her; with aged eyes aghast
185 From fright of dim espial. Safe at last,

---

4. I.e., soon to die.
5. Tolled when a person died ("passed away").
6. Possibly alluding to the tale that Merlin, in Arthurian legend a great wizard, lies bound for ages by a spell that he gave to an evil woman to buy her love.
7. The festival, or Mass, honoring St. Agnes.
8. A circular embroidery frame.

Through many a dusky gallery, they gain
The maiden's chamber, silken, hushed, and chaste;
Where Porphyro took covert, pleased amain.°   *greatly*
His poor guide hurried back with agues in her brain.

22

190   Her falt'ring hand upon the balustrade,
Old Angela was feeling for the stair,
When Madeline, St. Agnes' charmèd maid,
Rose, like a missioned spirit, unaware:
With silver taper's light, and pious care,
195   She turned, and down the aged gossip led
To a safe level matting. Now prepare,
Young Porphyro, for gazing on that bed;
She comes, she comes again, like ringdove frayed° and fled.   *affrighted*

23

Out went the taper as she hurried in;
200   Its little smoke, in pallid moonshine, died:
She closed the door, she panted, all akin
To spirits of the air, and visions wide:
No uttered syllable, or, woe betide!
But to her heart, her heart was voluble,
205   Paining with eloquence her balmy side;
As though a tongueless nightingale should swell
Her throat in vain, and die, heart-stifled, in her dell.

24

A casement high and triple-arched there was,
All garlanded with carven imag'ries
210   Of fruits, and flowers, and bunches of knot-grass,
And diamonded with panes of quaint device,
Innumerable of stains and splendid dyes,
As are the tiger-moth's deep-damasked wings;
And in the midst, 'mong thousand heraldries,
215   And twilight saints, and dim emblazonings,
A shielded scutcheon blushed with blood of queens and kings.[9]

25

Full on this casement shone the wintry moon,
And threw warm gules[1] on Madeline's fair breast,
As down she knelt for heaven's grace and boon;°   *gift*
220   Rose-bloom fell on her hands, together pressed,
And on her silver cross soft amethyst,
And on her hair a glory, like a saint:
She seemed a splendid angel, newly dressed,
Save wings, for heaven—Porphyro grew faint:
225   She knelt, so pure a thing, so free from mortal taint.

26

Anon his heart revives: her vespers done,
Of all its wreathèd pearls her hair she frees;
Unclasps her warmèd jewels one by one;
Loosens her fragrant bodice; by degrees
230   Her rich attire creeps rustling to her knees:
Half-hidden, like a mermaid in sea-weed,
Pensive awhile she dreams awake, and sees,
In fancy, fair St. Agnes in her bed,
But dares not look behind, or all the charm is fled.

---

9. A shield representing a coat of arms ("scutcheon") showed the red pigments ("blushed") indicating royal ancestry.
1. Heraldic red; here, in stained glass.

27

235 Soon, trembling in her soft and chilly nest,
  In sort of wakeful swoon, perplexed she lay,
  Until the poppied warmth of sleep oppressed
  Her soothéd limbs, and soul fatigued away;
  Flown, like a thought, until the morrow-day;
240 Blissfully havened both from joy and pain;
  Clasped like a missal where swart Paynims[2] pray;
  Blinded alike from sunshine and from rain,
As though a rose should shut, and be a bud again.

28

  Stol'n to this paradise, and so entranced,
245 Porphyro gazed upon her empty dress,
  And listened to her breathing, if it chanced
  To wake into a slumberous tenderness;
  Which when he heard, that minute did he bless,
  And breathed himself: then from the closet crept,
250 Noiseless as fear in a wide wilderness,
  And over the hushed carpet, silent, stepped,
And 'tween the curtains peeped, where, lo!—how fast she slept.

29

  Then by the bedside, where the faded moon
  Made a dim, silver twilight, soft he set
255 A table, and, half anguished, threw thereon
  A cloth of woven crimson, gold, and jet—
  O for some drowsy Morphean amulet![3]
  The boisterous, midnight, festive clarion,
  The kettledrum, and far-heard clarinet,
260 Affray his ears, though but in dying tone—
The hall door shuts again, and all the noise is gone.

30

  And still she slept an azure-lidded sleep,
  In blanchéd linen, smooth, and lavendered,
  While he from forth the closet brought a heap
265 Of candied apple, quince, and plum, and gourd;
  With jellies soother than the creamy curd,
  And lucent syrups, tinct° with cinnamon;   *tinctured*
  Manna and dates, in argosy transferred
  From Fez;[4] and spicéd dainties, every one,
270 From silken Samarcand to cedared Lebanon.[5]

31

  These delicates he heaped with glowing hand
  On golden dishes and in baskets bright
  Of wreathéd silver: sumptuous they stand
  In the retiréd quiet of the night,
275 Filling the chilly room with perfume light.—
  "And now, my love, my seraph° fair, awake!   *angel*
  Thou art my heaven, and I thine eremite:[6]
  Open thine eyes, for meek St. Agnes' sake,
Or I shall drowse beside thee, so my soul doth ache."

32

280 Thus whispering, his warm, unnervéd arm
  Sank in her pillow. Shaded was her dream
  By the dusk curtains: 'twas a midnight charm
  Impossible to melt as icéd stream:

---

2. Dark pagans.
3. An object, such as an engraved stone, exerting the power of Morpheus, god of sleep.
4. Morocco.

5. Places associated with ancient luxury and wealth.
6. Hermit, religious devotee.

The lustrous salvers° in the moonlight gleam;   *serving dishes*
Broad golden fringe upon the carpet lies:
It seemed he never, never could redeem
From such a steadfast spell his lady's eyes;
So mused awhile, entoiled in woofèd° fantasies.   *enwoven*

33
Awakening up, he took her hollow lute—
Tumultuous—and, in chords that tenderest be,
He played an ancient ditty, long since mute,
In Provence called "*La belle dame sans merci*"[7]
Close to her ear touching the melody;
Wherewith disturbed, she uttered a soft moan:
He ceased—she panted quick—and suddenly
Her blue affrayèd eyes wide open shone:
Upon his knees he sank, pale as smooth-sculptured stone.

34
Her eyes were open, but she still beheld,
Now wide awake, the vision of her sleep:
There was a painful change, that nigh expelled
The blisses of her dream so pure and deep,
At which fair Madeline began to weep,
And moan forth witless words with many a sigh;
While still her gaze on Porphyro would keep,
Who knelt, with joinèd hands and piteous eye,
Fearing to move or speak, she looked so dreamingly.

35
"Ah, Porphyro!" said she, "but even now
Thy voice was at sweet tremble in mine ear,
Made tunable with every sweetest vow;
And those sad eyes were spiritual and clear:
How changed thou art! how pallid, chill, and drear!
Give me that voice again, my Porphyro,
Those looks immortal, those complainings dear!
Oh leave me not in this eternal woe,
For if thou diest, my Love, I know not where to go."

36
Beyond a mortal man impassioned far
At these voluptuous accents, he arose,
Ethereal, flushed, and like a throbbing star
Seen mid the sapphire heaven's deep repose;
Into her dream he melted, as the rose
Blendeth its odor with the violet—
Solution sweet: meantime the frost-wind blows
Like Love's alarum° pattering the sharp sleet   *signal, call to arms*
Against the windowpanes; St. Agnes' moon hath set.

37
'Tis dark: quick pattereth the flaw-blown° sleet: *gust-blown*
"This is no dream, my bride, my Madeline!"
'Tis dark: the icèd gusts still rave and beat:
"No dream, alas! alas! and woe is mine!
Porphyro will leave me here to fade and pine.—
Cruel! what traitor could thee hither bring?
I curse not, for my heart is lost in thine,
Though thou forsakest a deceivèd thing—
A dove forlorn and lost with sick unprunèd[8] wing."

---

7. The lady beautiful but without mercy.   8. Unpreened; i.e., disarranged, rumpled.

38

335
"My Madeline! sweet dreamer! lovely bride!
Say, may I be for aye thy vassal blest?
Thy beauty's shield, heart-shaped and vermcil° dyed?   *vermilion*
Ah, silver shrine, here will I take my rest
After so many hours of toil and quest,
A famished pilgrim—saved by miracle.
340
Though I have found, I will not rob thy nest
Saving of thy sweet self; if thou think'st well
To trust, fair Madeline, to no rude infidel.

39

"Hark! 'tis an elfin-storm from faery land,
Of haggard° seeming, but a boon indeed: *wild, ugly*
345
Arise—arise! the morning is at hand—
The bloated wassaillers° will never heed—   *drunken revelers*
Let us away, my love, with happy speed;
There are no ears to hear, or eyes to see—
Drowned all in Rhenish and the sleepy mead:[9]
350
Awake! arise! my love, and fearless be,
For o'er the southern moors I have a home for thee."

40

She hurried at his words, beset with fears,
For there were sleeping dragons all around,
At glaring watch, perhaps, with ready spears—
355
Down the wide stairs a darkling way they found.—
In all the house was heard no human sound.
A chain-dropped lamp was flickering by each door;
The arras, rich with horseman, hawk, and hound,
Fluttered in the besieging wind's uproar;
360
And the long carpets rose along the gusty floor.

41

They glide, like phantoms, into the wide hall;
Like phantoms, to the iron porch, they glide;
Where lay the Porter, in uneasy sprawl,
With a huge empty flagon by his side:
365
The wakeful bloodhound rose, and shook his hide,
But his sagacious eye an inmate owns:°   *recognizes*
By one, and one, the bolts full easy slide:
The chains lie silent on the footworn stones;
The key turns, and the door upon its hinges groans.

42

370
And they are gone: aye, ages long ago
These lovers fled away into the storm.
That night the Baron dreamt of many a woe,
And all his warrior-guests, with shade and form
Of witch, and demon, and large coffin-worm,
375
Were long be-nightmared. Angela the old
Died palsy-twitched, with meager face deform;
The Beadsman, after thousand aves[1] told,
For aye unsought for slept among his ashes cold.

1819   1820

---

9. Rhine wine, and fermented honey and water.

1. As in *Ave Maria* (Hail Mary), a salutation to the Virgin.

La Belle Dame sans Merci[2]

O what can ail thee, Knight at arms,
　Alone and palely loitering?
The sedge has withered from the Lake
　And no birds sing!

5　O what can ail thee, Knight at arms,
　So haggard, and so woebegone?
The squirrel's granary is full
　And the harvest's done.

I see a lily on thy brow
10　With anguish moist and fever dew,
And on thy cheeks a fading rose
　Fast withereth too.

"I met a Lady in the Meads,°   *meadows*
　Full beautiful, a faery's child,
15　Her hair was long, her foot was light
　And her eyes were wild.

"I made a Garland for her head,
　And bracelets too, and fragrant Zone;°   *girdle*
She looked at me as she did love
20　And made sweet moan.

"I set her on my pacing steed
　And nothing else saw all day long,
For sidelong would she bend and sing
　A faery's song.

25　"She found me roots of relish sweet,
　And honey wild, and manna dew,
And sure in language strange she said
　'I love thee true.'

"She took me to her elfin grot
30　And there she wept and sighed full sore,
And there I shut her wild wild eyes
　With kisses four.

"And there she lulléd me asleep,
　And there I dreamed, Ah Woe betide!
35　The latest° dream I ever dreamt   *last*
　On the cold hill side.

"I saw pale Kings, and Princes too,
　Pale warriors, death-pale were they all;
They cried, 'La belle dame sans merci
40　Thee hath in thrall!'

2. The lady beautiful but without mercy.   This is an earlier (and widely preferred) version of a poem first published in 1820.

"I saw their starved lips in the gloam
   With horrid warning gapéd wide,
And I awoke, and found me here
   On the cold hill's side.

45 "And this is why I sojourn here,
      Alone and palely loitering;
   Though the sedge is withered from the Lake
      And no birds sing."

April 1819   1888

Ode to a Nightingale

1

My heart aches, and a drowsy numbness pains
   My sense, as though of hemlock[3] I had drunk,
Or emptied some dull opiate to the drains
   One minute past, and Lethe-wards[4] had sunk:
5 'Tis not through envy of thy happy lot,
      But being too happy in thine happiness—
   That thou, light-wingéd Dryad of the trees,
         In some melodious plot
   Of beechen green, and shadows numberless,
10   Singest of summer in full-throated ease.

2

O, for a draught of vintage! that hath been
   Cooled a long age in the deep-delvéd earth,
Tasting of Flora[5] and the country green,
   Dance, and Provençal song,[6] and sunburnt mirth!
15 O for a beaker full of the warm South,
      Full of the true, the blushful Hippocrene,[7]
   With beaded bubbles winking at the brim,
         And purple-stainéd mouth;
   That I might drink, and leave the world unseen,
20   And with thee fade away into the forest dim:

3

Fade far away, dissolve, and quite forget
   What thou among the leaves hast never known,
The weariness, the fever, and the fret
   Here, where men sit and hear each other groan;
25 Where palsy shakes a few, sad, last gray hairs,
      Where youth grows pale, and specter-thin, and dies,
   Where but to think is to be full of sorrow
         And leaden-eyed despairs,
   Where Beauty cannot keep her lustrous eyes,
30   Or new Love pine at them beyond tomorrow.

4

Away! away! for I will fly to thee,
   Not charioted by Bacchus and his pards,[8]
But on the viewless° wings of Poesy,   invisible
   Though the dull brain perplexes and retards:

3. Opiate made from a poisonous herb.
4. Towards the river Lethe, whose waters in Hades bring the dead forgetfulness.
5. Roman goddess of springtime and flowers.
6. Of the late-medieval troubadours of Provence, in southern France.

7. The fountain of the Muses (goddesses of poetry and the arts) on Mt. Helicon in Greece; its waters induce poetic inspiration.
8. "Bacchus": god of wine, often depicted in a chariot drawn by leopards ("pards").

35 Already with thee! tender is the night,
　　And haply the Queen-Moon is on her throne,
　　　Clustered around by all her starry Fays;°　　　　　　　*fairies*
　　　　But here there is no light,
　　　Save what from heaven is with the breezes blown
40　　Through verdurous glooms and winding mossy ways.
　　　　　　　　5
　　I cannot see what flowers are at my feet,
　　　Nor what soft incense hangs upon the boughs,
　　But, in embalméd° darkness, guess each sweet　　　　*perfumed*
　　　Wherewith the seasonable month endows
45　The grass, the thicket, and the fruit tree wild;
　　　White hawthorn, and the pastoral eglantine;⁹
　　　　Fast fading violets covered up in leaves;
　　　　　And mid-May's eldest child,
　　　The coming musk-rose, full of dewy wine,
50　　The murmurous haunt of flies on summer eves.
　　　　　　　　6
　　Darkling° I listen; and for many a time　　　　　　*in darkness*
　　I have been half in love with easeful Death,
　　Called him soft names in many a muséd rhyme,
　　　To take into the air my quiet breath;
55　Now more than ever seems it rich to die,
　　　To cease upon the midnight with no pain,
　　　　While thou art pouring forth thy soul abroad
　　　　　In such an ecstasy!
　　　Still wouldst thou sing, and I have ears in vain—
60　　To thy high requiem become a sod.
　　　　　　　　7
　　Thou wast not born for death, immortal Bird!
　　　No hungry generations tread thee down;
　　The voice I hear this passing night was heard
　　　In ancient days by emperor and clown:
65　Perhaps the selfsame song that found a path
　　　Through the sad heart of Ruth,¹ when, sick for home,
　　　　She stood in tears amid the alien corn;
　　　　　The same that ofttimes hath
　　　Charmed magic casements, opening on the foam
70　　Of perilous seas, in faery lands forlorn.
　　　　　　　　8
　　Forlorn! the very word is like a bell
　　　To toll me back from thee to my sole self!
　　Adieu! the fancy cannot cheat so well
　　　As she is famed to do, deceiving elf.
75　Adieu! adieu! thy plaintive anthem fades
　　　Past the near meadows, over the still stream,
　　　　Up the hill side; and now 'tis buried deep
　　　　　In the next valley-glades:
　　　Was it a vision, or a waking dream?
80　　Fled is that music:—Do I wake or sleep?

　　　　　　　　　　　　　　　　May 1819　　　　1820

---

9. Sweetbriar; wood roses.
1. In the Old Testament, a woman of great
loyalty and modesty who, as a stranger in
Judah, won a husband while gleaning in the
barley-fields ("the alien corn," line 67).

Ode on Melancholy

1

No, no, go not to Lethe,[2] neither twist
  Wolfsbane, tight-rooted, for its poisonous wine;
Nor suffer thy pale forehead to be kissed
  By nightshade,[3] ruby grape of Proserpine;[4]
5 Make not your rosary of yew-berries,[5]
  Nor let the beetle, nor the death-moth be
    Your mournful Psyche, nor the downy owl[6]
A partner in your sorrow's mysteries;
  For shade to shade will come too drowsily,
10   And drown the wakeful anguish of the soul.

2

But when the melancholy fit shall fall
  Sudden from heaven like a weeping cloud,
That fosters the droop-headed flowers all,
  And hides the green hill in an April shroud;
15 Then glut thy sorrow on a morning rose,
  Or on the rainbow of the salt sand-wave,
  Or on the wealth of globèd peonies;
Or if thy mistress some rich anger shows,
  Imprison her soft hand, and let her rave,
20   And feed deep, deep upon her peerless eyes.

3

She[7] dwells with Beauty—Beauty that must die;
  And Joy, whose hand is ever at his lips
Bidding adieu; and aching Pleasure nigh,
  Turning to Poison while the bee-mouth sips:
25 Aye, in the very temple of Delight
  Veiled Melancholy has her sov'reign shrine,
    Though seen of none save him whose strenuous tongue
Can burst Joy's grape against his palate fine;[8]
His soul shall taste the sadness of her might,
30   And be among her cloudy trophies[9] hung.

                May 1819   1820

Ode on a Grecian Urn

1

Thou still unravished bride of quietness,
  Thou foster child of silence and slow time,
Sylvan historian, who canst thus express
  A flowery tale more sweetly than our rhyme:
5 What leaf-fringed legend haunts about thy shape
  Of deities or mortals, or of both,

2. River whose waters in Hades bring forgetfulness to the dead.
3. "Nightshade" and "wolfsbane" are poisonous herbs from which sedatives and opiates were extracted.
4. Queen of Hades.
5. Symbols of mourning; often growing in cemeteries.
6. Beetles, moths, and owls have been traditionally associated with darkness, death and burial; "Psyche" means *Soul*, sometimes symbolized by a moth that escapes the mouth in sleep or at death.
7. The goddess Melancholy.
8. Keen, subtle.
9. Symbols of victory, such as banners, hung in religious shrines.

In Tempe or the dales of Arcady?[1]
What men or gods are these? What maidens loath?
What mad pursuit? What struggle to escape?
10   What pipes and timbrels? What wild ecstasy?

2

Heard melodies are sweet, but those unheard
Are sweeter; therefore, ye soft pipes, play on;
Not to the sensual ear, but, more endeared,
Pipe to the spirit ditties of no tone:
15 Fair youth, beneath the trees, thou canst not leave
Thy song, nor ever can those trees be bare;
Bold Lover, never, never canst thou kiss,
Though winning near the goal—yet, do not grieve;
She cannot fade, though thou hast not thy bliss,
20   Forever wilt thou love, and she be fair!

3

Ah, happy, happy boughs! that cannot shed
Your leaves, nor ever bid the Spring adieu;
And, happy melodist, unwearièd,
Forever piping songs forever new;
25 More happy love! more happy, happy love!
Forever warm and still to be enjoyed,
Forever panting, and forever young;
All breathing human passion far above,
That leaves a heart high-sorrowful and cloyed,
30   A burning forehead, and a parching tongue.

4

Who are these coming to the sacrifice?
To what green altar, O mysterious priest,
Lead'st thou that heifer lowing at the skies,
And all her silken flanks with garlands dressed?
35 What little town by river or sea shore,
Or mountain-built with peaceful citadel,
Is emptied of this folk, this pious morn?
And, little town, thy streets forevermore
Will silent be; and not a soul to tell
40   Why thou art desolate, can e'er return.

5

O Attic[2] shape! Fair attitude! with brede°   *woven pattern*
Of marble men and maidens overwrought,
With forest branches and the trodden weed;
Thou, silent form, dost tease us out of thought
45 As doth eternity: Cold Pastoral!
When old age shall this generation waste,
Thou shalt remain, in midst of other woe
Than ours, a friend to man, to whom thou say'st,
"Beauty is truth, truth beauty,"[3]—that is all
50   Ye know on earth, and all ye need to know.

                                        May 1819   1820

---

1. Tempe and Arcady (or Arcadia), in Greece, are traditional symbols of perfect pastoral landscapes.
2. Greek, especially Athenian.
3. The quotation marks around this phrase are absent from some other versions also having good authority. This discrepancy has led some readers to ascribe only this phrase to the voice of the Urn; others ascribe to the Urn the whole of the two concluding lines.

To Autumn

1

Season of mists and mellow fruitfulness,
  Close bosom-friend of the maturing sun;
Conspiring with him how to load and bless
  With fruit the vines that round the thatch-eaves run;
5 To bend with apples the mossed cottage-trees,
  And fill all fruit with ripeness to the core;
    To swell the gourd, and plump the hazel shells
  With a sweet kernel; to set budding more,
And still more, later flowers for the bees,
10 Until they think warm days will never cease,
    For Summer has o'er-brimmed their clammy cells.

2

Who hath not seen thee oft amid thy store?
  Sometimes whoever seeks abroad may find
Thee sitting careless on a granary floor,
15 Thy hair soft-lifted by the winnowing wind;[4]
Or on a half-reaped furrow sound asleep,
  Drowsed with the fume of poppies, while thy hook[5]
    Spares the next swath and all its twinéd flowers:
And sometimes like a gleaner thou dost keep
20 Steady thy laden head across a brook;
  Or by a cider-press, with patient look,
    Thou watchest the last oozings hours by hours.

3

Where are the songs of Spring? Aye, where are they?
  Think not of them, thou hast thy music too—
25 While barréd clouds bloom the soft-dying day,
  And touch the stubble-plains with rosy hue;
Then in a wailful choir the small gnats mourn
  Among the river sallows,° borne aloft   *low-growing willows*
    Or sinking as the light wind lives or dies;
30 And full-grown lambs loud bleat from hilly bourn;°   *field*
  Hedge crickets sing; and now with treble soft
  The redbreast whistles from a garden-croft;[6]
  And gathering swallows twitter in the skies.

                        September 19, 1819   1820

Bright Star

Bright star, would I were steadfast as thou art—
  Not in lone splendor hung aloft the night
And watching, with eternal lids apart,
  Like nature's patient, sleepless Eremite,°   *hermit, devotee*
5 The moving waters at their priestlike task
  Of pure ablution round earth's human shores,
Or gazing on the new soft fallen mask
  Of snow upon the mountains and the moors—

---

4. "Winnowing": blowing the grain clear of
the lighter chaff.
5. Small curved blade for cutting grain;
sickle.
6. Small field, as for a vegetable garden, near
a house.

No—yet still steadfast, still unchangeable,
10   Pillowed upon my fair love's ripening breast,
To feel forever its soft fall and swell,
     Awake forever in a sweet unrest,
Still, still to hear her tender-taken breath,
And so live ever—or else swoon to death.

                                    1819   1838

This Living Hand[7]

This living hand, now warm and capable
Of earnest grasping, would, if it were cold
And in the icy silence of the tomb,
So haunt thy days and chill thy dreaming nights
5 That thou wouldst wish thine own heart dry of blood
So in my veins red life might stream again,
And thou be conscience-calmed—see here it is—
I hold it towards you.

                                    1819?   1898

RALPH WALDO EMERSON
(1803–1882)

Concord Hymn

SUNG AT THE COMPLETION OF THE BATTLE MONUMENT,[1] JULY 4, 1837

By the rude bridge that arched the flood,
     Their flag to April's breeze unfurled,
Here once the embattled farmers stood
     And fired the shot heard round the world.

5 The foe long since in silence slept;
     Alike the conqueror silent sleeps;
And Time the ruined bridge has swept
     Down the dark stream which seaward creeps.

On this green bank, by this soft stream,
10   We set to-day a votive stone;
That memory may their deed redeem,
     When, like our sires, our sons are gone.

Spirit, that made those heroes dare
     To die, and leave their children free,
15 Bid Time and Nature gently spare
     The shaft we raise to them and thee.

                                    1837, 1876

---

7. Written on a manuscript page of Keats's
unfinished poem, *The Cap and Bells.*

1. Commemorating the battles of Lexington
and Concord, April 19, 1775.

The Rhodora

ON BEING ASKED, WHENCE IS THE FLOWER?

In May, when sea-winds pierced our solitudes,
I found the fresh Rhodora in the woods,
Spreading its leafless blooms in a damp nook,
To please the desert and the sluggish brook.
5   The purple petals, fallen in the pool,
Made the black water with their beauty gay;
Here might the red-bird come his plumes to cool,
And court the flower that cheapens his array.
Rhodora! if the sages ask thee why
10   This charm is wasted on the earth and sky,
Tell them, dear, that if eyes were made for seeing,
Then Beauty is its own excuse for being:
Why thou wert there, O rival of the rose!
I never thought to ask, I never knew;
15   But, in my simple ignorance, suppose
The self-same Power that brought me there brought you.

1834   1839, 1847

Hamatreya[2]

Bulkeley, Hunt, Willard, Hosmer, Meriam, Flint,[3]
Possessed the land which rendered to their toil
Hay, corn, roots, hemp, flax, apples, wool and wood.
Each of these landlords walked amidst his farm,
5   Saying, ' 'T is mine, my children's and my name's.
How sweet the west wind sounds in my own trees!
How graceful climb those shadows on my hill!
I fancy these pure waters and the flags°   *plants, grass*
Know me, as does my dog: we sympathize;
10   And, I affirm, my actions smack of the soil.'

Where are these men? Asleep beneath their grounds:
And strangers, fond as they, their furrows plough.
Earth laughs in flowers, to see her boastful boys
Earth proud, proud of the earth which is not theirs;
15   Who steer the plough, but cannot steer their feet
Clear of the grave.
They added ridge to valley, brook to pond,
And sighed for all that bounded their domain;
'This suits me for a pasture, that's my park;
20   We must have clay, lime, gravel, granite-ledge,
And misty lowland, where to go for peat.
The land is well—lies fairly to the south.
'T is good, when you have crossed the sea and back,
To find the sitfast acres where you left them.'
25   Ah! the hot owner sees not Death, who adds
Him to his land, a lump of mould the more.
Hear what the Earth says:

---

2. A variant of the Hindu name *Maitreya.*   3. First settlers of Concord, Massachusetts.

Earth-song

Mine and yours;
Mine, not yours.
Earth endures;
Stars abide—
Shine down in the old sea;
Old are the shores;
But where are old men?
I who have seen much,
Such have I never seen.

The lawyer's deed
Ran sure,
In tail,[4]
To them, and to their heirs
Who shall succeed,
Without fail,
Forevermore.

Here is the land,
Shaggy with wood,
With its old valley,
Mound and flood.
But the heritors?
Fled like the flood's foam.
The lawyer, and the laws,
And the kingdom,
Clean swept herefrom.

They called me theirs.
Who so controlled me;
Yet every one
Wished to stay, and is gone,
How am I theirs,
If they cannot hold me,
But I hold them?

60   When I heard the Earth-song,
I was no longer brave;
My avarice cooled
Like lust in the chill of the grave.

1847

Ode

INSCRIBED TO W. H. CHANNING[5]

Though loath to grieve
The evil time's sole patriot,
I cannot leave
My honied thought
5   For the priest's cant,
Or statesman's rant.

---

4. I.e., entailed; to *entail* is to limit by legal
means (usually a will) the inheritance of an
estate to a specified line of heirs.

5. Unitarian clergyman, transcendentalist, and
activist in social causes, particularly the anti-
slavery movement.

If I refuse
My study for their politique,
10   Which at the best is trick,
The angry Muse
Puts confusion in my brain.

But who is he that prates
Of the culture of mankind,
Of better arts and life?
15   Go, blindworm, go,
Behold the famous States
Harrying Mexico
With rifle and with knife!⁶

Or who, with accent bolder,
20   Dare praise the freedom-loving mountaineer?
I found by thee, O rushing Contoocook!⁷
And in thy valleys, Agiochook!⁸
The jackals of the Negro-holder.

The God who made New Hampshire
25   Taunted the lofty land
With little men;
Small bat and wren
House in the oak:
If earth-fire cleave

30   The upheaved land, and bury the folk,
The southern crocodile would grieve.
Virtue palters;° Right is hence;   *hesitates, equivocates*
Freedom praised, but hid;
Funeral eloquence
35   Rattles the coffin-lid.

What boots thy zeal,
O glowing friend,
That would indignant rend
The northland from the south?
40   Wherefore? to what good end?
Boston Bay and Bunker Hill
Would serve things still;
Things are of the snake.

The horseman serves the horse,
45   The neatherd serves the neat,⁹
The merchant serves the purse,
The eater serves his meat;
'T is the day of the chattel,
Web to weave, and corn to grind;
50   Things are in the saddle,
And ride mankind.

6. A reference to the war between the United
States and Mexico (1846–48) chiefly over the
question of the boundaries of Texas. To some
Americans, the United States' position was
immoral.

7. Part of the Merrimack River in New
Hampshire.
8. The White Mountains of New Hampshire.
9. Archaic terms for *cowherd* and *cow*.

There are two laws discrete,
Not reconciled,
Law for man, and law for things;
55   The last builds town and fleet,
But it runs wild,
And doth the man unking.

'T is fit the forest fall,
The steep be graded,
60   The mountain tunnelled,
The sand shaded,
The orchard planted,
The glebe tilled,
The prairie granted,
65   The steamer built.

Let man serve law for man;
Live for friendship, live for love,
For truth's and harmony's behoof;°   *benefit*
The state may follow how it can,
70   As Olympus follows Jove.

   Yet do not I implore
The wrinkled shopman to my surrounding woods,
Nor bid the unwilling senator
Ask votes of thrushes in the solitudes.
75   Every one to his chosen work;
Foolish hands may mix and mar;
Wise and sure the issues are.
Round they roll till dark is light,
Sex to sex, and even to odd;
80   The over-god
Who marries Right to Might,
Who peoples, unpeoples,
He who exterminates
Races by stronger races,
85   Black by white faces,
Knows to bring honey
Out of the lion;[1]
Grafts gentlest scion
On pirate and Turk.

90   The Cossack eats Poland,[2]
Like stolen fruit;
Her last noble is ruined,
Her last poet mute:
Straight, into double band
95   The victors divide;
Half for freedom strike and stand;—
The astonished Muse finds thousands at her side.

1847

1. The allusion in lines 83–87 is to Samson, who killed a lion and returned later to find the carcass filled with honey (Judges xiv.5–10).

2. Russian military despotism, established in Poland after the popular insurrections of 1830–31, was challenged by a new Polish uprising (lines 94–96) in 1846.

Brahma[3]

If the red slayer think he slays,
  Or if the slain think he is slain,
They know not well the subtle ways
  I keep, and pass, and turn again.

5 Far or forgot to me is near;
  Shadow and sunlight are the same;
The vanished gods to me appear;
  And one to me are shame and fame.

They reckon ill who leave me out;
10 When me they fly, I am the wings;
I am the doubter and the doubt,
  And I the hymn the Brahmin sings.

The strong gods pine for my abode,
  And pine in vain the sacred Seven,[4]
15 But thou, meek lover of the good!
  Find me, and turn thy back on heaven.

1856   1857, 1867

Days

Daughters of Time, the hypocritic Days,
Muffled and dumb like barefoot dervishes,
And marching single in an endless file,
Bring diadems and fagots in their hands.
5 To each they offer gifts after his will,
Bread, kingdom, stars, and sky that holds them all.

I, in my pleached garden,[5] watched the pomp,
Forgot my morning wishes, hastily
Took a few herbs and apples, and the Day
10 Turned and departed silent. I, too late,
Under her solemn fillet° saw the scorn.

               hair band
1857, 1867

HENRY WADSWORTH LONGFELLOW
(1807–1882)

Mezzo Cammin[1]

WRITTEN AT BOPPARD ON THE RHINE AUGUST 25, 1842, JUST BEFORE
LEAVING FOR HOME

Half of my life is gone, and I have let
  The years slip from me and have not fulfilled
  The aspiration of my youth, to build
Some tower of song with lofty parapet.

---

3. The supreme God of Hindu mythology and, in later theological developments, the divine reality itself, once thought to comprehend the entire universe which is the manifestation of that reality.
4. Perhaps the seven saints high in the Brahman hierarchy, but lesser than Brahma.

5. To pleach is to entwine, plait, or arrange foliage artificially.
1. A phrase from the first line of Dante's *Divina Commedia:* "*Nel mezzo del cammin di nostra vita*" (midway upon the journey of our life).

5 Not indolence, nor pleasure, nor the fret
    Of restless passions that would not be stilled,
    But sorrow, and care that almost killed,[2]
    Kept me from what I may accomplish yet;
Though, halfway up the hill, I see the Past
10   Lying beneath me with its sounds and sights,
    A city in the twilight dim and vast,
With smoking roofs, soft bells, and gleaming lights,
    And hear above me on the autumnal blast
The cataract of Death far thundering from the heights.

                      1842   1846

Divina Commedia[3]

1

Oft have I seen at some cathedral door
    A laborer, pausing in the dust and heat,
    Lay down his burden, and with reverent feet
    Enter, and cross himself, and on the floor
5 Kneel to repeat his paternoster[4] o'er;
    Far off the noises of the world retreat;
    The loud vociferations of the street
    Become an undistinguishable roar.
So, as I enter here from day to day,
10   And leave my burden at this minster gate,
    Kneeling in prayer, and not ashamed to pray,
The tumult of the time disconsolate
    To inarticulate murmurs dies away,
    While the eternal ages watch and wait.

2

How strange the sculptures that adorn these towers!
    This crowd of statues, in whose folded sleeves
    Birds build their nests; while canopied with leaves
    Parvis[5] and portal bloom like trellised bowers,
5 And the vast minster seems a cross of flowers!
    But fiends and dragons on the gargoyled eaves
    Watch the dead Christ between the living thieves,
    And, underneath, the traitor Judas lowers!
Ah! from what agonies of heart and brain,
10   What exultations trampling on despair,
    What tenderness, what tears, what hate of wrong,
What passionate outcry of a soul in pain,
    Uprose this poem of the earth and air,
    This mediaeval miracle of song!

3

I enter, and I see thee in the gloom
    Of the long aisles, O poet saturnine![6]
    And strive to make my steps keep pace with thine.
    The air is filled with some unknown perfume;
5 The congregation of the dead make room
    For thee to pass; the votive tapers shine;
    Like rooks that haunt Ravenna's[7] groves of pine
    The hovering echoes fly from tomb to tomb.

2. Probably an allusion to the death of Longfellow's wife in 1835.
3. Divine Comedy.
4. Literally, the Latin "our father," the first words of the Lord's Prayer.
5. The court or portico in front of a church or cathedral.
6. A reference to Dante himself.
7. A city in northeastern Italy, much admired by Dante and in which he died after having fled Florence in 1301.

From the confessionals I hear arise
10   Rehearsals of forgotten tragedies,
    And lamentations from the crypts below;
And then a voice celestial that begins
    With the pathetic words, "Although your sins
    As scarlet be," and ends with "as the snow."[8]

4

With snow-white veil and garments as of flame,
    She stands before thee, who so long ago
    Filled thy young heart with passion and the woe
    From which thy song and all its splendors came;[9]
5 And while with stern rebuke she speaks thy name,
    The ice about thy heart melts as the snow
    On mountain heights, and in swift overflow
    Comes gushing from thy lips in sobs of shame.
Thou makest full confession; and a gleam,
10   As of the dawn on some dark forest cast,
    Seems on thy lifted forehead to increase;
Lethe and Eunoë[1]—the remembered dream
    And the forgotten sorrow—bring at last
    That perfect pardon which is perfect peace.

5

I lift mine eyes, and all the windows blaze
    With forms of saints and holy men who died,
    Here martyred and hereafter glorified;
    And the great Rose[2] upon its leaves displays
5 Christ's Triumph, and the angelic roundelays,
    With splendor upon splendor multiplied;
    And Beatrice again at Dante's side
    No more rebukes, but smiles her words of praise.
And then the organ sounds, and unseen choirs
10   Sing the old Latin hymns of peace and love
    And benedictions of the Holy Ghost;
And the melodious bells among the spires
    O'er all the housetops and through heaven above
    Proclaim the elevation of the Host![3]

6

O star of morning and of liberty![4]
    O bringer of the light, whose splendor shines
    Above the darkness of the Apennines,
    Forerunner of the day that is to be!
5 The voices of the city and the sea,
    The voices of the mountains and the pines,
    Repeat thy song, till the familiar lines
    Are footpaths for the thought of Italy!
Thy flame is blown abroad from all the heights,
10   Through all the nations, and a sound is heard,
    As of a mighty wind, and men devout,
Strangers of Rome, and the new proselytes,
    In their own language hear thy wondrous word,
    And many are amazed and many doubt.

                                              1864–67   1865–67

8. "Come now, and let us reason together,
saith the Lord: though your sins be as scarlet,
they shall be as white as snow" (Isaiah i.18).
9. A reference to Beatrice, who, whether as a
real person in his youth or as a vision, was
Dante's inspiration in *Vita Nuova* and *Divina
Commedia.*
1. In classical myth and literature, Lethe is
the river of forgetfulness; Eunoë, of good
memories.
2. A many-petaled rose is, in the *Paradiso*
section of *Divina Commedia,* Dante's vision of
Christ triumphant, with the Virgin and the
saints.
3. The consecrated bread in the Eucharist, or
communion sacrament.
4. A direct address to Dante as symbol of the
rising spirit of freedom in the Renaissance.

EDWARD FITZGERALD
(1809–1883)

The Rubáiyát of Omar Khayyám of Naishápúr[1]

1

Wake! For the Sun, who scattered into flight
The Stars before him from the Field of Night,
   Drives Night along with them from Heav'n, and strikes
The Sultán's Turret with a Shaft of Light.

2

5 Before the phantom of False morning died,
Methought a Voice within the Tavern cried,
   "When all the Temple is prepared within,
"Why nods the drowsy Worshipper outside?"

3

And, as the Cock crew, those who stood before
10 The Tavern shouted—"Open then the Door!
   "You know how little while we have to stay,
"And, once departed, may return no more."

4

Now the New Year[2] reviving old Desires,
The thoughtful Soul to Solitude retires,
15   Where the WHITE HAND OF MOSES on the Bough
Puts out, and Jesus from the Ground suspires.[3]

5

Irám[4] indeed is gone with all his Rose,
And Jamshýd's Sev'n-ringed Cup[5] where no one knows;
   But still a Ruby kindles in the Vine,
20 And many a Garden by the Water blows.

6

And David's lips are lockt; but in divine
High-piping Pehleví,[6] with "Wine! Wine! Wine!
   "Red Wine!"—the Nightingale cries to the Rose
That sallow cheek of hers to incarnadine.

7

25 Come, fill the Cup, and in the fire of Spring
Your Winter-garment of Repentance fling:
   The Bird of Time has but a little way
To flutter—and the Bird is on the Wing.

8

Whether at Naishápúr or Babylon,
30 Whether the Cup with sweet or bitter run,
   The Wine of Life keeps oozing drop by drop,
The Leaves of Life keep falling one by one.

1. Omar Khayyám, Persian poet, mathematician, and astronomer (ca. 1050–1132?), lived at Nishapur, in the province of Khurasan. FitzGerald translated his epigrammatic quatrains (*Rubáiyát*, plural of *ruba'i*, quatrain) which he first published in 1859; in three subsequent editions (the fourth edition is printed here) FitzGerald made many alterations of detail, arrangement, and number of stanzas.
2. "Beginning with the Vernal Equinox, it must be remembered" [FitzGerald's note].
3. The blossoming of trees is compared to the whiteness of Moses' hand as it is described in Exodus iv.6, and the sweetness of flowers to the sweetness of the breath of Jesus.
4. "A royal Garden now sunk somewhere in the Sands of Arabia" [FitzGerald's note].
5. In Persian mythology, Jamshýd was a king of the peris (celestial beings), who, because he had boasted of his immortality, was compelled to live on earth in human form for 700 years, becoming one of the kings of Persia. His cup, the invention of Kai-Kosru (line 38), another Persian king, great-grandson of Kai-Kobad (line 36), was decorated with signs enabling its possessor to foretell the future.
6. The ancient literary language of Persia.

9

Each Morn a thousand Roses brings, you say;
Yes, but where leaves the Rose of Yesterday?
35   And this first Summer month that brings the Rose
Shall take Jamshýd and Kaikobád away.

10

Well, let it take them! What have we to do
With Kaikobád the Great, or Kaikhosrú?
    Let Zál and Rustum[7] bluster as they will,
40 Or Hátim[8] call to Supper—heed not you.

11

With me along the strip of Herbage strown
That just divides the desert from the sown,
    Where name of Slave and Sultán is forgot—
And Peace to Mahmúd[9] on his golden Throne!

12

45 A Book of Verses underneath the Bough,
A Jug of Wine, a Loaf of Bread—and Thou
    Beside me singing in the Wilderness—
Oh, Wilderness were Paradise enow!

13

Some for the Glories of This World; and some
50 Sigh for the Prophet's[1] Paradise to come;
    Ah, take the Cash, and let the Credit go,
Nor heed the rumble of a distant Drum!

14

Look to the blowing Rose about us—"Lo,
"Laughing," she says, "into the world I blow,
55   "At once the silken tassel of my Purse
"Tear, and its Treasure on the Garden throw."

15

And those who husbanded the Golden grain,
And those who flung it to the winds like Rain,
    Alike to no such aureate Earth are turned
60 As, buried once, Men want dug up again.

16

The Worldly Hope men set their Hearts upon
Turns Ashes—or it prospers; and anon,
    Like Snow upon the Desert's dusty Face,
Lighting a little hour or two—is gone.

17

65 Think, in this battered Caravanserai°   *inn*
Whose Portals are alternate Night and Day,
    How Sultán after Sultán with his Pomp
Abode his destined Hour, and went his way.

18

They say the Lion and the Lizard keep
70 The Courts where Jamshýd gloried and drank deep:
    And Bahrám,[2] that great Hunter—the Wild Ass
Stamps o'er his Head, but cannot break his Sleep.

---

7. "The 'Hercules' of Persia, and Zál his Father" [FitzGerald's note].
8. Hátim Tai: a Persian chieftain, an archetype of oriental hospitality.
9. Sultan Máhmúd of Ghazni, in Afghan- istan (971–1031), renowned both as ruler and as the conqueror of India.
1. I.e., Mohammed's.
2. A Sassanian king who, according to legend, met his death while hunting the wild ass.

19

I sometimes think that never blows so red
The Rose as where some buried Caesar bled;
   That every Hyacinth the Garden wears
Dropt in her Lap from some once lovely Head.

20

And this reviving Herb whose tender Green
Fledges the river-lip on which we lean—
   Ah, lean upon it lightly! for who knows
From what once lovely Lip it springs unseen!

21

Ah, my Belovéd, fill the Cup that clears
TODAY of past Regrets and future Fears:
   Tomorrow!—Why, Tomorrow I may be
Myself with Yesterday's Sev'n thousand Years.

22

For some we loved, the loveliest and the best
That from his Vintage rolling Time hath prest,
   Have drunk their Cup a Round or two before,
And one by one crept silently to rest.

23

And we, that make merry in the Room
They left, and Summer dresses in new bloom,
   Ourselves must we beneath the Couch of Earth
Descend—ourselves to make a Couch—for whom?

24

Ah, make the most of what we yet may spend,
Before we too into the Dust descend;
   Dust into Dust, and under Dust to lie,
Sans Wine, sans Song, sans Singer, and sans End!

25

Alike for those who for TODAY prepare,
And those that after some TOMORROW stare,
   A Muezzín[3] from the Tower of Darkness cries,
"Fools! your Reward is neither Here nor There."

26

Why, all the Saints and Sages who discussed
Of the Two Worlds so wisely—they are thrust
   Like foolish Prophets forth; their Words to Scorn
Are scattered, and their Mouths are stopt with Dust.

27

Myself when young did eagerly frequent
Doctor and Saint, and heard great argument
   About it and about: but evermore
Came out by the same door where in I went.

28

With them the seed of Wisdom did I sow,
And with mine own hand wrought to make it grow;
   And this was all the Harvest that I reaped—
"I came like Water, and like Wind I go."

29

Into this Universe, and *Why* not knowing
Nor *Whence*, like Water willy-nilly flowing;
   And out of it, as Wind along the Waste,
I know not *Whither*, willy-nilly blowing.

3. The crier who calls the hours of prayer from tower or minaret.

30

What, without asking, hither hurried *Whence?*
And, without asking, *Whither* hurried hence!
   Oh, many a Cup of this forbidden Wine[4]
120 Must drown the memory of that insolence!

31

Up from Earth's Center through the Seventh Gate
I rose, and on the Throne of Saturn[5] sate,
   And many a Knot unraveled by the Road;
But not the Master-knot of Human Fate.

32

125 There was the Door to which I found no Key;
There was the Veil through which I might not see:
   Some little talk awhile of ME and THEE
There was—and then no more of THEE and ME.

33

Earth could not answer; nor the Seas that mourn
130 In flowing Purple, of their Lord forlorn;
   Nor rolling Heaven, with all his Signs revealed
And hidden by the sleeve of Night and Morn.

34

Then of the THEE IN ME who works behind
The Veil, I lifted up my hands to find
135   A lamp amid the Darkness; and I heard,
As from Without—"THE ME WITHIN THEE BLIND!"

35

Then to the Lip of this poor earthen Urn
I leaned, the Secret of my Life to learn:
   And Lip to Lip it murmured—"While you live,
140 "Drink! for, once dead, you never shall return."

36

I think the Vessel, that with fugitive
Articulation answered, once did live,
   And drink; and Ah! the passive Lip I kissed,
How many Kisses might it take—and give!

37

145 For I remember stopping by the way
To watch a Potter thumping his wet Clay:
   And with its all-obliterated Tongue
It murmured—"Gently, Brother, gently, pray!"

38

And has not such a Story from of Old
150 Down Man's successive generations rolled
   Of such a clod of saturated Earth
Cast by the Maker into Human mold?

39

And not a drop that from our Cups we throw
For Earth to drink of, but may steal below
155   To quench the fire of Anguish in some Eye
There hidden—far beneath, and long ago.

---

4. Alcohol is forbidden to Mohammedans.
5. "Lord of the Seventh Heaven" [FitzGerald's note]. In ancient astronomy, Saturn was the most remote of the seven known planets; hence, Omar had reached the bounds of astronomical knowledge.

40

As then the Tulip for her morning sup
Of Heav'nly Vintage from the soil looks up,
  Do you devoutly do the like, till Heav'n
160 To Earth invert you—like an empty Cup.

41

Perplext no more with Human or Divine,
Tomorrow's tangle to the winds resign,
  And lose your fingers in the tresses of
The Cypress-slender Minister of Wine.[6]

42

165 And if the Wine you drink, the Lip you press,
End in what All begins and ends in—Yes;
  Think then you are TODAY what YESTERDAY
You were—TOMORROW you shall not be less.

43

So when that Angel of the darker Drink
170 At last shall find you by the river-brink,
  And, offering his Cup, invite your Soul
Forth to your Lips to quaff—you shall not shrink.

44

Why, if the Soul can fling the Dust aside,
And naked on the Air of Heaven ride,
175   Were't not a Shame—were't not a Shame for him
In this clay carcase crippled to abide?

45

'Tis but a Tent where takes his one day's rest
A Sultán to the realm of Death addrest;
  The Sultán rises, and the dark Ferrásh[7]
180 Strikes, and prepares it for another Guest.

46

And fear not lest Existence closing your
Account, and mine, should know the like no more;
  The Eternal Sáki° from that Bowl has poured   *cup-bearer*
Millions of Bubbles like us, and will pour.

47

185 When You and I behind the Veil are past,
Oh, but the long, long while the World shall last,
  Which of our Coming and Departure heeds
As the Sea's self should heed a pebble-cast.

48

190 A Moment's Halt—a momentary taste
Of BEING from the Well amid the Waste—
  And Lo!—the phantom Caravan has reached
The NOTHING it set out from—Oh, make haste!

49

Would you that spangle of Existence spend
About THE SECRET—quick about it, Friend!
195   A Hair perhaps divides the False and True—
And upon what, prithee, may life depend?

---

6. The maidservant who pours the wine.   7. The servant charged with setting up and striking the tent.

50

A Hair perhaps divides the False and True;
Yes; and a single Alif[8] were the clue—
   Could you but find it—to the Treasure-house,
200 And peradventure to THE MASTER too;

51

Whose secret Presence, through Creation's veins
Running Quicksilver-like eludes your pains;
   Taking all shapes from Máh to Máhi;[9] and
They change and perish all—but He remains;

52

205 A moment guessed—then back behind the Fold
Immerst of Darkness round the Drama rolled
   Which, for the Pastime of Eternity,
He doth Himself contrive, enact, behold.

53

But if in vain, down on the stubborn floor
210 Of Earth, and up to Heav'n's unopening Door,
   You gaze TODAY, while You are You—how then
TOMORROW, You when shall be You no more?

54

Waste not your Hour, nor in the vain pursuit
Of This and That endeavor and dispute;
215   Better be jocund with the fruitful Grape
Than sadden after none, or bitter, Fruit.

55

You know, my Friends, with what a brave Carouse
I made a Second Marriage in my house;
   Divorced old barren Reason from my Bed,
220 'And took the Daughter of the Vine to Spouse.

56

For "Is" and "Is-not" though with Rule and Line,
And "UP-AND-DOWN" by Logic I define,
   Of all that one should care to fathom, I
Was never deep in anything but—Wine.

57

225 Ah, but my Computations, People say,
Reduced the Year to better reckoning?[1]—Nay,
   'Twas only striking from the Calendar
Unborn Tomorrow, and dead Yesterday.

58

And lately, by the Tavern Door agape,
230 Came shining through the Dusk an Angel Shape
   Bearing a Vessel on his Shoulder; and
He bid me taste of it; and 'twas—the Grape!

59

The Grape that can with Logic absolute
The Two-and-Seventy jarring Sects[2] confute:
235   The sovereign Alchemist that in a trice
Life's leaden metal into Gold transmute:

---

8. First letter of Arabic alphabet, consisting of a single vertical stroke.
9. From lowest to highest.

1. Omar was one of the learned men who had been charged with reforming the calendar.
2. "The 72 sects into which Islamism so soon split" [FitzGerald's note].

60

The mighty Mahmúd, Allah-breathing Lord,[3]
That all the misbelieving and black Horde
    Of Fears and Sorrows that infest the Soul
240 Scatters before him with his whirlwind Sword.

61

Why, be this Juice the growth of God, who dare
Blaspheme the twisted tendril as a Snare?
    A Blessing, we should use it, should we not?
And if a Curse—why, then, Who set it there?

62

245 I must abjure the Balm of Life, I must,
Scared by some After-reckoning ta'en on trust,
    Or lured with Hope of some Diviner Drink,
To fill the Cup—when crumbled into Dust!

63

Oh threats of Hell and Hopes of Paradise!
250 One thing at least is certain—*This* Life flies;
    One thing is certain and the rest is Lies;
The Flower that once has blown for ever dies.

64

Strange, is it not? that of the myriads who
Before us passed the door of Darkness through,
255   Not one returns to tell us of the Road,
Which to discover we must travel too.

65

The Revelations of Devout and Learned
Who rose before us, and as Prophets burned,
    Are all but Stories, which, awoke from Sleep
260 They told their comrades, and to Sleep returned.

66

I sent my Soul through the Invisible,
Some letter of that Afterlife to spell:
    And by and by my Soul returned to me,
And answered "I Myself am Heav'n and Hell:"

67

265 Heav'n but the Vision of fulfilled Desire,
And Hell the Shadow from a Soul on fire,
    Cast on the Darkness into which Ourselves,
So late emerged from, shall so soon expire.

68

We are no other than a moving row
270 Of Magic Shadow-shapes that come and go
    Round with the Sun-illumined Lantern held
In Midnight by the Master of the Show;

69

But helpless Pieces of the Game He plays
Upon his Checkerboard of Nights and Days;
275   Hither and thither moves, and checks, and slays,
And one by one back in the Closet lays.

70

The Ball no question makes of Ayes and Noes,
But Here or There as strikes the Player goes;
    And He that tossed you down into the Field,
280 *He* knows about it all—HE knows—HE knows!

---

3. "This alludes to Máhmúd's Conquest of India and its swarthy Idolators" [FitzGerald's note].

71

The Moving Finger writes; and, having writ,
Moves on: nor all your Piety nor Wit
   Shall lure it back to cancel half a Line,
Nor all your Tears wash out a Word of it.

72

285 And that inverted Bowl they call the Sky,
Whereunder crawling cooped we live and die,
   Lift not your hands to *It* for help—for It
As impotently moves as you or I.

73

With Earth's first Clay They did the Last Man knead,
290 And there of the Last Harvest sowed the Seed:
   And the first Morning of Creation wrote
What the Last Dawn of Reckoning shall read.

74

Yesterday *This* Day's Madness did prepare;
Tomorrow's Silence, Triumph, or Despair:
295   Drink! for you know not whence you came, nor why:
Drink! for you know not why you go, nor where.

75

I tell you this—When, started from the Goal,
Over the flaming shoulders of the Foal[4]
   Of Heav'n, Parwín and Mushtarí[5] they flung,
300 In my predestined Plot of Dust and Soul.

76

The Vine had struck a fiber: which about
If clings my Being—let the Dervish[6] flout;
   Of my Base metal may be filed a Key,
That shall unlock the Door he howls without.

77

305 And this I know: whether the one True Light
Kindle to Love, or Wrath consume me quite,
   One Flash of It within the Tavern caught
Better than in the Temple lost outright.

78

What! out of senseless Nothing to provoke
310 A conscious Something to resent the yoke
   Of unpermitted Pleasure, under pain
Of Everlasting Penalties, if broke!

79

What! from his helpless Creature be repaid
Pure Gold for what he lent him dross-allayed—
315   Sue for a Debt he never did contract,
And cannot answer—Oh the sorry trade!

80

Oh Thou, who didst with pitfall and with gin°   *trap*
Beset the Road I was to wander in,
   Thou wilt not with Predestined Evil round
320 Enmesh, and then impute my Fall to Sin!

---

4. The constellation known as the Colt (*Equuleus*) or Foal.
5. "The Pleiads and Jupiter" [FitzGerald's note]; Omar ascribes his fate to the position of the stars and planets at the time of his birth.
6. Member of any of several Muslim orders taking vows of austerity and poverty.

81

Oh Thou, who Man of baser Earth didst make,
And ev'n with Paradise devise the Snake:
    For all the Sin wherewith the Face of Man
Is blackened—Man's forgiveness give—and take!

82

325 As under cover of departing Day
Slunk hunger-stricken Ramazán[7] away,
    Once more within the Potter's house alone
I stood, surrounded by the Shapes of Clay.

83

Shapes of all Sorts and Sizes, great and small,
330 That stood along the floor and by the wall;
    And some loquacious Vessels were; and some
Listened perhaps, but never talked at all.

84

Said one among them—"Surely not in vain
"My substance of the common Earth was ta'en
335   "And to this Figure molded, to be broke,
"Or trampled back to shapeless Earth again."

85

Then said a Second—"Ne'er a peevish Boy
"Would break the Bowl from which he drank in joy;
    "And He that with his hand the Vessel made
340 "Will surely not in after Wrath destroy."

86

After a momentary silence spake
Some Vessel of a more ungainly Make;
    "They sneer at me for leaning all awry:
"What! did the Hand then of the Potter shake?"

87

345 Whereat some one of the loquacious Lot—
I think a Súfi° pipkin—waxing hot—   mystic
    "All this of Pot and Potter—Tell me then,
"Who is the Potter, pray, and who the Pot?"

88

"Why," said another, "Some there are who tell
350 "Of one who threatens he will toss to Hell
    "The luckless Pots he marred in making—Pish!
"He's a Good Fellow, and 'twill all be well."

89

"Well," murmured one, "Let whoso make or buy,
"My Clay with long Oblivion is gone dry:
355   "But fill me with the old familiar Juice,
"Methinks I might recover by and by."

90

So while the Vessels one by one were speaking,
The little Moon[8] looked in that all were seeking:
    And then they jogged each other, "Brother! Brother!
360 "Now for the Porter's shoulder-knot[9] a-creaking!"

---

7. The Mohammedans' annual thirty-day fast,
during which no food may be taken from dawn
to sunset.

8. The new moon, which signaled the end of
Ramazán.
9. The knot on the porter's shoulder-strap
from which the wine-jars were hung.

91

Ah, with the Grape my fading Life provide,
And wash the Body whence the Life has died,
   And lay men shrouded in the living Leaf,
By some not unfrequented Garden-side.

92

365 That ev'n my buried Ashes such a snare
Of Vintage shall fling up into the Air
   As not a True-believer passing by
But shall be overtaken unaware.

93

Indeed the Idols I have loved so long
370 Have done my credit in this World much wrong:
   Have drowned my Glory in a shallow Cup,
And sold my Reputation for a Song.

94

Indeed, indeed, Repentance oft before
I swore—but was I sober when I swore?
375   And then and then came Spring, and Rose-in-hand
My threadbare Penitence apieces tore.

95

And much as Wine has played the Infidel,
And robbed me of my Robe of Honor—Well,
   I wonder often what the Vintners buy
380 One half so precious as the stuff they sell.

96

Yet Ah, that Spring should vanish with the Rose!
That Youth's sweet-scented manuscript should close!
   The Nightingale that in the branches sang,
Ah whence, and whither flown again, who knows!

97

385 Would but the Desert of the Fountain yield
One glimpse—if dimly, yet indeed, revealed,
   To which the fainting Traveler might spring,
As springs the trampled herbage of the field!

98

Would but some wingéd Angel ere too late
390 Arrest the yet unfolded Roll of Fate,
   And make the stern Recorder otherwise
Enregister, or quite obliterate!

99

Ah Love! could you and I with Him conspire
To grasp this sorry Scheme of Things entire,
395   Would not we shatter it to bits—and then
Remold it nearer to the Heart's Desire!

100

Yon rising Moon that looks for us again—
How oft hereafter will she wax and wane;
   How oft hereafter rising look for us
400 Through this same Garden—and for *one* in vain!

101
And when like her, oh Sákí, you shall pass
Among the Guests Star-scattered on the Grass,
    And in your joyous errand reach the spot
Where I made One—turn down an empty Glass!

TAMÁM[10]

1859, 1879

EDGAR ALLAN POE
(1809–1849)

Sonnet—To Science

Science! true daughter of Old Time thou art!
    Who alterest all things with thy peering eyes.
Why preyest thou thus upon the poet's heart,
    Vulture, whose wings are dull realities?
5 How should he love thee? or how deem thee wise?
    Who wouldst not leave him in his wandering
To seek for treasure in the jeweled skies,
    Albeit he soared with an undaunted wing?
Hast thou not dragged Diana[1] from her car?
10   And driven the Hamadryad[2] from the wood
To seek a shelter in some happier star?
    Hast thou not torn the Naiad° from her flood,   *river nymph*
The Elfin from the green grass, and from me
The summer dream beneath the tamarind tree?[3]

1829   1829, 1845

To Helen

Helen, thy beauty is to me
    Like those Nicean barks of yore,
That gently, o'er a perfumed sea,
    The weary, way-worn wanderer bore
5   To his own native shore.

On desperate seas long wont to roam,
    Thy hyacinth hair,[4] thy classic face,
Thy Naiad airs have brought me home
    To the glory that was Greece
10 And the grandeur that was Rome.

Lo! in yon brilliant window-niche
    How statue-like I see thee stand!
    The agate lamp within thy hand,
Ah! Psyche,[5] from the regions which
15   Are Holy Land!

1823   1831, 1845

10. It is ended.
1. To the Romans, the virgin goddess of the hunt, revered for her chastity and protectiveness. Her "car" is the moon.
2. Wood nymph said to live and die with the tree she inhabits.
3. An oriental tree the fruit of which is used medicinally and for food.
4. Presumably, hair like that of the slain youth

Hyacinthus, beloved of Apollo.
5. Having lost her lover Cupid because she insisted on seeing him when he preferred to come to her unseen at night (she dropped oil accidentally from her lamp while he was sleeping), Psyche appealed for help in finding Cupid to Venus, who required, among other things, that Psyche bring back unopened a box from the underworld.

ALFRED, LORD TENNYSON
(1809–1892)

Song

1

A spirit haunts the year's last hours
Dwelling amid these yellowing bowers.
　　To himself he talks;
For at eventide, listening earnestly,
5　At his work you may hear him sob and sigh
　　In the walks;
　Earthward he boweth the heavy stalks
Of the moldering flowers.
　　Heavily hangs the broad sunflower
10　　　Over its grave i' the earth so chilly;
　　Heavily hangs the hollyhock,
　　　Heavily hangs the tiger-lily.

2

The air is damp, and hushed, and close,
As a sick man's room when he taketh repose
15　　An hour before death;
My very heart faints and my whole soul grieves
At the moist rich smell of the rotting leaves,
　　And the breath
Of the fading edges of box[1] beneath,
20　And the year's last rose.
　　Heavily hangs the broad sunflower
　　　Over its grave i' the earth so chilly;
　　Heavily hangs the hollyhock,
　　　Heavily hangs the tiger-lily.

1830

The Kraken [2]

Below the thunders of the upper deep,
Far far beneath in the abysmal sea,
His ancient, dreamless, uninvaded sleep
The Kraken sleepeth: faintest sunlights flee
5　About his shadowy sides: above him swell
Huge sponges of millennial growth and height;
And far away into the sickly light,
From many a wondrous grot and secret cell
Unnumbered and enormous polypi [3]
10　Winnow with giant fins the slumbering green.
There hath he lain for ages and will lie
Battening upon huge seaworms in his sleep,

1. Evergreen shrub used in formal gardening.
2. A mythical sea monster, called in an 18th-century *History of Norway* "the largest and most surprising of all the animal creation" (*O. E. D.*).
3. Octopus-like creatures.

Until the latter fire shall heat the deep; [4]
Then once by men and angels to be seen,
15 In roaring he shall rise and on the surface die.

1830

The Lotos-Eaters[2]

"Courage!" he[3] said, and pointed toward the land,
"This mounting wave will roll us shoreward soon."
In the afternoon they came unto a land
In which it seeméd always afternoon.
5 All round the coast the languid air did swoon,
Breathing like one that hath a weary dream.
Full-faced above the valley stood the moon;
And, like a downward smoke, the slender stream
Along the cliff to fall and pause and fall did seem.

10 A land of streams! some, like a downward smoke,
Slow-dropping veils of thinnest lawn,[4] did go;
And some through wavering lights and shadows broke,
Rolling a slumbrous sheet of foam below.
They saw the gleaming river seaward flow
15 From the inner land; far off, three mountain-tops,
Three silent pinnacles of aged snow,
Stood sunset-flushed; and, dewed with showery drops,
Up-clomb the shadowy pine above the woven copse.

The charméd sunset lingered low adown
20 In the red West; through mountain clefts the dale
Was seen far inland, and the yellow down
Bordered with palm, and many a winding vale
And meadow, set with slender galingale;[5]
A land where all things always seemed the same!
25 And round about the keel with faces pale,
Dark faces pale against that rosy flame,
The mild-eyed melancholy Lotos-eaters came.

Branches they bore of that enchanted stem,
Laden with flower and fruit, whereof they gave
30 To each, but whoso did receive of them
And taste, to him the gushing of the wave
Far far away did seem to mourn and rave
On alien shores; and if his fellow spake,
His voice was thin, as voices from the grave;
35 And deep-asleep he seemed, yet all awake,
And music in his ears his beating heart did make.

They sat them down upon the yellow sand,
Between the sun and moon upon the shore;
And sweet it was to dream of fatherland,
40 Of child, and wife, and slave; but evermore

4. At the end of the world, ". . . the elements shall melt with fervent heat, the earth also and the works that are therein shall be burned up" (II Peter iii.10). See also Revelation viii. 8–9: "And the second angel sounded, and as it were a great mountain burning with fire was cast into the sea: and the third part of the sea became blood; and there died the third part of the creatures which were in the sea. . . ."

2. In Greek legend, a people who ate the fruit of the lotos, the effect of which was to induce drowsy languor and forgetfulness. The visit of Odysseus and his men to their island is described in the *Odyssey*, IX.82–97.
3. I.e., Odysseus.
4. Sheer cotton fabric.
5. A reed-like plant, a species of sedge.

Most weary seemed the sea, weary the oar,
Weary the wandering fields of barren foam.
Then someone said, "We will return no more;"
And all at once they sang, "Our island home
45 Is far beyond the wave; we will no longer roam."

   Choric Song

          1
There is sweet music here that softer falls
Than petals from blown roses on the grass,
Or night-dews on still waters between walls
Of shadowy granite, in a gleaming pass;
50 Music that gentlier on the spirit lies,
Than tired eyelids upon tired eyes;
Music that brings sweet sleep down from the blissful skies.
Here are cool mosses deep,
And through the moss the ivies creep,
55 And in the stream the long-leaved flowers weep,
And from the craggy ledge the poppy hangs in sleep.

          2
Why are we weighed upon with heaviness,
And utterly consumed with sharp distress,
While all things else have rest from weariness?
60 All things have rest: why should we toil alone,
We only toil, who are the first of things,
And make perpetual moan,
Still from one sorrow to another thrown;
Nor ever fold our wings,
65 And cease from wanderings,
Nor steep our brows in slumber's holy balm;
Nor harken what the inner spirit sings,
"There is no joy but calm!"—
Why should we only toil, the roof and crown of things?

          3
70 Lo! in the middle of the wood,
The folded leaf is wooed from out the bud
With winds upon the branch, and there
Grows green and broad, and takes no care,
Sun-steeped at noon, and in the moon
75 Nightly dew-fed; and turning yellow
Falls, and floats adown the air.
Lo! sweetened with the summer light,
The full-juiced apple, waxing over-mellow,
80 Drops in a silent autumn night.
All its allotted length of days
The flower ripens in its place,
Ripens and fades, and falls, and hath no toil,
Fast-rooted in the fruitful soil.

          4
Hateful is the dark-blue sky,
85 Vaulted o'er the dark-blue sea.
Death is the end of life; ah, why
Should life all labor be?
Let us alone. Time driveth onward fast
And in a little while our lips are dumb.
90 Let us alone. What is it that will last?
All things are taken from us, and become
Portions and parcels of the dreadful past.

Let us alone. What pleasure can we have
To war with evil? Is there any peace
95 In ever climbing up the climbing wave?
All things have rest, and ripen toward the grave
In silence—ripen, fall, and cease:
Give us long rest or death, dark death, or dreamful ease.

5
How sweet it were, hearing the downward stream,
100 With half-shut eyes ever to seem
Falling asleep in a half-dream!
To dream and dream, like yonder amber light,
Which will not leave the myrrh-bush on the height;
To hear each other's whispered speech;
105 Eating the Lotos day by day,
To watch the crisping ripples on the beach,
And tender curving lines of creamy spray;
To lend our hearts and spirits wholly
To the influence of mild-minded melancholy;
110 To muse and brood and live again in memory,
With those old faces of our infancy
Heaped over with a mound of grass,
Two handfuls of white dust, shut in an urn of brass!

6
Dear is the memory of our wedded lives,
115 And dear the last embraces of our wives
And their warm tears; but all hath suffered change;
For surely now our household hearths are cold,
Our sons inherit us, our looks are strange,
And we should come like ghosts to trouble joy.
120 Or else the island princes[6] over-bold
Have eat our substance, and the minstrel sings
Before them of the ten years' war in Troy,
And our great deeds, as half-forgotten things.
Is there confusion in the little isle?[7]
125 Let what is broken so remain.
The Gods are hard to reconcile;
'Tis hard to settle order once again.
There *is* confusion worse than death,
Trouble on trouble, pain on pain,
130 Long labor unto aged breath,
Sore tasks to hearts worn out by many wars
And eyes grown dim with gazing on the pilot-stars.

7
But, propt on beds of amaranth[8] and moly,
How sweet—while warm airs lull us, blowing lowly—
135 With half-dropt eyelid still,
Beneath a heaven dark and holy,
To watch the long bright river drawing slowly
His waters from the purple hill—
To hear the dewy echoes calling
140 From cave to cave through the thick-twined vine—
To watch the emerald-colored water falling
Through many a woven acanthus-wreath divine!
Only to hear and see the far-off sparkling brine,
Only to hear were sweet, stretched out beneath the pine.

6. The princes who had remained behind in Ithaca while Odysseus was at Troy.
7. I.e., Ithaca.
8. A legendary flower, reputed not to fade; moly, an herb of magical properties.

8

145 The Lotos blooms below the barren peak,
The Lotos blows by every winding creek;
All day the wind breathes low with mellower tone;
Through every hollow cave and alley lone
Round and round the spicy downs the yellow Lotos-dust is blown.
150 We have had enough of action, and of motion we,
Rolled to starboard, rolled to larboard, when the surge was seething free,
Where the wallowing monster spouted his foam-fountains in the sea.
Let us swear an oath, and keep it with an equal mind,
In the hollow Lotos-land to live and lie reclined
155 On the hills like Gods together, careless of mankind.
For they lie beside their nectar, and the bolts are hurled
Far below them in the valleys, and the clouds are lightly curled
Round their golden houses, girdled with the gleaming world;
Where they smile in secret, looking over wasted lands,
160 Blight and famine, plague and earthquake, roaring deeps and fiery sands,
Clanging fights, and flaming towns, and sinking ships, and praying hands.
But they smile, they find a music centered in a doleful song
Steaming up, a lamentation and an ancient tale of wrong,
Like a tale of little meaning though the words are strong;
165 Chanted from an ill-used race of men that cleave the soil,
Sow the seed, and reap the harvest with enduring toil,
Storing yearly little dues of wheat, and wine and oil;
Till they perish and they suffer—some, 'tis whispered—down in hell
Suffer endless anguish, others in Elysian valleys dwell,
170 Resting weary limbs at last on beds of asphodel.[9]
Surely, surely, slumber is more sweet than toil, the shore
Than labor in the deep mid-ocean, wind and wave and oar;
O, rest ye, brother mariners, we will not wander more.

1832, 1842

Break, Break, Break

Break, break, break,
   On thy cold gray stones, O Sea!
And I would that my tongue could utter
   The thoughts that arise in me.

5 O, well for the fisherman's boy,
   That he shouts with his sister at play!
O, well for the sailor lad,
   That he sings in his boat on the bay!

And the stately ships go on
10   To their haven under the hill;
But O for the touch of a vanished hand,
   And the sound of a voice that is still!

Break, break, break,
   At the foot of thy crags, O Sea!
15 But the tender grace of a day that is dead
   Will never come back to me.

1834   1842

---

9. Any one of a number of plants of the lily family.

Songs from The Princess

Tears, Idle Tears

Tears, idle tears, I know not what they mean,
Tears from the depth of some divine despair
Rise in the heart, and gather to the eyes,
In looking on the happy autumn-fields,
5　And thinking of the days that are no more.

Fresh as the first beam glittering on a sail,
That brings our friends up from the underworld,
Sad as the last which reddens over one
That sinks with all we love below the verge;
10　So sad, so fresh, the days that are no more.

Ah, sad and strange as in dark summer dawns
The earliest pipe of half-awakened birds
To dying ears, when unto dying eyes
The casement slowly grows a glimmering square;
15　So sad, so strange, the days that are no more.

Dear as remembered kisses after death,
And sweet as those by hopeless fancy feigned
On lips that are for others; deep as love,
Deep as first love, and wild with all regret;
20　O Death in Life, the days that are no more!

1847

Now Sleeps the Crimson Petal

Now sleeps the crimson petal, now the white;
Nor waves the cypress in the palace walk;
Nor winks the gold fin in the porphyry font.
The firefly wakens; waken thou with me.

5　Now droops the milk-white peacock like a ghost,
And like a ghost she glimmers on to me.

Now lies the Earth all Danaë[1] to the stars,
And all thy heart lies open unto me.

Now slides the silent meteor on, and leaves
10　A shining furrow, as thy thoughts in me.

Now folds the lily all her sweetness up,
And slips into the bosom of the lake.
So fold thyself, my dearest, thou, and slip
Into my bosom and be lost in me.

1847

1. Daughter of a king of Argos in ancient Greece who, warned by an oracle that she would bear a son who would kill him, shut her up in a bronze chamber, where she was visited by Zeus in a shower of gold.

From In Memoriam A. H. H.[2]

OBIIT. MDCCCXXXIII

1

I held it truth, with him who sings
 To one clear harp in divers tones,[3]
 That men may rise on stepping-stones
Of their dead selves to higher things.

5 But who shall so forecast the years
 And find in loss a gain to match?
 Or reach a hand through time to catch
The far-off interest of tears?

Let Love clasp Grief lest both be drowned,
10 Let darkness keep her raven gloss.
 Ah, sweeter to be drunk with loss,
To dance with Death, to beat the ground,

Than that the victor Hours should scorn
 The long result of love, and boast,
15 "Behold the man that loved and lost,
But all he was is overworn."

2

Old yew, which graspest at the stones
 That name the underlying dead,
 Thy fibers net the dreamless head,
Thy roots are wrapt about the bones.

5 The seasons bring the flowers again,
 And bring the firstling to the flock;
 And in the dusk of thee the clock
Beats out the little lives of men.

O, not for thee the glow, the bloom,
10 Who changest not in any gale,
 Nor branding summer suns avail
To touch thy thousand years of gloom;

And gazing on thee, sullen tree,
 Sick for thy stubborn hardihood,
15 I seem to fail from out my blood
And grow incorporate into thee.

7

Dark house, by which once more I stand
 Here in the long unlovely street,[4]
 Doors, where my heart was used to beat
So quickly, waiting for a hand,

---

2. Arthur Henry Hallam (1811–33) had been Tennyson's close friend at Cambridge; they had traveled together in France and Germany; and Hallam had been engaged to the poet's sister. To his associates at Cambridge, Hallam had seemed to give the most brilliant promise of future greatness. In the summer of 1833 Hallam had been traveling on the Continent with his father, when he died of stroke at Vienna.
3. I.e., Goethe.
4. I.e., Wimpole St., where Hallam had been living after he left Cambridge.

5 A hand that can be clasped no more—
   Behold me, for I cannot sleep,
   And like a guilty thing I creep
At earliest morning to the door.

   He is not here; but far away
10   The noise of life begins again,
   And ghastly through the drizzling rain
On the bald street breaks the blank day.

      11
Calm is the morn without a sound,
   Calm as to suit a calmer grief,
   And only through the faded leaf
The chestnut pattering to the ground;

5 Calm and deep peace on this high wold,°   *upland plain*
   And on these dews that drench the furze,
   And all the silvery gossamers
That twinkle into green and gold;

   Calm and still light on yon great plain
10   That sweeps with all its autumn bowers,
   And crowded farms and lessening towers,
To mingle with the bounding main;

   Calm and deep peace in this wide air,
   These leaves that redden to the fall,
15   And in my heart, if calm at all,
If any calm, a calm despair;

   Calm on the seas, and silver sleep,
   And waves that sway themselves in rest,
   And dead calm in the noble breast
20 Which heaves but with the heaving deep.

      19
The Danube to the Severn gave
   The darkened heart that beat no more;[7]
   They laid him by the pleasant shore,
And in the hearing of the wave.

5 There twice a day the Severn fills;
   The salt sea-water passes by,
   And hushes half the babbling Wye,[8]
And makes a silence in the hills.

   The Wye is hushed nor moved along,
10   And hushed my deepest grief of all,
   When filled with tears that cannot fall,
I brim with sorrow drowning song.

   The tide flows down, the wave again
   Is vocal in its wooded walls;
15   My deeper anguish also falls,
And I can speak a little then.

7. Vienna, where Hallam died, is on the Danube; the Severn empties into the Bristol Channel near Clevedon, Somersetshire, Hallam's burial place.

8. The Wye, a tributary of the Severn, also runs into the Bristol Channel; the incoming tide deepens the river and makes it quiet, but as the tide ebbs the Wye once more becomes voluble.

50

Be near me when my light is low,
    When the blood creeps, and the nerves prick
    And tingle; and the heart is sick,
And all the wheels of being slow.

5 Be near me when the sensuous frame
    Is racked with pangs that conquer trust;
    And Time, a maniac scattering dust,
And Life, a Fury slinging flame.

Be near me when my faith is dry,
10   And men the flies of latter spring,
    That lay their eggs, and sting and sing
And weave their petty cells and die.

Be near me when I fade away,
    To point the term of human strife,
15   And on the low dark verge of life
The twilight of eternal day.

67

When on my bed the moonlight falls,
    I know that in thy place of rest
    By that broad water of the west
There comes a glory on the walls:[1]

5 Thy marble bright in dark appears,
    As slowly steals a silver flame
    Along the letters of thy name,
And o'er the number of thy years.

The mystic glory swims away,
10   From off my bed the moonlight dies;
    And closing eaves of wearied eyes
I sleep till dusk is dipped in gray;

And then I know the mist is drawn
    A lucid veil from coast to coast,
15   And in the dark church like a ghost
Thy tablet glimmers to the dawn.

88

Wild bird, whose warble, liquid sweet,
    Rings Eden through the budded quicks,[2]
    O, tell me where the senses mix,
O, tell me where the passions meet,

5 Whence radiate: fierce extremes employ
    Thy spirits in the darkening leaf,
    And in the midmost heart of grief
Thy passion clasps a secret joy;

And I—my harp would prelude woe—
10   I cannot all command the strings;
    The glory of the sum of things
Will flash along the chords and go.

---

1. Hallam's tomb was inside Clevedon Church, just south of Clevedon, Somersetshire, on a hill overlooking the Bristol Channel.
2. Hawthorn hedge-row.

95
By night we lingered on the lawn,
  For underfoot the herb was dry;
  And genial warmth; and o'er the sky
The silvery haze of summer drawn;

5 And calm that let the tapers burn
  Unwavering: not a cricket chirred;
  The brook alone far-off was heard,
And on the board the fluttering urn.[3]

  And bats went round in fragrant skies,
10 And wheeled or lit the filmy shapes
  That haunt the dusk, with ermine capes
And woolly breasts and beaded eyes;

  While now we sang old songs that pealed
  From knoll to knoll, where, couched at ease,
15 The white kine glimmered, and the trees
Laid their dark arms about the field.

  But when those others, one by one,
  Withdrew themselves from me and night,
  And in the house light after light
20 Went out, and I was all alone,

  A hunger seized my heart; I read
  Of that glad year which once had been,
  In those fallen leaves which kept their green,
The noble letters of the dead.

25 And strangely on the silence broke
  The silent-speaking words, and strange
  Was love's dumb cry defying change
To test his worth; and strangely spoke

  The faith, the vigor, bold to dwell
30 On doubts that drive the coward back,
  And keen through wordy snares to track
Suggestion to her inmost cell.

  So word by word, and line by line,
  The dead man touched me from the past,
35 And all at once it seemed at last
The living soul was flashed on mine,

  And mine in this was wound, and whirled
  About empyreal heights of thought,
  And came on that which is, and caught
40 The deep pulsations of the world,

  Eonian music[4] measuring out
  The steps of Time—the shocks of Chance—
  The blows of Death. At length my trance
Was canceled, stricken through with doubt.

---

3. I.e., on the table a tea- or coffee-urn heated by a fluttering flame beneath.

4. I.e., the rhythm of the universe which has persisted for eons.

45 Vague words! but ah, how hard to frame
      In matter-molded forms of speech,
      Or even for intellect to reach
    Through memory that which I became;

    Till now the doubtful dusk revealed
50   The knolls once more where, couched at ease,
      The white kine glimmered, and the trees
    Lain their dark arms about the field;

    And sucked from out the distant gloom
      A breeze began to tremble o'er
55   The large leaves of the sycamore,
    And fluctuate all the still perfume,

    And gathering freshlier overhead
      Rocked the full-foliaged elms, and swung
      The heavy-folded rose, and flung
60 The lilies to and fro, and said,

    "The dawn, the dawn," and died away;
      And East and West, without a breath,
      Mixt their dim lights, like life and death,
    To broaden into boundless day.

                    119
    Doors, where my heart was used to beat
      So quickly, not as one that weeps
      I come once more; the city sleeps;
    I smell the meadow in the street;

5   I hear a chirp of birds; I see
      Betwixt the black fronts long-withdrawn
      A light-blue lane of early dawn,
    And think of early days and thee,

    And bless thee, for thy lips are bland,
10   And bright the friendship of thine eyes;
      And in my thoughts with scarce a sigh
    I take the pressure of thine hand.

                    121
    Sad Hesper o'er the buried sun
      And ready, thou, to die with him,
      Thou watchest all things ever dim
    And dimmer, and a glory done.

5   The team is loosened from the wain,°   *wagon*
      The boat is drawn upon the shore;
      Thou listenest to the closing door,
    And life is darkened in the brain.

    Bright Phosphor, fresher for the night,
10   By thee the world's great work is heard
      Beginning, and the wakeful bird;
    Behind thee comes the greater light.

The market boat is on the stream,
　And voices hail it from the brink;
15　Thou hear'st the village hammer clink,
And see'st the moving of the team.

Sweet Hesper-Phosphor, double name[8]
　For what is one, the first, the last,
　Thou, like my present and my past,
20 Thy place is changed; thou art the same.

　　　130
Thy voice is on the rolling air;
　I hear thee where the waters run;
　Thou standest in the rising sun,
And in the setting thou art fair.

5 What are thou then? I cannot guess;
　But though I seem in star and flower
　To feel thee some diffusive power,
I do not therefore love thee less.

My love involves the love before;
10　My love is vaster passion now;
　Though mixed with God and Nature thou,
I seem to love thee more and more.

Far off thou art, but ever nigh;
　I have thee still, and I rejoice;
15　I prosper, circled with thy voice;
I shall not lose theee though I die.

　　　　　　　　　　　1833–50　　　　1850

The Eagle

FRAGMENT

He clasps the crag with crooked hands;
Close to the sun in lonely lands,
Ringed with the azure world, he stands.

The wrinkled sea beneath him crawls;
5 He watches from his mountain walls,
And like a thunderbolt he falls.

　　　　　　　　　　　　　　　　　1851

Tithonus[9]

The woods decay, the woods decay and fall,
The vapors weep their burthen to the ground,
Man comes and tills the field and lies beneath,
And after many a summer dies the swan.
5 Me only cruel immortality
Consumes; I wither slowly in thine arms,

---

8. Hesper, the evening star, and Phosphor, the
morning star, are both the planet Venus.
9. A Trojan prince beloved by Aurora (Greek
Eos), goddess of the dawn, who took him as
her spouse. She begged Zeus to grant him
eternal life, but forgot to ask also for the gift
of eternal youth.

Here at the quiet limit of the world,
A white-haired shadow roaming like a dream
The ever-silent spaces of the East,
Far-folded mists, and gleaming halls of morn.
   Alas! for this gray shadow, once a man—
So glorious in his beauty and thy choice,
Who madest him thy chosen, that he seemed
To his great heart none other than a God!
I asked thee, "Give me immortality."
Then didst thou grant mine asking with a smile,
Like wealthy men who care not how they give.
But thy strong Hours indignant worked their wills,
And beat me down and marred and wasted me,
And though they could not end me, left me maimed
To dwell in presence of immortal youth.
Immortal age beside immortal youth,
And all I was in ashes. Can thy love,
Thy beauty, make amends, though even now,
Close over us, the silver star[1] thy guide,
Shines in those tremulous eyes that fill with tears
To hear me? Let me go; take back thy gift.
Why should a man desire in any way
To vary from the kindly race of men,
Or pass beyond the goal of ordinance
Where all should pause, as is most meet for all?
   A soft air fans the cloud apart; there comes
A glimpse of that dark world where I was born.
Once more the old mysterious glimmer steals
From thy pure brows, and from thy shoulders pure,
And bosom beating with a heart renewed.
Thy cheek begins to redden through the gloom,
Thy sweet eyes brighten slowly close to mine,
Ere yet they blind the stars, and the wild team
Which love thee, yearning for thy yoke, arise,
And shake the darkness from their loosened manes,
And beat the twilight into flakes of fire.
   Lo! ever thus thou growest beautiful
In silence, then before thine answer given
Departest, and thy tears are on my cheek.
   Why wilt thou ever scare me with thy tears,
And make me tremble lest a saying learnt,
In days far-off, on that dark earth, be true?
"The Gods themselves cannot recall their gifts."
   Ay me! ay me! with what another heart
In days far-off, and with what other eyes
I used to watch—if I be he that watched—
The lucid outline forming round thee; saw
The dim curls kindle into sunny rings;
Changed with thy mystic change, and felt my blood
Glow with the glow that slowly crimsoned all
Thy presence and thy portals, while I lay,
Mouth, forehead, eyelids, growing dewy-warm
With kisses balmier than half-opening buds
Of April, and could hear the lips that kissed
Whispering I knew not what of wild and sweet,

10

15

20

25

30

35

40

45

50

55

60

---

1. I.e., the morning star.

Like that strange song I heard Apollo sing,
While Ilion like a mist rose into towers.[2]
  Yet hold me not for ever in thine East;
65 How can my nature longer mix with thine?
Coldly thy rosy shadows bathe me, cold
Are all thy lights, and cold my wrinkled feet
Upon thy glimmering thresholds, when the steam
Floats up from those dim fields about the homes
70 Of happy men that have the power to die,
And grassy barrows of the happier dead.
Release me, and restore me to the ground.
Thou seest all things, thou wilt see my grave;
Thou wilt renew thy beauty morn by morn,
75 I earth in earth forget these empty courts,
And thee returning on thy silver wheels.

1833, 1859   1860

Milton

ALCAICS[3]

O mighty-mouthed inventor of harmonies,
O skilled to sing of Time or Eternity,
  God-gifted organ-voice of England,
    Milton, a name to resound for ages;
5 Whose Titan[4] angels, Gabriel, Abdiel,[5]
Starred from Jehovah's gorgeous armories,
  Tower, as the deep-domed empyrëan
    Rings to the roar of an angel onset—
Me rather all that bowery loneliness,
10 The brooks of Eden mazily murmuring,
  And bloom profuse and cedar arches
    Charm, as a wanderer out in ocean,
Where some refulgent sunset of India
Streams o'er a rich ambrosial ocean isle,
15   And crimson-hued the stately palm-woods
    Whisper in odorous heights of even.

1863

To Virgil

WRITTEN AT THE REQUEST OF THE MANTUANS FOR THE NINETEENTH
CENTENARY OF VIRGIL'S DEATH[6]

1

Roman Virgil, thou that singest[7]
  Ilion's lofty temples robed in fire,
Ilion falling, Rome arising,
  wars, and filial faith, and Dido's pyre;[8]

---

2. According to legend, the walls and towers of Ilion (Troy) were raised by the sound of Apollo's song, as related by Ovid, *Heroides*, XVI.179.
3. The Alcaic ode, named after the Greek lyric poet Alcaeus, ca. 600 B.C. See Glossary, entry on Alcaic strophe, at the end of this anthology.
4. Gigantic in size and power.
5. "Gabriel": one of the seven archangels; in *Paradise Lost*, one of the four angels who guard Paradise and who oppose Satan's attacks on it. "Abdiel": in *Paradise Lost*, one of the faithful angels who resisted Satan's revolt, striking the first sword-blow against him.

6. The Roman poet Virgil was born near Mantua, in northern Italy, on October 19, 70 B.C., and died at Brundisium (modern Brindisi), on September 20, 19 B.C.
7. In the *Aeneid*, Virgil's last and greatest work: Aeneas, who fought against the Greeks in the Trojan War and who escaped after the fall of Troy (Ilion) with his father Anchises, was destined after his wanderings to be the founder of Rome.
8. Dido, Queen of Carthage, loved by Aeneas and deserted by him when he was ordered by Mercury to continue on his way and to fulfill his imperial mission: she immolates herself.

2

5   Landscape-lover, lord of language
         more than he that sang the Works and Days,[9]
     All the chosen coin of fancy
         flashing out from many a golden phrase;

3

     Thou that singest wheat and woodland,
10   tilth and vineyard, hive and horse and herd;
     All the charm of all the Muses
         often flowering in a lonely word;

4

     Poet of the happy Tityrus
         piping underneath his beechen bowers;[1]
15   Poet of the poet-satyr[2]
         whom the laughing shepherd bound with flowers;

5

     Chanter of the Pollio,[3] glorying
         in the blissful years again to be,
     Summers of the snakeless meadow,
20   unlaborious earth and oarless sea;

6

     Thou that seest Universal
         Nature moved by Universal Mind;
     Thou majestic in thy sadness
         at the doubtful doom of human kind;

7

25   Light among the vanished ages;
         star that gildest yet this phantom shore;
     Golden branch[4] amid the shadows,
         kings and realms that pass to rise no more;

8

     Now thy Forum roars no longer,
30   fallen every purple Caesar's dome—
     Though thine ocean-roll of rhythm
         sound forever of Imperial Rome—

9

     Now the Rome of slaves hath perished,
         and the Rome of freemen holds her place,[5]
35   I, from out the Northern Island
         sundered once from all the human race,

10

     I salute thee, Mantovano,°   *Mantuan*
         I that loved thee since my day began,
     Wielder of the stateliest measure
40   ever molded by the lips of man.

                                      1880   1883

---

9. The Greek poet Hesiod, whose didactic poem of occupations is here compared with Virgil's *Georgics,* descriptive of country life and farm pursuits.
1. In Virgil's *Eclogues* or Pastorals, especially the opening of *Eclogue* I.
2. Silenus, in *Eclogue* VI.
3. Gaius Asinus Pollio, Roman consul and man of letters, to whom Virgil dedicated the fourth Eclogue, in which he identifies the re-
turn of the world's golden age with the time of Pollio's consulate.
4. In the *Aeneid* VI.136 ff. Aeneas, prior to his journey to the underworld, is warned by the Sibyl that his safety depends on his finding and breaking off the golden bough which must be presented to Proserpine, goddess of the underworld.
5. Italy had finally achieved its freedom and unification in 1870.

Frater Ave Atque Vale[6]

Row us out from Desenzano, to your Sirmione row!
So they rowed, and there we landed—"O venusta Sirmio!"[7]
There to me through all the groves of olive in the summer glow,
There beneath the Roman ruin where the purple flowers grow,
5   Came that "Ave atque Vale" of the poet's hopeless woe,
Tenderest of Roman poets nineteen-hundred years ago,
"Frater Ave atque Vale"—as we wandered to and fro
Gazing at the Lydian laughter of the Garda Lake below[8]
Sweet Catullus's all-but-island, olive-silvery Sirmio!

1880   1885

Crossing the Bar

Sunset and evening star,
    And one clear call for me!
And may there be no moaning of the bar,
    When I put out to sea,

5   But such a tide as moving seems asleep,
    Too full for sound and foam,
When that which drew from out the boundless deep
    Turns again home.

Twilight and evening bell,
10   And after that the dark!
And may there be no sadness of farewell,
    When I embark;

For though from out our bourne of Time and Place
    The flood may bear me far,
15 I hope to see my Pilot face to face
    When I have crossed the bar.

1889

---

6. The title (Brother, hail and farewell) repeats the concluding phrase of poem number CI, in which Catullus records the journey to visit his brother's tomb in Asia Minor. Tennyson's poem, written on a visit to the little peninsula of Sirmio, on Lake Garda in Northern Italy, shortly after his own brother had died, echoes phrases from another poem (XXXI) in which Catullus describes his pleasure in returning to Sirmio after a long absence.
7. O lovely Sirmio.
8. Catullus's line, "And rejoice, O Lydian waves of the lake" (XXXI: 13) alludes to the old belief that the Estruscans of the Garda region had originated in Lydia, in Asia Minor.

ROBERT BROWNING
1812–1889

My Last Duchess[1]

FERRARA

That's my last duchess painted on the wall,
Looking as if she were alive. I call
That piece a wonder, now: Frà Pandolf's hands
Worked busily a day, and there she stands.
5   Will't please you sit and look at her? I said
"Frà Pandolf" by design, for never read
Strangers like you that pictured countenance,
The depth and passion of its earnest glance,
But to myself they turned (since none puts by
10   The curtain I have drawn for you, but I)
And seemed as they would ask me, if they durst,
How such a glance came there; so, not the first
Are you to turn and ask thus. Sir, 'twas not
Her husband's presence only, called that spot
15   Of joy into the Duchess' cheek: perhaps
Frà Pandolf chanced to say "Her mantle laps
"Over my lady's wrist too much," or "Paint
"Must never hope to reproduce the faint
"Half-flush that dies along her throat": such stuff
20   Was courtesy, she thought, and cause enough
For calling up that spot of joy. She had
A heart—how shall I say?—too soon made glad,
Too easily impressed; she liked whate'er
She looked on, and her looks went everywhere.
25   Sir, 'twas all one! My favor at her breast,
The dropping of the daylight in the West,
The bough of cherries some officious fool
Broke in the orchard for her, the white mule
She rode with round the terrace—all and each
30   Would draw from her alike the approving speech,
Or blush, at least. She thanked men—good! but thanked
Somehow—I know not how—as if she ranked
My gift of a nine-hundred-years-old name
With anybody's gift. Who'd stoop to blame
35   This sort of trifling? Even had you skill
In speech—which I have not—to make your will
Quite clear to such an one, and say, "Just this
"Or that in you disgusts me; here you miss,
"Or there exceed the mark"—and if she let
40   Herself be lessoned so, nor plainly set
Her wits to yours, forsooth, and made excuse,
—E'en then would be some stooping; and I choose

---

1. The events of Browning's poem parallel historical events, but its emphasis is rather on truth to Renaissance attitudes than on historic specificity. Alfonso II d'Este, Duke of Ferrara (born 1533), in Northern Italy, had married his first wife, daughter of Cosimo I de'Medici, Duke of Florence, in 1558, when she was fourteen; she died on April 21, 1561, under suspicious circumstances, and soon afterwards he opened negotiations for the hand of the niece of the Count of Tyrol, the seat of whose court was at Innsbruck, in Austria. "Fra Pandolf" and "Claus of Innsbruck" are types rather than specific artists.

Never to stoop. Oh sir, she smiled, no doubt,
Whene'er I passed her; but who passed without
45   Much the same smile? This grew; I gave commands;
Then all smiles stopped together. There she stands
As if alive. Will 't please you rise? We'll meet
The company below, then. I repeat,
The Count your master's known munificence
50   Is ample warrant that no just pretense
Of mine for dowry will be disallowed;
Though his fair daughter's self, as I avowed
At starting, is my object. Nay, we'll go
Together down, sir. Notice Neptune, though,
55   Taming a sea-horse, thought a rarity,
Which Claus of Innsbruck cast in bronze for me!

1842

Soliloquy of the Spanish Cloister

1

Gr-r-r—there go, my heart's abhorrence!
   Water your damned flower-pots, do!
If hate killed men, Brother Lawrence,
   God's blood, would not mine kill you!
5   What? your myrtle-bush wants trimming?
     Oh, that rose has prior claims—
Needs its leaden vase filled brimming?
     Hell dry you up with its flames!

2

At the meal we sit together:
10   *Salve tibi!*[2] I must hear
Wise talk of the kind of weather,
     Sort of season, time of year:
Not a plenteous cork-crop: scarcely
     Dare we hope oak-galls,[3] *I doubt:*
15   *What's the Latin name for "parsley"?*
     What's the Greek name for Swine's Snout?

3

Whew! We'll have our platter burnished,
     Laid with care on our own shelf!
With a fire-new spoon we're furnished,
20   And a goblet for ourself,
Rinsed like something sacrificial
     Ere 'tis fit to touch our chaps—
Marked with L for our initial!
     (He-he! There his lily snaps!)

4

25   *Saint,* forsooth! While brown Dolores
     Squats outside the Convent bank
With Sanchicha, telling stories,
     Steeping tresses in the tank,
Blue-black, lustrous, thick like horsehairs,
30   —Can't I see his dead eye glow,
Bright as 'twere a Barbary corsair's?[4]
     (That is, if he'd let it show!)

---

2. Hail to thee!
3. Growths produced on oak-leaves by gall-flies.

4. "Barbary corsair": Pirate from the Berber countries on the north coast of Africa.

5

When he finishes refection,°   *dinner*
    Knife and fork he never lays
35 Cross-wise, to my recollection,
        As do I, in Jesu's praise.
    I the Trinity illustrate,
        Drinking watered orange-pulp—
    In three sips the Arian[5] frustrate;
40   While he drains his at one gulp.

6

    Oh, those melons? If he's able
        We're to have a feast! so nice!
    One goes to the Abbot's table,
        All of us get each a slice.
45 How go on your flowers? None double?
        Not one fruit-sort can you spy?
    Strange! And I, too, at such trouble,
        Keep them close-nipped on the sly!

7

    There's a great text in Galatians,[6]
50   Once you trip on it, entails
    Twenty-nine distinct damnations,
        One sure, if another fails:
    If I trip him just a-dying,
        Sure of heaven as sure can be,
55 Spin him around and send him flying
        Off to hell, a Manichee?[7]

8

    Or, my scrofulous French novel
        On grey paper with blunt type!
    Simply glance at it, you grovel
60   Hand and foot in Belial's[8] gripe:
    If I double down its pages
        At the woeful sixteenth print,
    When he gathers his greengages,
        Ope a sieve and slip it in't?

9

65 Or, there's Satan! one might venture
        Pledge one's soul to him, yet leave
    Such a flaw in the indenture
        As he'd miss till, past retrieve,
    Blasted lay that rose-acacia
70   We're so proud of![9] *Hy, Zy, Hine*[1] . . .
    'St, there's vespers! *Plena gratiâ
    Ave, Virgo!*[2] Gr-r-r—you swine!

                                                        1842

---

5. Arius, a fourth-century Alexandrian heretic, denied the doctrine of the Trinity.
6. The line has sometimes been taken as referring to Galatians iii.10; but see Galatians v.14–15, with its ironic applicability to the spirit of the monologue, and also v.16–24.
7. The Manichean heresy, which the speaker hopes to lure Brother Lawrence into accepting, claimed that the world was divided between forces of good and forces of evil.
8. Hebrew personification of lawlessness,

hence one of the names for the Devil.
9. The speaker seems to say that, if all else fails, he might secure Brother Lawrence's damnation by pledging his own soul to the Devil in return—but being careful to leave a flaw in the contract that would invalidate it.
1. Possibly an incantation used in calling up the Devil.
2. "*Plena gratiâ / Ave, Virgo*": the speaker reverses the opening words of the *Ave Maria*: "Hail Mary, full of grace."

Home-Thoughts, From Abroad

1

Oh, to be in England
Now that April's there,
And whoever wakes in England
Sees, some morning, unaware,
5   That the lowest boughs and the brushwood sheaf
Round the elm-tree bole are in tiny leaf,
While the chaffinch sings on the orchard bough
In England—now!

2

And after April, when May follows,
10 And the whitethroat builds, and all the swallows!
Hark, where my blossomed pear-tree in the hedge
Leans to the field and scatters on the clover
Blossoms and dewdrops—at the bent spray's edge—
That's the wise thrush; he sings each song twice over,
15 Lest you should think he never could recapture
The first fine careless rapture!
And though the fields look rough with hoary dew
All will be gay when noontide wakes anew
The buttercups, the little children's dower
—Far brighter than this gaudy melon-flower!

1845

The Bishop Orders His Tomb at Saint Praxed's Church[2]

ROME, 15—

Vanity, saith the preacher, vanity![3]
Draw round my bed: is Anselm keeping back?
Nephews—sons mine . . . ah God, I know not! Well—
She, men would have to be your mother once,
5   Old Gandolf envied me, so fair she was!
What's done is done, and she is dead beside,
Dead long ago, and I am Bishop since,
And as she died so must we die ourselves,
And thence ye may perceive the world's a dream.
10 Life, how and what is it? As here I lie
In this state-chamber, dying by degrees,
Hours and long hours in the dead night, I ask
"Do I live, am I dead?" Peace, peace seems all.
Saint Praxed's ever was the church for peace;
15 And so, about this tomb of mine. I fought
With tooth and nail to save my niche, ye know:
—Old Gandolf cozened° me, despite my care;   *cheated*
Shrewd was that snatch from out the corner south
He graced his carrion with, God curse the same!
20 Yet still my niche is not so cramped but thence
One sees the pulpit o' the epistle-side,[4]

2. The church of Santa Prassede, in Rome, dedicated to a Roman virgin, dates from the fifth century but was rebuilt early in the ninth and restored at later times. The 16th-century Bishop who speaks here is a fictional figure, as is his predecessor, Gandolf.

3. An echo of Ecclesiastes i.2: "Vanity of vanities, saith the Preacher, vanity of vanities; all is vanity."
4. The right-hand side as one faces the altar, the side from which the Epistles of the New Testament were read.

And somewhat of the choir, those silent seats,
And up into the aery dome where live
The angels, and a sunbeam's sure to lurk:
25   And I shall fill my slab of basalt there,
And 'neath my tabernacle⁵ take my rest,
With those nine columns round me, two and two,
The odd one at my feet where Anselm stands:
Peach-blossom marble all, the rare, the ripe
30   As fresh-poured red wine of a mighty pulse.
—Old Gandolf with his paltry onion-stone,
Put me where I may look at him! True peach,
Rosy and flawless: how I earned the prize!
Draw close: that conflagration of my church
35   —What then? So much was saved if aught were missed!
My sons, ye would not be my death? Go dig
The white-grape vineyard where the oil-press stood,
Drop water gently till the surface sink,
And if ye find . . . Ah God, I know not, I! . . .
40   Bedded in store of rotten fig-leaves soft,
And corded up in a tight olive-frail,°   *olive basket*
Some lump, ah God, of *lapis lazuli*,⁶
Big as a Jew's head cut off at the nape,
Blue as a vein o'er the Madonna's breast . . .
45   Sons, all have I bequeathed you, villas, all,
That brave Frascati⁷ villa with its bath,
So, let the blue lump poise between my knees,
Like God the Father's globe on both his hands
Ye worship in the Jesu Church⁸ so gay,
50   For Gandolf shall not choose but see and burst!
Swift as a weaver's shuttle fleet our years:⁹
Man goeth to the grave, and where is he?
Did I say basalt for my slab, sons? Black—
'Twas ever antique-black I meant! How else
55   Shall ye contrast my frieze to come beneath?
The bas-relief in bronze ye promised me,
Those Pans and Nymphs ye wot of, and perchance
Some tripod, thyrsus,¹ with a vase or so,
The Saviour at his sermon on the mount,
60   Saint Praxed in a glory,² and one Pan
Ready to twitch the Nymph's last garment off,
And Moses with the tables . . . but I know
Ye mark me not! What do they whisper thee,
Child of my bowels, Anselm? Ah, ye hope
65   To revel down my villas while I gasp
Bricked o'er with beggar's moldy travertine³
Which Gandolf from his tomb-top chuckles at!
Nay, boys, ye love me—all of jasper, then!
'T is jasper ye stand pledged to, lest I grieve
70   My bath must needs be left behind, alas!
One block, pure green as a pistachio-nut,

5. Canopy over his tomb.
6. A vivid blue stone, one of the so-called hard stones, used for ornament.
7. A resort town in the mountains.
8. The splendid baroque church, Il Gesù. The sculptured group of the Trinity includes a terrestrial globe carved from the largest known block of lapis lazuli.
9. See Job vii.6 ("My days are swifter than a weaver's shuttle, and are spent without hope").
1. A staff ornamented with ivy or vine-leaves, carried by followers of Bacchus, the Roman god of wine and revelry.
2. Rays of gold, signifying sanctity, around the head or body of the saint portrayed.
3. Ordinary limestone used in building.

There's plenty jasper somewhere in the world—
And have I not Saint Praxed's ear to pray
Horses for ye, and brown Greek manuscripts,
75 And mistresses with great smooth marbly limbs?
—That's if ye carve my epitaph aright,
Choice Latin, picked phrase, Tully's[4] every word,
No gaudy ware like Gandolf's second line—
Tully, my masters? Ulpian[5] serves his need!
80 And then how I shall lie through centuries,
And hear the blessed mutter of the mass,
And see God made and eaten all day long,[6]
And feel the steady candle-flame, and taste
Good strong thick stupefying incense-smoke!
85 For as I lie here, hours of the dead night,
Dying in state and by such slow degrees,
I fold my arms as if they clasped a crook,[7]
And stretch my feet forth straight as stone can point,
And let the bedclothes, for a mortcloth,[8] drop
90 Into great laps and folds of sculptor's-work:
And as yon tapers dwindle, and strange thoughts
Grow, with a certain humming in my ears,
About the life before I lived this life,
And this life too, popes, cardinals and priests,
95 Saint Praxed at his sermon on the mount,[9]
Your tall pale mother with her talking eyes,
And new-found agate urns as fresh as day,
And marble's language, Latin pure, discreet,
—Aha, ELUCESCEBAT[1] quoth our friend?
100 No Tully, said I, Ulpian at the best!
Evil and brief hath been my pilgrimage.
All *lapis*, all, sons! Else I give the Pope
My villas! Will ye ever eat my heart?
Ever your eyes were as a lizard's quick,
105 They glitter like your mother's for my soul,
Or ye would heighten my impoverished frieze,
Piece out its starved design, and fill my vase
With grapes, and add a vizor and a Term,[2]
And to the tripod ye would tie a lynx
110 That in his struggle throws the thyrsus down,
To comfort me on my entablature
Whereon I am to lie till I must ask
"Do I live, am I dead?" There, leave me, there!
For ye have stabbed me with ingratitude
115 To death—ye wish it—God, ye wish it! Stone—
Gritstone, a-crumble! Clammy squares which sweat
As if the corpse they keep were oozing through—
And no more *lapis* to delight the world!
Well, go! I bless ye. Fewer tapers there,
120 But in a row: and, going, turn your backs
—Ay, like departing altar-ministrants,

---

4. Familiar name for Cicero (Marcus Tullius Cicero).
5. His Latin would be stylistically inferior to that of Cicero.
6. Refers to the doctrine of transubstantiation.
7. I.e., the Bishop's crozier, with its emblematic resemblance to a shepherd's crook.
8. The pall with which the coffin is draped.
9. As the Bishop's mind wanders, he attributes Christ's Sermon on the Mount to Santa Prassede.
1. A word from Gandolf's epitaph (a form of the Latin verb meaning "to shine forth"); the Bishop claims that this form is inferior to *elucebat*, which Cicero would have used.
2. "Vizor": a mask; "Term": a pillar adorned with a bust. Both are motifs of classical sculpture imitated by the Renaissance.

And leave me in my church, the church for peace,
That I may watch at leisure if he leers—
Old Gandolf, at me, from his onion-stone,
125 As still he envied me, so fair she was!

1845, 1849

Fra Lippo Lippi[3]

I am poor brother Lippo, by your leave!
You need not clap your torches to my face.
Zooks, what's to blame? you think you see a monk!
What, 'tis past midnight, and you go the rounds,
5 And here you catch me at an alley's end
Where sportive ladies leave their doors ajar?
The Carmine's my cloister:[4] hunt it up,
Do—harry out, if you must show your zeal,
Whatever rat, there, haps on his wrong hole,
10 And nip each softling of a wee white mouse,
Weke, weke, that's crept to keep him company!
Aha, you know your betters! Then, you'll take
Your hand away that's fiddling on my throat,
And please to know me likewise. Who am I?
15 Why, one, sir, who is lodging with a friend
Three streets off—he's a certain . . . how d'ye call?
Master—a . . . Cosimo of the Medici,[5]
I' the house that caps the corner. Boh! you were best!
Remember and tell me, the day you're hanged,
20 How you affected such a gullet's-gripe![6]
But you, sir, it concerns you that your knaves
Pick up a manner nor discredit you:
Zooks, are we pilchards,° that they sweep the streets   *fish*
And count fair prize what comes into their net?
25 He's Judas to a tittle, that man is![7]
Just such a face! Why, sir, you make amends.
Lord, I'm not angry! Bid your hangdogs go
Drink out this quarter-florin to the health
Of the munificent House that harbors me
30 (And many more beside, lads! more beside!)
And all's come square again. I'd like his face—
His, elbowing on his comrade in the door
With the pike and lantern—for the slave that holds
John Baptist's head a-dangle by the hair
35 With one hand ("Look you, now," as who should say)
And his weapon in the other, yet unwiped!
It's not your chance to have a bit of chalk,
A wood-coal or the like? or you should see!
Yes, I'm the painter, since you style me so.
40 What, brother Lippo's doings, up and down,
You know them and they take you? like enough!

3. Florentine painter (ca. 1406–69), whose life Browning knew from Vasari's *Lives of the Most Eminent Painters, Sculptors, and Architects,* and from other sources, and whose paintings he had learned to know at first hand during his years in Florence.
4. Fra Lippo had entered the Carmelite cloister while still a boy. He gave up monastic vows on June 6, 1421, but was clothed by the monastery until 1431 and was called "Fra Filippo" in documents until his death.
5. Cosimo de'Medici (1389–1464), Fra Lippo's wealthy patron and an important political power in Florence.
6. I.e., grip on my throat.
7. Of one of the watchmen who have arrested him, he says he looks exactly like Judas.

I saw the proper twinkle in your eye—
'Tell you, I liked your looks at very first.
Let's sit and set things straight now, hip to haunch.
45   Here's spring come, and the nights one makes up bands
To roam the town and sing out carnival,
And I've been three weeks shut within my mew,[8]
A-painting for the great man, saints and saints
And saints again. I could not paint all night—
50   Ouf! I leaned out of window for fresh air.
There came a hurry of feet and little feet,
A sweep of lute-strings, laughs, and whifts of song—
Flower o' the broom,
Take away love, and our earth is a tomb!
55   *Flower o' the quince,*
I let Lisa go, and what good in life since?
Flower o' the thyme—and so on. Round they went.
Scarce had they turned the corner when a titter
Like the skipping of rabbits by moonlight—three slim shapes,
60   And a face that looked up . . . zooks, sir, flesh and blood,
That's all I'm made of! Into shreds it went,
Curtain and counterpane and coverlet,
All the bed-furniture—a dozen knots,
There was a ladder! Down I let myself,
65   Hands and feet, scrambling somehow, and so dropped,
And after them. I came up with the fun
Hard by Saint Laurence,[9] hail fellow, well met—
Flower o' the rose,
If I've been merry, what matter who knows?
70   And so as I was stealing back again
To get to bed and have a bit of sleep
Ere I rise up to-morrow and go work
On Jerome knocking at his poor old breast[1]
With his great round stone to subdue the flesh,
75   You snap me of the sudden. Ah, I see!
Though your eye twinkles still, you shake your head—
Mine's shaved—a monk, you say—the sting's in that!
If Master Cosimo announced himself,
Mum's the word naturally; but a monk!
80   Come, what am I a beast for? tell us, now!
I was a baby when my mother died
And father died and left me in the street.
I starved there, God knows how, a year or two
On fig-skins, melon-parings, rinds and shucks,
85   Refuse and rubbish. One fine frosty day,
My stomach being empty as your hat,
The wind doubled me up and down I went.
Old Aunt Lapaccia trussed me with one hand,
(Its fellow was a stinger as I knew)
90   And so along the wall, over the bridge,
By the straight cut to the convent. Six words there,
While I stood munching my first bread that month:
"So, boy, you're minded," quoth the good fat father
Wiping his own mouth, 't was refection-time—
95   "To quit this very miserable world?

8. I.e., within the confines of my quarters (in the Medici palace).
9. The church of San Lorenzo, not far from the Medici palace.
1. I.e., on a painting of St. Jerome in the Desert.

"Will you renounce" . . . "the mouthful of bread?" thought I;
By no means! Brief, they made a monk of me;
I did renounce the world, its pride and greed,
Palace, farm, villa, shop and banking-house,
Trash, such as these poor devils of Medici
Have given their hearts to—all at eight years old.
Well, sir, I found in time, you may be sure,
'T was not for nothing—the good bellyful,
The warm serge and the rope that goes all round,
And day-long blessed idleness beside!
"Let's see what the urchin's fit for"—that came next.
Not overmuch their way, I must confess.
Such a to-do! They tried me with their books:
Lord, they'd have taught me Latin in pure waste!
Flower o' the clove,
All the Latin I construe is, "amo" I love!
But, mind you, when a boy starves in the streets
Eight years together, as my fortune was,
Watching folk's faces to know who will fling
The bit of half-stripped grape-bunch he desires,
And who will curse or kick him for his pains—
Which gentleman processional and fine,
Holding a candle to the Sacrament,
Will wink and let him lift a plate and catch
The droppings of the wax to sell again,
Or holla for the Eight[2] and have him whipped—
How say I? nay, which dog bites, which lets drop
His bone from the heap of offal in the street—
Why, soul and sense of him grow sharp alike,
He learns the look of things, and none the less
For admonition from the hunger-pinch.
I had a store of such remarks, be sure,
Which, after I found leisure, turned to use.
I drew men's faces on my copy-books,
Scrawled them within the antiphonary's[3] marge,
Joined legs and arms to the long music-notes,
Found eyes and nose and chin for A's and B's,
And made a string of pictures of the world
Betwixt the ins and outs of verb and noun,
On the wall, the bench, the door. The monks looked black.
"Nay," quoth the Prior, "turn him out, d'ye say?
"In no wise. Lose a crow and catch a lark.
"What if at last we get our man of parts,
"We Carmelites, like those Camaldolese[4]
"And Preaching Friars,[5] to do our church up fine
"And put the front on it that ought to be!"
And hereupon he bade me daub away.
Thank you! my head being crammed, the walls a blank,
Never was such prompt disemburdening.
First, every sort of monk, the black and white,
I drew them, fat and lean: then, folk at church,
From good old gossips waiting to confess
Their cribs of barrel-droppings, candle-ends—
To the breathless fellow at the altar-foot,

2. The Florentine magistrates.
3. The book containing the antiphons, or re-
sponses chanted in the liturgy.
4. Members of a religious order at Camaldoli,
in the Apennines.
5. I.e., Dominicans.

150 Fresh from his murder, safe and sitting there
With the little children round him in a row
Of admiration, half for his beard and half
For that white anger of his victim's son
Shaking a fist at him with one fierce arm,
155 Signing[6] himself with the other because of Christ
(Whose sad face on the cross sees only this
After the passion of a thousand years)
Till some poor girl, her apron o'er her head,
(Which the intense eyes looked through) came at eve
160 On tiptoe, said a word, dropped in a loaf,
Her pair of earrings and a bunch of flowers
(The brute took growling), prayed, and so was gone.
I painted all, then cried " 'Tis ask and have;
"Choose, for more's ready!"—laid the ladder flat,
165 And showed my covered bit of cloister-wall.
The monks closed in a circle and praised loud
Till checked, taught what to see and not to see,
Being simple bodies—"That's the very man!
"Look at the boy who stoops to pat the dog!
170 "That woman's like the Prior's niece who comes
"To care about his asthma: it's the life!"
But there my triumph's straw-fire flared and funked;
Their betters took their turn to see and say:
The Prior and the learned pulled a face
175 And stopped all that in no time. "How? what's here?
"Quite from the mark of painting, bless us all!
"Faces, arms, legs and bodies like the true
"As much as pea and pea! it's devil's-game!
"Your business is not to catch men with show,
180 "With homage to the perishable clay,
"But lift them over it, ignore it all,
"Make them forget there's such a thing as flesh.
"Your business is to paint the souls of men—
"Man's soul, and it's a fire, smoke . . . no, it's not . . .
185 "It's vapor done up like a new-born babe—
"(In that shape when you die it leaves your mouth)
"It's . . . well, what matters talking, it's the soul!
"Give us no more of body than shows soul!
"Here's Giotto,[7] with his Saint a-praising God,
190 "That sets us praising—why not stop with him?
"Why put all thoughts of praise out of our head
"With wonder at lines, colors, and what not?
"Paint the soul, never mind the legs and arms!
"Rub all out, try at it a second time.
195 "Oh, that white smallish female with the breasts,
"She's just my niece . . . Herodias,[8] I would say—
"Who went and danced and got men's heads cut off!
"Have it all out!" Now, is this sense, I ask?
A fine way to paint soul, by painting body
200 So ill, the eye can't stop there, must go further
And can't fare worse! Thus, yellow does for white
When what you put for yellow's simply black,

6. Making the sign of the cross with one hand, because of the image of Christ on the altar.
7. The great Florentine painter (1267–1337).
8. Sister-in-law of the tetrarch Herod. She had demanded that John the Baptist be imprisoned: when her daughter Salome so pleased the king with her dancing that he promised her anything she asked, Herodias instructed her to ask for the head of a Baptist on a platter (Matthew xiv.1–12).

And any sort of meaning looks intense
When all beside itself means and looks nought.
205 Why can't a painter lift each foot in turn,
Left foot and right foot, go a double step,
Make his flesh liker and his soul more like,
Both in their order? Take the prettiest face,
The Prior's niece . . . patron-saint—is it so pretty
210 You can't discover if it means hope, fear,
Sorrow or joy? won't beauty go with these?
Suppose I've made her eyes all right and blue,
Can't I take breath and try to add life's flash,
And then add soul and heighten them threefold?
215 Or say there's beauty with no soul at all—
(I never saw it—put the case the same—)
If you get simple beauty and nought else,
You get about the best thing God invents:
That's somewhat: and you'll find the soul you have missed,
220 Within yourself, when you return him thanks.
"Rub all out!" Well, well, there's my life, in short,
And so the thing has gone on ever since.
I'm grown a man no doubt, I've broken bounds:
You should not take a fellow eight years old
225 And make him swear to never kiss the girls.
I'm my own master, paint now as I please—
Having a friend, you see, in the Corner-house![9]
Lord, it's fast holding by the rings in front—
Those great rings serve more purposes than just
230 To plant a flag in, or tie up a horse!
And yet the old schooling sticks, the old grave eyes
Are peeping o'er my shoulder as I work,
The heads shake still—"It's art's decline, my son!
"You're not of the true painters, great and old;
235 "Brother Angelico's the man, you'll find;
"Brother Lorenzo[1] stands his single peer:
"Fag on at flesh, you'll never make the third!"
Flower o' the pine,
You keep your mistr . . . . manners, and I'll stick to mine!
240 I'm not the third, then: bless us, they must know!
Don't you think they're the likeliest to know,
They with their Latin? So, I swallow my rage,
Clench my teeth, suck my lips in tight, and paint
To please them—sometimes do and sometimes don't;
245 For, doing most, there's pretty sure to come
A turn, some warm eve finds me at my saints—
A laugh, a cry, the business of the world—
(Flower o' the peach,
Death for us all, and his own life for each!)
250 And my whole soul revolves, the cup runs over,
The world and life's too big to pass for a dream,
And I do these wild things in sheer despite,
And play the fooleries you catch me at,
In pure rage! The old mill-horse, out at grass
255 After hard years, throws up his stiff heels so,
Although the miller does not preach to him
The only good of grass is to make chaff.

---

9. I.e., the Medici palace.

1. Fra Angelico (1387–1455), and Fra
Lorenzo Monaco (1370–1425).

What would men have? Do they like grass or no—
May they or mayn't they? all I want's the thing
260 Settled for ever one way. As it is,
You tell too many lies and hurt yourself:
You don't like what you only like too much,
You do like what, if given you at your word,
You find abundantly detestable.
265 For me, I think I speak as I was taught;
I always see the garden and God there
A-making man's wife: and, my lesson learned,
The value and significance of flesh,
I can't unlearn ten minutes afterwards.

270   You understand me: I'm a beast, I know.
But see, now—why, I see as certainly
As that the morning-star's about to shine,
What will hap some day. We've a youngster here
Comes to our convent, studies what I do,
275 Slouches and stares and lets no atom drop:
His name is Guidi—he'll not mind the monks—
They call him Hulking Tom,[2] he lets them talk—
He picks my practice up—he'll paint apace,
I hope so—though I never live so long,
280 I know what's sure to follow. You be judge!
You speak no Latin more than I, belike;
However, you're my man, you've seen the world
—The beauty and the wonder and the power,
The shapes of things, their colors, lights and shades,
285 Changes, surprises—and God made it all!
—For what? Do you feel thankful, ay or no,
For this fair town's face, yonder river's line,
The mountain round it and the sky above,
Much more the figures of man, woman, child,
290 These are the frame to? What's it all about?
To be passed over, despised? or dwelt upon,
Wondered at? oh, this last of course!—you say.
But why not do as well as say, paint these
Just as they are, careless what comes of it?
295 God's works—paint anyone, and count it crime
To let a truth slip. Don't object, "His works
"Are here already; nature is complete:
"Suppose you reproduce her (which you can't)
"There's no advantage! you must beat her, then."
300 For, don't you mark? we're made so that we love
First when we see them painted, things we have passed
Perhaps a hundred times nor cared to see;
And so they are better, painted—better to us,
Which is the same thing. Art was given for that;
305 God uses us to help each other so,
Lending our minds out. Have you noticed, now,
Your cullion's hanging face? A bit of chalk,
And trust me but you should, though! How much more,
If I drew higher things with the same truth!

---

2. The painter Tommaso Guidi (1401–28), known as Masaccio (from *Tomasaccio*, meaning "Big Tom" or "Hulking Tom"). The series of frescoes which he painted in Santa Maria del Carmine, of key importance in the history of Florentine painting, was completed by Fra Lippo's son, Filippino Lippi, and it is in fact more likely that Fra Lippo learned from Masaccio than that he saw him as a promising newcomer.

310 That were to take the Prior's pulpit-place,
    Interpret God to all of you! Oh, oh,
    It makes me mad to see what men shall do
    And we in our graves! This world's no blot for us,
    Nor blank; it means intensely, and means good:
315 To find its meaning is my meat and drink.
    "Ay, but you don't so instigate to prayer!"
    Strikes in the Prior: "when your meaning's plain
    "It does not say to folk—remember matins,
    "Or, mind you fast next Friday!" Why, for this
320 What need of art at all? A skull and bones,
    Two bits of stick nailed crosswise, or, what's best,
    A bell to chime the hour with, does as well.
    I painted a Saint Laurence six months since
    At Prato,[3] splashed the fresco in fine style:
325 "How looks my painting, now the scaffold's down?"
    I ask a brother: "Hugely," he returns—
    "Already not one phiz of your three slaves
    "Who turn the Deacon off his toasted side,[4]
    "But's scratched and prodded to our heart's content,
330 "The pious people have so eased their own
    "With coming to say prayers there in a rage:
    "We get on fast to see the bricks beneath.
    "Expect another job this time next year,
    "For pity and religion grow i' the crowd—
355 "Your painting serves its purpose!" Hang the fools!
    —That is—you'll not mistake an idle word
    Spoke in a huff by a poor monk, God wot,
    Tasting the air this spicy night which turns
    The unaccustomed head like Chianti wine!
340 Oh, the church knows! don't misreport me, now!
    It's natural a poor monk out of bounds
    Should have his apt word to excuse himself:
    And hearken how I plot to make amends.
    I have bethought me: I shall paint a piece
345 . . . There's for you! Give me six months, then go, see
    Something in Sant' Ambrogio's![5] Bless the nuns!
    They want a cast o' my office. I shall paint
    God in the midst, Madonna and her babe,
    Ringed by a bowery flowery angel-brood,
350 Lilies and vestments and white faces, sweet
    As puff on puff of grated orris-root
    When ladies crowd to Church at midsummer.
    And then i' the front, of course a saint or two—
    Saint John, because he saves the Florentines,[6]
355 Saint Ambrose, who puts down in black and white
    The convent's friends and gives them a long day,
    And Job, I must have him there past mistake,
    The man of Uz (and Us without the z,
    Painters who need his patience). Well, all these
360 Secured at their devotion, up shall come
    Out of a corner when you least expect,

3. Smaller town near Florence, where Fra Lippo painted some of his most important pictures.
4. Saint Lawrence was martyred by being roasted on a gridiron; according to legend, he urged his executioners to turn him over, saying that he was done on one side.
5. Fra Lippo painted the *Coronation of the Virgin*, here described, for the high altar of Sant' Ambrogio in 1447.
6. San Giovanni is the patron saint of Florence.

As one by a dark stair into a great light,
Music and talking, who but Lippo! I!
Mazed, motionless and moonstruck—I'm the man!
365   Back I shrink—what is this I see and hear?
I, caught up with my monk's-things by mistake,
My old serge gown and rope that goes all round,
I, in this presence, this pure company!
Where's a hole, where's a corner for escape?
370   Then steps a sweet angelic slip of a thing
Forward, puts out a soft palm—"Not so fast!"
—Addresses the celestial presence, "nay—
"He made you and devised you, after all,
"Though he's none of you! Could Saint John there draw—
375   "His camel-hair[7] make up a painting-brush?
"We come to brother Lippo for all that,
"*Iste perfecit opus!*"[8] So, all smile—
I shuffle sideways with my blushing face
Under the cover of a hundred wings
380   Thrown like a spread of kirtles[9] when you're gay
And play hot cockles,[1] all the doors being shut,
Till, wholly unexpected, in there pops
The hothead husband! Thus I scuttle off
To some safe bench behind, not letting go
285   The palm of her, the little lily thing
That spoke the good word for me in the nick,
Like the Prior's niece . . . Saint Lucy, I would say.
And so all's saved for me, and for the church
A pretty picture gained. Go, six months hence!
390   Your hand, sir, and good-bye: no lights, no lights!
The street's hushed, and I know my own way back,
Don't fear me! there's the gray beginning. Zooks!

1855

A Toccata of Galuppi's[2]

1

Oh Galuppi, Baldassare, this is very sad to find!
I can hardly misconceive you; it would prove me deaf and blind;
But although I take your meaning, 'tis with such a heavy mind!

2

Here you come with your old music, and here's all the good it brings.
5   What, they lived once thus at Venice where the merchants were the kings,
Where Saint Mark's is, where the Doges used to wed the sea with rings?[3]

3

Ay, because the sea's the street there; and 'tis arched by . . . what you call
. . . Shylock's bridge[4] with houses on it, where they kept the carnival:
I was never out of England—it's as if I saw it all.

7. John the Baptist is often portrayed wearing a rough robe of camel's hair, in accord with Mark i.6.
8. It is more likely that the figure which Browning took to be that of the painter is that of the patron, the Very Reverend Francesco Marenghi, who ordered the painting in 1441, and that the words on the scroll before him ("*Is [te] perfecit opus*," This man accomplished the work) refer to the commissioning of the project.
9. Women's gowns or skirts.
1. A game in which a blindfolded player must guess who has struck him.
2. The poem presents the reflections of a 19th-century Englishman, as he plays a toccata by the 18th-century Venetian composer Baldassare Galuppi. (A toccata is a "touch-piece," the word derived from the Italian verb *toccare*, to touch: "a composition intended to exhibit the touch and exhibition of the performer," and hence often having the character of "showy improvisation" [*Grove's Dictionary of Music and Musicians*]. In stanzas 7–9, the quoted words represent the thoughts, feelings, or casual remarks of the earlier Venetian audience, now dispersed by death.
3. Each year the Doge, chief magistrate of the Venetian republic, threw a ring into the sea with the ceremonial words, "We wed thee, O sea, in sign of true and everlasting dominion."
4. The Rialto Bridge over the Grand Canal.

4

¹⁰ Did young people take their pleasure when the sea was warm in May?
Balls and masks begun at midnight, burning ever to mid-day,
When they made up fresh adventures for the morrow, do you say?

5

Was a lady such a lady, cheeks so round and lips so red—
On her neck the small face bouyant, like a bellflower on its bed,
¹⁵ O'er the breast's superb abundance where a man might base his head?

6

Well, and it was graceful of them—they'd break talk off and afford
—She, to bite her mask's black velvet—he, to finger on his sword,
While you sat and played Toccatas, stately at the clavichord?⁵

7

What? Those lesser thirds so plaintive, sixths diminished, sigh on sigh,
²⁰ Told them something? Those suspensions, those solutions—"Must we die?"
Those commiserating sevenths—"Life might last! we can but try!"

8

"Were you happy?" "Yes." "And are you still as happy?" "Yes. And you?"
"Then, more kisses!" "Did *I* stop them, when a million seemed so few?"
Hark, the dominant's persistence till it must be answered to!

9

²⁵ So, an octave struck the answer. Oh, they praised you, I dare say!
"Brave Galuppi! that was music! good alike at grave and gay!
"I can always leave off talking when I hear a master play!"

10

Then they left you for their pleasure: till in due time, one by one,
Some with lives that came to nothing, some with deeds as well undone,
³⁰ Death stepped tacitly and took them where they never see the sun.

11

But when I sit down to reason, think to take my stand nor swerve,
While I triumph o'er a secret wrung from nature's close reserve,
In you come with your cold music⁶ till I creep through every nerve.

12

Yes, you, like a ghostly cricket, creaking where a house was burned:
³⁵ "Dust and ashes, dead and done with, Venice spent what Venice earned.
"The soul, doubtless, is immortal—where a soul can be discerned.

13

"Yours for instance: you know physics, something of geology,
"Mathematics are your pastime; souls shall rise in their degree;
"Butterflies may dread extinction—you'll not die, it cannot be!

14

⁴⁰ "As for Venice and her people, merely born to bloom and drop,
"Here on earth they bore their fruitage, mirth and folly were the crop:
"What of soul was left, I wonder, when the kissing had to stop?

15

"Dust and ashes!" So you creak it, and I want the heart to scold.
Dear dead women, with such hair, too—what's become of all the gold
⁴⁵ Used to hang and brush their bosoms? I feel chilly and grown old.

ca. 1847   1855

---

5. "A keyboard instrument, precursor of the piano" [Webster].

6. In stanzas 12–15, the quoted words are the words he imagines the composer as speaking to him.

Memorabilia

1

Ah, did you once see Shelley plain,
    And did he stop and speak to you
And did you speak to him again?
    How strange it seems and new!

2

5 But you were living before that,
    And also you are living after;
And the memory I started at—
    My starting moves your laughter.

3

I crossed a moor, with a name of its own
10   And a certain use in the world no doubt,
Yet a hand's-breadth of it shines alone
    'Mid the blank miles round about:

4

For there I picked up on the heather
    And there I put inside my breast
15 A moulted feather, an eagle-feather!
    Well, I forget the rest.

1855

Two in the Campagna[7]

1

I wonder do you feel today
    As I have felt since, hand in hand,
We sat down on the grass, to stray
    In spirit better through the land,
5 This morn of Rome and May?

2

For me, I touched a thought, I know,
    Has tantalized me many times,
(Like turns of thread the spiders throw
    Mocking across our path) for rhymes
10 To catch at and let go.

3

Help me to hold it! First it left
    The yellowing fennel,[8] run to seed
There, branching from the brickwork's cleft,
    Some old tomb's ruin: yonder weed
15 Took up the floating weft,°   *spider-web*

4

Where one small orange cup amassed
    Five beetles—blind and green they grope
Among the honey-meal: and last,
    Everywhere on the grassy slope
20 I traced it. Hold it fast!

---

7. The grassy, rolling countryside around Rome;
it was malarial, and hence semi-deserted, until
Mussolini reclaimed the Pontine marshes.

8. A yellow-flowered plant, whose aromatic
seeds are used as a condiment.

5

The champaign[9] with its endless fleece
  Of feathery grasses everywhere!
Silence and passion, joy and peace,
  An everlasting wash of air—
25 Rome's ghost since her decease.

6

Such life here, through such lengths of hours,
  Such miracles performed in play,
Such primal naked forms of flowers,
  Such letting nature have her way
30 While heaven looks from its towers!

7

How say you? Let us, O my dove,
  Let us be unashamed of soul,
As earth lies bare to heaven above!
  How is it under our control
35 To love or not to love?

8

I would that you were all to me,
  You that are just so much, no more.
Nor yours nor mine, nor slave nor free!
  Where does the fault lie? What the core
40 O' the wound, since wound must be?

9

I would I could adopt your will,
  See with your eyes, and set my heart
Beating by yours, and drink my fill
  At your soul's springs—your part my part
45 In life, for good and ill.

10

No. I yearn upward, touch you close,
  Then stand away. I kiss your cheek,
Catch your soul's warmth—I pluck the rose
  And love it more than tongue can speak—
50 Then the good minute goes.

11

Already how am I so far
  Out of that minute? Must I go
Still like the thistle-ball, no bar,
  Onward, whenever light winds blow,
55 Fixed by no friendly star?

12

Just when I seemed about to learn!
  Where is the thread now? Off again!
The old trick! Only I discern—
  Infinite passion, and the pain
60 Of finite hearts that yearn.

1855

---

9. I.e., grassland—here, the Campagna itself.

HENRY DAVID THOREAU
(1817–1862)

I Am a Parcel of Vain Strivings Tied

I am a parcel of vain strivings tied
 By a chance bond together,
 Dangling this way and that, their links
 Were made so loose and wide,
5   Methinks,
 For milder weather.

A bunch of violets without their roots,
 And sorrel intermixed,
 Encircled by a wisp of straw
10   Once coiled about their shoots,
 The law
 By which I'm fixed.

A nosegay which Time clutched from out
 Those fair Elysian fields,[1]
15 With weeds and broken stems, in haste,
 Doth make the rabble rout
 That waste
 The day he yields.

And here I bloom for a short hour unseen,
20   Drinking my juices up,
 With no root in the land
 To keep my branches green,
 But stand
 In a bare cup.

                                        1841

The Inward Morning

Packed in my mind lie all the clothes
 Which outward nature wears,
And in its fashion's hourly change
 It all things else repairs.

5 In vain I look for change abroad,
 And can no difference find,
Till some new ray of peace uncalled
 Illumes my inmost mind.

What is it gilds the trees and clouds,
10   And paints the heavens so gay,
But yonder fast-abiding light
 With its unchanging ray?

---

1. In Greek mythology, the home of the blessed in the afterlife.

Lo, when the sun streams through the wood,
  Upon a winter's morn,
15 Where'er his silent beams intrude
  The murky night is gone.

How could the patient pine have known
  The morning breeze would come,
Or humble flowers anticipate
20   The insect's noonday hum,

Till the new light with morning cheer
  From far streamed through the aisles,
And nimbly told the forest trees
  For many stretching miles?

25 I've heard within my inmost soul
  Such cheerful morning news,
In the horizon of my mind
  Have seen such orient hues,

As in the twilight of the dawn,
30   When the first birds awake,
Are heard within some silent wood,
  Where they the small twigs break,

Or in the eastern skies are seen,
  Before the sun appears,
35 The harbingers of summer heats
  Which from afar he bears.

1842,   1849

HERMAN MELVILLE
(1819–1891)

Shiloh[5]

A REQUIEM (APRIL 1862)

Skimming lightly, wheeling still,
  The swallows fly low
Over the field in clouded days,
  The forest-field of Shiloh—
5 Over the field where April rain
Solaced the parched one stretched in pain
Through the pause of night
That followed the Sunday fight
  Around the church of Shiloh—
10 The church so lone, the log-built one,
That echoed to many a parting groan
    And natural prayer
  Of dying foemen mingled there—

---

5. The battle at Shiloh church in Tennessee on April 6 and 7, 1862, was one of the bloodiest
of the Civil War.

Foemen at morn, but friends at eve—
15   Fame or country least their care:
(What like a bullet can undeceive!)
    But now they lie low,
While over them the swallows skim,
    And all is hushed at Shiloh.

1866

The Maldive Shark

About the Shark, phlegmatical one,
Pale sot of the Maldive sea,
The sleek little pilot-fish, azure and slim,
How alert in attendance be.
5   From his saw-pit of mouth, from his charnel of maw,
They have nothing of harm to dread,
But liquidly glide on his ghastly flank
Or before his Gorgonian[6] head;
Or lurk in the port of serrated teeth
10   In white triple tiers of glittering gates,
And there find a haven when peril's abroad,
An asylum in jaws of the Fates!
They are friends; and friendly they guide him to prey,
Yet never partake of the treat—
15   Eyes and brains to the dotard lethargic and dull,
Pale ravener of horrible meat.

1888

WALT WHITMAN
(1819–1892)

Vigil Strange I Kept on the Field One Night

Vigil strange I kept on the field one night;
When you my son and my comrade dropt at my side that day,
One look I but gave which your dear eyes return'd with a look I shall never
    forget,
One touch of your hand to mine O boy, reach'd up as you lay on the ground,
5   Then onward I sped in the battle, the even-contested battle,
Till late in the night reliev'd to the place at last again I made my way,
Found you in death so cold dear comrade, found your body son of respond-
    ing kisses, (never again on earth responding,)
Bared your face in the starlight, curious the scene, cool blew the moderate
    night-wind,
Long there and then in vigil I stood, dimly around me the battle-field
    spreading,
10   Vigil wondrous and vigil sweet there in the fragrant silent night,
But not a tear fell, not even a long-drawn sigh, long I gazed,
Then on the earth partially reclining sat by your side leaning my chin in my
    hands,
Passing sweet hours, immortal and mystic hours with you dearest comrade—
    not a tear, not a word,

6. In classical mythology, Gorgon was one of
three sisters (Medusa was another) whose
face and snake-entwined hair could turn the
viewer to stone; hence, a thing so frightening
as to freeze its beholder.

Vigil of silence, love and death, vigil for you my son and my soldier,
15 As onward silently stars aloft, eastward new ones upward stole,
Vigil finally for you brave boy, (I could not save you, swift was your death,
I faithfully loved you and cared for you living, I think we shall surely meet again,)
Till at latest lingering of the night, indeed just as the dawn appear'd,
My comrade I wrapt in his blanket, envelop'd well his form,
20 Folded the blanket well, tucking it carefully over head and carefully under feet,
And there and then and bathed by the rising sun, my son in his grave, in his rude-dug grave I deposited,
Ending my vigil strange with that, vigil of night and battle-field dim,
Vigil for boy of responding kisses, (never again on earth responding,)
Vigil for comrade swiftly slain, vigil I never forget, how as day brighten'd,
25 I rose from the chill ground and folded my soldier well in his blanket,
And buried him where he fell.

1865   1867

Beat! Beat! Drums!

Beat! beat! drums! blow! bugles! blow!
Through the windows—through doors—burst like a ruthless force,
Into the solemn church, and scatter the congregation,
Into the school where the scholar is studying;
5 Leave not the bridegroom quiet—no happiness must he have now with his bride,
Nor the peaceful farmer any peace, ploughing his field or gathering his grain,
So fierce you whirr and pound you drums—so shrill you bugles blow.

Beat! beat! drums!—blow! bugles! blow!
Over the traffic of cities—over the rumble of wheels in the streets;
10 Are beds prepared for sleepers at night in the houses? no sleepers must sleep in those beds,
No bargainers' bargains by day—no brokers or speculators—would they continue?
Would the talkers be talking? would the singer attempt to sing?
Would the lawyer rise in the court to state his case before the judge?
Then rattle quicker, heavier drums—you bugles wilder blow.
15 Beat! beat! drums!—blow! bugles! blow!
Make no parley—stop for no expostulation,
Mind not the timid—mind not the weeper or prayer,
Mind not the old man beseeching the young man,
Let not the child's voice be heard, nor the mother's entreaties,
20 Make even the trestles to shake the dead where they lie awaiting the hearses,
So strong you thump O terrible drums—so loud you bugles blow.

1861   1867

Out of the Cradle Endlessly Rocking

Out of the cradle endlessly rocking,
Out of the mocking-bird's throat, the musical shuttle,
Out of the Ninth-month[1] midnight,
Over the sterile sands and the fields beyond, where the child leaving his bed wander'd alone, bareheaded, barefoot,

---

1. The Quaker designation for September may here also suggest the human cycle of fertility and birth, in contrast with "sterile sands" in the next line.

5   Down from the shower'd halo,
Up from the mystic play of shadows twining and twisting as if they were
     alive,
Out from the patches of briers and blackberries,
From the memories of the bird that chanted to me,
From your memories sad brother, from the fitful risings and fallings I heard,
10 From under that yellow half-moon late-risen and swollen as if with tears,
From those beginning notes of yearning and love there in the mist,
From the thousand responses of my heart never to cease,
From the myriad thence-arous'd words,
From the word stronger and more delicious than any,
15 From such as now they start the scene revisiting,
As a flock, twittering, rising, or overhead passing,
Borne hither, ere all eludes me, hurriedly,
A man, yet by these tears a little boy again,
Throwing myself on the sand, confronting the waves,
20 I, chanter of pains and joys, uniter of here and hereafter,
Taking all hints to use them, but swiftly leaping beyond them,
A reminiscence sing.

Once Paumanok,[2]
When the lilac-scent was in the air and Fifth-month grass was growing,
25 Up this seashore in some briers,
Two feather'd guests from Alabama, two together,
And their nest, and four light-green eggs spotted with brown,
And every day the he-bird to and fro near at hand,
And every day the she-bird crouch'd on her nest, silent, with bright eyes,
30 And every day I, a curious boy, never too close, never disturbing them,
Cautiously peering, absorbing, translating.

Shine! shine! shine!
Pour down your warmth, great sun!
While we bask, we two together.

35 *Two together!*
Winds blow south, or winds blow north,
Day come white, or night come black,
Home, or rivers and mountains from home,
Singing all time, minding no time,
40 *While we two keep together.*

Till of a sudden,
May-be kill'd, unknown to her mate,
One forenoon the she-bird crouch'd not on the nest,
Nor return'd that afternoon, nor the next,
45 Nor ever appear'd again.

And thenceforward all summer in the sound of the sea,
And at night under the full of the moon in calmer weather,
Over the hoarse surging of the sea,
Or flitting from brier to brier by day,
50 I saw, I heard at intervals the remaining one, the he-bird,
The solitary guest from Alabama.

2. The Indian name for Long Island.

Blow! blow! blow!
Blow up sea-winds along Paumanok's shore;
I wait and I wait till you blow my mate to me.

55   Yes, when the stars glisten'd,
All night long on the prong of a moss-scallop'd stake,
Down almost amid the slapping waves,
Sat the lone singer wonderful causing tears.

He call'd on his mate,
60   He pour'd forth the meanings which I of all men know.

Yes my brother I know,
The rest might not, but I have treasur'd every note,
For more than once dimly down to the beach gliding,
Silent, avoiding the moonbeams, blending myself with the shadows,
65   Recalling now the obscure shapes, the echoes, the sounds and sights after
their sorts,
The white arms out in the breakers tirelessly tossing,
I, with bare feet, a child, the wind wafting my hair,
Listen'd long and long.

Listen'd to keep, to sing, now translating the notes,
70   Following you my brother.

Soothe! soothe! soothe!
Close on its wave soothes the wave behind,
And again another behind embracing and lapping, every one close,
But my love soothes not me, not me.

75   *Low hangs the moon, it rose late,*
It is lagging—O I think it is heavy with love, with love.

O madly the sea pushes upon the land,
With love, with love.

O night! do I not see my love fluttering out among the breakers?
80   *What is that little black thing I see there in the white?*

Loud! loud! loud!
Loud I call to you, my love!

High and clear I shoot my voice over the waves,
Surely you must know who is here, is here,
85   *You must know who I am, my love.*

Low-hanging moon!
What is that dusky spot in your brown yellow?
O it is the shape, the shape of my mate!
O moon do not keep her from me any longer.

90   *Land! land! O land!*
Whichever way I turn, O I think you could give me my mate back again if
you only would,
For I am almost sure I see her dimly whichever way I look.

O rising stars!
Perhaps the one I want so much will rise, will rise with some of you.

95 *O throat! O trembling throat!*
Sound clearer through the atmosphere!
Pierce the woods, the earth,
Somewhere listening to catch you must be the one I want.

Shake out carols!
100 *Solitary here, the night's carols!*
Carols of lonesome love! death's carols!
Carols under that lagging, yellow, waning moon!
O under that moon where she droops almost down into the sea!
O reckless despairing carols.

105 *But soft! sink low!*
Soft! let me just murmur,
And do you wait a moment you husky-nois'd sea,
For somewhere I believe I heard my mate responding to me,
So faint, I must be still, be still to listen,
110 *But not altogether still, for then she might not come immediately to me.*

Hither my love!
Here I am! here!
With this just-sustain'd note I announce myself to you,
This gentle call is for you my love, for you.

115 *Do not be decoy'd elsewhere,*
That is the whistle of the wind, it is not my voice,
That is the fluttering, the fluttering of the spray,
Those are the shadows of leaves.

O darkness! O in vain!
120 *O I am very sick and sorrowful.*

O brown halo in the sky near the moon, drooping upon the sea!
O troubled reflection in the sea!
O throat! O throbbing heart!
And I singing uselessly, uselessly all the night.

125 *O past! O happy life! O songs of joy!*
In the air, in the woods, over fields,
Loved! loved! loved! loved! loved!
But my mate no more, no more with me!
We two together no more.

130 The aria sinking,
All else continuing, the stars shining,
The winds blowing, the notes of the bird continuous echoing,
With angry moans the fierce old mother incessantly moaning,
On the sands of Paumanok's shore gray and rustling,
135 The yellow half-moon enlarged, sagging down, drooping, the face of the sea
almost touching,
The boy ecstatic, with his bare feet the waves, with his hair the atmosphere
dallying,

The love in the heart long pent, now loose, now at last tumultuously bursting,
The aria's meaning, the ears, the soul, swiftly depositing,
The strange tears down the cheeks coursing,
140 The colloquy there, the trio, each uttering,
The undertone, the savage old mother incessantly crying,
To the boy's soul's questions sullenly timing, some drown'd secret hissing,
To the outsetting bard.

Demon or bird! (said the boy's soul,)
145 Is it indeed toward your mate you sing? or is it really to me?
For I, that was a child, my tongue's use sleeping, now I have heard you,
Now in a moment I know what I am for, I awake,
And already a thousand singers, a thousand songs, clearer, louder and more
    sorrowful than yours,
A thousand warbling echoes have started to life within me, never to die.

150 O you singer solitary, singing by yourself, projecting me,
O solitary me listening, never more shall I cease perpetuating you,
Never more shall I escape, never more the reverberations,
Never more the cries of unsatisfied love be absent from me,
Never again leave me to be the peaceful child I was before what there in the
    night,
155 By the sea under the yellow and sagging moon,
The messenger there arous'd, the fire, the sweet hell within,
The unknown want, the destiny of me.

O give me the clew! (it lurks in the night here somewhere,)
O if I am to have so much, let me have more!

160 A word then, (for I will conquer it,)
The word final, superior to all,
Subtle, sent up—what is it?—I listen;
Are you whispering it, and have been all the time, you sea-waves?
Is that it from your liquid rims and wet sands?

165 Whereto answering, the sea,
Delaying not, hurrying not,
Whisper'd me through the night, and very plainly before daybreak,
Lisp'd to me the low and delicious word death,
And again death, death, death, death,
170 Hissing melodious, neither like the bird nor like my arous'd child's heart,
But edging near as privately for me rustling at my feet,
Creeping thence steadily up to my ears and laving me softly all over,
Death, death, death, death, death.

Which I do not forget,
175 But fuse the song of my dusky demon and brother,
That he sang to me in the moonlight on Paumanok's gray beach,
With the thousand responsive songs at random,
My own songs awaked from that hour,
And with them the key, the word up from the waves,
180 The word of the sweetest song and all songs,
That strong and delicious word which, creeping to my feet,
(Or like some old crone rocking the cradle, swathed in sweet garments, bend-
    ing aside,)
The sea whisper'd me.

1859   1881

The Dalliance of the Eagles

Skirting the river road, (my forenoon walk, my rest,)
Skyward in air a sudden muffled sound, the dalliance of the eagles,
The rushing amorous contact high in space together,
The clinching interlocking claws, a living, fierce, gyrating wheel,
5   Four beating wings, two beaks, a swirling mass tight grappling,
In tumbling turning clustering loops, straight downward falling,
Till o'er the river pois'd, the twain yet one, a moment's lull,
A motionless still balance in the air, then parting, talons loosing,
Upward again on slow-firm pinions slanting, their separate diverse flight,
10   She hers, he his, pursuing.

                                1880   1881

When Lilacs Last in the Dooryard Bloom'd

1

When lilacs last in the dooryard bloom'd,
And the great star early droop'd in the western sky in the night,
I mourn'd, and yet shall mourn with ever-returning spring.

Ever-returning spring, trinity sure to me you bring,
5   Lilac blooming perennial and drooping star in the west,
And thought of him I love.

2

O powerful western fallen star!
O shades of night—O moody, tearful night!
O great star disappear'd—O the black murk that hides the star!
10   O cruel hands that hold me powerless—O helpless soul of me!
O harsh surrounding cloud that will not free my soul.

3

In the dooryard fronting an old farm-house near the white-wash'd palings,
Stands the lilac-bush tall-growing with heart-shaped leaves of rich green,
With many a pointed blossom rising delicate, with the perfume strong I love,
15   With every leaf a miracle—and from this bush in the dooryard,
With delicate-color'd blossoms and heart-shaped leaves of rich green,
A sprig with its flower I break.

4

In the swamp in secluded recesses,
A shy and hidden bird is warbling a song.

20   Solitary the thrush,
The hermit withdrawn to himself, avoiding the settlements,
Sings by himself a song.

Song of the bleeding throat,
Death's outlet song of life, (for well dear brother I know,
25   If thou wast not granted to sing thou would'st surely die.)

5

Over the breast of the spring, the land, amid cities,
Amid lanes and through old woods, where lately the violets peep'd from the
        ground, spotting the gray debris,
Amid the grass in the fields each side of the lanes, passing the endless grass,
Passing the yellow-spear'd wheat, every grain from its shroud in the dark-
        brown fields uprisen,
30   Passing the apple-tree blows of white and pink in the orchards,
Carrying a corpse to where it shall rest in the grave,
Night and day journeys a coffin.

6

Coffin that passes through lanes and streets,[3]
Through day and night with the great cloud darkening the land,
35   With the pomp of the inloop'd flags with the cities draped in black,
With the show of the States themselves as of crape-veil'd women standing,
With processions long and winding and the flambeaus of the night,
With the countless torches lit, with the silent sea of faces and the unbared
      heads,
With the waiting depot, the arriving coffin, and the sombre faces,
40   With dirges through the night, with the thousand voices rising strong and
      solemn,
With all the mournful voices of the dirges pour'd around the coffin,
The dim-lit churches and the shuddering organs—where amid these you
      journey,
With the tolling tolling bells' perpetual clang,
Here, coffin that slowly passes,
45   I give you my sprig of lilac.

7

(Nor for you, for one alone,
Blossoms and branches green to coffins all I bring,
For fresh as the morning, thus would I chant a song for you O sane and
      sacred death.

All over bouquets of roses,
50   O death, I cover you over with roses and early lilies,
But mostly and now the lilac that blooms the first,
Copious I break, I break the sprigs from the bushes,
With loaded arms I come, pouring for you,
For you and the coffins all of you O death.)

8

55   O western orb sailing the heaven,
Now I know what you must have meant as a month since I walk'd,
As I walk'd in silence the transparent shadowy night,
As I saw you had something to tell as you bent to me night after night,
As you droop'd from the sky low down as if to my side, (while the other
      stars all look'd on,)
60   As we wander'd together the solemn night, (for something I know not what
      kept me from sleep,)
As the night advanced, and I saw on the rim of the west how full you were
      of woe,
As I stood on the rising ground in the breeze in the cool transparent night,
As I watch'd where you pass'd and was lost in the netherward black of the
      night,
As my soul in its trouble dissatisfied sank, as where you sad orb,
65   Concluded, dropt in the night, and was gone.

9

Sing on there in the swamp,
O singer bashful and tender, I hear your notes, I hear your call,
I hear, I come presently, I understand you,
But a moment I linger, for the lustrous star has detain'd me,
70   The star my departing comrade holds and detains me.

10

O how shall I warble myself for the dead one there I loved?
And how shall I deck my song for the large sweet soul that has gone?

---

3. The funeral cortège of Lincoln traveled from Washington to Springfield, Illinois, stopping
at cities and towns all along the way for the people to honor the murdered President.

And what shall my perfume be for the grave of him I love?
Sea-winds blown from east and west,
75 Blown from the Eastern sea and blown from the Western sea, till there on
the prairies meeting,
These and with these and the breath of my chant,
I'll perfume the grave of him I love.

11

O what shall I hang on the chamber walls?
And what shall the pictures be that I hang on the walls,
80 To adorn the burial-house of him I love?

Pictures of growing spring and farms and homes,
With the Fourth-month eve at sundown, and the gray smoke lucid and
bright,
With floods of the yellow gold of the gorgeous, indolent, sinking sun, burn-
ing, expanding the air,
With the fresh sweet herbage under foot, and the pale green leaves of the
trees prolific,
85 In the distance the flowing glaze, the breast of the river, with a wind-dapple
here and there,
With ranging hills on the banks, with many a line against the sky, and
shadows,
And the city at hand with dwellings so dense, and stacks of chimneys,
And all the scenes of life and the workshops, and the workmen homeward
returning.

12

Lo, body and soul—this land,
90 My own Manhattan with spires, and the sparkling and hurrying tides, and
the ships,
The varied and ample land, the South and the North in the light, Ohio's
shores and flashing Missouri,
And ever the far-spreading prairies cover'd with grass and corn.

Lo, the most excellent sun so calm and haughty,
The violet and purple morn with just-felt breezes,
95 The gentle soft-born measureless light,
The miracle spreading bathing all, the fulfill'd noon,
The coming eve delicious, the welcome night and the stars,
Over my cities shining all, enveloping man and land.

13

Sing on, sing on you gray-brown bird,
100 Sing from the swamps, the recesses, pour your chant from the bushes,
Limitless out of the dusk, out of the cedars and pines.

Sing on dearest brother, warble your reedy song,
Loud human song, with voice of uttermost woe.

O liquid and free and tender!
105 O wild and loose to my soul—O wondrous singer!
You only I hear—yet the star holds me, (but will soon depart,)
Yet the lilac with mastering odor holds me.

14

Now while I sat in the day and look'd forth,
In the close of the day with its light and the fields of spring, and the farmers
preparing their crops,
110 In the large unconscious scenery of my land with its lakes and forests,
In the heavenly aerial beauty, (after the perturb'd winds and the storms,)

Under the arching heavens of the afternoon swift passing, and the voices of
    children and women.
The many-moving sea-tides, and I saw the ships how they sail'd,
And the summer approaching with richness, and the fields all busy with
    labor,
115   And the infinite separate houses, how they all went on, each with its meals
    and minutia of daily usages,
And the streets how their throbbings throbb'd, and the cities pent—lo, then
    and there,
Falling upon them all and among them all, enveloping me with the rest,
Appear'd the cloud, appear'd the long black trail,
And I knew death, its thought, and the sacred knowledge of death.

120   Then with the knowledge of death as walking one side of me,
And the thought of death close-walking the other side of me,
And I in the middle as with companions, and as holding the hands of
    companions,
I fled forth to the hiding receiving night that talks not,
Down to the shores of the water, the path by the swamp in the dimness,
125   To the solemn shadowy cedars and ghostly pines so still.

And the singer so shy to the rest receiv'd me,
The gray-brown bird I know receiv'd us comrades three,
And he sang the carol of death, and a verse for him I love.

From deep secluded recesses,
130   From the fragrant cedars and the ghostly pines so still,
Came the carol of the bird.

And the charm of the carol rapt me,
As I held as if by their hands my comrades in the night,
And the voice of my spirit tallied the song of the bird.

135   *Come lovely and soothing death,*
Undulate round the world, serenely arriving, arriving,
In the day, in the night, to all, to each,
Sooner or later delicate death.

Prais'd be the fathomless universe,
140   *For life and joy, and for objects and knowledge curious,*
And for love, sweet love—but praise! praise! praise!
For the sure-enwinding arms of cool-enfolding death.

Dark mother always gliding near with soft feet,
Have none chanted for thee a chant of fullest welcome?
145   *Then I chant it for thee, I glorify thee above all,*
I bring thee a song that when thou must indeed come, come unfalteringly.

Approach strong deliveress,
When it is so, when thou hast taken them I joyously sing the dead,
Lost in the loving floating ocean of thee,
150   *Laved in the flood of thy bliss O death.*

From me to thee glad serenades,
Dances for thee I propose saluting thee, adornments and feastings for thee,
And the sights of the open landscape and the high-spread sky are fitting,
And life and the fields, and the huge and thoughtful night.

155   *The night in silence under many a star,*
The ocean shore and the husky whispering wave whose voice I know,
And the soul turning to thee O vast and well-veil'd death,
And the body gratefully nestling close to thee.

Over the tree-tops I float thee a song,
160   *Over the rising and sinking waves, over the myriad fields and the prairies*
wide,
Over the dense-pack'd cities all and the teeming wharves and ways,
I float this carol with joy, with joy to thee O death.

15
To the tally of my soul,
Loud and strong kept up the gray-brown bird,
165   With pure deliberate notes spreading filling the night.

Loud in the pines and cedars dim,
Clear in the freshness moist and the swamp-perfume,
And I with my comrades there in the night.

While my sight that was bound in my eyes unclosed,
170   As to long panoramas of visions.

And I saw askant the armies,
I saw as in noiseless dreams hundreds of battle-flags,
Borne through the smoke of the battles and pierc'd with missiles I saw them,
And carried hither and yon through the smoke, and torn and bloody,
175   And at last but a few shreds left on the staffs, (and all in silence,)
And the staffs all splinter'd and broken.

I saw battle-corpses, myriads of them,
And the white skeletons of young men, I saw them,
I saw the debris and debris of all the slain soldiers of the war,
180   But I saw they were not as was thought,
They themselves were fully at rest, they suffer'd not,
The living remain'd and suffer'd, the mother suffer'd,
And the wife and the child and the musing comrade suffer'd,
And the armies that remain'd suffer'd.

16
185   Passing the visions, passing the night,
Passing, unloosing the hold of my comrades' hands,
Passing the song of the hermit bird and the tallying song of my soul,
Victorious song, death's outlet song, yet varying ever-altering song,
As low and wailing, yet clear the notes, rising and falling, flooding the night,
190   Sadly sinking and fainting, as warning and warning, and yet again bursting
with joy,
Covering the earth and filling the spread of the heaven,
As that powerful psalm in the night I heard from recesses,
Passing, I leave thee lilac with heart-shaped leaves,
I leave thee there in the door-yard, blooming, returning with spring.

195 I cease from my song for thee,
From my gaze on thee in the west, fronting the west, communing with thee,
O comrade lustrous with silver face in the night.

Yet each to keep and all, retrievements out of the night,
The song, the wondrous chant of the gray-brown bird,
200 And the tallying chant, the echo arous'd in my soul,
With the lustrous and drooping star with the countenance full of woe,
With the holders holding my hand nearing the call of the bird,
Comrades mine and I in the midst, and their memory ever to keep, for the
   dead I loved so well,
For the sweetest, wisest soul of all my days and lands—and this for his dear
   sake,
205 Lilac and star and bird twined with the chant of my soul,
There in the fragrant pines and the cedars dusk and dim.

1865–66   1881

A Noiseless Patient Spider

A noiseless patient spider,
I mark'd where on a little promontory it stood isolated,
Mark'd how to explore the vacant vast surrounding,
It launch'd forth filament, filament, filament, out of itself,
5 Ever unreeling them, ever tirelessly speeding them.

And you O my soul where you stand,
Surrounded, detached, in measureless oceans of space,
Ceaselessly musing, venturing, throwing, seeking the spheres to connect
   them,
Till the bridge you will need be form'd, till the ductile anchor hold,
10 Till the gossamer thread you fling catch somewhere, O my soul.

1868   1881

MATTHEW ARNOLD
(1822–1888)

The Forsaken Merman

Come, dear children, let us away;
Down and away below!
Now my brothers call from the bay,
Now the great winds shoreward blow,
5 Now the salt tides seaward flow;
Now the wild white horses play,
Champ and chafe and toss in the spray.
Children dear, let us away!
This way, this way!

10 Call her once before you go—
Call once yet!
In a voice that she will know:
"Margaret! Margaret!"

15　Children's voices should be dear
　　(Call once more) to a mother's ear;
　　Children's voices, wild with pain—
　　Surely she will come again!
　　Call her once and come away;
　　This way, this way!
20　"Mother dear, we cannot stay!
　　The wild white horses foam and fret."
　　Margaret! Margaret!

　　Come, dear children, come away down;
　　Call no more!
25　One last look at the white-walled town,
　　And the little gray church on the windy shore;
　　Then come down!
　　She will not come though you call all day;
　　Come away, come away!

30　Children dear, was it yesterday
　　We heard the sweet bells over the bay?
　　In the caverns where we lay,
　　Through the surf and through the swell,
　　The far-off sound of a silver bell?
35　Sand-strewn caverns, cool and deep,
　　Where the winds are all asleep;
　　Where the spent lights quiver and gleam,
　　Where the salt weed sways in the stream,
　　Where the sea-beasts, ranged all round,
40　Feed in the ooze of their pasture-ground;
　　Where the sea-snakes coil and twine,
　　Dry their mail and bask in the brine;
　　Where great whales come sailing by,
　　Sail and sail, with unshut eye,
45　Round the world for ever and aye?
　　When did music come this way?
　　Children dear, was it yesterday?

　　Children dear, was it yesterday
　　(Call yet once) that she went away?
50　Once she sate with you and me,
　　On a red gold throne in the heart of the sea,
　　And the youngest sate on her knee.
　　She combed its bright hair, and she tended it well,
　　When down swung the sound of a far-off bell.
55　She sighed, she looked up through the clear green sea;
　　She said: "I must go, for my kinsfolk pray
　　In the little gray church on the shore today.
　　'Twill be Easter-time in the world—ah me!
　　And I lose my poor soul, Merman! here with thee."
60　I said: "Go up, dear heart, through the waves;
　　Say thy prayer, and come back to the kind sea-caves!"
　　She smiled, she went up through the surf in the bay.
　　Children dear, was it yesterday?

　　Children dear, were we long alone?
65　"The sea grows stormy, the little ones moan;
　　Long prayers," I said, "in the world they say;
　　Come!" I said; and we rose through the surf in the bay.

We went up the beach, by the sandy down
Where the sea-stocks bloom, to the white-walled town;
70   Through the narrow paved streets, where all was still,
To the little gray church on the windy hill.
From the church came a murmur of folk at their prayers,
But we stood without in the cold blowing airs.
We climbed on the graves, on the stones worn with rains,
75   And we gazed up the aisle through the small leaded panes.
She sate by the pillar; we saw her clear:
"Margaret, hist! come quick, we are here!
Dear heart," I said, "we are long alone;
The sea grows stormy, the little ones moan."
80   But, ah, she gave me never a look,
For her eyes were sealed to the holy book!
Loud prays the priest; shut stands the door.
Come away, children, call no more!
Come away, come down, call no more!

85   Down, down, down!
Down to the depths of the sea!
She sits at her wheel in the humming town,
Singing most joyfully.
Hark what she sings: "O joy, O joy,
90   For the humming street, and the child with its toy!
For the priest, and the bell, and the holy well;
For the wheel where I spun,
And the blessed light of the sun!"
And so she sings her fill.
95   Singing most joyfully,
Till the spindle drops from her hand,
And the whizzing wheel stands still.
She steals to the window, and looks at the sand,
And over the sand at the sea;
100 And her eyes are set in a stare;
And anon there breaks a sigh,
And anon there drops a tear,
From a sorrow-clouded eye,
And a heart sorrow-laden,
105 A long, long sigh;
For the cold strange eyes of a little Mermaiden
And the gleam of her golden hair.

     Come away, away children;
Come children, come down!
110 The hoarse wind blows coldly;
Lights shine in the town.
She will start from her slumber
When gusts shake the door;
She will hear the winds howling,
115 Will hear the waves roar.
We shall see, while above us
The waves roar and whirl,
A ceiling of amber,
A pavement of pearl.
120 Singing: "Here came a mortal,
But faithless was she!

And alone dwell for ever
The kings of the sea."

But, children, at midnight,
125 When soft the winds blow,
When clear falls the moonlight,
When spring-tides are low;
When sweet airs come seaward
From heaths starred with broom,
130 And high rocks throw mildly
On the blanched sands a gloom;
Up the still, glistening beaches,
Up the creeks we will hie,
Over banks of bright seaweed
135 The ebb-tide leaves dry.
We will gaze, from the sand-hills,
At the white, sleeping town;
At the church on the hill-side—
And then come back down.
140 Singing: "There dwells a loved one,
But cruel is she!
She left lonely for ever
The kings of the sea."

1849

To Marguerite

Yes! in the sea of life enisled,
With echoing straits between us thrown,
Dotting the shoreless watery wild,
We mortal millions live *alone*.
5 The islands feel the enclasping flow,
And then their endless bounds they know.

But when the moon their hollows lights,
And they are swept by balms of spring,
And in their glens, on starry nights,
10 The nightingales divinely sing;
And lovely notes, from shore to shore,
Across the sounds and channels pour—

Oh! then a longing like despair
Is to their farthest caverns sent;
15 For surely once, they feel, we were
Parts of a single continent!
Now round us spreads the watery plain—
Oh might our marges meet again!

Who ordered, that their longing's fire
20 Should be, as soon as kindled, cooled?
Who renders vain their deep desire?—
A God, a God their severance ruled!
And bade betwixt their shores to be
The unplumbed, salt, estranging sea.

1852

Thyrsis

A MONODY,[1] TO COMMEMORATE THE AUTHOR'S FRIEND, ARTHUR HUGH
CLOUGH, WHO DIED AT FLORENCE, 1861[2]

How changed is here each spot man makes or fills!
  In the two Hinkseys[3] nothing keeps the same;
    The village street its haunted mansion lacks,
    And from the sign is gone Sibylla's name,[4]
5   And from the roofs the twisted chimney-stacks—
      Are ye too changed, ye hills?
  See, 'tis no foot of unfamiliar men
    Tonight from Oxford up your pathway strays!
  Here came I often, often, in old days—
10 Thyrsis and I; we still had Thyrsis then.

Runs it not here, the track by Childsworth Farm,
  Past the high wood, to where the elm-tree crowns
    The hill behind whose ridge the sunset flames?
  The signal-elm, that looks on Ilsley Downs,
15   The Vale, the three lone weirs,° the youthful Thames?   *river-dams*
      This winter-eve is warm,
  Humid the air! leafless, yet soft as spring,
    The tender purple spray on corpse and briers!
  And that sweet city with her dreaming spires,
20 She needs not June for beauty's heightening,

Lovely all times she lies, lovely tonight!
  Only, methinks, some loss of habit's power
    Befalls me wandering through this upland dim.
  Once passed I blindfold here, at any hour;
25   Now seldom come I, since I came with him.
      That single elm-tree bright
  Against the west—I miss it! is it gone?
    We prized it dearly; while it stood, we said,
  Our friend, the Gypsy-Scholar, was not dead;
30 While the tree lived, he in these fields lived on.

Too rare, too rare, grow now my visits here,
  But once I knew each field, each flower, each stick;
    And with the country-folk acquaintance made
  By barn in threshing-time, by new-built rick.
35   Here, too, our shepherd-pipes we first assayed.
      Ah me! this many a year
  My pipe is lost, my shepherd's holiday!

1. Species of poem in which a single mourner
laments.
2. The friendship between Arnold and Clough
(1819–61), himself a distinguished poet, had
been at its closest while they were at Oxford,
and Arnold chooses as the framework for his
poem a visit to Oxford—at least in reminis-
cence—and more specifically to a hill above the
town crowned by the signal-elm. The tree had
had a particular significance for them, since
they connected it with the continuing symbolic
presence in the countryside of the Scholar-
Gypsy and his lonely faithfulness to an ideal
of truth-seeking. (See Arnold's poem *The
Scholar-Gypsy* and his note to it, above.) As
the name Thyrsis (and later, Corydon) indi-
cates, Arnold is adopting the conventions of
the Greek and Latin pastoral elegy for his
poem.
3. Two villages (North and South Hinksey)
near Oxford.
4. Sibylla Kerr, a tavern-keeper when Arnold
and Clough were students.

Needs must I lose them, needs with heavy heart
Into the world and wave of men depart;
40   But Thyrsis of his own will went away.[5]

It irked him to be here, he could not rest.
He loved each simple joy the country yields,
He loved his mates; but yet he could not keep,
For that a shadow loured on the fields,
45   Here with the shepherds and the silly° sheep.   innocent
Some life of men unblest
He knew, which made him droop; and filled his head.
He went; his piping took a troubled sound
Of storms that rage outside our happy ground;
50   He could not wait their passing, he is dead.

So, some tempestuous morn in early June,
When the year's primal burst of bloom is o'er,
Before the roses and the longest day—
When garden-walks and all the grassy floor
55   With blossoms red and white of fallen May
And chestnut-flowers are strewn—
So have I heard the cuckoo's parting cry,
From the wet field, through the vext garden-trees,
Come with the volleying rain and tossing breeze:
60   *The bloom is gone, and with the bloom go I!*

Too quick despairer, wherefore wilt thou go?
Soon will the high Midsummer pomps come on,
Soon will the musk carnations break and swell,
Soon shall we have gold-dusted snapdragon,
65   Sweet-William with his homely cottage-smell,
And stocks in fragrant blow;
Roses that down the alleys shine afar,
And open, jasmine-muffled lattices,
And groups under the dreaming garden-trees,
70   And the full moon, and the white evening-star.

He hearkens not! light comer, he is flown!
What matters it? next year he will return,
And we shall have him in the sweet spring-days,
With whitening hedges, and uncrumpling fern,
75   And bluebells trembling by the forest-ways,
And scent of hay new-mown.
But Thyrsis never more we swains shall see;
See him come back, and cut a smoother reed,
And blow a strain the world at last shall heed—
80   For Time, not Corydon, hath conquered thee!

Alack, for Corydon no rival now!
But when Sicilian shepherds lost a mate,
Some good survivor with his flute would go,

5. Clough resigned his fellowship at Oxford in 1848, rather than subscribe to the Thirty-nine Articles of the Anglican Church.

85   Piping a ditty sad for Bion's fate;[6]
      And cross the unpermitted ferry's flow,[7]
        And relax Pluto's brow,
      And make leap up with joy the beauteous head
        Of Proserpine, among whose crownéd hair
        Are flowers first opened on Sicilian air,
90   And flute his friend, like Orpheus,[8] from the dead.

     O easy access to the hearer's grace
      When Dorian[9] shepherds sang to Proserpine!
        For she herself had trod Sicilian fields,
      She knew the Dorian water's gush divine,
95   She knew each lily white which Enna yields,
         Each rose with blushing face;
      She loved the Dorian pipe, the Dorian strain.
        But ah, of our poor Thames she never heard!
        Her foot the Cumner cowslips never stirred;
100 And we should tease her with our plaint in vain!

    Well! wind-dispersed and vain the words will be,
      Yet, Thyrsis, let me give my grief its hour
        In the old haunt, and find our tree-topped hill!
      Who, if not I, for questing here hath power?
105   I know the wood which hides the daffodil,
        I know the Fyfield tree,
      I know what white, what purple fritillaries°   *flowers*
        The grassy harvest of the river-fields,
        Above by Ensham, down by Sandford, yields,
110 And what sedged brooks are Thames's tributaries;

    I know these slopes; who knows them if not I?
      But many a dingle° on the loved hillside,   *valley*
        With thorns once studded, old, white-blossomed trees,
      Where thick the cowslips grew, and far descried
115   High towered the spikes of purple orchises,
        Hath since our day put by
      The coronals of that forgotten time;[1]
        Down each green bank hath gone the ploughboy's team,
        And only in the hidden brookside gleam
120 Primroses, orphans of the flowery prime.

    Where is the girl, who by the boatman's door,
      Above the locks, above the boating throng,
        Unmoored our skiff when through the Wytham flats,
      Red loosestrife and blond meadow-sweet among
125   And darting swallows and light water-gnats,
        We tracked the shy Thames shore?
      Where are the mowers, who, as the tiny swell
        Of our boat passing heaved the river-grass,
        Stood with suspended scythe to see us pass?
130 They all are gone, and thou art gone as well!

6. Greek pastoral poet of the first century B.C. who lived in Sicily and who was mourned in *Lament for Bion*, sometimes ascribed to his pupil Moschus.
7. The ferry across the River Styx to Hades, ruled over by Pluto and his queen, Proserpine, whom he had abducted while she was gathering flowers in the fields near Enna, in Sicily. She spent half of each year in the underworld and half on earth.
8. Orpheus, because of the power and charm of his music, had been permitted to attempt to lead his wife, Eurydice, back from the dead.
9. One of the ancient Greek lyrical modes, characterized by simplicity and nobility.
1. I.e., the flowers that once crowned them.

Yes, thou art gone! and round me too the night
  In ever-nearing circle weaves her shade.
    I see her veil draw soft across the day,
  I feel her slowly chilling breath invade
35   The cheek grown thin, the brown hair sprent° with grey;   *sprinkled*
      I feel her finger light
  Laid pausefully upon life's headlong train;
    The foot less prompt to meet the morning dew,
    The heart less bounding at emotion new,
40 And hope, once crushed, less quick to spring again.

And long the way appears, which seemed so short
  To the less practiced eye of sanguine youth;
    And high the mountain-tops, in cloudy air,
  The mountain-tops where is the throne of Truth,
45   Tops in life's morning-sun so bright and bare!
      Unbreachable the fort
  Of the long-battered world uplifts its wall;
    And strange and vain the earthly turmoil grows,
    And near and real the charm of thy repose,
50 And night as welcome as a friend would fall.

But hush! the upland hath a sudden loss
  Of quiet!—Look, adown the dusk hillside,
    A troop of Oxford hunters going home,
  As in old days, jovial and talking, ride!
55   From hunting with the Berkshire hounds they come.
      Quick! let me fly, and cross
  Into yon farther field!—'Tis done; and see,
    Backed by the sunset, which doth glorify
    The orange and pale violet evening-sky,
60 Bare on its lonely ridge, the Tree! the Tree!

I take the omen! Eve lets down her veil,
  The white fog creeps from bush to bush about,
    The west unflushes, the high stars grow bright,
  And in the scattered farms the lights come out.
165   I cannot reach the signal-tree to-night,
      Yet, happy omen, hail!
  Hear it from thy broad lucent Arno-vale[2]
    (For there thine earth-forgetting eyelids keep
    The morningless and unawakening sleep
170 Under the flowery oleanders pale),

Hear it, O Thyrsis still our tree is there!
  Ah, vain! These English fields, this upland dim,
    These brambles pale with mist engarlanded,
  That lone, sky-pointing tree, are not for him;
175   To a boon southern country he is fled,
      And now in happier air,
  Wandering with the great Mother's train divine[3]
    (And purer or more subtle soul than thee,
    I trow, the mighty Mother doth not see)
180 Within a folding of the Apennine,[4]

2. Clough is buried in the Protestant cemetery in Florence, through which city the Arno flows.

3. Possibly the devotees of Demeter, the Earth Mother.
4. The Apennines are a mountain range in Italy.

Thou hearest the immortal chants of old!
  Putting his sickle to the perilous grain
    In the hot cornfield of the Phrygian king,
  For thee the Lityerses-song again
185   Young Daphnis with his silver voice doth sing;[5]
      Sings his Sicilian fold,
  His sheep, his hapless love, his blinded eyes—
  And how a call celestial round him rang,
  And heavenward from the fountain-brink he sprang,
190 And all the marvel of the golden skies.

  There thou art gone, and me thou leavest here
    Sole in these fields! yet will I not despair.
  Despair I will not, while I yet descry
    Neath the mild canopy of English air
195   That lonely tree against the western sky.
      Still, still these slopes, 'tis clear,
  Our Gypsy-Scholar haunts, outliving thee!
  Fields where soft sheep from cages pull the hay,
  Woods with anemonies in flower till May,
200 Know him a wanderer still; then why not me?

  A fugitive and gracious light he seeks,
    Shy to illumine; and I seek it too.
  This does not come with houses or with gold,
    With place, with honor, and a flattering crew;
205   'Tis not in the world's market bought and sold—
      But the smooth-slipping weeks
  Drop by, and leave its seeker still untired;
  Out of the heed of mortals he is gone,
  He wends unfollowed, he must house alone;
210 Yet on he fares, by his own heart inspired.

  Thou too, O Thyrsis, on like quest wast bound;
    Thou wanderest with me for a little hour!
  Men gave thee nothing; but this happy quest,
    If men esteemed thee feeble, gave thee power,
215   If men procured thee trouble, gave thee rest.
      And this rude Cumner ground,
  Its fir-topped Hurst, its farms, its quiet fields,
  Here cam'st thou in thy jocund youthful time,
  Here was thine height of strength, thy golden prime!
220 And still the haunt beloved a virtue yields.

  What though the music of thy rustic flute
    Kept not for long its happy, country tone;
    Lost it too soon, and learnt a stormy note

5. "Daphnis, the ideal Sicilian shepherd of Greek pastoral poetry, was said to have followed into Phrygia his mistress Piplea, who had been carried off by robbers, and to have found her in the power of the king of Phrygia, Lityerses. Lityerses used to make strangers try a contest with him in reaping corn, and to put them to death if he overcame them. Hercules arrived in time to save Daphnis, took upon himself the reaping-contest with Lityerses, overcame him, and slew him. The Lityerses-song connected with this tradition was, like the Linus-song, one of the early plaintive strains of Greek popular poetry, and used to be sung by corn-reapers. Other traditions represented Daphnis as beloved by a nymph who exacted from him an oath to love no one else. He fell in love with a princess, and was struck blind by the jealous nymph. Mercury, who was his father, raised him to heaven, and made a fountain spring up in the place from which he ascended. At this fountain the Sicilians offered yearly sacrifices. —See Servius, *Comment. in Virgil. Bucol.,* v.20 and viii.68" [Arnold's note].

Of men contention-tost, of men who groan,
225   Which tasked thy pipe too sore, and tired thy throat—
      It failed, and thou wast mute!
Yet hadst thou alway visions of our light,
    And long with men of care thou couldst not stay,
    And soon thy foot resumed its wandering way,
230 Left human haunt, and on alone till night.

Too rare, too rare, grow now my visits here!
    'Mid city-noise, not, as with thee of yore,
      Thyrsis! in reach of sheep-bells is my home.
    —Then through the great town's harsh, heart-wearying roar,
235   Let in thy voice a whisper often come,
      To chase fatigue and fear:
    Why faintest thou? I wandered till I died.
    Roam on! The light we sought is shining still.
    Dost thou ask proof? Our tree yet crowns the hill,
240 *Our Scholar travels yet the loved hillside.*

                                1866

Dover Beach

The sea is calm tonight.
The tide is full, the moon lies fair
Upon the straits; on the French coast the light
Gleams and is gone; the cliffs of England stand,
5 Glimmering and vast, out in the tranquil bay.
Come to the window, sweet is the night-air!
Only, from the long line of spray
Where the sea meets the moon-blanched land,
Listen! you hear the grating roar
10 Of pebbles which the waves draw back, and fling,
At their return, up the high strand,
Begin, and cease, and then again begin,
With tremulous cadence slow, and bring
The eternal note of sadness in.

15 Sophocles long ago
Heard it on the Aegean, and it brought
Into his mind the turbid ebb and flow
Of human misery;[6] we
Find also in the sound a thought,
20 Hearing it by this distant northern sea.

The Sea of Faith
Was once, too, at the full, and round earth's shore
Lay like the folds of a bright girdle furled.
But now I only hear
25 Its melancholy, long, withdrawing roar,
Retreating, to the breath
Of the night-wind, down the vast edges drear
And naked shingles[7] of the world.

---

6. Compare Sophocles' *Antigone*, lines 583–91.   7. Beaches covered with water-worn small stones and pebbles.

Ah, love, let us be true
30 To one another! for the world, which seems
    To lie before us like a land of dreams,
    So various, so beautiful, so new,
    Hath really neither joy, nor love, nor light,
    Nor certitude, nor peace, nor help for pain;
35 And we are here as on a darkling plain
    Swept with confused alarms of struggle and flight,
    Where ignorant armies clash by night.

1867

Palladium[8]

Set where the upper streams of Simois flow[9]
Was the Palladium, high 'mid rock and wood;
And Hector was in Ilium,[1] far below,
And fought, and saw it not—but there it stood!

5   It stood, and sun and moonshine rained their light
    On the pure columns of its glen-built hall.
    Backward and forward rolled the waves of fight
    Round Troy—but while this stood, Troy could not fall.

    So, in its lovely moonlight, lives the soul.
10 Mountains surround it, and sweet virgin air;
    Cold plashing, past it, crystal waters roll;
    We visit it by moments, ah, too rare!

    We shall renew the battle in the plain
    Tomorrow; red with blood will Xanthus[2] be,
15 Hector and Ajax will be there again,
    Helen will come upon the wall to see.

    Then we shall rust in shade, or shine in strife,
    And fluctuate 'twixt blind hopes and blind despairs,
    And fancy that we put forth all our life,
20 And never know how with the soul it fares.

    Still doth the soul, from its lone fastness high,
    Upon our life a ruling effluence send.
    And when it fails, fight as we will, we die;
    And while it lasts, we cannot wholly end.

1867

8. The image of the goddess Pallas Athena (or, as perhaps here, the temple in which the image was housed), believed to guarantee the safety of the city which possessed it.
9. In the *Iliad*, a river near Troy (Ilium).
1. Hector, the Trojan hero, son of Priam and Hecuba; brother of Paris whose abduction of the beautiful Helen from her husband Men-elaus, brother of the Greek king Agamemnon, had caused the war between Greeks and Trojans. Ajax, second only to Achilles among the Greek heroes, fought in single combat with Hector in the tenth year of the war.
2. In the *Iliad*, the Scamander river (called Xanthus by the gods).

DANTE GABRIEL ROSSETTI
(1828–1882)

The Blessed Damozel[1]

The blessed damozel leaned out
  From the gold bar of Heaven;
Her eyes were deeper than the depth
  Of waters stilled at even;
5 She had three lilies in her hand,
  And the stars in her hair were seven.

Her robe, ungirt from clasp to hem,
  No wrought flowers did adorn,
But a white rose of Mary's gift,
10 For service meetly worn;
Her hair that lay along her back
  Was yellow like ripe corn.°   *wheat, grain*

Herseemed she scarce had been a day
  One of God's choristers;
15 The wonder was not yet quite gone
  From that still look of hers;
Albeit, to them she left, her day
  Had counted as ten years.

(To one, it is ten years of years.
20 . . . Yet now, and in this place,
Surely she leaned o'er me—her hair
  Fell all about my face. . . .
Nothing: the autumn fall of leaves.
  The whole year sets apace.)

25 It was the rampart of God's house
  That she was standing on;
By God built over the sheer depth
  The which is Space begun;
So high, that looking downward thence
30 She scarce could see the sun.

It lies in Heaven, across the flood
  Of ether, as a bridge.
Beneath, the tides of day and night
  With flame and darkness ridge
35 The void, as low as where this earth
  Spins like a fretful midge.

---

1. Older form of *damsel*, meaning "young un-
married lady," preferred by Romantic and
later writers because it avoids the simpler,
homelier associations of *damsel*.

Around her, lovers, newly met
  In joy no sorrow claims,
Spoke evermore among themselves
40   Their rapturous new names;
And the souls mounting up to God
  Went by her like thin flames.

And still she bowed herself and stooped
  Out of the circling charm;
45 Until her bosom must have made
  The bar she leaned on warm,
And the lilies lay as if asleep
  Along her bended arm.

From the fixed place of Heaven she saw
50 Time like a pulse shake fierce
Through all the worlds. Her gaze still strove
  Within the gulf to pierce
Its path; and now she spoke as when
  The stars sang in their spheres.

55 The sun was gone now; the curled moon
  Was like a little feather
Fluttering far down the gulf; and now
  She spoke through the still weather.
Her voice was like the voice the stars
60 Had when they sang together.

(Ah sweet! Even now, in that bird's song,
  Strove not her accents there,
Fain to be hearkened? When those bells
  Possessed the midday air,
65 Strove not her steps to reach my side
  Down all the echoing stair?)

"I wish that he were come to me,
  For he will come," she said.
"Have I not prayed in Heaven?—on earth,
70 Lord, Lord, has he not prayed?
Are not two prayers a perfect strength?
  And shall I feel afraid?

"When round his head the aureole clings,
  And he is clothed in white,
75 I'll take his hand and go with him
  To the deep wells of light;
We will step down as to a stream,
  And bathe there in God's sight.

"We two will stand beside that shrine,
80 Occult, withheld, untrod,
Whose lamps are stirred continually
  With prayer sent up to God;
And see our old prayers, granted, melt
  Each like a little cloud.

85   "We two will lie i' the shadow of
      That living mystic tree
    Within whose secret growth the Dove
      Is sometimes felt to be,
    While every leaf that His plumes touch
90   Saith His Name audibly.

    "And I myself will teach to him,
      I myself, lying so,
    The songs I sing here; which his voice
      Shall pause in, hushed and slow,
95   And find some knowledge at each pause,
      Of some new thing to know."

    (Alas! We two, we two, thou say'st!
      Yea, one wast thou with me
    That once of old. But shall God lift
100   To endless unity
    The soul whose likeness with thy soul
      Was but its love for thee?)

    "We two," she said, "will seek the groves
      Where the lady Mary is,
105   With her five handmaidens, whose names
      Are five sweet symphonies,
    Cecily, Gertrude, Magdalen,
      Margaret and Rosalys.

    "Circlewise sit they, with bound locks
110   And foreheads garlanded;
    Into the fine cloth white like flame
      Weaving the golden thread,
    To fashion the birth-robes for them
      Who are just born, being dead.

115   "He shall fear, haply, and be dumb:
      Then will I lay my cheek
    To his, and tell about our love,
      Not once abashed or weak:
    And the dear Mother will approve
120   My pride, and let me speak.

    "Herself shall bring us, hand in hand,
      To Him round whom all souls
    Kneel, the clear-ranged unnumbered heads
      Bowed with their aureoles:
125   And angels meeting us shall sing
      To their citherns and citoles.[2]

    "There will I ask of Christ the Lord
      Thus much for him and me:—
    Only to live as once on earth

---

2. Antique musical instruments: the cithern (17th century), a guitar-like instrument with wire strings; the citole, a stringed instrument dating from the 13th–15th century.

130   With Love—only to be,
As then awhile, forever now
    Together, I and he."

She gazed and listened and then said,
    Less sad of speech than mild,
135   "All this is when he comes." She ceased.
    The light thrilled towards her, filled
With angels in strong level flight.
    Her eyes prayed, and she smiled.

(I saw her smile.) But soon their path
140   Was vague in distant spheres:
And then she cast her arms along
    The golden barriers,
And laid her face between her hands,
    And wept. (I heard her tears.)

                                        1846   1850

Sudden Light

I have been here before,
    But when or how I cannot tell:
I know the grass beyond the door,
    The sweet keen smell,
5   The sighing sound, the lights around the shore.

You have been mine before,
    How long ago I may not know:
But just when at that swallow's soar
    Your neck turned so,
10   Some veil did fall—I knew it all of yore.

Has this been thus before?
    And shall not thus time's eddying flight
Still with our lives our love restore
    In death's despite,
15   And day and night yield one delight once more?

                                        1854   1863

The Woodspurge

The wind flapped loose, the wind was still,
Shaken out dead from tree and hill:
I had walked on at the wind's will—
I sat now, for the wind was still.

5   Between my knees my forehead was—
My lips, drawn in, said not Alas!
My hair was over in the grass,
My naked ears heard the day pass.

My eyes, wide open, had the run
10   Of some ten weeds to fix upon;
Among those few, out of the sun,
The woodspurge flowered, three cups in one.

From perfect grief there need not be
Wisdom or even memory:
15   One thing then learnt remains to me—
The woodspurge has a cup of three.

1856   1870

From The House of Life

19. Silent Noon

Your hands lie open in the long fresh grass—
    The finger-points look through like rosy blooms:
    Your eyes smile peace. The pasture gleams and glooms
'Neath billowing skies that scatter and amass.
5   All round our nest, far as the eye can pass,
    Are golden kingcup-fields with silver edge
    Where the cow-parsley skirts the hawthorn-hedge.
'Tis visible silence, still as the hour-glass.

Deep in the sun-searched growths the dragonfly
10   Hangs like a blue thread loosened from the sky:
    So this winged hour is dropt to us from above.
Oh! clasp we to our hearts, for deathless dower,
This close-companioned inarticulate hour
    When twofold silence was the song of love.

70. The Hill Summit

This feast-day of the sun, his altar there
    In the broad west has blazed for vesper-song;
    And I have loitered in the vale too long
And gaze now a belated worshipper.
5   Yet may I not forget that I was 'ware,
    So journeying, of his face at intervals
    Transfigured where the fringed horizon falls,
A fiery bush with coruscating hair.

And now that I have climbed and won this height,
10   I must tread downward through the sloping shade
And travel the bewildered tracks till night.
    Yet for this hour I still may here be stayed
    And see the gold air and the silver fade
And the last bird fly into the last night.

83. Barren Spring

Once more the changed year's turning wheel returns:
    And as a girl sails balanced in the wind,
    And now before and now again behind
Stoops as it swoops, with cheek that laughs and burns—
5   So Spring comes merry towards me here, but earns
    No answering smile from me, whose life is twined
    With the dead boughs that winter still must bind,
And whom to-day the Spring no more concerns.

Behold, this crocus is a withering flame;
10   This snowdrop, snow; this apple-blossom's part
    To breed the fruit that breeds the serpent's art.
Nay, for these Spring-flowers, turn thy face from them,
    Nor gaze till on the year's last lily-stem
    The white cup shrivels round the golden heart.

91. *Lost on Both Sides*

As when two men have loved a woman well,
  Each hating each, through Love's and Death's deceit;
  Since not for either this stark marriage-sheet
And the long pauses of this wedding-bell;
5 Yet o'er her grave the night and day dispel
    At last their feud forlorn, with cold and heat;
    Nor other than dear friends to death may fleet
The two lives left that most of her can tell:

So separate hopes, which in a soul had wooed
10 The one same Peace, strove with each other long,
    And Peace before their faces perished since:
So through that soul, in restless brotherhood,
  They roam together now, and wind among
    Its bye-streets, knocking at the dusty inns.

97. *A Superscription*

Look in my face; my name is Might-have-been;
  I am also called No-more, Too-late, Farewell;
  Unto thine ear I hold the dead-sea shell
Cast up thy Life's foam-fretted feet between;
5 Unto thine eyes the glass where that is seen
  Which had Life's form and Love's, but by my spell
  Is now a shaken shadow intolerable,
Of ultimate things unuttered the frail screen.

Mark me, how still I am! But should there dart
10 One moment through thy soul the soft surprise
  Of that winged Peace which lulls the breath of sighs,
Then shalt thou see me smile, and turn apart
  Thy visage to mine ambush at thy heart
  Sleepless with cold commemorative eyes.

                    1847–80   1870, 1881

EMILY DICKINSON
(1830–1886)

89

Some things that fly there be—
Birds—Hours—the Bumblebee—
Of these no Elegy.

Some things that stay there be—
5 Grief—Hills—Eternity—
Nor this behooveth me.

There are that resting, rise.
Can I expound the skies?
How still the Riddle lies!

                    1859?   1890

187

How many times these low feet staggered—
Only the soldered mouth can tell—
Try—can you stir the awful rivet—
Try—can you lift the hasps of steel!

5   Stroke the cool forehead—hot so often—
Lift—if you care— the listless hair—
Handle the adamantine° fingers   *rigid, unmovable*
Never a thimble—more—shall wear—

Buzz the dull flies—on the chamber window—
10 Brave—shines the sun through the freckled pane—
Fearless—the cobweb swings from the ceiling—
Indolent Housewife—in Daises—lain!

                              1860?   1890

214

I taste a liquor never brewed—
From Tankards scooped in Pearl—
Not all the Frankfort Berries[1]
Yield such an Alcohol!

5   Inebriate of Air—am I—
And Debauchee of Dew—
Reeling—thro endless summer days—
From inns of Molten Blue—

When "Landlords" turn the drunken Bee
10 Out of the Foxglove's door—
When Butterflies—renounce their "dram"—
I shall but drink the more!

Till Seraphs swing their snowy Hats—
And Saints—to windows run—
15 To see the little Tippler
From Manzanilla[2] come!

                          1860?   1861, 1890

216

Safe in their Alabaster Chambers—
Untouched by Morning
And untouched by Noon—
Sleep the meek members of the Resurrection—
5   Rafter of satin,
And Roof of stone.

1. Wine grapes from the vicinity of Frankfort and the Rhine in Germany.   2. Name of a sherry wine from the Guadalquivar River area in Spain, and also the name of towns in Trinidad, Mexico, and Panama.

402   *Emily Dickinson*

Light laughs the breeze
In her Castle above them—
Babbles the Bee in a stolid Ear,
Pipe the Sweet Birds in ignorant cadence—
Ah, what sagacity perished here!

1859 version   1862

216³

Safe in their Alabaster Chambers—
Untouched by Morning—
And untouched by Noon—
Lie the meek members of the Resurrection—
Rafter of Satin—and Roof of Stone!

Grand go the Years—in the Crescent—above them—
Worlds scoop their Arcs—
And Firmaments—row—
Diadems—drop—and Doges—surrender—
Soundless as dots—on a Disc of Snow—

1861 version   1890

287

A Clock stopped—
Not the Mantel's—
Geneva's farthest skill⁴
Cant put the puppet bowing—
That just now dangled still—

An awe came on the Trinket!
The Figures hunched, with pain—
Then quivered out of Decimals—
Into Degreeless Noon—

It will not stir for Doctor's—
This Pendulum of snow—
The Shopman importunes it—
While cool—concernless No—

Nods from the Gilded pointers—
Nods from the Seconds slim—
Decades of Arrogance between
The Dial life—
And Him—

1861?   1896

---

3. This poem has been familiar to readers of
Emily Dickinson in a three-stanza version
which we now know was never her concep-
tion of the poem. Thomas H. Johnson's ac-
count of the composition of the poem traces
Emily's characteristic trying and re-trying of
various articulations of her poetic idea. The
1859 version was sent to Sue Dickinson,
Emily's sister-in-law, for advice, and Sue
evidently did not like it much. The notes be-
tween the two women (they lived in adjoining
houses) show Emily's labors over the poem,
and her 1861 version was an attempt to meet
her own and Sue's exactions. Professor John-
son believes Emily Dickinson was never fully
satisfied with the poem. It was printed once
during her lifetime (1862) in the 1859 version,
but when she began her famous correspondence
with Thomas W. Higginson, the literary critic
and editor, she sent a modified version of the
1861 poem. When Higginson edited Emily
Dickinson's poetry for posthumous publica-
tion (1890), he combined the two versions, and
it is this three-stanza poem that readers had
known as Emily's until Johnson's definitive
edition of the poems in 1955.
4. Geneva, Switzerland, is traditionally famous
for watch-making.

303

The Soul selects her own Society—
Then—shuts the Door—
To her divine Majority—
Present no more—

5   Unmoved—she notes the Chariots—pausing—
At her low Gate—
Unmoved—an Emperor be kneeling
Upon her Mat—

I've known her—from an ample nation—
10 Choose One—
Then—close the Valves of her attention—
Like Stone—

                              1862?   1890

341

After great pain, a formal feeling comes—
The Nerves sit ceremonious, like Tombs—
The stiff Heart questions was it He, that bore,
And Yesterday, or Centuries before?

5   The Feet, mechanical, go round—
Of Ground, or Air, or Ought—°   *nothing, a void*
A Wooden way
Regardless grown,
A Quartz contentment, like a stone—

10 This is the Hour of Lead—
Remembered, if outlived,
As Freezing persons, recollect the Snow—
First—Chill—then Stupor—then the letting go—

                              1862?   1929

357

God is a distant—stately Lover—
Woos, as He states us—by His Son—
Verily, a Vicarious Courtship—
"Miles", and "Priscilla", were such an One[5]—

5   But, lest the Soul—like fair "Priscilla"
Choose the Envoy—and spurn the Groom—
Vouches, with hyperbolic archness—
"Miles", and "John Alden" were Synonyme—

                              1862?   1891, 1929

---

5. Allusion to the story in Longfellow's   John Alden to speak for him. Priscilla falls
Courtship of Miles Standish, where Miles   in love with John himself.
wishes to court Priscilla Mullins but sends

449

I died for Beauty—but was scarce
Adjusted. in the Tomb
When One who died for Truth, was lain
In an adjoining Room—

5   He questioned softly "Why I failed"?
"For Beauty", I replied—
"And I—for Truth—Themself are One—
We Brethren, are", He said—

And so, as Kinsmen, met a Night—
10   We talked between the Rooms—
Until the Moss had reached our lips—
And covered up—our names—

                                        1862?   1890

465

I heard a Fly buzz—when I died—
The Stillness in the Room
Was like the Stillness in the Air—
Between the Heaves of Storm—

5   The Eyes around—had wrung them dry—
And Breaths were gathering firm
For that last Onset—when the King
Be witnessed—in the Room—

I willed my Keepsakes—Signed away
10   What portion of me be
Assignable—and then it was
There interposed a Fly—

With Blue—uncertain stumbling Buzz—
Between the light—and me—
15   And then the Windows failed—and then
I could not see to see—

                                        1862?   1896

510

It was not Death, for I stood up,
And all the Dead, lie down—
It was not Night, for all the Bells
Put out their Tongues, for Noon.

5   It was not Frost, for on my Flesh
I felt Siroccos[6]—crawl—
Nor Fire—for just my Marble feet
Could keep a Chancel, cool—

---

6. Hot, moist southeasterly winds usually associated with the Libyan desert.

And yet, it tasted, like them all,
10   The Figures I have seen
Set orderly, for Burial,
Reminded me, of mine—

As if my life were shaven,
And fitted to a frame,
15   And could not breathe without a key,
And 'twas like Midnight, some—

When everything that ticked—has stopped—
And Space stares all around—
Or Grisly frosts—first Autumn morns,
20   Repeal the Beating Ground—

But, most, like Chaos—Stopless—cool—
Without a Chance, or Spar—
Or even a Report of Land—
To justify—Despair.

                                        1862   1891

528

Mine—by the Right of the White Election!
Mine—by the Royal Seal!
Mine—by the Sign in the Scarlet prison—
Bars—cannot conceal!

5   Mine—here—in Vision—and in Veto!
Mine—by the Grave's Repeal—
Titled—Confirmed—
Delirious Charter!
Mine—long as Ages steal!

                                        1862?   1890

640

I cannot live with You—
It would be Life—
And Life is over there—
Behind the Shelf

5   The Sexton keeps the Key to—
Putting up
Our Life—His Porcelain—
Like a Cup—

Discarded of the Housewife—
10   Quaint—or Broke—
A newer Sevres[7] pleases—
Old Ones crack—

---

7. A fine and expensive French porcelain.

I could not die—with You—
For One must wait
15 To shut the Other's Gaze down—
You—could not—

And I—Could I stand by
And see You—freeze—
Without my Right of Frost—
20 Death's privilege?

Nor could I rise—with You—
Because Your Face
Would put out Jesus'—
That New Grace

25 Glow plain—and foreign
On my homesick Eye—
Except that You than He
Shone closer by—

They'd judge Us—How—
30 For You—served Heaven—You know,
Or sought to—
I could not—

Because You saturated Sight—
And I had no more Eyes
35 For sordid excellence
As Paradise

And were You lost, I would be—
Though My Name
Rang loudest
40 On the Heavenly fame—

And were You—saved—
And I—condemned to be
Where You were not—
That self—were Hell to Me—

45 So We must meet apart—
You there—I—here—
With just the Door ajar
That Oceans are—and Prayer—
And that White Sustenance—
50 Despair—

                                    1862?   1890

712

Because I could not stop for Death—
He kindly stopped for me—
The Carriage held but just Ourselves—
And Immortality.

5   We slowly drove—He knew no haste
And I had put away
My labor and my leisure too,
For His Civility—

We passed the School, where Children strove
10   At Recess—in the Ring—
We passed the Fields of Gazing Grain—
We passed the Setting Sun—

Or rather—He passed Us—
The Dews drew quivering and chill—
15   For only Gossamer, my Gown—
My Tippet[8]—only Tulle—

We paused before a House that seemed
A Swelling of the Ground—
The Roof was scarcely visible—
20   The Cornice—in the Ground—

Since then—'tis Centuries—and yet
Feels shorter than the Day
I first surmised the Horses Heads
Were toward Eternity—

1863?   1890

1068

Further in Summer than the Birds
Pathetic from the Grass
A minor Nation celebrates
Its unobtrusive Mass.

5   No Ordinance[9] be seen
So gradual the Grace
A pensive Custom it becomes
Enlarging Loneliness.

Antiquest felt at Noon
10   When August burning low
Arise this spectral Canticle[1]
Repose to typify.

Remit as yet no Grace
No Furrow on the Glow
15   Yet a Druidic[2] Difference
Enhances Nature now.

1866?   1891

8. A woman's short cape or cloak.
9. A prescribed religious or ceremonial practice, as applied to the sacrament of the Lord's Supper.

1. A hymn or song used by the church in public services.
2. Pertaining to the mysterious religious practices of Celtic priest-magicians.

1463

A Route of Evanescence
With a revolving Wheel—
A Resonance of Emerald—
A Rush of Cochineal°—   *scarlet*
5 And every Blossom on the Bush
Adjusts its tumbled Head—
The mail from Tunis, probably,
An easy Morning's Ride—

                                        1879   1891, 1891

CHRISTINA ROSSETTI
(1830–1894)

Song

When I am dead, my dearest,
  Sing no sad songs for me;
Plant thou no roses at my head,
  Nor shady cypress tree:
5 Be the green grass above me
    With showers and dewdrops wet:
And if thou wilt, remember,
  And if thou wilt, forget.

I shall not see the shadows,
10   I shall not feel the rain;
I shall not hear the nightingale
  Sing on as if in pain:
And dreaming through the twilight
  That doth not rise nor set,
15 Haply I may remember,
  And haply may forget.

                                        1848   1862

Remember

Remember me when I am gone away,
  Gone far away into the silent land;
  When you can no more hold me by the hand,
Nor I half turn to go yet turning stay.
5 Remember me when no more day by day
  You tell me of our future that you planned:
  Only remember me: you understand
It will be late to counsel then or pray.
Yet if you should forget me for a while
10 And afterwards remember, do not grieve:
  For if the darkness and corruption leave
  A vestige of the thoughts that once I had,
Better by far you should forget and smile
  Than that you should remember and be sad.

                                        1849   1862

Uphill

Does the road wind uphill all the way?
    Yes, to the very end.
Will the day's journey take the whole long day?
    From morn to night, my friend.

5   But is there for the night a resting-place?
    A roof for when the slow dark hours begin.
May not the darkness hide it from my face?
    You cannot miss that inn.

Shall I meet other wayfarers at night?
10   Those who have gone before.
Then must I knock, or call when just in sight?
    They will not keep you standing at that door.

Shall I find comfort, travel-sore and weak?
    Of labor you shall find the sum.
15 Will there be beds for me and all who seek?
    Yea, beds for all who come.

                           1858   1862

In an Artist's Studio

One face looks out from all his canvases,
    One selfsame figure sits or walks or leans:
    We found her hidden just behind those screens,
5   That mirror gave back all her loveliness.
A queen in opal or in ruby dress,
    A nameless girl in freshest summer-greens,
    A saint, an angel—every canvas means
The same one meaning, neither more nor less.
He feeds upon her face by day and night,
10   And she with true kind eyes looks back on him,
Fair as the moon and joyful as the light:
    Not wan with waiting, not with sorrow dim;
Not as she is, but was when hope shone bright;
Not as she is, but as she fills his dream.

                           1856   1896

ALGERNON CHARLES SWINBURNE
(1837–1909)

Chorus from *Atalanta in Calydon*

Before the Beginning of Years

Before the beginning of years
    There came to the making of man
Time, with a gift of tears;
    Grief, with a glass that ran;
5   Pleasure, with pain for leaven;
    Summer, with flowers that fell;

Remembrance fallen from heaven,
   And madness risen from hell;
Strength without hands to smite;
10   Love that endures for a breath:
Night, the shadow of light,
   And life, the shadow of death.
And the high gods took in hand
   Fire, and the falling of tears,
15 And a measure of sliding sand
   From under the feet of the years;
And froth and drift of the sea;
   And dust of the laboring earth;
And bodies of things to be
20   In the houses of death and of birth;
And wrought with weeping and laughter,
   And fashioned with loathing and love
With life before and after
   And death beneath and above,
25 For a day and a night and a morrow,
   That his strength might endure for a span
With travail and heavy sorrow,
   The holy spirit of man.
From the winds of the north and the south
30   They gathered as unto strife;
They breathed upon his mouth,
   They filled his body with life;
Eyesight and speech they wrought
   For the veils of the soul therein,
35 A time for labor and thought,
   A time to serve and to sin;
They gave him light in his ways,
   And love, and a space for delight,
And beauty and length of days,
40   And night, and sleep in the night.
His speech is a burning fire;
   With his lips he travaileth;
In his heart is a blind desire,
   In his eyes foreknowledge of death;
45 He weaves, and is clothed with derision;
   Sows, and he shall not reap;
His life is a watch or a vision
   Between a sleep and a sleep.

1865

The Garden of Proserpine[1]

Here, where the world is quiet;
   Here, where all trouble seems
Dead winds' and spent waves' riot
   In doubtful dreams of dreams;

1. Persephone, in Roman mythology Proser-
pine, the daughter of Zeus and Demeter, had
been abducted by Hades (the Roman Pluto),
god of the underworld, over which she ruled
with him thereafter as his queen.

5   I watch the green field growing
    For reaping folk and sowing,
    For harvest-time and mowing,
        A sleepy world of streams.

    I am tired of tears and laughter,
10   And men that laugh and weep;
    Of what may come hereafter
    For men that sow to reap:
    I am weary of days and hours,
    Blown buds of barren flowers,
15 Desires and dreams and powers
        And everything but sleep.

    Here life has death for neighbor,
        And far from eye or ear
    Wan waves and wet winds labor,
20   Weak ships and spirits steer;
    They drive adrift, and whither
    They wot not who make thither;
    But no such winds blow hither,
        And no such things grow here.

25 No growth of moor or coppice,
        No heather-flower or vine,
    But bloomless buds of poppies,
        Green grapes of Proserpine,
    Pale beds of blowing rushes
30 Where no leaf blooms or blushes
    Save this whereout she crushes
        For dead men deadly wine.

    Pale, without name or number,
        In fruitless fields of corn,°   *wheat*
35 They bow themselves and slumber
        All night till light is born;
    And like a soul belated,
    In hell and heaven unmated,
    By cloud and mist abated
40   Comes out of darkness morn.

    Though one were strong as seven,
        He too with death shall dwell,
    Nor wake with wings in heaven,
        Nor weep for pains in hell;
45 Though one were fair as roses,
    His beauty clouds and closes;
    And well though love reposes,
        In the end it is not well.

    Pale, beyond porch and portal,
50   Crowned with calm leaves, she stands
    Who gathers all things mortal
        With cold immortal hands;
    Her languid lips are sweeter
    Than love's who fears to greet her
55 To men that mix and meet her
        From many times and lands.

She waits for each and other,
  She waits for all men born;
Forgets the earth her mother,
60   The life of fruits and corn;
And spring and seed and swallow
Take wing for her and follow
Where summer song rings hollow
  And flowers are put to scorn.

65 There go the loves that wither,
    The old loves with wearier wings;
And all dead years draw thither,
    And all disastrous things;
Dead dreams of days forsaken,
70 Blind buds that snows have shaken,
  Wild leaves that winds have taken,
    Red strays of ruined springs.

We are not sure of sorrow,
  And joy was never sure;
75 Today will die tomorrow;
    Time stoops to no man's lure;[2]
And love, grown faint and fretful,
With lips but half regretful
Sighs, and with eyes forgetful
80   Weeps that no love endure.

From too much love of living,
  From hope and fear set free,
We thank with brief thanksgiving
  Whatever gods may be
85 That no life lives for ever;
That dead men rise up never;
That even the weariest river
  Winds somewhere safe to sea.

Then star nor sun shall waken,
90   Nor any change of light:
Nor sound of waters shaken,
  Nor any sound or sight:
Nor wintry leaves nor vernal,
Nor days nor things diurnal;
95 Only the sleep eternal
  In an eternal night.

1866

The Sundew

A little marsh-plant, yellow green,
And pricked at lip with tender red.
Tread close, and either way you tread
Some faint black water jets between
5 Lest you should bruise the curious head.

---

2. In falconry, the lure is a device used to recall the hawk to the falconer's wrist.

A live thing maybe; who shall know?
The summer knows and suffers it;
For the cool moss is thick and sweet
Each side, and saves the blossom so
10   That it lives out the long June heat.

The deep scent of the heather burns
About it; breathless though it be,
Bow down and worship; more than we
Is the least flower whose life returns,
15   Least weed renascent in the sea.

We are vexed and cumbered in earth's sight
With wants, with many memories;
These see their mother what she is,
Glad-growing, till August leave more bright
20   The apple-colored cranberries.

Wind blows and bleaches the strong grass,
Blown all one way to shelter it
From trample of stayed kine, with feet
Felt heavier than the moorhen was,
25   Strayed up past patches of wild wheat.

You call it sundew: how it grows,
If with its color it have breath,
If life taste sweet to it, if death
Pain its soft petal, no man knows:
30   Man has no sight or sense that saith.

My sundew, grown of gentle days,
In these green miles the spring begun
Thy growth ere April had half done
With the soft secret of her ways
35   Or June made ready for the sun.

O red-lipped mouth of marsh-flower,
I have a secret halved with thee.
The name that is love's name to me
Thou knowest, and the face of her
40   Who is my festival to see.

The hard sun, as thy petals knew,
Colored the heavy moss-water:
Thou wert not worth green midsummer
Nor fit to live to August blue,
45   O sundew, not remembering her.

                                1862   1866

A Forsaken Garden

In a coign of the cliff between lowland and highland,
    At the sea-down's edge between windward and lee,
Walled round with rocks as an inland island,
    The ghost of a garden fronts the sea.

5 A girdle of brushwood and thorn encloses
    The steep square slope of the blossomless bed
Where the weeds that grew green from the graves of its roses
    Now lie dead.

The fields fall southward, abrupt and broken,
10   To the low last edge of the long lone land.
If a step should sound or a word be spoken,
    Would a ghost not rise at the strange guest's hand?
So long have the grey bare walks lain guestless,
    Through branches and briars if a man make way,
15 He shall find no life but the sea-wind's, restless
    Night and day.

The dense hard passage is blind and stifled
    That crawls by a track none turn to climb
To the strait waste place that the years have rifled
20   Of all but the thorns that are touched not of time.
The thorns he spares when the rose is taken;
    The rocks are left when he wastes the plain.
The wind that wanders, the weeds wind-shaken,
    These remain.

25 Not a flower to be pressed of the foot that falls not;
    As the heart of a dead man the seed-plots are dry;
From the thicket of thorns whence the nightingale calls not,
    Could she call, there were never a rose to reply.
Over the meadows that blossom and wither
30   Rings but the note of a sea-bird's song;
Only the sun and the rain come hither
    All year long.

The sun burns sere° and the rain dishevels   *dry*
    One gaunt bleak blossom of scentless breath.
35 Only the wind here hovers and revels
    In a round where life seems barren as death.
Here there was laughing of old, there was weeping,
    Haply, of lovers none ever will know,
Whose eyes went seaward a hundred sleeping
40   Years ago.

Heart handfast in heart as they stood, "Look thither,"
    Did he whisper? "look forth from the flowers to the sea,
For the foam-flowers endure when the rose-blossoms wither,
    And men that love lightly may die—but we?"
45 And the same wind sang and the same waves whitened,
    And or ever the garden's last petals were shed,
In the lips that had whispered, the eyes that had lightened,
    Love was dead.

Or they loved their life through, and then went whither?
50   And were one to the end—but what end who knows?
Love deep as the sea as a rose must wither,
    As the rose-red seaweed that mocks the rose.
Shall the dead take thought for the dead to love them?
    What love was ever as deep as a grave?
55 They are loveless now as the grass above them
    Or the wave.

All are at one now, roses and lovers,
    Not known of the cliffs and the fields and the sea.
Not a breath of the time that has been hovers
60   In the air now soft with a summer to be.
Not a breath shall there sweeten the seasons heerafter
    Of the flowers or the lovers that laugh now or weep,
When as they that are free now of weeping and laughter
        We shall sleep.

65 Here death may deal not again for ever;
    Here change may come not till all change end.
From the graves they have made they shall rise up never,
    Who have left nought living to ravage and rend.
Earth, stones, and thorns of the wild ground growing,
70   While the sun and the rain live, these shall be;
Till a last wind's breath upon all these blowing
        Roll the sea.

Till the slow sea rise and the sheer cliff crumble,
    Till terrace and meadow the deep gulfs drink,
75 Till the strength of the waves of the high tides humble
    The fields that lessen, the rocks that shrink,
Here now in his triumph where all things falter,
    Stretched out on the spoils that his own hand spread,
As a god self-slain on his own strange altar,
80   Death lies dead.

                                    1876   1878

THOMAS HARDY
(1840–1928)

I Look into My Glass

I look into my glass,
And view my wasting skin,
And say, "Would God it came to pass
My heart had shrunk as thin!"

5 For then, I, undistrest
By hearts grown cold to me,
Could lonely wait my endless rest
With equanimity.

But Time, to make me grieve,
10 Part steals, lets part abide;
And shakes this fragile frame at eve
With throbbings of noontide.

                                    1898

Drummer Hodge[1]

1

They throw in drummer Hodge, to rest
    Uncoffined—just as found:
His landmark is a kopje-crest[2]
    That breaks the veldt around;
5 And foreign constellations west
    Each night above his mound.

2

Young Hodge the Drummer never knew—
    Fresh from his Wessex home—
The meaning of the broad Karoo,
10   The Bush, the dusty loam,
And why uprose to nightly view
    Strange stars amid the gloam.

3

Yet portion of that unknown plain
    Will Hodge forever be;
15 His homely Northern breast and brain
    Grow to some Southern tree,
And strange-eyed constellations reign
    His stars eternally.

1902

A Broken Appointment

You did not come,
And marching Time drew on, and wore me numb.
Yet less for loss of your dear presence there
Than that I thus found lacking in your make
5 That high compassion which can overbear
Reluctance for pure lovingkindness' sake
Grieved I, when, as the hope-hour stroked its sum,
    You did not come.

You love not me,
10 And love alone can lend you loyalty;
—I know and knew it. But, unto the store
Of human deeds divine in all but name,
Was it not worth a little hour or more
To add yet this: Once you, a woman, came
15 To soothe a time-torn man; even though it be
    You love not me?

1902

The Self-Unseeing

Here is the ancient floor,
Footworn and hollowed and thin,
Here was the former door
Where the dead feet walked in.

1. The poem presents an incident from the Boer War (1899–1902) and when first published bore the note: "One of the Drummers killed was a native of a village near Casterbridge," i.e., Dorchester, the principal city of the region of southern England to which, in his novels and poems, Hardy gave its medieval name of Wessex.

2. In Afrikaans, the language of the Dutch settlers in South Africa, the crest of a small hill. The veldt (line 4) is open country, unenclosed pasture land; the Karoo (line 9), barren tracts of plateau-land.

5   She sat here in her chair,
    Smiling into the fire;
    He who played stood there,
    Bowing it higher and higher.

10   Childlike, I danced in a dream;
    Blessings emblazoned that day;
    Everything glowed with a gleam;
    Yet we were looking away!

1902

The Rejected Member's Wife

    We shall see her no more
        On the balcony,
    Smiling, while hurt, at the roar
        As of surging sea
5   From the stormy sturdy band
        Who have doomed her lord's cause,
    Though she waves her little hand
        As it were applause.

    Here will be candidates yet,
10   And candidates' wives,
    Fervid with zeal to set
        Their ideals on our lives:
    Here will come market-men
        On the market-days,
15   Here will clash now and then
        More such party assays.

    And the balcony will fill
        When such times are renewed,
    And the throng in the street will thrill
20   With today's mettled mood;
    But she will no more stand
        In the sunshine there,
    With that wave of her white-gloved hand,
        And that chestnut hair.

January 1906   1909

The Convergence of the Twain

LINES ON THE LOSS OF THE TITANIC[4]

1
    In a solitude of the sea
    Deep from human vanity,
And the Pride of Life that planned her, stilly couches she.

2
    Steel chambers, late the pyres
    Of her salamandrine fires,[5]
Cold currents thrid,° and turn to rhythmic tidal lyres.   *thread*

---

4. The White Star liner R.M.S. *Titanic* was sunk, with great loss of life, as the result of collision with an iceberg on its maiden voyage from Southampton to New York on April 15, 1912.

5. The ship's fires, which burn though immersed in water, are compared to the salamander, a lizard-like creature which according to fable could live in the midst of fire.

3
Over the mirrors meant
To glass the opulent
The sea-worm crawls—grotesque, slimed, dumb, indifferent.

4
10   Jewels in joy designed
To ravish the sensuous mind
Lie lightless, all their sparkles bleared and black and blind.

5
Dim moon-eyed fishes near
Gaze at the gilded gear
15   And query: "What does this vaingloriousness down here?"

6
Well: while was fashioning
This creature of cleaving wing,
The Immanent Will that stirs and urges everything

7
Prepared a sinister mate
20   For her—so gaily great—
A Shape of Ice, for the time far and dissociate.

8
And as the smart ship grew
In stature, grace, and hue,
In shadowy silent distance grew the Iceberg too.

9
25   Alien they seemed to be:
No mortal eye could see
The intimate welding of their later history,

10
Or sign that they were bent
By paths coincident
30   On being anon twin halves of one august event,

11
Till the Spinner of the Years
Said "Now!" And each one hears,
And consummation comes, and jars two hemispheres.

1912

Channel Firing

That night your great guns, unawares,
Shook all our coffins as we lay,
And broke the chancel window-squares,
We thought it was the Judgment-day

5   And sat upright. While drearisome
Arose the howl of wakened hounds:
The mouse let fall the altar-crumb,
The worms drew back into the mounds,

The glebe cow[6] drooled. Till God called, "No;
10   It's gunnery practice out at sea
Just as before you went below;
The world is as it used to be:

---

6. Cow pastured on the glebe, a piece of land attached to a vicarage or rectory.

"All nations striving strong to make
Red war yet redder. Mad as hatters
15 They do no more for Christés sake
Than you who are helpless in such matters.

"That this is not the judgment-hour
For some of them's a blessed thing,
For if it were they'd have to scour
20 Hell's floor for so much threatening. . . .

"Ha, ha. It will be warmer when
I blow the trumpet (if indeed
I ever do; for you are men,
And rest eternal sorely need)."

25 So down we lay again. "I wonder,
Will the world ever saner be,"
Said one, "than when He sent us under
In our indifferent century!"

And many a skeleton shook his head.
30 "Instead of preaching forty year,"
My neighbor Parson Thirdly said,
"I wish I had stuck to pipes and beer."

Again the guns disturbed the hour,
Roaring their readiness to avenge,
35 As far inland as Stourton Tower,
And Camelot, and starlit Stonehenge.[7]

April 1914   1914

The Voice

Woman much missed, how you call to me, call to me,
Saying that now you are not as you were
When you had changed from the one who was all to me,
But as at first, when our day was fair.

5 Can it be you that I hear? Let me view you, then,
Standing as when I drew near to the town
Where you would wait for me: yes, as I knew you then,
Even to the original air-blue gown!

Or is it only the breeze, in its listlessness
10 Traveling across the wet mead to me here,
You being ever dissolved to wan wistlessness,°   *heedlessness*
Heard no more again far or near?

Thus I; faltering forward,
Leaves around me falling,
15 Wind oozing thin through the thorn from norward,
And the woman calling.

December 1912   1914

7. Stourton Tower, built in 1772, and locally known as "Alfred's Tower," stands on the highest point of the estate of Stourhead, in Wiltshire, close to the Somersetshire border. Camelot, the seat of King Arthur's court, has been variously associated with Winchester and with certain places in Somersetshire. Stonehenge is a circular grouping of megalithic monuments on Salisbury Plain, Wiltshire, dating back to the late Neolithic or early Bronze age.

In Time of "The Breaking of Nations"[8]

1

Only a man harrowing clods
  In a slow silent walk
With an old horse that stumbles and nods
  Half asleep as they stalk.

2

5 Only thin smoke without flame
  From the heaps of couch-grass;
Yet this will go onward the same
  Though Dynasties pass.

3

Yonder a maid and her wight
10   Come whispering by:
War's annals will cloud into night
  Ere their story die.

1915   1916

Afterwards

When the Present has latched its postern° behind my tremulous stay,   back gate
  And the May month flaps its glad green leaves like wings,
Delicate-filmed as new-spun silk, will the neighbors say,
  "He was a man who used to notice such things"?

5 If it be in the dusk when, like an eyelid's soundless blink,
  The dewfall-hawk comes crossing the shades to alight
Upon the wind-warped upland thorn, a gazer may think,
  "To him this must have been a familiar sight."

If I pass during some nocturnal blackness, mothy and warm,
10   When the hedgehog travels furtively over the lawn,
One may say, "He strove that such innocent creatures should come to no harm,
  But he could do little for them; and now he is gone."

If, when hearing that I have been stilled at last, they stand at the door,
  Watching the full-starred heavens that winter sees,
15 Will this thought rise on those who will meet my face no more,
  "He was one who had an eye for such mysteries"?

And will any say when my bell of quittance is head in the gloom,
  And a crossing breeze cuts a pause in its outrollings,
Till they rise again, as they were a new bell's boom,
20   "He hears it not now, but used to notice such things"?

1917

<hr />

8. See Jeremiah li.20: "Thou art my battle ax and weapons of war: for with thee will I break in pieces the nations, and with thee will I destroy kingdoms."

Jezreel

ON ITS SEIZURE BY THE ENGLISH UNDER ALLENBY, SEPTEMBER 1918[9]

Did they catch as it were in a Vision at shut of the day—
When their cavalry smote through the ancient Esdraelon Plain,
And they crossed where the Tishbite[1] stood forth in his enemy's way—
His gaunt mournful Shade as he bade the King haste off amain?

5   On war-men at this end of time—even on Englishmen's eyes—
Who slay with their arms of new might in the long-ago place,
Flashed he who drove furiously?[2] . . . Ah, did the phantom arise
Of that queen, of that proud Tyrian woman who painted her face?[3]

Faintly marked they the words "Throw her down!" from the night eerily,
10 Specter-spots of the blood of her body on some rotten wall?
And the thin note of pity that came: "A King's daughter is she,"
As they passed where she trodden was once by the chargers' footfall?

Could such be the hauntings of men of today, at the cease
Of pursuit, at the dusk-hour, ere slumber their senses could seal?
15 Enghosted seers, kings—one on horseback who asked "Is it peace?"[4] . . .
Yea, strange things and spectral may men have beheld in Jezreel!
                           September 24, 1918   1918

The Children and Sir Nameless

Sir Nameless, once of Athelhall, declared:
"These wretched children romping in my park
Trample the herbage till the soil is bared,
And yap and yell from early morn till dark!
5 Go keep them harnessed to their set routines:
Thank God I've none to hasten my decay;
For green remembrance there are better means
Than offspring, who but wish their sires away."

Sir Nameless of that mansion said anon:
10 "To be perpetuate for my mightiness
Sculpture must image me when I am gone."
—He forthwith summoned carvers there express
To shape a figure stretching seven-odd feet
(For he was tall) in alabaster stone,
15 With shield, and crest, and casque, and sword complete:
When done a statelier work was never known.

Three hundred years hied; Church-restorers came,
And, no one of his lineage being traced,
They thought an effigy so large in frame
20 Best fitted for the floor. There it was placed,

9. Towards the end of World War I, in the autumn of 1918, General Allenby, commanding the Egyptian Expeditionary Force, won the final victory against the Turks when his cavalry swept through the plain of Esdraelon, called in Hebrew *Emeq Yizre'el*, the plain of Jezreel: the plain lies southeast of Haifa, in northern Israel. In biblical times the city of Jezreel was the location of the palace of Ahab, the wicked king of Israel, and his wife Jezebel.
1. The prophet Elijah (I Kings xvii), implacable enemy of King Ahab (I Kings xvi. 29–34).
2. II Kings ix.20. Jehu was anointed King of Israel by Elisha, Elijah's successor.
3. II Kings ix.30–37.
4. II Kings ix.17.

Under the seats for schoolchildren. And they
Kicked out his name, and hobnailed off his nose;
And, as they yawn through sermon-time, they say,
"Who was this old stone man beneath our toes?"

1922

No Buyers

A STREET SCENE

A load of brushes and baskets and cradles and chairs
    Labors along the street in the rain:
With it a man, a woman, a pony with whiteybrown hairs.
    The man foots in front of the horse with a shambling sway
5   At a slower tread than a funeral train,
    While to a dirge-like tune he chants his wares,
Swinging a Turk's-head brush (in a drum-major's way
      When the bandsmen march and play).

A yard from the back of the man is the whiteybrown pony's nose:
10 He mirrors his master in every item of pace and pose:
      He stops when the man stops, without being told,
    And seems to be eased by a pause; too plainly he's old,
      Indeed, not strength enough shows
      To steer the disjointed wagon straight,
15   Which wriggles left and right in a rambling line,
    Deflected thus by its own warp and weight,
    And pushing the pony with it in each incline.

    The woman walks on the pavement verge,
      Parallel to the man:
20   She wears an apron white and wide in span,
And carries a like Turk's head, but more in nursing-wise:
      Now and then she joins in his dirge,
    But as if her thoughts were on distant things.
    The rain clams her apron till it clings.
25 So, step by step, they move with their merchandise,
      And nobody buys.

1925

GERARD MANLEY HOPKINS
(1844–1889)

The Alchemist in the City

My window shows the travelling clouds,
Leaves spent, new seasons, alter'd sky,
The making and the melting crowds:
The whole world passes; I stand by.

5 They do not waste their meted hours,
But men and masters plan and build:
I see the crowning of their towers,
And happy promises fulfill'd.

And I—perhaps if my intent
10   Could count on prediluvian age,[1]
The labours I should then have spent
Might so attain their heritage,

But now before the pot can glow
With not to be discover'd gold,
15   At length the bellows shall not blow,
The furnace shall at last be cold.

Yet it is now too late to heal
The incapable and cumbrous shame
Which makes me when with men I deal
20   More powerless than the blind or lame.

No, I should love the city less
Even than this my thankless lore;
But I desire the wilderness
Or weeded landslips of the shore.

25   I walk my breezy belvedere
To watch the low or levant sun,
I see the city pigeons veer,
I mark the tower swallows run

Between the tower-top and the ground
30   Below me in the bearing air;
Then find in the horizon-round
One spot and hunger to be there.

And then I hate the most that lore
That holds no promise of success;
35   Then sweetest seems the houseless shore,
Then free and kind the wilderness.

Or ancient mounds that cover bones,
Or rocks where rockdoves do repair
And trees of terebinth[2] and stones
40   And silence and a gulf of air.

There on a long and squarèd height
After the sunset I would lie,
And pierce the yellow waxen light
With free long looking, ere I die.

1865   1948

The Habit of Perfection

Elected Silence, sing to me
And beat upon my whorlèd ear,
Pipe me to pastures still and be
The music that I care to hear.

---

1. I.e., age as great as the ages attained by men who lived before the Flood (Genesis v).

2. A European tree which yields turpentine.

5 Shape nothing, lips; be lovely-dumb:
It is the shut, the curfew sent
From there where all surrenders come
Which only makes you eloquent.

Be shellèd, eyes, with double dark
10 And find the uncreated light:[3]
This ruck and reel which you remark
Coils, keeps, and teases simple sight.

Palate, the hutch of tasty lust,
Desire not to be rinsed with wine:
15 The can° must be so sweet, the crust   *tankard, cup*
So fresh that come in fasts divine!

Nostrils, your careless breath that spend
Upon the stir and keep of pride,
What relish shall the censers[4] send
20 Along the sanctuary side!

O feel-of-primrose hands, O feet
That want the yield of plushy sward,
But you shall walk the golden street
And you unhouse and house the Lord.[5]

25 And, Poverty, be thou the bride
And now the marriage feast begun,
And lily-coloured clothes provide
Your spouse not laboured-at nor spun.[6]

1866   1918

God's Grandeur

The world is charged with the grandeur of God.
    It will flame out, like shining from shook foil;[7]
    It gathers to a greatness, like the ooze of oil
Crushed.[8] Why do men then now not reck his rod?
5 Generations have trod, have trod, have trod;
    And all is seared with trade; bleared, smeared with toil;
    And wears man's smudge and shares man's smell: the soil
Is bare now, nor can foot feel, being shod.

And for all this, nature is never spent;
10   There lives the dearest freshness deep down things;
And though the last lights off the black West went
    Oh, morning, at the brown brink eastward, springs—
Because the Holy Ghost over the bent
    World broods with warm breast and with ah! bright wings.

1877   1895

3. W. H. Gardner, in his notes to the poem, explains "uncreated light" as "the *lux increata* of the Schoolmen, the creative energy of God's mind."
4. Vessels in which incense is burned.
5. I.e., the hands will open and close the pyx, the vessel containing the host, the consecrated bread, used in the sacrament.
6. See Matthew vi.28–29: "* * * Consider the lilies of the field, how they grow; they toil not, neither do they spin."
7. In a letter to Robert Bridges (January 4, 1883), Hopkins says: "* * * I mean foil in its sense of leaf or tinsel, and no other word whatever will give the effect I want. Shaken goldfoil gives off broad glares like sheet lightning and also, and this is true of nothing else, owing to its zigzag dints and crossings and network of small many cornered facets, a sort of fork lightning too."
8. I.e., as when olives are crushed for their oil.

The Windhover[9]

TO CHRIST OUR LORD

I caught this morning morning's minion,° king-   *darling, favorite*
dom of daylight's dauphin,[1] dapple-dawn-drawn Falcon, in his riding
Of the rolling level underneath him steady air, and striding
High there, how he rung upon the rein of a wimpling° wing   *rippling*
5   In his ecstasy! then off, off forth on swing,
As a skate's heel sweeps smooth on a bow-bend: the hurl and gliding
Rebuffed the big wind. My heart in hiding
Stirred for a bird,—the achieve of, the mastery of the thing!

Brute beauty and valour and act, oh, air, pride, plume, here
Buckle![2] AND the fire that breaks from thee then, a billion
10   Times told lovelier, more dangerous, O my chevalier![3]

No wonder of it: shéer plód makes plough down sillion°   *furrow*
Shine, and blue-bleak embers, ah my dear,
Fall, gall themselves, and gash gold-vermilion.
                                                    1877   1918

Pied Beauty[4]

Glory be to God for dappled things—
For skies of couple-colour as a brinded° cow;   *streaked, brindled*
For rose-moles all in stipple upon trout that swim;
Fresh-firecoal chestnut-falls;[5] finches' wings;
5   Landscape plotted and pieced—fold, fallow and plough;[6]
And áll trádes, their gear and tackle and trim.
All things counter, original, spare, strange;
Whatever is fickle, freckled (who knows how?)
With swift, slow; sweet, sour; adazzle, dim;
10   He fathers-forth whose beauty is past change:
                    Praise him.
                                        1877   1918

Felix Randal

Felix Randal the farrier,° O is he dead then? my duty all ended,   *blacksmith*
Who have watched his mould of man, big-boned and hardy-handsome
Pining, pining, till time when reason rambled in it and some
Fatal four disorders, fleshed there, all contended?

---

9. "A name for the kestral [a species of small hawk], from its habit of hovering or hanging with its head to the wind" [O.E.D.].
1. The eldest son of the king of France was called the *dauphin:* hence, the word here means heir to a splendid, kingly condition.
2. The word "buckle" brings to a single focus the several elements of line 8, in both their literal sense, as descriptive of a single, sudden movement of the airborne bird, and in their symbolic sense as descriptive of Christ and with further reference to the poet himself and the lesson he draws from his observation. It may be read either as indicative or imperative,

and in one or another of its possible meanings: "to fasten," "to join closely," "to equip for battle," "to grapple with, engage," but also "to cause to bend, give way, crumple."
3. Knight, nobleman, champion.
4. Having two or more colors, in patches or blotches.
5. W. H. Gardner cites a note from Hopkins's *Journals:* "Chestnuts as bright as coals or spots of vermilion."
6. The land makes a pattern of varicolored patches by reason of its several uses, as for pasture, or being left fallow for a season, or being plowed and sown.

5 Sickness broke him. Impatient, he cursed at first, but mended
Being anointed and all; though a heavenlier heart began some
Months earlier, since I had our sweet reprieve and ransom
Tendered to him.[7] Ah well, God rest him all road ever he offended![8]

This seeing the sick endears them to us, us too it endears.
10 My tongue had taught thee comfort, touch had quenched thy tears,
Thy tears that touched my heart, child, Felix, poor Felix Randal;

How far from then forethought of, all thy more boisterous years,
When thou at the random[9] grim forge, powerful amidst peers,
Didst fettle[1] for the great grey drayhorse his bright and battering sandal!

1880   1918

Spring and Fall

TO A YOUNG CHILD

Márgarét, áre you gríeving
Over Goldengrove unleaving?
Leáves, líke the things of man, you
With your fresh thoughts care for, can you?
5 Áh! ás the heart grows older
It will come to such sights colder
By and by, nor spare a sigh
Though worlds of wanwood leafmeal lie;[2]
And yet you *will* weep and know why.
10 Now no matter, child, the name:
Sórrow's spríngs áre the same.
Nor mouth had, no nor mind, expressed
What heart heard of, ghost° guessed: **spirit, soul**
It ís the blight man was born for,
15 It is Margaret you mourn for.

1880   1893

Inversnaid [4]

This darksome burn,° horseback brown,   *stream*
His rollrock highroad roaring down,
In coop° and in comb° the fleece of his foam   *hollow/crest*
Flutes and low to the lake falls home.

5 A windpuff-bonnet of fáwn-fróth
Turns and twindles [5] over the broth
Of a pool so pitchblack, féll-frówning,
It rounds and rounds Despair to drowning.

7. I.e., since I had a priest visit him to hear his confession and give absolution.
8. I.e., for any way in which he may have offended.
9. Ramshackle, as applied to the forge itself; but also meaning that the man's life as a blacksmith was merely one casual earthly life as opposed to the sure way of Christian salvation.
1. To line or cover with a refractory material; hence, to shoe.
2. "Wanwood": *pale* or *dim*—the groves are pale because of their light-colored autumn foliage, or dim because of the filtered light.

"Leafmeal" (a word coined by Hopkins by analogy with *piecemeal*): *leaf by leaf*, or *leaf mold*—in the first sense, the foliage lies about the grove, having fallen leaf by leaf; in the second, foliage gradually decays to leaf mold.
4. Town in the Scottish Highlands.
5. The editors of *The Poems of Gerard Manley Hopkins*, Fourth Edition, say that *twindles* "seems to be a portmanteau coinage inscaping 'twists,' 'twitches,' and 'dwindles' . . . but possibly verbal use of obs. 'twindle' (twin) is intended, to suggest the splitting of a whirl-pool into two."

Degged° with dew, dappled with dew   *sprinkled*
10 Are the groins of the braes° that the brook treads through,   *steep banks*
    Wiry heathpacks,° flitches [6] of fern,   *heather*
    And the beadbonny [7] ash that sits over the burn.

    What would the world be, once bereft
    Of wet and of wildness? Let them be left,
15 O let them be left, wildness and wet;
    Long live the weeds and the wilderness yet.

                                            1881   1918

[As Kingfishers Catch Fire, Dragonflies Draw Flame]

As kingfishers catch fire, dragonflies draw flame;[3]
    As tumbled over rim in roundy wells
    Stones ring; like each tucked° string tells, each hung bell's   *touched, plucked*
Bow swung finds tongue to fling out broad its name;
5 Each mortal thing does one thing and the same:
    Deals out that being indoors each one dwells;[4]
    Selves[5]—goes itself; *myself* it speaks and spells,
Crying *What I do is me: for that I came.*

    I say more: the just man justices;
10   Keeps gráce: thát keeps all his goings graces;
    Acts in God's eye what in God's eye he is—
    Chríst. For Christ plays in ten thousand places,
    Lovely in limbs, and lovely in eyes not his
    To the Father through the features of men's faces.

                                            1882?   1918

[No Worst, There Is None. Pitched Past Pitch of Grief]

No worst, there is none. Pitched past pitch of grief,
More pangs will, schooled at forepangs, wilder wring.
Comforter, where, where is your comforting?
Mary, mother of us, where is your relief?
5 My cries heave, herds-long; huddle in a main, a chief-
woe, world-sorrow; on an age-old anvil wince and sing—
Then lull, then leave off. Fury had shrieked 'No ling-
ering! Let me be fell:° force° I must be brief'.   *fierce, deadly/perforce*
O the mind, mind has mountains; cliffs of fall
10 Frightful, sheer, no-man-fathomed. Hold them cheap
May who ne'er hung there. Nor does long our small
Durance deal with that steep or deep. Here! creep,
Wretch, under a comfort serves in a whirlwind: all
Life death does end and each day dies with sleep.

                                            1885   1918

---

6. *Ibid.*: "ragged, russet flakes, tufts or clumps."
7. With clusters of bright beadlike berries.
3. I.e., as their bright colors flash in the light.

4. I.e., gives utterance to the essential nature that dwells within ("indoors") each individual being.
5. I.e., gives being to its own individuality.

[I Wake and Feel the Fell of Dark, Not Day.]

I wake and feel the fell[6] of dark, not day.
What hours, O what black hoürs we have spent
This night! what sights you, heart, saw; ways you went!
And more must, in yet longer light's delay.

5   With witness I speak this. But where I say
Hours I mean years, mean life. And my lament
Is cries countless, cries like dead letters sent
To dearest him that lives alas! away.

I am gall, I am heartburn. God's most deep decree
10 Bitter would have me taste: my taste was me;
Bones built in me, flesh filled, blood brimmed the curse.

Selfyeast of spirit a dull dough sours. I see
The lost are like this, and their scourge to be
As I am mine, their sweating selves, but worse.

                                        1885   1918

[My Own Heart Let Me More Have Pity On]

My own heart let me more have pity on; let
Me live to my sad self hereafter kind,
Charitable; not live this tormented mind
With this tormented mind tormenting yet.

5   I cast for comfort I can no more get
By groping round my comfortless, than blind
Eyes in their dark can day or thirst can find
Thirst's all-in-all in all a world of wet.[7]

Soul, self; come, poor Jackself,[8] I do advise
10 You, jaded, let be; call off thoughts awhile
Elsewhere; leave comfort root-room;[9] let joy size
At God knows when to God knows what;[1] whose smile
's not wrung,[2] see you; unforeseen times rather—as skies
Betweenpie mountains[3]—lights a lovely mile.

                                        1885   1918

6. "Fell" is capable of being read in a number of senses: as "the hide or hairy skin of a beast," or, in an obsolete or rare sense, as "gall, bitterness; hence, animosity, rancor" [O.E.D.], or possibly as the adjective *fell*—fierce, savage, cruel—used as a noun.
7. I.e., as shipwrecked persons adrift without drinking water cannot quench their thirst, even though they are surrounded by "wet." The noun *world* is common to all three instances: the speaker's "comfortless" world, the blind man's "dark" world, the "world of wet" in which the shipwrecked are adrift.

8. The humble self—"Jack" used in a pitying, deprecating sense (as in *jack-of-all-trades*).
9. Room for its roots to grow.
1. "Size" (line 11): grow, increase in size; "At God knows when": at unpredictable times; "to God knows what": until it reaches an unpredictable condition.
2. Cannot be forced, but must come as it will.
3. "Betweenpie" (a verb of Hopkins's invention [see *Pied Beauty*]): the brightness of skies seen between mountains, which makes a variegated patterning of light and dark.

That Nature is a Heraclitean[4] Fire and of the comfort of the Resurrection

Cloud-puffball, torn tufts, tossed pillows | flaunt forth, then
   chevy° on an air-   *race, scamper*
built thoroughfare: heaven-roysterers, in gay-gangs | they throng;
   they glitter in marches.
Down roughcast, down dazzling whitewash, | wherever an elm arches,
Shivelights[5] and shadowtackle[6] in long | lashes lace, lance, and pair.
5 Delightfully the bright wind boisterous | ropes, wrestles, beats earth bare
Of yestertempest's creases; | in pool and rutpeel parches
Squandering ooze to squeezed | dough, crust, dust; stanches, starches
Squadroned masks and manmarks | treadmire toil there
Footfretted in it. Million-fuelèd, | nature's bonfire burns on.
10 But quench her bonniest, dearest | to her, her clearest-selvèd spark
Man, how fast his firedint,[7] | his mark on mind, is gone!
Both are in an unfathomable, all is in an enormous dark
Drowned. O pity and indig | nation! Manshape, that shone
Sheer off, disseveral, a star, | death blots black out; nor mark
15   Is any of him at all so stark
But vastness blurs and time | beats level. Enough! the Resurrection,
A heart's-clarion! Away grief's gasping, | joyless days, dejection.
      Across my foundering deck shone
A beacon, an eternal beam. | Flesh fade, and mortal trash
20 Fall to the residuary worm; | world's wildfire, leave but ash:
      In a flash, at a trumpet crash,
I am at once what Christ is, | since he was what I am, and
This Jack,[8] joke, poor potsherd, | patch, matchwood, immortal diamond,
      Is immortal diamond.

                                  1888   1918

A. E. HOUSMAN
(1859–1936)

Loveliest of Trees, the Cherry Now

Loveliest of trees, the cherry now
Is hung with bloom along the bough,
And stands about the woodland ride
Wearing white for Eastertide.

---

4. Heraclitus of Ephesus (flourished 500 b.c.)
was the founder of an important school of pre-
Socratic philosophy who taught that the
world had its origin in fire and would end in
fire. "He is best known for his doctrine of
perpetual change and impermanence in nature
* * * ." For him the principle of the universe
was "a law of opposites, whose conflicts were
controlled by eternal justice and whose con-
trary tensions produced the apparent stability
of being. Fire, the underlying primary sub-
stance, is the prototype of the world, which
is an 'ever-living fire with measures of it
kindling and measures of it going out.' Fire
passes by combustion through the fiery water-
spout * * * into water and earth; and the
reverse process occurs simultaneously, when
part of the earth liquefies and passes by evapo-
ration and 'exhalation' as fuel into fire. Thus
are constituted a 'way up' and a 'way down,'
a two-way process of interchange between the
elements, with approximate balance of
'measures.' 'All is perpetual flux and nothing
abides.' " [A. J. D. Porteous, in *Chambers's
Encyclopedia*].
5. Light in splinters, fragments.
6. Shadows in complicated shapes, as of ship's
ropes, tackle, gear.
7. Hopkins's compound, meaning the mark
made by the flame of man's spirit, the spirit's
power to make its mark.
8. Common mortal like "poor Jackself" in
My Own Heart Let Me More Have Pity On.

5   Now, of my threescore years and ten,
       Twenty will not come again,
     And take from seventy springs a score,
       It only leaves me fifty more.

     And since to look at things in bloom
10   Fifty springs are little room,
     About the woodlands I will go
       To see the cherry hung with snow.

                              1896

Reveille

Wake: the silver dusk returning
    Up the beach of darkness brims,
And the ship of sunrise burning
    Strands upon the eastern rims.

5   Wake: the vaulted shadow shatters,
       Trampled to the floor it spanned,
    And the tent of night in tatters
       Straws° the sky-pavilioned land.   *strews*

    Up, lad, up, 'tis late for lying:
10   Hear the drums of morning play;
    Hark, the empty highways crying
       "Who'll beyond the hills away?"

    Towns and countries woo together,
       Forelands beacon, belfries call;
15   Never lad that trod on leather
       Lived to feast his heart with all.

    Up, lad; thews° that lie and cumber   *limbs*
       Sunlit pallets never thrive;
    Morns abed and daylight slumber
20   Were not meant for man alive.

    Clay lies still, but blood's a rover;
       Breath's a ware that will not keep.
    Up, lad: when the journey's over
       There'll be time enough to sleep.

                              1896

To an Athlete Dying Young

The time you won your town the race
We chaired you through the market-place;
Man and boy stood cheering by,
And home we brought you shoulder-high.

5   Today, the road all runners come,
Shoulder-high we bring you home,
And set you at your threshold down,
Townsman of a stiller town.

Smart lad, to slip betimes away
10 From fields where glory does not stay
And early though the laurel grows
It withers quicker than the rose.

Eyes the shady night has shut
Cannot see the record cut,
15 And silence sounds no worse than cheers
After earth has stopped the ears:

Now you will not swell the rout
Of lads that wore their honors out,
Runners whom renown outran
20 And the name died before the man.

So set, before its echoes fade,
The fleet foot on the sill of shade,
And hold to the low lintel up
The still-defended challenge-cup.

25 And round that early-laureled head
Will flock to gaze the strengthless dead,
And find unwithered on its curls
The garland briefer than a girl's.

1896

With Rue My Heart Is Laden

With rue my heart is laden
For golden friends I had,
For many a rose-lipt maiden
And many a lightfoot lad.

5 By brooks too broad for leaping
The lightfoot boys are laid;
The rose-lipt girls are sleeping
In fields where roses fade.

1896

"Terence,[1] This Is Stupid Stuff . . ."

"Terence, this is stupid stuff:
You eat your victuals fast enough;
There can't be much amiss, 'tis clear,
To see the rate you drink your beer.
5 But oh, good Lord, the verse you make,
It gives a chap the belly-ache.
The cow, the old cow, she is dead;
It sleeps well, the hornéd head:
We poor lads, 'tis our turn now
10 To hear such tunes as killed the cow.
Pretty friendship 'tis to rhyme
Your friends to death before their time
Moping melancholy mad:
Come, pipe a tune to dance to, lad."

1. Housman had at first planned to call the volume in which this poem appeared *The Poems of Terence Hearsay.*

15 Why, if 'tis dancing you would be,
There's brisker pipes than poetry.
Say, for what were hop-yards meant,
Or why was Burton built on Trent?[2]
Oh many a peer of England brews
20 Livelier liquor than the Muse,
And malt does more than Milton can
To justify God's ways to man.
Ale, man, ale's the stuff to drink
For fellows whom it hurts to think:
25 Look into the pewter pot
To see the world as the world's not.
And faith, 'tis pleasant till 'tis past:
The mischief is that 'twill not last.
Oh I have been to Ludlow[3] fair
30 And left my necktie God knows where,
And carried halfway home, or near,
Pints and quarts of Ludlow beer:
Then the world seemed none so bad,
And I myself a sterling lad;
35 And down in lovely muck I've lain,
Happy till I woke again.
Then I saw the morning sky:
Heigho, the tale was all a lie;
The world, it was the old world yet,
40 I was I, my things were wet,
And nothing now remained to do
But begin the game anew.

  Therefore, since the world has still
Much good, but much less good than ill,
45 And while the sun and moon endure
Luck's a chance, but trouble's sure,
I'd face it as a wise man would,
And train for ill and not for good.
'Tis true, the stuff I bring for sale
50 Is not so brisk a brew as ale:
Out of a stem that scored the hand
I wrung it in a weary land.
But take it: if the smack is sour,
The better for the embittered hour;
55 It should do good to heart and head
When your soul is in my soul's stead;
And I will friend you, if I may,
In the dark and cloudy day.

  There was a king reigned in the East:
60 There, when kings will sit to feast,
They get their fill before they think
With poisoned meat and poisoned drink.
He gathered all that springs to birth
From the many-venomed earth;
65 First a little, thence to more,

---

2. Burton-on-Trent, a town in Staffordshire
whose principal industry is the brewing of ale.

3. A town in Shropshire.

He sampled all her killing store;
And easy, smiling, seasoned sound,
Sate the king when healths went round.
They put arsenic in his meat
70 And stared aghast to watch him eat;
They poured strychnine in his cup
And shook to see him drink it up:
They shook, they stared as white's their shirt:
Them it was their poison hurt.
75 —I tell the tale that I heard told.
Mithridates, he died old.[4]

1896

Eight O'clock

He stood, and heard the steeple
    Sprinkle the quarters on the morning town.
One, two, three, four, to market-place and people
    It tossed them down.

5   Strapped, noosed, nighing his hour,
    He stood and counted them and cursed his luck;
And then the clock collected in the tower
    Its strength, and struck.

1922

The Oracles[5]

'Tis mute, the word they went to hear on high Dodona mountain
    When winds were in the oakenshaws and all the cauldrons tolled,
And mute's the midland navel-stone beside the singing fountain,
    And echoes list to silence now where gods told lies of old.

5   I took my question to the shrine that has not ceased from speaking,
    The heart within, that tells the truth and tells it twice as plain;
And from the cave of oracles I heard the priestess shrieking
    That she and I should surely die and never live again.

Oh priestess, what you cry is clear, and sound good sense I think it;
10   But let the screaming echoes rest, and froth your mouth no more.
'Tis true there's better booze than brine, but he that drowns must drink it;
    And oh, my lass, the news is news that men have heard before.

4. Mithridates VI, king of Pontus in Asia Minor in the first century B.C., produced in himself an immunity to certain poisons by administering them to himself in small, gradual doses.
5. It was a feature of the Greek religion that the gods could be consulted through their oracles. Questions concerning the future or asking advice in matters of conduct, both political and moral, were presented at the shrine of the oracle, and the answers—usually vague, ambiguous, or incoherent—were interpreted by a priest. The two most famous oracles, both alluded to in Housman's poem, were that of Zeus at Dodona, in Epirus, and that of Apollo at Delphi. At Dodona the answers came from the oak sacred to Zeus, either through the sound of the wind in its leaves or from the sound of a spring which gushed up at its roots; this temple contained a large cauldron, renowned for its echoes. At Delphi, where the answers were given by the Pythia, a divinely inspired priestess who uttered her pronouncements in an incoherent frenzy, there was a stone called the Omphalos, or navel, supposed to be the central point of the earth.

The King with half the East at heel is marched from lands of morning;
 Their fighters drink the rivers up, their shafts benight the air.
15 *And he that stands will die for nought, and home there's no returning.*
 The Spartans on the sea-wet rock sat down and combed their hair.[6]

1922

Revolution

West and away the wheels of darkness roll,
  Day's beamy banner up the east is borne,
Specters and fears, the nightmare and her foal,
  Drown in the golden deluge of the morn.

5 But over sea and continent from sight
  Safe to the Indies has the earth conveyed
The vast and moon-eclipsing cone of night,
  Her towering foolscap of eternal shade.

See, in mid heaven the sun is mounted; hark,
10 The belfries tingle to the noonday chime.
'Tis silent, and the subterranean dark
  Has crossed the nadir,[7] and begins to climb.

1922

Stars, I Have Seen Them Fall

Stars, I have seen them fall,
  But when they drop and die
No star is lost at all
  From all the star-sown sky.
5 The toil of all that be
  Helps not the primal fault;
It rains into the sea,
  And still the sea is salt.

1936

---

6. Xerxes (the "King," line 13), the leader of the Persian forces who were to defeat the Greeks, including a small body of unyielding Spartans, at the battle of Thermopylae. The details of the last stanza may be referred to Herodotus' account of the battle and the events leading up to it in Book VII of his *History.* The Athenians had twice consulted the oracle at Delphi, but even the predictions of defeat, which "struck fear into their hearts, failed to persuade them to fly from Greece. They had the courage to remain faithful to their land, and await the coming of the foe." Of Xerxes' army, Herodotus asks, "* * * Was there a nation in all Asia which Xerxes did not bring with him against Greece? Or was there a river, except those of unusual size, which sufficed for his troops to drink?" At one point, Xerxes had sent a spy to observe the Greeks; the Spartans, who happened to hold the outer guard, "were seen by the spy, some of them engaged in gymnastic exercises, others combing their long hair," which struck Xerxes as laughable. He "had no means of surmising the truth—namely, that the Spartans were preparing to do or die manfully * * *"

7. "The point of the heavens diametrically opposite to the zenith; the point directly under the observer" [O.E.D.].

RUDYARD KIPLING
(1865–1936)

Tommy[1]

I went into a public-'ouse to get a pint o' beer,
The publican° 'e up an' sez, "We serve no red-coats here."   bar-keeper
The girls be'ind the bar they laughed an' giggled fit to die,
I outs into the street again an' to myself sez I:
5   O it's Tommy this, an' Tommy that, an' "Tommy, go away";
     But it's "Thank you, Mister Atkins," when the band begins to play—
     The band begins to play, my boys, the band begins to play,
     O it's "Thank you, Mister Atkins," when the band begins to play.

I went into a theater as sober as could be,
10 They gave a drunk civilian room, but 'adn't none for me;
They sent me to the gallery or round the music-'alls,[2]
But when it comes to fightin', Lord! they'll shove me in the stalls!
     For it's Tommy this, an' Tommy that, an' "Tommy, wait outside";
     But its "Special train for Atkins" when the trooper's on the tide—
15   The troopship's on the tide, my boys, the troopship's on the tide,
     O it's "Special train for Atkins" when the trooper's on the tide.

Yes, makin' mock o' uniforms that guard you while you sleep
Is cheaper than them uniforms, an' they're starvation cheap;
An' hustlin' drunken soldiers when they're goin' large a bit
20 Is five times better business than paradin' in full kit.
     Then it's Tommy this, an' Tommy that, an' "Tommy, 'ow's yer soul?"
     But it's "Thin red line of 'eroes"[3] when the drums begin to roll—
     The drums begin to roll, my boys, the drums begin to roll,
     O it's "Thin red line of 'eroes" when the drums begin to roll.

25 We aren't no thin red 'eroes, nor we aren't no blackguards too,
But single men in barricks, most remarkable like you;
An' if sometimes our conduck isn't all your fancy paints,
Why, single men in barricks don't grow into plaster saints;
     While it's Tommy this, an' Tommy that, an' "Tommy, fall be'ind,"
30   But it's "Please to walk in front, sir," when there's trouble in the wind—
     There's trouble in the wind, my boys, there's trouble in the wind,
     O it's "Please to walk in front, sir," when there's trouble in the wind.

You talk o' better food for us, an' schools, an' fires, an' all:
We'll wait for extry rations if you treat us rational.
35 Don't mess about the cook-room slops, but prove it to our face
The Widow's Uniform[4] is not the soldier-man's disgrace.
     For it's Tommy this, an' Tommy that, an' "Chuck him out, the brute!"
     But it's "Savior of 'is country" when the guns begin to shoot;
     An' it's Tommy this, an' Tommy that, an' anything you please;
40   An' Tommy ain't a bloomin' fool—you bet that Tommy sees!

1890

1. Derived from "Thomas Atkins," as the typical name for a soldier in the British army.
2. Cheaper seats in a theater, in the balcony; the best seats, in the orchestra, are the stalls.
3. W. H. Russell, a London *Times* correspondent, had used the phrase "thin red line tipped with steel" to describe the 93rd Highlanders infantry regiment as they stood to meet the advancing Russian cavalry at Balaclava (1854), in the Crimean War.
4. I.e., the queen's uniform. In his poems and stories Kipling occasionally referred to Queen Victoria as "The Widow at Windsor."

The Recall

I am the land of their fathers.
In me the virtue stays.
I will bring back my children,
After certain days.

5   Under their feet in the grasses
My clinging magic runs.
They shall return as strangers.
They shall remain as sons.

Over their heads in the branches
10 Of their new-bought, ancient trees,
I weave an incantation
And draw them to my knees.

Scent of smoke in the evening,
Smell of rain in the night—
15 The hours, the days and the seasons,
Order their souls aright,

Till I make plain the meaning
Of all my thousand years—
Till I fill their hearts with knowledge,
20 While I fill their eyes with tears.

                                                                    1909

WILLIAM BUTLER YEATS[1]
(1865–1939)

The Lamentation of the Old Pensioner

Although I shelter from the rain
Under a broken tree,
My chair was nearest to the fire
In every company
5   That talked of love or politics,
Ere time transfigured me.

Though lads are making pikes° again   *weapons*
For some conspiracy,
And crazy rascals rage their fill
10 At human tyranny,
My contemplations are of Time
That has transfigured me.

1. In providing footnotes to Yeats's poems, the principle has been (as throughout this anthology) to give necessary background information without entering into interpretation or including biographical information for its own sake. With Yeats, however, the line dividing these areas from each other is not always easy to maintain, since the poems often make direct use of detail from Yeats's life and develop ideas and images that can be fully understood only by reference to other poems of Yeats's or to his prose. Although the notes are sometimes detailed, they are intended to provide a minimum background of essential matter, and to provide it, wherever possible, by citing complementary or explanatory passages from Yeats's own writings.

There's not a woman turns her face
Upon a broken tree,
15 And yet the beauties that I loved
Are in my memory;
I spit into the face of Time
That has transfigured me.

1892

Easter 1916[4]

I have met them at close of day
Coming with vivid faces
From counter or desk among gray
Eighteenth-century houses.
5 I have passed with a nod of the head
Or polite meaningless words,
Or have lingered awhile and said
Polite meaningless words,
And thought before I had done
10 Of a mocking tale or a gibe
To please a companion
Around the fire at the club,
Being certain that they and I
But lived where motley is worn:
15 All changed, changed utterly:
A terrible beauty is born.

That woman's days were spent
In ignorant good will,
Her nights in argument
20 Until her voice grew shrill.
What voice more sweet than hers
When, young and beautiful,
She rode to harriers?[5]
This man had kept a school
25 And rode our wingèd horse;[6]
This other his helper and friend
Was coming into his force;
He might have won fame in the end,
So sensitive his nature seemed,
30 So daring and sweet his thought.
This other man I had dreamed
A drunken, vainglorious lout.[7]
He had done most bitter wrong
To some who are near my heart,
35 Yet I number him in the song;

---

4. An Irish Nationalist uprising had been planned for Easter Sunday 1916, and although the German ship which was bringing munitions had been intercepted by the British, attempts to postpone the uprising failed; it began in Dublin on Easter Monday. "Fifteen hundred men seized key points and an Irish republic was proclaimed from the General Post Office. After the initial surprise prompt British military action was taken, and when over 300 lives had been lost the insurgents were forced to surrender on 29 April * * * The seven signatories of the republican proclamation, including [Pádraic] Pearse and [James] Connolly, and nine others were shot after court martial between 3 and 12 May; 75 were reprieved and over 2000 held prisoners" [From

"Ireland: History," by D. B. Quinn, in *Chambers's Encyclopedia*].
5. Countess Constance Georgina Markiewicz, *née* Gore-Booth, about whom Yeats wrote *On a Political Prisoner* and a later poem, *In Memory of Eva Gore-Booth and Con Markiewicz*.
6. Pádraic Pearse, headmaster of St. Enda's School, and a prolific writer of poems, plays, and stories as well as of essays on Irish politics and Gaelic literature. "This other" was Thomas MacDonough, also a schoolteacher.
7. Major John MacBride, who had married Maud Gonne (the woman with whom Yeats had for years been hopelessly in love) in 1903 and separated from her in 1905.

He, too, has resigned his part
In the casual comedy;
He, too, has been changed in his turn,
Transformed utterly:
40   A terrible beauty is born.

Hearts with one purpose alone
Through summer and winter seem
Enchanted to a stone
To trouble the living stream.
45   The horse that comes from the road,
The rider, the birds that range
From cloud to tumbling cloud,
Minute by minute they change;
A shadow of cloud on the stream
50   Changes minute by minute;
A horse-hoof slides on the brim,
And a horse plashes within it;
The long-legged moor-hens dive,
And hens to moor-cocks call;
55   Minute by minute they live:
The stone's in the midst of all.

Too long a sacrifice
Can make a stone of the heart.
O when may it suffice?
60   That is Heaven's part, our part
To murmur name upon name,
As a mother names her child
When sleep at last has come
On limbs that had run wild.
65   What is it but nightfall?
No, no, not night but death;
Was it needless death after all?
For England may keep faith
For all that is done and said.
70   We know their dream; enough
To know they dreamed and are dead;
And what if excess of love
Bewildered them till they died?
I write it out in a verse—
75   MacDonagh and MacBride
And Connolly and Pearse
Now and in time to be,
Wherever green is worn,
Are changed, changed utterly:
80   A terrible beauty is born.

September 25, 1916   1916

The Wild Swans at Coole[8]

The trees are in their autumn beauty,
The woodland paths are dry,
Under the October twilight the water
Mirrors a still sky;
5 Upon the brimming water among the stones
Are nine-and-fifty swans.

The nineteenth autumn has come upon me
Since I first made my count;[9]
I saw, before I had well finished,
10 All suddenly mount
And scatter wheeling in great broken rings
Upon their clamorous wings.

I have looked upon those brilliant creatures,
And now my heart is sore.
15 All's changed since I, hearing at twilight,
The first time on this shore,
The bell-beat of their wings above my head,
Trod with a lighter tread.

Unwearied still, lover by lover,
20 They paddle in the cold
Companionable streams or climb the air;
Their hearts have not grown old;
Passion or conquest, wander where they will,
Attend upon them still.

25 But now they drift on the still water,
Mysterious, beautiful;
Among what rushes will they build,
By what lake's edge or pool
Delight men's eyes when I awake some day
30 To find they have flown away?

1917

The Scholars

Bald heads forgetful of their sins,
Old, learned, respectable bald heads
Edit and annotate the lines
That young men, tossing on their beds,
5 Rhymed out in love's despair
To flatter beauty's ignorant ear.

All shuffle there; all cough in ink;
All wear the carpet with their shoes;
All think what other people think;
10 All know the man their neighbor knows.
Lord, what would they say
Did their Catullus walk that way?

1917

8. Coole Park, the estate in western Ireland
of Lady Augusta Gregory, Yeats's patroness
and friend.

9. Yeats had first visted Coole Park in 1897;
the poem was written in October 1916.

On a Political Prisoner[1]

She that but little patience knew,
From childhood on, had now so much
A gray gull lost its fear and flew
Down to her cell and there alit,
5   And there endured her fingers' touch
And from her fingers ate its bit.

Did she in touching that lone wing
Recall the years before her mind
Became a bitter, an abstract thing,
10   Her thought some popular enmity:
Blind and leader of the blind
Drinking the foul ditch where they lie?

When long ago I saw her ride
Under Ben Bulben[2] to the meet,
15   The beauty of her countryside
With all youth's lonely wildness stirred,
She seemed to have grown clean and sweet
Like any rock-bred, sea-borne bird:

Sea-borne, or balanced on the air
20   When first it sprang out of the nest
Upon some lofty rock to stare
Upon the cloudy canopy,
While under its storm-beaten breast
Cried out the hollows of the sea.

1921

The Second Coming

Turning and turning in the widening gyre[3]
The falcon cannot hear the falconer;
Things fall apart; the center cannot hold;
Mere anarchy is loosed upon the world,
5   The blood-dimmed tide is loosed, and everywhere
The ceremony of innocence is drowned;
The best lack all conviction, while the worst
Are full of passionate intensity.

Surely some revelation is at hand;
10   Surely the Second Coming is at hand;
The Second Coming! Hardly are those words out

1. The Countess Constance Georgina Markie-
wicz, *née* Gore-Booth, who was imprisoned in
Holloway Gaol for her part in the Easter Re-
bellion of 1916.
2. Mountain in County Sligo, in the West of
Ireland, where Yeats spent large parts of his
childhood and youth.
3. The gyre—the cone whose shape is traced
in the falcon's sweep upward and out in widen-
ing circles from the falconer who should con-
trol its flight—involves a reference to the
geometrical figure of the interpenetrating

cones, the "fundamental symbol" Yeats used
to diagram his cyclical view of history. (See
the opening pages of "The Great Wheel," in
A Vision [1937]). He saw the cycle of Greco-
Roman civilization as having been brought
to a close by the advent of Christianity, and
in the violence of his own times—"the growing
murderousness of the world"—he saw signs
that the 2000-year cycle of Christianity was
itself about to end, and to be replaced by a
system anithetical to it.

When a vast image out of *Spiritus Mundi*[4]
Troubles my sight: somewhere in sands of the desert
A shape with lion body and the head of a man,[5]
15   A gaze blank and pitiless as the sun,
Is moving its slow thighs, while all about it
Reel shadows of the indignant desert birds.
The darkness drops again; but now I know
That twenty centuries of stony sleep
20   Were vexed to nightmare by a rocking cradle,
And what rough beast, its hour come round at last,
Slouches towards Bethlehem to be born?

1921

A Prayer for My Daughter [8]

Once more the storm is howling, and half hid
Under this cradle-hood and coverlid
My child sleeps on. There is no obstacle
But Gregory's wood and one bare hill
5   Whereby the haystack- and roof-leveling wind,
Bred on the Atlantic, can be stayed;
And for an hour I have walked and prayed
Because of the great gloom that is in my mind.

I have walked and prayed for this young child an hour
10   And heard the sea-wind scream upon the tower,
And under the arches of the bridge, and scream
In the elms above the flooded stream;
Imagining in excited reverie
That the future years had come,
15   Dancing to a frenzied drum,
Out of the murderous innocence of the sea.

May she be granted beauty and yet not
Beauty to make a stranger's eye distraught,
Or hers before a looking glass, for such,
20   Being made beautiful overmuch,
Consider beauty a sufficient end,
Lose natural kindness and maybe
The heart-revealing intimacy
That chooses right, and never find a friend.

4. Or *Anima Mundi,* the Great Memory. "Before the mind's eye, whether in sleep or waking, came images that one was to discover presently in some book one had never read, and after looking in vain for explanation to the current theory of forgotten personal memory, I came to believe in a great memory passing on from generation to generation * * * Our daily thought was certainly but the line of foam at the shallow edge of a vast luminous sea" [*Per Amica Silentia Lunae,* "Anima Mundi," § ii].
5. In the Introduction to his play *The Resurrection* (in *Wheels and Butterflies,* 1935),

Yeats describes the way in which the sphinx image had first manifested itself to him: "Our civilisation was about to reverse itself, or some new civilisation about to be born from all that our age had rejected * * *; because we had worshipped a single god it would worship many * * * Had I begun *On Baile's Strand* or not when I began to imagine, as always at my left side just out of the range of the sight, a brazen winged beast (afterwards described in my poem *The Second Coming*) that I associated with laughing, ecstatic destruction?"
8. Yeats's daughter, Anne Butler Yeats, was born on February 26, 1919.

25   Helen [1] being chosen found life flat and dull
      And later had much trouble from a fool,
      While that great Queen,[2] that rose out of the spray,
      Being fatherless could have her way
      Yet chose a bandy-leggèd smith for man.
30   It's certain that fine women eat
      A crazy salad with their meat,
      Whereby the Horn of Plenty is undone.

      In courtesy I'd have her chiefly learned;
      Hearts are not had as a gift but hearts are earned
35   By those that are not entirely beautiful;
      Yet many, that have played the fool
      For beauty's very self, has charm made wise,
      And many a poor man that has roved,
      Loved and thought himself beloved,
40   From a glad kindness cannot take his eyes.

      May she become a flourishing hidden tree
      That all her thoughts may like the linnet [3] be,
      And have no business but dispensing round
      Their magnanimities of sound,
45   Nor but in merriment begin a chase,
      Nor but in merriment a quarrel.
      Oh, may she live like some green laurel
      Rooted in one dear perpetual place.

      My mind, because the minds that I have loved,
50   The sort of beauty that I have approved,
      Prosper but little, has dried up of late,
      Yet knows that to be choked with hate
      May well be of all evil chances chief.
      If there's no hatred in a mind
55   Assault and battery of the wind
      Can never tear the linnet from the leaf.

      An intellectual hatred is the worst,
      So let her think opinions are accursed.
      Have I not seen the loveliest woman born [4]
60   Out of the mouth of Plenty's horn,
      Because of her opinionated mind
      Barter that horn and every good
      By quiet natures understood
      For an old bellows full of angry wind?

---

1. Helen of Troy, whose beauty was legendary. The daughter of Zeus and Leda, she married Menelaus, brother of the Greek leader, Agamemnon. She was abducted by Paris, son of the king of Troy; the Greeks undertook an expedition to Troy to bring her back, besieged the city for ten years, and finally took it. Helen was reunited with Menelaus.
2. Aphrodite, Greek goddess of love. "Fatherless" in the sense that, in Hesiod's version of the myth, "she sprang from the foam (*aphros*) of the sea that gathered about the severed member of Uranus when Cronos . . . mutilated him" (*Oxford Companion to Classical Literature*). She was married to Hephaestus, the smith, lame from birth, who forged thunderbolts for the gods.
3. Small European bird of the finch family.
4. Doubtless Maud Gonne, whom Yeats had loved hopelessly since meeting her in 1889, and who had married Major John MacBride in 1903; often to Yeats's dismay, she was a very daring activist in the cause of Irish liberation.

65 Considering that, all hatred driven hence,
The soul recovers radical innocence
And learns at last that it is self-delighting,
Self-appeasing, self-affrighting,
And that its own sweet will is Heaven's will;
70 She can, though every face should scowl
And every windy quarter howl
Or every bellows burst, be happy still.

And may her bridegroom bring her to a house
Where all's accustomed, ceremonious;
75 For arrogance and hatred are the wares
Peddled in the thoroughfares.
How but in custom and in ceremony
Are innocence and beauty born?
Ceremony's a name for the rich horn,
80 And custom for the spreading laurel tree.

                                  1919   1921

Leda and the Swan[6]

A sudden blow: the great wings beating still
Above the staggering girl, her thighs caressed
By the dark webs, her nape caught in his bill,
He holds her helpless breast upon his breast.

5 How can those terrified vague fingers push
The feathered glory from her loosening thighs?
And how can body, laid in that white rush,
But feel the strange heart beating where it lies?

A shudder in the loins engenders there
10 The broken wall, the burning roof and tower
And Agamemnon dead.
                              Being so caught up,
So mastered by the brute blood of the air,
Did she put on his knowledge with his power
15 Before the indifferent beak could let her drop?

                                  1923   1924

6. Leda, possessed by Zeus in the guise of a swan, gave birth to Helen of Troy and the twins Castor and Pollux. (Leda was also the mother of Clytemnestra, Agamemnon's wife, who murdered him on his return from the war at Troy.) Helen's abduction by Paris from her husband, Menelaus, brother of Agamemnon, was the cause of the Trojan war. Yeats saw Leda as the recipient of an annunciation that would found Greek civilization, as the Annunciation to Mary would found Christianity.

Sailing to Byzantium[7]

1

That is no country for old men. The young
In one another's arms, birds in the trees
—Those dying generations—at their song,
The salmon-falls, the mackerel-crowded seas,
5 Fish, flesh, or fowl, commend all summer long
Whatever is begotten, born, and dies.
Caught in that sensual music all neglect
Monuments of unaging intellect.

2

An aged man is but a paltry thing,
10 A tattered coat upon a stick, unless
Soul clap its hands and sing, and louder sing
For every tatter in its mortal dress,
Nor is there singing school but studying
Monuments of its own magnificence;
15 And therefore I have sailed the seas and come
To the holy city of Byzantium.

3

O sages standing in God's holy fire
As in the gold mosaic of a wall,
Come from the holy fire, perne in a gyre,[8]
20 And be the singing-masters of my soul.
Consume my heart away; sick with desire
And fastened to a dying animal
It knows not what it is; and gather me
Into the artifice of eternity.

4

25 Once out of nature I shall never take
My bodily form from any natural thing,
But such a form as Grecian goldsmiths make
Of hammered gold and gold enameling

7. Of the ancient city of Byzantium—on the site of modern Istanbul, capital of the Eastern Roman Empire, and the center, especially in the fifth and sixth centuries, of highly developed and characteristic forms of art and architecture—Yeats made a many-faceted symbol, which, since it is a symbol, should not be brought within the limits of too narrowly specific interpretation. Byzantine painting and the mosaics which decorated its churches (Yeats had seen later derivatives of these mosaics in Italy, at Ravenna and elsewhere) were stylized and formal, making no attempt at the full naturalistic rendering of human forms, so that the city and its art can appropriately symbolize a way of life in which art is frankly accepted and proclaimed as artifice. As artifice, as a work of the intellect, this art is not subject to the decay and death which overtake the life of "natural things." But while such an opposition of artifice and nature is central to the poem, there are references to Byzantium in Yeats's prose which suggest the wider range of meaning that the city held for him. In *A Vision*, particularly, he makes of it an exemplar of a civilization which had achieved "Unity of Being": "I think if I could be given a month of Antiquity and leave to spend it where I chose, I would spend it in Byzantium a little before Justinian [who ruled at Byzantium from 527 to 565] opened St. Sophia and closed the Academy of Plato. I think I could find in some little wine-shop some philosophical worker in mosaic who could answer all my questions, the supernatural descending nearer to him than to Plotinus even, for the pride of his delicate skill would make what was an instrument of power to princes and clerics, a murderous madness in the mob, show as a lovely flexible presence like that of a perfect human body * * * I think that in early Byzantium, maybe never before or since in recorded history, religious, aesthetic and practical life were one, that architect and artificers * * * spoke to the multitude and the few alike. The painter, the mosaic worker, the worker in gold and silver, the illuminator of sacred books, were almost impersonal, almost perhaps without the consciousness of individual design, absorbed in their subject-matter and that the vision of a whole people."
8. Out of the noun *pern* (usually *pirn*), a weaver's bobbin, spool, or reel, Yeats makes a verb meaning to move in the spiral pattern taken by thread being unwound from a bobbin or being wound upon it. Here the speaker entreats the sages to descend to him in this manner, to come down into the gyres of history, the cycles of created life, out of their eternity in "the simplicity of fire" where is "all music and all rest." (For "the two realities, the terrestrial and the condition of fire," see *Per Amica Silentia Lunae*, "Anima Mundi," § x.)

To keep a drowsy Emperor awake;
30 Or set upon a golden bough to sing
To lords and ladies of Byzantium
Of what is past, or passing, or to come.

1927

Among School Children

1

I walk through the long schoolroom questioning;
A kind old nun in a white hood replies;
The children learn to cipher and to sing,
To study reading-books and histories,
5 To cut and sew, be neat in everything
In the best modern way—the children's eyes
In momentary wonder stare upon
A sixty-year-old smiling public man.

2

I dream of a Ledaean body,[9] bent
10 Above a sinking fire, a tale that she
Told of a harsh reproof, or trivial event
That changed some childish day to tragedy—
Told, and it seemed that our two natures blent
Into a sphere from youthful sympathy,
15 Or else, to alter Plato's parable,
Into the yoke and white of the one shell.[10]

3

And thinking of that fit of grief or rage
I look upon one child or t'other there
And wonder if she stood so at that age—
20 For even daughters of the swan can share
Something of every paddler's heritage—
And had that color upon cheek or hair,
And thereupon my heart is driven wild:
She stands before me as a living child.

4

25 Her present image floats into the mind—
Did Quattrocento finger[1] fashion it
Hollow of cheek as though it drank the wind
And took a mess of shadows for its meat?
And I though never of Ledaean kind
30 Had pretty plumage once—enough of that,
Better to smile on all that smile, and show
There is a comfortable kind of old scarecrow.

5

What youthful mother, a shape upon her lap
Honey of generation had betrayed,[2]
35 And that must sleep, shriek, struggle to escape

9. I.e., the body of a woman the poet has known and loved and who has seemed to him as beautiful as Leda or her daughter, Helen of Troy.
10. In Plato's *Symposium*, one of the speakers, to explain the origin of human love, recounts the legend according to which human beings were originally double their present form until Zeus, fearful of their power, decided to cut them in two, which he did "as men cut sorb-apples in two when they are preparing them for pickling, or as they cut eggs in two with a hair." Since then, "each of us is * * * but the half of a human being, * * * each is forever seeking his missing half."

1. I.e., the hand of an Italian artist of the fifteenth century.
2. In a note to the poem, Yeats says: "I have taken the 'honey of generation' from Porphyry's essay on 'The Cave of the Nymphs' but find no warrant in Porphyry for considering it the 'drug' that destroys the 'recollection' of pre-natal freedom * * * " In the essay explaining the symbolism of a passage from the Thirteenth Book of the *Odyssey*, Porphyry (ca. A.D. 232–305) makes such statements as that "the sweetness of honey signifies * * * the same thing as the pleasure arising from copulation," the pleasure "which draws souls downward to generation."

As recollection or the drug decide,
Would think her son, did she but see that shape
With sixty or more winters on its head,
A compensation for the pang of his birth,
40   Or the uncertainty of his setting forth?
                    6
Plato thought nature but a spume that plays
Upon a ghostly paradigm of things;[3]
Solider Aristotle played the taws
Upon the bottom of a king of kings;[4]
45   World-famous golden-thighed Pythagoras
Fingered upon a fiddle-stick or strings
What a star sang and careless Muses heard:[5]
Old clothes upon old sticks to scare a bird.
                    7
Both nuns and mothers worship images,
50   But those the candles light are not as those
That animate a mother's reveries,
But keep a marble or a bronze repose.
And yet they too break hearts—O Presences
That passion, piety or affection knows,
55   And that all heavenly glory symbolize—
O self-born mockers of man's enterprise;
                    8
Labor is blossoming or dancing where
The body is not bruised to pleasure soul,
Nor beauty born out of its own despair,
60   Nor blear-eyed wisdom out of midnight oil.
O chestnut-tree, great-rooted blossomer,
Are you the leaf, the blossom or the bole?
O body swayed to music, O brightening glance,
How can we know the dancer from the dance?

                                            1927

At Algeciras[6]—A Meditation Upon Death

The heron-billed pale cattle-birds
That feed on some foul parasite
Of the Moroccan flocks and herds
Cross the narrow straits to light
5   In the rich midnight of the garden trees
Till the dawn break upon those mingled seas.
Often at evening when a boy
Would I carry to a friend—

---

3. In Plato's idealistic philosophy the world of nature, of appearances, that we know is but the copy of a world of ideal, permanently enduring prototypes.
4. The philosophy of Aristotle differed most markedly from that of Plato in that it emphasized the systematic investigation of verifiable phenomena. Aristotle was tutor to the son of King Philip of Macedonia, later Alexander the Great. "Played the taws": whipped.
5. A Greek philosopher (sixth century B.C.), about whom clustered many legends even in his own lifetime, as that he was the incarnation of Apollo, that he had a golden hip- or thigh-bone, and so on. Central to the Pythagorean school of philosophy (along with the doctrine of the transmigration of souls) was the premise that the universe is mathematically regular, which premise had as one of its starting points the Pythagoreans' observations of the exact mathematical relationships underlying musical harmony.
6. A town in Spain, lying across the Straits of Gibraltar (where Atlantic and Mediterranean waters meet) from Spanish Morocco.

Hoping more substantial joy
10 Did an older mind commend—
Not such as are in Newton's metaphor,[7]
But actual shells of Rosses' level shore.[8]

Greater glory in the sun,
An evening chill upon the air,
15 Bid imagination run
Much on the Great Questioner;
What He can question, what if questioned I
Can with a fitting confidence reply.

November 1928   1929

Byzantium[5]

The unpurged images of day recede;
The Emperor's drunken soldiery are abed;
Night resonance recedes, night-walkers' song
After great cathedral gong;
5 A starlit or a moonlit dome disdains[6]
All that man is,
All mere complexities,
The fury and the mire of human veins.

Before me floats an image, man or shade,
10 Shade more than man, more image than a shade;
For Hades' bobbin bound in mummy-cloth
May unwind the winding path;[7]
A mouth that has no moisture and no breath
Breathless mouths may summon;[8]
15 I hail the superhuman;
I call it death-in-life and life-in-death.

7. " 'I seem to have been only like a boy playing on the seashore and diverting myself in now and then finding a smoother pebble, or a prettier shell, than ordinary, whilst the great ocean of truth lay all undiscovered before me' " [Newton, in Brewster's *Memoirs of the Life, Writings and Discoveries of Sir Isaac Newton*, vol. 2, chapter 27].
8. Rosses Point, on Sligo Bay, in the west of Ireland.
5. Under the heading "Subject for a Poem, April 30th," Yeats wrote in his *1930 Diary:* "Describe Byzantium as it is in the system [that is, his system in *A Vision*] towards the end of the first Christian millennium. A walking mummy. Flames at the street corners where the soul is purified, birds of hammered gold singing in the golden trees, in the harbor [dolphins], offering their backs to the wailing dead that they may carry them to Paradise."
6. If the dome is seen as "starlit" at the dark of the moon and as "moonlit" at the full, then these terms may be seen as referring to Phase 1 and Phase 15, respectively, of the twenty-eight phases of the moon in the system of *A Vision*. As Michael Robartes says in *The Phases of the Moon*, "* * * There's no human life at the full or the dark," these being "the superhuman phases," opposite to one another

on the Wheel of Being. Phase 1 is the phase of complete objectivity, the soul being "completely absorbed by its supernatural environment," waiting to be formed, in a state of "complete plasticity." Phase 15 is the state of complete subjectivity, when the soul is completely absorbed in an achieved state, "a phase of complete beauty." Thus, the world of "mere complexities," the world in which man is in a state of becoming, is banished from the poem at the beginning, as the "unpurged images of day" have been banished.
7. The soul and/or body of the dead. The comparison to the bobbin or spindle is at first visual, to describe the figure of the dead, wrapped in a winding-sheet or mummy-cloth, but it also emphasizes the idea that the soul may unwind the thread of its fate by retracing its path, returning to the world to serve as guide, instructor, inspiration.
8. The two lines have been read in two different ways, depending on which of the two phrases ("a mouth * * * " or "breathless mouths * * * ") is seen as subject and which as object of "may summon." Taking "breathless mouths" as subject: mouths of the living, breathless with the intensity of the act of invocation, may call up the mouths of the dead to instruct them.

Miracle, bird or golden handiwork,
More miracle than bird or handiwork,
Planted on the starlit golden bough,
20   Can like the cocks of Hades crow,[9]
Or, by the moon embittered, scorn aloud
In glory of changeless metal
Common bird or petal
And all complexities of mire or blood.

25   At midnight on the Emperor's pavement flit
Flames that no faggot feeds, nor steel has lit,
Nor storm disturbs, flames begotten of flame,
Where blood-begotten spirits come
And all complexities of fury leave,
30   Dying into a dance,
An agony of trance,
An agony of flame that cannot singe a sleeve.

Astraddle on the dolphin's mire and blood,
Spirit after spirit! The smithies break the flood.
35   The golden smithies of the Emperor!
Marbles of the dancing floor
Break bitter furies of complexity,
Those images that yet
Fresh images beget,
That dolphin-torn, that gong-tormented sea.

                                        1930   1932

Lapis Lazuli[1]

(FOR HARRY CLIFTON)

I have heard that hysterical women say
They are sick of the palette and fiddle-bow,
Of poets that are always gay,
For everybody knows or else should know
5   That if nothing drastic is done
Aeroplane and Zeppelin will come out,
Pitch like King Billy[2] bomb-balls in
Until the town lie beaten flat.

All perform their tragic play,
10   There struts Hamlet, there is Lear,
That's Ophelia, that Cordelia;
Yet they, should the last scene be there,

---

9. A symbol of rebirth and resurrection. In a book on Roman sculpture which Yeats is believed to have known, *Apotheosis and After Life* (1915), Mrs. Arthur Strong says: "* * * The great vogue of the cock on later Roman tombstones is due * * * to the fact that as herald of the sun he becomes by an easy transition the herald of rebirth and resurrection." In the next sentence she mentions another visual symbol which figures in the poem's last stanza: "The dolphins and marine monsters, another frequent decoration, form a mystic escort of the dead to the Islands of the Blest * * *"
1. A deep-blue semi-precious stone. In a letter dated July 6, 1935, Yeats wrote, "* * *

Someone has sent me a present of a great piece [of lapis lazuli] carved by some Chinese sculptor into the semblance of a mountain with temple, trees, paths and an ascetic and pupil about to climb the mountain. Ascetic, pupil, hard stone, eternal theme of the sensual east. The heroic cry in the midst of despair. But no, I am wrong, the east has its solutions always and therefore knows nothing of tragedy. It is we, not the east, that must raise the heroic cry."
2. At the Battle of the Boyne on July 1, 1690, William III, king of England since 1689, had defeated the forces of the deposed king, James II.

The great stage curtain about to drop,
If worthy their prominent part in the play,
15   Do not break up their lines to weep.
They know that Hamlet and Lear are gay;
Gaiety transfiguring all that dread.
All men have aimed at, found and lost;
Black out; Heaven blazing into the head:
20   Tragedy wrought to its uttermost.
Though Hamlet rambles and Lear rages,
And all the drop-scenes drop at once
Upon a hundred thousand stages,
It cannot grow by an inch or an ounce.

25   On their own feet they came, or on shipboard,
Camelback, horseback, ass-back, mule-back,
Old civilizations put to the sword.
Then they and their wisdom went to rack:
No handiwork of Callimachus,[3]
30   Who handled marble as if it were bronze,
Made draperies that seemed to rise
When sea-wind swept the corner, stands;
His long lamp-chimney shaped like the stem
Of a slender palm, stood but a day;
35   All things fall and are built again,
And those that build them again are gay.

Two Chinamen, behind them a third,
Are carved in lapis lazuli,
Over them flies a long-legged bird,
40   A symbol of longevity;
The third, doubtless a serving-man,
Carries a musical instrument.

Every discoloration of the stone,
Every accidental crack or dent,
45   Seems a water-course or an avalanche,
Or lofty slope where it still snows
Though doubtless plum or cherry-branch
Sweetens the little half-way house
Those Chinamen climb towards, and I
50   Delight to imagine them seated there;
There, on the mountain and the sky,
On all the tragic scene they stare.
One asks for mournful melodies;
Accomplished fingers begin to play.
55   Their eyes mid many wrinkles, their eyes,
Their ancient, glittering eyes, are gay.

1938

3. Greek sculptor of the fifth century B.C., of whom Yeats says in *A Vision* that only one example of his work remains, a marble chair, and goes on to mention "that bronze lamp [in the Erechtheum, a temple of the guardian deities of Athens] shaped like a palm, known to us by a description in Pausanias * * *"

Long-Legged Fly

That civilization may not sink,
Its great battle lost,
Quiet the dog, tether the pony
To a distant post;
5 Our master Caesar is in the tent
Where the maps are spread,
His eyes fixed upon nothing,
A hand under his head.
Like a long-legged fly upon the stream
10 *His mind moves upon silence.*

That the topless towers be burnt
And men recall that face,[4]
Move most gently if move you must
In this lonely place.
15 She thinks, part woman, three parts a child,
That nobody looks; her feet
Practice a tinker shuffle
Picked up on a street.
Like a long-legged fly upon the stream
20 *Her mind moves upon silence.*

That girls at puberty may find
The first Adam in their thought,
Shut the door of the Pope's chapel,[5]
Keep those children out.
25 There on that scaffolding reclines
Michael Angelo.
With no more sound than the mice make
His hand moves to and fro.
Like a long-legged fly upon the stream
30 *His mind moves upon silence.*

1939

Under Ben Bulben[6]

1

Swear by what the sages spoke
Round the Mareotic Lake[7]
That the Witch of Atlas knew,
Spoke and set the cocks a-crow.[8]

---

4. An echo of Marlowe's lines on Helen of Troy in *Dr. Faustus:* "Was this the face that launched a thousand ships, / And burnt the topless towers of Ilium?"
5. On the ceiling of the Sistine Chapel, so called because it was built under Pope Sixtus IV, Michelangelo painted a series of biblical scenes, including the creation of Adam.
6. A mountain in County Sligo, in the west of Ireland, which overlooks Drumcliff Churchyard, where Yeats is buried. The last three lines of the poem are carved on his tombstone.
7. Lake Mareotis, a salt lake in northern Egypt, near which the members of the Thebaid, among them St. Anthony (A.D. 251–356) had withdrawn to contemplation. About the The-

baid, in his *1930 Diary,* Yeats wrote, "* * * men went on pilgrimage to Saint Anthony that they might learn about their spiritual states, what was about to happen and why it happened, and Saint Anthony would reply neither out of traditional casuistry nor common sense but from spiritual powers."
8. In Shelley's poem *The Witch of Atlas,* the protagonist, a spirit of love, beauty, and freedom, visits Egypt and the Mareotic Lake in the course of her magic journeyings. The knowledge and belief that Yeats describes as common to her and to the sages "set the cocks a-crow" in the sense that, like "the cocks of Hades" and the golden bird in *Byzantium,* they summon to a spiritual rebirth.

5   Swear by those horsemen, by those women
    Complexion and form prove superhuman,
    That pale, long-visaged company
    That air in immortality
    Completeness of their passions won;
10 Now they ride the wintry dawn
    Where Ben Bulben sets the scene.[9]

    Here's the gist of what they mean.

2

    Many times man lives and dies
    Between his two eternities,
15 That of race and that of soul,
    And ancient Ireland knew it all.
    Whether man die in his bed
    Or the rifle knocks him dead,
    A brief parting from those dear
20 Is the worst man has to fear.
    Though gravediggers' toil is long,
    Sharp their spades, their muscles strong,
    They but thrust their buried men
    Back in the human mind again.

3

25 You that Mitchel's prayer have heard,
    "Send war in our time, O Lord!"[1]
    Know that when all words are said
    And a man is fighting mad,
    Something drops from eyes long blind,
30 He completes his partial mind,
    For an instant stands at ease,
    Laughs aloud, his heart at peace.
    Even the wisest man grows tense
    With some sort of violence
35 Before he can accomplish fate,
    Know his work or choose his mate.

4

    Poet and sculptor, do the work,
    Nor let the modish painter shirk
    What his great forefathers did,
40 Bring the soul of man to God,
    Make him fill the cradles right.

    Measurement began our might:[2]
    Forms a stark Egyptian thought,
    Forms that gentler Phidias wrought.
45 Michael Angelo left a proof
    On the Sistine Chapel roof,
    Where but half-awakened Adam

---

9. In another late poem, *Alternative Song for the Severed Head in "The King of the Great Clock Tower,"* Yeats re-introduces some of the Irish mythological or legendary heroes and heroines who figure in his early poems—Cuchulain, Niam, and others—with whom the supernatural riders of these lines may be identified.
1. John Mitchel (1815–75), the Irish patriot, wrote in his *Jail Journal, or Five Years in British Prisons* (published in New York, 1854): "Czar, I bless thee, I kiss the hem of thy garment. I drink to thy health and longevity. Give us war in our time, O Lord" [Quoted by T. R. Henn, *The Lonely Tower*].
2. The achievements of Western civilization—now, according to the poem, being challenged or destroyed—began with the exact mathematical rules which the Egyptians followed in working out the proportions of their sculptured figures—rules which Phidias (line 44), the great Greek sculptor of the fifth century B.C., used, and which have been implicit in the greatest Western art up to the present, when "confusion [falls] upon our thought."

Can disturb globe-trotting Madam
Till her bowels are in heat,
50 Proof that there's a purpose set
Before the secret working mind:
Profane perfection of mankind.

Quattrocento[3] put in paint
On backgrounds for a God or Saint
55 Gardens where a soul's at ease;
Where everything that meets the eye,
Flowers and grass and cloudless sky,
Resemble forms that are or seem
When sleepers wake and yet still dream,
60 And when it's vanished still declare,
With only bed and bedstead there,
That heavens had opened.

Gyres[4] run on;
When that greater dream had gone
65 Calvert and Wilson, Blake and Claude,
Prepared a rest for the people of God,
Palmer's phrase, but after that[5]
Confusion fell upon our thought.

5
Irish poets, learn your trade,
70 Sing whatever is well made,
Scorn the sort now growing up
All out of shape from toe to top,
Their unremembering hearts and heads
Base-born products of base beds.
75 Sing the peasantry, and then
Hard-riding country gentlemen,
The holiness of monks, and after
Porter-drinkers' randy laughter;
Sing the lords and ladies gay
80 That were beaten into the clay
Through seven heroic centuries;
Cast your mind on other days
That we in coming days may be
Still the indomitable Irishry.

6
85 Under bare Ben Bulben's head
In Drumcliff churchyard Yeats is laid.
An ancestor was rector there
Long years ago, a church stands near,
By the road an ancient cross.
90 No marble, no conventional phrase;
On limestone quarried near the spot
By his command these words are cut:

Cast a cold eye
On life, on death.
95 *Horseman, pass by!*

September 4, 1938   1939

3. The Italian fifteenth century.
4. I.e., the cycles of history.
5. The verse paragraph assembles five artists
who had provided Yeats with images and with
ideals of what art should be. Claude Lorrain
(1600–82), the great French landscape painter,
was a central standard for landscape painters
up to the early 19th century, including those
mentioned here, especially Richard Wilson
(1714–82). Edward Calvert (1799–1883) and
Samuel Palmer (1805–81), visionaries, land-
scape painters, and engravers, had found in-
spiration in many aspects of Blake's life and
work.

EDWIN ARLINGTON ROBINSON
(1869–1935)

Reuben Bright

Because he was a butcher and thereby
Did earn an honest living (and did right),
I would not have you think that Reuben Bright
Was any more a brute than you or I;
5 For when they told him that his wife must die,
He stared at them, and shook with grief and fright,
And cried like a great baby half that night,
And made the women cry to see him cry.

And after she was dead, and he had paid
10 The singers and the sexton and the rest,
He packed a lot of things that she had made
Most mournfully away in an old chest
Of hers, and put some chopped-up cedar boughs
In with them, and tore down the slaughter-house.

1897

Miniver Cheevy

Miniver Cheevy, child of scorn,
    Grew lean while he assailed the seasons;
He wept that he was ever born,
    And he had reasons.

5 Miniver loved the days of old
    When swords were bright and steeds were prancing;
The vision of a warrior bold
    Would set him dancing.

Miniver sighed for what was not,
10   And dreamed, and rested from his labors;
He dreamed of Thebes and Camelot,
    And Priam's neighbors.[1]

Miniver mourned the ripe renown
    That made so many a name so fragrant;
15 He mourned Romance, now on the town,
    And Art, a vagrant.

Miniver loved the Medici,[2]
    Albeit he had never seen one;
He would have sinned incessantly
20   Could he have been one.

1. Thebes was a Greek city, anciently famous in history and legend; Camelot is said to have been the site of King Arthur's court; Priam was king of Troy during the Trojan War.

2. A family of merchant-princes of the Italian Renaissance, rulers of Florence for nearly two centuries; they were known both for cruelty and for their support of learning and art.

Miniver cursed the commonplace
    And eyed a khaki suit with loathing;
He missed the medieval grace
    Of iron clothing.

25   Miniver scorned the gold he sought,
    But sore annoyed was he without it;
Miniver thought, and thought, and thought,
    And thought about it.

Miniver Cheevy, born too late,
30   Scratched his head and kept on thinking;
Miniver coughed, and called it fate,
    And kept on drinking.

New England

1910

Here where the wind is always north-north-east
And children learn to walk on frozen toes,
Wonder begets an envy of all those
Who boil elsewhere with such a lyric yeast
5   Of love that you will hear them at a feast
Where demons would appeal for some repose,
Still clamoring where the chalice overflows
And crying wildest who have drunk the least.

Passion is here a soilure of the wits,
10   We're told, and Love a cross for them to bear;
Joy shivers in the corner where she knits
And Conscience always has the rocking-chair,
Cheerful as when she tortured into fits
The first cat that was ever killed by Care.

1925

PAUL LAURENCE DUNBAR
(1872–1906)

Ere Sleep Comes Down to Soothe the Weary Eyes

Ere sleep comes down to soothe the weary eyes,
    Which all the day with ceaseless care have sought
The magic gold which from the seeker flies;
    Ere dreams put on the gown and cap of thought,
5   And make the waking world a world of lies—
    Of lies most palpable, uncouth, forlorn,
That say life's full of aches and tears and sighs—
    Oh, how with more than dreams the soul is torn,
Ere sleep comes down to soothe the weary eyes.

10   Ere sleep comes down to soothe the weary eyes,
    How all the griefs and heartaches we have known
Come up like pois'nous vapors that arise
    From some base witch's caldron, when the crone,
To work some potent spell, her magic plies.

15 The past which held its share of bitter pain,
Whose ghost we prayed that Time might exorcise,
Comes up, is lived and suffered o'er again,
Ere sleep comes down to soothe the weary eyes.

Ere sleep comes down to soothe the weary eyes,
20 What phantoms fill the dimly lighted room;
What ghostly shades in awe-creating guise
Are bodied forth within the teeming gloom.
What echoes faint of sad and soul-sick cries,
And pangs of vague inexplicable pain
25 That pay the spirit's ceaseless enterprise,
Come thronging through the chambers of the brain,
Ere sleep comes down to soothe the weary eyes.

Ere sleep comes down to soothe the weary eyes,
Where ranges forth the spirit far and free?
30 Through what strange realms and unfamiliar skies
Tends her far course to lands of mystery?
To lands unspeakable—beyond surmise,
Where shapes unknowable to being spring,
Till, faint of wing, the Fancy fails and dies
35 Much wearied with the spirit's journeying,
Ere sleep comes down to soothe the weary eyes.

Ere sleep comes down to soothe the weary eyes,
How questioneth the soul that other soul—
The inner sense which neither cheats nor lies,
40 But self exposes unto self, a scroll
Full writ with all life's acts unwise or wise,
In characters indelible and known;
So, trembling with the shock of sad surprise,
The soul doth view its awful self alone,
45 Ere sleep comes down to soothe the weary eyes.

When sleep comes down to seal the weary eyes,
The last dear sleep whose soft embrace is balm,
And whom sad sorrow teaches us to prize
For kissing all our passions into calm,
50 Ah, then, no more we heed the sad world's cries,
Or seek to probe th' eternal mystery,
Or fret our souls at long-withheld replies,
At glooms through which our visions cannot see,
When sleep comes down to seal the weary eyes.

1896

When Malindy Sings

G'way an' quit dat noise, Miss Lucy—
Put dat music book away;
What's de use to keep on tryin'?
Ef you practise twell you're gray,
5 You cain't sta't no notes a-flyin'
Lak de ones dat rants and rings
F'om de kitchen to de big woods
When Malindy sings.

10 You ain't got de nachel o'gans
        Fu' to make de soun' come right,
    You ain't got de tu'ns an' twistin's
        Fu' to make it sweet an' light.
    Tell you one thing now, Miss Lucy,
        An' I'm tellin' you fu' true,
15 When hit comes to raal right singin',
        'T ain't no easy thing to do.

    Easy 'nough fu' folks to hollah,
        Lookin' at de lines an' dots,
    When dey ain't no one kin sence it,
20   An' de chune comes in, in spots;
    But fu' real melojous music,
        Dat jes' strikes yo' hea't and clings,
    Jes' you stan' an' listen wif me
        When Malindy sings.

25 Ain't you nevah hyeahd Malindy?
        Blessed soul, tek up de cross!
    Look hyeah, ain't you jokin', honey?
        Well, you don't know whut you los'.
    Y' ought to hyeah dat gal a-wa'blin',
30   Robins, la'ks, an' all dem things,
    Heish dey moufs an' hides dey face.
        When Malindy sings.

    Fiddlin' man jes' stop his fiddlin',
        Lay his fiddle on de she'f;
35 Mockin'-bird quit tryin' to whistle,
        'Cause he jes' so shamed hisse'f.
    Folks a-playin' on de banjo
        Draps dey fingahs on de strings—
    Bless yo' soul—fu' gits to move em,
40   When Malindy sings.

    She jes' spreads huh mouf and hollahs,
        "Come to Jesus," twell you hyeah
    Sinnahs' tremblin' steps and voices
        Timid-lak a-drawin' neah;
45 Den she tu'ns to "Rock of Ages,"
        Simply to de cross she clings,
    An' you fin' yo' teahs a-drappin'
        When Malindy sings.

    Who dat says dat humble praises
50   Wif de Master nevah counts?
    Heish yo' mouf, I hyeah dat music,
        Ez hit rises up an' mounts—
    Floatin' by de hills an' valleys,
        Way above dis buryin' sod,
55 Ez hit makes its way in glory
        To de very gates of God!

    Oh, hit's sweetah dan de music
        Of an edicated band;
    An' hit's dearah dan de battle's

60   Song o' triumph in de lan'.
    It seems holier dan evenin'
        When de solemn chu'ch bell rings,
    Ez I sit an' ca'mly listen
        While Malindy sings.

65   Towsah, stop dat ba'kin', hyeah me!
        Mandy, mek dat chile keep still;
    Don't you hyeah de echoes callin'
        F'om de valley to de hill?
    Let me listen, I can hyeah it,
70   Th'oo de bresh of angels' wings,
    Sof' an' sweet, "Swing Low,
        Sweet Chariot,"
    Ez Malindy sings.

                                              1896

WALTER DE LA MARE
(1873–1956)

The Keys of Morning

    While at her bedroom window once,
        Learning her task for school,
    Little Louisa lonely sat
        In the morning clear and cool,
5   She slanted her small bead-brown eyes
        Across the empty street,
    And saw Death softly watching her
        In the sunshine pale and sweet.

    His was a long lean sallow face;
10   He sat with half-shut eyes,
    Like an old sailor in a ship
        Becalmed 'neath tropic skies.
    Beside him in the dust he had set
        His staff and shady hat;
15   These, peeping small, Louisa saw
        Quite clearly where she sat—
    The thinness of his coal-black locks,
        His hands so long and lean
    They scarcely seemed to grasp at all
20   The keys that hung between:
    Both were of gold, but one was small,
        And with this last did he
    Wag in the air, as if to say,
        "Come hither, child, to me!"

25   Louisa laid her lesson book
        On the cold window-sill;
    And in the sleepy sunshine house
        Went softly down, until
    She stood in the half-opened door,
30   And peeped. But strange to say,
    Where Death just now had sunning sat
        Only a shadow lay:

Just the tall chimney's round-topped cowl,
   And the small sun behind,
35 Had with its shadow in the dust
   Called sleepy Death to mind.
But most she thought how strange it was
   Two keys that he should bear,
And that, when beckoning, he should wag
40   The littlest in the air.

                                                     1912

Goodbye

The last of last words spoken is Goodbye—
The last dismantled flower in the weed-grown hedge,
The last thin rumor of a feeble bell far ringing,
The last blind rat to spurn the mildewed rye.

5 A hardening darkness glasses the haunted eye,
Shines into nothing the watcher's burnt-out candle,
Wreathes into scentless nothing the wasting incense,
Faints in the outer silence the hunting-cry.

Love of its muted music breathes no sigh,
10 Thought in her ivory tower gropes in her spinning,
Toss on in vain the whispering trees of Eden,
Last of all last words spoken is Goodbye.

                                                   1921

Away

There is no sorrow
Time heals never;
No loss, betrayal,
Beyond repair.
5 Balm for the soul, then,
Though grave shall sever
Lover from loved
And all they share;
See, the sweet sun shines,
10 The shower is over,
Flowers preen their beauty,
The day how fair!
Brood not too closely
On love, or duty;
15 Friends long forgotten
May wait you where
Life with death
Brings all to an issue;
None will long mourn for you,
20 Pray for you, miss you,
Your place left vacant,
You not there.

                                                   1938

ROBERT FROST
(1874–1963)

Mending Wall

Something there is that doesn't love a wall,
That sends the frozen-ground-swell under it
And spills the upper boulders in the sun,
And makes gaps even two can pass abreast.
5 The work of hunters is another thing:
I have come after them and made repair
Where they have left not one stone on a stone,
But they would have the rabbit out of hiding,
To please the yelping dogs. The gaps I mean,
10 No one has seen them made or heard them made,
But at spring mending-time we find them there.
I let my neighbor know beyond the hill;
And on a day we meet to walk the line
And set the wall between us once again.
15 We keep the wall between us as we go.
To each the boulders that have fallen to each.
And some are loaves and some so nearly balls
We have to use a spell to make them balance:
'Stay where you are until our backs are turned!'
20 We wear our fingers rough with handling them.
Oh, just another kind of outdoor game,
One on a side. It comes to little more:
There where it is we do not need the wall:
He is all pine and I am apple orchard.
25 My apple trees will never get across
And eat the cones under his pines, I tell him.
He only says, 'Good fences make good neighbors.'
Spring is the mischief in me, and I wonder
If I could put a notion in his head:
30 '*Why* do they make good neighbors? Isn't it
Where there are cows? But here there are no cows.
Before I built a wall I'd ask to know
What I was walling in or walling out,
And to whom I was like to give offense.
35 Something there is that doesn't love a wall,
That wants it down.' I could say 'Elves' to him,
But it's not elves exactly, and I'd rather
He said it for himself. I see him there,
Bringing a stone grasped firmly by the top
40 In each hand, like an old-stone savage armed.
He moves in darkness as it seems to me,
Not of woods only and the shade of trees.
He will not go behind his father's saying,
And he likes having thought of it so well
45 He says again, 'Good fences make good neighbors.'

1914

The Wood-Pile

Out walking in the frozen swamp one gray day,
I paused and said, 'I will turn back from here.
No, I will go on farther—and we shall see.'
The hard snow held me, save where now and then
5 One foot went through. The view was all in lines
Straight up and down of tall slim trees
Too much alike to mark or name a place by
So as to say for certain I was here
Or somewhere else: I was just far from home.
10 A small bird flew before me. He was careful
To put a tree between us when he lighted,
And say no word to tell me who he was
Who was so foolish as to think what *he* thought.
He thought that I was after him for a feather—
15 The white one in his tail; like one who takes
Everything said as personal to himself.
One flight out sideways would have undeceived him.
And then there was a pile of wood for which
I forgot him and let his little fear
20 Carry him off the way I might have gone,
Without so much as wishing him good-night.
He went behind it to make his last stand.
It was a cord of maple, cut and split
And piled—and measured, four by four by eight.
25 And not another like it could I see.
No runner tracks in this year's snow looped near it.
And it was older sure than this year's cutting,
Or even last year's or the year's before.
The wood was gray and the bark warping off it
30 And the pile somewhat sunken. Clematis
Had wound strings round and round it like a bundle.
What held it, though, on one side was a tree
Still growing, and on one a stake and prop,
These latter about to fall. I thought that only
35 Someone who lived in turning to fresh tasks
Could so forget his handiwork in which
He spent himself, the labor of his axe,
And leave it there far from a useful fireplace
To warm the frozen swamp as best it could
40 With the slow smokeless burning of decay.

1914

The Oven Bird

There is a singer everyone has heard,
Loud, a mid-summer and a mid-wood bird,
Who makes the solid tree trunks sound again.
He says that leaves are old and that for flowers
5 Mid-summer is to spring as one to ten.
He says the early petal-fall is past
When pear and cherry bloom went down in showers
On sunny days a moment overcast;
And comes that other fall we name the fall.

¹⁰ He says the highway dust is over all.
The bird would cease and be as other birds
But that he knows in singing not to sing.
The question that he frames in all but words
Is what to make of a diminished thing.

1916

Birches

When I see birches bend to left and right
Across the lines of straighter darker trees,
I like to think some boy's been swinging them.
But swinging doesn't bend them down to stay
⁵ As ice-storms do. Often you must have seen them
Loaded with ice a sunny winter morning
After a rain. They click upon themselves
As the breeze rises, and turn many-colored
As the stir cracks and crazes their enamel.
¹⁰ Soon the sun's warmth makes them shed crystal shells
Shattering and avalanching on the snowcrust—
Such heaps of broken glass to sweep away
You'd think the inner dome of heaven had fallen.
They are dragged to the withered bracken by the load,
¹⁵ And they seem not to break; though once they are bowed
So low for long, they never right themselves:
You may see their trunks arching in the woods
Years afterwards, trailing their leaves on the ground
Like girls on hands and knees that throw their hair
²⁰ Before them over their heads to dry in the sun.
But I was going to say when Truth broke in
With all her matter of fact about the ice-storm
I should prefer to have some boy bend them
As he went out and in to fetch the cows—
²⁵ Some boy too far from town to learn baseball,
Whose only play was what he found himself,
Summer or winter, and could play alone.
One by one he subdued his father's trees
By riding them down over and over again
³⁰ Until he took the stiffness out of them,
And not one but hung limp, not one was left
For him to conquer. He learned all there was
To learn about not launching out too soon
And so not carrying the tree away
³⁵ Clear to the ground. He always kept his poise
To the top branches, climbing carefully
With the same pains you use to fill a cup
Up to the brim, and even above the brim.
Then he flung outward, feet first, with a swish,
⁴⁰ Kicking his way down through the air to the ground.
So was I once myself a swinger of birches.
And so I dream of going back to be.
It's when I'm weary of considerations,
And life is too much like a pathless wood
⁴⁵ Where your face burns and tickles with the cobwebs
Broken across it, and one eye is weeping
From a twig's having lashed across it open.

I'd like to get away from earth awhile
And then come back to it and begin over.
50 May no fate willfully misunderstand me
And half grant what I wish and snatch me away
Not to return. Earth's the right place for love:
I don't know where it's likely to go better.
I'd like to go by climbing a birch tree,
55 And climb black branches up a snow-white trunk
Toward heaven, till the tree could bear no more,
But dipped its top and set me down again.
That would be good both going and coming back.
One could do worse than be a swinger of birches.

1916

Range-Finding

The battle rent a cobweb diamond-strung
And cut a flower beside a ground bird's nest
Before it stained a single human breast.
The stricken flower bent double and so hung.
5 And still the bird revisited her young.
A butterfly its fall had dispossessed
A moment sought in air his flower of rest,
Then lightly stooped to it and fluttering clung.
On the bare upland pasture there had spread
10 O'ernight 'twixt mullein stalks a wheel of thread
And straining cables wet with silver dew.
A sudden passing bullet shook it dry.
The indwelling spider ran to greet the fly,
But finding nothing, sullenly withdrew.

1916

The Hill Wife

I. *Loneliness*
HER WORD

One ought not to have to care
    So much as you and I
Care when the birds come round the house
    To seem to say good-by;

5 Or care so much when they come back
    With whatever it is they sing;
The truth being we are as much
    Too glad for the one thing

As we are too sad for the other here—
10   With birds that fill their breasts
But with each other and themselves
    And their built or driven nests.

II. *House Fear*

Always—I tell you this they learned—
Always at night when they returned
To the lonely house from far away,

To lamps unlighted and fire gone gray,
5 They learned to rattle the lock and key
To give whatever might chance to be,
Warning and time to be off in flight:
And preferring the out- to the in-door night,
They learned to leave the housedoor wide
10 Until they had lit the lamp inside.

III. The Smile
HER WORD

I didn't like the way he went away.
That smile! It never came of being gay.
Still he smiled—did you see him?—I was sure!
Perhaps because we gave him only bread
5 And the wretch knew from that that we were poor.
Perhaps because he let us give instead
Of seizing from us as he might have seized.
Perhaps he mocked at us for being wed,
Or being very young (and he was pleased
10 To have a vision of us old and dead).
I wonder how far down the road he's got.
He's watching from the woods as like as not.

IV. The Oft-Repeated Dream

She had no saying dark enough
    For the dark pine that kept
Forever trying the windowlatch
    Of the room where they slept.

5 The tireless but ineffectual hands
    That with every futile pass
Made the great tree seem as a little bird
    Before the mystery of glass!

It never had been inside the room,
10   And only one of the two
Was afraid in an oft-repeated dream
    Of what the tree might do.

V. The Impulse

It was too lonely for her there,
    And too wild,
And since there were but two of them,
    And no child,

5 And work was little in the house,
    She was free,
And followed where he furrowed field,
    Or felled tree.

She rested on a log and tossed
10   The fresh chips,
With a song only to herself
    On her lips.

And once she went to break a bough
　　Of black alder.
15　She strayed so far she scarcely heard
　　When he called her—

And didn't answer—didn't speak—
　　Or return.
She stood, and then she ran and hid
20　　In the fern.

He never found her, though he looked
　　Everywhere,
And he asked at her mother's house
　　Was she there.

25　Sudden and swift and light as that
　　The ties gave,
And he learned of finalities
　　Besides the grave.

　　　　　　　　　　　　　　　1916

The Aim Was Song

Before man came to blow it right
　　The wind once blew itself untaught,
And did its loudest day and night
　　In any rough place where it caught.

5　Man came to tell it what was wrong:
　　It hadn't found the place to blow;
It blew too hard—the aim was song.
　　And listen—how it ought to go!

He took a little in his mouth,
10　　And held it long enough for north
To be converted into south,
　　And then by measure blew it forth.

By measure. It was word and note,
　　The wind the wind had meant to be—
15　A little through the lips and throat.
　　The aim was song—the wind could see.

　　　　　　　　　　　　　　　1923

Stopping by Woods on a Snowy Evening

Whose woods these are I think I know,
His house is in the village, though;
He will not see me stopping here
To watch his woods fill up with snow.

5　My little horse must think it queer
To stop without a farmhouse near
Between the woods and frozen lake
The darkest evening of the year.

He gives his harness bells a shake
10 To ask if there is some mistake.
The only other sound's the sweep
Of easy wind and downy flake.

The woods are lovely, dark, and deep,
But I have promises to keep,
15 And miles to go before I sleep,
And miles to go before I sleep.

1923

To Earthward

Love at the lips was touch
As sweet as I could bear;
And once that seemed too much;
I lived on air

5   That crossed me from sweet things,
The flow of—was it musk
From hidden grapevine springs
Downhill at dusk?

I had the swirl and ache
10 From sprays of honeysuckle
That when they're gathered shake
Dew on the knuckle.

I craved strong sweets, but those
Seemed strong when I was young;
15 The petal of the rose
It was that stung.

Now no joy but lacks salt
That is not dashed with pain
And weariness and fault;
20 I crave the stain

Of tears, the aftermark
Of almost too much love,
The sweet of bitter bark
And burning clove.

25 When stiff and sore and scarred
I take away my hand
From leaning on it hard
In grass and sand,

The hurt is not enough:
30 I long for weight and strength
To feel the earth as rough
To all my length.

1923

Spring Pools

These pools that, though in forests, still reflect
The total sky almost without defect,
And like the flowers beside them, chill and shiver,
Will the flowers beside them soon be gone,
5 And yet not out by any brook or river,
But up by roots to bring dark foliage on.
The trees that have it in their pent-up buds
To darken nature and be summer woods—
Let them think twice before they use their powers
10 To blot out and drink up and sweep away
These flowery waters and these watery flowers
From snow that melted only yesterday.

1928

West-running Brook

"Fred, where is north?"

                    "North? North is there, my love.
The brook runs west."

                    "West-running Brook then call it."
(West-running Brook men call it to this day.)
"What does it think it's doing running west
5 When all the other country brooks flow east
To reach the ocean? It must be the brook
Can trust itself to go by contraries
The way I can with you—and you with me—
Because we're—we're—I don't know what we are.
What are we?"

                    "Young or new?"

10   "We must be something.
We've said we two. Let's change that to we three.
As you and I are married to each other,
We'll both be married to the brook. We'll build
Our bridge across it, and the bridge shall be
15 Our arm thrown over it asleep beside it.
Look, look, it's waving to us with a wave
To let us know it hears me."

                    "Why, my dear,
That wave's been standing off this jut of shore—"
(The black stream, catching on a sunken rock,
20 Flung backward on itself in one white wave,
And the white water rode the black forever,
Not gaining but not losing, like a bird
White feathers from the struggle of whose breast
Flecked the dark stream and flecked the darker pool

25 Below the point, and were at last driven wrinkled
In a white scarf against the far-shore alders.)
"That wave's been standing off this jut of shore
Ever since rivers, I was going to say,
Were made in heaven. It wasn't waved to us."

30 "It wasn't, yet it was. If not to you
It was to me—in an annunciation."

"Oh, if you take it off to lady-land,
As't were the country of the Amazons[1]
We men must see you to the confines of
35 And leave you there, ourselves forbid to enter—
It is your brook! I have no more to say."

"Yes, you have, too. Go on. You thought of something."

"Speaking of contraries, see how the brook
In that white wave runs counter to itself.
40 It is from that in water we were from
Long, long before we were from any creature.
Here we, in our impatience of the steps,
Get back to the beginning of beginnings,
The stream of everything that runs away.
45 Some say existence like a Pirouot
And Pirouette, forever in one place,
Stands still and dances, but it runs away;
It seriously, sadly, runs away
To fill the abyss's void with emptiness.
50 It flows beside us in this water brook,
But it flows over us. It flows between us
To separate us for a panic moment.
It flows between us, over us, and *with* us.
And it is time, strength, tone, light, life and love—
55 And even substance lapsing unsubstantial;
The universal cataract of death
That spends to nothingness—and unresisted,
Save by some strange resistance in itself,
Not just a swerving, but a throwing back,
60 As if regret were in it and were sacred.
It has this throwing backward on itself
So that the fall of most of it is always
Raising a little, sending up a little.
Our life runs down in sending up the clock.
65 The brook runs down in sending up our life.
The sun runs down in sending up the brook.
And there is something sending up the sun.
It is this backward motion toward the source,
Against the stream, that most we see ourselves in,
70 The tribute of the current to the source.
It is from this in nature we are from.
It is most us."

---

1. Legendary female warriors who inhabited a country without men.

"Today will be the day
You said so."

"No, today will be the day
You said the brook was called West-running Brook."

75 "Today will be the day of what we both said."

1928

A Lone Striker

The swinging mill bell changed its rate
To tolling like the count of fate,
And though at that the tardy ran,
One failed to make the closing gate.
5   There was a law of God or man
That on the one who came too late
The gate for half an hour be locked,
His time be lost, his pittance docked.
He stood rebuked and unemployed.
10 The straining mill began to shake.
The mill, though many–many-eyed,
Had eyes inscrutably opaque;
So that he couldn't look inside
To see if some forlorn machine
15 Was standing idle for his sake.
(He couldn't hope its heart would break.)

And yet he thought he saw the scene:
The air was full of dust of wool.
A thousand yarns were under pull,
20 But pull so slow, with such a twist,
All day from spool to lesser spool,
It seldom overtaxed their strength;
They safely grew in slender length.
And if one broke by any chance,
25 The spinner saw it at a glance.
The spinner still was there to spin.
That's where the human still came in.
Her deft hand showed with finger rings
Among the harp-like spread of strings.
30 She caught the pieces end to end
And, with a touch that never missed,
Not so much tied as made them blend.
Man's ingenuity was good.
He saw it plainly where he stood,
35 Yet found it easy to resist.

He knew another place, a wood,
And in it, tall as trees, were cliffs;
And if he stood on one of these,
'Twould be among the tops of trees,
40 Their upper branches round him wreathing,
Their breathing mingled with his breathing.
If—if he stood! Enough of ifs!

He knew a path that wanted walking;
He knew a spring that wanted drinking;
45 A thought that wanted further thinking;
A love that wanted re-renewing.
Nor was this just a way of talking
To save him the expense of doing.
With him it boded action, deed.

50 The factory was very fine;
He wished it all the modern speed.
Yet, after all, 'twas not divine,
That is to say, 'twas not a church.
He never would assume that he'd
55 Be any institution's need.
But he said then and still would say
If there should ever come a day
When industry seemed like to die
Because he left it in the lurch,
60 Or even merely seemed to pine
For want of his approval, why,
Come get him—they knew where to search.

1936

The Strong Are Saying Nothing

The soil now gets a rumpling soft and damp,
And small regard to the future of any weed.
The final flat of the hoe's approval stamp
Is reserved for the bed of a few selected seed.

5 There is seldom more than a man to a harrowed piece.
Men work alone, their lots plowed far apart,
One stringing a chain of seed in an open crease,
And another stumbling after a halting cart.

To the fresh and black of the squares of early mould
10 The leafless bloom of a plum is fresh and white;
Though there's more than a doubt if the weather is not too cold
For the bees to come and serve its beauty aright.

Wind goes from farm to farm in wave on wave,
But carries no cry of what is hoped to be.
15 There may be little or much beyond the grave,
But the strong are saying nothing until they see.

1936

Neither Out Far Nor In Deep

The people along the sand
All turn and look one way.
They turn their back on the land.
They look at the sea all day.

5 As long as it takes to pass
A ship keeps raising its hull;
The wetter ground like glass
Reflects a standing gull.

The land may vary more;
10   But wherever the truth may be—
The water comes ashore,
And the people look at the sea.

They cannot look out far.
They cannot look in deep.
15   But when was that ever a bar
To any watch they keep?

1936

Design

I found a dimpled spider, fat and white,
On a white heal-all,[2] holding up a moth
Like a white piece of rigid satin cloth—
Assorted characters of death and blight
5   Mixed ready to begin the morning right,
Like the ingredients of a witches' broth—
A snow-drop spider, a flower like froth,
And dead wings carried like a paper kite.

What had that flower to do with being white,
10   The wayside blue and innocent heal-all?
What brought the kindred spider to that height,
Then steered the white moth thither in the night?
What but design of darkness to appall?—
If design govern in a thing so small.

1936

Never Again Would Birds' Song Be the Same

He would declare and could himself believe
That the birds there in all the garden round
From having heard the daylong voice of Eve
Had added to their own an oversound,
5   Her tone of meaning but without the words.
Admittedly an eloquence so soft
Could only have had an influence on birds
When call or laughter carried it aloft.
Be that as may be, she was in their song.
10   Moreover her voice upon their voices crossed
Had now persisted in the woods so long
That probably it never would be lost.
Never again would birds' song be the same.
And to do that to birds was why she came.

1942

The Gift Outright

The land was ours before we were the land's.
She was our land more than a hundred years
Before we were her people. She was ours
In Massachusetts, in Virginia,
5   But we were England's, still colonials,

---

2. One of a variety of plants thought to have curative powers.

Possessing what we still were unpossessed by,
Possessed by what we now no more possessed.
Something we were withholding made us weak
Until we found it was ourselves
10 We were withholding from our land of living,
And forthwith found salvation in surrender.
Such as we were we gave ourselves outright
(The deed of gift was many deeds of war)
To the land vaguely realizing westward,
15 But still unstoried, artless, unenhanced,
Such as she was, such as she would become.

1942

Directive

Back out of all this now too much for us,
Back in a time made simple by the loss
Of detail, burned, dissolved, and broken off
Like graveyard marble sculpture in the weather,
5 There is a house that is no more a house
Upon a farm that is no more a farm
And in a town that is no more a town.
The road there, if you'll let a guide direct you
Who only has at heart your getting lost,
10 May seem as if it should have been a quarry—
Great monolithic knees the former town
Long since gave up pretense of keeping covered.
And there's a story in a book about it:
Besides the wear of iron wagon wheels
15 The ledges show lines ruled southeast northwest,
The chisel work of an enormous Glacier
That braced his feet against the Arctic Pole.
You must not mind a certain coolness from him
Still said to haunt this side of Panther Mountain.
20 Nor need you mind the serial ordeal
Of being watched from forty cellar holes
As if by eye pairs out of forty firkins.
As for the woods' excitement over you
That sends light rustle rushes to their leaves,
25 Charge that to upstart inexperience.
Where were they all not twenty years ago?
They think too much of having shaded out
A few old pecker-fretted apple trees.
Make yourself up a cheering song of how
30 Someone's road home from work this once was,
Who may be just ahead of you on foot
Or creaking with a buggy load of grain.
The height of the adventure is the height
Of country where two village cultures faded
35 Into each other. Both of them are lost.
And if you're lost enough to find yourself
By now, pull in your ladder road behind you
And put a sign up CLOSED to all but me.
Then make yourself at home. The only field
40 Now left's no bigger than a harness gall.
First there's the children's house of make believe,
Some shattered dishes underneath a pine,
The playthings in the playhouse of the children.

Weep for what little things could make them glad.
45   Then for the house that is no more a house,
But only a belilaced cellar hole,
Now slowly closing like a dent in dough.
This was no playhouse but a house in earnest.
Your destination and your destiny's
50   A brook that was the water of the house,
Cold as a spring as yet so near its source,
Too lofty and original to rage.
(We know the valley streams that when aroused
Will leave their tatters hung on barb and thorn.)
55   I have kept hidden in the instep arch
Of an old cedar at the waterside
A broken drinking goblet like the Grail
Under a spell so the wrong ones can't find it,
So can't get saved, as Saint Mark says they mustn't.[3]
60   (I stole the goblet from the children's playhouse.)
Here are your waters and your watering place.
Drink and be whole again beyond confusion.

                                                    1947

[In Winter in the Woods . . .]

In winter in the woods alone
Against the trees I go.
I mark a maple for my own
And lay the maple low.

5   At four o'clock I shoulder axe
And in the afterglow
I link a line of shadowy tracks
Across the tinted snow.

I see for Nature no defeat
10   In one tree's overthrow
Or for myself in my retreat
For yet another blow.

                                                    1962

EDWARD THOMAS
(1878–1917)

The Owl

Downhill I came, hungry, and yet not starved;
Cold, yet had heat within me that was proof
Against the North wind; tired, yet so that rest
Had seemed the sweetest thing under a roof.

5   Then at the inn I had food, fire, and rest,
Knowing how hungry, cold, and tired was I.
All of the night was quite barred out except
An owl's cry, a most melancholy cry

---

3. Cf. Mark iv.11–12, in which Christ says, "To you has been given the secret of the kingdom of God. but for those outside everything is in parables; so that they may indeed see but not perceive, and may indeed hear but not understand; lest they should turn again, and be forgiven." *The Grail:* the holy grail, a cup used by Jesus at the last supper, the object of many quests in Arthurian romance.

10   Shaken out long and clear upon the hill,
No merry note, nor cause of merriment,
But one telling me plain what I escaped
And others could not, that night, as in I went.

And salted was my food, and my repose,
Salted and sobered, too, by the bird's voice
15   Speaking for all who lay under the stars,
Soldiers and poor, unable to rejoice.

1917

Melancholy

The rain and wind, the rain and wind, raved endlessly.
On me the Summer storm, and fever, and melancholy
Wrought magic, so that if I feared the solitude
Far more I feared all company: too sharp, too rude,
5   Had been the wisest or the dearest human voice.
What I desired I knew not, but whate'er my choice
Vain it must be, I knew. Yet naught did my despair
But sweeten the strange sweetness, while through the wild air
All day long I heard a distant cuckoo calling
10   And, soft as dulcimers, sounds of near water falling,
And, softer, and remote as if in history,
Rumors of what had touched my friends, my foes, or me.

1917

Lights Out

I have come to the borders of sleep,
The unfathomable deep
Forest where all must lose
Their way, however straight,
5   Or winding, soon or late;
They cannot choose.

Many a road and track
That, since the dawn's first crack,
Up to the forest brink,
10   Deceived the travelers,
Suddenly now blurs,
And in they sink.

Here love ends,
Despair, ambition ends;
15   All pleasure and all trouble,
Although most sweet or bitter,
Here ends in sleep that is sweeter
Than tasks most noble.

There is not any book
20   Or face of dearest look
That I would not turn from now
To go into the unknown
I must enter, and leave, alone,
I know not how.

25   The tall forest towers;
Its cloudy foliage lowers
Ahead, shelf above shelf;
Its silence I hear and obey
That I may lose my way
30   And myself.

1917

The Dark Forest

Dark is the forest and deep, and overhead
Hang stars like seeds of light
In vain, though not since they were sown was bred
Anything more bright.

5   And evermore mighty multitudes ride
About, nor enter in;
Of the other multitudes that dwell inside
Never yet was one seen.

The forest foxglove is purple, the marguerite
10   Outside is gold and white,
Nor can those that pluck either blossom greet
The others, day or night.

1918

Good-Night

The skylarks are far behind that sang over the down;
I can hear no more those suburb nightingales;
Thrushes and blackbirds sing in the gardens of the town
In vain: the noise of man, beast, and machine prevails.

5   But the call of children in the unfamiliar streets
That echo with a familiar twilight echoing,
Sweet as the voice of nightingale or lark, completes
A magic of strange welcome, so that I seem a king

Among man, beast, machine, bird, child, and the ghost
10   That in the echo lives and with the echo dies.
The friendless town is friendly; homeless, I am not lost;
Though I know none of these doors, and meet but strangers' eyes.
Never again, perhaps, after tomorrow, shall
I see these homely streets, these church windows alight,
15   Not a man or woman or child among them all:
But it is All Friends' Night, a traveler's good-night.

1918

The Gypsy

A fortnight before Christmas Gypsies were everywhere:
Vans were drawn up on wastes, women trailed to the fair.
"My gentleman," said one, "you've got a lucky face."
"And you've a luckier," I thought, "if such a grace
5   And impudence in rags are lucky." "Give a penny

For the poor baby's sake." "Indeed I have not any
Unless you can give change for a sovereign,² my dear."
"Then just half a pipeful of tobacco can you spare?"
I gave it. With that much victory she laughed content.
10 I should have given more, but off and away she went
With her baby and her pink sham flowers to rejoin
The rest before I could translate to its proper coin
Gratitude for her grace. And I paid nothing then,
As I pay nothing now with the dipping of my pen
15 For her brother's music when he drummed the tambourine
And stamped his feet, which made the workmen passing grin,
While his mouth-organ changed to a rascally Bacchanal dance
"Over the hills and far away." This and his glance
Outlasted all the fair, farmer, and auctioneer,
20 Cheap-jack,° balloon-man, drover with crooked stick, and steer,   *peddler*
Pig, turkey, goose, and duck, Christmas corpses to be.
Not even the kneeling ox had eyes like the Romany.°   *gypsy*
That night he peopled for me the hollow wooded land,
More dark and wild than stormiest heavens, that I searched and scanned
25 Like a ghost new-arrived. The gradations of the dark
Were like an underworld of death, but for the spark
In the Gypsy boy's black eyes as he played and stamped his tune,
"Over the hills and far away," and a crescent moon.

1918

WALLACE STEVENS
(1879–1955)

The Snow Man

One must have a mind of winter
To regard the frost and the boughs
Of the pine-trees crusted with snow;

And have been cold a long time
5 To behold the junipers shagged with ice,
The spruces rough in the distant glitter

Of the January sun; and not to think
Of any misery in the sound of the wind,
In the sound of a few leaves,

10 Which is the sound of the land
Full of the same wind
That is blowing in the same bare place
For the listener, who listens in the snow,
And, nothing himself, beholds
15 Nothing that is not there and the nothing that is.

1923

2. Formerly, a British gold coin, value one pound, so called because it bore the effigy of the ruler on one face.

The Emperor of Ice-Cream

Call the roller of big cigars,
The muscular one, and bid him whip
In kitchen cups concupiscent curds.
Let the wenches dawdle in such dress
5   As they are used to wear, and let the boys
Bring flowers in last month's newspapers.
Let be be finale of seem.
The only emperor is the emperor of ice-cream.

Take from the dresser of deal.
10 Lacking the three glass knobs, that sheet
On which she embroidered fantails [1] once
And spread it so as to cover her face.
If her horny feet protrude, they come
To show how cold she is, and dumb.
15 Let the lamp affix its beam.
The only emperor is the emperor of ice-cream.

1923

Sunday Morning

1

Complacencies of the peignoir, and late
Coffee and oranges in a sunny chair,
And the green freedom of a cockatoo
Upon a rug mingle to dissipate
5   The holy hush of ancient sacrifice.
She dreams a little, and she feels the dark
Encroachment of that old catastrophe,
As a calm darkens among water-lights.
The pungent oranges and bright, green wings
10 Seem things in some procession of the dead,
Winding across wide water, without sound.
The day is like wide water, without sound,
Stilled for the passing of her dreaming feet
Over the seas, to silent Palestine,
15 Dominion of the blood and sepulchre.

2

Why should she give her bounty to the dead?
What is divinity if it can come
Only in silent shadows and in dreams?
Shall she not find in comforts of the sun,
20 In pungent fruit and bright, green wings, or else
In any balm or beauty of the earth,
Things to be cherished like the thought of heaven?
Divinity must live within herself:
Passions of rain, or moods in falling snow;
25 Grievings in loneliness, or unsubdued
Elations when the forest blooms; gusty
Emotions on wet roads on autumn nights;
All pleasures and all pains, remembering
The bough of summer and the winter branch.
30 These are the measures destined for her soul.

1. That is, fantail pigeons.

3

Jove in the clouds had his inhuman birth.
No mother suckled him, no sweet land gave
Large-mannered motions to his mythy mind
He moved among us, as a muttering king,
35 Magnificent, would move among his hinds,°   shepherds
Until our blood, commingling, virginal,
With heaven, brought such requital to desire
The very hinds discerned it, in a star.
Shall our blood fail? Or shall it come to be
40 The blood of paradise? And shall the earth
Seem all of paradise that we shall know?
The sky will be much friendlier then than now,
A part of labor and a part of pain,
And next in glory to enduring love,
45 Not this dividing and indifferent blue.

4

She says, "I am content when wakened birds,
Before they fly, test the reality
Of misty fields, by their sweet questionings;
But when the birds are gone, and their warm fields
50 Return no more, where, then, is paradise?"
There is not any haunt of prophecy,
Nor any old chimera of the grave,
Neither the golden underground, nor isle
Melodious, where spirits gat them home,
55 Nor visionary south, nor cloudy palm
Remote on heaven's hill, that has endured
As April's green endures; or will endure
Like her remembrance of awakened birds,
Or her desire for June and evening, tipped
60 By the consummation of the swallow's wings.

5

She says, "But in contentment I still feel
The need of some imperishable bliss."
Death is the mother of beauty; hence from her,
Alone, shall come fulfilment to our dreams
65 And our desires. Although she strews the leaves
Of sure obliteration on our paths,
The path sick sorrow took, the many paths
Where triumph rang its brassy phrase, or love
Whispered a little out of tenderness,
70 She makes the willow shiver in the sun
For maidens who were wont to sit and gaze
Upon the grass, relinquished to their feet.
She causes boys to pile new plums and pears
On disregarded plate.[1] The maidens taste
75 And stray impassioned in the littering leaves.

6

Is there no change of death in paradise?
Does ripe fruit never fall? Or do the boughs
Hang always heavy in that perfect sky,
Unchanging, yet so like our perishing earth,
80 With rivers like our own that seek for seas

1. "Plate is used in the sense of so-called
family plate. Disregarded refers to the disuse
into which things fall that have been possessed
for a long time. I mean, therefore, that death
releases and renews" [*Letters of Wallace
Stevens*, New York, 1966, pp. 183–184].

They never find, the same receding shores
That never touch with inarticulate pang?
Why set the pear upon those river-banks
Or spice the shores with odors of the plum?
85   Alas, that they should wear our colors there,
The silken weavings of our afternoons,
And pick the strings of our insipid lutes!
Death is the mother of beauty, mystical,
Within whose burning bosom we devise
90   Our earthly mothers waiting, sleeplessly.

7

Supple and turbulent, a ring of men
Shall chant in orgy on a summer morn
Their boisterous devotion to the sun,
Not as a god, but as a god might be,
95   Naked among them, like a savage source.
Their chant shall be a chant of paradise,
Out of their blood, returning to the sky;
And in their chant shall enter, voice by voice,
The windy lake wherein their lord delights,
100   The trees, like serafin,° and echoing hills,   *celestial beings*
That choir among themselves long afterward.
They shall know well the heavenly fellowship
Of men that perish and of summer morn.
And whence they came and whither they shall go
105   The dew upon their feet shall manifest.

8

She hears, upon that water without sound,
A voice that cries, "The tomb in Palestine
Is not the porch of spirits lingering.
It is the grave of Jesus, where he lay."
110   We live in an old chaos of the sun,
Or old dependency of day and night,
Or island solitude, unsponsored, free,
Of that wide water, inescapable.
Deer walk upon our mountains, and the quail
115   Whistle about us their spontaneous cries;
Sweet berries ripen in the wilderness;
And, in the isolation of the sky,
At evening, casual flocks of pigeons make
Ambiguous undulations as they sink,
120   Downward to darkness, on extended wings.

                                                                    1915   1923

The Bird with the Coppery, Keen Claws

Above the forest of the parakeets,
A parakeet of parakeets prevails,
A pip of life amid a mort° of tails.   *great quantity*

(The rudiments of tropics are around,
5   Aloe[2] of ivory, pear of rusty rind.)
His lids are white because his eyes are blind.

---

2. Plants of the lily family.

He is not paradise of parakeets,
Of his gold ether, golden alguazil,°   *bailiff, sheriff*
Except because he broods there and is still.

10 Panache[3] upon panache, his tails deploy
Upward and outward, in green-vented forms,
His tip a drop of water full of storms.

But though the turbulent tinges undulate
As his pure intellect applies its laws,
15 He moves not on his coppery, keen claws.

He munches a dry shell while he exerts
His will, yet never ceases, perfect cock,
To flare, in the sun-pallor of his rock.

                                                              1923

The Idea of Order at Key West

She sang beyond the genius of the sea.
The water never formed to mind or voice,
Like a body wholly body, fluttering
Its empty sleeves; and yet its mimic motion
5 Made constant cry, caused constantly a cry,
That was not ours although we understood,
Inhuman, of the veritable ocean.

The sea was not a mask. No more was she.
The song and water were not medleyed sound
10 Even if what she sang was what she heard,
Since what she sang was uttered word by word.
It may be that in all her phrases stirred
The grinding water and the gasping wind;
But it was she and not the sea we heard.
15 For she was the maker of the song she sang.
The ever-hooded, tragic-gestured sea
Was merely a place by which she walked to sing.
Whose spirit is this? we said, because we knew
It was the spirit that we sought and knew
20 That we should ask this often as she sang.

If it was only the dark voice of the sea
That rose, or even colored by many waves;
If it was only the outer voice of sky
And cloud, of the sunken coral water-walled,
25 However clear, it would have been deep air,
The heaving speech of air, a summer sound
Repeated in a summer without end
And sound alone. But it was more than that,
More even than her voice, and ours, among
30 The meaningless plungings of water and the wind,
Theatrical distances, bronze shadows heaped
On high horizons, mountainous atmospheres
Of sky and sea.

---

3. Tuft or plume of feathers.

It was her voice that made
35 The sky acutest at its vanishing.
She measured to the hour its solitude.
She was the single artificer of the world
In which she sang. And when she sang, the sea,
Whatever self it had, became the self
40 That was her song, for she was the maker. Then we,
As we beheld her striding there alone,
Knew that there never was a world for her
Except the one she sang and, singing, made.

Ramon Fernandez,[4] tell me, if you know,
45 Why, when the singing ended and we turned
Toward the town, tell why the glassy lights,
The lights in the fishing boats at anchor there,
As the night descended, tilting in the air,
Mastered the night and portioned out the sea,
50 Fixing emblazoned zones and fiery poles,
Arranging, deepening, enchanting night.

Oh! Blessed rage for order, pale Ramon,
The maker's rage to order words of the sea,
Words of the fragrant portals, dimly-starred,
55 And of ourselves and of our origins,
In ghostlier demarcations, keener sounds.

1935

The House Was Quiet and the World Was Calm

The house was quiet and the world was calm.
The reader became the book; and summer night

Was like the conscious being of the book.
The house was quiet and the world was calm.

5 The words were spoken as if there was no book,
Except that the reader leaned above the page,

Wanted to lean, wanted much most to be
The scholar to whom his book is true, to whom

The summer night is like a perfection of thought.
10 The house was quiet because it had to be.

The quiet was part of the meaning, part of the mind:
The access of perfection to the page.

And the world was calm. The truth in a calm world,
In which there is no other meaning, itself

15 Is calm, itself is summer and night, itself
Is the reader leaning late and reading there.

1947

<hr>

4. Stevens pointed out to two of his correspondents that in choosing this name he had simply combined two common Spanish names at random, without conscious reference to Ramon Fernandez the critic: "Ramon Fernandez was not intended to be anyone at all."

WILLIAM CARLOS WILLIAMS
(1883–1963)

The Young Housewife

At ten A.M. the young housewife
moves about in negligee behind
the wooden walls of her husband's house.
I pass solitary in my car.

5   Then again she comes to the curb
to call the ice-man, fish-man, and stands
shy, uncorseted, tucking in
stray ends of hair, and I compare her
to a fallen leaf.

10   The noiseless wheels of my car
rush with a crackling sound over
dried leaves as I bow and pass smiling.

1917

The Red Wheelbarrow

so much depends
upon

a red wheel
barrow

5   glazed with rain
water

beside the white
chickens.

1923

Queen-Ann's-Lace

Her body is not so white as
anemone petals nor so smooth—nor
so remote a thing. It is a field
of the wild carrot taking
5   the field by force; the grass
does not raise above it.
Here is no question of whiteness,
white as can be, with a purple mole
at the center of each flower.
10   Each flower is a hand's span
of her whiteness. Wherever
his hand has lain there is
a tiny purple blemish. Each part
is a blossom under his touch
15   to which the fibres of her being
stem one by one, each to its end,
until the whole field is a

white desire, empty, a single stem,
a cluster, flower by flower,
20   a pious wish to whiteness gone over—
or nothing.

1925

Poem

As the cat
climbed over
the top of

the jamcloset
5   first the right
forefoot

carefully
then the hind
stepped down

10   into the pit of
the empty
flowerpot

1934

The Yachts

contend in a sea which the land partly encloses
shielding them from the too-heavy blows
of an ungoverned ocean which when it chooses

tortures the biggest hulls, the best man knows
5   to pit against its beatings, and sinks them pitilessly.
Mothlike in mists, scintillant in the minute

brilliance of cloudless days, with broad bellying sails
they glide to the wind tossing green water
from their sharp prows while over them the crew crawls

10   ant-like, solicitously grooming them, releasing,
making fast as they turn, lean far over and having
caught the wind again, side by side, head for the mark.

In a well guarded arena of open water surrounded by
lesser and greater craft which, sycophant, lumbering
15   and flittering follow them, they appear youthful, rare

as the light of a happy eye, live with the grace
of all that in the mind is fleckless, free and
naturally to be desired. Now the sea which holds them

is moody, lapping their glossy sides, as if feeling
20   for some slightest flaw but fails completely.
Today no race. Then the wind comes again. The yachts

move, jockeying for a start, the signal is set and they
are off. Now the waves strike at them but they are too
well made, they slip through, though they take in canvas.

25   Arms with hands grasping seek to clutch at the prows.
      Bodies thrown recklessly in the way are cut aside.
      It is a sea of faces about them in agony, in despair

      until the horror of the race dawns staggering the mind,
      the whole sea become an entanglement of watery bodies
30   lost to the world bearing what they cannot hold. Broken,

      beaten, desolate, reaching from the dead to be taken up
      they cry out, failing, failing! their cries rising
      in waves still as the skillful yachts pass over.

                                                        1935

The Dance

      In Breughel's[3] great picture, The Kermess,
      the dancers go round, they go round and
      around, the squeal and the blare and the
      tweedle of bagpipes, a bugle and fiddles
5   tipping their bellies (round as the thick-
      sided glasses whose wash they impound)
      their hips and their bellies off balance
      to turn them. Kicking and rolling about
      the Fair Grounds, swinging their butts, those
10   shanks must be sound to bear up under such
      rollicking measures, prance as they dance
      in Breughel's great picture, The Kermess.

                                                        1944

The Ivy Crown

      The whole process is a lie,
             unless,
                          crowned by excess,
      it break forcefully,
5   one way or another,
                          from its confinement—
      or find a deeper well.
             Antony and Cleopatra
                          were right;
10   they have shown
             the way. I love you
                          or I do not live
      at all.

      Daffodil time
15   is past. This is
                          summer, summer!
      the heart says,
             and not even the full of it.
                          No doubts
20   are permitted—
             though they will come
                          and may

---

3. Pieter Breughel (died 1569), Flemish painter of peasant life.

before our time
                    overwhelm us.
                             We are only mortal
but being mortal
                    can defy our fate.
                             We may
by an outside chance
                    even win! We do not
                             look to see
jonquils and violets
                    come again
                             but there are,
still,
                    the roses!

Romance has no part in it.
                    The business of love is
                             cruelty *which,*
by our wills,
                    we transform
                             to live together.
It has its seasons,
                    for and against,
                             whatever the heart
fumbles in the dark
                    to assert
                             toward the end of May.
Just as the nature of briars
                    is to tear flesh,
                             I have proceeded
through them.
                    Keep
                             the briars out,
they say.
                    You cannot live
                             and keep free of
briars.

Children pick flowers.
                    Let them.
                             Though having them
in hand
                    they have no further use for them
                             but leave them crumpled
at the curb's edge.

At our age the imagination
                    across the sorry facts
                             lifts us
to make roses
                    stand before thorns.
                             Sure
love is cruel
                    and selfish
                             and totally obtuse—
at least, blinded by the light,
                    young love is.
                             But we are older,

> I to love
> > and you to be loved,
> > > we have,
80
> no matter how,
> > by our wills survived
> > > to keep
> the jeweled prize
85
> > always
> > > at our finger tips.
> We will it so
> > and so it is
> > > past all accident.

1955

D. H. LAWRENCE
(1885–1930)

Baby Running Barefoot

When the white feet of the baby beat across the grass
The little white feet nod like white flowers in a wind,
They poise and run like puffs of wind that pass
Over water where the weeds are thinned.

5 And the sight of their white playing in the grass
Is winsome as a robin's song, so fluttering;
Or like two butterflies that settle on a glass
Cup for a moment, soft little wing-beats uttering.

And I wish that the baby would tack across here to me
10 Like a wind-shadow running on a pond, so she could stand
With two little bare white feet upon my knee
And I could feel her feet in either hand

Cool as syringa buds in morning hours,
Or firm and silken as young peony flowers.

1916

Piano

Softly, in the dusk, a woman is singing to me;
Taking me back down the vista of years, till I see
A child sitting under the piano, in the boom of the tingling strings
And pressing the small, poised feet of a mother who smiles as she sings.

5 In spite of myself, the insidious mastery of song
Betrays me back, till the heart of me weeps to belong
To the old Sunday evenings at home, with winter outside
And hymns in the cozy parlor, the tinkling piano our guide.

So now it is vain for the singer to burst into clamor
10 With the great black piano appassionato. The glamour
Of childish days is upon me, my manhood is cast
Down in the flood of remembrance, I weep like a child for the past.

1918

Reading a Letter

She sits on the recreation ground
    Under an oak whose yellow buds dot the pale blue sky.
The young grass twinkles in the wind, and the sound
    Of the wind in the knotted buds makes a canopy.

5 So sitting under the knotted canopy
    Of the wind, she is lifted and carried away as in a balloon
Across the insensible void, till she stoops to see
    The sandy desert beneath her, the dreary platoon.

She knows the waste all dry beneath her, in one place
10   Stirring with earth-colored life, ever turning and stirring.
But never the motion has a human face
    Nor sound, only intermittent machinery whirring.

And so again, on the recreation ground
    She alights a stranger, wondering, unused to the scene;
15 Suffering at sight of the children playing around,
    Hurt at the chalk-colored tulips, and the evening-green.

                                               1918

Snake

A snake came to my water-trough
On a hot, hot day, and I in pajamas for the heat,
To drink there.

In the deep, strange-scented shade of the great dark carob-tree
5 I came down the steps with my pitcher
And must wait, must stand and wait, for there he was at the trough before
    me.

He reached down from a fissure in the earth-wall in the gloom
And trailed his yellow-brown slackness soft-bellied down, over the edge of
    the stone trough
And rested his throat upon the stone bottom,
10 And where the water had dripped from the tap, in a small clearness,
He sipped with his straight mouth,
Softly drank through his straight gums, into his slack long body,
Silently.

Someone was before me at my water-trough,
15 And I, like a second comer, waiting.

He lifted his head from his drinking, as cattle do,
And looked at me vaguely, as drinking cattle do,
And flickered his two-forked tongue from his lips, and mused a moment,
And stooped and drank a little more,
20 Being earth-brown, earth-golden from the burning bowels of the earth
On the day of Sicilian July, with Etna smoking.

The voice of my education said to me
He must be killed,
For in Sicily the black, black snakes are innocent, the gold are venomous.

25 And voices in me said, If you were a man
    You would take a stick and break him now, and finish him off.

    But must I confess how I liked him,
    How glad I was he had come like a guest in quiet, to drink at my water-
        trough

    And depart peaceful, pacified, and thankless,
30 Into the burning bowels of this earth?

    Was it cowardice, that I dared not kill him?
    Was it perversity, that I longed to talk to him?
    Was it humility, to feel so honored?
    I felt so honored.

    And yet those voices:
35 *If you were not afraid, you would kill him!*

    And truly I was afraid, I was most afraid,
    But even so, honored still more
    That he should seek my hospitality
    From out the dark door of the secret earth.

40 He drank enough
    And lifted his head, dreamily, as one who has drunken,
    And flickered his tongue like a forked night on the air, so black,
    Seeming to lick his lips,
    And looked around like a god, unseeing, into the air,
45 And slowly turned his head,
    And slowly, very slowly, as if thrice adream,
    Proceeded to draw his slow length curving round
    And climb again the broken bank of my wall-face.

    And as he put his head into that dreadful hole,
50 And as he slowly drew up, snake-easing his shoulders, and entered farther,
    A sort of horror, a sort of protest against his withdrawing into that horrid
        black hole,
    Deliberately going into the blackness, and slowly drawing himself after,
    Overcame me now his back was turned.

    I looked round, I put down my pitcher,
55 I picked up a clumsy log
    And threw it at the water-trough with a clatter.

    I think it did not hit him,
    But suddenly that part of him that was left behind convulsed in undignified
        haste
    Writhed like lightning, and was gone
60 Into the black hole, the earth-lipped fissure in the wall-front,
    At which, in the intense still noon, I stared with fascination.

    And immediately I regretted it.
    I thought how paltry, how vulgar, what a mean act!
    I despised myself and the voices of my accursed human education.

65 And I thought of the albatross[1]
And I wished he would come back, my snake.

For he seemed to me again like a king,
Like a king in exile, uncrowned in the underworld,
Now due to be crowned again.

70 And so, I missed my chance with one of the lords
Of life.
And I have something to expiate;
A pettiness.

Taormina.
1923

Bavarian Gentians

Not every man has gentians in his house
in Soft September, at slow, sad Michaelmas.

Bavarian gentians, big and dark, only dark
darkening the daytime, torch-like with the smoking blueness of Pluto's gloom,
5 ribbed and torch-like, with their blaze of darkness spread blue
down flattening into points, flattened under the sweep of white day
torch-flower of the blue-smoking darkness, Pluto's dark-blue daze,
black lamps from the halls of Dis,[2] burning dark blue,
giving off darkness, blue darkness, as Demeter's pale lamps give off light,
10 lead me then, lead the way.

Reach me a gentian, give me a torch!
let me guide myself with the blue, forked torch of this flower
down the darker and darker stairs, where blue is darkened on blueness
even where Persephone goes, just now, from the frosted September
15 to the sightless realm where darkness is awake upon the dark
and Persephone herself is but a voice
or a darkness invisible enfolded in the deeper dark
of the arms Plutonic, and pierced with the passion of dense gloom,
among the splendor of torches of darkness, shedding darkness on the lost
bride and her groom.

1932

The Ship of Death[3]

1

Now it is autumn and the falling fruit
and the long journey towards oblivion.

The apples falling like great drops of dew
to bruise themselves an exit from themselves.

5 And it is time to go, to bid farewell
to one's own self, and find an exit
from the fallen self.

1. In Coleridge's *Rime of the Ancient Mariner.*
2. Another Roman name for Pluto (Greek Hades), ruler of the underworld. He had abducted Persephone (Roman Proserpine) the daughter of Demeter (Roman Ceres), goddess of growing vegetation and living nature; Persephone ruled with him as queen of the underworld, but returned to spend six months of each year with her mother in the world above.
3. In *Etruscan Places,* the book which describes his visit to the Etruscan painted tombs in Central Italy, in the spring of 1927, Lawrence mentions that originally, before the tombs were pillaged, there would be found in the last chamber among "the sacred treasures of the dead, the little bronze ship that should bear [the soul of the dead] over to the other world * * * "

2

Have you built your ship of death, O have you?
O build your ship of death, for you will need it.

10 The grim frost is at hand, when the apples will fall
    thick, almost thundrous, on the hardened earth.

    And death is on the air like a smell of ashes!
    Ah! can't you smell it?

    And in the bruised body, the frightened soul
15 finds itself shrinking, wincing from the cold
    that blows upon it through the orifices.

                    3
    And can a man his own quietus make
    with a bare bodkin?[4]

    With daggers, bodkins, bullets, man can make
20 a bruise or break of exit for his life;
    but is that a quietus, O tell me, is it quietus?

    Surely not so! for how could murder, even self-murder
    ever a quietus make?

                    4
    O let us talk of quiet that we know,
25 that we can know, the deep and lovely quiet
    of a strong heart at peace!

    How can we this, our own quietus, make?
                    5
    Build then the ship of death, for you must take
    the longest journey, to oblivion.

30 And die the death, the long and painful death
    that lies between the old self and the new.

    Already our bodies are fallen, bruised, badly bruised,
    already our souls are oozing through the exit
    of the cruel bruise.

35 Already the dark and endless ocean of the end
    is washing in through the breaches of our wounds,
    already the flood is upon us.

    Oh build your ship of death, your little ark
    and furnish it with food, with little cakes, and wine
40 for the dark flight down oblivion.
                    6
    Piecemeal the body dies, and the timid soul
    has her footing washed away, as the dark flood rises.

    We are dying, we are dying, we are all of us dying
    and nothing will stay the death-flood rising within us
45 and soon it will rise on the world, on the outside world.

---

4. From *Hamlet*, III.i.75–6.

We are dying, we are dying, piecemeal our bodies are dying
and our strength leaves us,
and our soul cowers naked in the dark rain over the flood,
cowering in the last branches of the tree of our life.

7

50 We are dying, we are dying, so all we can do
is now to be willing to die, and to build the ship
of death to carry the soul on the longest journey.

A little ship, with oars and food
and little dishes, and all accoutrements
55 fitting and ready for the departing soul.

Now launch the small ship, now as the body dies
and life departs, launch out, the fragile soul
in the fragile ship of courage, the ark of faith
with its store of food and little cooking pans
60 and change of clothes,
upon the flood's black waste
upon the waters of the end
upon the sea of death, where still we sail
darkly, for we cannot steer, and have no port.

65 There is no port, there is nowhere to go
only the deepening blackness darkening still
blacker upon the soundless, ungurgling flood
darkness at one with darkness, up and down
and sideways utterly dark, so there is no direction any more.
70 and the little ship is there; yet she is gone.
She is not seen, for there is nothing to see her by.
She is gone! gone! and yet
somewhere she is there.
Nowhere!

8

75 And everything is gone, the body is gone
completely under, gone, entirely gone.
The upper darkness is heavy as the lower,
between them the little ship
is gone
80 she is gone.

It is the end, it is oblivion.

9

And yet out of eternity, a thread
separates itself on the blackness,
a horizontal thread
85 that fumes a little with pallor upon the dark.

Is it illusion? or does the pallor fume
A little higher?
Ah wait, wait, for there's the dawn,
the cruel dawn of coming back to life
90 out of oblivion.

Wait, wait, the little ship
drifting, beneath the deathly ashy gray
of a flood-dawn.

95 Wait, wait! even so, a flush of yellow
and strangely, O chilled wan soul, a flush of rose.

A flush of rose, and the whole thing starts again.
                    10
The flood subsides, and the body, like a worn sea-shell
emerges strange and lovely.
And the little ship wings home, faltering and lapsing
100 on the pink flood,
and the frail soul steps out, into her house again
filling the heart with peace.

Swings the heart renewed with peace
even of oblivion.

105 Oh build your ship of death, oh build it!
for you will need it.
For the voyage of oblivion awaits you.

                                                    1932

EZRA POUND
(1885–1972)

Portrait d'Une Femme[3]

Your mind and you are our Sargasso Sea,[4]
London has swept about you this score years
And bright ships left you this or that in fee:
Ideas, old gossip, oddments of all things,
5 Strange spars of knowledge and dimmed wares of price.
Great minds have sought you—lacking someone else.
You have been second always. Tragical?
No. You preferred it to the usual thing:
One dull man, dulling and uxorious,
10 One average mind—with one thought less, each year.
Oh, you are patient, I have seen you sit
Hours, where something might have floated up.
And now you pay one. Yes, you richly pay.
You are a person of some interest, one comes to you
15 And takes strange gain away:
Trophies fished up; some curious suggestion;
Fact that leads nowhere; and a tale or two,
Pregnant with mandrakes,[5] or with something else
That might prove useful and yet never proves,
20 That never fits a corner or shows use,
Or finds its hour upon the loom of days:
The tarnished, gaudy, wonderful old work;
Idols and ambergris[6] and rare inlays,
These are your riches, your great store; and yet

---

3. Portrait of a Lady.
4. A region of the North Atlantic partially covered with accumulations of floating gulf-weed.
5. A plant, of narcotic properties, and some-

times believed to be aphrodisiac, whose forked root was traditionally thought to resemble the human body.
6. Secretion of the whale, used in perfumery.

25 For all this sea-hoard of deciduous things,
    Strange woods half sodden, and new brighter stuff:
    In the slow float of differing light and deep,
    No! there is nothing! In the whole and all,
    Nothing that's quite your own.
                    Yet this is you.

                                                    1912

The Garden

En robe de parade.[7]
            —SAMAIN

    Like a skein of loose silk blown against a wall
    She walks by the railing of a path in Kensington Gardens,[8]
    And she is dying piecemeal
            of a sort of emotional anemia.

5   And round about there is a rabble
    Of the filthy, sturdy, unkillable infants of the very poor.
    They shall inherit the earth.

    In her is the end of breeding.
    Her boredom is exquisite and excessive.
10 She would like some one to speak to her,
    And is almost afraid that I
            will commit that indiscretion.

                                                    1916

The Study in Aesthetics

    The very small children in patched clothing,
    Being smitten with an unusual wisdom,
    Stopped in their play as she passed them
    And cried up from their cobbles:

5   *Guarda! Ahi, guarda! ch' è be' a!*[9]

    But three years after this
    I heard the young Dante, whose last name I do not know—
    For there are, in Sirmione,[1] twenty-eight young Dantes
        and thirty-four Catulli;
    And there had been a great catch of sardines,
10 And his elders
    Were packing them in the great wooden boxes
    For the market in Brescia, and he
    Leapt about, snatching at the bright fish
    And getting in both of their ways;
15 And in vain they commanded him to *sta fermo!*[2]
    And when they would not let him arrange
    The fish in the boxes

---

7. "Dressed as for a state occasion." The phrase is from a poem by the French poet Albert Samain (1858–1900), *The Infanta.*
8. Extensive public gardens in the residential district west of Hyde Park, London.

9. *"Be'a: bella"* [Pound's note]. Look! Ah, look! how beautiful she is!
1. Town on Lake Garda, in northern Italy.
2. Stand still!

He stroked those which were already arranged,
Murmuring for his own satisfaction
20 This identical phrase:

                    Ch' è be' a.

And at this I was mildly abashed.

                                          1916

Ts' ai Chi'h[3]

The petals fall in the fountain,
        the orange-colored rose-leaves,
Their ochre clings to the stone.

                                          1916

In a Station of the Metro

The apparition of these faces in the crowd;
Petals on a wet, black bough.

                                          1916

Simulacra[6]

Why does the horse-faced lady of just the unmentionable age
Walk down Longacre[7] reciting Swinburne to herself, inaudibly?
Why does the small child in the soiled-white imitation fur coat
Crawl in the very black gutter beneath the grape stand?
5 Why does the really handsome young woman approach me in Sackville
        Street[8]
Undeterred by the manifest age of my trappings?

                                          1916

The River-Merchant's Wife: a Letter

While my hair was still cut straight across my forehead
I played about the front gate, pulling flowers.
You came by on bamboo stilts, playing horse,
You walked about my seat, playing with blue plums.
5 And we went on living in the village of Chokan:
Two small people, without dislike or suspicion.

At fourteen I married My Lord you.
I never laughed, being bashful.
Lowering my head, I looked at the wall.
10 Called to, a thousand times, I never looked back.

---

3. Ts'ai Chi'h, or more usually Ts'ao Chih, is the name of a Chinese poet who lived from 192–232, and Pound's using it as the title of his poem perhaps indicates that in it he is adopting the mode of Ts'ao Chih's "five-character poems," or even translating one of them.

6. A simulacrum is an image, or an imitation, a sham representation of something.
7. Street in the Covent Garden district of London.
8. Runs into Picadilly, not far from Picadilly Circus.

At fifteen I stopped scowling,
I desired my dust to be mingled with yours
Forever and forever and forever.
Why should I climb the look out?

15   At sixteen you departed,
You went into far Ku-to-yen, by the river of swirling eddies,
And you have been gone five months.
The monkeys make sorrowful noise overhead.

You dragged your feet when you went out.
20   By the gate now, the moss is grown, the different mosses,
Too deep to clear them away!
The leaves fall early this autumn, in wind.
The paired butterflies are already yellow with August
Over the grass in the West garden;
25   They hurt me. I grow older.
If you are coming down through the narrows of the river Kiang,
Please let me know beforehand,
And I will come out to meet you
                    As far as Cho-fu-Sa.

                                        By *Rihaku*[9]
                                        1915

Hugh Selwyn Mauberley

LIFE AND CONTACTS [5]

I. E. P. Ode Pour L'Election de son Sepulchre [6]

For three years, out of key with his time,
He strove to resuscitate the dead art
Of poetry; to maintain "the sublime"
In the old sense. Wrong from the start—

5   No, hardly, but seeing he had been born
In a half savage country, out of date;
Bent resolutely on wringing lilies from the acorn;
Capaneus;[7] trout for factitious° bait;   *false; artificial*

"Ἴδμεν γάρ τοι πάνθ' ὅσ' ἐνὶ Τροίῃ [8]
10   Caught in the unstopped ear;
Giving the rocks small lee-way
The chopped seas held him, therefore, that year.

---

9. *Rihaku* is the transcription from the Japanese of the name of one of the greatest of the Chinese poets of the T'ang Dynasty, Li Po (ca. 700–762).
5. *Hugh Selwyn Mauberley* (*Life and Contacts*) comprises two sets of poems; the first, reprinted here, consists of thirteen poems; the second consists of five poems, headed "Mauberley/1920." There are many connections not only among the poems in each set, but also between the two sets. The entire volume bore an epigraph from the fourth Eclogue of the 3rd-century Latin poet Nemesianus: *Vocat aestus in umbram* ("The heat urges us into the shade").
6. Cf. Pierre Ronsard (1524–1585), Odes IV, iv, *"De l'élection de son sépulchre"* ["Concerning the choice of his tomb"], in which the poet describes the kind of burial place, and the kind of fame, he would like to have.
7. In classical mythology, one of the Seven against Thebes, heroes who led an expedition against Thebes in an unsuccessful attempt to get one of their number, Polynices, on the throne. Capaneus, climbing on the walls and defying even Zeus to harm him, was struck by a thunderbolt.
8. Idmen gár toi pánth'hós enì Troíei, from the song sung by the Sirens to lure Odysseus's ship onto the rocks: "For we know everything which [the Greeks and the Trojans have suffered] in Troy [by the will of the Gods]." (*Odyssey* xii, 184 ff.) Circe had told Odysseus how to avoid the danger: his men must have their ears stopped with wax, after they have bound him hand and foot—he alone hears their song.

His true Penelope [9] was Flaubert,[1]
He fished by obstinate isles;
15 Observed the elegance of Circe's [2] hair
Rather than the mottoes on sundials.

Unaffected by "the march of events,"
He passed from men's memory in *l'an trentiesme*
De son eage; [3] the case presents
20 No adjunct to the Muses' diadem.

II

The age demanded an image
Of its accelerated grimace,
Something for the modern stage,
Not, at any rate, an Attic [4] grace;

5 Not, not certainly, the obscure reveries
Of the inward gaze;
Better mendacities
Than the classics in paraphrase!

The "age demanded" chiefly a mold in plaster,
10 Made with no loss of time,
A prose kinema,[5] not, not assuredly, albaster
Or the "sculpture" of rhyme.

III

The tea-rose tea-gown, etc.
Supplants the mousseline of Cos,[6]
The pianola "replaces"
Sappho's barbitos.[7]

5 Christ follows Dionysus,[8]
Phallic and ambrosial
Made way for macerations; [9]
Caliban casts out Ariel.[1]

All things are a flowing,
10 Sage Heracleitus says; [2]
But a tawdry cheapness
Shall outlast our days.

9. The faithful wife to whom Odysseus returned after the ten years of adventure that followed the ten-year siege of Troy.
1. French realist novelist (1821–1880), a meticulous craftsman, author of *Madame Bovary, L'Education sentimentale,* etc.
2. An enchantress, living on the island of Aeaea, with whom Odysseus stayed for a year. She turned his men into swine, but he was able to resist her spell with the help of the herb moly, given to him by Hermes.
3. From the part satiric, part elegiac poem *"Le grand testament"* (1461), in which the French poet François Villon (1431–1489?), writing in prison, reviews his life, castigates his enemies, thinks of his friends, etc.: "In the thirtieth year of my age,/When I have drunk down all my shame . . ."
4. Athenian—of simple, pure, classical style.

5. Transliteration of the Greek word for "motion," a root word in the early term for motion pictures, "cinematograph."
6. The muslin worn in ancient times by the women of the Greek island of Cos.
7. The Greek poetess, born on the island of Lesbos c. 612 B.C. *Barbitos* (Greek): lyre.
8. The god of an ecstatic, emotional religion among the early Greeks, as well as the god of wine (later Bacchus).
9. Mortifications of the flesh.
1. Two figures from Shakespeare's *The Tempest,* Caliban almost an animal, Ariel totally spiritual.
2. Heraclitus of Ephesus, the early Greek philosopher (fl. c. 500 B.C.), whose central doctrine was that all things are in a state of flux ("everything flows").

Even the Christian beauty
Defects—after Samothrace; [3]
15   We see τὸ καλὸν [4]
Decreed in the market place.

Faun's flesh is not to us,
Nor the saint's vision.
We have the press for wafer;
20   Franchise for circumcision.

All men, in law, are equals.
Free of Pisistratus,[5]
We choose a knave or an eunuch
To rule over us.

25   O bright Apollo,
τίν ἄνδρα, τίν ἥρωα, τίνα θεὸν,[6]
What god, man, or hero
Shall I place a tin wreath upon!

IV

These fought in any case,
and some believing,
                    pro domo,[7] in any case . . .

Some quick to arm,
5   some for adventure,
some from fear of weakness,
some from fear of censure,
some for love of slaughter, in imagination,
learning later . . .
10   some in fear, learning love of slaughter;

Died some, pro patria,
                    non "dulce" non "et decor" . . .[8]
walked eye-deep in hell
believing in old men's lies, then unbelieving
15   came home, home to a lie,
home to many deceits,
home to old lies and new infamy;
usury age-old and age-thick
and liars in public places.

20   Daring as never before, wastage as never before.
Young blood and high blood,
fair cheeks, and fine bodies;

3. An Aegean island where was found the masterpiece of Hellenistic sculpture, the Winged Victory (early 2nd century B.C.?), now in the Louvre. That Pound has this feature of Samothrace in mind here is given at least slight support by the fact that the Winged Victory figures in a prose piece by Remy de Gourmont, "*Stratagèmes*," which has a role in Poem XI of this sequence.
4. Tò kalón (Greek): "The Beautiful."
5. Athenian tyrant (in the sense of absolute ruler, but without later connotations of one who rules cruelly or oppressively), d. 527 B.C. "His long rule weakened the grip of the aristocrats upon their followers, encouraged individualism in many circles, and brought the cultural enlightenment and financial prosperity in which a movement towards democracy became possible" (*Oxford Classical Dictionary*).
6. Part of a line from the second Olympic ode of the Greek poet Pindar (518–438 B.C.), transliterated : tín ándra, tín héroa, tína theòn [keladésimon]: "What man, what hero, what god [shall we celebrate]?"
7. From the Latin phrase *pro domo sua*, "for one's own home."
8. The famous line from one of Horace's *Odes* (III.ii.13): *Dulce et decorum est pro patria mori* ("Sweet and fitting it is to die for one's country").

fortitude as never before

frankness as never before,
25 disillusions as never told in the old days,
hysterias, trench confessions,
laughter out of dead bellies.

V

There died a myriad,
And of the best, among them,
For an old bitch gone in the teeth,
For a botched civilization,

5   Charm, smiling at the good mouth,
Quick eyes gone under earth's lid,

For two gross of broken statues,
For a few thousand battered books.

Yeux Glauques [9]

Gladstone [1] was still respected,
When John Ruskin produced
"King's Treasuries"; [2] Swinburne
And Rossetti still abused.

5   Fetid Buchanan [3] lifted up his voice
When that faun's head of hers
Became a pastime for
Painters and adulterers.

The Burne-Jones cartons [4]
10 Have preserved her eyes;
Still, at the Tate, they teach
Cophetua to rhapsodize;

Thin like brook water,
With a vacant gaze.
15 The English Rubaiyat was stillborn [5]
In those days.

The thin, clear gaze, the same
Still darts out faunlike from the half-ruined face,
Questing and passive. . . .

9. French, "sea-green eyes." Pound's poem focuses on the eyes of Elizabeth Siddal, wife of D. G. Rossetti and the model used for many of his paintings as well as for those of other Pre-Raphaelite painters, including Burne-Jones, in whose painting "King Cophetua and the Beggar Maid" (1884; now in the Tate Gallery, London; see stanza 3 below) she appears as the beggar maid (painted from studies made earlier; Elizabeth Siddal died in 1862). William Michael Rossetti described her as "Tall, finely formed, with a lofty neck, and regular yet somewhat uncommon features, greenish-blue unsparkling eyes. . . ."
1. William Ewart Gladstone was Prime Minister for four separate terms between 1868 and 1894.
2. John Ruskin's *Sesame and Lilies,* consisting of two parts ("Sesame: Of Kings' Treasuries" and "Lilies: Of Queens' Gardens") was published in 1865, with a drawing by Burne-Jones on the title page. Its subject was "the treasures hidden in books; . . . the way we find them and the way we lose them," the way we lose them being through a Philistine indifference to art, religion, and moral purpose.
3. Robert W. Buchanan's controversial attack on Swinburne, Morris, and Rossetti, but especially Rossetti, appeared pseudonymously in *The Contemporary Review* for October 1871.
4. For "cartoons," in the sense of preliminary studies from which a finished painting is made.
5. FitzGerald's translation of *The Rubáiyát of Omar Khayyám* was first published in 1859. It did not sell and was remaindered at a penny a copy outside the publisher's shop, where Swinburne and Rossetti discovered it and bought several copies to give away; returning to buy more, they found that the price had begun to go up.

20   "Ah, poor Jenny's case" . . .[6]

Bewildered that a world
Shows no surprise
At her last maquero's [7]
Adulteries.

"Siena Mi Fe'; Disfecemi Maremma"[8]

Among the pickled fetuses and bottled bones,
Engaged in perfecting the catalogue,
I found the last scion of the
Senatorial families of Strasbourg, Monsieur Verog.[9]

5   For two hours he talked of Gallifet; [1]
Of Dowson; of the Rhymers' Club; [2]
Told me how Johnson (Lionel) died [3]
By falling from a high stool in a pub . . .

But showed no trace of alcohol
10   At the autopsy, privately performed—
Tissue preserved—the pure mind
Arose toward Newman [4] as the whiskey warmed.

Dowson found harlots cheaper than hotels;
Headlam [5] for uplift; Image [6] impartially imbued
15   With raptures for Bacchus, Terpsichore and the Church.
So spoke the author of "The Dorian Mood,"

M. Verog, out of step with the decade,
Detached from his contemporaries,
Neglected by the young,
20   Because of these reveries.

---

6. Buchanan's criticism of Rossetti had discussed one poem in particular, "Jenny," claiming that its scene had appealed to the poet less for human tenderness than for its "inherent quality of animalism." The poem presents the thoughts of a young man who has gone with Jenny, a prostitute, to her room after a dance and spends the night with her sleeping head resting on his knee. It has an epigraph from *The Merry Wives of Windsor*: "'Vengence of Jenny's case! Fie on her! Never name her, child!'—Mrs. Quickly." Shakespeare has her continue, ". . . if she be a whore." The Jenny of Rossetti's poem has nothing to do with Elizabeth Siddal, but one phrase describing Jenny—"whose eyes are as blue as the skies"—may be the link, in Pound's poem, between Jenny and the eyes of Rossetti's wife and model.
7. For the French slang term for pimp, *"maquereau."*
8. "Siena made me; the Maremma undid me." (*Purgatorio*, V. 133.) Words spoken to Dante by the spirit of Pia de' Tolomei, encountered in Purgatory among those who have repented only at the last moment and without absolution. Although innocent, she had been imprisoned by her husband in a fortress in the Maremma, and died there, either by poison or from malaria. The line carries with it the idea of exile from one's native place; the subject of Pound's poem had been born in Alsace.
9. Pound's model for Verog was Victor Gustav Plarr (1863–1929) friend of such Nineties poets as Yeats, Ernest Dowson, and Lionel Johnson, like them a member of the Rhymers' Club. Besides his own poems (*In the Dorian Mood*, 1896) and biographical work arising out of his post as librarian to the Royal College of Surgeons, he published a brief memoir of Ernest Dowson, covering the years of their friendship (1888–1897).
1. Gallifet (1830–1909), a French general who distinguished himself at the head of the *Chasseurs d'Afrique* at the battle of Sedan, in the Franco-Prussian War, 1870.
2. Founded in 1891, it consisted of from 12 to 14 members who met at the Cheshire Cheese in Fleet St., London, for literary discussion.
3. Lionel Johnson (1867–1902) was received into the Church of Rome in 1891 and published his first collection of poems in 1895. He died from an injury sustained by falling in the street.
4. John Henry Cardinal Newman (1801–1890), who joined the Church of Rome in 1845, author of *Apologia pro Vita Sua* (1864–65).
5. Rev. Stewart Headlam (1847–1924), liberal clergyman who for many years a vicar in the East End of London, writer on social and religious questions; although he scarcely knew Wilde, he had helped post bail for him at the time of his arrest in 1895.
6. Selwyn Image (1849–1930), artist, poet, and clergyman; his work had appeared in such Nineties periodicals as *The Hobby Horse* and *The Savoy*. Bacchus is the Roman god of wine, Terpsichore the Greek muse of the dance.

Brennbaum [7]

The skylike limpid eyes,
The circular infant's face,
The stiffness from spats to collar
Never relaxing into grace;

5 The heavy memories of Horeb, Sinai [8] and the 'forty
      years,[9]
Showed only when the daylight fell
Level across the face
Of Brennbaum "The Impeccable."

Mr. Nixon [1]

In the cream gilded cabin of his steam yacht
Mr. Nixon advised me kindly, to advance with fewer
Dangers of delay. "Consider
               Carefully the reviewer.

5 "I was as poor as you are;
"When I began I got, of course,
"Advance on royalties, fifty at first," said Mr. Nixon,
"Follow me, and take a column,
"Even if you have to work free.

10 "Butter reviewers. From fifty to three hundred
"I rose in eighteen months;
"The hardest nut I had to crack
"Was Dr. Dundas.

"I never mentioned a man but with the view
15 "Of selling my own works.
"The tip's a good one, as for literature
"It gives no man a sinecure.

"And no one knows, at sight, a masterpiece.
"And give up verse, my boy,
20 "There's nothing in it."

.   .   .   .

Likewise a friend of Bloughram's once advised me:
Don't kick against the pricks,
Accept opinion. The "Nineties" tried your game
And died, there's nothing in it.

---

7. The model for Brennbaum is pretty clearly
Max Beerbohm, brilliant satirist in his books
(*Zuleika Dobson*, 1911, and *A Christmas Gar-
land*, 1912), but even more widely known for
his satiric drawings and caricatures of the
literary and political great. He was known as
"The Incomparable Max," but Pound, in an
essay on Remy de Gourmont, calls him "the
impeccable Beerbohm." The Beerbohms were
of German descent, however, not Jewish.
8. The young Moses, keeping Jethro's sheep,
led them "to the backside of the desert, and
came to the mountain of God, even to Horeb,"
where the angel of the Lord appeared to him
out of the burning bush (Exodus iii.1–2).
On the top of Mt. Sinai, Moses received the

Ten Commandments from God (Exodus xix.
20 ff.).
9. The 40 years spent by the Israelites in the
wilderness, after the Exodus from Egypt.
1. This portrait of the calculatingly successful
writer is generally thought to refer to Arnold
Bennett (1867–1931), the novelist, who did
indeed own a yacht. "Dr. Dundas" and the
"friend of Bloughram's" are stock figures not
susceptible of identification, but in the latter
there may be intended a reference to the wily
arguments of the bishop, in Browning's
"Bishop Blougram's Apology," who lives on
the Church whose doctrines he does not en-
tirely believe.

X

Beneath the sagging roof
The stylist [2] has taken shelter,
Unpaid, uncelebrated,
At last from the world's welter

5   Nature receives him;
With a placid and uneducated mistress
He exercises his talents
And the soil meets his distress.

The haven from sophistications and contentions
10   Leaks through its thatch;
He offers succulent cooking;
The door has a creaking latch.

XI

"Conservatrix of Milésien" [3]
Habits of mind and feeling,
Possibly. But in Ealing [4]
With the most bank-clerkly of Englishmen?

5   No, "Milésian" is an exaggeration.
No instinct has survived in her
Older than those her grandmother
Told her would fit her station.

XII

"Daphne with her thighs in bark
Stretches toward me her leafy hands,"[5]—
Subjectively. In the stuffed-satin drawing room
I await The Lady Valentine's commands,

5   Knowing my coat has never been
Of precisely the fashion
To stimulate, in her,
A durable passion;

Doubtful, somewhat, of the value
10   Of well-gowned approbation
Of literary effort,
But never of The Lady Valentine's vocation:

Poetry, her border of ideas,
The edge, uncertain, but a means of blending
15   With other strata
Where the lower and higher have ending;

2. In direct contrast with the preceding portrait, this one may be based on Ford Madox Ford (1873–1939), experimental novelist, editor of *The English Review*, and interested in the theory of "The New Novel" as practiced by James and Conrad. The poem depicts his circumstances at one particular period in his life.
3. Pound was fond of a phrase which occurs in a story by Remy de Gourmont, *"Stratagemes," in Histoires magiques*. Riffling through his recollections of women he has possessed, the narrator thinks of the role of knowingly induced pain in lovemaking; women who know how to bite, he says, shouldn't be despised, they are *conservatrices de traditions milésiennes* ("preservers of Milesian traditions")—Milesian from Miletus, ancient Greek city in Asia Minor and the native city of one Aristides (c. 100 B.C.), the writer or collector of a lost group of erotic stories, stories in what has come to be called "the Milesian genre."
4. Staid residential district in West London.
5. The first two lines translate two lines from Gautier's *"Le Château du souvenir"* ("The Castle of Memory"): the speaker is in a salon decorated with the exploits of Apollo. (Daphne, pursued by Apollo, was turned into a laurel to enable her to escape; the tree became sacred to Apollo, its leaves the symbol of literary honor.)

A hook to catch the Lady Jane's attention,
A modulation toward the theatre,
Also, in the case of revolution,
20   A possible friend and comforter.

. . . .

Conduct, on the other hand, the soul
"Which the highest cultures have nourished"
To Fleet St.[6] where
Dr. Johnson [7] flourished;

25   Beside this thoroughfare
The sale of half-hose has
Long since superseded the cultivation
Of Pierian [8] roses.

Envoi (1919)

Go, dumb-born book,
Tell her that sang me once that song of Lawes: [9]
Hadst thou but song
As thou hast subjects known,
5   *Then were there cause in thee that should condone*
Even my faults that heavy upon me lie,
And build her glories their longevity.

Tell her that sheds
Such treasure in the air,
10 *Recking naught else but that her graces give*
Life to the moment,
I would bid them live
As roses might, in magic amber laid,
Red overwrought with orange and all made
15 *One substance and one color*
Braving time.

Tell her that goes
With song upon her lips
But sings not out the song, nor knows
20 *The maker of it, some other mouth,*
May be as fair as hers,
Might, in new ages, gain her worshipers,
When our two dusts with Waller's shall be laid,
Siftings on siftings in oblivion,
25 *Till change hath broken down*
All things save Beauty alone.

1920

6. The center of London journalism.
7. Dr. Samuel Johnson (1709–1784), the great critic after whom the latter half of the 18th century is known as "The Age of Johnson," and who participated in many journalistic enterprises, both as contributor (for example, to *The Gentlemen's Magazine*) and as founder (of *The Rambler*).
8. Pieria was a district on the northern slopes of Mt. Olympus, where the cult of the Muses originated.
9. Henry Lawes (1596–1662), the composer who had set to music "Go, lovely rose," the best known poem of the Cavalier poet Edmund Waller (1606–1687), the phrasing and movement of which are echoed in this poem.

H. D. (Hilda Doolittle)
(1886–1961)

Sea Rose

Rose, harsh rose,
marred and with stint of petals,
meager flower, thin,
sparse of leaf,

5   more precious
than a wet rose
single on a stem—
you are caught in the drift.

Stunted, with small leaf,
10   you are flung on the sand,
you are lifted
in the crisp sand
that drives in the wind.

Can the spice-rose
15   drip such acrid fragrance
hardened in a leaf?

1916

Helen [1]

All Greece hates
the still eyes in the white face,
the luster as of olives
where she stands,
5   And the white hands.

All Greece reviles
the wan face when she smiles,
hating it deeper still
when it grows wan and white,
10   remembering past enchantments
and past ills.

Greece sees unmoved,
God's daughter,[2] born of love,
the beauty of cool feet
15   and slenderest knees,
could love indeed the maid,
only if she were laid,
white ash amid funereal cypresses.

1924

1. Helen of Troy, whose abduction by Paris
led to the Trojan War and ultimately to the
defeat of Troy by Greece.

2. Helen was said to be the daughter of Zeus,
ruler of the gods, and Leda, a mortal woman.

ROBINSON JEFFERS
(1887–1962)

Shine, Perishing Republic

While this America settles in the mold of its vulgarity, heavily thickening to
  empire,
And protest, only a bubble in the molten mass, pops and sighs out, and the
  mass hardens,

I sadly smiling remember that the flower fades to make fruit, the fruit rots
  to make earth.
Out of the mother; and through the spring exultances, ripeness and
  decadence; and home to the mother.

5 You making haste haste on decay: not blameworthy; life is good, be it
     stubbornly long or suddenly
A mortal splendor: meteors are not needed less than mountains: shine,
  perishing republic.

But for my children, I would have them keep their distance from the
  thickening center; corruption
Never has been compulsory, when the cities lie at the monster's feet there
  are left the mountains.

And boys, be in nothing so moderate as in love of man, a clever servant,
  insufferable master.
10 There is the trap that catches noblest spirits, that caught—they say—God,
      when he walked on earth.

                                                                    1924

Hurt Hawks

                1
The broken pillar of the wing jags from the clotted shoulder,
The wing trails like a banner in defeat,
No more to use the sky forever but live with famine
And pain a few days: cat nor coyote
5 Will shorten the week of waiting for death, there is game without talons.
He stands under the oak-bush and waits
The lame feet of salvation; at night he remembers freedom
And flies in a dream, the dawns ruin it.
He is strong and pain is worse to the strong, incapacity is worse.
10 The curs of the day come and torment him
At distance, no one but death the redeemer will humble that head,
The intrepid readiness, the terrible eyes.
The wild God of the world is sometimes merciful to those
That ask mercy, not often to the arrogant.
15 You do not know him, you communal people, or you have forgotten him;
Intemperate and savage, the hawk remembers him;
Beautiful and wild, the hawks, and men that are dying, remember him.

2

I'd sooner, except the penalties, kill a man than a hawk; but
  the great redtail°   *red-tailed hawk*
Had nothing left but unable misery
20 From the bone too shattered for mending, the wing that trailed under
  his talons when he moved.
We had fed him six weeks, I gave him freedom,
He wandered over the foreland hill and returned in the evening,
  asking for death,
Not like a beggar, still eyed with the old
Implacable arrogance. I gave him the lead gift in the twilight. What
  fell was relaxed,
25 Owl-downy, soft feminine feathers; but what
Soared: the fierce rush: the night-herons by the flooded river cried
  fear at its rising
Before it was quite unsheathed from reality.

1928

MARIANNE MOORE
(1887–1972)

Poetry

I, too, dislike it: there are things that are important beyond all this fiddle.
  Reading it, however, with a perfect contempt for it, one discovers in
  it after all, a place for the genuine.
    Hands that can grasp, eyes
5   that can dilate, hair that can rise
      if it must, these things are important not because a

high-sounding interpretation can be put upon them but because they are
  useful. When they become so derivative as to become unintelligible,
  the same thing may be said for all of us, that we
10   do not admire what
    we cannot understand: the bat
      holding on upside down or in quest of something to

eat, elephants pushing, a wild horse taking a roll, a tireless wolf under
  a tree, the immovable critic twitching his skin like a horse that feels
  a flea, the base-
15 ball fan, the statistician—
    nor is it valid
      to discriminate against "business documents and

school-books"; 1 all these phenomena are important. One must make a
  distinction
  however: when dragged into prominence by half poets, the result is
    not poetry,

<hr>

1. *"Diary of Tolstoy* (Dutton), p. 84. 'Where the boundary between prose and poetry lies, I shall never be able to understand. The question is raised in manuals of style, yet the answer to it lies beyond me. Poetry is verse: prose is not verse. Or else poetry is everything with the exception of business documents and school books'" [Moore's note].

20   nor till the poets among us can be
       "literalists of
         the imagination" [2]—above
           insolence and triviality and can present

    for inspection, "imaginary gardens with real toads in them," shall we have
25   it. In the meantime, if you demand on the one hand,
       the raw material of poetry in
         all its rawness and
         that which is on the other hand
           genuine, you are interested in poetry.

                                             1921

No Swan So Fine

"No water so still as the
    dead fountains of Versailles."[1] No swan,
with swart blind look askance
and gondoliering legs,[2] so fine
5   as the chintz china one with fawn-
brown eyes and toothed gold
collar on to show whose bird it was.

Lodged in the Louis Fifteenth
    candelabrum-tree[3] of cockscomb-
10   tinted buttons, dahlias,
sea-urchins, and everlastings,[4]
    it perches on the branching foam
of polished sculptured
flowers—at ease and tall. The king is dead.

                                     1932, 1951

Peter

    Strong and slippery,
built for the midnight grass-party
confronted by four cats, he sleeps his time away—
the detached first claw on the foreleg corresponding
5   to the thumb, retracted to its tip; the small tuft of fronds
or katydid-legs above each eye numbering all units
in each group; the shadbones[5] regularly set about the mouth
to droop or rise in unison like porcupine-quills.
He lets himself be flattened out by gravity,
10   as seaweed is tamed and weakened by the sun,
compelled when extended, to lie stationary.
Sleep is the result of his delusion that one must
do as well as one can for oneself,
sleep—epitome of what is to him the end of life.

2. "Yeats: *Ideas of Good and Evil* (A. H. Bullen), p. 182. 'The limitation of [Blake's] view was from the very intensity of his vision; he was a too literal realist of imagination, as others are of nature; and because he believed that the figures seen by the mind's eye, when exalted by inspiration, were "eternal existences," symbols of divine essences, he hated every grace of style that might obscure their lineaments'" [Moore's note].
1. Famed palace of French kings in the late 17th and early 18th centuries, now a museum.
2. Italian gondoliers paddle from the stern to propel their gondolas.
3. "A pair of Louis XV candelabra with Dresden figures of swans belonging to Lord Balfour" [Moore's note].
4. Plants whose flowers may be dried without losing their form or color; also, the flowers from such plants.
5. Long, very fine bones of the shad fish.

15 Demonstrate on him how the lady placed a forked stick
   on the innocuous neck-sides of the dangerous southern snake.
   One need not try to stir him up; his prune-shaped head
   and alligator-eyes are not party to the joke.
   Lifted and handled, he may be dangled like an eel
20 or set up on the forearm like a mouse;
   his eyes bisected by pupils of a pin's width,
   are flickeringly exhibited, then covered up.
   May be? I should have said might have been;
   when he has been got the better of in a dream—
25 as in a fight with nature or with cats, we all know it.
   Profound sleep is not with him a fixed illusion.
   Springing about with froglike accuracy, with jerky cries
   when taken in hand, he is himself again;
   to sit caged by the rungs of a domestic chair
30 would be unprofitable—human. What is the good of hypocrisy?
   it is permissible to choose one's employment,
   to abandon the nail, or roly-poly,
   when it shows signs of being no longer a pleasure,
   to score the nearby magazine with a double line of strokes.
35 He can talk but insolently says nothing. What of it?
   When one is frank, one's very presence is a compliment.
   It is clear that he can see the virtue of naturalness,
   that he does not regard the published fact as a surrender.
   As for the disposition invariably to affront,
40 an animal with claws should have an opportunity to use them.
   The eel-like extension of trunk into tail is not an accident.
   To leap, to lengthen out, divide the air, to purloin, to pursue.
   To tell the hen: fly over the fence, go in the wrong way
   in your perturbation—this is life;
45 to do less would be nothing but dishonesty.

1935

EDWIN MUIR
(1887–1959)

The Animals

They do not live in the world,
Are not in time and space.
From birth to death hurled
No word do they have, not one
5 To plant a foot upon,
Were never in any place.

For with names the world was called
Out of the empty air,[3]
With names was built and walled,

---

3. Genesis i.5, i.8, and i.10 illustrate the naming of the elements of the world as they were created ("And God called the light Day, and the darkness he called Night. . . . And God called the firmament Heaven. . . . And God called the dry land Earth. . . .")

10 Line and circle and square,
    Dust and emerald;
    Snatched from deceiving death
    By the articulate breath.

    But these have never trod
15 Twice the familiar track,
    Never never turned back
    Into the memoried day.
    All is new and near
    In the unchanging Here
20 Of the fifth great day of God,[4]
    That shall remain the same,
    Never shall pass away.

    On the sixth day we came.

                                              1952

The Brothers [8]

    Last night I watched my brothers play,
    The gentle and the reckless one,
    In a field two yards away.
    For half a century they were gone
5   Beyond the other side of care
    To be among the peaceful dead.
    Even in a dream how could I dare
    Interrogate that happiness
    So wildly spent yet never less?
10 For still they raced about the green
    And were like two revolving suns;
    A brightness poured from head to head,
    So strong I could not see their eyes
    Or look into their paradise.
15 What were they doing, the happy ones?
    Yet where I was they once had been.

    I thought, How could I be so dull,
    Twenty thousand days ago,
    Not to see they were beautiful?
20 I asked them, Were you really so
    As you are now, that other day?
    And the dream was soon away.

    For then we played for victory
    And not to make each other glad.
25 A darkness covered every head,

4. Genesis i.20–25 describes the creation of the fish of the sea, the fowls of the air, and the beasts of the earth on the fifth day.
8. Two of Muir's three brothers had died before he himself was 18, and what he says of them here, in a poem completed toward the end of his own life, and which records a dream-vision of his brothers during their life together in Orkney, shares in what he has to say in his *Autobiography* (1954) about the sources of his poetry: "I must have been influenced by something, since we all are, but when I try to find out what it was that influenced me, I can only think of the years of childhood which I spent on my father's farm in the little island of Wyre in Orkney, and the beauty I apprehended then, before I knew there was beauty. These years had come alive, after being forgotten for so long, and when I wrote about horses they were my father's plow-horses as I saw them when I was four or five: and a poem on Achilles pursuing Hector round the walls of Troy was really a resuscitation of the afternoon when I ran away, in real terror, from another boy as I returned from school."

Frowns twisted the original face,
And through that mask we could not see
The beauty and the buried grace.

I have observed in foolish awe
30   The dateless mid-days of the law
And seen indifferent justice done
By everyone on everyone.
And in a vision I have seen
My brothers playing on the green.

                                          1956   1960

T. S. ELIOT
(1888–1965)

The Love Song of J. Alfred Prufrock

S'io credesse che mia risposta fosse
A persona che mai tornasse al mondo,
Questa fiamma staria senza piu scosse.
Ma perciocche giammai di questo fondo
Non torno vivo alcun, s'i'odo il vero,
Senza tema d'infamia ti rispondo.[1]

Let us go then, you and I,
When the evening is spread out against the sky
Like a patient etherized upon a table;
Let us go, through certain half-deserted streets,
5   The muttering retreats
Of restless nights in one-night cheap hotels
And sawdust restaurants with oyster-shells:
Streets that follow like a tedious argument
Of insidious intent
10   To lead you to an overwhelming question. . .
Oh, do not ask, "What is it?"
Let us go and make our visit.

In the room the women come and go
Talking of Michelangelo.

15   The yellow fog that rubs its back upon the window-panes
The yellow smoke that rubs its muzzle on the window-panes
Licked its tongue into the corners of the evening,
Lingered upon the pools that stand in drains,
Let fall upon its back the soot that falls from chimneys,
20   Slipped by the terrace, made a sudden leap,
And seeing that it was a soft October night,
Curled once about the house, and fell asleep.

1. Dante, *Inferno*, XXVII.61–66. These words
are spoken by Guido da Montefeltro, whom
Dante and Virgil have encountered in the
Eighth Chasm, that of the False Counselors,
where each spirit is concealed within a flame
which moves as the spirit speaks: "If I
thought my answer were given/to anyone who
would ever return to the world,/this flame
would stand still without moving any further./
But since never from this abyss/has anyone
ever returned alive, if what I hear is true,/
without fear of infamy I answer thee."

And indeed there will be time
For the yellow smoke that slides along the street,
25   Rubbing its back upon the window-panes;
There will be time, there will be time
To prepare a face to meet the faces that you meet;
There will be time to murder and create,
And time for all the works and days[2] of hands
30   That lift and drop a question on your plate;
Time for you and time for me,
And time yet for a hundred indecisions,
And for a hundred visions and revisions,
Before the taking of a toast and tea.

35   In the room the women come and go
Talking of Michelangelo.

And indeed there will be time
To wonder, "Do I dare?" and, "Do I dare?"
Time to turn back and descend the stair,
40   With a bald spot in the middle of my hair—
[They will say: "How his hair is growing thin!"]
My morning coat, my collar mounting firmly to the chin,
My necktie rich and modest, but asserted by a simple pin—
[They will say: "But how his arms and legs are thin!"]
45   Do I dare
Disturb the universe?
In a minute there is time
For decisions and revisions which a minute will reverse.

For I have known them all already, known them all:
50   Have known the evenings, mornings, afternoons,
I have measured out my life with coffee spoons;
I know the voices dying with a dying fall
Beneath the music from a farther room.
     So how should I presume?

55   And I have known the eyes already, known them all—
The eyes that fix you in a formulated phrase,
And when I am formulated, sprawling on a pin,
When I am pinned and wriggling on the wall,
Then how should I begin
60   To spit out all the butt-ends of my days and ways?
     And how should I presume?

And I have known the arms already, known them all—
Arms that are braceleted and white and bare
[But in the lamplight, downed with light brown hair!]
65   Is it perfume from a dress
That makes me so digress?
Arms that lie along a table, or wrap about a shawl.
     And should I then presume?
     And how should I begin?

          . . . . . .

70   Shall I say, I have gone at dusk through narrow streets
And watched the smoke that rises from the pipes
Of lonely men in shirt-sleeves, leaning out of windows? . . .

---

2. Possibly alludes to the title of a didactic work on the seasonal pursuits of country life, *Works and Days*, by the Greek poet Hesiod (eighth century B.C.).

I should have been a pair of ragged claws
Scuttling across the floors of silent seas.

. . . .

75 And the afternoon, the evening, sleeps so peacefully!
Smoothed by long fingers,
Asleep . . . tired . . . or it malingers,
Stretched on the floor, here beside you and me.
Should I, after tea and cakes and ices,
80 Have the strength to force the moment to its crisis?
But though I have wept and fasted, wept and prayed,
Though I have seen my head [grown slightly bald] brought in upon a
        platter,[3]
I am no prophet—and here's no great matter;
I have seen the moment of my greatness flicker,
85 And I have seen the eternal Footman hold my coat, and snicker,
And in short, I was afraid.

And would it have been worth it, after all,
After the cups, the marmalade, the tea,
Among the porcelain, among some talk of you and me,
90 Would it have been worth while,
To have bitten off the matter with a smile,
To have squeezed the universe into a ball
To roll it toward some overwhelming question,
To say: "I am Lazarus,[4] come from the dead,
95 Come back to tell you all, I shall tell you all"—
If one, settling a pillow by her head,
        Should say: "That is not what I meant at all.
        That is not it, at all."

And would it have been worth it, after all,
100 Would it have been worth while,
After the sunsets and the dooryards and the sprinkled streets,
After the novels, after the teacups, after the skirts that trail along the floor—
And this, and so much more?—
It is impossible to say just what I mean!
105 But as if a magic lantern threw the nerves in patterns on a screen:
Would it have been worth while
If one, settling a pillow or throwing off a shawl,
And turning toward the window, should say:
        "That is not it at all,
110   That is not what I meant, at all."

. . . .

No! I am not Prince Hamlet, nor was meant to be;
Am an attendant lord, one that will do
To swell a progress,[5] start a scene or two,
Advise the prince; no doubt, an easy tool,
115 Deferential, glad to be of use,
Politic, cautious, and meticulous;
Full of high sentence,° but a bit obtuse;   *sententiousness*
At times, indeed, almost ridiculous—
Almost, at times, the Fool.

---

3. See the story of the martyrdom of St. John
the Baptist (Matthew xiv.1–12), whose head
was presented to Salome on a plate at the order
of the tetrarch Herod.
4. See John xi, and xii 1–2.
5. In Elizabethan sense: state journey.

120 I grow old . . . I grow old . . .
  I shall wear the bottoms of my trousers rolled.

  Shall I part my hair behind? Do I dare to eat a peach?
  I shall wear white flannel trousers, and walk upon the beach.
  I have heard the mermaids singing, each to each.

125 I do not think that they will sing to me.

  I have seen them riding seaward on the waves
  Combing the white hair of the waves blown back
  When the wind blows the water white and black.

  We have lingered in the chambers of the sea
130 By sea-girls wreathed with seaweed red and brown
  Till human voices wake us, and we drown.

1917

Preludes

1

  The winter evening settles down
  With smell of steaks in passageways.
  Six o'clock.
  The burnt-out ends of smoky days.
5 And now a gusty shower wraps
  The grimy scraps
  Of withered leaves about your feet
  And newspapers from vacant lots;
  The showers beat
10 On broken blinds and chimney-pots,
  And at the corner of the street
  A lonely cab-horse steams and stamps.
  And then the lighting of the lamps.

2

  The morning comes to consciousness
15 Of faint stale smells of beer
  From the sawdust-trampled street
  With all its muddy feet that press
  To early coffee-stands.
  With the other masquerades
20 That time resumes,
  One thinks of all the hands
  That are raising dingy shades
  In a thousand furnished rooms.

3

  You tossed a blanket from the bed,
25 You lay upon your back, and waited;
  You dozed, and watched the night revealing
  The thousand sordid images
  Of which your soul was constituted;
  They flickered against the ceiling.
30 And when all the world came back
  And the light crept up between the shutters
  And you heard the sparrows in the gutters,
  You had such a vision of the street
  As the street hardly understands;

35 Sitting along the bed's edge, where
    You curled the papers from your hair,
    Or clasped the yellow soles of feet
    In the palms of both soiled hands.

4

    His soul stretched tight across the skies
40 That fade behind a city block,
    Or trampled by insistent feet
    At four and five and six o'clock;
    And short square fingers stuffing pipes,
    And evening newspapers, and eyes
45 Assured of certain certainties,
    The conscience of a blackened street
    Impatient to assume the world.

    I am moved by fancies that are curled
    Around these images, and cling:
50 The notion of some infinitely gentle
    Infinitely suffering thing.

    Wipe your hand across your mouth, and laugh;
    The worlds revolve like ancient women
    Gathering fuel in vacant lots.

                                                      1917

Sweeney Among the Nightingales

ὤμοι, πέπληγμαι καιρίαν πληγὴν ἔσω.[3]

    Apeneck Sweeney spreads his knees
    Letting his arms hang down to laugh,
    The zebra stripes along his jaw
    Swelling to maculate° giraffe.   *spotted*

5   The circles of the stormy moon
    Slide westward toward the River Plate,[4]
    Death and the Raven[5] drift above
    And Sweeney guards the hornéd gate.[6]

    Gloomy Orion[7] and the Dog
10 Are veiled; and hushed the shrunken seas;
    The person in the Spanish cape
    Tries to sit on Sweeney's knees

    Slips and pulls the table cloth
    Overturns a coffee-cup,
15 Reorganized upon the floor
    She yawns and draws a stocking up;

    The silent man in mocha brown
    Sprawls at the window-sill and gapes;
    The waiter brings in oranges
20 Bananas figs and hothouse grapes;

3. Aeschylus, *Agamemnon*, line 1343. Aga-
memnon's cry, heard from inside the palace,
as Clytemnestra strikes her first blow: "Oh, I
have been struck a direct deadly blow, within!"
4. Rio de la Plata, an estuary of the Paraná
and Uruguay rivers, between Uruguay and
Argentina.
5. The southern constellation Corvus.

6. In Greek legend, dreams came to mortals
through two sets of gates: the gates of horn,
for dreams which were true, the gates of
ivory, for dreams which were untrue.
7. A constellation in which is seen the figure
of a hunter, with belt and sword; near it, the
dog-star, Sirius, represents the hunter's dog.

The silent vertebrate in brown
Contracts and concentrates, withdraws;
Rachel *née* Rabinovitch
Tears at the grapes with murderous paws;

25 She and the lady in the cape
Are suspect, thought to be in league;
Therefore the man with heavy eyes
Declines the gambit, shows fatigue,

Leaves the room and reappears
30 Outside the window, leaning in,
Branches of wistaria
Circumscribe a golden grin;

The host with someone indistinct
Converses at the door apart,
35 The nightingales are singing near
The Convent of the Sacred Heart,

And sang within the bloody wood
When Agamemnon cried aloud,
And let their liquid siftings fall
40 To stain the stiff dishonored shroud.

1919

The Waste Land[2]

"Nam Sibyllam quidem Cumis ego ipse oculis meis vidi
in ampulla pendere, et cum illi pueri dicerent: Σίβυλλα τί
θέλεις; respondebat illa: ἀποθανεῖν θέλω."[3]

FOR EZRA POUND
il miglior fabbro.[4]

I. The Burial of the Dead[5]

April is the cruelest month, breeding
Lilacs out of the dead land, mixing
Memory and desire, stirring
Dull roots with spring rain.
5 Winter kept us warm, covering
Earth in forgetful snow, feeding
A little life with dried tubers.

2. On its first publication in book form, T. S. Eliot provided *The Waste Land* with notes directing the reader to the sources of many of its allusions and explaining certain phases of its plan. Eliot's notes are included below. His general note to the poem is as follows: "Not only the title, but the plan and a good deal of the incidental symbolism of the poem were suggested by Miss Jessie L. Weston's book on the Grail legend: *From Ritual to Romance* (Cambridge). Indeed, so deeply am I indebted, Miss Weston's book will elucidate the difficulties of the poem much better than my notes can do; and I recommend it (apart from the great interest of the book itself) to any who think such elucidation of the poem worth the trouble. To another work of anthropology I am indebted in general, one which has influenced our generation profoundly; I mean *The Golden Bough* [by Sir James Frazer; 12 volumes, 1890–1915]; I have used especially the two volumes *Adonis, Attis,*

Osiris. Anyone who is acquainted with these works will immediately recognize in the poem certain references to vegetation ceremonies."
3. "For indeed I myself have seen, with my own eyes, the Sibyl hanging in a bottle at Cumae, and when those boys would say to her: 'Sibyl, what do you want?' she would reply, 'I want to die.'" From the *Satyricon* of Petronius (d. A.D. 66), chapter 48. According to legend the Sibyl, a prophetess who was immortal but subject to the withering of age, was kept in a bottle or cage suspended in the temple of Hercules at Cumae (near Naples).
4. "The better craftsman." The poet Guido Guinizelli, encountered by Dante in Purgatory, answers the latter's praise of him with praise of his predecessor, the Provençal poet Arnaut Daniel, as being "the better craftsman in the maternal tongue" (*Purgatorio,* XXVI.117).
5. From the burial service of the Anglican Church.

Summer surprised us, coming over the Starnbergersee[6]
With a shower of rain; we stopped in the colonnade,
10   And went on in sunlight, into the Hofgarten,
And drank coffee, and talked for an hour.
Bin gar keine Russin, stamm' aus Litauen, echt deutsch.[7]
And when we were children, staying at the archduke's,
My cousin's, he took me out on a sled,
15   And I was frightened. He said, Marie,
Marie, hold on tight. And down we went.
In the mountains, there you feel free.
I read, much of the night, and go south in the winter.

What are the roots that clutch, what branches grow
20   Out of this stony rubbish? Son of man,[8]
You cannot say, or guess, for you know only
A heap of broken images, where the sun beats,
And the dead tree gives no shelter, the cricket no relief,[9]
And the dry stone no sound of water. Only
25   There is shadow under this red rock,
(Come in under the shadow of this red rock),
And I will show you something different from either
Your shadow at morning striding behind you
Or your shadow at evening rising to meet you;
30   I will show you fear in a handful of dust.
               Frisch weht der Wind
               Der Heimat zu
               Mein Irisch Kind,
               Wo weilest du?[1]
35   "You gave me hyacinths first a year ago;
"They called me the hyacinth girl."
—Yet when we came back, late, from the Hyacinth garden,
Your arms full, and your hair wet, I could not
Speak, and my eyes failed, I was neither
40   Living nor dead, and I knew nothing,
Looking into the heart of light, the silence.
Oed' und leer das Meer.[2]

Madame Sosostris,[3] famous clairvoyante,
Had a bad cold, nevertheless
45   Is known to be the wisest woman in Europe,
With a wicked pack of cards.[4] Here, said she,

6. Lake a few miles south of Munich. The Hofgarten (line 10) is a public garden in Munich, partly surrounded by a colonnaded walk.
7. "I am by no means a Russian, I come from Lithuania, am really German."
8. "Cf. Ezekiel II, i" [Eliot's note].
9. "Cf. Ecclesiastes XII, v" [Eliot's note].
1. "V. *Tristan und Isolde,* I, verses 5–8" [Eliot's note]. The sailor's song from Wagner's opera: "Fresh blows the wind/Towards home./My Irish child,/Where are you lingering?"
2. "Id. III, verse 24" [Eliot's note]. "Empty and waste the sea": that is, the ship bringing Isolde back to the dying Tristan is nowhere in sight.
3. An invented, generic name for a fortune-teller, perhaps meant to have Egyptian overtones.
4. "I am not familiar with the exact constitution of the Tarot pack of cards, from which I have obviously departed to suit my own convenience. The Hanged Man, a member of the traditional pack, fits my purpose in two ways: because he is associated in my mind with the Hanged God of Frazer, and because

I associate him with the hooded figure in the passage of the disciples to Emmaus in Part V. The Phoenician Sailor and the Merchant appear later; also the 'crowds of people,' and Death by Water is executed in Part IV. The Man with Three Staves (an authentic member of the Tarot pack) I associate, quite arbitrarily, with the Fisher King himself" [Eliot's note]. The tarot cards are playing-cards, whose origin goes back to the 14th century in Italy, still in use both for playing and for fortune-telling, as here. The Hanged Man hangs by one foot from the top bar of a trapeze-like construction. The individual figures which the fortune-teller refers to as appearing on her cards have subtle and complex relations to figures who appear in the poem on other levels and to the three principal figures of the Fisher King myth (the impotent King of the waste land, the Deliverer, and the Woman). Besides the relationships which Eliot suggests in his note above, "Belladonna, * * * the lady of situations," looks ahead to the neurotic woman of the opening lines of Part II. The Hanged Man, whom Madame Sosostris cannot find, is the fertility god whose death would bring new life to his people.

Is your card, the drowned Phoenician Sailor,
(Those are pearls that were his eyes.[5] Look!)
Here is Belladonna, the Lady of the Rocks,
50   The lady of situations.
Here is the man with three staves, and here the Wheel,
And here is the one-eyed merchant, and this card,
Which is blank, is something he carries on his back,
Which I am forbidden to see. I do not find
55   The Hanged Man. Fear death by water.
I see crowds of people, walking round in a ring.
Thank you. If you see dear Mrs. Equitone,
Tell her I bring the horoscope myself:
One must be so careful these days.

60   Unreal City,[6]
Under the brown fog of a winter dawn,
A crowd flowed over London Bridge, so many,
I had not thought death had undone so many.[7]
Sighs, short and infrequent, were exhaled,[8]
65   And each man fixed his eyes before his feet.
Flowed up the hill and down King William Street,
To where Saint Mary Woolnoth kept the hours
With a dead sound on the final stroke of nine.[9]
There I saw one I knew, and stopped him, crying: "Stetson!
70   "You who were with me in the ships at Mylae![1]
"That corpse you planted last year in your garden,
"Has it begun to sprout? Will it bloom this year?
"Or has the sudden frost disturbed its bed?
"Oh keep the Dog far hence, that's friend to men,
75   "Or with his nails he'll dig it up again![2]
"You! hypocrite lecteur!—mon semblable,—mon frère!"[3]

II. A Game of Chess[4]

The Chair she sat in, like a burnished throne,[5]
Glowed on the marble, where the glass
Held up by standards wrought with fruited vines

5. From Ariel's song in Shakespeare's *The Tempest*, I.ii, "Full fathom five thy father lies."
6. "Cf. Baudelaire: 'Fourmillante cité, cité pleine de rêves,/Où le spectre en plein jour raccroche le passant' " [Eliot's note]. The lines are from *Les Sept vieillards* (*The Seven Old Men*), one of the poems in *Les Fleurs du mal* (1857): "Swarming city, city filled with dreams,/Where the specter in broad daylight accosts the passerby."
7. "Cf. Inferno III, 55–57: 'si lunga tratta/di gente, ch' io non avrei mai creduto/che morte tanta n'avesse disfatta' " [Eliot's note]. On his arrival in the Inferno, Dante sees the vast crowd of those who "lived without infamy and without praise, * * * such a long procession of people, that I would never have believed that death had undone so many."
8. "Cf. Inferno IV, 25–27: 'Quivi, secondo che per ascoltare,/non avea pianto, ma' che di sospiri,/che l'aura eterna facevan tremare' " [Eliot's note]. Descending into the first circle of Hell, peopled by those whose virtues did not outweigh the fact that they had not been baptized, or that they had lived before the advent of Christ, Dante hears a noise of lamentation: "Here, if one trusted to hearing, there was no weeping but so many sighs as caused the everlasting air to tremble."
9. "A phenomenon which I have often noticed" [Eliot's note]. King William Street leads into London Bridge; St. Mary Woolnoth stood in an angle formed by that street and Lombard Street. These and other London place-names

in the poem refer to the East End—the City, the usual name for London's financial and business center.
1. Sicilian seaport, near which the Romans gained a naval victory over the Carthaginians in 260 B.C.
2. "Cf. the Dirge in Webster's *White Devil*" [Eliot's note]. The Dirge begins, "Call for the robin redbreast and the wren," and ends, "But keep the wolf far thence, that's foe to men;/For with his nails he'll dig them up again."
3. "V. Baudelaire, Preface to *Fleurs du Mal*" [Eliot's note]. Baudelaire's prefatory poem is entitled *To the Reader*, and it takes him through a list of the evils which beset him— foolishness, error, sin, miserliness—evoking at the end the most monstrous vice of all, Ennui: "You, reader, know the delicate monster,/ —Hypocritical reader,—my counterpart,—my brother!"
4. The title alludes to two plays by Thomas Middleton (1570–1627), *A Game at Chesse* and *Women Beware Women*, both of which involve sexual intrigue. In the second, a game of chess is used to mark a seduction, the moves in the game paralleling the steps in the seduction.
5. "Cf. *Antony and Cleopatra*, II, ii, l. 190" [Eliot's note]. Enobarbus' long description of Cleopatra's first meeting with Antony on the River Cydnus begins: "The barge she sat in, like a burnished throne/Burned on the water * * *"

⁸⁰ From which a golden Cupidon peeped out
(Another hid his eyes behind his wing)
Doubled the flames of sevenbranched candelabra
Reflecting light upon the table as
The glitter of her jewels rose to meet it,
⁸⁵ From satin cases poured in rich profusion;
In vials of ivory and colored glass
Unstoppered, lurked her strange synthetic perfumes,
Unguent, powdered, or liquid—troubled, confused
And drowned the sense in odors; stirred by the air
⁹⁰ That freshened from the window, these ascended
In fattening the prolonged candle-flames,
Flung their smoke into the laquearia,⁶
Stirring the pattern on the coffered ceiling.
Huge sea-wood fed with copper
⁹⁵ Burned green and orange, framed by the colored stone,
In which sad light a carvéd dolphin swam.
Above the antique mantel was displayed
As though a window gave upon the sylvan scene⁷
The change of Philomel, by the barbarous king⁸
¹⁰⁰ So rudely forced; yet there the nightingale⁹
Filled all the desert with inviolable voice
And still she cried, and still the world pursues,
"Jug Jug" to dirty ears.
And other withered stumps of time
¹⁰⁵ Were told upon the walls; staring forms
Leaned out, leaning, hushing the room enclosed.
Footsteps shuffled on the stair.
Under the firelight, under the brush, her hair
Spread out in fiery points
¹¹⁰ Glowed into words, then would be savagely still.

"My nerves are bad to-night. Yes, bad. Stay with me.
"Speak to me. Why do you never speak. Speak.
    "What are you thinking of? What thinking? What?
"I never know what you are thinking. Think."

¹¹⁵ I think we are in rats' alley¹
Where the dead men lost their bones.

"What is that noise?"
                    The wind under the door.²
"What is that noise now? What is the wind doing?"

---

6. "Laquearia. V. *Aeneid*, I, 726: dependent lychni laquearibus aureis/Incensi, et noctem flammis funalia vincunt" [Eliot's note]. "Laquearia" are the panels of a coffered ceiling, and the two lines read: "Glowing lamps hang from the gold-paneled ceiling, and the torches conquer the darkness with their flames." They come from the description of the banquet hall in Dido's palace at Carthage, just after Dido has been inspired by Venus with the passion for Aeneas, her guest, which will end (as Cleopatra's passion for Antony was to end) in her suicide.
7. "Sylvan scene. V. Milton, *Paradise Lost*, IV, 140" [Eliot's note]. The phrase occurs in the description of Eden as it looks to Satan when he sees it for the first time.
8. "V. Ovid, *Metamorphoses*, VI, Philomela"

[Eliot's note]. In Ovid's version of the myth, Tereus, king of Thrace, is married to Procne but falls in love with her sister, Philomela, whom he ravishes; he cuts out her tongue to silence her, but she weaves her story into an embroidered cloth. Procne avenges herself and her sister by murdering her child, Itys, and serving his flesh to his father at a banquet. The sisters are saved, as the maddened king pursues them, by being changed to birds: Procne into a swallow, Philomela into a nightingale.
9. "Cf. Part III, l. 204" [Eliot's note].
1. "Cf. Part III, l. 195" [Eliot's note].
2. "Cf. Webster: 'Is the wind in that door still?'" [Eliot's note], referring to John Webster's play, *The Devil's Law Case*, III.ii. 162.

120   Nothing again nothing.
                 "Do
"You know nothing? Do you see nothing? Do you remember
"Nothing?"

         I remember
125 Those are pearls that were his eyes.[3]
"Are you alive, or not? Is there nothing in your head?"

                                        But
O O O O that Shakespeherian Rag—
It's so elegant
130 So intelligent
"What shall I do now? What shall I do?"
"I shall rush out as I am, and walk the street
"With my hair down, so. What shall we do tomorrow?
"What shall we ever do?"
135   The hot water at ten.
And if it rains, a closed car at four.
And we shall play a game of chess,
Pressing lidless eyes and waiting for a knock upon the door.[4]

When Lil's husband got demobbed,° I said—   *demobilized*
140 I didn't mince my words, I said to her myself,
HURRY UP PLEASE ITS TIME[5]
Now Albert's coming back, make yourself a bit smart.
He'll want to know what you done with that money he gave you
To get yourself some teeth. He did, I was there.
145 You have them all out, Lil, and get a nice set,
He said, I swear, I can't bear to look at you.
And no more can't I, I said, and think of poor Albert,
He's been in the army four years, he wants a good time,
And if you don't give it him, there's others will, I said.
150 Oh is there, she said. Something o' that, I said.
Then I'll know who to thank, she said, and give me a straight look.
HURRY UP PLEASE ITS TIME
If you don't like it you can get on with it, I said.
Others can pick and choose if you can't.
155 But if Albert makes off, it won't be for lack of telling.
You ought to be ashamed, I said, to look so antique.
(And her only thirty-one.)
I can't help it, she said, pulling a long face,
It's them pills I took, to bring it off, she said.
160 (She's had five already, and nearly died of young George.)
The chemist° said it would be all right, but I've never been the same. *druggist*
You *are* a proper fool, I said.
Well, if Albert won't leave you alone, there it is, I said,
What you get married for if you don't want children?
165 HURRY UP PLEASE ITS TIME
Well, that Sunday Albert was home, they had a hot gammon,°   *smoked ham*
And they asked me in to dinner, to get the beauty of it hot—
HURRY UP PLEASE ITS TIME
HURRY UP PLEASE ITS TIME

3. See Part I, line 48 and note.
4. "Cf. the game of chess in Middleton's
Women Beware Women" [Eliot's note].

5. A typical injunction of a London bartender,
telling his customers that it is closing-time.

170 Goonight Bill. Goonight Lou. Goonight May. Goonight.
Ta ta. Goonight. Goonight.
Good night, ladies, good night, sweet ladies, good night, good night.[6]

III. The Fire Sermon[7]

The river's tent is broken: the last fingers of leaf
Clutch and sink into the wet bank. The wind
175 Crosses the brown land, unheard. The nymphs are departed.
Sweet Thames, run softly, till I end my song.[8]
The river bears no empty bottles, sandwich papers,
Silk handkerchiefs, cardboard boxes, cigarette ends
Or other testimony of summer nights. The nymphs are departed.
180 And their friends, the loitering heirs of city directors;
Departed, have left no addresses.
By the waters of Leman I sat down and wept[9] . . .
Sweet Thames, run softly till I end my song,
Sweet Thames, run softly, for I speak not loud or long.
185 But at my back in a cold blast I hear[1]
The rattle of the bones, and chuckle spread from ear to ear.
A rat crept softly through the vegetation
Dragging its slimy belly on the bank
While I was fishing in the dull canal
190 On a winter evening round behind the gashouse
Musing upon the king my brother's wreck[2]
And on the king my father's death before him.
White bodies naked on the low damp ground
And bones cast in a little low dry garret,
195 Rattled by the rat's foot only, year to year.
But at my back from time to time I hear[3]
The sound of horns and motors, which shall bring[4]
Sweeney to Mrs. Porter in the spring.
O the moon shone bright on Mrs. Porter[5]
200 And on her daughter
They wash their feet in soda water
Et O ces voix d'enfants, chantant dans la coupole![6]

---

6. Compare Ophelia's speech, *Hamlet*, IV.v. 71–72: "Good night, ladies, good night. Sweet ladies, good night, good night."
7. The title is that of the Buddha's Fire Sermon (see Eliot's note to line 308, below), in which he preached that "all things are on fire, * * * with the fire of passion, * * * with the fire of hatred, with the fire of infatuation; with birth, old age, death, sorrow, lamentation, misery, grief, and despair are they on fire," and that the disciple must conceive "an aversion for the eye," for all the senses, "for impressions received by the mind; and whatever sensation, pleasant, unpleasant, or indifferent, originates in dependence on impressions received by the mind," so that he may become divested of passion and hence be free and know that he is free and that "he is no more of this world."
8. "V. Spenser, *Prothalamion*" [Eliot's note]. The line is the refrain from Spenser's marriage-song, whose picture of "the silver-streaming Thames," its nymphs, and the London through which it flows are to be contrasted in detail with the same things as they are presented in Eliot's poem.
9. An echo of Psalm 137: "By the rivers of Babylon, there we sat down, yea, we wept, when we remembered Zion." Lac Léman is the Lake of Geneva, and *The Waste Land* is said to have been written at Lausanne, on its shore. *Leman* is also an archaic word for lover, mistress, or paramour.
1. Echoes Marvell's *To his Coy Mistress:* "But at my back I always hear/Time's winged chariot hurrying near."

2. "Cf. *The Tempest*, I, ii" [Eliot's note]. Ferdinand, in Shakespeare's play, just after hearing Ariel's song, "Come unto these yellow sands," and just before Ariel sings "Full fathom five thy father lies," the song inspired by the death by drowning of Ferdinand's father, describes himself as "sitting on a bank,/Weeping again the King my father's wreck./This music crept by me upon the waters."
3. "Cf. Marvell, *To His Coy Mistress*" [Eliot's note].
4. "Cf. Day, *Parliament of Bees:* 'When of the sudden, listening, you shall hear,/A noise of horns and hunting, which shall bring/Actaeon to Diana in the spring'" [Eliot's note]. The young Actaeon, discovering Diana bathing with her nymphs, was changed by the goddess to a stag, which his hounds set upon and killed.
5. "I do not know the origin of the ballad from which these lines are taken: it was reported to me from Sydney, Australia" [Eliot's note]. The ballad was popular with Australian soldiers in World War I. Sweeney (line 198) is the figure of vulgar, thoughtless sexual enterprise who figures in Eliot's *Sweeney among the Nightingales* and *Sweeney Agonistes*.
6. "V. Verlaine, *Parsifal*" [Eliot's note]. Quoted is the concluding line of Verlaine's sonnet (1886), which treats ironically Parsifal's conquering of some forms of fleshly temptation, only to be haunted—even in his purity—by others: "And, O those children's voices singing in the dome!"

Twit twit twit
Jug jug jug jug jug jug
205   So rudely forc'd.
Tereu[7]

Unreal City[8]
Under the brown fog of a winter noon
Mr. Eugenides, the Smyrna merchant
210   Unshaven, with a pocket full of currants
C.i.f. London: documents at sight,[9]
Asked me in demotic French[1]
To luncheon at the Cannon Street Hotel[2]
Followed by a weekend at the Metropole.

215   At the violet hour, when the eyes and back
Turn upward from the desk, when the human engine waits
Like a taxi throbbing waiting,
I Tiresias, though blind, throbbing between two lives,[3]
Old man with wrinkled female breasts, can see
220   At the violet hour, the evening hour that strives
Homeward, and brings the sailor home from sea,[4]
The typist home at teatime, clears her breakfast, lights
Her stove, and lays out food in tins.
Out of the window perilously spread
225   Her drying combinations touched by the sun's last rays,
On the divan are piled (at night her bed)
Stockings, slippers, camisoles, and stays.

7. These four lines reproduce the mode in which Elizabethan poets indicated the song of the nightingale, including "Tereu"—also a form of the name of Philomela's ravisher, Tereus. See Part II, lines 99–103.
8. See note to Part I, line 60.
9. "The currants were quoted at a price 'carriage and insurance free to London'; and the Bill of Lading etc. were to be handed to the buyer upon payment of the sight draft" [Eliot's note].
1. Here, simply "bad French."
2. Before the Second World War, a very large hotel in London's commercial district. The Metropole is probably the large hotel at Brighton, the beach-resort.
3. "Tiresias, although a mere spectator and not indeed a 'character,' is yet the most important personage in the poem, uniting all the rest. Just as the one-eyed merchant, seller of currants, melts into the Phoenician sailor, and the latter is not wholly distinct from Ferdinand Prince of Naples, so all the women are one woman, and the two sexes meet in Tiresias. What Tiresias *sees*, in fact, is the substance of the poem. The whole passage from Ovid is of great anthropological interest * * *" [Eliot's note]. Mythology offers three separate accounts of the reasons why Tiresias was blinded by a goddess and then granted a seer's power by Zeus. Ovid's version is contained in a passage (*Metamorphoses*, III.322 ff.) which Eliot's note cites in Latin, and which runs as follows in Golding's verse translation:
    They say that Jove, disposed to mirth as he and Juno sat
    A-drinking nectar after meat in sport and pleasant rate,
    Did fall a-jesting with his wife, and said: "A greater pleasure
    In Venus' games ye women have than men beyond all measure."
    She answered, no. To try the truth, they both of them agree
    The wise Tiresias in this case indifferent judge to be,

Who both the man's and woman's joys by trial understood,
For finding once two mighty snakes engend'-ring in a wood,
He struck them overthwart the backs, by means whereof behold
(As strange a thing to be of truth as ever yet was told)
He being made a woman straight, seven winter livéd so.
The eighth he finding them again did say unto them tho:
"And if to strike ye have such power as for to turn their shape
That are the givers of the stripe, before you hence escape,
One stripe now shall I lend you more." He struck them as beforne
And straight returned his former shape in which he first was born.
Tiresias therefore being ta'en to judge this jesting strife,
Gave sentence on the side of Jove; the which the queen his wife
Did take a great deal more to heart than needed, and in spite
To wreak her teen upon her judge, bereft him of his sight;
But Jove (for to the gods it is unlawful to undo
The things which other of the gods by any means have do)
Did give him sight in things to come for loss of sight of eye,
And so his grievous punishment with honor did supply.
4. "This may not appear as exact as Sappho's lines, but I had in mind the 'longshore' or 'dory' fisherman, who returns at nightfall" [Eliot's note]. Sappho's poem (Number 120 in E. Diehl, *Anthologia Lyrica*), may be translated as follows: "Hesperus, all things you bring, as many as light-bringing morning has scattered abroad./You bring the sheep,/You bring the goat, you bring the child to its mother."

I Tiresias, old man with wrinkled dugs
Perceived the scene, and foretold the rest—
230   I too awaited the expected guest.
He, the young man carbuncular,[5] arrives,
A small house agent's clerk, with one bold stare,
One of the low on whom assurance sits
As a silk hat on a Bradford[6] millionaire.
235   The time is now propitious, as he guesses,
The meal is ended, she is bored and tired,
Endeavors to engage her in caresses
Which still are unreproved, if undesired.
Flushed and decided, he assaults at once;
240   Exploring hands encounter no defense;
His vanity requires no response,
And makes a welcome of indifference.
(And I Tiresias have foresuffered all
Enacted on this same divan or bed;
245   I who have sat by Thebes below the wall[7]
And walked among the lowest of the dead.)
Bestows one final patronizing kiss,
And gropes his way, finding the stairs unlit . . .

She turns and looks a moment in the glass,
250   Hardly aware of her departed lover;
Her brain allows one half-formed thought to pass:
"Well now that's done: and I'm glad it's over."
When lovely woman stoops to folly and[8]
Paces about her room again, alone,
255   She smoothes her hair with automatic hand,
And puts a record on the gramophone.

"This music crept by me upon the waters"[9]
And along the Strand, up Queen Victoria Street.
O City city, I can sometimes hear
260   Beside a public bar in Lower Thames Street,
The pleasant whining of a mandolin
And a clatter and a chatter from within
Where fishmen lounge at noon: where the walls
Of Magnus Martyr[1] hold
265   Inexplicable splendor of Ionian white and gold.

---

5. Afflicted with carbuncles, a boil-like inflammation.
6. A manufacturing town in the English Midlands.
7. The blind Theban seer (see note to line 218 above) was supposed to have lived three times as long as the average man, and his prophecies enter the lives of many legendary citizens of Thebes, including those of Oedipus and his family.
8. "V. Goldsmith, the song in *The Vicar of Wakefield*" [Eliot's note]. ("When lovely woman stoops to folly/And finds too late that men betray/What charm can soothe her melancholy,/What art can wash her guilt away?/The only art her guilt to cover,/To hide her shame from every eye,/To give repentance to her lover/And wring his bosom

—is to die.")
9. "V. *The Tempest,* as above" [Eliot's note]. See note to line 191 above.
1. "The interior of St. Magnus Martyr is to my mind one of the finest among Wren's interiors. See *The Proposed Demolition of Nineteen City Churches:* (P. S. King & Son, Ltd.)" [Eliot's note]. Again in this passage (lines 257–265) it is the busy commercial East End of London that is evoked. The church of St. Magnus Martyr stands just below London Bridge, in Lower Thames Street, which skirts the north bank of the Thames between London Bridge and the Tower of London. The phrase "O City city" apostrophizes both the *City* of London, a relatively small area of the metropolis which contains its business wealth, and the generic total city.

The river sweats[2]
Oil and tar
The barges drift
With the turning tide
270   Red sails
Wide
To leeward, swing on the heavy spar.
The barges wash
Drifting logs
275   Down Greenwich reach
Past the Isle of Dogs.[3]
          Weialala leia
          Wallala leialala

Elizabeth and Leicester[4]
280   Beating oars
The stern was formed
A gilded shell
Red and gold
The brisk swell
285   Rippled both shores
Southwest wind
Carried down stream
The peal of bells
White towers
290   Weialala leia
          Wallala leialala

"Trams and dusty trees.
Highbury bore me.[5] Richmond and Kew
Undid me. By Richmond I raised my knees
295   Supine on the floor of a narrow canoe."

"My feet are at Moorgate,[6] and my heart
Under my feet. After the event
He wept. He promised 'a new start.'
I made no comment. What should I resent?"

300   "On Margate Sands.[7]
I can connect
Nothing with nothing.

2. "The song of the (three) Thames-daughters begins here. From line 292 to 306 inclusive they speak in turn. V. *Götterdämmerung*, III,i: the Rhine-daughters" [Eliot's note]. Lines 277–278 repeat the refrain of the Rhine-maidens in Wagner's music-drama.
3. A tongue of land extending into the Thames opposite Greenwich.
4. "V. Froude, [*Reign of*] *Elizabeth*, Vol. I, ch. iv, letter of De Quadra to Philip of Spain: 'In the afternoon we were in a barge, watching the games on the river. (The queen) was alone with the Lord Robert and myself on the poop, when they began to talk nonsense, and went so far that Lord Robert at last said, as I was on the spot there was no reason why they should not be married if the queen pleased' " [Eliot's note]. Sir Robert Dudley (1532?–88), Earl of Leicester, was a favorite of the queen.

5. "Cf. Purgatorio, V, 133: Ricorditi di me, che son la Pia;/Siena mi fe', disfecemi Maremma" [Eliot's note]. Pia de' Tolomei, whom Dante encounters in Purgatory, after telling her story, says: "Pray, when you have returned to the world and are rested from your long journey, * * * remember me, who am la Pia; Siena made me, the Maremma unmade me"; she had been shut up by her husband in one of his castles, La Pietra in Maremma, and was there done to death by his orders. Highbury is a residential suburb in North London; Richmond is the object of a pleasant excursion up the river from London; Kew is another excursion point, chiefly because of its botanical gardens.
6. A humble district in East London.
7. A beach resort in Kent, where the Thames Estuary broadens into the Channel.

The broken fingernails of dirty hands.
My people humble people who expect
305   Nothing."
                    la la

To Carthage then I came[8]

Burning burning burning burning[9]
O Lord Thou pluckest me out[1]
310   O Lord Thou pluckest

burning

IV. Death by Water

Phlebas the Phoenician, a fortnight dead,
Forgot the cry of gulls, and the deep sea swell
And the profit and loss.
315   A current under sea
Picked his bones in whispers. As he rose and fell
He passed the stages of his age and youth
Entering the whirlpool.
                    Gentile or Jew
320   O you who turn the wheel and look to windward,
Consider Phlebas, who was once handsome and tall as you.

V. What the Thunder Said[2]

After the torchlight red on sweaty faces
After the frosty silence in the gardens
After the agony in stony places
325   The shouting and the crying
Prison and palace and reverberation
Of thunder of spring over distant mountains
He who was living is now dead
We who were living are now dying
330   With a little patience

Here is no water but only rock
Rock and no water and the sandy road
The road winding above among the mountains
Which are mountains of rock without water
335   If there were water we should stop and drink
Amongst the rock one cannot stop or think
Sweat is dry and feet are in the sand
If there were only water amongst the rock
Dead mountain mouth of carious teeth that cannot spit
340   Here one can neither stand nor lie nor sit
There is not even silence in the mountains
But dry sterile thunder without rain
There is not even solitude in the mountains

8. "V. St. Augustine's *Confessions:* 'to Carthage then I came, where a cauldron of unholy loves sang all about mine ears'" [Eliot's note].
9. "The complete text of the Buddha's Fire Sermon (which corresponds in importance to the Sermon on the Mount) from which these words are taken, will be found translated in the late Henry Clarke Warren's *Buddhism in Translation* (Harvard Oriental Series). Mr. Warren was one of the great pioneers of Buddhist studies in the Occident" [Eliot's

note].
1. "From St. Augustine's *Confessions* again. The collocation of these two representatives of eastern and western asceticism, as the culmination of this part of the poem, is not an accident" [Eliot's note].
2. "In the first part of Part V three themes are employed: the journey to Emmaus, the approach to the Chapel Perilous (see Miss Weston's book) and the present decay of eastern Europe" [Eliot's note]. For the title of Part V, see note to line 401, below.

But red sullen faces sneer and snarl
345 From doors of mudcracked houses
                    If there were water
    And no rock
    If there were rock
    And also water
350 And water
    A spring
    A pool among the rock
    If there were the sound of water only
    Not the cicada
355 And dry grass singing
    But sound of water over a rock
    Where the hermit-thrust sings in the pine trees[3]
    Drip drop drip drop drop drop drop
    But there is no water

360 Who is the third who walks always beside you?
    When I count, there are only you and I together[4]
    But when I look ahead up the white road
    There is always another one walking beside you
    Gliding wrapt in a brown mantle, hooded
365 I do not know whether a man or a woman
    —But who is that on the other side of you?

    What is that sound high in the air[5]
    Murmur of maternal lamentation
    Who are those hooded hordes swarming
370 Over endless plains, stumbling in cracked earth
    Ringed by the flat horizon only
    What is the city over the mountains
    Cracks and reforms and bursts in the violet air
    Falling towers
375 Jerusalem Athens Alexandria
    Vienna London
    Unreal

    A woman drew her long black hair out tight
    And fiddled whisper music on those strings
380 And bats with baby faces in the violet light
    Whistled, and beat their wings
    And crawled head downward down a blackened wall
    And upside down in air were towers
    Tolling reminiscent bells, that kept the hours
385 And voices singing out of empty cisterns and exhausted wells.

---

3. "This is * * * the hermit-thrush which I have heard in Quebec Province * * * Its 'water-dripping song' is justly celebrated" [Eliot's note].
4. "The following lines were stimulated by the account of one of the Antarctic expeditions (I forget which, but I think one of Shackleton's): it was related that the party of explorers, at the extremity of their strength, had the constant delusion that there was *one more member* than could actually be counted" [Eliot's note]. And compare at this point the journey of two of Christ's disciples to Emmaus, after the Crucifixion; on the way "they talked together of all these things which had happened. And * * * while they communed together and reasoned, Jesus himself drew near and went with them. But their eyes were holden that they should not know him." Luke xxiv.13–16.
5. Eliot's note to lines 366–376 quotes a passage from Hermann Hesse's *Blick ins Chaos* (*A Glimpse into Chaos*) which may be translated as follows: "Already half Europe, already at least half of Eastern Europe is on the road to Chaos, drives drunken in holy madness along the abyss and sings the while, sings drunk and hymn-like as Dmitri Karamazov sang. The bourgeois laughs, offended, at these songs, the saint and the prophet hear them with tears."

In this decayed hole among the mountains
In the faint moonlight, the grass is singing
Over the tumbled graves, about the chapel
There is the empty chapel, only the wind's home.
390 It has no windows, and the door swings,
Dry bones can harm no one.
Only a cock stood on the rooftree
Co co rico co co rico
In a flash of lightning. Then a damp gust
395 Bringing rain

Ganga[6] was sunken, and the limp leaves
Waited for rain, while the black clouds
Gathered far distant, over Himavant.
The jungle crouched, humped in silence.
400 Then spoke the thunder
     DA
Datta:[7] what have we given?
My friend, blood shaking my heart
The awful daring of a moment's surrender
405 Which an age of prudence can never retract
By this, and this only, we have existed
Which is not to be found in our obituaries
Or in memories draped by the beneficent spider[8]
Or under seals broken by the lean solicitor
410 In our empty rooms
     DA
Dayadhvam: I have heard the key[9]
Turn in the door once and turn once only
We think of the key, each in his prison
415 Thinking of the key, each confirms a prison
Only at nightfall, ethereal rumors
Revive for a moment a broken Coriolanus[1]
     DA
Damyata: The boat responded
420 Gaily, to the hand expert with sail and oar
The sea was calm, your heart would have responded
Gaily, when invited, beating obedient
To controlling hands

6. The River Ganges. Himavant is a peak in the Himalayas.
7. " 'Datta, dayadhvam, damyata' (Give, sympathize, control). The fable of the meaning of the Thunder is found in the *Brihadaranyaka—Upanishad*, 5, [ii] * * * [Eliot's note]. The relevant chapter of this Upanishad tells how "the three-fold offspring of Prajápati, gods, men and Asuras [demons]" in turn asked their father to tell them their duty. He replies with the one letter *Da,* which each of the three interprets differently. The gods say, " 'We do comprehend. Restrain your desires, hast thou said to us.' " The men: " 'Be liberal, hast thou said to us.' " The Asuras: " 'Be clement, hast thou said to us.' " In each case, Prajápati answers, " 'Om! you have fully comprehended.' The same is repeated by a divine voice with the force of thunder, the syllables *Da, Da, Da,* meaning, Be restrained (*damyata*), be liberal (*datta*), and be clement (*dayadhvam*).
8. "Cf. Webster, *The White Devil*, V, vi: '. . . they'll remarry/Ere the worm pierce your winding-sheet, ere the spider/Make a thin curtain for your epitaphs' " [Eliot's note].
9. "Cf. *Inferno*, XXXIII, 46: 'ed io sentii chiavar l'uscio di sotto/ all' orribile torre.' Also F. H. Bradley, *Appearance and Reality*, p. 346. 'My external sensations are no less private to myself than are my thoughts or my feelings. In either case my experience falls within my own circle, a circle closed on the outside; and, with all its elements alike, every sphere is opaque to the others which surround it. . . . In brief, regarded as an existence which appears in a soul, the whole world for each is peculiar and private to that soul' " [Eliot's note]. The lines from Dante are from the section of the *Inferno* in which Count Ugolino of Pisa recounts his imprisonment with his little sons in the Hunger Tower, where they were left to starve: "and I heard them turning the key in the door of the dreadful tower, below."
1. The Roman hero of Shakespeare's tragedy, *Coriolanus*, the symbol of a truly great man whose greatness is tragically destroyed when he seeks to be utterly self-sufficient.

I sat upon the shore
425 Fishing, with the arid plain behind me[2]
Shall I at least set my lands in order?
London Bridge is falling down falling down falling down
Poi s'ascose nel foco che gli affina[3]
Quando fiam uti chelidon[4]—O swallow swallow
430 *Le Prince d'Aquitaine à la tour abolie*[5]
These fragments I have shored against my ruins
Why then Ile fit you. Hieronymo's mad againe.[6]
Datta. Dayadhvam. Damyata.
        Shantih   shantih   shantih[7]

                                                  1922

JOHN CROWE RANSOM
(1888–1974)

Bells for John Whiteside's Daughter

There was such speed in her little body,
And such lightness in her footfall,
It is no wonder her brown study
Astonishes us all.

5 Her wars were bruited in our high window.
We looked among orchard trees and beyond
Where she took arms against her shadow,
Or harried unto the pond

The lazy geese, like a snow cloud
10 Dripping their snow on the green grass,
Tricking and stopping, sleepy and proud,
Who cried in goose, Alas,

For the tireless heart within the little
Lady with rod that made them rise
15 From their noon apple-dreams and scuttle
Goose-fashion under the skies!

But now go the bells, and we are ready,
In one house we are sternly stopped
To say we are vexed at her brown study,
20 Lying so primly propped.

                                                  1924

2. "V. Weston: *From Ritual to Romance;* chapter on the Fisher King" [Eliot's note].
3. "V. *Purgatorio,* XXVI, 148. ' "Ara vos prec per aquella valor/que vos guida al som de l'escalina,/sovegna vos a temps de ma dolor."/Poi s'ascose nel foco che gli affina' " [Eliot's note]. Arnaut Daniel, the late-12th-century poet, encountered among the lustful in Purgatory, after recounting his story, concludes with the lines quoted: " 'And so I pray you, by that Virtue which guides you to the top of the stair, be reminded in time of my pain.' Then he hid himself in the fire that purifies them."
4. "V. *Pervigilium Veneris.* Cf. Philomela in Parts I and II" [Eliot's note]. The quoted line ("When shall I become as the swallow?") is from a late Latin poem (*The Vigil of Venus*) celebrating the spring festival of Venus. It alludes to the Procne-Philomela-

Tereus myth, but makes Philomela the swallow.
5. "V. Gérard de Nerval, Sonnet *El Desdichado*" [Eliot's note]. The poem (*The Disinherited*) describes "the man of shadows,—the widower,—the unconsoled,/The prince of Aquitania in the abandoned tower:/My only star is dead,—and my starred lute/Carries as its emblem the black sun of Melancholy * * *"
6. "V. Kyd's *Spanish Tragedy*" [Eliot's note]. The subtitle of Kyd's *Spanish Tragedy* (1594) is *Hieronymo's Mad Againe.* Hieronymo, driven mad by his son's death, "fits" the parts in a court masque so that in the course of it he kills his son's murderers.
7. "Shantih. Repeated as here, a formal ending to an Upanishad. 'The Peace which passeth understanding' is our nearest equivalent to this word" [Eliot's note].

Dead Boy

The little cousin is dead, by foul subtraction,
A green bough from Virginia's aged tree,
And none of the county kin like the transaction,
Nor some of the world of outer dark, like me.

5   A boy not beautiful, nor good, nor clever,
A black cloud full of storms too hot for keeping,
A sword beneath his mother's heart—yet never
Woman bewept her babe as this is weeping.

A pig with a pasty face, so I had said,
10   Squealing for cookies, kinned by poor pretense
With a noble house. But the little man quite dead,
I see the forbears' antique lineaments.

The elder men have strode by the box of death
To the wide flag porch, and muttering low send round
15   The bruit° of the day. O friendly waste of breath!   news, report
Their hearts are hurt with a deep dynastic wound.

He was pale and little, the foolish neighbors say;
The first-fruits, saith the Preacher, the Lord hath taken;
But this was the old tree's late branch wrenched away,
20   Grieving the sapless limbs, the shorn and shaken.

                                                            1927

CLAUDE McKAY
(1890–1948)

If We Must Die

If we must die, let it not be like hogs
Hunted and penned in an inglorious spot,
While round us bark the mad and hungry dogs,
Making their mock at our accurséd lot.
5   If we must die, O let us nobly die,
So that our precious blood may not be shed
In vain; then even the monsters we defy
Shall be constrained to honor us though dead!
O kinsmen we must meet the common foe!
10   Though far outnumbered let us show us brave,
And for their thousand blows deal one deathblow!
What though before us lies the open grave?
Like men we'll face the murderous, cowardly pack,
Pressed to the wall, dying, but fighting back!

                                                            1922

HUGH MACDIARMID (C. M. Grieve)
(1892–   )

The Innumerable Christ

"Other stars may have their Bethlehem, and their Calvary too."
—PROFESSOR J. Y. SIMPSON

Wha kens° on whatna° Bethlehems — *knows/what kind of*
Earth twinkles like a star the nicht,
An' whatna shepherds lift their heids
 In its unearthly licht?° — *light*

5 'Yont a' the stars oor een° can see — *eyes*
An' farther than their lichts can fly,
I' mony an unco warl'° the nicht° — *strange world/night*
 The fatefu' bairnies° cry. — *babies*

I' mony an unco warl' the nicht
10 The lift° gaes black as pitch at noon, — *sky*
An' sideways on their chests the heids
 O' endless Christs roll doon.

An' when the earth's as cauld's the mune
An' a its folk are lang syne° deid, — *since*
15 On coontless stars the Babe maun° cry — *may*
 An' the Crucified maun bleed.

1925

Parley of Beasts

Auld Noah was at hame wi' them a',
The lion and the lamb,
Pair by pair they entered the Ark
And he took them as they cam'.

5 If twa o' ilka° beist there is — *every*
Into this room sud° come, — *should*
Wad° I cud welcome them like him, — *would*
And no' staun' gowpin' dumb!

Be chief° wi' them and they wi' me — *very friendly*
10 And a' wi' ane anither
As Noah and his couples were
There in the Ark thegither.

It's fain I'd mell° wi' tiger and tit, — *mix*
Wi' elephant and eel,
15 But noo-a-days e'en wi' ain's se° — *one's own self*
At hame it's hard to feel.

1926

Bubblyjock°   *turkey*

It's hauf ° like a bird and hauf like a bogle °   *half/goblin*
And juist stands in the sun there and bouks.°   *hiccups*
It's a wunder its heid disna burst
The way it's aye raxin' its chouks.³

5   Syne° it twists its neck like a serpent   *then*
But canna get oot a richt note
For the bubblyjock swallowed the bagpipes
And the blether ° stuck in its throat.   *bladder*
1926

ARCHIBALD MacLEISH
(1892–   )

You, Andrew Marvell¹

And here face down beneath the sun
And here upon earth's noonward height
To feel the always coming on
The always rising of the night

5   To feel creep up the curving east
The earthy chill of dusk and slow
Upon those under lands the vast
And ever climbing shadow grow

And strange at Ecbatan² the trees
10   Take leaf by leaf the evening strange
The flooding dark about their knees
The mountains over Persia change

And now at Kermanshah the gate
Dark empty and the withered grass
15   And through the twilight now the late
Few travelers in the westward pass

And Baghdad darken and the bridge
Across the silent river gone
And through Arabia the edge
20   Of evening widen and steal on

And deepen on Palmyra's street
The wheel rut in the ruined stone
And Lebanon fade out and Crete
High through the clouds and overblown

3. "The way it's always stretching its throat."
1. Andrew Marvell (1621–1678) wrote *To His Coy Mistress*, the poem to which MacLeish specifically alludes.
2. The poet's thoughts, following the daily path of the sun, move westward, from Ecbatana, once the capital of Media Magna (part of Persia), on to Kermanshah, Baghdad, Palmyra, Sicily, and so on.

25 And over Sicily the air
Still flashing with the landward gulls
And loom and slowly disappear
The sails above the shadowy hulls

And Spain go under and the shore
30 Of Africa the gilded sand
And evening vanish and no more
The low pale light across that land

Nor now the long light on the sea
And here face downward in the sun
35 To feel how swift how secretly
The shadow of the night comes on. . . .

1930

Empire Builders

The Museum Attendant:

This is *The Making of America in Five Panels*:

This is Mister Harriman[3] making America:
Mister-Harriman-is-buying-the-Union-Pacific-at-Seventy:
The Sante Fe is shining on his hair.

5 This is Commodore Vanderbilt[4] making America:
Mister-Vanderbilt-is-eliminating-the short-interest-in-Hudson:
Observe the carving on the rocking chair.

This is J. P. Morgan[5] making America:
(The Tennessee Coal is behind to the left of the Steel Company.)
10 Those in mauve are braces he is wearing.

This is Mister Mellon[6] making America:
Mister-Mellon-is-represented-as-a-symbolic-figure-in-aluminum-
Strewing-bank-stocks-on-a-burnished-stair.

This is the Bruce is the Barton[7] making America:
15 Mister-Barton-is-selling-us-Doctor's-Deliciousest-Dentifrice.
This is he in beige with the canary.

You have just beheld the Makers making America:
This is The Making of America in Five Panels:
America lies to the west-southwest of the switch-tower:
20 There is nothing to see of America but land.

---

3. Edward H. Harriman (1848–1909), American railroad magnate and one of those called "robber barons" in the period.
4. Cornelius Vanderbilt (1794–1872), financier and railroad magnate.
5. J. P. Morgan (1837–1913), banker and financier.
6. Andrew Mellon (1885–1937), financier, one-time Secretary of the Treasury and, like Harriman, Vanderbilt, and Morgan, a man of enormous wealth and power.
7. Bruce Barton (1886–   ), pioneer American advertising executive who made extraordinary use of that profession in his religious writings.

The Original Document under the Panel Paint:

"To Thos. Jefferson Esq. his obd't serv't
M. Lewis: captain: detached:
                    Sir:

  Having in mind your repeated commands in this matter,
25 And the worst half of it done and the streams mapped,

  And we here on the back of this beach beholding the
  Other ocean—two years gone and the cold

  Breaking with rain for the third spring since St. Louis,
  The crows at the fishbones on the frozen dunes,

30 The first cranes going over from south north,
  And the river down by a mark of the pole since the morning,

  And time near to return, and a ship (Spanish)
  Lying in for the salmon: and fearing chance or the

  Drought or the Sioux should deprive you of these discoveries—
35 Therefore we send by sea in this writing.

                                        Above the
  Platte[8] there were long plains and a clay country:
  Rim of the sky far off, grass under it,

  Dung for the cook fires by the sulphur licks.
40 After that there were low hills and the sycamores,

  And we poled up by the Great Bend in the skiffs:
  The honey bees left us after the Osage River.[9]

  The wind was west in the evenings, and no dew and the
  Morning Star larger and whiter than usual—

45 The winter rattling in the brittle haws.
  The second year there was sage and the quail calling.

  All that valley is good land by the river:
  Three thousand miles and the clay cliffs and

  Rue and beargrass by the water banks
50 And many birds and the brant going over and tracks of

  Bear, elk, wolves, marten: the buffalo
  Numberless so that the cloud of their dust covers them:

  The antelope fording the fall creeks, and the mountains and
  Grazing lands and the meadow lands and the ground

55 Sweet and open and well-drained.
                                  We advise you to
  Settle troops at the forks and to issue licenses:

---

8. A river in Nebraska.   9. The Great Bend and Osage are rivers in
                                 Kansas.

Many men will have living on these lands.
There is wealth in the earth for them all and the wood standing
60 And wild birds on the water where they sleep.
There is stone in the hills for the towns of a 'great people . . ."

You have just beheld the Makers Making America:

They screwed her scrawny and gaunt with their seven-year panics:
They bought her back on their mortgages old-whore-cheap:
65 They fattened their bonds at her breasts till the thin blood ran from them.

Men have forgotten how full clear and deep
The Yellowstone moved on the gravel and the grass grew
When the land lay waiting for her westward people!

1933

WILFRED OWEN
(1893–1918)

Strange Meeting

It seemed that out of battle I escaped
Down some profound dull tunnel, long since scooped
Through granites which titanic wars had groined.
Yet also there encumbered sleepers groaned,
5 Too fast in thought or death to be bestirred.
Then, as I probed them, one sprang up, and stared
With piteous recognition in fixed eyes,
Lifting distressful hands as if to bless.
And by his smile, I knew that sullen hall,
10 By his dead smile I knew we stood in Hell.
With a thousand pains that vision's face was grained;
Yet no blood reached there from the upper ground,
And no guns thumped, or down the flues made moan.
"Strange friend," I said, "here is no cause to mourn."
15 "None," said that other, "save the undone years,
The hopelessness. Whatever hope is yours,
Was my life also; I went hunting wild
After the wildest beauty in the world,
Which lies not calm in eyes, or braided hair,
20 But mocks the steady running of the hour,
And if it grieves, grieves richlier than here.
For of my glee might many men have laughed,
And of my weeping something had been left,
Which must die now. I mean the truth untold,
25 The pity of war, the pity war distilled.
Now men will go content with what we spoiled.
Or, discontent, boil bloody, and be spilled.
They will be swift with swiftness of the tigress,
None will break ranks, though nations trek from progress.
30 Courage was mine, and I had mystery,
Wisdom was mine, and I had mastery:

To miss the march of this retreating world
Into vain citadels that are not walled.
Then, when much blood had clogged their chariot wheels
35 I would go up and wash them from sweet wells,
Even with truths that lie too deep for taint.
I would have poured my spirit without stint
But not through wounds; not on the cess° of war.   *waste*
Foreheads of men have bled where no wounds were.
40 I am the enemy you killed, my friend.
I knew you in this dark; for so you frowned
Yesterday through me as you jabbed and killed.
I parried; but my hands were loath and cold.
Let us sleep now. . . ."

                                        1919   1920

The Parable of the Old Man and the Young

So Abram rose,[1] and clave the wood, and went,
And took the fire with him, and a knife.
And as they sojourned both of them together,
Isaac the first-born spake and said, My Father,
5 Behold the preparations, fire and iron,
But where the lamb for this burnt offering?
Then Abram bound the youth with belts and straps,
And builded parapets and trenches there,
And stretchèd forth the knife to slay his son.
10 When lo! an angel called him out of heaven,
Saying, Lay not thy hand upon the lad,
Neither do anything to him. Behold,
A ram, caught in a thicket by its horns;
Offer the Ram of Pride instead of him.
15 But the old man would not so, but slew his son,
And half the seed of Europe, one by one.

                                                          1920

Anthem for Doomed Youth

What passing-bells for these who die as cattle?
    Only the monstrous anger of the guns.
    Only the stuttering rifles' rapid rattle
Can patter out their hasty orisons.°   *prayers*
5 No mockeries now for them; no prayers nor bells,
    Nor any voice of mourning save the choirs—
The shrill, demented choirs of wailing shells;
    And bugles calling for them from sad shires.

What candles may be held to speed them all?
10   Not in the hands of boys, but in their eyes
Shall shine the holy glimmers of good-byes.
    The pallor of girls' brows shall be their pall;
Their flowers the tenderness of patient minds,
And each slow dusk a drawing-down of blinds.

                                        1917   1920

1. See Genesis xxii.1–14. God tested Abraham by commanding him to sacrifice his son Isaac, sending a ram to be sacrificed instead when it was clear that the God-fearing Abraham would obey the command.

Futility

Move him into the sun—
Gently its touch awoke him once,
At home, whispering of fields unsown.
Always it woke him, even in France,
5   Until this morning and this snow.
If anything might rouse him now
The kind old sun will know.

Think how it wakes the seeds—
Woke, once, the clays of a cold star.
10 Are limbs, so dear-achieved, are sides,
Full-nerved—still warm—too hard to stir?
Was it for this the clay grew tall?
—O what made fatuous sunbeams toil
To break earth's sleep at all?

                                    1918   1920

E. E. CUMMINGS
(1894–1963)

in Just-

in Just-
spring   when the world is mud-
luscious the little
lame balloonman

5   whistles   far   and wee

and eddieandbill come
running from marbles and
piracies and it's
spring

10 when the world is puddle-wonderful

the queer
old balloonman whistles
far   and   wee
and bettyandisbel come dancing

15 from hop-scotch and jump-rope and

it's
spring
and
        the

20   goat-footed
balloonMan   whistles
far
and
wee   1923

O sweet spontaneous

O sweet spontaneous
earth how often have
the
doting

5   fingers of
prurient philosophers pinched
and
poked

thee
10 , has the naughty thumb
of science prodded
thy

beauty   . how
often have religions taken
15 thee upon their scraggy knees
squeezing and

buffeting thee that thou mightest conceive
gods
          (but
20 true

to the incomparable
couch of death thy
rhythmic
lover

25   thou answerest

them only with

                spring)

                                    1923

the Cambridge ladies who live in furnished souls

the Cambridge ladies who live in furnished souls
are unbeautiful and have comfortable minds
(also, with the church's protestant blessings
daughters, unscented shapeless spirited)
5 they believe in Christ and Longfellow, both dead,
are invariably interested in so many things—
at the present writing one still finds
delighted fingers knitting for the is it Poles?
perhaps. While permanent faces coyly bandy
10 scandal of Mrs. N and Professor D
. . . . the Cambridge ladies do not care, above
Cambridge if sometimes in its box of
sky lavender and cornerless, the
moon rattles like a fragment of angry candy

                                    1923

"next to of course god america i

"next to of course god america i
love you land of the pilgrims' and so forth oh
say can you see by the dawn's early my
country 'tis of centuries come and go
5   and are no more what of it we should worry
in every language even deafanddumb
thy sons acclaim your glorious name by gorry
by jingo by gee by gosh by gum
why talk of beauty what could be more beau-
10   tiful than these heroic happy dead
who rushed like lions to the roaring slaughter
they did not stop to think they died instead
then shall the voice of liberty be mute?"

He spoke. And drank rapidly a glass of water

1926

since feeling is first

since feeling is first
who pays any attention
to the syntax of things
will never wholly kiss you;
wholly to be a fool
5   while Spring is in the world

my blood approves,
and kisses are a better fate
than wisdom
lady i swear by all flowers. Don't cry
10 —the best gesture of my brain is less than
your eyelids' flutter which says

we are for each other: then
laugh, leaning back in my arms
for life's not a paragraph

15 And death i think is no parenthesis

1926

somewhere i have never travelled, gladly beyond

somewhere i have never travelled,gladly beyond
any experience, your eyes have their silence:
in your most frail gesture are things which enclose me,
or which i cannot touch because they are too near

5   your slightest look easily will unclose me
though i have closed myself as fingers,
you open always petal by petal myself as Spring opens
(touching skilfully,mysteriously)her first rose

or if your wish be to close me,i and
my life will shut very beautifully,suddenly,
as when the heart of this flower imagines
the snow carefully everywhere descending;

nothing which we are to perceive in this world equals
the power of your intense fragility:whose texture
compels me with the colour of its countries,
rendering death and forever with each breathing

(i do not know what it is about you that closes
and opens;only something in me understands
the voice of your eyes is deeper than all roses)
nobody,not even the rain,has such small hands

1931

anyone lived in a pretty how town

anyone lived in a pretty how town
(with up so floating many bells down)
spring summer autumn winter
he sang his didn't he danced his did.

Women and men(both little and small)
cared for anyone not at all
they sowed their isn't they reaped their same
sun moon stars rain

children guessed(but only a few
and down they forgot as up they grew
autumn winter spring summer)
that noone loved him more by more

when by now and tree by leaf
she laughed his joy she cried his grief
bird by snow and stir by still
anyone's any was all to her

someones married their everyones
laughed their cryings and did their dance
(sleep wake hope and then)they
said their nevers they slept their dream

stars rain sun moon
(and only the snow can begin to explain
how children are apt to forget to remember
with up so floating many bells down)

one day anyone died i guess
(and noone stooped to kiss his face)
busy folk buried them side by side
little by little and was by was

all by all and deep by deep
and more by more they dream their sleep
noone and anyone earth by april
wish by spirit and if by yes.

Women and men (both dong and ding)
summer autumn winter spring
35 reaped their sowing and went their came
sun moon stars rain

1940

JEAN TOOMER
(1894–1967)

Face

Hair—
silver-gray,
like streams of stars,
Brows—
5 recurved canoes
quivered by the ripples blown by pain,
Her eyes—
mist of tears
condensing on the flesh below
10 And her channeled muscles
are cluster grapes of sorrow
purple in the evening sun
nearly ripe for worms.

1923

Georgia Dusk

The sky, lazily disdaining to pursue
    The setting sun, too indolent to hold
    A lengthened tournament for flashing gold,
Passively darkens for night's barbecue,

5 A feast of moon and men and barking hounds,
    An orgy for some genius of the South
    With blood-hot eyes and cane-lipped scented mouth,
Surprised in making folksongs from soul sounds.

The sawmill blows its whistle, buzz-saws stop,
10   And silence breaks the bud of knoll and hill,
    Soft settling pollen where plowed lands fulfill
Their early promise of a bumper crop.

Smoke from the pyramidal sawdust pile
    Curls up, blue ghosts of trees, tarrying low
15   Where only chips and stumps are left to show
The solid proof of former domicile.

Meanwhile, the men, with vestiges of pomp,
    Race memories of king and caravan,
    High-priests, an ostrich, and a juju-man,°   *witch-doctor*
20 Go singing through the footpaths of the swamp.

Their voices rise . . the pine trees are guitars,
  Strumming, pine-needles fall like sheets of rain . .
  Their voices rise . . the chorus of the cane
Is caroling a vesper to the stars.

25 O singers, resinous and soft your songs
  Above the sacred whisper of the pines,
  Give virgin lips to cornfield concubines,
Bring dreams of Christ to dusky cane-lipped throngs.

1923

ROBERT GRAVES
(1895–   )

The Cool Web

Children are dumb to say how hot the day is,
How hot the scent is of the summer rose,
How dreadful the black wastes of evening sky,
How dreadful the tall soldiers drumming by.

5 But we have speech, to chill the angry day,
And speech to dull the rose's cruel scent.
We spell away the overhanging night,
We spell away the soldiers and the fright.

There's a cool web of language winds us in,
10 Retreat from too much joy or too much fear:
We grow sea-green at last and coldly die
In brininess and volubility.

But if we let our tongues lose self-possession,
Throwing off language and its watery clasp
15 Before our death, instead of when death comes,
Facing the wide glare of the children's day,
Facing the rose, the dark sky and the drums,
We shall go mad no doubt and die that way.

1927

Warning to Children

Children, if you dare to think
Of the greatness, rareness, muchness,
Fewness of this precious only
Endless world in which you say
5 You live, you think of things like this:
Blocks of slate enclosing dappled
Red and green, enclosing tawny
Yellow nets, enclosing white
And black acres of dominoes,
10 Where a neat brown paper parcel
Tempts you to untie the string.

In the parcel a small island,
On the island a large tree,
On the tree a husky fruit.
15 Strip the husk and pare the rind off:
In the kernel you will see
Blocks of slate enclosed by dappled
Red and green, enclosed by tawny
Yellow nets, enclosed by white
20 And black acres of dominoes,
Where the same brown paper parcel—
Children, leave the string alone!
For who dares undo the parcel
Finds himself at once inside it,
25 On the island, in the fruit,
Blocks of slate about his head,
Finds himself enclosed by dappled
Green and red, enclosed by yellow
Tawny nets, enclosed by black
30 And white acres of dominoes,
With the same brown paper parcel
Still unopened on his knee.
And, if he then should dare to think
Of the fewness, muchness, rareness,
35 Greatness of this endless only
Precious world in which he says
He lives—he then unties the string.

1929

The Frog and the Golden Ball

She let her golden ball fall down the well
    And begged a cold frog to retrieve it;
For which she kissed his ugly, gaping mouth—
    Indeed, he could scarce believe it.

5 And seeing him transformed to his princely shape,
    Who had been by hags enchanted,
She knew she could never love another man
    Nor by any fate be daunted.

But what would her royal father and mother say?
10   They had promised her in marriage
To a cousin whose wide kingdom marched with theirs,
    Who rode in a jeweled carriage.

'Our plight, dear heart, would appear past human hope
    To all except you and me: to all
15 Who have never swum as a frog in a dark well
    Or have lost a golden ball.'

'What then shall we do now?' she asked her lover.
    He kissed her again, and said:
'Is magic of love less powerful at your Court
20   Than at this green well-head?'

1965

HART CRANE
(1899–1932)

At Melville's Tomb

Often beneath the wave, wide from this ledge
The dice[3] of drowned men's bones he saw bequeath
An embassy. Their numbers as he watched,
Beat on the dusty shore and were obscured.

5   And wrecks passed without sound of bells,
The calyx[4] of death's bounty giving back
A scattered chapter, livid hieroglyph,
The portent wound in corridors of shells.

Then in the circuit calm of one vast coil,
10 Its lashings charmed and malice reconciled,
Frosted eyes there were that lifted altars;
And silent answers crept across the stars.

Compass, quadrant and sextant[5] contrive
No farther tides . . . High in the azure steeps
15 Monody shall not wake the mariner.
This fabulous shadow only the sea keeps.

1926

From The Bridge

Proem: To Brooklyn Bridge

How many dawns, chill from his rippling rest
The seagull's wings shall dip and pivot him,
Shedding white rings of tumult, building high
Over the chained bay waters Liberty—

5   Then, with inviolate curve, forsake our eyes
As apparitional as sails that cross
Some page of figures to be filed away;
—Till elevators drop us from our day . . .

I think of cinemas, panoramic sleights
10 With multitudes bent toward some flashing scene
Never disclosed, but hastened to again,
Foretold to other eyes on the same screen;

And Thee,[3] across the harbor, silver-paced
As though the sun took step of thee, yet left
15 Some motion ever unspent in thy stride—
Implicitly thy freedom staying thee!

3. Small, broken pieces.
4. Chalice, or cup-like container.
5. Instruments of measurement: the compass for describing circles or determining geo-graphic directions; the quadrant and sextant for measuring angles and reckoning altitudes.
3. I.e., Brooklyn Bridge.

Out of some subway scuttle, cell or loft
A bedlamite° speeds to thy parapets,   *madman*
Tilting there momently, shrill shirt ballooning,
20 A jest falls from the speechless caravan.

Down Wall, from girder into street noon leaks,
A rip-tooth of the sky's acetylene,
All afternoon the cloud-flown derricks turn . . .
Thy cables breathe the North Atlantic still.

25 And obscure as that heaven of the Jews,
Thy guerdon . . . Accolade thou dost bestow
Of anonymity time cannot raise:
Vibrant reprieve and pardon thou dost show.

O harp and altar, of the fury fused,
30 (How could mere toil align thy choiring strings!)
Terrific threshold of the prophet's pledge,
Prayer of pariah, and the lover's cry—

Again the traffic lights that skim thy swift
Unfractioned idiom, immaculate sigh of stars,
35 Beading thy path—condense eternity:
And we have seen night lifted in thine arms.

Under thy shadow by the piers I waited;
Only in darkness is thy shadow clear.
The City's fiery parcels all undone,
40 Already snow submerges an iron year . . .

O Sleepless as the river under thee,
Vaulting the sea, the prairies' dreaming sod,
Unto us lowliest sometime sweep, descend
And of the curveship lend a myth to God.

1930

Royal Palm

Green rustlings, more-than-regal charities
Drift coolly from that tower of whispered light.
Amid the noontide's blazed asperities
I watched the sun's most gracious anchorite

5 Climb up as by communings, year on year
Uneaten of the earth or aught earth holds,
And the gray trunk, that's elephantine, rear
Its frondings sighing in ethereal folds.

Forever fruitless, and beyond that yield
10 Of sweat the jungle presses with hot love
And tendril till our deathward breath is sealed—
It grazes the horizons, launched above

Mortality—ascending emerald-bright,
A fountain at salute, a crown in view—
15 Unshackled, casual of its azured height,
As though it soared suchwise through heaven too.

1933

ALLEN TATE
(1899–   )

Ode to the Confederate Dead

Row after row with strict impunity
The headstones yield their names to the element,
The wind whirrs without recollection;
In the riven troughs the splayed leaves
5   Pile up, of nature the casual sacrament
To the seasonal eternity of death;
Then driven by the fierce scrutiny
Of heaven to their election in the vast breath,
They sough the rumor of mortality.

10   Autumn is desolation in the plot
Of a thousand acres where these memories grow
From the inexhaustible bodies that are not
Dead, but feed the grass row after rich row.
Think of the autumns that have come and gone!
15   Ambitious November with the humors of the year,
With a particular zeal for every slab,
Staining the uncomfortable angels that rot
On the slabs, a wing chipped here, an arm there:
The brute curiosity of an angel's stare
20   Turns you, like them, to stone,
Transforms the heaving air
Till plunged to a heavier world below
You shift your sea-space blindly
Heaving, turning like the blind crab.

25   Dazed by the wind, only the wind
            The leaves flying, plunge

You know who have waited by the wall
The twilight certainty of an animal,
Those midnight restitutions of the blood
30   You know—the immitigable° pines, the smoky frieze   *unvarying*
Of the sky, the sudden call: you know the rage,
The cold pool left by the mounting flood,
Of muted Zeno and Parmenides.[1]
You who have waited for the angry resolution
35   Of those desires that should be yours tomorrow,
You know the unimportant shrift of death
And praise the vision
And praise the arrogant circumstance
Of those who fall
40   Rank upon rank, hurried beyond decision—
Here by the sagging gate, stopped by the wall.

            Seeing, seeing only the leaves
            Flying, plunge and expire

1. Zeno and Parmenides were Greek philosophers of the Eleatic school who, among other beliefs, held that what is various and changeable, all "development," is a delusive phantom. "To be imagined and to be able to exist are the same thing, and there is no development."

Turn your eyes to the immoderate past,
45 Turn to the inscrutable infantry rising
Demons out of the earth—they will not last.
Stonewall, Stonewall, and the sunken fields of hemp,
Shiloh, Antietam, Malvern Hill, Bull Run.[2]
50 Lost in that orient of the thick and fast
You will curse the setting sun.

       Cursing only the leaves crying
       Like an old man in a storm

You hear the shout, the crazy hemlocks point
55 With troubled fingers to the silence which
Smothers you, a mummy, in time.
         The hound bitch
Toothless and dying, in a musty cellar
Hears the wind only.

60   Now that the salt of their blood
Stiffens the saltier oblivion of the sea,
Seals the malignant purity of the flood,
What shall we who count our days and bow
Our heads with a commemorial woe
65 In the ribboned coats of grim felicity,
What shall we say of the bones, unclean,
Whose verdurous anonymity will grow?

The ragged arms, the ragged heads and eyes
Lost in these acres of the insane green?
70 The gray lean spiders come, they come and go;
In a tangle of willows without light
The singular screech-owl's tight
Invisible lyric seeds the mind
With the furious murmur of their chivalry.

75   We shall say only the leaves
      Flying, plunge and expire

We shall say only the leaves whispering
In the improbable mist of nightfall
That flies on multiple wing:
80 Night is the beginning and the end
And in between the ends of distraction
Waits mute speculation, the patient curse
That stones the eyes, or like the jaguar leaps
For his own image in a jungle pool, his victim.

85 What shall we say who have knowledge
Carried to the heart? Shall we take the act
To the grave? Shall we, more hopeful, set up the grave
In the house? The ravenous grave?

       Leave now
90 The shut gate and the decomposing wall:
The gentle serpent, green in the mulberry bush,
Riots with his tongue through the hush—
Sentinel of the grave who counts us all!

                                 1928

2. Names of important Civil War battles.

LANGSTON HUGHES
(1902–1967)

The Weary Blues

Droning a drowsy syncopated tune,
Rocking back and forth to a mellow croon,
    I heard a Negro play.
Down on Lenox Avenue[1] the other night
5   By the pale dull pallor of an old gas light
        He did a lazy sway. . . .
        He did a lazy sway. . . .
To the tune o' those Weary Blues.
With his ebony hands on each ivory key
10 He made that poor piano moan with melody.
        O Blues!
Swaying to and fro on his rickety stool
He played that sad raggy tune like a musical fool.
        Sweet Blues!
15 Coming from a black man's soul.
        O Blues!
In a deep song voice with a melancholy tone
I heard that Negro sing, that old piano moan—
        "Ain't got nobody in all this world,
20   Ain't got nobody but ma self.
        I's gwine to quit ma frownin'
        And put ma troubles on the shelf."
Thump, thump, thump, went his foot on the floor.
He played a few chords then he sang some more—
25   "I got the Weary Blues
        And I can't be satisfied.
        Got the Weary Blues
        And can't be satisfied—
        I ain't happy no mo'
30   And I wish that I had died."
And far into the night he crooned that tune.
The stars went out and so did the moon.
The singer stopped playing and went to bed
While the Weary Blues echoed through his head.
35 He slept like a rock or a man that's dead.

1926

The Negro Speaks of Rivers

(TO W. E. B. DU BOIS)[2]

I've known rivers:
I've known rivers ancient as the world and older than the
    flow of human blood in human veins.

My soul has grown deep like the rivers.

1. A main thoroughfare in the heart of Harlem.
2. The American historian, educator, and Negro leader (1868–1963).

5   I bathed in the Euphrates when dawns were young.
I built my hut near the Congo and it lulled me to sleep.
I looked upon the Nile and raised the pyramids above it.
I heard the singing of the Mississippi when Abe Lincoln
      went down to New Orleans, and I've seen its muddy
10   bosom turn all golden in the sunset.

I've known rivers:
Ancient, dusky rivers.

My soul has grown deep like the rivers.

                                  1926

Harlem

What happens to a dream deferred?

    Does it dry up
    like a raisin in the sun?
    Or fester like a sore—
5   And then run?
    Does it stink like rotten meat?
    Or crust and sugar over—
    like a syrupy sweet?

    Maybe it just sags
10   like a heavy load.

    Or does it explode?

                                    1951

EARLE BIRNEY
(1904–   )

Bushed

He invented a rainbow but lightning struck it
shattered it into the lake-lap of a mountain
so big his mind slowed when he looked at it

Yet he built a shack on the shore
5 learned to roast porcupine belly and
wore the quills on his hatband

At first he was out with the dawn
whether it yellowed bright as wood-columbine
or was only a fuzzed moth in a flannel of storm
10 But he found the mountain was clearly alive
sent messages whizzing down every hot morning
boomed proclamations at noon and spread out
a white guard of goat
before falling asleep on its feet at sundown

15 When he tried his eyes on the lake   ospreys[1]
    would fall like valkyries[2]
    choosing the cut-throat
    He took then to waiting
    till the night smoke rose from the boil of the sunset

20 But the moon carved unknown totems
    out of the lakeshore
    owls in the beardusky woods derided him
    moosehorned cedars circled his swamps and tossed
    their antlers up to the stars
25 Then he knew   though the mountain slept   the winds
    were shaping its peak to an arrowhead
    poised

    And now he could only
    bar himself in and wait
30 for the great flint to come singing into his heart

                                                                1952

A Walk in Kyoto[3]

    All week   the maid tells me   bowing
    her doll's body at my mat   is Boys' Day
    Also please Man's Day   and gravely
    bends deeper   The magnolia sprig in my alcove
5   is it male?   The ancient discretions of Zen were not shaped
    for my phallic western eye   There is so much discretion
    in this small bowed body of an empire
    the wild hair of waterfalls combed straight
    in the ricefields   the inn-maid retreating
10 with the face of a shut flower   I stand hunched
    and clueless like a castaway in the shoals of my room

    When I slide my parchment door to stalk awkward
    through Lilliput[4] gardens framed and untouchable
    as watercolors   the streets look much the same
15 the Men are being pulled past on the strings of their engines
    the legs of the Boys are revolved by a thousand pedals
    and all the faces as taut and unfestive as Moscow's
    or Chicago's   or mine

    Lord Buddha helps us all there is vigor enough
20 in these islands and in all islands reefed and resounding
    with cities   But the pitch is high as the ping
    of cicadas°   those small strained motors concealed   *locusts*
    in the propped pines by the dying river   and only
    male as the stretched falsetto of actors mincing
25 the women's roles in *kabuki*[5]   or female only
    as the lost heroes womanized in the Ladies' Opera
    Where in these alleys jammed with competing waves
    of signs in two tongues and three scripts[6]
    can the simple song of a man be heard?

1. Sea-hawks.
2. In Norse mythology, one of the 13 warrior-maidens of Odin; they selected the heroes who were to die in battle, and afterwards carried them to Valhalla.
3. City in Japan, its capital until 1869.
4. In Swift's *Gulliver's Travels*, a country in-habited by tiny people; to them, Gulliver was a giant.
5. Stylized popular drama of Japan, developed chiefly in the 17th century. Both male and female roles were performed by male actors.
6. That is, English and the ideogrammic and phonetic writing systems of Japanese.

30 By the shoguns'[7] palace   the Important Cultural Property
stripped for tiptoeing schoolgirls   I stare at the staring
penned carp that flail on each other's backs
to the shrunk pool's edge for the crumb this nonfish
tossed   Is this the Day's one parable?
35 Or under that peeling pagoda the five hundred tons
of hermaphrodite Word?

At the inn I prepare to surrender again my defeated
shoes to the bending maid   But suddenly the closed
lotus opens to a smile and she points
40 over my shoulder   above the sagging tiles   to where
tall in the bare sky and huge as Gulliver
a carp is rising   golden and fighting
thrusting its paper body up from the fist
of a small boy on an empty roof   higher
45 and higher   into the endless winds of the world

Kyoto & Hong Kong 1958   1962

WILLIAM EMPSON
(1906–)

To an Old Lady[1]

Ripeness is all; her in her cooling planet
Revere; do not presume to think her wasted.
Project her no projectile, plan nor man it;
Gods cool in turn, by the sun long outlasted.

5 Our earth alone given no name of god
Gives, too, no hold for such a leap to aid her;
Landing, you break some palace and seem odd;
Bees sting their need, the keeper's queen invader.

10 No, to your telescope; spy out the land;
Watch while her ritual is still to see,
Still stand her temples emptying in the sand
Whose waves o'erthrew their crumbled tracery;

Still stand uncalled-on her soul's appanage;[2]
Much social detail whose successor fades,
15 Wit used to run a house and to play bridge,
And tragic fervor, to dismiss her maids.

Years her precession do not throw from gear.
She reads a compass certain of her pole;
Confident, finds no confines on her sphere,
20 Whose failing crops are in her sole control.

---

7. The chief military commanders, members of a quasi-dynasty holding virtual rule of Japan from 1192 to 1869.
1. "First three words from *King Lear. Our earth* without a god's name such as the other planets have is compared to some body of people (absurd to say 'the present generation') without fundamental beliefs as a basis for action. When a hive needs a new queen and the keeper puts one in the bees sometimes kill her. *Her precession* is some customary movement of the planet, meant to suggest the dignity of "procession." The unconfined surface of her sphere is like the universe in being finite but unbounded, but I failed to get that into the line" [Empson's note].
2. Natural attribute or accomplishment.

Stars how much further from me fill my night.
Strange that she too should be inaccessible,
Who shares my sun. He curtains her from sight,
And but in darkness is she visible.

1935

Legal Fiction³

Law makes long spokes of the short stakes of men.
Your well fenced out real estate of mind
No high flat of the nomad citizen
Looks over, or train leaves behind.

5 Your rights extend under and above your claim
Without bound; you own land in heaven and hell;
Your part of earth's surface and mass the same,
Of all cosmos' volume, and all stars as well.

Your rights reach down where all owners meet, in hell's
10 Pointed exclusive conclave, at earth's center
(Your spun farm's root still on that axis dwells);
And up, through galaxies, a growing sector.

You are nomad yet; the lighthouse beam you own
Flashes, like Lucifer,⁴ through the firmament.
15 Earth's axis varies; your dark central cone
Wavers a candle's shadow, at the end.

1935

W. H. AUDEN
(1907–1973)

As I Walked Out One Evening

As I walked out one evening,
    Walking down Bristol Street,
The crowds upon the pavement
    Were fields of harvest wheat.

5 And down by the brimming river
    I heard a lover sing
Under an arch of the railway:
    "Love has no ending.

"I'll love you, dear, I'll love you
10   Till China and Africa meet,
And the river jumps over the mountain
    And the salmon sing in the street,

"I'll love you until the ocean
    Is folded and hung up to dry
15 And the seven stars go squawking
    Like geese about the sky.

---

3. "Legal fiction" as used here means the as-
sumption that ownership of land extends into
the earth beneath and into the air above.
4. The morning star.

The years shall run like rabbits,
   For in my arms I hold
The Flower of the Ages,
20   And the first love of the world."

But all the clocks in the city
   Began to whirr and chime:
"O let not Time deceive you,
   You cannot conquer Time.

25 "In the burrows of the Nightmare
   Where Justice naked is,
Time watches from the shadow
   And coughs when you would kiss.

"In headaches and in worry
30   Vaguely life leaks away,
And Time will have his fancy
   Tomorrow or today.

"Into many a green valley
   Drifts the appalling snow;
35 Time breaks the threaded dances
   And the diver's brilliant bow.

"O plunge your hands in water,
   Plunge them in up to the wrist;
Stare, stare in the basin
40   And wonder what you've missed.

"The glacier knocks in the cupboard,
   The desert sighs in the bed,
And the crack in the teacup opens
   A lane to the land of the dead.

45 "Where the beggars raffle the banknotes
   And the Giant is enchanting to Jack,
And the Lily-white Boy is a Roarer,
   And Jill goes down on her back.

"O look, look in the mirror,
50   O look in your distress;
Life remains a blessing
   Although you cannot bless.

"O stand, stand at the window
   As the tears scald and start;
55 You shall love your crooked neighbor
   With your crooked heart."

It was late, late in the evening,
   The lovers they were gone;
The clocks had ceased their chiming,
60   And the deep river ran on.

1940

Musée des Beaux Arts[1]

About suffering they were never wrong,
The Old Masters: how well they understood
Its human position; how it takes place
While someone else is eating or opening a window or just walking dully along;
5 How, when the aged are reverently, passionately waiting
For the miraculous birth, there always must be
Children who did not specially want it to happen, skating
On a pond at the edge of the wood:
They never forgot
10 That even the dreadful martyrdom must run its course
Anyhow in a corner, some untidy spot
Where the dogs go on with their doggy life and the torturer's horse
Scratches its innocent behind on a tree.

In Breughel's *Icarus*,[2] for instance: how everything turns away
15 Quite leisurely from the disaster; the ploughman may
Have heard the splash, the forsaken cry,
But for him it was not an important failure; the sun shone
As it had to on the white legs disappearing into the green
Water; and the expensive delicate ship that must have seen
20 Something amazing, a boy falling out of the sky,
Had somewhere to get to and sailed calmly on.

1940

Law Like Love

Law, say the gardeners, is the sun,
Law is the one
All gardeners obey
Tomorrow, yesterday, today.

5 Law is the wisdom of the old
The impotent grandfathers feebly scold;
The grandchildren put out a treble tongue,
Law is the senses of the young.

Law, says the priest with a priestly look,
10 Expounding to an unpriestly people,
Law is the words in my priestly book,
Law is my pulpit and my steeple.

Law, says the judge as he looks down his nose,
Speaking clearly and most severely,
15 Law is as I've told you before,
Law is as you know I suppose,
Law is but let me explain it once more,
Law is The Law.

1. The Museum of Fine Arts in Brussels, where hangs the painting of The Fall of Icarus, by Pieter Brueghel (ca. 1525–69) described in the poem.
2. Daedalus, the greatly skilled Athenian craftsman, constructed for Minos, king of Crete, a labyrinth in which the Minotaur was kept; but Daedalus was himself imprisoned in it with his son Icarus. He made wings of feathers and wax, with which they flew away; but Icarus flew too near the sun, the wax melted, and he fell into the sea.

Yet law-abiding scholars write;
20 Law is neither wrong nor right,
   Law is only crimes
   Punished by places and by times,
   Law is the clothes men wear
   Anytime, anywhere,
25 Law is Goodmorning and Goodnight.

   Others say, Law is our Fate;
   Others say, Law is our State;
   Others say, others say
   Law is no more
30 Law has gone away.

   And always the loud angry crowd
   Very angry and very loud
   Law is We,
   And always the soft idiot softly Me.

35 If we, dear, know we know no more
   Than they about the Law,
   If I no more than you
   Know what we should and should not do
   Except that all agree
40 Gladly or miserably
   That the Law is
   And that all know this,
   If therefore thinking it absurd
   To identify Law with some other word,
45 Unlike so many men
   I cannot say Law is again,
   No more than they can we suppress
   The universal wish to guess
   Or slip out of our own position
50 Into an unconcerned condition.
   Although I can at least confine
   Your vanity and mine
   To stating timidly
   A timid similarity,
55 We shall boast anyway:
   Like love I say.

   Like love we don't know where or why,
   Like love we can't compel or fly,
   Like love we often weep,
60 Like love we seldom keep.

1940

Our Bias

The hour-glass whispers to the lion's roar,
The clock-towers tell the gardens day and night,
How many errors Time has patience for,
How wrong they are in being always right.

5 Yet Time, however loud its chimes or deep,
However fast its falling torrent flows,
Has never put one lion off his leap
Nor shaken the assurance of a rose.

For they, it seems, care only for success:
10 While we choose words according to their sound
And judge a problem by its awkwardness;

And time with us was always popular.
When have we not preferred some going round
To going straight to where we are?

1940

The Shield of Achilles[3]

She looked over his shoulder
For vines and olive trees,
Marble well-governed cities
And ships upon untamed seas,
5 But there on the shining metal
His hands had put instead
An artificial wilderness
And a sky like lead.

A plain without a feature, bare and brown,
10 No blade of grass, no sign of neighborhood,
Nothing to eat and nowhere to sit down,
Yet, congregated on its blankness, stood
An unintelligible multitude,
A million eyes, a million boots in line,
15 Without expression, waiting for a sign.

Out of the air a voice without a face
Proved by statistics that some cause was just
In tones as dry and level as the place:
No one was cheered and nothing was discussed;
20 Column by column in a cloud of dust
They marched away enduring a belief
Whose logic brought them, somewhere else, to grief.

She looked over his shoulder
For ritual pieties,
25 White flower-garlanded heifers,
Libation and sacrifice,
But there on the shining metal
Where the altar should have been,
She saw by his flickering forge-light
30 Quite another scene.

3. Achilles, the chief Greek hero in the war with Troy, loses his armor when his great friend Patroclus, wearing it, is slain by Hector. While Achilles is mourning the death of his friend, his mother, the goddess Thetis, goes to Olympus to entreat Hephaestos to make new armor for him: both she and Hephaestos pity Achilles because he is fated to die soon and because his life has not been happy. The splendid shield, incorporating gold and silver as well as less precious metals, is described at length in Book XVIII of the *Iliad* (lines 478–608), the scenes depicted on it constituting an epitome of the universe and the lives of men. Hephaestos portrays on it the earth, the heavens, the sea, and the planets; a city in peace (with a wedding and a trial-at-law) and a city at war; scenes from country life, including a harvest feast and a grape-gathering; scenes from animal life and the joyful life of young men and maidens. Around all these scenes, closing them in as the outer border, flows the ocean.

Barbed wire enclosed an arbitrary spot
  Where bored officials lounged (one cracked a joke)
And sentries sweated for the day was hot:
  A crowd of ordinary decent folk
35 Watched from without and neither moved nor spoke
As three pale figures were led forth and bound
To three posts driven upright in the ground.

The mass and majesty of this world, all
  That carries weight and always weighs the same
40 Lay in the hands of others; they were small
  And could not hope for help and no help came:
What their foes liked to do was done, their shame
Was all the worst could wish; they lost their pride
And died as men before their bodies died.

45   She looked over his shoulder
         For athletes at their games,
       Men and women in a dance
         Moving their sweet limbs
       Quick, quick, to music,
50   But there on the shining shield
       His hands had set no dancing-floor
         But a weed-choked field.

A ragged urchin, aimless and alone,
  Loitered about that vacancy, a bird
55 Flew up to safety from his well-aimed stone:
  That girls are raped, that two boys knife a third,
Were axioms to him, who'd never heard
Of any world where promises were kept,
Or one could weep because another wept.

60   The thin-lipped armorer,
         Hephaestos hobbled away,
       Thetis of the shining breasts
         Cried out in dismay
       At what the god had wrought
65   To please her son, the strong
       Iron-hearted man-slaying Achilles
         Who would not live long.

                                        1955

LOUIS MacNEICE
(1907–1963)

The Sunlight on the Garden

The sunlight on the garden
Hardens and grows cold,
We cannot cage the minute
Within its nets of gold,
5 When all is told
We cannot beg for pardon.

Our freedom as free lances
Advances towards its end;
The earth compels, upon it
10 Sonnets and birds descend;
And soon, my friend,
We shall have no time for dances.

The sky was good for flying
Defying the church bells
15 And every evil iron
Siren and what it tells:
The earth compels,
We are dying, Egypt, dying[1]

And not expecting pardon,
20 Hardened in heart anew,
But glad to have sat under
Thunder and rain with you,
And grateful too
For sunlight on the garden.

1938

London Rain

The rain of London pimples
The ebony street with white
And the neon-lamps of London
Stain the canals of night
5 And the park becomes a jungle
In the alchemy of night.

My wishes turn to violent
Horses black as coal—
The randy mares of fancy,
10 The stallions of the soul—
Eager to take the fences
That fence about my soul.

Across the countless chimneys
The horses ride and across
15 The country to the channel
Where warning beacons toss,
To a place where God and No-God
Play at pitch and toss.

Whichever wins I am happy
20 For God will give me bliss
But No-God will absolve me
From all I do amiss
And I need not suffer conscience
If the world was made amiss.

---

1. From *Antony and Cleopatra*, IV.xv.41, Antony's speech to Cleopatra, "I am dying, Egypt, dying."

25 Under God we can reckon
On pardon when we fall
But if we are under No-God
Nothing will matter at all,
Adultery and murder
30 Will count for nothing at all.

So reinforced by logic
As having nothing to lose
My lust goes riding horseback
To ravish where I choose,
35 To burgle all the turrets
Of beauty as I choose.

But now the rain gives over
Its dance upon the town,
Logic and lust together
40 Come dimly tumbling down,
And neither God nor No-God
Is either up or down.

The argument was wilful,
The alternatives untrue,
45 We need no metaphysics
To sanction what we do
Or to muffle us in comfort
From what we did not do.

Whether the living river
50 Began in bog or lake,
The world is what was given,
The world is what we make.
And we only can discover
Life in the life we make.

55 So let the water sizzle
Upon the gleaming slates,
There will be sunshine after
When the rain abates
And rain returning duly
60 When the sun abates.

My wishes now come homeward,
Their gallopings in vain,
Logic and lust are quiet
And again it starts to rain;
65 Falling asleep I listen
To the falling London rain.

1941

THEODORE ROETHKE
(1908–1963)

Root Cellar

Nothing would sleep in that cellar, dank as a ditch,
Bulbs broke out of boxes hunting for chinks in the dark,
Shoots dangled and drooped,
Lolling obscenely from mildewed crates,
5   Hung down long yellow evil necks, like tropical snakes.
And what a congress of stinks!
Roots ripe as old bait,
Pulpy stems, rank, silo-rich,
Leaf-mold, manure, lime, piled against slippery planks.
10 Nothing would give up life:
Even the dirt kept breathing a small breath.

1948

My Papa's Waltz

The whiskey on your breath
Could make a small boy dizzy;
But I hung on like death:
Such waltzing was not easy.

5   We romped until the pans
Slid from the kitchen shelf;
My mother's countenance
Could not unfrown itself.

The hand that held my wrist
10 Was battered on one knuckle;
At every step you missed
My right ear scraped a buckle.

You beat time on my head
With a palm caked hard by dirt,
15 Then waltzed me off to bed
Still clinging to your shirt.

1948

The Waking

I wake to sleep, and take my waking slow.
I feel my fate in what I cannot fear.
I learn by going where I have to go.

We think by feeling. What is there to know?
5   I hear my being dance from ear to ear.
I wake to sleep, and take my waking slow.

Of those so close beside me, which are you?
God bless the Ground! I shall walk softly there,
And learn by going where I have to go.

¹⁰ Light takes the Tree; but who can tell us how?
The lowly worm climbs up a winding stair;
I wake to sleep, and take my waking slow.

Great Nature has another thing to do
To you and me; so take the lively air,
¹⁵ And, lovely, learn by going where to go.

This shaking keeps me steady. I should know.
What falls away is always. And is near.
I wake to sleep, and take my waking slow.
I learn by going where I have to go.

1953

I Knew a Woman

I knew a woman, lovely in her bones,
When small birds sighed, she would sigh back at them;
Ah, when she moved, she moved more ways than one:
The shapes a bright container can contain!
⁵ Of her choice virtues only gods should speak,
Or English poets who grew up on Greek
(I'd have them sing in chorus, cheek to cheek).

How well her wishes went! She stroked my chin,
She taught me Turn, and Counter-turn, and Stand;¹
¹⁰ She taught me Touch, that undulant white skin;
I nibbled meekly from her proffered hand;
She was the sickle; I, poor I, the rake,
Coming behind her for her pretty sake
(But what prodigious mowing we did make).

¹⁵ Love likes a gander, and adores a goose:
Her full lips pursed, the errant note to seize;
She played it quick, she played it light and loose,
My eyes, they dazzled at her flowing knees;
Her several parts could keep a pure repose,
²⁰ Or one hip quiver with a mobile nose
(She moved in circles, and those circles moved).

Let seed be grass, and grass turn into hay:
I'm martyr to a motion not my own;
What's freedom for? To know eternity.
²⁵ I swear she cast a shadow white as stone.
But who would count eternity in days?
These old bones live to learn her wanton ways:
(I measure time by how a body sways).

1958

The Far Field

1

I dream of journeys repeatedly:
Of flying like a bat deep into a narrowing tunnel,
Of driving alone, without luggage, out a long peninsula,
The road lined with snow-laden second growth,
⁵ A fine dry snow ticking the windshield,

1. Literary terms, for the three parts of the Pindaric ode.

Alternate snow and sleet, no on-coming traffic,
And no lights behind, in the blurred side-mirror,
The road changing from glazed tarface to a rubble of stone,
Ending at last in a hopeless sand-rut,
10 Where the car stalls,
Churning in a snowdrift
Until the headlights darken.

                2

At the field's end, in the corner missed by the mower,
Where the turf drops oﬂ into a grass-hidden culvert,
15 Haunt of the cat-bird, nesting-place of the field-mouse,
Not too far away from the ever-changing flower-dump,
Among the tin cans, tires, rusted pipes, broken machinery,—
One learned of the eternal;
And in the shrunken face of a dead rat, eaten by rain and ground-beetles
20 (I found it lying among the rubble of an old coal bin)
And the tom-cat, caught near the pheasant-run,
Its entrails strewn over the half-grown flowers,
Blasted to death by the night watchman.

I suffered for birds, for young rabbits caught in the mower,
25 My grief was not excessive.
For to come upon warblers in early May
Was to forget time and death:
How they filled the oriole's elm, a twittering restless cloud, all one morning,
And I watched and watched till my eyes blurred from the bird shapes,—
30 Cape May, Blackburnian, Cerulean—
Moving, elusive as fish, fearless,
Hanging, bunched like young fruit, bending the end branches,
Still for a moment,
Then pitching away in half-flight,
35 Lighter than finches,
While the wrens bickered and sang in the half-green hedgerows,
And the flicker drummed from his dead tree in the chicken-yard.

—Or to lie naked in sand,
In the silted° shallows of a slow river,   *sedimented*
40 Fingering a shell,
Thinking:
Once I was something like this, mindless,
Or perhaps with another mind, less peculiar;
Or to sink down to the hips in a mossy quagmire;[2]
45 Or, with skinny knees, to sit astride a wet log,
Believing:
I'll return again,
As a snake or a raucous bird,
Or, with luck, as a lion.

50 I learned not to fear infinity,
The far field, the windy cliffs of forever,
The dying of time in the white light of tomorrow,
The wheel turning away from itself,
The sprawl of the wave,
55 The on-coming water.

2. Soft, wet land.

3

The river turns on itself,
The tree retreats into its own shadow.
I feel a weightless change, a moving forward
As of water quickening before a narrowing channel
⁶⁰ When banks converge, and the wide river whitens;
Or when two rivers combine, the blue glacial torrent
And the yellowish-green from the mountainy upland,—
At first a swift rippling between rocks,
Then a long running over flat stones

⁶⁵ Before descending to the alluvial plain,[3]
To the clay banks, and the wild grapes hanging from the elmtrees.
The slightly trembling water
Dropping a fine yellow silt where the sun stays;
And the crabs bask near the edge,
⁷⁰ The weedy edge, alive with small snakes and bloodsuckers—
I have come to a still, but not a deep center,
A point outside the glittering current;
My eyes stare at the bottom of a river,
At the irregular stones, iridescent sandgrains,
⁷⁵ My mind moves in more than one place,
In a country half-land, half-water.

I am renewed by death, thought of my death,
The dry scent of a dying garden in September,
The wind fanning the ash of a low fire.
⁸⁰ What I love is near at hand,
Always, in earth and air.

4

The lost self changes,
Turning toward the sea,
A sea-shape turning around—
⁸⁵ An old man with his feet before the fire,
In robes of green, in garments of adieu.

A man faced with his own immensity
Wakes all the waves, all their loose wandering fire.
The murmur of the absolute, the why
⁹⁰ Of being born fails on his naked ears.
His spirit moves like monumental wind
That gentles on a sunny blue plateau.
He is the end of things, the final man.

All finite things reveal infinitude:
⁹⁵ The mountain with its singular bright shade
Like the blue shine on freshly frozen snow,
The after-light upon ice-burdened pines;
Odor of basswood on a mountain-slope,
A scent beloved of bees;
¹⁰⁰ Silence of water above a sunken tree:
The pure serene of memory in one man—
A ripple widening from a single stone
Winding around the waters of the world.

1964

3. Sand or soil built up from the deposits of running water.

ROBERT HAYDEN
(1913–   )

Mourning Poem for the Queen of Sunday

Lord's lost Him His mockingbird,
His fancy warbler;
Satan sweet-talked her,
four bullets hushed her.
5   Who would have thought
she'd end that way?

Four bullets hushed her. And the world a-clang with evil.
Who's going to make old hardened sinner men tremble now
and the righteous rock?
10   Oh who and oh who will sing Jesus down
to help with struggling and doing without and being colored
all through blue Monday?
Till way next Sunday?

All those angels
15   in their cretonne clouds and finery
the true believer saw
when she rared back her head and sang,
all those angels are surely weeping.
Who would have thought
20   she'd end that way?

Four holes in her heart. The gold works wrecked.
But she looks so natural in her big bronze coffin
among the Broken Hearts and Gates-Ajar,
it's as if any moment she'd lift her head
25   from its pillow of chill gardenias
and turn this quiet into shouting Sunday
and make folks forget what she did on Monday.

Oh, Satan sweet-talked her,
and four bullets hushed her.
30   Lord's lost Him His diva,
His fancy warbler's gone.
Who would have thought,
who would have thought she'd end that way?

1966

JOHN BERRYMAN
(1914–1972)

The Ball Poem

What is the boy now, who has lost his ball,
What, what is he to do? I saw it go
Merrily bouncing, down the street, and then
Merrily over—there it is in the water!
5   No use to say "O there are other balls":
An ultimate shaking grief fixes the boy
As he stands rigid, trembling, staring down
All his young days into the harbor where
His ball went. I would not intrude on him,
10   A dime, another ball, is worthless. Now
He senses first responsibility
In a world of possessions. People will take balls,
Balls will be lost always, little boy,
And no one buys a ball back. Money is external.
15   He is learning, well behind his desperate eyes,
The epistemology of loss, how to stand up
Knowing what every man must one day know
And most know many days, how to stand up.
And gradually light returns to the street,
20   A whistle blows, the ball is out of sight,
Soon part of me will explore the deep and dark
Floor of the harbor . . . I am everywhere,
I suffer and move, my mind and my heart move
With all that move me, under the water
25   Or whistling, I am not a little boy.

1958

The Dream Songs [2]

1

Huffy Henry hid   the day,
unappeasable Henry sulked.
I see his point,—a trying to put things over.
It was the thought that they thought
5   they could *do* it made Henry wicked & away.
But he should have come out and talked.

All the world like a woolen lover
once did seem on Henry's side.
Then came a departure.
10   Thereafter nothing fell out as it might or ought.
I don't see how Henry, pried
open for all the world to see, survived.

2. "[The Dream Songs are] essentially about an imaginary character (not the poet, not me) named Henry, a white American in early middle age sometimes in blackface, who has suffered an irreversible loss and talks about himself sometimes in the first person, sometimes in the third, sometimes even in the second; he has a friend, never named, who addresses him as Mr. Bones and variants thereof" [Berryman's note].

What he has now to say is a long
wonder the world can bear & be.
15 Once in a sycamore I was glad
all at the top, and I sang.
Hard on the land wears the strong sea
and empty grows every bed.

1964

29

There sat down, once, a thing on Henry's heart
so heavy, if he had a hundred years
& more, & weeping, sleepless, in all them time
Henry could not make good.
5 Starts again always in Henry's ears
the little cough somewhere, an odor, a chime.

And there is another thing he has in mind
like a grave Sienese[3] face a thousand years
would fail to blur the still profiled reproach of. Ghastly,
10 with open eyes, he attends, blind.
All the bells say: too late. This is not for tears;
thinking.

But never did Henry, as he thought he did,
end anyone and hacks her body up
15 and hide the pieces, where they may be found.
He knows: he went over everyone, & nobody's missing.
Often he reckons, in the dawn, them up.
Nobody is ever missing.

1964

53

He lay in the middle of the world, and twitcht.
More Sparine for Pelides,[4]
human (half) & down here as he is,
with probably insulting mail to open
5 and certainly unworthy words to hear
and his unforgivable memory.

—I seldom *go* to *films*. They are too exciting,
said the Honourable Possum.[5]
—It takes me so long to read the 'paper,
10 said to me one day a novelist hot as a firecracker,[6]
because I have to identify myself with everyone in it,
including the corpses, pal.

Kierkegaard[7] wanted a society, to refuse to read 'papers,
and that was not, friends, his worst idea.
15 Tiny Hardy, toward the end, refused to say *anything*,
a programme adopted early on by long Housman,
and Gottfried Benn[8]
said:—We are using our own skins for wallpaper and we cannot win.

1964

3. Of Siena, a center of Italian painting dur-
ing the 13th century.
4. Another name for Achilles, Greek hero of
the Trojan war and son of the mortal king
Peleus and the sea nymph Thetis, with whom
Henry "with his plights & gripes/as bad as
achilles" is compared in Dream Song 14.
Sparine is a tranquilizing drug.

5. T. S. Eliot, who wrote *Old Possum's Book
of Practical Cats.*
6. Berryman identified him as his friend, Saul
Bellow.
7. Søren Kierkegaard (1813–1855), Swedish
existentialist philosopher.
8. (1886–1956), German poet.

375. *His Helplessness*

I know a young lady's high-piled ashen hair
and she is miserable, threatened a thoroughfare
for pants in their desire
fondless: she drinks too dear, & feels put down,
"no one is friendly to me" she scribbles here,
of all them griefs the crown

having been her lay by her father agèd ten
from which she grew up slowly into the world of men
who headed ha for her.
She put her soul in jeopardy with pills
a week ago, she writes—Henry would offer,
only it's thousands of miles,

help to the delicate lady far in her strait,
counsel she needs, needs one to pace her fate.
I cannot spot a hole,
& I look with my heart, in her darkness over there:
dark shroud the clouds on her disordered soul
whose last letter flew like a prayer.

1968

382

At Henry's bier let some thing fall out well:
enter there none who somewhat has to sell,
the music ancient & gradual,
the voices solemn but the grief subdued,
no hairy jokes but everybody's mood
subdued, subdued,

until the Dancer comes, in a short short dress
hair black & long & loose, dark dark glasses,
uptilted face,
pallor & strangeness, the music changes
to "Give!" & "Ow!" and how! the music changes,
she kicks a backward limb

on tiptoe, pirouettes, & she is free
to the knocking music, sails, dips, & suddenly
returns to the terrible gay
occasion hopeless & mad, she weaves, it's hell,
she flings to her head a leg, bobs, all is well,
she dances Henry away.

1968

RANDALL JARRELL
(1914–1965)

Nestus Gurley

Sometimes waking, sometimes sleeping,
Late in the afternoon, or early
In the morning, I hear on the lawn,
On the walk, on the lawn, the soft quick step,
5 The sound half song, half breath: a note or two
That with a note or two would be a tune.
It is Nestus Gurley.

It is an old
Catch or snatch or tune
10 In the Dorian mode:[1] the mode of the horses
That stand all night in the fields asleep
Or awake, the mode of the cold
Hunter, Orion, wheeling upside-down,
All space and stars, in cater-cornered Heaven.
15 When, somewhere under the east,
The great march begins, with birds and silence;
When, in the day's first triumph, dawn
Rides over the houses, Nestus Gurley
Delivers to me my lot.

20 As the sun sets, I hear my daughter say:
"He has four routes and makes a hundred dollars."
Sometimes he comes with dogs, sometimes with children,
Sometimes with dogs and children.
He collects, today.
25 I hear my daughter say:
"Today Nestus has got on his derby."
And he says, after a little: "It's two-eighty."
"How could it be two-eighty?"
"Because this month there're five Sundays: it's two-eighty."

30 He collects, delivers. Before the first, least star
Is lost in the paling east; at evening
While the soft, side-lit, gold-leafed day
Lingers to see the stars, the boy Nestus
Delivers to me the Morning Star, the Evening Star
35 —Ah no, only the Morning *News,* the Evening *Record*
Of what I have done and what I have not done
Set down and held against me in the Book
Of Death, on paper yellowing
Already, with one morning's sun, one evening's sun.

---

1. The scale pattern to which ancient Greek philosophers ascribed a "manly and strong" character.

40 Sometimes I only dream him. He brings then
    News of a different morning, a judgment not of men.
    The bombers have turned back over the Pole,
    Having met a star. . . . I look at that new year
    And, waking, think of our Moravian Star
45 Not lit yet, and the pure beeswax candle
    With its red flame-proofed paper pompom
    Not lit yet, and the sweetened
    Bun we brought home from the love-feast, still not eaten,
    And the song the children sang: *O Morning Star—*

50 And at this hour, to the dew-hushed drums
    Of the morning, Nestus Gurley
    Marches to me over the lawn; and the cat Elfie,
    Furred like a musk-ox, coon-tailed, gold-leaf-eyed,
    Looks at the paper boy without alarm
55 But yawns, and stretches, and walks placidly
    Across the lawn to his ladder, climbs it, and begins to purr.

    I let him in,
    Go out and pick up from the grass the paper hat
    Nestus has folded: this tricorne fit for a Napoleon
60 Of our days and institutions, weaving
    Baskets, being bathed, receiving
    Electric shocks, Rauwolfia.[2] . . . I put it on
    —Ah no, only unfold it.
    There is dawn inside; and I say to no one
65 About—
              it is a note or two
    That with a note or two would—
                             say to no one
    About nothing: "He delivers dawn."

70 When I lie coldly
    —Lie, that is, neither with coldness nor with warmth—
    In the darkness that is not lit by anything,
    In the grave that is not lit by anything
    Except our hope: the hope
75 That is not proofed against anything, but pure
    And shining as the first, least star
    That is lost in the east on the morning of Judgment—
    May I say, recognizing the step
    Or tune or breath. . . .
80   recognizing the breath,
    May I say, "It is Nestus Gurley."

                                        1960

2. A plant whose substance is sometimes used in the treatment of certain mental disorders.

HENRY REED
(1914–   )

From Lessons of the War

TO ALAN MICHELL

Vixi duellis nuper idoneus
Et militavi non sine gloria[1]

1. *Naming of Parts*

Today we have naming of parts. Yesterday,
We had daily cleaning. And tomorrow morning,
We shall have what to do after firing. But today,
Today we have naming of parts. Japonica[2]
5   Glistens like coral in all of the neighboring gardens,
    And today we have naming of parts.

This is the lower sling swivel. And this
Is the upper sling swivel, whose use you will see,
When you are given your slings. And this is the piling swivel,
10   Which in your case you have not got. The branches
Hold in the gardens their silent, eloquent gestures,
    Which in our case we have not got.

This is the safety-catch, which is always released
With an easy flick of the thumb. And please do not let me
15   See anyone using his finger. You can do it quite easy
If you have any strength in your thumb. The blossoms
Are fragile and motionless, never letting anyone see
    Any of them using their finger.

And this you can see is the bolt. The purpose of this
20   Is to open the breech, as you see. We can slide it
Rapidly backwards and forwards: we call this
Easing the spring. And rapidly backwards and forwards
The early bees are assaulting and fumbling the flowers:
    They call it easing the Spring.

25   They call it easing the Spring: it is perfectly easy
If you have any strength in your thumb: like the bolt,
And the breech, and the cocking-piece, and the point of balance,
Which in our case we have not got; and the almond-blossom
Silent in all of the gardens and the bees going backwards and forwards,
30   For today we have naming of parts.

---

1. The opening lines of a poem by Horace (III.26), but with Horace's word *"puellis"* (girls) changed to *"duellis"* (war, battles): "Lately I have lived in the midst of battles, creditably enough,/And have soldiered, not without glory."
2. The flowering quince (*Cydonia japonica*), a shrub with brilliant scarlet flowers.

2. *Judging Distances*

Not only how far away, but the way that you say it
Is very important. Perhaps you may never get
The knack of judging a distance, but at least you know
How to report on a landscape: the central sector,
35 The right of arc and that, which we had last Tuesday,
      And at least you know

That maps are of time, not place, so far as the army
Happens to be concerned—the reason being,
Is one which need not delay us. Again, you know
40 There are three kinds of tree, three only, the fir and the poplar,
And those which have bushy tops to; and lastly
      That things only seem to be things.

A barn is not called a barn, to put it more plainly,
Or a field in the distance, where sheep may be safely grazing.
45 You must never be over-sure. You must say, when reporting:
At five o'clock in the central sector is a dozen
Of what appear to be animals; whatever you do,
      Don't call the bleeders *sheep.*

I am sure that's quite clear; and suppose, for the sake of example,
50 The one at the end, asleep, endeavors to tell us
What he sees over there to the west, and how far away,
After first having come to attention. There to the west,
On the fields of summer the sun and the shadows bestow
      Vestments of purple and gold.

55 The still white dwellings are like a mirage in the heat,
And under the swaying elms a man and a woman
Lie gently together. Which is, perhaps, only to say
That there is a row of houses to the left of arc,
And that under some poplars a pair of what appear to be humans
60   Appear to be loving.

Well that, for an answer, is what we might rightly call
Moderately satisfactory only, the reason being,
Is that two things have been omitted, and those are important.
The human beings, now: in what direction are they,
65 And how far away, would you say? And do not forget
      There may be dead ground[3] in between.

There may be dead ground in between; and I may not have got
The knack of judging a distance; I will only venture
A guess that perhaps between me and the apparent lovers,
70 (Who, incidentally, appear by now to have finished,)
At seven o'clock from the houses, is roughly a distance
      Of about one year and a half.

                                                        1946

---

3. Military: "Space that cannot be reached   point" [Webster's Third New International
by fire from a given weapon or a given   Dictionary].

DYLAN THOMAS
(1914–1953)

The Force That
Through the Green Fuse
Drives the Flower

The force that through the green fuse drives the flower
Drives my green age; that blasts the roots of trees
Is my destroyer.
And I am dumb to tell the crooked rose
5   My youth is bent by the same wintry fever.

The force that drives the water through the rocks
Drives my red blood; that dries the mouthing streams
Turns mine to wax.
And I am dumb to mouth unto my veins
10   How at the mountain spring the same mouth sucks.

The hand that whirls the water in the pool
Stirs the quicksand; that ropes the blowing wind
Hauls my shroud sail.
And I am dumb to tell the hanging man
15   How of my clay is made the hangman's lime.

The lips of time leech to the fountain head;
Love drips and gathers, but the fallen blood
Shall calm her sores.
And I am dumb to tell a weather's wind
20   How time has ticked a heaven round the stars.

And I am dumb to tell the lover's tomb
How at my sheet goes the same crooked worm.

1934

After the Funeral

(IN MEMORY OF ANN JONES) [1]

After the funeral, mule praises, brays,
Windshake of sailshaped ears, muffle-toed tap
Tap happily of one peg in the thick
Grave's foot, blinds down the lids, the teeth in black,
5   The spittled eyes, the salt ponds in the sleeves,
Morning smack of the spade that wakes up sleep,
Shakes a desolate boy who slits his throat
In the dark of the coffin and sheds dry leaves,

1. Ann [Williams] Jones was Dylan Thomas'
aunt, his mother's sister, who had married
a tenant farmer; their rented farm was Fern
Hill. She died in 1933.

That breaks one bone to light with a judgment clout,
10 After the feast of tear-stuffed time and thistles
In a room with a stuffed fox and a stale fern,
I stand, for this memorial's sake, alone
In the sniveling hours with dead, humped Ann
Whose hooded, fountain heart once fell in puddles
15 Round the parched worlds of Wales and drowned each sun
(Though this for her is a monstrous image blindly
Magnified out of praise; her death was a still drop;
She would not have me sinking in the holy
Flood of her heart's fame; she would lie dumb and deep
20 And need no druid [2] of her broken body).
But I, Ann's bard on a raised hearth, call all
The seas to service that her wood-tongued virtue
Babble like a bellbuoy over the hymning heads,
Bow down the walls of the ferned and foxy woods
25 That her love sing and swing through a brown chapel,
Bless her bent spirit with four, crossing birds.
Her flesh was meek as milk, but this skyward statue
With the wild breast and blessed and giant skull
Is carved from her in a room with a wet window
30 In a fiercely mourning house in a crooked year.
I know her scrubbed and sour humble hands
Lie with religion in their cramp, her threadbare
Whisper in a damp word, her wits drilled hollow,
Her fist of a face died clenched on a round pain;
35 And sculptured Ann is seventy years of stone.
These cloud-sopped, marble hands, this monumental
Argument of the hewn voice, gesture and psalm,
Storm me forever over her grave until
The stuffed lung of the fox twitch and cry Love
40 And the strutting fern lay seeds on the black sill.

1939

The Hunchback in the Park

The hunchback in the park
A solitary mister
Propped between trees and water
From the opening of the garden lock
5 That lets the trees and water enter
Until the Sunday somber bell at dark[1]

Eating bread from a newspaper
Drinking water from the chained cup
That the children filled with gravel
10 In the fountain basin where I sailed my ship
Slept at night in a dog kennel
But nobody chained him up.

2. Priest, among ancient Celts of Gaul or Britain, also magician or soothsayer.

1. The bell that warns visitors that the park gates are about to be closed for the night.

Like the park birds he came early
Like the water he sat down
15 And Mister they called Hey mister
The truant boys from the town
Running when he had heard them clearly
On out of sound

Past lake and rockery
20 Laughing when he shook his paper
Hunchbacked in mockery
Through the loud zoo of the willow groves
Dodging the park keeper
With his stick that picked up leaves.

25 And the old dog sleeper
Alone between nurses and swans
While the boys among willows
Made the tigers jump out of their eyes
To roar on the rockery stones
30 And the groves were blue with sailors

Made all day until bell time
A woman figure without fault
Straight as a young elm
Straight and tall from his crooked bones
35 That she might stand in the night
After the locks and chains

All night in the unmade park
After the railings and shrubberies
The birds the grass the trees the lake
40 And the wild boys innocent as strawberries
Had followed the hunchback
To his kennel in the dark.

1942

The Conversation of Prayer

The conversation of prayers about to be said
By the child going to bed and the man on the stairs
Who climbs to his dying love in her high room,
The one not caring to whom in his sleep he will move
5 And the other full of tears that she will be dead,

Turns in the dark on the sound they know will arise
Into the answering skies from the green ground,
From the man on the stairs and the child by his bed.
The sound about to be said in the two prayers
10 For the sleep in a safe land and the love who dies

Will be the same grief flying. Whom shall they calm?
Shall the child sleep unharmed or the man be crying?
The conversation of prayers about to be said

Turns on the quick and the dead, and the man on the stairs
15 Tonight shall find no dying but alive and warm

In the fire of his care his love in the high room.
And the child not caring to whom he climbs his prayer
Shall drown in a grief as deep as his true grave,
And mark the dark eyed wave, through the eyes of sleep,
20 Dragging him up the stairs to one who lies dead.

1946

Fern Hill

Now as I was young and easy under the apple boughs
About the lilting house and happy as the grass was green,
      The night above the dingle starry,
         Time let me hail and climb
5   Golden in the heydays of his eyes,
And honored among wagons I was prince of the apple towns
And once below a time I lordly had the trees and leaves
         Trail with daisies and barley
      Down the rivers of the windfall light.

10 And as I was green and carefree, famous among the barns
About the happy yard and singing as the farm was home,
      In the sun that is young once only,
         Time let me play and be
            Golden in the mercy of his means,
15 And green and golden I was huntsman and herdsman, the calves
Sang to my horn, the foxes on the hills barked clear and cold,
         And the sabbath rang slowly
      In the pebbles of the holy streams.

All the sun long it was running, it was lovely, the hay
20 Fields high as the house, the tunes from the chimneys, it was air
         And playing, lovely and watery
            And fire green as grass.
      And nightly under the simple stars
As I rode to sleep the owls were bearing the farm away,
25 All the moon long I heard, blessed among stables, the night-jars
         Flying with the ricks, and the horses
            Flashing into the dark.

And then to awake, and the farm, like a wanderer white
With the dew, come back, the cock on his shoulder: it was all
30   Shining, it was Adam and maiden,
            The sky gathered again
      And the sun grew round that very day.
So it must have been after the birth of the simple light
In the first, spinning place, the spellbound horses walking warm
35   Out of the whinnying green stable
            On to the fields of praise.

And honored among foxes and pheasants by the gay house
Under the new made clouds and happy as the heart was long,
    In the sun born over and over,
40   I ran my heedless ways,
    My wishes raced through the house high hay
And nothing I cared, at my sky blue trades, that time allows
In all his tuneful turning so few and such morning songs
    Before the children green and golden
45   Follow him out of grace,

Nothing I cared, in the lamb white days, that time would take me
Up to the swallow thronged loft by the shadow of my hand,
    In the moon that is always rising,
      Nor that riding to sleep
50   I should hear him fly with the high fields
And wake to the farm forever fled from the childless land.
Oh as I was young and easy in the mercy of his means,
    Time held me green and dying
    Though I sang in my chains like the sea.

                                    1946

GWENDOLYN BROOKS
(1917–   )

my dreams, my works, must wait till after hell

I hold my honey and I store my bread
In little jars and cabinets of my will.
I label clearly, and each latch and lid
I bid, Be firm till I return from hell.
5 I am very hungry. I am incomplete.
And none can tell when I may dine again.
No man can give me any word but Wait,
The puny light. I keep eyes pointed in;
Hoping that, when the devil days of my hurt
10 Drag out to their last dregs and I resume
On such legs as are left me, in such heart
As I can manage, remember to go home,
My taste will not have turned insensitive
To honey and bread old purity could love.

                                    1945

We Real Cool

    The Pool Players.
    Seven at the Golden Shovel.

We real cool. We
Left school. We

5   Lurk late. We
    Strike straight. We

    Sing sin. We
    Thin gin. We

    Jazz June. We
10 Die soon.

                             1960

Boy Breaking Glass

TO MARC CRAWFORD FROM WHOM THE COMMISSION

Whose broken window is a cry of art
(success, that winks aware
as elegance, as a treasonable faith)
is raw: is sonic: is old-eyed première.
5 Our beautiful flaw and terrible ornament.
    Our barbarous and metal little man.

    "I shall create! If not a note, a hole.
    If not an overture, a desecration."

    Full of pepper and light
10 and Salt and night and cargoes.

    "Don't go down the plank
    if you see there's no extension.
    Each to his grief, each to
    his loneliness and fidgety revenge.

15 Nobody knew where I was and now I am no longer there."

    The only sanity is a cup of tea.
    The music is in minors.

    Each one other
    is having different weather.

20 "It was you, it was you who threw away my name!
    And this is everything I have for me."

    Who has not Congress, lobster, love, luau,
    the Regency Room, the Statue of Liberty,
    runs. A sloppy amalgamation.
25 A mistake.
    A cliff.
    A hymn, a snare, and an exceeding sun.

                             1968

ROBERT LOWELL
(1917–   )

The Quaker Graveyard in Nantucket

(FOR WARREN WINSLOW, DEAD AT SEA)

*Let man have dominion over the fishes of the
sea and the fowls of the air and the beasts and the
whole earth, and every creeping creature that
moveth upon the earth.*[2]

1

A brackish reach of shoal off Madaket[3]
The sea was still breaking violently and night
Had steamed into our North Atlantic Fleet,
When the drowned sailor clutched the drag-net. Light
5 Flashed from his matted head and marble feet,
He grappled at the net
With the coiled, hurdling muscles of his thighs:
The corpse was bloodless, a botch of reds and whites,
Its open, staring eyes
10 Were lusterless dead-lights
Or cabin-windows on a stranded hulk
Heavy with sand.[4] We weight the body, close
Its eyes and heave it seaward whence it came,
Where the heel-headed dogfish barks its nose
15 On Ahab's[5] void and forehead; and the name
Is blocked in yellow chalk.
Sailors, who pitch this portent at the sea
Where dreadnaughts shall confess
Its hell-bent deity,
20 When you are powerless
To sand-bag this Atlantic bulwark, faced
By the earth-shaker, green, unwearied, chaste
In his steel scales: ask for no Orphean lute
To pluck life back.[6] The guns of the steeled fleet
25 Recoil and then repeat
The hoarse salute.

2

Whenever winds are moving and their breath
Heaves at the roped-in bulwarks of this pier,
The terns and sea-gulls tremble at your death
30 In these home waters. Sailor, can you hear
The Pequod's sea wings, beating landward, fall
Headlong and break on our Atlantic wall
Off 'Sconset,[7] where the yawing S-boats° splash   *sailboats*
The bellbuoy, with ballooning spinnakers,
35 As the entangled, screeching mainsheet clears

2. Genesis i.26.
3. Name of a small settlement, and a bay, on Nantucket Island, Massachusetts.
4. Lines 1–12 are based on the opening chapter of Thoreau's *Cape Cod.*
5. Captain Ahab, who is protagonist of Herman Melville's *Moby Dick* (1851) and a recurring presence in this sequence of poems, sailed from Nantucket on the *Pequod* in pursuit of the white whale.

6. Orpheus went to the underworld to recover his wife Eurydice and so charmed its queen, Persephone, by his playing on the lyre that she allowed him to lead Eurydice up from Hades, on condition that he not look back before the end of the journey: he did look back, and Eurydice vanished forever. The "earth-shaker" is Poseidon, god of the sea.
7. Siasconset, a town on Nantucket.

The blocks: off Madaket, where lubbers lash
The heavy surf and throw their long lead squids
For blue-fish? Sea-gulls blink their heavy lids
Seaward. The winds' wings beat upon the stones,
40   Cousin, and scream for you and the claws rush
At the sea's throat and wring it in the slush
Of this old Quaker graveyard where the bones
Cry out in the long night for the hurt beast
Bobbing by Ahab's whaleboats in the East.

3

45   All you recovered from Poseidon died
With you, my cousin, and the harrowed brine
Is fruitless on the blue beard of the god,
Stretching beyond us to the castles in Spain,
Nantucket's westward haven. To Cape Cod
50   Guns, cradled on the tide,
Blast the eelgrass about a waterclock
Of bilge and backwash, roil the salt and sand
Lashing earth's scaffold, rock
Our warships in the hand
55   Of the great God, where time's contrition blues
Whatever it was these Quaker sailors lost

In the mad scramble of their lives. They died
When time was open-eyed,
Wooden and childish; only bones abide
60   There, in the nowhere, where their boats were tossed
Sky-high, where mariners had fabled news
Of IS, the whited monster. What it costs
Them is their secret. In the sperm-whale's slick
I see the Quakers drown and hear their cry:
65   "If God himself had not been on our side,
If God himself had not been on our side,
When the Atlantic rose against us, why,
Then it had swallowed us up quick."

4

This is the end of the whaleroad and the whale
70   Who spewed Nantucket bones on the thrashed swell
And stirred the troubled waters to whirlpools
To send the Pequod packing off to hell:
This is the end of them, three-quarters fools,
Snatching at straws to sail
75   Seaward and seaward on the turntail whale,
Spouting out blood and water as it rolls,
Sick as a dog to these Atlantic shoals:
Clamavimus, O depths.[8] Let the sea-gulls wail

For water, for the deep where the high tide
80   Mutters to its hurt self, mutters and ebbs.
Waves wallow in their wash, go out and out,
Leave only the death-rattle of the crabs,
The beach increasing, its enormous snout
Sucking the ocean's side.
85   This is the end of running on the waves;

---

8. "We have cried * * * ": Psalms cxxx.1— "Out of the depths have I cried unto thee, O Lord."

We are poured out like water. Who will dance
The mast-lashed master of Leviathans
Up from this field of Quakers in their unstoned graves?
                    5
When the whale's viscera go and the roll
90 Of its corruption overruns this world
Beyond tree-swept Nantucket and Wood's Hole[9]
And Martha's Vineyard, Sailor, will your sword
Whistle and fall and sink into the fat?
In the great ash-pit of Jehoshaphat[1]
95 The bones cry for the blood of the white whale,
The fat flukes arch and whack about its ears,
The death-lance churns into the sanctuary, tears
The gun-blue swingle, heaving like a flail,
And hacks the coiling life out: it works and drags
100 And rips the sperm-whale's midriff into rags,
Gobbets of blubber spill to wind and weather,
Sailor, and gulls go round the stoven timbers
Where the morning stars sing out together
And thunder shakes the white surf and dismembers
105 The red flag hammered in the mast-head.[2] Hide,
Our steel, Jonas Messias,[3] in Thy side.

6. *Our Lady of Walsingham*[4]

There once the penitents took off their shoes
And then walked barefoot the remaining mile;
And the small trees, a stream and hedgerows file
110 Slowly along the munching English lane,
Like cows to the old shine, until you lose
Track of your dragging pain.
The stream flows down under the druid tree,
Shiloah's whirlpools gurgle and make glad
115 The castle of God. Sailor, you were glad
And whistled Sion[5] by that stream. But see:

---

9. Harbor and township in southern Massachusetts, north of the island of Martha's Vineyard, which lies to the west of Nantucket.
1. Identified by some commentators as an image for the Day of Judgment, when the world will end in fire.
2. As was the flag in the concluding chapter of *Moby Dick.*
3. For the juxtaposition of Jonah with the Messiah, see the words of Jesus in Matthew xii.39–41, and especially: "For as Jonas was three days and three nights in the whale's belly; so shall the Son of man be three days and three nights in the heart of the earth" [See Robert Lowell, *Poesie 1943–1952*, ed. Rolando Anzilotti, p. 86].
4. Walsingham is a small town in Norfolk, England; a shrine to the Virgin Mary, built in the 11th century, was an object of pilgrimage until it was destroyed in the Reformation. Lowell points out in a prefatory note to *Lord Weary's Castle* that "'Our Lady of Walsingham' is an adaptation of several paragraphs from E. I. Watkin's *Catholic Art and Culture*" which describe the present Roman Catholic shrine. The passage is in part as follows: "Now once again pilgrims visit her image erected in a mediaeval chapel, where, it is said, they took off their shoes to walk barefoot the remaining mile to the shrine. * * * The road to the chapel is a quiet country lane shaded with trees, and lined on one side by a hedgerow. On the other, a stream flows down beneath the trees, the water symbol of the Holy Spirit, 'the waters of Shiloah that go softly,' the 'flow of the river making glad the city of God.' Within the chapel, an attractive example of Decorated achitecture, near an altar of mediaeval fashion, is seated Our Lady's image. It is too small for its canopy, and is not superficially beautiful. 'Non est species neque decor,' there is no comeliness of charm in that expressionless face with heavy eyelids. But let us look carefully, and allow the image, as every work of art should be allowed, to speak to us in its own language. We become aware of an inner beauty more impressive than outward grace. That expressionless countenance expresses what is beyond expression. It is the countenance of one whose spirit dwells in a region beyond emotion and thought, the centre of which mystical writers speak. Mary is beyond joy and sorrow. For her spirit is in God, and she knows as He knows, receiving His knowledge. No longer the Mother of Sorrows nor yet of the human joy of the crib, she understands the secret counsel of God to whose accomplishment Calvary and Bethlehem alike ministered. Therefore her peace, the central peace of God, is beyond the changes of earthly experience. And the inscrutability of that illegible countenance is the inscrutability of the Divine Will made known to her."
5. Sion, or Zion, was a hill in Jerusalem, the residence of King David and his successors: the heavenly city.

Our Lady, too small for her canopy,
Sits near the altar. There's no comeliness
At all or charm in that expressionless
120 Face with its heavy eyelids. As before,
This face, for centuries a memory,
Non est species, neque decor,
Expressionless, expresses God: it goes
Past castled Sion. She knows what God knows,
125 Not Calvary's Cross nor crib at Bethlehem
Now, and the world shall come to Walsingham.

                    7
The empty winds are creaking and the oak
Splatters and splatters on the cenotaph,[6]
The boughs are trembling and a gaff°   *spar*
130 Bobs on the untimely stroke
Of the greased wash exploding on a shoal-bell
In the old mouth of the Atlantic. It's well;
Atlantic, you are fouled with the blue sailors,
Sea-monsters, upward angel, downward fish:[7]
135 Unmarried and corroding, spare of flesh
Mart once of supercilious, wing'd clippers,
Atlantic, where your bell-trap guts its spoil
You could cut the brackish winds with a knife
Here in Nantucket, and cast up the time
140 When the Lord God formed man from the sea's slime
And breathed into his face the breath of life,
And blue-lung'd combers lumbered to the kill.
The Lord survives the rainbow of His will.[8]

                                                    1946

After the Surprising Conversions[9]

September twenty-second, Sir: today
I answer. In the latter part of May,

---

6. An empty tomb, or monument erected to the dead but not containing their remains; often for those lost at sea.
7. From Milton, *Paradise Lost,* I.462–63: "Dagon his name, sea monster, upward man/ And downward fish * * * "
8. See Genesis ix.11–17, especially "I do set my bow in the cloud, and it shall be for a token of a covenant between me and the earth."
9. The poem takes its departure from an account by Jonathan Edwards (1703–58) of a resurgence of religious enthusiasm that took place in and around Northampton, Massachusetts, during several months of 1734–35. Edwards's *Narrative of Surprising Conversions,* in the form of a letter to the Rev. Dr. Colman of Boston, dated Nov. 6, 1736, traces the revival from its beginnings through its decline. One passage towards the end of the letter (see *The Works of President Edwards,* New York, 1851, III, 69–72) figures prominently in the poem:
"In the latter part of May, it began to be very sensible that the Spirit of God was gradually withdrawing from us, and after this time Satan seemed to be more let loose, and raged in a dreadful manner. The first instance wherein it appeared, was a person's putting an end to his life by cutting his throat. He was a gentleman of more than common understanding, of strict morals, religious in his behavior, and a useful, honorable person in the town; but was of a family that are exceeding prone to melancholy, and his mother was killed with it. He had, from the beginning of this extraordinary time, been exceedingly concerned about the state of his soul, and there were some things in his experience, that appeared very hopefully, but he durst entertain no hope concerning his own good estate. Towards the latter end of his time, he grew much discouraged, and melancholy grew amain upon him, till he was wholly overpowered by it, and was, in great measure, past a capacity of receiving advice, or being reasoned with to any purpose: the devil took the advantage, and drove him into despairing thoughts. He was kept awake nights meditating upon terror, so that he had scarce any sleep at all, for a long time together. And it was observable at last, that he was scarcely well capable of managing his ordinary business, and was judged delirious by the coroner's inquest. The news of this extraordinarily affected the minds of people here, and struck them as it were with astonishment. After this, multitudes in this and other towns seemed to have it strongly suggested to them, and pressed upon them, to do as this person had done. And many that seemed to be under no melancholy, some pious persons, that had no special darkness or doubts about the goodness of their state, nor were under any special trouble or concern of mind about any thing spiritual or temporal, yet had it urged upon them, as if somebody had spoken to them, *Cut your own throat, now is a good opportunity.* Now! Now! So that they were obliged to fight with all their might to resist it, and yet no reason suggested to them why they should do it." Elsewhere, Edwards identified the man as his uncle, Joseph Hawley, who cut his throat on June 1, 1735.

Hard on ou Lord's Ascension, it began
To be more sensible.° A gentleman   *evident*
5   Of more than common understanding, strict
In morals, pious in behavior, kicked
Against our goad. A man of some renown,
An useful, honored person in the town,
He came of melancholy parents; prone
10   To secret spells, for years they kept alone—
His uncle, I believe, was killed of it:
Good people, but of too much or little wit.
I preached one Sabbath on a text from Kings;
He showed concernment for his soul. Some things
15   In his experience were hopeful. He
Would sit and watch the wind knocking a tree
And praise this countryside our Lord has made.
Once when a poor man's heifer died, he laid
A shilling on the doorsill; though a thirst
20   For loving shook him like a snake, he durst
Not entertain much hope of his estate
In heaven. Once we saw him sitting late
Behind his attic window by a light
That guttered on his Bible; through that night
25   He meditated terror, and he seemed
Beyond advice or reason, for he dreamed
That he was called to trumpet Judgment Day
To Concord. In the latter part of May
He cut his throat. And though the coroner
30   Judged him delirious, soon a noisome° stir   *noxious, disgusting*
Palsied our village. At Jehovah's nod
Satan seemed more let loose amongst us: God
Abandoned us to Satan, and he pressed
Us hard, until we thought we could not rest
35   Till we had done with life. Content was gone.
All the good work was quashed. We were undone.
The breath of God had carried out a planned
And sensible withdrawal from this land;
The multitude, once unconcerned with doubt,
40   Once neither callous, curious nor devout,
Jumped at broad noon, as though some peddler groaned
At it in its familiar twang: "My friend,
Cut your own throat. Cut your own throat. Now! Now!"
September twenty-second, Sir, the bough
45   Cracks with the unpicked apples, and at dawn
The small-mouth bass breaks water, gorged with spawn.

1946

Skunk Hour

(FOR ELIZABETH BISHOP) [5]

Nautilus Island's hermit
heiress still lives through winter in her Spartan cottage;
her sheep still graze above the sea.

5. In his essay "On 'Skunk Hour'" (see *Robert Lowell: A Collection of Critical Essays*, ed. T. Parkinson, 1968), Lowell says that his poem is modeled on Elizabeth Bishop's poem *The Armadillo*, that both poems "use short line stanzas, start with drifting description and end with a single animal."

Her son's a bishop. Her farmer
is first selectman [6] in our village;
she's in her dotage.

Thirsting for
the hierarchic privacy
of Queen Victoria's century,
she buys up all
the eyesores facing her shore,
and lets them fall.

The season's ill—
we've lost our summer millionaire,
who seemed to leap from an L. L. Bean [7]
catalogue. His nine-knot yawl
was auctioned off to lobstermen.
A red fox stain covers Blue Hill.[8]

And now our fairy
decorator brightens his shop for fall;
his fishnet's filled with orange cork,
orange, his cobbler's bench and awl;
there is no money in his work,
he'd rather marry.

One dark night,
my Tudor Ford climbed the hill's skull;
I watched for love-cars. Lights turned down,
they lay together, hull to hull,
where the graveyard shelves on the town. . . .
My mind's not right.

A car radio bleats,
"Love, O careless Love. . . ." I hear
my ill-spirit sob in each blood cell,
as if my hand were at its throat. . . .
I myself am hell; [8a]
nobody's here—

only skunks, that search
in the moonlight for a bite to eat.
They march on their soles up Main Street:
white stripes, moonstruck eyes' red fire
under the chalk-dry and spar spire
of the Trinitarian Church.

I stand on top
of our back steps and breathe the rich air—
a mother skunk with her column of kittens swills the garbage pail.
She jabs her wedge-head in a cup
of sour cream, drops her ostrich tail,
and will not scare.

1957   1959

6. Elected member of the administrative body (Board of Selectmen) of many New England towns.
7. A mail-order dealer in hunting, fishing, and camping specialties in Freeport, Me.
8. In his essay Lowell says: "The red fox stain was merely meant to describe the rusty reddish color of autumn on Blue Hill, a Maine mountain near where we were living." 8a. Possibly an allusion to *Paradise Lost*, IV. 75, where Lucifer says, "Which way I fly is Hell; myself am Hell."

The Public Garden[7]

Burnished, burned-out, still burning as the year
you lead me to our stamping ground.
The city and its cruising cars surround
the Public Garden. All's alive—
5　the children crowding home from school at five,
punting a football in the bricky air,
the sailors and their pick-ups under trees
with Latin labels. And the jaded flock
of swanboats paddles to its dock.
10　The park is drying.
Dead leaves thicken to a ball
inside the basin of a fountain, where
the heads of four stone lions stare
and suck on empty fawcets. Night
15　deepens. From the arched bridge, we see
the shedding park-bound mallards, how they keep
circling and diving in the lanternlight,
searching for something hidden in the muck.
And now the moon, earth's friend, that cared so much
20　for us, and cared so little, comes again—
always a stranger! As we walk,
it lies like chalk
over the waters. Everything's aground.
Remember summer? Bubbles filled
25　the fountain, and we splashed. We drowned
in Eden, while Jehovah's grass-green lyre
was rustling all about us in the leaves
that gurgled by us, turning upside down . . .
The fountain's failing waters flash around
30　the garden. Nothing catches fire.

1964

For the Union Dead[8]

"Relinquunt Omnia Servare Rem Publicam."

The old South Boston Aquarium stands
in a Sahara of snow now. Its broken windows are boarded.
The bronze weathervane cod has lost half its scales.
The airy tanks are dry.

5　Once my nose crawled like a snail on the glass;
my hand tingled
to burst the bubbles
drifting from the noses of the cowed, compliant fish.

---

7. A small park next to the Common in Boston, Massachusetts, containing flower-beds, walks, greensward, and a pond on which, during the summer, open pleasure-boats decorated with large artificial swans, circulate.
8. At the edge of Boston Common, across from the Massachusetts State House, stands a monument to Colonel Robert Gould Shaw (1837–63) and the Negro troops of the 54th Massachusetts regiment whom he was leading in the assault on Fort Wagner, South Carolina, when he was killed on July 18, 1863. The memorial, by Augustus St. Gaudens, representing Shaw in equestrian high-relief, with his troops, was dedicated in 1897. In the upper right it bears the motto of the Society of the Cincinnati (slightly altered in the epigraph to Lowell's poem), *"Omnia relinquit servare rempublicam,"* "He leaves all else to serve the republic."

My hand draws back. I often sigh still
10 for the dark downward and vegetating kingdom
of the fish and reptile. One morning last March,
I pressed against the new barbed and galvanized

fence on the Boston Common. Behind their cage,
yellow dinosaur steamshovels were grunting
15 as they cropped up tons of mush and grass
to gouge their underworld garage.

Parking spaces luxuriate like civic
sandpiles in the heart of Boston.
A girdle of orange, Puritan-pumpkin colored girders
20 braces the tingling Statehouse,

shaking over the excavations, as it faces Colonel Shaw
and his bell-cheeked Negro infantry
on St. Gaudens' shaking Civil War relief,
propped by a plank splint against the garage's earthquake.

25 Two months after marching through Boston,
half the regiment was dead;
at the dedication,
William James could almost hear the bronze Negroes breathe.

Their monument sticks like a fishbone
30 in the city's throat.
Its Colonel is as lean
as a compass-needle.

He has an angry wrenlike vigilance,
a greyhound's gentle tautness;
35 he seems to wince at pleasure,
and suffocate for privacy.

He is out of bounds now. He rejoices in man's lovely,
peculiar power to choose life and die—
when he leads his black soldiers to death,
40 he cannot bend his back.

On a thousand small town New England greens,
the old white church holds their air
of sparse, sincere rebellion; frayed flags
quilt the graveyards of the Grand Army of the Republic

45 The stone statues of the abstract Union Soldier
grow slimmer and younger each year—
wasp-waisted, they doze over muskets
and muse through their sideburns . . .

Shaw's father wanted no monument
50 except the ditch,
where his son's body was thrown
and lost with his "niggers."

The ditch is nearer.
There are no statutes for the last war here;
on Boylston Street, a commerical photograph
55 shows Hiroshima boiling

over a Mosler Safe, the "Rock of Ages"
that survived the blast. Space is nearer.
When I crouch to my television set,
the drained faces of Negro school-children rise like balloons.

60   Colonel Shaw
is riding on his bubble,
he waits
for the blessèd break.

The Aquarium is gone. Everywhere,
65   giant finned cars nose forward like fish;
a savage servility
slides by on grease.

1964

Dolphin

My Dolphin, you only guide me by surprise,
forgetful as Racine, the man of craft,
drawn through his maze of iron composition
by the incomparable wandering voice of Phèdre.[3]
5   When I was troubled in mind, you made for my body
caught in its hangman's-knot of sinking lines,
the glassy bowing and scraping of my will. . . .
I have sat and listened to too many
words of the collaborating muse,
10   and plotted perhaps too freely with my life,
not avoiding injury to others,
not avoiding injury to myself—
to ask compassion . . . this book,[4] half fiction,
an eelnet made by man for the eel fighting—

15   my eyes have seen what my hand did.

1973

MARGARET AVISON
(1918–   )

Thaw

Sticky inside their winter suits
the Sunday children stare at pools
in pavement and black ice where roots
of sky in moodier sky dissolve.

5   An empty coach train runs along
the thin and sooty river flats
and stick and straw and random stones
steam faintly when its steam departs.

3. The heroine of Jean Racine's tragedy *Phèdre* (1677), of which Lowell has published a verse translation (*Phaedra*, 1961).   4. This poem stands at the end of the volume of poems entitled *The Dolphin* (1973).

Lime-water and licorice light
10 wander the tumbled streets. A few
sparrows gather. A dog barks out
under the dogless pale pale blue.

Move your tongue along a slat
of a raspberry box from last year's crate.
15 Smell a saucepantilt of water
on the coal-ash in your grate.

Think how the Black Death [1] made men dance,
and from the silt of centuries
the proof is now scraped bare that once
20 Troy fell and Pompeii scorched and froze.[2]

A boy alone out in the court
whacks with his hockey stick, and whacks
in the wet, and the pigeons flutter, and rise,
and settle back.

1960

The Dumbfounding

When you walked here,
took skin, muscle, hair,
eyes, larynx, we
withheld all honor: "His house is clay,
5 how can he tell us of his far country?"

Your not familiar pace
in flesh, across the waves,
woke only our distrust.
Twice-torn we cried "A ghost"
10 and only on our planks counted you fast.

Dust wet with your spittle [4]
cleared mortal trouble.
We called you a blasphemer,
a devil-tamer.

15 The evening you spoke of going away
we could not stay.
All legions massed. You had to wash, and rise,
alone, and face
out of the light, for us.

20 You died.
We said,
"The worst is true, our bliss
has come to this."

When you were seen by men
25 in holy flesh again
we hoped so despairingly for such report
we closed their windpipes for it.

1. A form of bubonic plague which ravaged
Europe in the 14th century.
2. Troy was sacked and burned by the Greeks
at the end of the Trojan War; Pompeii was
destroyed by the eruption of Vesuvius in 79
A.D.
4. In Mark vii.33 and viii.23, Jesus is re-
ported to have healed dumbness and blindness
with his spittle.

Now you have sought
and seek, in all our ways, all thoughts,
30   streets, musics—and we make of these a din
trying to lock you out, or in,
to be intent. And dying.

Yet you are
constant and sure,
35   the all-lovely, all-men's-way
to that far country.

Winning one, you again
all ways would begin
life: to make new
40   flesh, to empower
the weak in nature
to restore
or stay the sufferer;

lead through the garden to
45   trash, rubble, hill,
where, the outcast's outcast, you
sound dark's uttermost, strangely light-brimming, until
time be full.

1966

HOWARD NEMEROV
(1920–   )

The Goose Fish

On the long shore, lit by the moon
To show them properly alone,
Two lovers suddenly embraced
So that their shadows were as one.
5   The ordinary night was graced
For them by the swift tide of blood
That silently they took at flood,
And for a little time they prized
    Themselves emparadised.

10   Then, as if shaken by stage-fright
Beneath the hard moon's bony light,
They stood together on the sand
Embarrassed in each other's sight
But still conspiring hand in hand,
15   Until they saw, there underfoot,
As though the world had found them out,
The goose fish turning up, though dead,
    His hugely grinning head.

There in the china light he lay,
20   Most ancient and corrupt and gray
They hesitated at his smile,

Wondering what it seemed to say
To lovers who a little while
Before had thought to understand,
25 By violence upon the sand,
The only way that could be known
    To make a world their own.

It was a wide and moony grin
Together peaceful and obscene;
30 They knew not what he would express,
So finished a comedian
He might mean failure or success,
But took it for an emblem of
Their sudden, new and guilty love
35 To be observed by, when they kissed,
    That rigid optimist.

So he became their patriarch,
Dreadfully mild in the half-dark.
His throat that the sand seemed to choke,
40 His picket teeth, these left their mark
But never did explain the joke
That so amused him, lying there
While the moon went down to disappear
Along the still and tilted track
45   That bears the zodiac.

1960

RICHARD WILBUR
(1921–   )

First Snow in Alsace

The snow came down last night like moths
Burned on the moon; it fell till dawn,
Covered the town with simple cloths.

Absolute snow lies rumpled on
5 What shellbursts scattered and deranged,
Entangled railings, crevassed lawn.

As if it did not know they'd changed,
Snow smoothly clasps the roofs of homes
Fear-gutted, trustless and estranged.

10 The ration stacks are milky domes;
Across the ammunition pile
The snow has climbed in sparkling combs.

You think: beyond the town a mile
Or two, this snowfall fills the eyes
15 Of soldiers dead a little while.

Persons and persons in disguise,
Walking the new air white and fine,
Trade glances quick with shared surprise.

At children's windows, heaped, benign,
20 As always, winter shines the most,
And frost makes marvelous designs.

The night guard coming from his post,
Ten first-snows back in thought, walks slow
And warms him with a boyish boast:

25 He was the first to see the snow.

1947

Objects

Meridians are a net
Which catches nothing; that sea-scampering bird
The gull, though shores lapse every side from sight, can yet
Sense him to land, but Hanno[1] had not heard

5 Hesperidean song,[2]
Had he not gone by watchful periploi:[3]
Chalk rocks, and isles like beasts, and mountain stains along
The water-hem, calmed him at last nearby

The clear high hidden chant
10 Blown from the spellbound coast, where under drifts
Of sunlight, under plated leaves, they guard the plant
By praising it. Among the wedding gifts

Of Herë, were a set
Of golden McIntoshes, from the Greek
15 Imagination. Guard and gild what's common, and forget
Uses and prices and names; have objects speak.

There's classic and there's quaint,
And then there is that devout intransitive eye
Of Pieter de Hooch:[4] see feinting from his plot of paint
20 The trench of light on boards, the much-mended dry

Courtyard wall of brick,
And sun submerged in beer, and streaming in glasses,
The weave of a sleeve, the careful and undulant tile. A quick
Change of the eye and all this calmly passes

25 Into a day, into magic.
For is there any end to true textures, to true
Integuments; do they ever desist from tacit, tragic
Fading away? Oh maculate, cracked, askew,

1. Carthaginian navigator who led an expedition down the west coast of Africa in the fifth century B.C.
2. The Hesperides were sweet-voiced nymphs who guarded the golden apples ("McIntoshes") given by Ge to Hera for her marriage to Zeus (see lines 12–14).
3. Plural of *periplus*, a voyage or trip around an island or a coast.
4. Pieter de Hooch (1629–ca. 1677), Dutch genre painter.

Gay-pocked and potsherd world
³⁰ I voyage, where in every tangible tree
I see afloat among the leaves, all calm and curled,
The Cheshire smile⁵ which sets me fearfully free.

1947

The Death of a Toad

A toad the power mower caught,
Chewed and clipped of a leg, with a hobbling hop has got
  To the garden verge, and sanctuaried him
  Under the cineraria leaves, in the shade
⁵   Of the ashen heartshaped leaves, in a dim,
    Low, and a final glade.

The rare original heartsblood goes,
Spends on the earthen hide, in the folds and wizening, flows
  In the gutters of the banked and staring eyes. He lies
¹⁰ As still as if he would return to stone,
    And soundlessly attending, dies
    Toward some deep monotone,

Toward misted and ebullient seas
And cooling shores, toward lost Amphibia's emperies.⁶
¹⁵ Day dwindles, drowning, and at length is gone
    In the wide and antique eyes, which still appear
    To watch, across the castrate lawn,
    The haggard daylight steer.

1950, 1957

PHILIP LARKIN
(1922–   )

Wants

Beyond all this, the wish to be alone:
However the sky grows dark with invitation-cards
However we follow the printed directions of sex
However the family is photographed under the flagstaff—
⁵ Beyond all this, the wish to be alone.

Beneath it all, desire of oblivion runs:
Despite the artful tensions of the calendar,
The life insurance, the tabled fertility rites,
The costly aversion of the eyes from death—
¹⁰ Beneath it all, desire of oblivion runs.

1955

5. In *Alice in Wonderland,* when the Cheshire   6. I.e., the land of amphibians.
cat disappeared, its smile lingered.

Church Going

Once I am sure there's nothing going on
I step inside, letting the door thud shut.
Another church: matting, seats, and stone,
And little books; sprawlings of flowers, cut
5   For Sunday, brownish now; some brass and stuff
Up at the holy end; the small neat organ;
And a tense, musty, unignorable silence,
Brewed God knows how long. Hatless, I take off
My cycle-clips in awkward reverance,

10 Move forward, run my hand around the font.
From where I stand, the roof looks almost new—
Cleaned, or restored? Somone would know: I don't.
Mounting the lectern, I peruse a few
Hectoring large-scale verses, and pronounce
15 "Here endeth" much more loudly than I'd meant.
The echoes snigger briefly. Back at the door
I sign the book, donate an Irish sixpence,
Reflect the place was not worth stopping for.

Yet stop I did: in fact I often do,
20 And always end much at a loss like this,
Wondering what to look for; wondering, too,
When churches fall completely out of use
What we shall turn them into, if we shall keep
25 A few cathedrals chronically on show,
Their parchment, plate and pyx[1] in locked cases,
And let the rest rent-free to rain and sheep.
Shall we avoid them as unlucky places?

Or, after dark, will dubious women come
30 To make their children touch a particular stone;
Pick simples° for a cancer; or on some   *herbs*
Advised night see walking a dead one?
Power of some sort or other will go on
In games, in riddles, seemingly at random;
35 But superstition, like belief, must die,
And what remains when disbelief has gone?
Grass, weedy pavement, brambles, buttress, sky,

A shape less recognizable each week,
A purpose more obscure. I wonder who
40 Will be the last, the very last, to seek
This place for what it was; one of the crew
That tap and jot and know what rood-lofts were?
Some ruin-bibber, randy for antique,
Or Christmas-addict, counting on a whiff
45 Of gown-and-bands and organ-pipes and myrrh?
Or will he be my representative,

Bored, uninformed, knowing the ghostly silt
Dispersed, yet tending to this cross of ground
Through suburb scrub because it held unspilt
50 So long and equably what since is found
Only in separation—marriage, and birth,

1. The vessel in which the Host is kept.

And death, and thoughts of these—for whom was built
This special shell? For, though I've no idea
What this accoutred frowsty barn is worth,
55   It pleases me to stand in silence here;

A serious house on serious earth it is,
In whose blent air all our compulsions meet,
Are recognized, and robed as destinies.
And that much never can be obsolete,
60   Since someone will forever be surprising
A hunger in himself to be more serious,
And gravitating with it to this ground,
Which, he once heard, was proper to grow wise in,
If only that so many dead lie round.

1955

Myxomatosis [2]

Caught in the center of a soundless field
While hot inexplicable hours go by
What trap is this? Where were its teeth concealed?
You seem to ask.
        I make a sharp reply,
5   Then clean my stick. I'm glad I can't explain
Just in what jaws you were to suppurate:
You may have thought things would come right again
If you could only keep quite still and wait.

1955

Days

What are days for?
Days are where we live.
They come, they wake us
Time and time over.
5   They are to be happy in:
Where can we live but days?

Ah, solving that question
Brings the priest and the doctor
In their long coats
10   Running over the fields.

1964

Talking in Bed

Talking in bed ought to be easiest,
Lying together there goes back so far,
An emblem of two people being honest.

Yet more and more time passes silently.
5   Outside, the wind's incomplete unrest
Builds and disperses clouds about the sky,

2. An infectious and fatal disease of rabbits, artificially introduced into Great Britain and Australia in recent years to keep down the rabbit population.

And dark towns heap up on the horizon.
None of this cares for us. Nothing shows why
At this unique distance from isolation

10 It becomes still more difficult to find
Words at once true and kind,
Or not untrue and not unkind.

                                              1964

JAMES DICKEY
(1923–   )

At Darien Bridge

The sea here used to look
As if many convicts had built it,

Standing deep in their ankle chains,
Ankle-deep in the water, to smite

5 The land and break it down to salt.
I was in this bog as a child

When they were all working all day
To drive the pilings down.

I thought I saw the still sun
10 Strike the side of a hammer in flight

And from it a sea bird be born
To take off over the marshes.

As the gray climbs the side of my head
And cuts my brain off from the world,

15 I walk and wish mainly for birds,
For the one bird no one has looked for

To spring again from a flash
Of metal, perhaps from the scratched

Wedding band on my ring finger.
20 Recalling the chains of their feet,

I stand and look out over grasses
At the bridge they built, long abandoned,

Breaking down into water at last,
And long, like them, for freedom

25 Or death, or to believe again
That they worked on the ocean to give it

The unchanging, hopeless look
Out of which all miracles leap.

                                              1964

Buckdancer's Choice

So I would hear out those lungs,
The air split into nine levels,
Some gift of tongues of the whistler

In the invalid's bed: my mother,
5 Warbling all day to herself
The thousand variations of one song;

It is called Buckdancer's Choice.
For years, they have all been dying
Out, the classic buck-and-wing² men

10 Of traveling minstrel shows;
With them also an old woman
Was dying of breathless angina,³

Yet still found breath enough
To whistle up in my head
15 A sight like a one-man band,

Freed black, with cymbals at heel,
An ex-slave who thrivingly danced
To the ring of his own clashing light

Through the thousand variations of one song
20 All day to my mother's prone music,
The invalid's warbler's note,

While I crept close to the wall
Sock-footed, to hear the sounds alter,
Her tongue like a mockingbird's break

25 Through stratum after stratum of a tone
Proclaiming what choices there are
For the last dancers of their kind,

For ill women and for all slaves
Of death, and children enchanted at walls
30 With a brass-beating glow underfoot,

Not dancing but nearly risen
Through barnlike, theaterlike houses
On the wings of the buck and wing.

1965

---

2. A dance associated with American minstrel shows, and similar to a clog dance. The dancer's feet (sometimes he beats his own rhythm on a tambourine) make movements like wings.
3. A respiratory disease usually related to heart ailments.

DENISE LEVERTOV
(1923–   )

Triple Feature

Innocent decision: to enjoy.
And the pathos
of hopefulness, of his solicitude:

5 —he in mended serape,
she having plaited carefully
magenta ribbons into her hair,
the baby a round half-hidden shape
slung in her rebozo,° and the young son steadfastly   *shawl*
gripping a fold of her skirt,
10 pale and severe under a
handed-down sombrero—

          all regarding
the stills with full attention, preparing
to pay and go in—
15 to worlds of shadow-violence, half-
familiar, warm with popcorn, icy
with strange motives, barbarous splendors!

                                        1959

From the Roof

This wild night, gathering the washing as if it were flowers
          animal vines twisting over the line and
          slapping my face lightly, soundless merriment
          in the gesticulations of shirtsleeves,
5 I recall out of my joy a night of misery

walking in the dark and the wind over broken earth,
          halfmade foundations and unfinished
          drainage trenches and the spaced-out
                    circles of glaring light
10   marking streets that were to be,
walking with you but so far from you,

and now alone in October's
first decision towards winter, so close to you—
          my arms full of playful rebellious linen, a freighter
15   going down-river two blocks away, outward bound,
          the green wolf-eyes of the Harborside Terminal
                    glittering on the Jersey shore,
and a train somewhere under ground bringing you towards me
to our new living-place from which we can see

20 a river and its traffic (the Hudson and the
hidden river, who can say which it is we see, we see
something of both. Or who can say

the crippled broom-vendor yesterday, who passed
just as we needed a new broom, was not
25   one of the Hidden Ones?)
                Crates of fruit are unloading
                across the street on the cobbles,
                and a brazier flaring
                to warm the men and burn trash. He wished us
30   luck when we bought the broom. But not luck
brought us here. By design

clear air and cold wind polish
the river lights, by design
we are to live now in a new place.

                                                    1961

The Victors

In June the bush we call
alder was heavy, listless,
its leaves studded with galls,

growing wherever we didn't
5   want it. We cut it
savagely, hunted it from the pasture, chopped it

away from the edge of the wood.
In July, still everywhere, it appeared
wearing green berries.

10   Anyway it must go. It takes
the light and air and the good of the earth
from flowers and young trees.

But now in August
its berries are red. Do the birds
15   eat them?   Swinging

clusters of red, the hedges are full of them,
red-currant red, a graceful
ornament or a merry smile.

                                                    1964

O Taste and See

The world is
not with us enough.[1]
O taste and see

the subway Bible poster said,
5   meaning The Lord,[2] meaning
if anything all that lives
to the imagination's tongue,

---

1. Cf. Wordsworth's sonnet, *The World Is Too Much with Us,* above.   2. "O taste and see that the Lord is good" (Psalms xxxiv.8).

grief, mercy, language,
tangerine, weather, to
10   breathe them, bite,
savor, chew, swallow, transform

into our flesh our
deaths, crossing the street, plum, quince,
living in the orchard and being

15   hungry, and plucking
the fruit.

1964

Tenebrae [3]

(FALL OF 1967) [4]

Heavy, heavy, heavy, hand and heart.
We are at war,
bitterly, bitterly at war.

And the buying and selling
5   buzzes at our heads, a swarm
of busy flies, a kind of innocence.

Gowns of gold sequins are fitted,
sharp-glinting. What harsh rustlings
of silver moiré° there are,   *watered silk*
10   to remind me of shrapnel splinters.

And weddings are held in full solemnity
not of desire but of etiquette,
the nuptial pomp of starched lace;
a grim innocence.

15   And picnic parties return from the beaches
burning with stored sun in the dusk;
children promised a TV show when they get home
fall asleep in the backs of a million station wagons,
sand in their hair, the sound of waves
20   quietly persistent at their ears.
They are not listening.

Their parents at night
dream and forget their dreams.
They wake in the dark
25   and make plans. Their sequin plans
glitter into tomorrow.
They buy, they sell.

---

3. *Tenebrae* (Latin, darkness), are church services for the last three days of Holy Week, to commemorate the sufferings and death of Christ; candles lighted at the beginning of the service are extinguished one by one after each psalm, in memory of the darkness at the time of the crucifixion.
4. The fall of 1967 witnessed the march on the Pentagon, in protest against the continuing presence of American troops in Vietnam.

They fill freezers with food.
Neon signs flash their intentions
30   into the years ahead.

And at their ears the sound
of the war. They are
not listening, not listening.

                                                              1972

KENNETH KOCH
(1925–   )

Permanently

One day the Nouns were clustered in the street.
An Adjective walked by, with her dark beauty.
The Nouns were struck, moved, changed.
The next day a Verb drove up, and created the Sentence.

5   Each Sentence says one thing—for example, "Although it was a dark rainy day
      when the Adjective walked by, I shall remember the pure and sweet
      expression on her face until the day I perish from the green, effective
      earth."
Or, "Will you please close the window, Andrew?"
Or, for example, "Thank you, the pink pot of flowers on the window sill has
      changed color recently to a light yellow, due to the heat from the boiler
      factory which exists nearby."

In the springtime the Sentences and the Nouns lay silently on the grass.
A lonely Conjunction here and there would call, "And! But!"
10   But the Adjective did not emerge.

As the adjective is lost in the sentence,
So I am lost in your eyes, ears, nose, and throat—
You have enchanted me with a single kiss
Which can never be undone
15   Until the destruction of language.

                                                              1962

You Were Wearing

You were wearing your Edgar Allan Poe printed cotton blouse.
In each divided up square of the blouse was a picture of Edgar Allan Poe.
Your hair was blonde and you were cute. You asked me, "Do most boys think
      that most girls are bad?"
I smelled the mould of your seaside resort hotel bedroom on your hair held
      in place by a John Greenleaf Whittier clip.
5   "No," I said, "it's girls who think that boys are bad." Then we read
      Snowbound together
And ran around in an attic, so that a little of the blue enamel was scraped off
      my George Washington, Father of His Country, shoes.

Mother was walking in the living room, her Strauss Waltzes comb in her hair.
We waited for a time and then joined her, only to be served tea in cups
    painted with pictures of Herman Melville
As well as with illustrations from his book *Moby Dick* and from his novella,
    Benito Cereno.
Father came in wearing his Dick Tracy necktie: "How about a drink,
    everyone?"
I said, "Let's go outside a while." Then we went onto the porch and sat on
    the Abraham Lincoln swing.
You sat on the eyes, mouth, and beard part, and I sat on the knees.
In the yard across the street we saw a snowman holding a garbage can lid
    smashed into a likeness of the mad English king, George the Third.

1962

A. R. AMMONS
(1926–   )

Corsons Inlet [1]

I went for a walk over the dunes again this morning
to the sea,
then turned right along
    the surf
₅   rounded a naked headland
                    and returned

    along the inlet shore:

it was muggy sunny, the wind from the sea steady and high,
crisp in the running sand,
₁₀   some breakthroughs of sun
    but after a bit

continuous overcast:

the walk liberating, I was released from forms,
from the perpendiculars,
₁₅   straight lines, blocks, boxes, binds
of thought
into the hues, shadings, rises, flowing bends and blends
        of sight:

                I allow myself eddies of meaning:
₂₀ yield to a direction of significance
running
like a stream through the geography of my work:
    you can find
in my sayings
₂₅   swerves of action
            like the inlet's cutting edge:
        there are dunes of motion,
organizations of grass, white sandy paths of remembrance
in the overall wandering of mirroring mind:

---

1. Located in southeast New Jersey.

30 but Overall is beyond me: is the sum of these events
    I cannot draw, the ledger I cannot keep, the accounting
    beyond the account:

    in nature there are few sharp lines: there are areas of
    primrose
35   more or less dispersed;
    disorderly orders of bayberry; between the rows
    of dunes,
    irregular swamps of reeds,
    though not reeds alone, but grass, bayberry, yarrow, all . . .
40 predominantly reeds:

    I have reached no conclusions, have erected no boundaries,
    shutting out and shutting in, separating inside
       from outside: I have
       drawn no lines:
45   as

    manifold events of sand
    change the dune's shape that will not be the same shape
    tomorrow,

    so I am willing to go along, to accept
50 the becoming
    thought, to stake off no beginnings or ends, establish
       no walls:

    by transitions the land falls from grassy dunes to creek
    to undercreek: but there are no lines, though
55   change in that transition is clear
       as any sharpness: but "sharpness" spread out,
    allowed to occur over a wider range
    than mental lines can keep:

    the moon was full last night: today, low tide was low:
60 black shoals of mussels exposed to the risk
    of air
    and, earlier, of sun,
    waved in and out with the waterline, waterline inexact,
    caught always in the event of change:
65   a young mottled gull stood free on the shoals
       and ate
    to vomiting: another gull, squawking possession, cracked a crab,
    picked out the entrails, swallowed the soft-shelled legs, a ruddy
    turnstone running in to snatch leftover bits:

70 risk is full: every living thing in
    siege: the demand is life, to keep life: the small
    white blacklegged egret, how beautiful, quietly stalks and spears
       the shallows, darts to shore
          to stab—what? I couldn't
75   see against the black mudflats—a frightened
       fiddler crab?

       the news to my left over the dunes and
    reeds and bayberry clumps was
80   fall: thousands of tree swallows
       gathering for flight:

an order held
in constant change: a congregation
rich with entropy: nevertheless, separable, noticeable
as one event,
85   not chaos: preparations for
flight from winter,
cheet, cheet, cheet, cheet, wings rifling the green clumps,
beaks
at the bayberries
90   a perception full of wind, flight, curve,
sound:
the possibility of rule as the sum of rulelessness:
the "field" of action
with moving, incalculable center:

95   in the smaller view, order tight with shape:
blue tiny flowers on a leafless weed: carapace of crab:
snail shell:
pulsations of order
in the bellies of minnows: orders swallowed,
100   broken down, transferred through membranes
to strengthen larger orders: but in the large view, no
lines or changeless shapes: the working in and out, together
and against, of millions of events: this,
so that I make
105   no form
formlessness:

orders as summaries, as outcomes of actions override
or in some way result, not predictably (seeing me gain
the top of a dune,
110   the swallows
could take flight—some other fields of bayberry
could enter fall
berryless) and there is serenity:

no arranged terror: no forcing of image, plan,
115   or thought:
no propaganda, no humbling of reality to precept:

terror pervades but is not arranged, all possibilities
of escape open: no route shut, except in
the sudden loss of all routes:

120   I see narrow orders, limited tightness, but will
not run to that easy victory:
still around the looser, wider forces work:
I will try
to fasten into order enlarging grasps of disorder, widening
125   scope, but enjoying the freedom that
Scope eludes my grasp, that there is no finality of vision,
that I have perceived nothing completely,
that tomorrow a new walk is a new walk.

1965

ROBERT CREELEY
(1926–   )

Heroes

In all those stories the hero
is beyond himself into the next
thing, be it those labors
of Hercules,[1] or Aeneas going into death.

5   I thought the instant of the one humanness
in Virgil's plan of it
was that it was of course human enough to die,
yet to come back, as he said, *hoc opus, hic labor est.*[2]

That was the Cumaean Sibyl speaking.
10   This is Robert Creeley, and Virgil
is dead now two thousand years, yet Hercules
and the *Aeneid,* yet all that industrious wis-

dom lives in the way the mountains
and the desert are waiting
15   for the heroes, and death also
can still propose the old labors.

1959

The World

I wanted so ably
to reassure you, I wanted
the man you took to be me,

to comfort you, and got
5 up, and went to the window,
pushed back, as you asked me to,

the curtain, to see
the outline of the trees
in the night outside.

10 The light, love,
the light we felt then,
grayly, was it, that

came in, on us, not
merely my hands or yours,
15 or a wetness so comfortable,

but in the dark then
as you slept, the gray
figure came so close

1. Who represents superhuman strength and
courage, as revealed in his legendary 12
labors.
2. From Virgil's *Aeneid,* VI. The full quota-
tion (in John Dryden's translation): "Smooth
the descent and easy is the way:/But, to re-
turn, and view the cheerful skies—/In this
the task and mighty labor lies." It is spoken
by the Cumaean Sibyl, a prophetic priestess,
in advising Aeneas to visit the Underworld to
seek counsel in his god-appointed task of
founding Rome.

and leaned over,
20   between us, as you
slept, restless, and

my own face had to
see it, and be seen by it,
the man it was, your

25   gray lost tired bewildered
brother, unused, untaken—
hated by love, and dead,

but not dead, for an
instant, saw me, myself
30   the intruder, as he was not.

I tried to say, it is
all right, she is
happy, you are no longer

needed. I said,
35   he is dead, and he
went as you shifted

and woke, at first afraid,
then knew by my own knowing
what had happened—

40   and the light then
of the sun coming
for another morning
in the world.

1969

ALLEN GINSBERG
(1926–   )

To Aunt Rose

Aunt Rose—now—might I see you
with your thin face and buck tooth smile and pain
        of rheumatism—and a long black heavy shoe
            for your bony left leg
5   limping down the long hall in Newark on the running carpet
            past the black grand piano
                in the day room
                    where the parties were
        and I sang Spanish loyalist songs
10   in a high squeaky voice
                (hysterical) the committee listening
            while you limped around the room
                collected the money—

Aunt Honey, Uncle Sam, a stranger with a cloth arm
15   in his pocket
          and huge young bald head
             of Abraham Lincoln Brigade[1]

—your long sad face
          your tears of sexual frustration
20   (what smothered sobs and bony hips
                under the pillows of Osborne Terrace)
—the time I stood on the toilet seat naked
          and you powdered my thighs with Calomine
             against the poison ivy—my tender
25   and shamed first black curled hairs
what were you thinking in secret heart then
             knowing me a man already—
and I an ignorant girl of family silence on the thin pedestal
             of my legs in the bathroom—Museum of Newark.
30   Aunt Rose
Hitler is dead, Hitler is in Eternity; Hitler is with
             Tamburlane and Emily Brontë

Though I see you walking still, a ghost on Osborne Terrace
             down the long dark hall to the front door
35   limping a little with a pinched smile
             in what must have been a silken
                flower dress
          welcoming my father, the Poet, on his visit to Newark
             —see you arriving in the living room
40   dancing on your crippled leg
             and clapping hands his book
                had been accepted by Liveright

Hitler is dead and Liveright's gone out of business
The Attic of the Past and *Everlasting Minute* are out of print
45   Uncle Harry sold his last silk stocking
          Claire quit interpretive dancing school
             Buba[2] sits a wrinkled monument in Old
                Ladies Home blinking at new babies

last time I saw you was the hospital
50   pale skull protruding under ashen skin
             blue veined unconscious girl
                in an oxygen tent
          the war in Spain has ended long ago
          Aunt Rose

                              Paris 1958   1961

1. A group of American volunteers, led by Martin Wolff, in the Spanish Civil War of the 1930's.   2. Yiddish for "Grandmother."

JAMES MERRILL
(1926–   )

Willowware [1] Cup

Mass hysteria, wave after breaking wave
Blueblooded Cantonese upon these shores

Left the gene pool Lux-opaque and smoking
With dimestore mutants. One turned up today.

5   Plum in bloom, pagoda, blue birds, plume of willow—
Almost the replica of a prewar pattern—

The same boat bearing the gnat-sized lovers away,
The old bridge now bent double where her father signals

Feebly, as from flypaper, minding less and less.
10 Two smaller retainers with lanterns light him home.

Is that a scroll he carries? He must by now be immensely
Wise, and have given up earthly attachments, and all that.

Soon, of these May mornings, rising in mist, he will ask
Only to blend—like ink in flesh, blue anchor

15 Needled upon drunkenness while its destroyer
Full steam departs, the stigma throbbing, intricate—

Only to blend into a crazing [2] texture.
You are far away. The leaves tell what they tell.

But this lone, chipped vessel, if it fills,
20 Fills for you with something warm and clear.

Around its inner horizon the old odd designs
Crowd as before, and seem to concentrate on you.

They represent, I fancy, a version of heaven
In its day more trouble to mend than to replace:

25 Steep roofs aslant, minutely tiled;
Tilted honeycombs, thunderhead blue.

1972

1. Blue-and-white dinnerware picturing a Chinese scene including a willow tree and a bridge.
2. Developing a mesh of fine superficial cracks.

GALWAY KINNELL
(1927–   )

The Correspondence School Instructor Says Goodbye to His Poetry Students

Goodbye, lady in Bangor, who sent me
snapshots of yourself, after definitely hinting
you were beautiful; goodbye,
Miami Beach urologist, who enclosed plain
5   brown envelopes for the return of your *very*
"Clinical Sonnets"; goodbye, manufacturer
of brassieres on the Coast, whose eclogues
give the fullest treatment in literature yet
to the sagging breast motif; goodbye, you in San Quentin,
10   who wrote, "Being German my hero is Hitler,"
instead of "Sincerely yours," at the end of long,
neat-scripted letters demolishing
the pre-Raphaelites: [2]

I swear to you, it was just my way
15   of cheering myself up, as I licked
the stamped, self-addressed envelopes,
the game I had
of trying to guess which one of you, this time,
had poisoned his glue. I did care.
20   I did read each poem entire.
I did say what I thought was the truth
in the mildest words I knew. And now,
in this poem, or chopped prose, not any better,
I realize, than those troubled lines
25   I kept sending back to you,
I have to say I am relieved it is over:
at the end I could feel only pity
for that urge toward more life
your poems kept smothering in words, the smell
30   of which, days later, would tingle
in your nostrils as new, God-given impulses
to write.

Goodbye,
you who are, for me, the postmarks again
35   of shattered towns—Xenia, Burnt Cabins, Hornell—
their loneliness
given away in poems, only their solitude kept.

1968

2. A group of English poets and painters, among them Dante Gabriel Rossetti and William Morris, whose aim was to restore to art the aesthetic principles of the early Italian Renaissance—that is, before Raphael (1483–1520), the great painter.

W. S. MERWIN
(1927–   )

The Drunk in the Furnace

For a good decade
The furnace stood in the naked gully, fireless
And vacant as any hat. Then when it was
No more to them than a hulking black fossil
5   To erode unnoticed with the rest of the junk-hill
By the poisonous creek, and rapidly to be added
    To their ignorance.

They were afterwards astonished
To confirm, one morning, a twist of smoke like a pale
10   Resurrection, staggering out of its chewed hole,
And to remark then other tokens that someone,
Cozily bolted behind the eye-holed iron
Door of the drafty burner, had there established
    His bad castle.

15   Where he gets his spirits
It's a mystery. But the stuff keeps him musical:
Hammer-and-anviling with poker and bottle
To his jugged bellowings, till the last groaning clang
As he collapses onto the rioting
20   Springs of a litter of car-seats ranged on the grates,
    To sleep like an iron pig.

In their tar-paper church
On a text about stoke-holes that are sated never
25   Their Reverend lingers. They nod and hate trespassers.
When the furnace wakes, though, all afternoon
Their witless offspring flock like piped rats to its siren
Crescendo, and agape on the crumbling ridge
    Stand in a row and learn.

1960

For the Anniversary of My Death

Every year without knowing it I have passed the day
When the last fires will wave to me
And the silence will set out
Tireless traveler
5   Like the beam of a lightless star

Then I will no longer
Find myself in life as in a strange garment
Surprised at the earth
And the love of one woman
10   And the shamelessness of men
As today writing after three days of rain
Hearing the wren sing and the falling cease
And bowing not knowing to what

1967

CHARLES TOMLINSON
(1927–   )

The View

The woods are preparing to wait out winter.
  Gusts blow with an earnest of all there is to be done
Once frost will have entered the apple and the sun.
  Of the view, there is no tale to tell you.
5 Its history is incidental. One would not date
  The window that stands open like a gate
In the opposing house-face. It is dark inside.
  The façade is a dirty white, and yet it seems
The right color to stand there between
10 The dull green of the foreground trees
Still bearing leaves, and the autumnal glare
  From the others framing it, foregoing theirs.
The dark of the window square might be
  A mineshaft of pure shadow, a way
15 Through to the heart of the hill—the black
  Center, if center there were where
Sight must travel such drops and intervals,
  And an undulation of aspens along the slope
Is turning the wind to water and to light,
20 Unpivoting place amid its shaken coins,
While under a shuddering causeway, a currency,
  The season is dragging at all the roots of the view.

1969

Stone Speech

Crowding this beach
are milkstones, white
teardrops; flints
edged out of flinthood
5 into smoothness chafe
against grainy ovals,
pitted pieces, nosestones,
stoppers and saddles;
veins of orange
10 inlay black beads:
chalk-swaddled babyshapes,
tiny fists, facestones
and facestone's brother
skullstone, roundheads
15 pierced by a single eye,
purple finds, all
rubbing shoulders:
a mob of grindings,
groundlings, scatterings
20 from a million necklaces
mined under sea-hills, the pebbles
are as various as the people.

1972

JAMES WRIGHT
(1927–   )

A Note Left in Jimmy Leonard's Shack

Near the dry river's water-mark we found
    Your brother Minnegan,
Flopped like a fish against the muddy ground.
Beany, the kid whose yellow hair turns green,
5   Told me to find you, even in the rain,
    And tell you he was drowned.

I hid behind the chasis on the bank,
    The wreck of someone's Ford:
I was afraid to come and wake you drunk:
10   You told me once the waking up was hard,
    The daylight beating at you like a board.
    Blood in my stomach sank.

Beside, you told him never to go out
    Along the river-side
15   Drinking and singing, clattering about.
You might have thrown a rock at me and cried
I was to blame, I let him fall in the road
    And pitch down on his side.

Well, I'll get hell enough when I get home
20   For coming up this far,
Leaving the note, and running as I came.
I'll go and tell my father where you are.
You'd better go find Minnegan before
    Policemen hear and come.

25   Beany went home, and I got sick and ran,
    You old son of a bitch.
You better hurry down to Minnegan;
He's drunk or dying now, I don't know which,
Rolled in the roots and garbage like a fish,
30   The poor old man.

1959

A Blessing

Just off the highway to Rochester, Minnesota,
Twilight bounds softly forth on the grass.
And the eyes of those two Indian ponies
Darken with kindness.
5 They have come gladly out of the willows
To welcome my friend and me.
We step over the barbed wire into the pasture
Where they have been grazing all day, alone.
They ripple tensely, they can hardly contain their happiness
10 That we have come.
They bow shyly as wet swans. They love each other.
There is no loneliness like theirs.

At home once more,
They begin munching the young tufts of spring in the darkness.
15 I would like to hold the slenderer one in my arms,
For she has walked over to me
And nuzzled my left hand.
She is black and white,
Her mane falls wild on her forehead,
20 And the light breeze moves me to caress her long ear
That is delicate as the skin over a girl's wrist.
Suddenly I realize
That if I stepped out of my body I would break
Into blossom.

1963

THOM GUNN
(1929–   )

On the Move
'Man, you gotta Go.'

The blue jay scuffling in the bushes follows
Some hidden purpose, and the gust of birds
That spurts across the field, the wheeling swallows,
Have nested in the trees and undergrowth.
5 Seeking their instinct, or their poise, or both,
One moves with an uncertain violence
Under the dust thrown by a baffled sense
Or the dull thunder of approximate words.

On motorcycles, up the road, they come:
10 Small, black, as flies hanging in heat, the Boys,
Until the distance throws them forth, their hum
Bulges to thunder held by calf and thigh.
In goggles, donned impersonality,
In gleaming jackets trophied with the dust,
15 They strap in doubt—by hiding it, robust—
And almost hear a meaning in their noise.

Exact conclusion of their hardiness
Has no shape yet, but from known whereabouts
They ride, direction where the tires press.
20 They scare a flight of birds across the field:
Much that is natural, to the will must yield.
Men manufacture both machine and soul,
And use what they imperfectly control
To dare a future from the taken routes.

25 It is a part solution, after all.
One is not necessarily discord
On earth; or damned because, half animal,
One lacks direct instinct, because one wakes
Afloat on movement that divides and breaks.
30 One joins the movement in a valueless world,
Choosing it, till, both hurler and the hurled,
One moves as well, always toward, toward.

A minute holds them, who have come to go:
The self-defined, astride the created will
35 They burst away; the towns they travel through
Are home for neither bird nor holiness,
For birds and saints complete their purposes.
At worst, one is in motion; and at best,
Reaching no absolute, in which to rest,
40 One is always nearer by not keeping still.

California   1957

From the Wave

It mounts at sea, a concave wall
    Down-ribbed with shine,
And pushes forward, building tall
    Its steep incline.

5   Then from their hiding rise to sight
    Black shapes on boards
Bearing before the fringe of white
    It mottles towards.

Their pale feet curl, they poise their weight
10   With a learn'd skill.
It is the wave they imitate
    Keeps them so still.

The marbling bodies have become
    Half wave, half men,
15 Grafted it seems by feet of foam
    Some seconds, then,

Late as they can, they slice the face
    In timed procession:
Balance is triumph in this place,
20   Triumph possession.

The mindless heave of which they rode
    A fluid shelf
Breaks as they leave it, falls and, slowed,
    Loses itself.

25 Clear, the sheathed bodies slick as seals
    Loosen and tingle;
And by the board the bare foot feels
    The suck of shingle.

They paddle in the shallows still;
30   Two splash each other;
Then all swim out to wait until
    The right waves gather.

1971

ADRIENNE RICH
(1929–   )

Planetarium

(THINKING OF CAROLINE HERSCHEL, 1750–1848,
ASTRONOMER, SISTER OF WILLIAM; [1] AND OTHERS)

A woman in the shape of a monster
a monster in the shape of a woman
the skies are full of them

5   a woman   "in the snow
among the Clocks and instruments
or measuring the ground with poles"

in her 98 years to discover
8 comets

she whom the moon ruled
10 like us
levitating into the night sky
riding the polished lenses

Galaxies of women, there
doing penance for impetuousness
15 ribs chilled
in those spaces   of the mind

An eye,
    "virile, precise and absolutely certain"
    from the mad webs of Uranisborg [2]
20   encountering the NOVA

every impulse of light exploding
from the core
as life flies out of us
    Tycho whispering at last
25   "Let me not seem to have lived in vain"

What we see, we see
and seeing is changing

the light that shrivels a mountain
and leaves a man alive

30 Heartbeat of the pulsar
heart sweating through my body

The radio impulse
pouring in from Taurus [3]

1. Famous astronomer (1738–1822).   (1546–1601), the Danish astronomer.
2. The observatory built by Tycho Brahe 3. The constellation "The Bull."

I am bombarded yet   I stand

35 I have been standing all my life in the
direct path of a battery of signals
the most accurately transmitted most
untranslateable language in the universe
I am a galactic cloud so deep   so invo-
40 luted that a light wave could take 15
years to travel through me   And has
taken   I am an instrument in the shape
of a woman trying to translate pulsations
into images   for the relief of the body
45 and the reconstruction of the mind.

1971

Diving into the Wreck

First having read the book of myths,
and loaded the camera,
and checked the edge of the knife-blade,
I put on
5   the body-armor of black rubber
the absurd flippers
the grave and awkward mask.
I am having to do this
not like Cousteau with his
10 assiduous team
aboard the sun-flooded schooner
but here alone.

There is a ladder.
The ladder is always there
15 hanging innocently
close to the side of the schooner.
We know what it is for,
we who have used it.
otherwise
20 it is a piece of maritime floss
some sundry equipment.

I go down.
Rung after rung and still
25 the oxygen immerses me
the blue light
the clear atoms
of our human air.
I go down.
My flippers cripple me,
30 I crawl like an insect down the ladder
and there is no one
to tell me when the ocean
will begin.

First the air is blue and then
35 it is bluer and then green and then
black I am blacking out and yet

my mask is powerful
it pumps my blood with power
the sea is another story
40   the sea is not a question of power
I have to learn alone
to turn my body without force
in the deep element.

And now: it is easy to forget
45   what I came for
among so many who have always
lived here
swaying their crenellated fans
between the reefs
50   and besides
you breathe differently down here.

I came to explore the wreck.
The words are purposes.
The words are maps.
55   I came to see the damage that was done
and the treasures that prevail.
I stroke the beam of my lamp
slowly along the flank
of something more permanent
60   than fish or weed

the thing I came for:
the wreck and not the story of the wreck
the thing itself and not the myth
the drowned face always staring
65   toward the sun
the evidence of damage
worn by salt and sway into this threadbare beauty
the ribs of the disaster
curving their assertion
70   among the tentative haunters.

This is the place.
And I am here, the mermaid whose dark hair
streams black, the merman in his armored body.
We circle silently
75   about the wreck
we dive into the hold.
I am she: I am he

whose drowned face sleeps with open eyes
whose breasts still bear the stress
80   whose silver, copper, vermeil cargo lies
obscurely inside barrels
half-wedged and left to rot
we are the half-destroyed instruments
that once held to a course
85   the water-eaten log
the fouled compass

We are, I am, you are
by cowardice or courage
the one who find our way
90   back to this scene
carrying a knife, a camera
a book of myths
in which
our names do not appear.

1973

TED HUGHES
(1930–   )

The Bull Moses

A hoist up and I could lean over
The upper edge of the high half-door,
My left foot ledged on the hinge, and look in at the byre's [1]
Blaze of darkness: a sudden shut-eyed look
5   Backward into the head.
                              Blackness is depth
Beyond star. But the warm weight of his breathing,
The ammoniac reek of his litter, the hotly-tongued
Mash of his cud, steamed against me.
Then, slowly, as onto the mind's eye—
10   The brow like masonry, the deep-keeled neck:
Something come up there onto the brink of the gulf,
Hadn't heard of the world, too deep in itself to be called to,
Stood in sleep. He would swing his muzzle at a fly
But the square of sky where I hung, shouting, waving,
15   Was nothing to him; nothing of our light
Found any reflection in him.
                              Each dusk the farmer led him
Down to the pond to drink and smell the air,
And he took no pace but the farmer
Led him to take it, as if he knew nothing
20   Of the ages and continents of his fathers,
Shut, while he wombed, to a dark shed
And steps between his door and the duckpond;
The weight of the sun and the moon and the world hammered
To a ring of brass through his nostrils.
                              He would raise
25   His streaming muzzle and look out over the meadows,
But the grasses whispered nothing awake, the fetch
Of the distance drew nothing to momentum
In the locked black of his powers. He came strolling gently back,
Paused neither toward the pigpens on his right,
30   Nor toward the cow-byres on his left: something
Deliberate in his leisure, some beheld future
Founding in his quiet.
                              I kept the door wide,
Closed it after him and pushed the bolt.

1960

1. Cattle-shed's.

November

The month of the drowned dog. After long rain the land
Was sodden as the bed of an ancient lake,
Treed with iron and birdless. In the sunk lane
The ditch—a seep silent all summer—

5   Made brown foam with a big voice: that, and my boots
On the lane's scrubbed stones, in the gulleyed leaves,
Against the hill's hanging silence;
Mist silvering the droplets on the bare thorns

Slower than the change of daylight.
10   In a let of the ditch a tramp was bundled asleep:
Face tucked down into beard, drawn in
Under its hair like a hedgehog's. I took him for dead,

But his stillness separated from the death
Of the rotting grass and the ground. A wind chilled,
15   And a fresh comfort tightened through him,
Each hand stuffed deeper into the other sleeve.

His ankles, bound with sacking and hairy band,
Rubbed each other, resettling. The wind hardened;
A puff shook a glittering from the thorns,
20   And again the rains' dragging gray columns

Smudged the farms. In a moment
The fields were jumping and smoking; the thorns
Quivered, riddled with the glassy verticals.
I stayed on under the welding cold

25   Watching the tramp's face glisten and the drops on his coat
Flash and darken. I thought what strong trust
Slept in him—as the trickling furrows slept,
And the thorn-roots in their grip on darkness;

And the buried stones, taking the weight of winter;
30   The hill where the hare crouched with clenched teeth.
Rain plastered the land till it was shining
Like hammered lead, and I ran, and in the rushing wood

Shuttered by a black oak leaned.
The keeper's gibbet° had owls and hawks   *gallows*
35   By the neck, weasels, a gang of cats, crows:
Some, stiff, weightless, twirled like dry bark bits

In the drilling rain. Some still had their shape,
Had their pride with it; hung, chins on chests,
Patient to outwait these worst days that beat
40   Their crowns bare and dripped from their feet.

1960

Crow Alights[2]

Crow saw the herded mountains, steaming in the morning.
And he saw the sea
Dark-spined, with the whole earth in its coils.
He saw the stars, fuming away into the black, mushrooms of the nothing
    forest, clouding their spores, the virus of God.
5 And he shivered with the horror of Creation.

In the hallucination of the horror
He saw this shoe, with no sole, rain-sodden,
Lying on a moor.
And there was this garbage can, bottom rusted away,
10 A playing place for the wind, in a waste of puddles.

There was this coat, in the dark cupboard,
                in the silent room, in the silent house.
There was this face, smoking its cigarette between the dusk window and
    the fire's embers.

Near the face, this hand, motionless.

15 Near the hand, this cup.

Crow blinked. He blinked. Nothing faded.

He stared at the evidence.

Nothing escaped him. (Nothing could escape.)

                                    1971

JON SILKIN
(1930–   )

Death of a Son

(WHO DIED IN A MENTAL HOSPITAL AGED ONE)

Something has ceased to come along with me.
Something like a person: something very like one.
    And there was no nobility in it
        Or anything like that.

5   Something was there like a one year
Old house, dumb as stone. While the near buildings
    Sang like birds and laughed
        Understanding the pact

    They were to have with silence. But he
10 Neither sang nor laughed. He did not bless silence
    Like bread, with words.
        He did not forsake silence.

2. This poem is from *Crow: from the life and Songs of the Crow* (1971), a cycle of 60-odd poems with a common protagonist, Crow, whose role and character as reflector of experience are defined by the entire sequence.

But rather, like a house in mourning
Kept the eye turned in to watch the silence while
15   The other houses like birds
              Sang around him.

And the breathing silence neither
Moved nor was still.

              I have seen stones: I have seen brick
20 But this house was made up of neither bricks nor stone
              But a house of flesh and blood
                  With flesh of stone

          And bricks for blood. A house
Of stones and blood in breathing silence with the other
25   Birds singing crazy on its chimneys.
              But this was silence,

          This was something else, this was
Hearing and speaking though he was a house drawn
              Into silence, this was
30   Something religious in his silence,

          Something shining in his quiet,
This was different this was altogether something else:
              Though he never spoke, this
                  Was something to do with death.

35   And then slowly the eye stopped looking
Inward. The silence rose and became still.
The look turned to the outer place and stopped,
          With the birds still shrilling around him.
              And as if he could speak

40 He turned over on his side with his one year
Red as a wound
He turned over as if he could be sorry for this
And out of his eyes two great tears rolled, like stones, and he died.

                                                    1954

The Strawberry Plant

The rootless strawberry plant
Moves across the soil. It hops
Six inches. Has no single location,
Or root.
5   You cannot point to its origin,
Or parent. It shoots out
A pipe, and one more plant
Consolidates its ground.
It puts out crude petals, loosely met.
10 As if the business of flowering
Were to be got over. Their period is brief.
Even then, the fruit is green,
Swart, hairy. Its petals invite tearing
And are gone quickly,
15 As if they had been. The fruit swells,
Reddens, becomes succulent.

Propagation through the devouring
Appetite of another.
Is sweet, seeded, untruculent;
20   Slugs like it, all over.
It is nubile° to the lips,   *marriageable*
And survives even them. And teeth,
Insane with edible fury,
Of the loving kind.

1965

GARY SNYDER
(1930–   )

Mid-August at Sourdough Mountain [1] Lookout

Down valley a smoke haze
Three days heat, after five days rain
Pitch glows on the fir-cones
Across rocks and meadows
5   Swarms of new flies.

I cannot remember things I once read
A few friends, but they are in cities.
Drinking cold snow-water from a tin cup
Looking down for miles
10   Through high still air.

1959

Myths and Texts: Burning

17

the text

Sourdough mountain called a fire in:
Up Thunder Creek, high on a ridge.
Hiked eighteen hours, finally found
A snag and a hundred feet around on fire:
5   All afternoon and into night
Digging the fire line
Falling the burning snag
It fanned sparks down like shooting stars
Over the dry woods, starting spot-fires
10   Flaring in wind up Skagit valley
From the Sound.[3]
Toward morning it rained.
We slept in mud and ashes,
Woke at dawn, the fire was out,
15   The sky was clear, we saw
The last glimmer of the morning star.

---

1. The setting of this and others of Snyder's   3. Puget Sound, in the state of Washington.
poems is the Pacific Northwest.

                    the myth

     Fire up Thunder Creek and the mountain—
                       troy's burning! [4]
     The cloud mutters
     The mountains are your mind.
5   The woods bristle there,
     Dogs barking and children shrieking
     Rise from below.

     Rain falls for centuries
     Soaking the loose rocks in space
10   Sweet rain, the fire's out
     The black snag glistens in the rain
     & the last wisp of smoke floats up
     Into the absolute cold
     Into the spiral whorls of fire
15   The storms of the Milky Way
     "Buddha incense in an empty world"
     Black pit cold and light-year
     Flame tongue of the dragon
     Licks the sun

20   The sun is but a morning star

                                            1960

        The Levels

     wild cat kittens
     born in the ceiling
          play sky gods
     thundering over the room.
5   was it claude in the night?
     was it thieves?

          above our northbound steps
     the wild cat brood walks west

     a hawk sails over the roof
10   a snake went under the floor

          how can hawks hunt in the rain?

     I walk through the hallway:
     the soul of a great-bellied cloud.

                                            1967

        Civilization

     Those are the people who do complicated things.

          they'll grab us by the thousands
          and put us to work.

---

4. Alludes to the catastrophic destruction of Troy by the Greeks, as described in Homer's *Iliad* and Virgil's *Aeneid*.

World's going to hell, with all these
5   villages and trails.
Wild duck flocks aren't
        what they used to be.
Aurochs [5] grow rare.

Fetch me my feathers and amber

✿

10 A small cricket
on the typescript page of
"Kyoto born in spring song"
grooms himself
in time with *The Well-Tempered Clavier.*[6]
15 I quit typing and watch him thru a glass.
How well articulated! How neat!

Nobody understands the ANIMAL KINGDOM.

✿

When creeks are full
The poems flow
20 When creeks are down
We heap stones.

1970

SYLVIA PLATH
(1932–1963)

Lady Lazarus [1]

I have done it again.
One year in every ten
I manage it—

A sort of walking miracle, my skin
5 Bright as a Nazi lampshade,
My right foot

A paperweight,
My face a featureless, fine
Jew linen.

10 Peel off the napkin
O my enemy.
Do I terrify?—

The nose, the eye pits, the full set of teeth?
The sour breath
15 Will vanish in a day.

---

5. A species of European bison.
6. J. S. Bach's collection of 48 preludes and fugues for harpsichord.

1. Lazarus was raised by Jesus from the dead (John xi.1–44).

Soon, soon the flesh
The grave cave ate will be
At home on me

And I a smiling woman.
20   I am only thirty.
And like the cat I have nine times to die.

This is Number Three.
What a trash
To annihilate each decade.

25   What a million filaments.
The peanut-crunching crowd
Shoves in to see

Them unwrap me hand and foot—
The big strip tease.
30   Gentleman, ladies,

These are my hands,
My knees.
I may be skin and bone,

Nevertheless, I am the same, identical woman.
35   The first time it happened I was ten.
It was an accident.

The second time I meant
To last it out and not come back at all.
I rocked shut

40   As a seashell.
They had to call and call
And pick the worms off me like sticky pearls.

Dying
Is an art, like everything else.
45   I do it exceptionally well.

I do it so it feels like hell.
I do it so it feels real.
I guess you could say I've a call.

It's easy enough to do it in a cell.
50   It's easy enough to do it and stay put.
It's the theatrical

Comeback in broad day
To the same place, the same face, the same brute
Amused shout:

55   "A miracle!"
That knocks me out.
There is a charge

For the eyeing of my scars, there is a charge
For the hearing of my heart—
60   It really goes.

And there is a charge, very large charge,
For a word or a touch
Or a bit of blood

Or a piece of my hair or my clothes.
65   So, so, Herr Doktor.
So, Herr Enemy.

I am your opus,
I am your valuable,
The pure gold baby

70   That melts to a shriek.
I turn and burn.
Do not think I underestimate your great concern.

Ash, ash—
You poke and stir.
75   Flesh, bone, there is nothing there—

A cake of soap,
A wedding ring,
A gold filling.

Herr God, Herr Lucifer,
80   Beware
Beware.

Out of the ash
I rise with my red hair
And I eat men like air.

1965

Tulips

The tulips are too excitable, it is winter here.
Look how white everything is, how quiet, how snowed-in.
I am learning peacefulness, lying by myself quietly
As the light lies on these white walls, this bed, these hands.
5   I am nobody; I have nothing to do with explosions.
I have given my name and my day-clothes up to the nurses
And my history to the anaesthetist and my body to surgeons.

They have propped my head between the pillow and the sheet-cuff
Like an eye between two white lids that will not shut.
10   Stupid pupil, it has to take everything in.
The nurses pass and pass, they are no trouble,
They pass the way gulls pass inland in their white caps,
Doing things with their hands, one just the same as another,
So it is impossible to tell how many there are.

15 My body is a pebble to them, they tend it as water
    Tends to the pebbles it must run over, smoothing them gently.
    They bring me numbness in their bright needles, they bring me sleep.
    Now I have lost myself I am sick of baggage—
    My patent leather overnight case like a black pillbox,
20 My husband and child smiling out of the family photo;
    Their smiles catch onto my skin, little smiling hooks.

    I have let things slip, a thirty-year-old cargo boat
    Stubbornly hanging on to my name and address.
    They have swabbed me clear of my loving associations.
25 Scared and bare on the green plastic-pillowed trolley
    I watched my tea-set, my bureaus of linen, my books
    Sink out of sight, and the water went over my head.
    I am a nun now, I have never been so pure.

    I didn't want any flowers, I only wanted
30 To lie with my hands turned up and be utterly empty.
    How free it is, you have no idea how free—
    The peacefulness is so big it dazes you,
    And it asks nothing, a name tag, a few trinkets.
    It is what the dead close on, finally; I imagine them
35 Shutting their mouths on it, like a Communion tablet.

    The tulips are too red in the first place, they hurt me.
    Even through the gift paper I could hear them breathe
    Lightly, through their white swaddlings, like an awful baby.
    Their redness talks to my wound, it corresponds.
40 They are subtle: they seem to float, though they weigh me down,
    Upsetting me with their sudden tongues and their color,
    A dozen red lead sinkers round my neck.

    Nobody watched me before, now I am watched.
    The tulips turn to me, and the window behind me
45 Where once a day the light slowly widens and slowly thins,
    And I see myself, flat, ridiculous, a cut-paper shadow
    Between the eye of the sun and the eyes of the tulips,
    And I have no face, I have wanted to efface myself.
    The vivid tulips eat my oxygen.

50 Before they came the air was calm enough,
    Coming and going, breath by breath, without any fuss.
    Then the tulips filled it up like a loud noise.
    Now the air snags and eddies round them the way a river
    Snags and eddies round a sunken rust-red engine.
55 They concentrate my attention, that was happy
    Playing and resting without committing itself.

    The walls, also, seem to be warming themselves.
    The tulips should be behind bars like dangerous animals;
    They are opening like the mouth of some great African cat,
60 And I am aware of my heart: it opens and closes
    Its bowl of red blooms out of sheer love of me.
    The water I taste is warm and salt, like the sea,
    And comes from a country far away as health.

                                                    1965

IMAMU AMIRI BARAKA (LeRoi Jones)
(1934–   )

In Memory of Radio

Who has ever stopped to think of the divinity of Lamont Cranston?[1]
(Only Jack Kerouac, that I know of: & me.
The rest of you probably had on WCBS and Kate Smith,
Or something equally unattractive.)

5   What can I say?
It is better to have loved and lost
Than to put linoleum in your living rooms?

Am I a sage or something?
Mandrake's hypnotic gesture of the week?
10   (Remember, I do not have the healing powers of Oral Roberts . . .
I cannot, like F. J. Sheen, tell you how to get saved *& rich!*
I cannot even order you to gaschamber satori like Hitler or Goody Knight

& Love is an evil word.
15   Turn it backwards/see, what I mean?
An evol word. & besides
Who understands it?
I certainly wouldn't like to go out on that kind of limb.

Saturday mornings we listened to *Red Lantern* & his undersea folk.
20   At 11, *Let's Pretend*/& we did/& I, the poet, still do, Thank God!

What was it he used to say (after the transformation, when he was safe
& invisible & the unbelievers couldn't throw stones?) "Heh, heh, heh,
Who knows what evil lurks in the hearts of men? The Shadow knows."

O, yes he does
25   O, yes he does.
An evil word it is,
This Love.

                                                                1961

The New World

The sun is folding, cars stall and rise
beyond the window. The workmen leave
the street to the bums and painters' wives
pushing their babies home. Those who realize
5   how fitful and indecent consciousness is
stare solemnly out on the emptying street.
The mourners and soft singers. The liars,
and seekers after ridiculous righteousness. All
my doubles, and friends, whose mistakes cannot
10   be duplicated by machines, and this is all of our
arrogance. Being broke or broken, dribbling

---

1. The hero of the radio serial "The Shadow." The poem refers to prominent characters and personalities that Jones would have heard on radio as a boy. Jack Kerouac (1922–1969) was a novelist of the "Beat Generation."

at the eyes. Wasted lyricists, and men
who have seen their dreams come true, only seconds
after they knew those dreams to be horrible conceits
15 and plastic fantasies of gesture and extension,
shoulders, hair and tongues distributing misinformation
about the nature of the understanding. No one is that simple
or priggish, to be alone out of spite and grown strong
in its practice, mystics in two-pants suits. Our style,
20 and discipline, controlling the method of knowledge.
Beatniks, like Bohemians, go calmly out of style. And boys
are dying in Mexico, who did not get the word.
The lateness of their fabrication: mark their holes
with filthy needles. The lust of the world. This will not
25 be news. The simple damning lust,
                float flat magic in low changing
                evenings. Shiver your hands
                in dance. Empty all of me for
                knowing, and will the danger
30   of identification,

                Let me sit and go blind in my dreaming
                and be that dream in purpose and device.

                A fantasy of defeat, a strong strong man
                older, but no wiser than the defect of love.

                            1969

DON L. LEE
(1942–   )

The Revolutionary Screw

(FOR MY BLACKSISTERS)

brothers,
i
under/overstand
the situation:

5 i mean—
      u bes hitten the man hard
      all day long.
a stone revolutionary, "a full time revolutionary."
      tellen the man how bad u is
10   & what u goin ta do
      & how u goin ta do it.

it must be a bitch
to be able to do all that
talken. (& not one irregular breath fr/yr/mouth)
15 being so
foreful & all
to the man's face (the courage)
& u not even cracken a smile (realman).

i know,
20 the sisters just don't
understand the
pressure u is under.

&
when u ask for a piece
25 of leg/
it's not for yr/self
but for
yr/people——it keeps u going
& anyway us is a revolutionary
30 & she wd be doin
a revolutionary thing.

that sister dug it
from the beginning,
had an early-eye.
35 i mean
she really had it together
when she said:
              go fuck yr/self nigger.

now
40 that was
revolutionary.

                                        1969

NIKKI GIOVANNI
(1943-   )

Nikki-Rosa

childhood remembrances are always a drag
if you're Black
you always remember things like living in Woodlawn [1]
with no inside toilet
5 and if you become famous or something
they never talk about how happy you were to have your mother
all to your self and
how good the water felt when you got your bath from one of those
big tubs that folk in chicago barbecue in
10 and somehow when you talk about home
it never gets across how much you
understood their feelings
as the whole family attended meetings about Hollydale
and even though you remember
15 your biographers never understand
your father's pain as he sells his stock
and another dream goes
and though you're poor it isn't poverty that
concerns you
20 and though they fought a lot
it isn't your father's drinking that makes any difference

---

1. A black suburb of Cincinnati, Ohio.

but only that everybody is together and you
and your sister have happy birthdays and very good christmasses
and I really hope no white person ever has cause to write about me
25   because they never understand Black love is Black wealth and they'll
probably talk about my hard childhood and never understand that
all the while I was quite happy.

1968

A Poem for Carol

(MAY SHE ALWAYS WEAR RED RIBBONS)

when i was very little
though it's still true today
there were no sidewalks in lincoln heights [2]
and the home we had on jackson street
5   was right next to a bus stop and a sewer
which didn't really ever become offensive
but one day from the sewer a little kitten
with one eye gone
came crawling out
10   though she never really came into our yard but just
sort of hung by to watch the folk
my sister who was always softhearted but able
to act effectively started taking milk
out to her while our father would only say
15   don't bring *him* home and everyday
after school i would rush home to see if she was still
there and if gary had fed her but i could never
bring myself to go near her
she was so loving
20   and so hurt and so singularly beautiful and i knew
i had nothing to give that would
replace her one gone eye

and if i had named her which i didn't i'm sure
i would have called her carol

1972

MICHAEL ONDAATJE
(1945–   )

Elizabeth [1]

Catch, my Uncle Jack said
and oh I caught this huge apple
red as Mrs Kelly's bum.
It's red as Mrs Kelly's bum, I said
5   and Daddy [2] roared
and swung me on his stomach with a heave.
Then I hid the apple in my room
till it shrunk like a face
growing eyes and teeth ribs.

---

2. A black suburb of Cincinnati.   England.
1. Elizabeth I (1533–1603), Queen of   2. Henry VIII (1491–1547).

10 Then Daddy took me to the zoo
he knew the man there
they put a snake around my neck
and it crawled down the front of my dress.
I felt its flicking tongue
15 dripping onto me like a shower.
Daddy laughed and said Smart Snake
and Mrs Kelly with us scowled.

In the pond where they kept the goldfish
Philip³ and I broke the ice with spades
20 and tried to spear the fishes;
we killed one and Philip ate it,
then he kissed me
with raw saltless fish in his mouth.

My sister Mary's got bad teeth
25 and said I was lucky, then she said
I had big teeth, but Philip said I was pretty.
He had big hands that smelled.

I would speak of Tom,⁴ soft laughing,
who danced in the mornings round the sundial
30 teaching me the steps from France, turning
with the rhythm of the sun on the warped branches,
who'd hold my breast and watch it move like a snail
leaving his quick urgent love in my palm.
And I kept his love in my palm till it blistered.

35 When they axed his shoulders and neck
the blood moved like a branch into the crowd.
And he staggered with his hanging shoulder
cursing their thrilled cry, wheeling,
waltzing in the French style to his knees
40 holding his head with the ground,
blood settling on his clothes like a blush;
this way
when they aimed the thud into his back.

And I find cool entertainment now
45 with white young Essex,⁵ and my nimble rhymes.

1967

Letters & Other Worlds

> *"for there was no more darkness for him and,
> no doubt like Adam before the fall, he could
> see in the dark"*

My father's body was a globe of fear
His body was a town we never knew
He hid that he had been where we were going
His letters were a room he seldom lived in
5 In them the logic of his love could grow

3. Philip II (1527–1598), King of Spain. In 1554 he came to England to become husband of Queen Mary I (1516–1558), Elizabeth's half-sister, and in 1559 he proposed marriage to Elizabeth herself, in vain.
4. Thomas, Lord Seymour (1508–1549), who married Henry VIII's widow Catherine Parr, and upon her death offered to marry Elizabeth. This was taken as signifying political ambition, and he was executed for treason.
5. Robert Devereux, Earl of Essex (1566–1601), became the queen's favorite in 1587; he was executed for treason.

My father's body was a town of fear
He was the only witness to its fear dance
He hid where he had been that we might lose him
His letters were a room his body scared

10 He came to death with his mind drowning.
On the last day he enclosed himself
in a room with two bottles of gin, later ·
fell the length of his body
so that brain blood moved
15 to new compartments
that never knew the wash of fluid
and he died in minutes of a new equilibrium.

His early life was a terrifying comedy
and my mother divorced him again and again.
20 He would rush into tunnels magnetized
by the white eye of trains
and once, gaining instant fame,
managed to stop a Perahara [6] in Ceylon
—the whole procession of elephants dancers
25 local dignitaries—by falling
dead drunk onto the street.
As a semi-official, and semi-white at that,
the act was seen as a crucial
turning point in the Home Rule Movement
30 and led to Ceylon's independence in 1948.

(My mother had done her share too—
her driving so bad
she was stoned by villagers
whenever her car was recognized)

35 For 14 years of marriage
each of them claimed he or she
was the injured party.
Once on the Colombo docks
saying goodbye to a recently married couple
40 my father, jealous
at my mother's articulate emotion,
dove into the waters of the harbor
and swam after the ship waving farewell.
My mother pretending no affiliation
45 mingled with the crowd back to the hotel.

Once again he made the papers
though this time my mother
with a note to the editor
corrected the report—saying he was drunk
50 rather than broken hearted at the parting of friends.
The married couple received both editions
of *The Ceylon Times* when their ship reached Aden.[7]

---

6. Or Anuradhapura Perahera, an annual
Ceylonese religious festival commemorating
the birth of Vishnu, one of the three primary
Hindu gods. On its fifth and final day the
festival culminates in nocturnal processions
such as that described here, the elephants
bearing shrines and relics.
7. A country southwest of Arabia, then a
British colony.

And then in his last years
he was the silent drinker,
55 the man who once a week
disappeared into his room with bottles
and stayed there until he was drunk
and until he was sober.

There speeches, head dreams, apologies,
60 the gentle letters, were composed.
With the clarity of architects
he would write of the row of blue flowers
his new wife had planted,
the plans for electricity in the house,
65 how my half-sister fell near a snake
and it had awakened and not touched her.
Letters in a clear hand of the most complete empathy
his heart widening and widening and widening
to all manner of change in his children and friends
70 while he himself edged
into the terrible acute hatred
of his own privacy
till he balanced and fell
the length of his body
75 the blood screaming in
the empty reservoir of bones
the blood searching in his head without metaphor

                                                    1973

We're at the Graveyard

Stuart Sally Kim and I
watching still stars
or now and then sliding stars
like hawk spit to the trees.
5 Up there the clear charts,
the systems' intricate branches
which change with hours and solstices,
the bone geometry of moving from there, to there.

And down here—friends
10 whose minds and bodies
shift like acrobats to each other.
When we leave, they move
to an altitude of silence.

So our minds shape
15 and lock the transient,
parallel these bats
who organize the air
with thick blinds of travel.
Sally is like grey snow in the grass.
20 Sally of the beautiful bones
pregnant below stars.

                                                    1973

Prosody

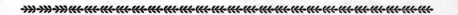

Commentary*

Prosody is the description of those formal patterns of sound, such as meter and rhyme, to which poems are systematically accommodated. The term refers, by extension, to irregular systems of rhythm such as **free verse**.

SCANSION AND METER

Metrical analysis (scansion) employs certain signs written above the line of verse in order to make its rhythmic structure visible. The meter or length of a line is measured in rhythmic units; that is, by the number of feet that a given line contains. A **foot** normally consists of two or three syllables, only one of which is strongly stressed. Hence, lines are measured as *monometer* (at least one stressed accent; *dimeter* (two); *trimeter* (three); and by the two commonest measures, *tetrameter* (four) and *pentameter* (five); as well as by *hexameter* (six) and *heptameter* (seven).

The following signs denote the main features of meter and accent:

⌣ = An unstressed syllable.

╱ = A stressed syllable.

| = A division between one foot and the next.

|| = A significant pause or **caesura**. (Since the visible end of a line often indicates a caesura, the double bar is not usually inserted there.)

╲ or ⌣̇ = A stress between heavy and light; for precision in metrical analysis it is often useful.

In the lines that follow, the first is scored to show the normal meter, using only two degrees of stress; the second exhibits a possible spoken reading. Most practiced readers of verse will carry the first pattern in their minds while actually reading along with and sometimes in contrast to the first:

Hŏw frésh, | ŏh Lórd, | hŏw swéet | ănd cléan |
Hów frésh, | ŏh Lórd, | hów swéet | ănd cléan |
(Herbert)

Ăll thís | thĕ wórld | wĕll knóws; | yĕt nóne | knŏws wéll |
Áll thís | thĕ wórld | wĕll knóws; | yĕt nóne | knóws wéll |
(Shakespeare)

For several centuries most verse in English has availed itself of this dual system, by which syllables are counted according to rule and accents are permitted to be diversified. No other prosodic system has superseded this, despite much experimentation.

PROSODY BASED ON NATIVE CADENCES

The oldest recorded English poetry was void of rhyme, and of meter as we are familiar with it, and relied instead on a system of *alliteration* and accentual balance. A fragment of medieval verse, modernized in vocabulary but with the alliteration and phrasing intact, reads

* **Boldface** type denotes a glossary entry.

> And you *lovely ladies,*   with your *long fingers,*
> Who would have *silk and* satin   to *sew* on occasion
> *Chas*ubles for *chap*lains   to the *church's honor,*
> *Wives* and *widows* too,   *wool* and *flax* spin

(Italics added)

When stanzaic lyrics came into the literature, with end-rhyme partly displacing alliteration and partly existing alongside it, the cadences in them were often various and free. The exquisite first stanza of one medieval lyric (p 22) would naturally be read

> Ĭ síng ŏf ă máydĕn
> Thăt iš mákĕléss;
> Kíng ŏf állĕ kíngĕs
> Tŏ hĕr són shĕ chés.

The stresses falling two by two and the answering alliteration of *may*den, *make*less; *King, kinges;* and (more remotely) *sing, son* suggest the old prosody, while the rhyme, the stanzaic arrangement, and the reversed rhythm in the third line reflect new influences.

The freedom claimed in these earlier centuries was sought again by some of the 19th-century poets, rebelling against strict metrical regularity. A fertile inventor of freer rhythms was Walt Whitman, who composed lines such as

> Oút of the crádle éndlessly rócking,
> Oút of the mócking-bird's thróat, the músical shúttle,
> Oút of the Nínth-month mídnight,
> Óver the stérile sánds and the fíelds beyónd where the chíld
>   léaving his béd wánder'd alóne, báreheaded, bárefoot . . .

Such freedom is congenial to English poetry because our language falls naturally into phrases, like "Out of the cradle || endlessly rocking," which can be either balanced against each other or strung together in loosely rhythmic sequences. Modern poets who have adopted freer rhythms have occasionally (like Gerard Manley Hopkins) revived some features of Old English poetry and often (like Theodore Roethke) used cadences recalling Whitman's.

SYLLABIC METER

The principal conventions of English prosody nevertheless remain the traditional meters. These meters, deriving from cultural borrowings, are not altogether natural to English and must be mastered anew, with some degree of difficulty, by each generation of readers.

The basis for conventional English metrics, ever since late-medieval and Renaissance poets began to imitate French and Italian models, has been the line of a fixed number of syllables. But such lines do not of themselves approach self-sufficiency in English, as they do in the poetry of the Romance languages. The English ear cannot count syllables unless they are differentiated according to some regular system. The preceding sentence, which happens to contain thirty syllables, is divisible into three parts:

> The English ear cannot count syllables
> Unless they are differentiated
> According to some regular system.

But only by adding up on the fingers can a reader tell that each of these lines is ten syllables long, even though the first and third of these lines approximate a familiar metrical pattern.

For metrical purposes, a syllable is normally regarded as the basic unit of pronunciation, and consists of a vowel sound alone or a vowel with attendant consonants: *a-way; oh; syl-la-ble*. (Sometimes *m*, *n* and *l* are counted as vowel sounds, as in *riddle* and *prism*—ri-dl, pri-zm). In words of two or more syllables one syllable is almost always more strongly accented than the others: *sýl-lă-blĕ, phó-tŏ-grăph*. A word of one syllable, however, may be counted either as a stressed or as an unstressed accent, depending on the emphasis of the phrase in which it appears: *hé wĭll nŏt; hĕ wíll nŏt; hĕ wĭll nót*. Connective monosyllables such as *and, but, or, of, to*, etc., are not usually stressed, however.

Four different feet, two of them disyllabic and two trisyllabic, are the constituent units of most English verse from the 16th through the 19th centuries. The first and most common disyllabic foot is the **iambic**. (⌣ ´), which consists of an unaccented syllable followed by an accented. Four successive iambs yield Thomas Wyatt's line,

Fŏrgét | nŏt yét | thĕ tríed | ĭntént. |

The other disyllabic foot—the **trochaic** foot or trochee (´ ⌣)—consists of an accented syllable followed by an unaccented. It is the unit of Robert Burns's line,

Hád wĕ névĕr lóved săe kíndlў |

Sequences, whether of iambic or trochaic feet, are heard as a continuous alternation of stressed and unstressed syllables, but it is easy to lose the sense of whether iambs or trochees are the constituent units. Iambic and trochaic lines are not, in fact, always distinguishable from each other except in the first foot and the last. In Ben Jonson's lines,

Quéen aňd húntreš, cháste aňd fáir,
Nów thĕ sún iš laíd tŏ sleép,

the meter may be defined either as iambic with an initial unaccented syllable missing or as trochaic with a final unaccented syllable missing. Despite occasional ambiguities, however, the concepts of iamb and trochee are useful for descriptive analysis.

The more common of the two trisyllabic feet is the anapest (⌣ ⌣ ´), in which two unaccented syllables are followed by an accented one, as in Byron's line

Wĭth thĕ déw | ŏn hĭs brów | aňd thĕ rúst | ŏn hĭs máil. |

The dactyl (´ ⌣ ⌣), finally, is an accented syllable followed by two unaccented. A dactylic meter of six feet—reminiscent of the meter of Homer and Virgil—is found in Longfellow's *Evangeline*, one line of which reads

Bláck wĕre hĕr | éyes aš thĕ | bérrў thăt | gróws ŏn thĕ | thórn bў thĕ | wáysĭde. |

Anapests and dactyls, like iambs and trochees, may become indistinguishable in a sustained sequence, though sequences of the trisyllabic feet are indicated, very naturally, by accents falling on every third syllable rather than on every second. Such sequences can absorb some disyllabic feet without losing their essential character. In the following lines from Swinburne, a generally anapestic-dactylic progression absorbs occasional iambs as it goes:

> Swéet iš thě tréadĭng ŏf wíne, aňd swéet thě féet ŏf thě dóve;
> Bŭt ă góodlĭěr gíft iš thíne thăn foám ŏf thě grápes ŏr lóve.

Even in verse written in these traditional patterns, the differentiation of meters is seen to be partly an abstract exercise. The English language resists perfect accommodation to feet of a fixed number of syllables.

VARIATIONS WITHIN A FOOT

In detail the phenomenon of accentuation is less simple than these definitions imply. A single long word, like *disestablishmentarian,* contains several scarcely accented syllables as well as syllables having different degrees of positive stress. Accents supplying semantic emphasis ("But Jack is *táller* than Jill") also introduce diversity. A succession of iambic feet, therefore, is seldom in practice a series of closely similar entities. We demand of it only that some of the even numbered syllables show a higher degree of accent than the syllables adjoining them.

Something of the diversity of the iamb is apparent even in so regular a poem as Gray's *Elegy Written in a Country Churchyard*:

> Thě cúr | fěw tólls | thě knéll | ŏf párt | ĭng dáy, |
>
> Thě lów | ĭng hérd | wĭnd slów | ly̆ ó'er | thě léa,

In the first line the degree of accent distinguishing the even-numbered syllables is approximately constant. In the second line, however, the word *wind* resists being sunk into an unaccented position, and *o'er*, though in strong position, is rather weakly stressed. Such variations are made possible by the several degrees of accentuation natural to English.

When a syllable is accented, it tends also to be raised in pitch and to be lengthened. Any of these characteristics (stress, pitch, or length) or combination of them, can signal a metrical accent. By a flexible use of these variations, a poet can save regular meters from mechanical sameness. In particular, two sound patterns can be made apparent simultaneously. Hence rather free "organic" rhythms can be combined with conventional meter. The concluding line of a Shakespeare sonnet, for example, shows a regular iambic beat:

> Tŏ lóve | thăt wéll | whĭch thóu | mušt léave | ĕre lóng. |

Yet the sense of the line, as patterns of alliteration and syntax direct us to it, seems concentrated in three consecutive monosyllables near the beginning of the line and three at the end: *lóve thàt wéll . . . léave ère lóng*. Both phrases are part of a balanced scheme of meaning as well as of a sequence of iambs. It is impossible to attain a satisfactory reading by recipe. Ideally, one builds the metrical principle into his consciousness, rather as the accomplished musician builds in the principle of an exact regular beat and diversifies it in expressive performance.

CAESURA

Another source of variation within the standard measures is the interruption or delaying of the flow of the meter by means of **caesuras**. Such pauses or suspensions—short or long—often appear near the middle of a line or at the end, but may fall wherever the sense and emphasis of the line require. Jonson's invocation to Shakespeare is a favorable example; the punctuation accurately defines the pauses:

> I therefore will begin. || Soul.of the age! ||
> The applause! || delight! || the wonder of our stage! ||
> My Shakespeare, || rise; || I will not lodge thee by
> Chaucer or Spenser, || or bid Beaumont lie
> A little further || to make thee a room . . .

The third and fourth lines are not end-stopped, that is, do not provide the more usual end-of-line caesuras. Such variations assist the expression of meaning as well as supplying cadences of phrase that in no way impair the metrical pattern. In free verse, caesuras are often of crucial weight, simply because they appear so frequently as marking the end of a line and because no other definite accentual pattern may be readily apparent.

SUBSTITUTIONS FOR FEET IN A LINE

Thus far it has been tacitly assumed that every line embodies, however variously, the precise accentual pattern which the meter requires. But some transfers of accent within lines have become nearly as conventional as the meter itself. Chief among these is an initial trochee in place of an iamb, as in Shakespeare's line

> Áge căn | nŏt wí | thĕr hér, | nŏr cús | tŏm stále

It is permissible as well to resume on a trochee, in lieu of an iamb, after a caesura in the line. Ben Jonson included this line in a sequence of iambics:

> Áll thăt | Ĭ ám | ĭn árts, | áll thăt | Ĭ knów.

Another common variation involves transferring an accent normally belonging to one syllable to the next, as in the beginning of Dryden's line,

> Ănd thĕ | lóng gló | riĕs óf | măjés | tĭc Róme.

This pattern was often used by Dryden, Pope, and their contemporaries to lend finality to the last line of a verse paragraph.

Such substitutions will sometimes appear elsewhere than in the initial feet. Poets depart from metrical norms here and there whenever they can gain an intelligible end thereby. Shakespeare, wanting to break into sudden expostulation, begins a sonnet with the highly irregular line,

> Lét mĕ | nót tŏ | thĕ már | riăge ŏf | trúe mínds

Milton, to introduce a wailful repetition into the first line of his elegy, begins *Lycidas* thus:

> Yĕt ońce | móre, Ŏ | yĕ láu | rĕls, ańd | ońce móre

And Gerard Manley Hopkins, to underscore his feeling for the immanence of God in Nature, ventures a sonnet chiefly iambic but incorporating also features of alliterative verse:

> The wórld is chárged with the grándeur of Gód.
> It will fláme oút, like shíning from shóok fóil

METER AS A GUIDE TO INTERPRETATION

Because meter strongly affects emphasis, one can discover, or perhaps invent, relationships between the readings given and a regular meter. In Milton's line above, the iambic norm suggests that we modify the reading "*once more . . .* and *once more,*" in the *direction* of "*once* more . . . and once *more,*" enhancing its interest and possibly its lamenting quality. In Hopkins' second line, an iambic undertone proposes that the in-dwelling grandeur will not only "*flame out,*" but that it "*will* flame *out,*" *is intent* on flaming out.

Where no such particular effects are assignable, the pull exerted on the language by the metrical standard still renders it fit for stirring utterance. To dispense with such norms, Robert Frost once wrote, is like playing tennis without a net. But many modern poets do not accept his analogy.

RHYME

Where rhyming comes from, nobody knows. Almost everyone meets it first in children's verses—counting rhymes, nursery rhymes, spells, and riddles. Quite possibly it simply inheres in the playful possibilities of language, and quite as possibly in its origins it is tied to magic—to the hope that certain mysterious combinations of concordant sounds can cast spells. Since rhyme is a kind of accurate non-sense, it carries into poetry something irrational but not meaningless. It can suggest mirth and sorrow, anger and blessing. Yet in itself it is little more than a game.

In prosody rhyme refers to a close, but not identical, correspondence of vowel and consonant sounds that occur at the end of separate lines of verse (though rhyming—"internal rhyming"—may also take place within a single line). "**Rhyme proper,**" the ordinary rule of rhyme, requires a close matching of accented vowel sounds and also of the consonants and vowels (unaccented) that may follow.

rude	be *mute*	*sing*ing	re*lation*
brood	dis*pute*	*spring*ing	sen*sation*

When lines end on the accented rhyme (*rude/brood*) it is called "masculine"; otherwise (*singing/springing*) "feminine." "**Rime riche**"—rhyming the same word or sound (*grate/great*)—is not accounted proper rhyme. Patterns of successive rhymes from line to line are exceedingly various and are functional in defining **stanza** forms. Some such forms, to be found among the selections in this anthology, are described in the glossary: the **ballad stanza,** **ottava rima, rhyme royal,** the **Spenserian stanza,** the **tercet,** and **terza rima,** apply to stanzas; while **ballade, rondel, sestina, sonnet,** and **villanelle** pertain to whole poems. In analyzing the rhyme scheme, the first rhyming sound at the end of a line is denoted "a," the next different rhyme sound "b." The recurrence of the first rhyme is again "a," and so forth. Hence a stanza of Tennyson's that rhymes plain/bowers/towers/main is described as having the rhyme scheme abba.

Various departures from the rules of rhyme proper are allowable within its framework, or occur *de facto* as a result of changes in pronunciation. For example, "hours" rhymed with "yours" in Chaucer's time, and "care" with "were" in Pope's, and there are many differences between standard American and standard English pronunciation. But "close" rhymes such as climb/dine are not allowed, since the sounds *m* and *n* do not precisely match. In comic or grotesque poems rhyming has more liberty, and Byron can rhyme a funny stanza (*Don Juan*, Canto I, stanza 130) with potatoes/grinning/apparatus/beginning/gratis/spinning/late/grate, which make up a perfectly good **ottava rima:** abababcc.

Other uses of the sound of words are **alliteration, onomatopoeia,** and the rhyming devices described above when they occur elsewhere than at the ends of lines.

Half-rhyme (or "slant rhyme") is much rarer than rhyme proper but follows fairly exact rules and is of two kinds: (1) Assonantal rhyme matches the accented vowels but not the consonants (glaze/stain or seen/feet); (2) Somewhat more common, consonantal rhyme varies the vowels but matches the consonants, particularly those following the vowels: peer/pare, reach/touch, shun/man.

Milton thought rhyme too trivial for a solemn epic, but rhyming has given much delight to writers and readers. It has no single or definable effect. It may in itself amuse, or it may support or counterpoint a poem's mood and meaning.

FREE VERSE

That the last 200 pages of this book contain more **free verse** than all the preceding ones correctly indicates how widespread the abandonment of traditional versification has become during the past century. This is not without precedent; Examples of unusually varied rhythmic patterns are found in Spenser, Milton, and Blake. As the term implies, free verse defies exact definition, yet free verse poems, though departing from the traditional rules of prosody, still show most of the other familiar poetic conventions. With respect to imagery, figures of speech, and dialectic of thought, free verse poems are often quite traditional. Although usually devoid of rhyme patterns, they sometimes employ partial or irregular rhyme, and although not strictly stanzaic they are often composed in stanzalike sections. The line of verse is often a major rhythmic unit.

What free verse is free *of* is fixed patterns of alternating accents, though fragments of the traditional meters are common. Poems in free verse afford a wide spectrum of forms, both visible and audible, from the long-lined cadences of Whitman, Jeffers, and Roethke to the syllabic regularities of Marianne Moore and the lean, laconic one-sentence poems of William Carlos Williams.

Free verse poems need not be deficient in rhythm nor in other sources of formal order. To reinterpret Frost's analogy between verse and tennis, it may be said that in free verse a poet devises for each poem new and often exacting ground rules as demanding as the regular meters. Although the wide variety of free verse forms defies simple codification, the familiar methods of prosodic analysis can usually be adapted to the scansion of free verse.

ALEXANDER W. ALLISON
ARTHUR J. CARR

Glossary*

ACCENT: Metrical accent is the regularly recurring stress or beat of measured poetry, the emphasis which falls on one syllable of a **foot** and defines the **meter** by its placement within the foot.

ALCAIC STROPHE: A stanza named for the Greek poet Alcaeus. A scheme for it, which ignores permissible **quantitative** variants but includes the conventionally overlaid pattern of stresses, is

```
– | ´ ˘ | ´ – || ´ ˘ ˘ | ´ ˘ | ´
– | ´ ˘ | ´ – || ´ ˘ ˘ | ´ ˘ | ´
      – | ´ ˘ | ´ – | ´ ˘ | ´ ˘
      ´ ˘ ˘ | ´ ˘ ˘ | ´ ˘ | ´ ˘
```

Tennyson imitated this strophe in his ode *Milton* (p. 351). Robert Frost was influenced by the meter of the first two lines in his *The Strong Are Saying Nothing*. See Commentary, "Quantitative Meter."

ALEXANDRINE: A twelve-syllable line; in English always a line of six iambic feet. It forms the last line of the **Spenserian stanza** and is an occasional variant for the second line of the **Heroic couplet**.

ALLITERATION: The close repetition of initial sounds: *from stem to stern*. Loosely, any close phonetic recurrence: *immemorial elms*.

ALLITERATIVE VERSE: A verse form distinguished by regular recurrence of the initial sounds of stressed syllables within the line. The alliteration lights, typically, on two principal words in the first half-line and one in the second half-line. For illustration, see Commentary, "Prosody Based on Native Cadences."

ANACRUSIS: The prefixing of an unstressed syllable or syllables to a line of which they form no metrical part:

> Spórt thăt wrínklĕd Cáre dĕrídes,
> Ănd Laúghtĕr hóldĭng bóth hĭs sídes.

ANAPEST: A metrical foot made up of two unaccented syllables followed by an accented. See Commentary, "Syllabic Feet."

ANTISTROPHE: The second of two corresponding metrical divisions; in Greek choral recitation, the response to the strophe. See **ode**.

ASSONANCE: Similarity of sounds; particularly, as distinguished from **rhyme**, the similarity of like vowels followed by unlike consonants: *cat, map; holy, story*.

BALLAD STANZA: A four-line stanza of which the first and third lines are iambic tetrameter and the second and fourth lines are iambic trimeter, the second and fourth lines rhyming. The meter of the ballad stanza, called also common meter, is often varied in practice, as witness medieval folk ballads (pp. 32–50), and literary ballads like Coleridge's *Rime of the Ancient Mariner*.

---

* Cross-references are in **boldface** type.

BALLADE: A poem commonly of three eight-line stanzas with all stanzas following the rhyme-scheme *ababbcbc*, concluded by a four-line **envoy** rhyming *bcbc*. Chaucer wrote ballades, as did some late-nineteenth-century poets.

BLANK VERSE: Unrhymed iambic pentameter. The meter of Shakespeare's plays, Milton's *Paradise Lost* and Wordsworth's *Prelude*.

BURDEN: The refrain of a song, as (typically) of a **carol**. The burden of a familiar Christmas carol is

> Hark! the herald angels sing
> Glory to the newborn King!

In musical performance a burden is usually sung through once before the first stanza. In this text, therefore, as in most others, it is printed in that position.

CADENCE: A rhythm or unit of rhythmic progression; distinguished from Meter as not necessarily regular. Walt Whitman wrote in cadences rather than in meters.

CAESURA: Normally, in English poetry, a break occurring in the middle of a line of five or more feet. Represented by the symbol ||:

> To err is human, || to forgive, divine.

Sometimes used for any break within the line. In classical prosody, caesuras occurred whenever a word ended within a foot.

CAROL: A song or hymn of joy; now usually a Christmas song with a burden. Example: *The Corpus Christi Carol* (p. 25).

CATALEXIS: The dropping of one or two unaccented syllables from the end of a line—necessarily, in practice, a trochaic line or a dactylic. The first of the following lines represents a normal trochaic tetrameter; the second is the same meter with catalexis:

> Dust thou | art to | dust re | turnest
> Was not | spoken | of the | soul.

Normal lines, like the first line above, are sometimes distinguished as *acatalectic* (*not* catalectic).

CLOSED COUPLET: A **couplet** self-contained in syntax and sense.

COMMON METER: The meter of the **ballad stanza.**

COUPLET: Two successive lines of the same meter and length, usually rhyming with each other. Couplets sometimes constitute two-line stanzas.

DACTYL: A metrical foot made up of an accented syllable followed by two unaccented. See Commentary, "Syllabic Feet."

DIMETER: A verse line of two feet.

DISTICH: A **couplet.**

DOUBLE RHYME: **Feminine rhyme. See rhyme.**

ELISION: The running together of vowels in adjacent words, for the sake of eliminating a syllable: th'eternal, as happy'as I.

END-RHYME: Rhyme occurring at the ends of poetic lines.

END-STOP: The conclusion of a line, a couplet, or (occasionally) a longer metrical unit, with a period or other clear pause.

ENJAMBMENT: The running of one line into another. Lines not enjambed are **end-stopped.**

ENVOY (*Envoi*): A stanza, usually of four or five lines, concluding a
ballade, a sestina, or some other such form; normally interlaced with the
foregoing stanzas by its rhyme-scheme.

EPODE: The third division of the Pindaric ode, contrasting metrically with
the strophe and antistrophe. See ode.

EYE-RHYME: Words or terminal syllables spelled alike but pronounced
differently: *some, home.*

FEMININE ENDING: A final unstressed syllable appended to an iambic or
anapestic line:

To be | or nót | to be, | that is | the quéstion.

FEMININE RHYME: A double or disyllabic rhyme: *nation, station.* See rhyme.

FOOT: A group of two or three syllables constituting the unit of a metrical
line. Normally, in English, an iamb, trochee, anapest or dactyl.

FOURTEENER: A line of fourteen syllables and seven iambic feet. A pair of
fourteeners is often resolvable into common meter.

FREE VERSE: Verse without a regular metrical pattern.

HEROIC COUPLET: An iambic pentameter couplet, usually end-stopped and
often containing interior patterns of balance. Called Heroic because, for
a century after the Restoration (1660), it was the accustomed form for
English translations of classical epics (called heroic poems) and for
native mock-heroic verse.

HEXAMETER: A verse line of six feet.

IAMB: A metrical foot made up of an unaccented syllable followed by an
accented. See Commentary, "Syllabic Feet."

ICTUS: The metrical accent, or some other rhythmic beat.

INTERNAL RHYME: Rhyme occurring within the line of verse:

And all is *seared* with trade; *bleared, smeared* with toil.
(Gerard Manley Hopkins, *God's Grandeur,* line 6, p. 424)

ITALIAN SONNET: See sonnet.

LEONINE RHYME: A scheme in which the word preceding the caesura rhymes
with the last word of the line:

I bring fresh *showers* || for the thirsting *flowers,*
(Percy Bysshe Shelley, *The Cloud* [p. 284], line 1. Italics added).

MADRIGAL: A brief lyric, averaging eight or ten lines, suitable for part sing-
ing. Popular in Elizabethan England. Example: Fletcher's *Take, O, Take
Those Lips Away.*

MEASURE: Meter; sometimes specifically quantitative meter.

METER: The pattern of arrangement in poetic lines having a regularly meas-
urable phonetic structure. The traditional meters are identified by (1)
the names of the constituent feet, as iambic, trochaic, anapestic, dactylic;
and (2) the number of feet per line, as trimeter, tetrameter, pentameter.
Examples: iambic pentameter, trochaic tetrameter.

MONOMETER: A verse line of one foot.

OCTAVE: An eight-line stanza (as of the ballade) or self-sufficient part of a
stanza (like the first division of the Italian sonnet).

OCTOSYLLABIC: Containing eight syllables; a variant designation for iambic tetrameter. Octosyllabic couplets are very frequent: Marlowe's *The Passionate Shepherd to His Love* (p. 77), Marvell's *To His Coy Mistress* (p. 153); Swift's verse narratives.

ODE: An exalted lyric which enlarges upon a serious theme. The regular or Pindaric ode, a legacy of Greek choral song, is divided into sections, each with a **strophe**, a metrically identical **antistrophe,** and a contrasting epode. (These three parts may, in English odes, be called the turn, the counterturn, and the stand.) The irregular ode (like Wordsworth's *Intimations of Immortality* [p. 241]) reproduces the internal elaborateness of the Pindaric strophe but dispenses with regular strophic recurrence. The Horatian ode (of which Keats's *Ode to a Nightingale* [p. 314] is a somewhat distant derivative) employs a uniform stanza throughout.

ONOMATOPOEIA: The formation of words or phrases whose sound is designed to imitate that of the object described: "The moan of doves in immemorial elms, / And murmuring of innumerable bees." (Tennyson, "Come Down, O Maid," lines 30–31.)

OTTAVA RIMA: A stanza of eight iambic pentameter lines rhyming *abababcc.* The medium of Italian heroic romance, it is used lyrically by William Butler Yeats in *Among School Children* (p. 445).

PENTAMETER: A verse line of five feet.

PROSODY: The scientific study of those formal patterns of sound, like meter and rhyme, to which poems are systematically accommodated; comprehending by extension such irregular phonetic systems as the cadences of Walt Whitman and the **"sprung rhythm"** of Gerard Manley Hopkins.

PYRRHIC FOOT: A foot of two unaccented syllables; bearing the name of a quantitative foot of two short syllables. Example: the third foot of

The slíngs | ånd ár | rŏws ŏf | oútrá | geŏus fórtune.

QUANTITATIVE METER: The metrical system of classical poetry, based on a division of syllables into those of long and short duration. It is the basis for English meter, which is based on degrees of stress rather than duration.

QUATRAIN: A four-line stanza or division of a stanza. Still used also in its original sense, a four-line poem.

REFRAIN: A line or phrase of regular recurrence, appended typically to the several stanzas of a stanzaic poem. Refrains may be the same throughout, or similar but with progressive variations. They may also repeat the last line or phrase of each successive stanza. A vestige of choral response, they attach most naturally to songs. Compare **burden.**

RHYME: A concurrence of terminal sounds, usually those at the ends of lines (End-rhyme). Masculine rhymes, which are the rule, coincide in the vowel, and in the final consonant(s) if any, of stressed terminal syllables: *strife, life;* com*pel, bell.* A feminine ending (*q.v.*) adds an identical unstressed syllable. Triple rhymes add yet another such syllable: *glorious,* vic*torious.* Imperfect rhymes (variously called slant rhymes, off-rhymes and half-rhymes) normally entail either identical vowels or identical consonants, but not both: *hats, pets; ice, prize; fear, four.*

RHYME ROYAL: A seven-line iambic pentameter stanza rhyming *ababbcc.* Wyatt's *They Flee From Me* is a (metrically loose) example.

RHYTHM: A regular or at least clearly progressive sequence of sound patterns, as distinguished by recurrence of beat or stress; normally, in poetry, the verbal embodiment of an abstract metrical norm. It is a comprehensive term: there are both prose rhythms (or **cadences**) and poetic rhythms (or **meters**).

RONDEL: A fourteen-line poem rhyming *abbaababbaab*. The medial lines (seven and eight) and the final lines (thirteen and fourteen) repeat lines one and two. Charles d' Orléans employed the form.

RUN-ON: Enjambed; see **enjambment**.

SAPPHIC STROPHE: A stanza named for the Greek poetess Sappho. A scheme for it, which ignores permissible **quantitative** variants but includes the conventionally overlaid pattern of stresses, is

$$\acute{-}\, \smile\, |\, \acute{-}\, -\, |\, \acute{-}\, \|\, \smile\, \smile\, |\, \acute{-}\, \smile\, |\, \acute{-}\, \smile$$
$$\acute{-}\, \smile\, |\, \acute{-}\, -\, |\, \acute{-}\, \|\, \smile\, \smile\, |\, \acute{-}\, \smile\, |\, \acute{-}\, \smile$$
$$\acute{-}\, \smile\, |\, \acute{-}\, -\, |\, \acute{-}\, \|\, \smile\, \smile\, |\, \acute{-}\, \smile\, |\, \acute{-}\, \smile$$
$$\acute{-}\, \smile\, \smile\, |\, \acute{-}\, \smile$$

Isaac Watts imitated this strophe in *The Day of Judgment* (p. 177), and Algernon Swinburne in *Sapphics*.

SCANSION: The analysis of poetic lines to determine the meter, the variations upon it, and the deviations from it. (See Commentary, "Variations Within a Foot" and "Substitutions for Feet in a Line.")

SEPTET: A seven-line stanza, like that of **rhyme royal**.

SESTET: The last six lines of an Italian sonnet (see **sonnet**); occasionally some other six-line division of a poem.

SESTINA: A poem of six six-line stanzas with a three-line **envoy**. The lines of the several stanzas employ, in a regular permutation, the same six terminal words: each stanza after the first picks up successively the terminal words of lines 6, 1, 5, 2, 4, and 3 of the stanza before it. The envoy incorporates all six terminal words. Sir Philip Sidney's *Ye Goatherd Gods* is a double sestina (see poem and title note, p. 71).

SKELTONICS: Loosely rhythmic lines of two or three accents each, rhyming on the same word for as many as six lines together. Exemplified by their inventor, John Skelton (pp. 29–30).

SONNET: A fourteen-line lyric poem, almost always iambic pentameter, the form of which was first borrowed from Italy and which is still, in the variant clearly acknowledging that origin, called the Italian or Petrarchan sonnet. Italian sonnets are divided into an **octave** rhyming *abbaabba*, and a **sestet** rhyming *cdecde, cdcdcd*, or more or less as the poet pleases. Donne, Milton, and Wordsworth wrote Italian sonnets. The English or Shakespearean sonnet is divided into three **quatrains** and a **couplet**, which together rhyme *ababcdcdefefgg*. Spenser interlocked the rhymes of his quatrains: *ababbcbccdcd*. Gerard Manley Hopkins and others varied the sonnet form.

SPENSERIAN STANZA: A nine-line stanza, comprising eight lines of iambic pentameter and a final **Alexandrine**, and rhyming *ababbcbcc*. Invented by Edmund Spenser for his *Faerie Queene*; used also by Keats in *The Eve of St. Agnes* (p. 305).

SPONDEE: A foot of two accented syllables; bearing the name of the **quantitative** foot of two long syllables. (See Commentary, "Quantitative Meter.") Milton introduced a spondee into the fourth foot of the following line to suggest a clot of density in primordial chaos:

O'er bóg | or stéep, | through stráit, | rough, dénse, | or ráre, . . .

SPRUNG RHYTHM: A metrical system named and discussed by Gerard Manley Hopkins, and in part exemplified by his poetry, in which a foot consists of an accented syllable followed by a varying number of unaccented syllables, but in which all feet take up the same time interval.

STANZA: A group of lines conformed to a regular and typical scheme, usually of both meter and rhyme. It is the unit of larger poetic structures. Examples: *ottava rima*, the Spenserian stanza.

STROPHE: A stanza or, in verse not regularly stanzaic, a section of a poem accomplishing a clearly defined metrical movement. In Greek choral recitation, it is the first of two metrically identical divisions. See ode.

TERCET: A three-line stanza (or division of a stanza) in which all lines rhyme either with each other or with the lines of an adjoining tercet. Sestets rhyming *cdecde* contain two tercets.

TERZA RIMA: A three-line stanza concatenated with adjoining stanzas according to the formula *aba, bcb, cdc,* and so forth. The stanza of Dante's *Divine Comedy,* it was employed by Shelley in his *Ode to the West Wind* p. 282).

TETRAMETER: A verse line of four feet.

TRIMETER: A verse line of three feet.

TROCHEE: A metrical foot made up of an accented syllable followed by an unaccented. See Commentary, "Syllabic Feet."

VERSE: Metrical composition, or poetry in its metrical aspect; sometimes implying that the other functions of poetry are absent. More broadly, a line of poetry, with implicit reference to its meter. In popular hymnody, and erroneously in **prosody**, it is used as a synonym for **stanza**.

VILLANELLE: A poem made up of five **tercets**, all rhyming *aba*, and a concluding **quatrain**, rhyming *abaa*. Lines six, twelve and eighteen repeat line one; lines nine, fifteen and nineteen repeat line three. Theodore Roethke's *The Waking* is a nearly perfect villanelle.

Index

Index

650 Index